A CONCEPTUAL ENCYCLOPAEDIA OF GURU GRANTH SAHIB

A CONCEPTUAL ENCYCLOPAEDIA OF GURU GRANTH SAHIB

S.S. KOHLI

MANOHAR
2026

First published 1992
Reprinted 2026

ISBN 978-81-7304-006-1

Published by
Ajay Kumar Jain *for*
Manohar Publishers & Distributors
4753/23 Ansari Road, Daryaganj,
New Delhi 110 002

Printed at
Replika Press Pvt. Ltd.

Scheme of Transliteration

Vowels:

ਅ	ਆ	ਇ	ਈ	ਉ	ਊ
a	ā	i	ī	u	ū
ਏ	ਐ	ਓ	ਔ	ਅਂ	ਅੱ
e	ai	o	au	aṁ	ã

Consonants:

ਕ	ਖ	ਗ	ਘ	ਙ
k	kh	g	gh	ṅ
ਚ	ਛ	ਜ	ਝ	ਞ
c	ch	g	jh	ñ
ਟ	ਠ	ਡ	ਢ	ਣ
ṭ	ṭh	ḍ	ḍh	ṇ
ਤ	ਥ	ਦ	ਧ	ਨ
t	th	d	dh	n
ਪ	ਫ	ਬ	ਭ	ਮ
p	ph	b	bh	m
ਯ	ਰ	ਲ	ਵ	ੜ
y	r	l	v	ṛ
ਸ	ਹ	ਸ਼		
s	h	ṣ		

INTRODUCTION

I had been thinking of doing this encyclopaedic work on this youngest of the world scriptures ever since I completed my doctoral thesis entitled 'A Critical Study of the Adi Granth' in 1957. However, I could not start work on the project due to my pre-occupations as a Professor in Punjab University, Chandigarh, Director, Guru Nanak Foundation, New Delhi and Director of the Punjab State University Text Board, Chandigarh.

I had meanwhile published *A Critical Study of the Adi Granth, Outlines of Sikh Thought, Philosophy of Guru Nanak and Sikh Ethics.* These works gave me penetrating insight in the Sikh philosophy and religion. In the meantime a reprint of the classic *The Sacred Books of the East* (50 vols. set) edited by Max Muller also became available. The fiftieth volume is an index to forty-nine volumes of the series and has been compiled with commendable thoroughness and industry by Prof. Winternitz. In the preface to this volume Professor Macdonnel writes '*The Sacred Books of the East* include all the most important works of the seven non-Christian religions that have exercised a profound influence on the civilisations of the continent of Asia. Of the Indian religions, the Vedic-Brahmanic system here claims twenty-one volumes, Buddhist ten, and Jainism two. Eight volumes comprise translations of the sacred books of the Persians, two volumes represent Islam, and six the two main indigenous systems of China, Confucianism and Taoism'.

The series thus represents seven non-Christian religions and excludes 'Shintoism' and 'Sikhism'. Sikhism is the youngest world religion with followers all over the world and its scripture the 'Adi Granth' has several translations in English. With the project already in my mind and fresh impetus provided by Prof. 'Winternitz's work, I selected more than 1200 entries from the index volume appropriate for the study of Sikh scripture for my work and was able to start work on it in right earnest in 1986 with the award of a fellowship by the Indian Council of Philosophical Research. I now present the complete work for the discerning readers. I am conscious of the fact that there would be shortcomings here and there in a work like this and I leave it to better-equipped scholars to improve upon it.

II

The Enlightened Persons in various ages revealed their spiritual affinity with the Highest Being and recorded their experiences in the spiritual domain. They codified the injunctions, presenting the divine discipline, for the welfare of humanity. Every nation which received these divine revelations, was guided by them in succeeding centuries, setting its distinct tradition. At present there are eleven living religions in the world. A living religion has three distinct features. It has its own scripture, its own set of laws and a well-set tradition. Without these three factors, many religions which sprang up, have passed into oblivion. Out of the eleven living religions in the world, four are in the Indian sub-continent viz. Hinduism, Jainism, Buddhism and Sikhism, four in the Middle East viz. Zoroastrianism, Judaism, Christianity and Islam, two in China viz. Taoism and Confucianism and one in Japan i.e. Shintoism. Sikhism is the youngest of world-religions. Its founder Guru Nanak Dev was born in AD 1469. He undertook four long journeys during his life and visited all the prominent centres of major religions. He held meaningful dialogues with the divines and savants of those religions and incorporated his thoughts in the hymns composed by him. The Sikh scripture i.e. the *Adi Granth*, which includes the compositions of Sikh Gurus and the radical saints, is thus the acme and consummation of the religious and spiritual discipline. It contains the best of all religious ideals.

There are several points on which the *Adi Granth* differs from other scriptures of the world:

1– The *Adi Granth* is purely monotheistic. It accepts only One God and rejects all other deities, spirits, angels etc. Only God is Immortal. All the other deities are mortal and prone to death. "Why should we remember and serve others, who undergo birth and death" (Gujri M.3, p. 509). "He neither has father, nor mother, nor sons nor brothers" (Maru M.1, p. 1021). "He does not seek the advice of another and Does All by Himself whatever He wants to Do" (Gaund M.5, p. 863). Thus the *Adi Granth* does not believe like the New Testament in the Son of God and like the Holy Quran in a Prophet.

2– The religion of the *Adi Granth*, being free from inhibitions of any kind regarding the way of life and its adaptability in all the regions of the world vouches its universality. It is not a religion of the chosen people (like Judaism), but instead it is the religion of the entire humanity. It rises above all the regional barriers "The True Guru wishes the well-being of all the creation". (Var Gujri M.4, p. 302).

3– The *Adi Granth* rejects all ritualism, formalism and symbolism. The adherents of most of the religions perform various rites and ceremonies in order to appease their deities or achieve their objectives. Thus the priestcraft is rejected. All the intermediaries, exploiting the masses in the name of religion, have been brought under severe criticism. The *Adi Granth* has no belief in any sacrament.

4– The *Adi Granth* focuses all its attention on the unfoldment of the discipline for the attainment of the unity of the Jiva with Brahman. The emphasis has been laid on the adoption of godly qualities by the seeker.

5– The *Adi Granth* repudiates the prevalent theories of creation and scans the universe as the work of the Creator, Whose Existence Pulsates evereywhere in His Creation. All the beliefs regarding the origin of creation are wrong. The extent and expanse of creation of the Infinite Lord cannot be delimited. The created phenomena, from the minutest to the greatest, is under the surveillance of the Lord.

6– The *Adi Granth* lays great emphasis on honest and sincere labour. Its religion is the religion of workers and householders. Therefore, it decries renunciation and ascetic practices of all types.

7– The *Adi Granth* advocates the equality of all human beings, irrespective of birth and sex. The woman, is in no way, inferior to man. The *Adi Granth* rejects all distinctions of caste and colour. The *Varnashrama Dharma* of Hinduism, propagating the distinction of caste and advocating various stages of life, has been bitterly criticised. The untouchability, thus, becomes a slur on society.

8– The State has to play its part in the provision of food, shelter and clothing to the members of the society. There can be no devotion, if the individual is not carefree about his requirements.

9– The *Adi Granth* presents a balanced combination of action (karma), devotion (Bhakti) and knowledge (Gyan). It is, essentially, a religion of devotion. Whereas the body has to work for the well-being of the family and society, the mind has to remain in tune with the Lord. Service, is, thus, the motto of an adherent of the *Adi Granth*. His best service towards the Guru and the Lord is the remembrance of the Name. One must also share his earnings (preferably *tithe*)with the needy and deserving. The core of the teaching of the *Adi Granth* is *Nam Japna* (remembrance of the Name of the Lord), *Kirt Karni* (The honest labour) and *Wand Chhakna* (sharing of the earning with the needy and deserving).

10– The religion of the *Adi Granth* is most practical. The devotee overbrims with love and devotion. He visualises the Lord all around him in multifarious forms and guises. The whole world appears as a family to him. The Earth is an abode of *Dharma* for him. He passes his whole life under the dense shade of his Guru, who is *Dharma*-incarnate.

The UNIQUE ASPECT OF THE *ADI GRANTH*, as compared with other scriptures of the world, is its unique position, as an embodiment of the spirit of the Ten Sikh Gurus and the Saints, whose Word is included in it. It is the *Shabad Guru*. "The Book is the Abode of God" (Sarang M.5, p. 1226). It is Guru (Preceptor) of all times. Guru Gobind Singh, the tenth and the last Sikh Guru circumambulated and bowed his head before it, thereby ending the line of personal Guruship. Since AD 1708, it has attained the position of the "Eternal Guru". It receives veneration and shall ever receive veneration like the "LIVING GURU". No living Guru can take its place. Its WORD directs the devotee in all his functions, secular as well as spiritual.

III

The compilation of the Adi Granth began, when Guru Nanak Dev, during his travels, undertook to collect the *bani* (hymns) of like-minded saints in his note-book (*pothi*). This *pothi* was passed on to the second Guru and then to the third Guru. The third Guru, Guru Amar Das, got prepared under his personal supervision, through his grandson Sahansar Ram, four *pothis* which came in the possession of Baba Mohan and were known as the *pothis* of Baba Mohan. When Guru Arjan Dev, the fifth Guru compiled the *Adi Granth*, he went himself to take these *pothis*. The compilation of the *bani* of Guru Nanak Dev and like-minded saints was Herculian task for the fifth Guru. The bani of Guru Angad Dev, Guru Amar Das and Guru Ram Das had been preserved in the House of the Guru, but the bani of Guru Nanak Dev lay scattered far and wide because of his extensive travels. An order of the fifth Guru was circulated to all the Sikh centres, both inside and outside the country, for the collection of the *bani* of Guru Nanak Dev. The Sikh Sangats complied with the orders and sent available compositions of the first Guru. The Guru sent Bhai Paira to Ceylon for bringing the compositions of Guru Nanak Dev bound in a collection entitled "Pran Sangali".

It is said that the elder brother of Guru Arjan Dev, Prithi Chand by name, had also been trying to compose and get composed hymns and pass them as those of Guru Nanak Dev and other Gurus. In this way, he wanted to be recognised as a Guru. This also led Guru Arjan Dev to prepare an anthology of poetry of the preceding Sikh Gurus alongwith his own compositions. One day when he heard a hymn of Meharvan (the son of Prithi Chand) being sung by the bards, he told Bhai Gurdas that the genuine hymns be separated from the false ones. This was the beginning of the compilation of the *Granth Sahib.* Bhai Gurdas was the scribe, who wrote *Granth Sahib* in Gurmukhi script, which was one of the prevalent scripts in Punjab in those days.

Guru Arjan Dev collected all the material for the *Granth Sahib,* which came through several sources. The bards had left their panegyrics with the Gurus, whom they had met in their lives. The hymns of Guru Nanak Dev had been collected from far and near. The hymns of the succeeding Gurus had been there in the House of the Guru. The hymns of like-minded saints had been collected from their followers, though some of the hymns had been included in the *pothis* of Guru Nanak Dev and Baba Mohan. The saints had been travelling extensively throughout India. The Maharashtrian saint Namdev is said to have visited Punjab during his lifetime. There is a shrine in his name in village Ghuman in Gurdaspur district. Several other saints like Kabir, Ravidas etc. had been intimately known to the people of Punjab through their devotees and popular hymns. The Bhakti Movement had gained great momentum in this area because of the work being done by the Sikh Gurus. When the living saints came to know about the preparation of *Granth Sahib,* they came to meet the Guru and requested him to include their hymns also in the holy *Granth.* In the biography of the Guru, mention has been made of four such saints coming from Lahore namely Peelu, Chhajju, Kahna and Shah Hussain.

IV

After compiling the material from different sources for *Granth Sahib,* Guru Arjan Dev started the work of editing the great scripture. The compilation was over in AD 1601 and editing was completed in AD 1604. The very first consideration for the inclusion of the hymns of various saints for the new anthology was the ideology of Guru Nanak Dev. Some of the hymns of like-minded saints had already been collected by Guru Nanak Dev in his *pothi* and Guru Amar Das in *Baba Mohan dian Pothian*. Guru Arjan Dev had even dropped some of the hymns of the saints already compiled. Seven hymns of Kabir and two of Namdev, included in *Baba Mohan dian Pothian* were not included in *Granth Sahib.* The thoughts of the contemporary saints like Kahna, Peelu, Chhajju and Shah Hussain were not in consonance with the ideology of Guru Nanak Dev, therefore the hymns of these saints were not accepted. A large number of shlokas composed by the Gurus were interspersed in longer poems, especially Vars of the Gurus. Some shlokas were appended with the shlokas of Kabir and Farid for clarification and elaboration. The Yogic path of Pranayama and Asanas was not acceptable to Guru Nanak Dev, therefore the compositions of Gorakhnath and his disciples were left out. The saints who were traditionalists and believed in *Karma Kanda* and *Upasana Kanda* were also not considered. The compositions included in *Pran Sangali* and said to be the work of Guru Nanak Dev were closely scrutinised and everything connected with Hathyoga was left out from the purview of selection.

Another criterion besides the ideology was that of Ragas and Raganis (musical modes). Only *Japuji* in the beginning and Shlokas and Swayyas at the end of the anthology are free from any musical notation. The main body of the scripture has been divided into musical modes. The order of the poetry included in the *Adi Granth* is as follows:

I Part:

1– *Japuji,* the morning prayer

2– *Rahiras*, the evening prayer containing nine hymns of the Gurus

3– *Sohila*, the bed-time prayer containing five hymns of the Gurus

II Part: It contains hymns of the Gurus and saints in the following thirty-one Ragas and Raganis:

1– Sri Raga pronounced as *Srī Rāg*

2– Majh pronounced as *Mājh*

3– Gauri pronounced as *Gauṛī*

4– Asa pronounced as *Āsā*

5– Gujri pronounced as *Gūjrī*

6– Devgandhari pronounced as *Devgandhārī*

7– Bihagra pronounced as *Bihāgṛā*

8– Vadhans pronounced as Vadhans

9– Sorath pronounced as *Soraṭh*

10– Dhanasari pronouned as *Dhanāsarī*
11– Jaitsri pronounced as *Jaitsrī*
12– Todi pronounced as *Todī*
13– Bairari pronounced as *Bairāṛī*
14– Tilang pronounced as Tilang
15– Suhi pronounced as *Sūhī*
16– Bilawal pronounced as *Bilāwal*
17– Gond & Gaund pronounced as Gond & Gaund
18– Ramkali pronounced as *Rāmkalī*
19– Nat Narain pronounced as *Nat Nārāin*
20– Mali Gaura pronounced as *Mālī Gauṛā*
21– Maru pronounced as *Mārū*
22– Tukhari pronounced as *Tukhārī*
23– Kedara pronounced as *Kedārā*
24– Bhairo pronounced as Bhairo
25– Basant pronounced as Basant
26– Sarang/Sarag pronounced as Sārang/Sārag
27– Malar pronounced as *Malār*
28– Kanra pronounced as *Kānṛā*
29– Kalyan pronounced as *Kalyān*
30– Prabhati pronounced as *Prabhātī*
31– Jaijavanti pronounced as *Jaijāvantī*

In these Ragas and Raganis, the following order of hymns is observed:

1– Chaupade, Dupade, Tipade, Panchpade or Chhipade with the number of musical notation of the Raga/Ragani in serial order and the number of Mahla in serial order
2– Ashapadis with the number of musical notation of the Raga/Ragani in serial order and the number of Mahla in serial order
3– Solhe, if any, with the number of Mahla in serial order
4– Poems with special sub-headings with the number of Mahla and musical notation in serial order, which do not come under 1 and 2.
5– Chhants with the number of musical notation and the number of Mahla in serial order
6– Vars of the Gurus in serial order followed by Var written by bards, if any.
7– The hymns of the saints, mostly beginning with Kabir, followed by Namdev, Ravidas and other saint-poets. Dupade, Tipade, Chaupade, Panchpade, Chhipade, Ashtapade, Solhe are the

hymns containing two, three, four, five, six, eight and sixteen stanzas respectively.

III Part: Shlokas and Swayyas are given in the following order:.

1– Sahaskriti Shlokas
2– Gatha Shlokas
3– Phunhay Shlokas
4– Chaubolay
5– Shlokas of Kabir
6– Shlokas of Sheikh Farid
7– Swayyas of Guru Arjan Dev
8– Swayyas written by bards as panegyrics of the first, second, third, fourth and fifth Gurus in serial order
9– Shlokas in excess of Vars by the first, third, fourth and fifth Gurus in serial order
10– Shlokas of the ninth Guru
11– Mundavani (The seal) consisting of two Shlokas
12– Ragamala.

V

Three recensions of the Adi Granth

The original volume of *Granth Sahib* prepared by Guru Arjan Dev, with the scribe Bhai Gurdas, was installed by the Guru at Darbar Sahib (Golden Temple) at Amritsar. Baba Budha was the first high-priest (*Granthī*). This recension passed on from Guru Arjan Dev to Guru Hargobind and to his grandson Dhir Mal, the son of Baba Gurditta. His brother Har Rai became the Guru and Dhir Mal thought it advisable to take possession of *Granth Sahib*. Thenceforward, this recension remained in the family of Dhir Mal at Kartarpur and is still there. It is, therefore, known as *Kartarpur wali Bīṛ*.

The second recension is known as *Bhai Banno ki Bīṛ*, which was prepared, when Bhai Banno was taking the first recension for binding at Lahore. This second recension contains two additional hymns—one of Sur Das and the other of Mira Bai and several other poems after Mundavani (the seal). Guru Arjan Dev did not approve of the additions of Bhai Banno, which are thus considered apocryphal. This second recension is also called *Khārī Bīṛ*, which is still with the descendents of Bhai Banno.

When Dhir Mal was approached by Guru Gobind Singh to hand over *Granth Sahib*, he did not care for the request, but instead said tauntingly: "If you are the Guru, you prepare your own". The Guru had been busy in the battlefield for a long time. He had no human successor in view. He wanted to bestow Guruship on *Granth Sahib.* Therefore when he left Anandpur, he stayed at Damdama Sahib for some time. Bhai Mani Singh joined him there and worked as a scribe for the third recension. The Guru dictated and Bhai Mani Singh wrote. As the story goes, it was a miraculous feat, but it appears that a manuscript copy of the first recension was provided to him by the Sikhs. In this third recension, the additions made in the first recension are the hymns of the ninth Guru. In the Shlokas of the ninth Guru at the end of the holy Granth, there is one Shloka said to have been composed by Guru Gobind Singh.

VI

The Composers of the Divine Poetry of the Adi Granth:

It has been said of the Bible: "Human creatures took over the actual work of writing, but they all wrote under God's Guidance and Dictation, being moved by His Spirit. Some were judges and kings, some were learned, others were lowly labourers, herdsmen, fishermen etc. They were not professional writers, but men of action, servants and witnesses of Jehovah from all walks of life. They wrote over long stretch of years..." (*Equipped for every good work* published in 1946 by Watchtower Bible and Tract Society, Inc. International Bible Students Association, Brooklyn, New York, U.S.A., p. 10). The same can be said of the *Adi Granth*. Guru Nanak Dev has plainly said:

"Whatever Word I receive from the Lord, I pass it on in the same strain, O Lalo!" Thus the Word of God has been put forth in the *Adi Granth.* The Contributors were all types of men. Jaidev was a Brahmin, Pipa was a king, Namdev was a calico-printer,Trilochan was a Vaish, Sadhna was a butcher, Dhanna was a farmer, Sain was a barber, Kabir was a weaver, Ravidas was a cobbler and the Gurus were all Kshatriyas. They all composed the divine songs over a stretch of about six centuries. Jaidev, the Bengali saint of the twelfth century, is the oldest composer included in this holy Book. Namdev, the famous Maharashtrian saint belonged to the fourteenth century. Kabir, the Hindi poet of the Gangetic Valley, flourished in the fifteenth century. Guru Nanak Dev and his successors lived in the sixteenth and the seventeenth centuries.

The Pre-Nanak saints whose hymns have been included in the *Adi Granth* are Jaidev, the famous Bengali poet of *Gita Govinda* of the twelfth century (two hymns), Sheikh Farid (1173-1266), the famous Sufi saint of Chishti order (Four hymns and 112 Shalokas), Namdev, the Maharashtrian saint born in AD 1270 (60 hymns), Trilochan, another Maharashtrian, born in AD 1267 (4 hymns), Parmanand, another Maharashtrian (one hymn), Sadhna of Sind and contemporary of Namdev (one hymn), Beni (three hymns), Ramanand, the Guru of Kabir and others (one hymn), Dhanna, a farmer of Rajasthan, born in AD 1415 (four hymns), Pipa, the king of Gagaraungarh, born in A.D. 1425 (one hymn), Sain, a barber of Rewa and disciple of Ramananda (one hymn), Kabir (1398-1518) the weaver and disciple of Ramanand (292 hymns including Pauris of *Bawan Akhri, Thittin, Var Sat* and 249 Shlokas) and Ravidas, the cobbler and a disciple of Ramanand (41 hymns).

The Sikh Gurus whose verses have been included in the *Adi Granth* are Guru Nanak Dev (1469-1538), the first Guru and founder of Sikhism (974 hymns including Pauris and Shlokas), Guru Angad Dev (1504-1553), the second Sikh Guru (62 Shlokas), Guru Amar Das (1479-1574), the third Sikh Guru (907 hymns including Pauris and Shlokas), Guru Ram Das (1534-1581), the fourth Sikh Guru (679 hymns including Pauris and Shlokas), Guru Arjan Dev (1563-1606), the fifth Sikh Guru and compilar of the *Adi Granth* (2218 hymns including Pauris and Shlokas) and Guru Tegh Bahadur (1622-1675), the ninth Sikh Guru (59 hymns and 56 Shlokas).

The saints and bards of the times of the Sikh Gurus, whose verses have been included in the *Adi Granth* are: The Sufi saint Bhikhan of Uttar Pradesh, who died in the reign of Akbar (two hymns), Sur Das, born in 1528, and appointed the Governor of the province of Sandila by Akbar (two hymns), Sundar, the grandson of Guru Amar Das (One *Sad* of six Pauris), Mardana, the bard who accompanied Guru Nanak Dev during his travels (Three Shlokas), the bard Kal (46 Swayyas and three Sorathas), the bard Kalsahar (four Swayyas), the bard Tal (one Swayya), the bard Jalap (4 Swayyas), the bard Jal (one Swayya), the bard Kirat (8 Swayyas), the bard Sal (three Swayyas), the bard Bhal (one Swayya), the bard Nal (six Swayyas), the bard Bhikha (2 Swayyas), the bard Jalan (one Swayya), the bard Das (7 Swayyas, 3 Rad and 4 Jholnay), the bard Gayand (five Swayyas), the bard Sewak (7 Swayyas), the bard Mathura (ten Swayyas), the bard Bal (five Swayyas), the bard Harbans (2 Swayyas) and two bards Satta and Balwand (One Var containing eight Pauris). According to some scholars, the bards who composed Swayyas were not seventeen, but eleven only.

VII

The Language of the *Adi Granth*: Since the contributors of the *Adi Granth* belonged to different parts of the country, they used different languages and dialects in their compositions. The oldest specimen of the language in the *Adi Granth* are the two hymns of the saint Jaidev of Bengal. They are in Eastern Apabhramsa. The language used in Sahaskriti Shlokas is Western Apabhramsa. We also find the after-effects of Southern Apabhramas in the verses of Namdev. The main language of the *Adi Granth* is Sant-Bhasha (the saint-language), which has been used by the Sikh Gurus and the saint-poets. This language was becoming the *lingua franca* of the country. The peculiar characteristics of this language were: 1-The religious diction derived from Sanskrit and Prakrit works, 2-The affixes and case-terminations of the language of the area, in which the saint lived, 3-The analytical character of the language, 4-The mixed language because of the travels of the saints from one area to the other and 5-The influence of Persian and Arabic. Undoubtedly, the diction of Sant-Bhasha shows great indebtedness to Sanskrit and Prakirt, we can also notice the impact of Persian and Arabic. We find the use of Western Hindi in the verses of Kabir, Ravidas, Dhanna, Sain, Pipa, Bhikhan, and Guru Tegh Bahadur. The bards used Eastern Hindi except Mardana, Satta and Balwand. The first five Gurus also composed their hymns in Eastern Punjabi. The Western Punjabi *or* Lehndi was used by Sheikh Farid, Guru Arjan Dev and Satta and Balwand. "Jaitsri ki Var" of Guru Arjan Dev presents an interesting study of languages. Each Pauri of this Var is preceded by two Shlokas; the Pauri is written in Eastern Punjabi, the first Shloka in Sahaskriti and the second in Lehndi. Guru Arjan Dev also composed some verses in Sindhi in "Var Maru Dakhne". The use of Marathi endings can be observed in the verses of Namdev and Trilochan. Besides the above-mentioned languages and dialects, there are other languages, whose words and case-terminations are found. A close observation of the diction used in the *Adi Granth* shows that most of the languages used are *deshi* or corrupt formations.

Religious Philosophy of the Adi Granth: Means of Knowledge: The Sikh philosophy recognises three means of knowledge viz. perception, inference and scriptural testimony. The perception includes the perception of ordinary persons i.e. the contact of the soul with the sense-organs and objects through mind, the perception of the 'liberated souls' e.g. the Guru and the True Sikh and the Perception of God Himself. The world, according to Sikhism, is not a mere appearance, it is definitely real. Even, with the attainment of final beatitude, the world remains real. The Guru and the True Sikh perceive everywhere the grandeur of Brahman. God Perceives His Creation and Enjoys the Sport (*līlā*). The second source of knowledge i.e. inference is based on perceptual knowledge. It includes comparison and presumption as well. The third source of knowledge is *Shabda* or verbal testimony. The testimony may either be sacred or secular. Adopting the above-mentioned three sources of knowledge, the religious philosophy of the *Adi Granth* presents forth the following thoughts about *Brahman*, *Jiva* and *Maya*.

Brahman (God): Brahman is One without a second. His Name is Truth. He is the Creator. He is without Fear and Enmity. He is Immortal, Unborn and Self-Existent. He is Truth, Consciousness and Bliss. He is Omnipresent, Omnipotent and Omniscient. He is Changeless and Flawless. When He Wills, He becomes Many. He begins His Sport like a Juggler. He Creates the universe and brings the matter out of Himself. Before the creation, He is in abstract meditation (Sunn Samādhī) and devoid of Attributes (*Nirguna*) but after the creation, He, as Ishvara, manifests Himself as treasure-house of qualities (*Saguna*). He is Faultless, Good, Holy, Light, Primal-Cause and Essence, Beyond our cognizance, Pervasive and Everlasting. He does not Incarnate. All the gods and goddesses are His Creation. He is a *Purusha*, Who Creates the whole universe. There is no other separate Eternal Entity except Brahman. He is the Creator of the *Prakriti* of three *gunas* (qualities) i.e. *rajas* (activity), *tamas* (morbidity) and *sattva* (rhythm). He is *Purusha*, distinct from other Purushas (Jivas/souls). He is *Adi Purakh* (who is from the very beginning), *Sat Purakh* (Pervasive and Everlasting), *Kartā Purakh* (Creator), *Akāl Purakh* (Uninfluenced by Time) and *Niranjan Purakh* (without the influence of *Maya*).

Jīva: Jiva is a part and parcel of Brahman. It should not be mistaken for Brahman Himself. It has its own individuality, but since it is a part of Brahman, it carries the qualities of Brahman. It is immortal like Brahman, but works under the Will of Brahman. The physical body decays, but it continues for ever.

Māyā: According to the *Adi Granth, Prakriti* or *māyā* is not a separate Ultimate Reality. It has been created by God. It takes the individual away from God and thus leads him towards transmigration. When the influence of maya vanishes, the Jiva realises Brahman. When Brahman comes into contact with maya of three *gunas* (qualities), the process of creation begins. The unconscious matter and the finite selves, which exist in Brahman before the creation, join this process by a Gracious Act of His Will. Maya is the bondage for Jiva and its main functionary is ego. The three *gunas* are the resultant of ego or *Ahamkāra.*

Other aspects of the religious philosophy of Sikhism are given hereunder:

Creation: The Sikh Gurus are of the view that it is wrong to delimit the Creation of the Lord. Whereas the Lord Himself is without limits, His Creation cannot be considered within limits. There are countless universes and in them there are many species of diverse forms and colours. The Pauranic idea of eighty-four lakhs of species is found in the *Adi Granth.* There are lakhs and crores of upper and nether regions. Guru Nanak Dev says, "From God arose air, from air water, from water the three worlds, with His Light in every self". The theory of creation expounded by the Sikh Gurus resembles *Brahmparinamavada* of Ramanuja, which presents forth the Samkhyan theory of evolution, but emphasises that Prakriti is absolutely dependent upon God. Guru Nanak Dev says, "Nobody knows the exact time, when the universe was created except the Creator Himself".

Microcosm: The Truth (Brahman) is Immanent in the universe. The human body is its repository. The body is not merely a thing like other objects. It is an epitome of the universe. It is a microcosm, whereas the universe is macrocosm. Therefore whatever exists in the universe, also exists in the body of the human being. This implies that the same energy is in action, both in the human body and the vast cosmos, therefore the seeker should not get himself lost in the vastness of the cosmos and only concentrate himself on the Truth within his own body.

Karma: Every Jiva desires, thinks and acts. Every action has its associations in the past, present and future. Every action is like seed sown in the body, which is a field of action. When the seed of action is sown, the consequences must follow. A Jiva repeatedly experiences births and deaths becuse of his actions in this world. This is the thoery of Karma or the moral law of causation. There are two types of Karmas i.e. the higher karmas and the lower karmas. The works ordained by Shastric injunctions are considered lower karmas in the *Adi Granth.* Therefore they are rejected. The emphasis has been laid on the higher karmas, which lead one to the realisation of Brahman. The worldly karmas may be good or bad, virtuous or sinful. The remuneration of these karmas depends on their quality. Whatever one did in his previous births, that makes his present life. It is futile to slander others for the actions done. The fault lies in one's own actions. The karmas done under the influence of maya and ego are the cause of transmigration. The soul takes various physical forms according to its karmas. It experiences bondage, when it enters the field of action. Every action enchains him further. It tightens the noose round his neck. Transmigration ceases with the exhaustion of desire, but the desire (*Trishna*) comes to an end only, when we meet the True Guru, who is the Knower of Brahman and act according to his instructions. The Guru gives to the disciple the Name of the Lord, which is the panacea of all ills.

Grace: Though we get our body on account of our karmas, the release can only be obtained through the Grace of the Lord. The Grace of the Lord begins with our acceptance of the True Path in life. All the creation works under the *Hukam* or the Laws of God. These Laws are true for all times and work in all the three fields i.e. physical, moral and spiritual. All the creatures in the world are bound by these Laws. The Law of cause and effect operates in every field. The amount of the Grace of the Lord necessitates our accomplishments on the right Path. In fact, the Grace of the Lord is not the result of any whim of the Lord, it begins and matures with the beginning and maturity of our *Dharma*.

Virtue and Vice: In Sikhism, the performance of duty i.e. *Dharma* does not mean the observance of formal ritualism or the pursuance of the Shastric injunctions. The Sikh Gurus laid down a definite moral code, which enjoins a Sikh to do such actions as are called higher karmas. The practice of these higher karmas is the practice of virtues in life. The Sikh has to imbibe the godly qualities in his life. These qualities include Truth, Purity, Justice, Sweetness, Fearlessness, Mercy etc. The five major vices can be overcome with the practice of five virtues i.e. the lust can be overcome with self-contorl, anger with toleration, greed with contentment, worldly affection with devotion to duty and ego with modesty. The virtue and vice are both the Creation of God. Vice is a sin. It is impure and unclean. God is Pure. An individual becomes godlike to the extent he becomes pure. In a world vitiated by all types of ills, one should avoid indulgence to the extreme and also avoid self-mortification. On both the sides, one loses balance, therefore, the middle path is to be followed, which is the golden mean. One has neither to renounce the world or jump in the field of action like an unbridled horse. The foremost duty of an individual is to understand *Dharma* or the path of piety. The piety can be achieved by the control of our senses. The five senses of sight, hearing, taste, smell and touch are to be kept under discipline.

Ego: The path of ego is averse to the path of devotion. Modesty is a pre-requisite to the path of devotion. The path of ego is the path of destruction. Whosoever thinks high of himself, is reduced to dust in a moment. Ego is the principal and subtle vice. It is always present in a Jiva in one form or the other. It is the I-ness which spoils the fruit of great penances. The Truth or the Fourth State is never realised in ego. The Fourth State or the Supreme State (*Param Pad*) is an egoless state.

Mind and Intellect: The mind and intellect are the outer coverings of the soul undergoing transmigration. The light of mind is eclipsed by the dirt of ego, which has blackened it in the course of several births. The mind is puffed up with ego, but in its original form, the mind is identical with *Jivātmā* (soul). In order to control the mind, its reins should be tightened. It is not an easy job to bring the mind under control. The great sages have failed in their attempts. When the disciple follows the discipline ordained by the Guru, he comes to know the nature of mind. He realises that the mind is like an intoxicated elephant and only the goad of the Guru can give it a new life. The Grace of he Lord and Guru play a great part in the conquest of mind. When the mind is conquered, the Lord is realised and the whole world is conquered. The intellect makes one wise and educated. The education makes us realise the Truth. The Gurus are in favour of *Parā Vidyā* or the spiritual education. For them the verbal testimony is the vital source of knowledge. The *Granth* (*pothi*) is the Abode of the Lord. The education creates such intellect as helps us to subdue the mind and realise the Lord.

Death: Death is a reality. Whosoever is born, must die. Every moment that passes reduces the span of our life. The Jiva does not realise it. The soul is eternal. The death lays its hand only on the body, but nothing is destroyed. The air mixes with air, light in light, earth in earth. When the gross body dies, the subtle body of the soul consisting of vital breath (*Prāna*), mind and intellect lives. This subtle body also dies, when the state of final emancipation is realised. When, after death, the soul appears before *Dharmaraja* (the god of justice), a decision is taken about its future according to its actions in the material world. It may be sent to be reborn as an animal, a bird or an insect. It may even be sent to the higher planes of gods or it may be sent to be born again as a human being for its further development.

Health: The Sikh Religion recognises the human body as the abode of God. It is the temple of God, wherein the individual can see His Light. A healthy mind lives in a healthy body. The gods are said to have a burning desire for the human body, which is the only medium, through which the soul reaches the desired goal. Like other temples, the temple of human body has to be kept neat and clean with full veneration. It should be made a befitting house for the Lord. The cleanliness of mind and body takes the individual soul nearer God. The Gurus have laid emphasis on continence (*Sanyam*). Over-eating or gluttony is bad. Under-nourishment is still worse. A balanced diet is necessary for the upkeep of health. A hungry person cannot be a healthy constituent of society. He cannot even think of God. Such foods only should be eaten, which do not upset the physical and mental balance. Therefore the use of intoxicants has been strictly forbidden, which destroy our happiness, create pains in the body and bring up vices in the mind. For the upkeep of health, it is necessary to rise early in the morning. The Sikh of the Guru should eat less and sleep less.

Yoga: The beliefs and practices of contemporary Yogis were not liked by Guru Nanak Dev. He rejected outright all their formalism. He said, "Yoga does not consist in wearing patched quilt, in carrying staff and smearing the body with ashes. Yoga does not consist in wearing ear-rings, in cutting hair and playing on *Singhī* (a musical instrument). Yoga does not consist in going to the cremation ground and roaming about in the country..." According to the Guru, the true Yoga consists in the meditation on the Word and the repetition of the Name of the Lord. The Yogi remains unaffected by maya, just as the lotus remains above the surface of water. The Yoga of the Sikh Gurus is a balanced union of action, devotion and knowledge.

Bhakti: The real devotion of the Lord is His Love. There are two types of devotion (*Bhakti*) i.e. *Antarang* (inward) and *Behrang* (outward). The *Adi Granth* rejects the outward or formalistic devotion. It lays emphasis on the inward devotion of pure love. *Bhakti* is the real path towards *Nirvana*. The final emancipation can never be attained through learning and guises. The world is mad without Bhakti. Without Bhakti, the human being appears as a dog or a swine. The Bhakta (devotee) is full of undefiled fear and pure love; fear of the Omnipotent and love of the Merciful and Compassionate Lord. The Word of the

Guru is the treasure-house of devotion. Whosoever sings, listens or practises it, attains his objective. The Name of the Lord is instilled in his being and the union of the soul and the Higher Soul is achieved.

Guru and Name: In every walk of life, one needs a guide. Similar is the case in spiritual domain. For our spiritual uplift, we need a Guru or religious preceptor, who prepares us in thought, deed and action in order to make us a loving bride of the Lord. The Guru or Satguru is the kindly light, which sheds lustre on our path. The ten Gurus of the Sikhs are the ten manifestations of the Guru-soul. The last Sikh Guru Guru Gobind Singh, bestowed the status of the Guru on *Granth Sahib* (the *Adi Granth*). The Guru-Soul manifested itself in the form of *WORD, NAME* or *BĀNĪ*. The Word or the *mantra* of the Guru is the Guru himself, therefore the greatest service of the Guru consists in the repetition of the mantra with faith and love. None of the meritorious works equals the Name of the Lord. All the sins are washed away with it. The Name and ego cannot live at one plane. The Name saves the Jiva from the dreadful *Yama*. The true devotee remembers the Lord in all his actions and postures i.e. standing, sleeping or waking.

Holy Congregation: The holy congregation (*Sādh Sangat* or *Satsang*) of the Sikhs meets in a temple (*Gurdwaro*), where it recites the Name of the Lord and sings the *bānī* (composition) of the Guru from *Guru Granth Sahib*. This congregation is like a philosopher's stone, which turns ordinary people into gold. The member of this congregation is in love with the Name of the Lord and ultimately realises TRUTH (The Lord). This congregation is like a boat, which takes the inmate beyond the world-ocean, where there is no birth and death. The pure intellect dawns upon him and his overturned mind-lotus blossoms. He is cool, calm and content. All his desires are extinguished. The mind does not run in diverse directions and the Pure Abode of the Lord is achieved. The holy congregation is a school of the True Guru, where the devotee learns about the qualities of the Lord, which he has to imbibe within himself. The main function of *Sādh Sangat* is the remembrance of the Name of the Lord. For this purpose each disciple concentrates on WORD and the music of the sweet songs of the Guru not only helps him to drink deep the nectar of *bānī*, but also helps him in further spiritual flights. The singing of *Guru-bānī* is known as *Kīrtan*. Whosoever listens to or sings the *Kīrtan* of Hari, no trouble can come near him. *Kīrtan* is the food of divine love.

A True Sikh: The *Adi Granth* decries any distinction of caste. No devotee considers himself superior to any other. Humility and modesty are his specialities, therefore, the service of humanity is the main aim of his life. He is a saint, soldier and scholar, therefore the society of which he is a constituent is martial in spirit, saintly in character and scholarly in knowledge. The religion of the *Adi Granth* is the religion of activity. It enjoins every devotee to lead the life of a householder. It rejects *varnas* (castes) and *ashramas* (stages of life) and lays emphasis on equality and fraternity. The adherent of the discipline enunciated in the *Adi Granth* has to work and earn for himself and his family and is even in a position to give tithe (*daswandh*) for the good of others. Whereas, following the path of *Dharma*, he realises *Moksha* (final emancipation), he also makes appropriate use of *Artha* (material gains) and *Kāma* (worldly desires).

An Ideal Society: According to the *Adi Granth*, the responsibility of the society rests on the shoulders of the State. The king or the Chief of the State should be an ideal personality in whom all his subjects can repose confidence. He should be an humble servant of the poor. He should follow the democratic principles, without which his kingdom is sure to fall after some time. Woman is the most significant part of the society; she gives birth to the greatest individuals of society. She should receive the utmost reverence. She has an equal right to grow spiritually, equal right to attend religious congregations and recite divine hymns in the temples. As a daughter, sister, mother and wife, she should receive due respect.

Ceremonies: The Sikh Gurus have rejected the performance of all kinds of works, which result in ego and duality. For them all those actions are commendable which help us in the realisation of our ultimate objective i.e. the Union with the Lord. Guru Arjan Dev says, "All other works are useless except those about the Lord". There are no rituals and formal ceremonies which must be performed by the adherent of the *Adi Granth*. A Sikh is a saint and a saint has nothing else to do except to adore his Guru and follow his instructions. His primary function is the remembrance of the Name of the Lord. His Guru is *Guru Granth Sahib*, for whose instructions, he has to meet the holy congregation in the Gurdwara. He is also a householder. The male has to earn the bread for the family and the female has to look after the upkeep of the house and the welfare of the family. Thus a Sikh has to perform twin duties, the secular as well as divine. His secular duties also verge on the divine border because in every work, he has to seek the divine Grace. According to Guru Ram Das, whosoever calls himself a Sikh of the True Guru, gets up in the early hours of the morning and remembers the Name of the Lord. He takes a bath in the tank of nectar and under the instructions of the Guru recites the Name of Hari. In this way, he sheds off all his sins. He sings the *bānī* of the Guru and remembers the Name of the Lord, while sitting and standing. He works with his hands and feet and in his heart, he is attuned with the Lord.

God-Realisation: The *Adi Granth* considers God-realisation as the chief objective of human life. The human body is the only medium, through which the objective can be fulfilled. The qualities or virtues form the foundation on which the spiritual edifice can be raised. With these qualities, the self shines like a mirror, in which the Higher Soul manifests Itself. Selfless action, devotion and knowledge put us on the right pathway, because the Grace of the Lord begins at the very outset and the resultant is God-realisation. The Guru gives us knowledge; the Word given by him creates devotion and selfless action. By the Grace of the Lord, we meet the Guru and by the Grace of the Guru, we meet the Lord. The State of God-realisation is known as *Sahaj*. It is also known as *Chautha Pad* (the Fourth State) and *Param Pad* or the Supreme State. It is called the Fourth State because it is beyond the other three states of awakening (*Jāgrit*), dream (*Svapan*)and dreamless sleep (*Sushuptī*). It is also beyond the three qualities of *Rajas, Tamas* and *Sattva*, which are the constituents of *Maya*. There are some obstacles in the way of God-realisation and the remembrance of the Name of the Lord. These obstacles are idleness, worldly thoughts, sleep and the power to perform miracles. The Guru has cautioned the disciples about these ills. The Union of the soul and the Higher Soul is known as Yoga in Indian philosophy. The Yoga of the *Adi Granth* is called *Sahaj Yoga*, *Name-Yoga* or *Surt-Shabad Yoga*. The concept of *Nirvana* in Sikhism is different from that of other Indian religions. The Sikh has no desire to enter heaven. He even discards *Mukti* as defined in Shastras. He wants to remain always at the Feet of the Lord, filled with extreme devotion and love. God-realisation is the result of both effort and Grace. Guru Nanak Dev has mentioned five regions (*khands*) in the process of God-realisation. The first region is the region of *Dharma* (piety) and the fifth and the last is that of Truth. The maturity of pious actions leads the seeker to the second region called the region of knowledge (*Gyan*). In this region, he becomes aware of the vastness of the universe i.e. the infinite expanse of the creation. With the maturity of knowledge, the seeker enters the third region of Effort (*Saram*). In this region of beauty, his mind and intellect become superfine. This brings the seeker to the fourth region of Grace (*Karam*), where he attains the necessary spiritual strength to enter the fifth and the last region of TRUTH (*Sach*). In this region, the journey of the seeker comes to an end. He realises Truth i.e. GOD.

IX

In the preparation of this Encyclopaedia of the concepts of *Guru Granth Sahib* (the *Adi Granth*) various encyclopaedic works, Dictionaries and lexicons had to be consulted, besides other books of religion and philosophy, in English, Hindi and Punjabi. The literal import of the entries in English has been drawn from the two volume Shorter Oxford English Dictionary and that of the entries in Sanskrit from V.S. Apte's Sanskrit-English Dictionary. Appropriate quotations from the *Adi Granth* have been given in support of the interpretation of each entry. The translated version of each original quotation is mine. After each quotation, whereas the page number of the *Adi Granth* is given, the name of the Raga from which the quotation has been taken and also the number in the serial order of the Guru or the name of the saint-poet has been mentioned for the facility of the student or the researcher. The word *Mahlā* or "M" connotes the Guru, because the Gurus considered themselves as *Mahlās* or wives of the Lord. With M. (which stands for *Mahlā*), the number of the Guru in serial order has been given.

Though effort has been made to avoid repetition of quotations in the cross-entries, some repetition could not be avoided in the case of those quotations, which carry several ideas for various entries.

This dictionary is the first work of its own kind regarding the Sikh scripture. I am confident that it will be warmly received throughout the world. It will not only be useful to the Sikh intelligensia, but also to the students, scholars and researchers of comparative philosophy and religion.

My sincere thanks are due to the members of the Indian Council of Philosophical Research, New Delhi and its Director and Programme Officer for the financial help and the encouragement for the preparation of this work, to the authorities of the Panjab University and the librarian for allowing me the use of a carrel within the library, to my wife Dr. (Mrs.) Kulwant Kaur Kohli, for tracing and arranging the material in order and my son-in-law Dr. Inder Pal Singh, Registrar, E.N.T. Department, Wythenshawe Hospital, Manchester (U.K.) for getting the material typed and zeroxed.

1182, Sector 15–B,
Chandigarh – 160 015.

Surindar Singh Kohli

A

Abduction: The act of carrying off illegally or carrying another man's wife, child etc. There is no direct reference to abduction in the *Adi Granth*. Namdev (the Maharashtrian saint) while talking about adultery says that 'the blind one forsakes his own wife and transgresses with another woman' (Bhairo Namdev, p. 1165). In this case abduction is implied. The result of such an act, says Namdev, is 'the continuous burning of the sinner'. The *Adi Granth* decries violence and misappropriation. "Whatever belongs to the others is a cow for the Hindu and a hog for the Muslim: (Var Majh M.1, p. 141).

Abhai-Pad: State of Fearlessness; the Fourth or the Supreme State. This State has also been called *Turīā avasthā* or *Jīvan-Pad* (Jīvan-Padvī), the State of Real Life. In this State, because of the realisation of his Almighty Lord, the devotee becomes Fearless and is always absorbed in singing the Praises of the Lord (Maru M.5, p. 1000). When he realises this State of Fearlessness, all the three types of suffering (*Ādhi*, sufferings caused by mind, *Biādhi*, sufferings of the body, and *Upādhi*, sufferings caused by illusion) vanish away (Kedara Kabir, p. 1123). See: *Supreme State*.

Abhedatā: Spiritual unity. In order to convey the unity of the soul and the Over-soul, the instances of drop and ocean, ray and sun have been repeated several times (Bilawal M.5, p. 846). Ravidas addresses the Lord in the following manner: "What difference is there between Thee and me? It is like the golden bangle and the gold or like the wave and the ocean" (Sri Rag Ravidas, p. 93).

Abhiāgat: A beggar, who comes to beg at the door; a *Darvesh*. According to the *Adi Granth*, one cannot be called an *abhiāgat*, whose mind is without faith. The charity (alms) given to him are of no avail. The *abhiāgat* who seriously begs for God-realisation and Supreme State and also the person, who serves such a food, are very rare. One cannot be called an *abhiāgat*, who begs for food at the doors of others and adopts several guises for the sake of his belly. He is, indeed, an *abhiāgat*, who travels inwards into the soul and abides in his own home after realising the Lord. (Var Ramkali M.3, p. 949). See: *Darvesh*.

Abhimān: Pride; ego. See: *Aham, Ahamkāra*.

Ablutions: Ablutions in different forms are prevalent in several religions. The Muslim is required to wash his face and hands upto the elbows, wipe his head and his feet upto the ankles before prayer. This practice is known as *wuzū*, which is mentioned by Sheikh Farid in his Shlokas (p. 1381). In Hinduism, at the time of initiation, a Brahmin is required to sip water thrice, next wipe his mouth twice and lastly touch with water the centre of the head (Laws of Manu). The *Adi Granth* has no belief in such practices. Guru Nanak Dev says that the sacred rinsing consists in knowledge for the wise, self-control for a Yogi, contentment for a Brahmin, charity for a householder, justice for a king and concentration on Truth for the educated. (Var Sarang M. 4, Shalok M.1, p. 1240).

Abortion: There is no direct reference to abortion in the *Adi Granth*. There is, in abortion, a wilful destruction of the embryo, amounting to killing a developing *jīva*, which is considered a sin and a crime. The *Adi Granth* lays emphasis on mercy towards *jīvas* (Var Asa M.1, p. 468). Hence rejection of abortion is implied.

Abuse: Sweetness of tongue is considered a prominent virtue in Sikh Ethics. A wound inflicted by tongue is deeper than that of the sword. Guru Nanak Dev says, "Do not use abusive language, because that will create strife" (Vadhans M.1, p. 566). The defamers, informers, scandal-mongers and back-biters use abusive language. They ought to be punished. The Guru says, "The insipid words make the mind and body insipid, one who uses insipid words is punished in the Court of the Lord" (Var Asa M.1, p. 473).

Ācār: Conduct; practice; character; way of living. According to Guru Nanak Dev everything else is below Truth, but the truthful conduct (ācār) is above it (Sri Rag M.1, p. 62). Guru Arjan Dev recommends this conduct (ācār) for a devotee: Become a humble servant of the saints and see the Presence of the Lord everywhere. Give the fast colouring of the Name of the Lord to the beautiful mind and forsake all worldly wisdom (Asa M.5, p. 400).

Accident: An accident is an unforeseen contingency, which occurs by the Will of Providence. We may be thinking of going towards the west, but the hidden powers lead us towards the east (Gujri M.5, p. 469). Things occur unexpectedly. The crane may be sporting on the bank of a stream, but the falcon may dart unexpectedly from the blue and pounce upon it (Shlok Farid, p. 1383). The river takes its course by the Will of Providence (Shlok Farid, p. 1382).

Action: Every living being acts for the fulfilment of its requirements, in relation to time and space. The human being, being rational, makes use of his thinking faculty. He distinguishes between good and bad actions. The body is the field of actions. According to Indian philosophy, whatever one sows in the field, reaps the fruit accordingly (Sri Rag M. 5, p. 78). The actions of a person will stand witness in the Court of the Lord (Shlok Farid, p. 1383). Actions done in complete secrecy are known in all the four directions. One who practises virtues will be called virtuous and the sinful person will be known as sinner (Var Majh M.1, Shlok M. 2, p. 138).

Ādambar: Material effects; material decoration; material expanse. All the material expanse is false and short-lived (Var Asa M. 1, p. 468). The devotee experiences great bliss, when he comes to know of the arrival of the Lord and the bed is bedecked in preparation (Ādambar baniā)—(Asa M. 5, p. 459).

Adharma: This word is antonym of *Dharma*. According to Jainism, the characteristic of *Dharma* is motion, that of *Adharma* immobility. Moreover, *Dharma* and *Adharma* are substances alongwith space, time, matter and soul (*Uttaradhyayana*, Lecture XXVIII). The images of *Dharma* and *Adharma* are painted white and black respectively. In Nyaya, *Dharma* and *Adharma* are two of the twenty-four qualities. They pertain only to the soul. They are the peculiar causes of pleasure and pain respectively. They are imperceptible, but are inferred from reasoning and from transmigration. (Sanskrit-English Dictionary by V.S. Apte). *Dharma* means righteouness and *Adharma* unrighteousness. The *Adi Granth* lays stress on the ethical aspect of *Dharma* and *Adharma*. *Dharma* is godly and *Adharma* is ungodly; *Dharma* is virtuous and *Adharma* is sinful. The Guru says, "There is none so great as Hari, Who Contemplates only on *Dharma*. Why should one be fearful, when *Adharma* cannot strike? The True Lord administers True Justice and the sinner only suffers defeat" (Var Sri Rag M. 4, p. 90).

Adhibhuta: This word does not occur in the *Adi Granth*. According to Bhagavad Gita, it signifies all perishable things. The Supreme Spirit pervades in all matter, which is perishable. Thus the supreme Being in relation to matter is called *Adhibhuta*. He pervades all the elements (Gauri M. 5, p. 294).

Adhidaiva: This word does not occur in the *Adi Granth*. It signifies the Supreme Being in relation to the gods. The *Adi Granth* has no belief in gods. Countless Brahmas and Vishnus have been created by the Supreme Being (Swayyas M. 4, p. 1403).

Adhikārī: The deserving. In the *Adi Granth*, they are called truly deserving, whom the Lord Himself has given the opportunity to meet the True Guru and receive the Name of the Lord. Guru Amar Das says, "The people carry the load of vices and do not trade in virtues. The customer of virtues is very rare" (Var Maru M. 3, p. 1092). According to Guru Nanak Dev, if virtue is sold without a proper customer, it does not bring full value and when the proper customer comes in, real value is obtained. (Var Maru M.3, Shalok M. 1, p. 1086-87).

Adhyatma: This word signifies the manifestation of Supreme Being as individual self. The actions performed for the realisation of the self are known as *Adhyatma Karmas*. The *Adi Granth* lays great emphasis on such actions. The Guru says, "He whosoever performs *Adhyatma Karmas* day and night, (he) realises within his self the Pure Effulgence (Maru M. 1, p.1039). It is further said, "That person is truthful, who performs *Adhyatma Karmas*" (Gauri M. 1, p. 223).

Ādmī: (man, men). Ordinarily, the Persian word *Ādmī* means 'a man', but according to Guru Nanak Dev, *Ādmī* is *ik-damī* (of one breath), who is always uncertain about his next breath and is unaware about the time of his death (Dhanasari M. 1, p. 660).

Adoption: To take up from another and use as one's own. The adoption in Indian literature usually refers to the adoption of a son. The birth of a son in a Hindu family was considered most auspicious. If one did not have a son, he was considered excluded from happiness after death. Therefore the practice of adoption began in Hindu families. To be called "sonless" was considered an abuse. The use of the word "Nipoot" in the *Adi Granth* on page 856 may be noted. There has also been a practice of the adoption of successors or disciples by saints. A disciple of Gorakh Nath named Lohreepa has been called as *Gorakh-poot* i.e. the son of Gorakh (p. 939). Guru Angad Dev, the second Sikh Guru was adopted as successor by Guru Nanak Dev. Similarly Guru Amar Das and Guru Ram Das were adopted successors (See 'Var of Satta and Balwand' in Ramkali Raga on pages 966-68).

Adrishta: The Invisible Lord. It is a Qualifying Name of the Supreme Being, Who cannot be seen with physical eyes. It is said about Him that He is without any form, sign or colour (Sorath M. 1, p. 597).

Adultery: It is considered one of the principal sins in Sikhism. One should not see the beauty of another's wife with lustful eyes (Gauri M. 5, p. 274). For a moment's enjoyment one suffers for a million days. After appeasing his lust one repents again and again (Asa M. 5, p.

403). Adultery leads towards hell and many births (Sahaskriti Shlokas M. 5, p. 1358). The sinner keeps the lustful desire in his heart. He is unable to control his mind. Even the Yogis, *Jangams* and *Sannyasis* cannot escape this noose (Basant M. 9, p. 1186). After leaving his own wife and becoming a Yogi, one indulges in lust and makes love with another's wife. (Maru M. 1, p. 1013). Enjoying another's wealth, love of another's wife and back-biting is like eating poison; the enjoyment ends in grief (Malar M.1, p. 1255).

Advaita: Monism; non-duality. This doctrine of Vedanta asserts that Brahman is the only Reality, which is identified with *Atman*. According to it, the world is unreal. (*Brahm Satyam Jagan Mithyā Jivo Brahmaiva na Parā*). Whereas the *Adi Granth* accepts the Reality and All-Pervasiveness of Brahman, it does not agree with the idea of Unreality and illusory nature of the world. Guru Nanak Dev says, "The regions, the universes, the worlds, the forms are all real (Var Asa M. 1, p. 463). The Guru also says, "He (God) Himself is the Tablet, Himself the Pen and Himself the Writing. There is only One; why a second?" (Malar M. 1, p. 1291). Guru Arjan Dev says, "Whatever we see is Brahm, whatever we hear is Brahm (Brahman)" (Bilawal M. 5, p. 846). Vedantic monism, as advocated by Shankaracharya, lays emphasis on "Aham Brahm Asmi" (I am Brahman) and "Tat Tvam Asi" (Thou Art That), but the Guru's monism asserts "I have nothing which is mine, everything is Yours" (Shlok Kabir, p. 1375).

Āgama: Two words *Āgama* and *Nigama* are found together in the *Adi Granth*. *Āgama* means the tradition and is used for the non-Vedic Hindu texts. *Nigama* is used for pure Vedic texts. The term *Āgama* is applied to the religious works of Hindu sects. The Shakta Agamas numbering 77 are also known as Tantras. Shaivism has 28 Agamas and 108 minor Agamas known as Up-Agamas. Guru Amar Das says, "I have known the essence of *Āgama* and *Nigama* by the Grace of True Guru" (Maru M. 3, p. 1016). The Vaishnavas call their Agamas as *Panchratras*. The heterodox faiths i.e. Buddhism and Jainism have their own Agamas.

Age: A naturally distinct period or stage of life. The period of human life is divided into three stages viz. childhood, youth and old age. At ten one is in childhood, he attains youth at twenty; at thirty he is beautiful and at forty he is mature and at fifty he shows signs of weariness. The old age comes at sixty; at seventy one loses intellect, at eighty he loses strength and at ninety he is bed-ridden (Var Majh M. 1, p. 138).

The ninth Guru has clearly stated: Childhood, youth and old age are the three stages of life. All are futile, if not devoted to Hari (Shlok M. 9, p. 1428). Guru Arjan Dev says, "Remember, O human being, the Qualities of All-Pervading One, Who has brought you to the present state from the initial stage, Who has Created and Beautified you, Who has saved you from the fire of the womb, Who makes you love milk in your childhood, Who makes you enjoy pleasures and comforts in youth, Who gives you relatives to look after you in old age and serve you with food (Gauri M. 5, pp. 266-67).

Ages of the World: According to Puranas, the ages of the world have been divided into *Yugas, Mahayugas* and *Manvantaras*. A *Mahayuga* is composed of four *Yugas* and each *Manvantara* is composed of seventy-one *Mahayugas*. Four *Yugas* i.e. *Krta* (golden age), *Treta* (silver age), *Dvapara* (copper age) and *Kali* (iron age) have been mentioned in the *Adi Granth*. According to Guru Nanak Dev, the bead of the body with its chariot and charioteer changes in every *Yuga*; only the wise know it. In *Krta Yuga* (Satya Yuga), the chariot is of contentment and the charioteer of righteousness. In *Treta Yuga*, the chariot is of celibacy and charioteer of power. In *Dvapara*, the chariot is of austerity and charioteer of charity. In *Kali Yuga* the chariot is of fire and charioteer of falsehood (Var Asa M. 1, p. 470). In *Satya Yuga*, there were truth and contentment in human beings... everybody spoke truth. In *Treta Yuga* Dharma (the bull) lost one of its feet and duality took its place.... In *Dvapara Yuga* half of *Daya* (mercy) was left behind and another foot of Dharma was lost.... In *Kali Yuga* Dharma stands on one foot only (Manu). Satya Yuga, Treta and Dvapara are said to be of higher status, but Kali Yuga may be considered as the best of all the Yugas, because in this Yuga one is responsible only for his own actions. None suffers because of the actions of others (Asa M. 5, p. 406). The resultant of the experiences of the past four Yugas is one treasure for human beings. Celibacy, continence, pilgrimage were practised in earlier Yugas, but in Kali Yuga, the praiseworthy is only the Name of the Lord. Every Yuga has its own peculiar Dharma, you may search for it in the Vedas and Puranas (Bilawal M. 3, p. 797).

Agiān, Agiāntā: Ignorance; nescience. The Guru gives the antimony of knowledge in order to destroy the darkness of ignorance (Gauri Sukhmani M. 5, p. 293). See: *Avidyā*.

Agni: The god of fire. In the *Adi Granth*, Agni has also been named as *Baisantar Devata*. He contributes his share in the preparation of Pure

Food (Var Asa M. 1, p. 473). The god Agni is the personification of one of the five elements i.e. fire. In the evolutionary process of the world, fire takes its birth from air and its further evolute is water (Sri Rag M.1, p.19). The fire lies hidden in the wood. It is not satiated with any quantity of fuel. Philosophically, there are two fires, through which the human being has to pass; the first is the fire of mother's womb and the second is the fire of *maya* (Ramkali M. 3, Anand, p. 921). The *Adi Granth* has no belief in any god.

Agnosticism: According to this doctrine, the existence of anything beyond phenomena and/ or noumena is not and cannot be known. But the *Adi Granth* refutes this concept by saying that 'many struggle hard to find the limits of Brahman, but none can do so. Nobody knows this limit; the more we say, the more it expands (Japuji, p. 5). The *Adi Granth* believes in the concept of "Neti, Neti". The Creation of Infinite Lord cannot be finite (Japuji, p. 7).

Agriculture: Being an agricultural state, the poetry of the Punjab is full of images drawn from the occupation of agriculture. In the *Adi Granth*, the whole process of tilling, sowing, watering, harvesting etc. has been mentioned metaphorically. Just as the peasant sows the seed in his field and mows the harvest and does not leave any plant whether ripe or raw, similarly the death takes away everybody who is born (Asa M. 5, p. 375). Our body is a field of action (Sri Rag M. 5, p. 78). Whosoever's mind is the farmer, practical life his profession, effort, the water, body, the field, Name of the Lord, the seed, contentment, the leveller, modesty the hedge—the seed will sprout forth and grow, consider his house as fortunate (Sorath M. 1, p. 595). Someone cultivates, someone shears the crop, someone separates the grain from the chaff. But none can say who will consume the corn ultimately (Var Bilawal M. 4, Shlok M. 1, p. 854).

Aham, Ahamkāra: It is one of the five principal vices. The other four are lust, anger, greed and attachment. It is also called *Haumai* (I-ness). That person is considered a hero, who kills the tyrant named *Ahamkāra* (Var Sri Rag M. 3, p. 86). Anyone who indulges abundantly in ego (*Ahamkāra*) is reduced to dust in no time (Gauri M. 5, p. 268). The Vedas declare that God does not like ego (Var Maru M. 3, p. 1089). Therefore the Name of the Lord and the ego cannot reside at the same place (Vadhans M. 3, p. 560). *Haumai* (ego) is a destructive disease, but there is a remedy within it. The Word of the Guru can be practised by the Grace of the Lord (Var Asa M.1, p. 466). The king who is haughty about his status will fall into hell and become a dog. Whosoever is haughty about his youth, becomes worm in the faeces. Whosoever is haughty about the works performed by him, will undergo transmigration in various forms. Whosoever shows pride about his wealth and property, he is a fool and blind in ignorance (Gauri Sukhmani M. 5, p. 278). According to Samkhya, *Ahamkāra* is an evolute from *Mahat* (intellect), a principle resulting from the combination of *Purusha* and *Prakriti*. Five sense-organs, five organs of action, five *Tanmatras*, five *Mahabhutas* and the mind—all proceed from *Ahamkāra*. Therefore the creation may be said to have been caused by ego (*Ahamkāra*)—(Ramkali M.1, p. 946). About *Haumai* Guru Nanak Dev says, "One comes and goes in ego. One takes birth and dies in ego. One gives and takes in ego. One earns and loses in ego. One is truthful and false in ego. One is virtuous and sinful in ego. One rises to heaven and falls in hell in ego. One laughs and weeps in ego. One is emaciated and washed in ego. One loses his real self in ego. One is foolish and wise in ego and is not aware of *Moksha*. One is overpowered by *Maya* and illusion in ego. The creatures take birth in ego. If one understands the ego, he can realise the abode of the Lord. Without knowledge one wastes his life in fruitless discussion" (Var Asa M. 1, p. 466).

Ahimsā: Non-violence. In Indian thought, there is great emphasis on *Ahimsā*. The Buddhists declared: "*Ahimsā Parmo Dharma*" i.e. non-injury to living beings is the great path of righteousness. Non-injury contemplated here is not only by action, but also in thought and speech. *Ahimsā* implies mercy, which is considered a basic quality for the upkeep of Dharma (righteousness). He who does not injure anybody is received respectfully in the abode of the Lord (Var Gauri M. 5, p. 322). One should be merciful towards all the *jivas* from his heart of hearts (Ramkali M.1, p. 940). He who has faith in the Lord, he will do away with ego and forget violence and greed (Sarang M.1, p.1198).

Air: One of the five elements (*Mahābhūtas*). It is an evolute from *Ākāsha* (ether) and the fire is evolved from it (Sri Rag M.1, p. 19). The air which works in our body is known as *Prāna* (vital air). Without this air the body cannot function (Sri Rag M.1, p. 63). Since the air produces *Shabda*, it is called Guru (preceptor)—(Japuji, p. 8).

Ajapā Jāp: The effortless remembrance of the Name of the Lord. In the more mature stages, when the devotee can think of nothing else except the Name of the Lord, the Name is uttered through every pore of the body (Ramkali M.1, Siddh Goshta, p. 941). This advanced stage of the remembrance of the Name is known as *Ajāpa Jāp* i.e. the spontaneous remembrance.

Ajūnī: This word occurs in the *Mūl Mantra*, which portrays the Nature of Brahman. It means "Unborn" i.e. the Lord does not come in the womb. This implies that He is without father and mother. His other name is *Saibhang* (Swayyam-Bhū), which means that He is Self-Existent. He never incarnates.

Akāl: The Immortal and Non-Temporal Lord. This word occurs in *Mūl Mantra*. Brahman is Timeless Being. Time or *Kāl* has no influence on Him, therefore He is always the same (*Ik-ras*; *Ik-ves*). He is ever New and Fresh (*Nit Nawān*; *Navtan*).

Akāl Mūrat: Brahman; An entity on Whom Time and Death have no influence. All other gods and goddesses are prone to death. These two words occur together in the *Mūl Mantra*.

Akāl Purkh: A Purusha whom death cannot assail. This is an attribute of Brahman. All other Purushas (souls) are subject to birth and death. (Maru M.1, p. 1038).

Ākāsh: Sky; firmament; ether. According to the *Adi Granth*, there are lakhs of skies and nether-regions (Japuji, p. 5). *Ākāsh* is also one of the *Mahabhutas*, the other four being air, fire, water and earth. See: *Creation*.

Akirtghantā: Ungratefulness. The ungrateful *Jiva* forgets the Lord and undergoes transmigration (Var Jaitsri M. 5, p. 706). None can save the ungrateful person, who falls in a deep hell (Maru M. 5, p. 1086).

Akkhar: See: *Akshara*.

Akshara: This word has two meanings viz. 1-a syllable or a letter and 2-That which does not dissolve i.e. imperishable. OM (AUM) is considered the primal letter. This letter is the essence of three worlds (Ramkali M. 1, p. 930). *Akshara* is Imperishable (*Akheo*) God Himself (Var Majh M. 1, p. 150). Whatever is visible, is *Akshara* (Brahman)—(Gauri M. 1, p. 261). In *Japuji*, Guru Nanak Dev has said, "The Name is made up of *Aksharas*. Through *Aksharas* we sing praises and procure knowledge. With *Aksharas*, the verses are written and recited. The Writ on the head is composed of *Aksharas* (Japuji, p. 4).

Ālas: Idleness. One remains idle in the performance of good acts, but remains excited in vices (Var Gujri M. 5, p. 518). The self-willed person (*Manmukh*) is laid down with idleness, thereby suffering alone (Maru M. 1, p. 1011). According to the *Adi Granth*, he who remembers the Name of the Lord in the company of the saints, his malady of idleness is destroyed (Majh M. 5, p. 108). The man of God requests Him to remove the state of idleness, which puts obstacles in spiritual advancement (Asa M. 5, p. 460).

Allah: Arabic Name of God. It is considered the essential Name, while *Rabb* is considered an attribute of Supreme Being. Both the words *Allah* and *Rabb* have been used in the *Adi Granth*. In the *Quran*, the unity and greatness of Allah have been expressed. According to Islam, there are ninety-nine Names of God, which are based upon His Attributes. In the *Kalimah* (creed) it is said, "There is no deity but *Allah*", which expresses the Unity of the Supreme Being. Sheikh Farid, the Sufi saint, whose verses have been included in the *Adi Granth*, says, "Whatever *Allah* desires, is Good (p. 1383). Kabir says, "*Allah* is Unknowable" (p. 1350). "If *Allah* lives in a mosque, then who sustains all the other country?" (Prabhati Kabir, p. 1349). Guru Arjan Dev says, "*Allah*, Who resides in the heart and *prāna* of a *jīva*, should not be forgotten" (Bhairo M. 5, p. 1138).

Allegory: The poetry of the *Adi Granth* gives an allegorical description of the subtle spiritual domain. An individual is a journey-man. His destination is *Begam Purā* (the city of Bliss) or *Sac Khand* (the region of Truth) or *Amarā Purī* (the eternal habitation). The path leading to this city/region/habitation is hazardous. The traveller, who is blind, carries a big burden of sins and he has to cross desolate and thorny hills and dales (Suhi M.1, p. 729). The human body is a golden citadel, in which there is the nectar of Hari (Asa M. 4, p. 449).

Alms: The practice of begging alms is decried in the *Adi Granth*. Begging of the Praises of the Lord from the Guru is the real begging (Maru M. 5, p. 1018). If a person called Guru or *Pīr* goes abegging, no one should bow before him (Var Sarang M. 4, Shlok M. 1, p. 1245). It implies rejection of begging alms by *Sannyasis, Bhikshus, Sramanas, Darveshes* etc.

Altar: There had been practice of offering sacrifices to gods or burning incense for them. For this purpose an elevated place specially prepared for the sacrifice was used. Sikhism rejects the offering of sacrifices. The sacrifice that God requires us to perform is to be always ready for death and to become the dust of the feet of all others (Var Maru M. 5, p. 1102). If there is a talk about the Lord, what should be offered to Him? Our head be severed and given to Him as a seat (Vadhans M.1, p. 558). The Lord wants from us the sacrifice of our head, if we want to play the game of love (Shlok Varan te Vadhik M. 1, p. 1412).

Amal: Action. See: *Karma*.

Amarā Purī: The eternal habitation. The Pauranic concept about the eternal habitation is that of *Amarāvatī*, the capital of Indra on Mount Meru. The *Adi Granth* does not believe in the gods and their eternality. Only Brahman is Eternal; therefore His Abode is Eternal. This Abode has been called *Begam Purā* or the City of Bliss. Whosoever is blessed by the Lord will reside in *Amarā Purī* (Swayyas M. 4, p. 1398). Allegorically, *Amarā Purī* is *Sādh Sangat*, the company of the saints.

Amar Pad: The Immortal State or the Supreme State. He who is absorbed in the True Word and practises Truth; he who sings the Praises of the Lord, he abides in his own real home and attains the Immortal State. Then he is received reverently at the Gate of the True Lord. (Prabhati M.1, p.1342).

Ambrosia, Amrit: Nectar of Immortality. The Indian mystic tradition locates *Amrit* (Ambrosia) within the human body. The Yogis, who visualise the macrocosm, locate it in the *moon*, from where it trickles down through the channel called *Shankhanī* and passes out through the *tenth door* (*Dasam Dvār*). If the Yogi is unable to preserve it, it is dried up by the heat of the Sun. Though the yogic terminology has been used sometimes in the *Adi Granth*, the Sikh Gurus have their own concept of *Amrit*. According to them, the Name of the Lord is the real ambrosia. Guru Nanak Dev says, "The ambrosia for which you have come into this world, can only be obtained from the Guru. The ambrosia for which you wander in the world and undergo great troubles, in fact, lies within the body (Sorath M. 1, p. 598). The Guru has described the method of attainment of this *Amrit* in the following metaphorical way: "In the workshop of self-restraint, poise is the goldsmith, the intellect is the anvil and knowledge is the hammer; Fear of the Lord fans the fire of continuous effort, the vessel is of devotion, wherein melts the *Amrit*" (Japuji, p. 8). The initiation ceremony in Sikhism is known as *Amrit Chaknā* (the drinking of the nectar of immortality). By this ceremony, a Sikh becomes a *Singh* (lion) or the *Khalsa* (the Pure). The Name of the Omnipotent is instilled in the sweetened water, which turns it into *Amrit*, which gives both *Bhaktī* (devotion) and *Shaktī* (bravery) to the disciple.

Amrit: Nectar; ambrosia. See: *Ambrosia*.

Amrit Velā: The time when one gets intuned with the Lord, Who is the Fount of Ambrosia. The early hours of the morning are known as

Amrit Vela, which are considered most appropriate for concentration and meditation. Guru Nanak Dev says, "One should absorb himself in the True Name of the Lord in the early hours of the morning (*Amrit Velā*)" (Japuji, p.1). Sheikh Farid says, "If you do not awake in the later part of the night, consider yourself dead while living. If you have forgotten the Lord, the Lord has not forgotten you" (Shlok Farid, p. 1383).

Amulets: In order to ward off evils, mischief, diseases, witchcraft etc. a charm or a preservative is worn in order to ensure that no trouble would come to the wearer. Usually a *mantra* is worn by a Hindu and a *Tavīz* by a Muslim. The container is generally a very small metallic box, which is worn around the neck. The *Adi Granth* is against all types of formalism and symbolism, therefore the practice of wearing amulets is rejected. "The *mantra* of the Name of the Lord is the amulet of the disciple, which is his protecting armour" (Gaund M. 5, p. 868).

Amusements: An amusement is a pastime, play, game etc. It is a diversion to gain or waste time. The *Adi Granth* lays emphasis on the most advantageous use of time, therefore all diversions from the real objective of life are unnecessary and futile. There is no real comfort in seeing multi-faceted *maya* in diverse forms, in reading worldly wisdom in books and in becoming a chieftain or a king. There is no real comfort in riding on swift-footed horses and on elephants, lying in fragranted bed with beautiful wife, in enjoying song and drama. There is no real comfort in sitting on throne and soft cushions with courtiers, in eating all types of fruits, in strolling in beautiful gardens, in hunting and sporting in royal fashion. The mind is not comforted by such amusements (Gauri M. 5, p. 179). There is no comfort in earning more wealth, in seeing dance and drama, in going through many countries—all comforts lie in singing the Praises of Hari (Bhairo M. 5, p. 1147).

Anāhad: Limitless. This word comes together with *Shabda,* which conveys the continuous resounding of the celestial music, which the devotee hears at the time of God-realisation. See: *Anhad.*

Anāhat: Unassailable. This word comes together with *Shabda,* which conveys the unending and unassailable sound of the Celestial Music heard in the Abode of the Lord. See: *Anhat.*

Ananda: Bliss. This is one of the three basic attributes of Brahman. Whereas Brahman is *Sat* (Truth) and *Cit* (Conscious), He is also *Ananda* (Bliss). He is also called *Parmananda* (Supreme Bliss). The highest spiritual state, when one attains Unity with the Lord, is also the state of bliss. This state is realised with the help of True Guru (Ramkali M. 3, Ananda, p. 917). The disciple has to follow a discipline on the physical and mental planes in order to rise higher on the spiritual plane.

Ananta: Without end or limits. In Hindu mythology, this is the Name of Vishnu, also of Shesha Naga, of Krishna and his brother Balarama and of Shiva. But in the *Adi Granth*, it is used for God-Infinite, Limitless and Endless. It also occurs as *Anat* in the *Adi Granth*. God is symbolised as an ocean with countless (Anat) waves (Gauri Sukhmani M. 5, p. 275).

Anātam: That which is not the soul; Non-self. This word denotes negation of *Ātmā* (soul), therefore it is used for matter or objects, which are unreal and transitory.

Ancestors, Ancestor-Worship: Forefathers; Manes; Pitr. Ancient Hindus believed that the ancestors were sanctified by certain rites. They were satisfied by the recitation of scriptures. They could be presented with food, drink, garments etc. They were to be worshipped with oblations and libations. Daily offerings were to be made to them. Procreation of sons was considered a debt to them. They were considered the deities at a *Sraddha* (the funeral oblation and meal). Guru Nanak Dev rejected the ancestor-worship. He said, "If a robber robs a house and offers his loot in order to propitiate the ancestors; the robbed article is recognised in the other world and the manes are charged with theft. The hands of the mediator (i.e. Brahmin) are cut down—this is the Lord's Justice. Only that is received by one in the other world, which he earns honestly and gives in charity" (Var Asa M.1, p. 472). The Guru believed that only one's own actions were rewarded in the other world. The offerings to the manes do not reach them. Kabir was very emphatic on this point. "Nobody cares for the fathers, when they are alive. The offerings are made to them when they die. Even these offerings are not received by the manes, because they are eaten away by the crows and the dogs..." (Gauri Bairagan Kabir, p. 332).

Ancient One: In the *Adi Granth*, the *Ancient One*, the First One (Ādi), the First One in the cycle of *Yugas* (Ages) (Jugādi) is God Himself.

Andesā:Fear. See: *Fear*.

Andhā: Blind; Ignorant. Guru Amar Das says, "The ignorant people, who are blind, do not remember the Name of the Lord, and are absorbed in other works. They are punished in the abode of *Yama*." (Var Sorath M. 4, Shlok M. 3, p. 648). He may be called blind who performs vicious acts and whose mind has no eyes. (Var Malar M.1, p.1289). When the blind becomes a leader, he misdirects all his followers (Var Majh M.1, p.140). Those whose Guru is blind, the disciples also perform futile actions. They are self-willed and liers... (Var Ramkali M. 3, p. 951).

Angels: The Arabic equivalent for angel is *Malak*, whose plural is *malaik*. The Persian equivalent is *Farishtā*. In the six articles of Muslim faith, belief in angels is next to belief in God. There are four archangels namely *Gabrāil*, the angel of revelations, *Mikāil*, the patron of the Israelities, *Izrāil*, the angel of death and Isrāfīl, the angel, who will sound the trumpet at the last day. Two angels are said to record the good and evil actions. They are *Munkar* and *Nakīr*, who examine all the dead in their graves. Eight angles support the throne of God and nineteen are in charge of hell. The *Adi Granth* does not believe in angels. The words *Malak* or *Malak-ul-Maut* have been used for the god of death, who has also been called, following the folk-tradition, *Azrāil Firishtah*.

Anger: It is one of the five major vices, the other four being, lust, greed, attachment and ego. Anger and lust are the cause of the gradual destruction of the body (Ramkali M. 1, p. 932) and the wealth of virtues (Asa M. 1, p. 352). Guru Arjan Dev has addressed this vice in the following manner: "O Anger, the source of all quarrels, you do not take pity at all. You subdue your prey completely, who dances like a monkey (Sahaskriti Shlokas M. 5, p. 1358). This vice has been symbolised as a *Chandāl* (an outcast)—(Sri Rag M. 4, p. 40). The fool utters insipid words, which are the cause of fury, therefore such utterances should be avoided (Var Asa M. 1, p. 473). The anger can be overcome by sweet words and love.

Anhad, Anhad Nād, Anhad Shabda: Limitless Celestial Music. By remembering the Lord, the Limitless Music resounds (Gauri Sukhmani M. 5, p. 263). "Where the Divine Effulgence is visualised, the *Anhad Shabda* resounds there" (Sorath Namdev p. 657). "The mind was prevented from going out of the nine doors and it settled down within the tenth door in its own home, where the Anhad Shabda resounds throughout the day and night..." (Majh M. 3, p. 124).

Anhat: The Unassailable Celestial Music. The Perfect devotee following the discipline of the Guru, remembers the Name of the Lord. In his heart resounds the instrument of unassailable divine Music. (Gauri M.1, p. 228). Where there is the Light of the *Anhat* (Lord), all other lights appear dim. (Sorath Namdev, p. 657). In this quotation, there is mention of divine light instead of divine music.

Animals, Animal Sacrifices: According to the *Adi Granth*, God has Created the Universes of various types and kinds (Gauri Sukhmani M. 5, p. 275). There are traditionally four divisions of creation viz. *Jaruyuja* (viviporous), *Andaja* (oviporous), *Udbhijja* (germinating) and *Svedaja* (generated by heat and moisture). This is the division of organic production. *Udbhijja* is the vegetable creation. The first two divisions and the fourth division in various forms constitute the animal creation. Human being is a part of the first division, but he is considered the best of God's Creation. According to the law of Karma and transmigration, the human being, because of his actions, falls to the animal level and migrates to many forms. He may be born as a worm, a butterfly, an elephant, a fish, a deer, a bird, a crawling snake, a horse, a bull etc. (Gauri M. 5, p. 176). There are eighty-four lakhs of forms, some on land and some in water. There are worms in wood and stones. The strongest desire at the time of death gives a suitable animal body to the soul. One who thinks of sons at the time of death, is born as a pig. One who thinks of wealth, is born as a snake. One who thinks of a woman, is born as a prostitute (Gujri Trilochan, p. 526). At times, the saint-poets of the *Adi Granth*, have used the names of various four-legged animals and birds as symbols and metaphors. The swan is a symbol for a virtuous person and a crane for an evil one. The kings of the age have been depicted metaphorically as lions and their officials as dogs. When the human beings do not act as human beings, they are like animals. A person without devotion towards the Lord is like a dog or a swine (Shlok M. 9, p. 1428). Without love for the Lord, one becomes a four-legged, horned dumb bull (Gujri Kabir, p. 524). Without the remembrance of the Lord, one is like the worm of the faeces (Var Jaitsri M. 5, p. 707). An ant who remembers the Lord is better than a king with boundless riches (Japuji, p. 5). Similarly a sparrow is better than an elephant (Var Malar M.1, p. 1286). When a man dies, his body is of no use, but when an animal dies, his remains are useful in several ways (Gaund Kabir, p. 870). In Hinduism, there had been a tradition of animal sacrifices in order to propitiate gods, but the Sikh Gurus have decried such practices. Even a rhinoceros was killed as a sacrifice (Var Malar M.1, p. 1289). When we talk of mercy on *jivas*, then why should there be violence? How can a Brahmin remain pure, when he kills a he-goat? (Var Asa M. 1, p. 471).

Anna, Annahomas: It is written in Maitrayana Brahman/Upanishad: "From food (*Anna*) are born all creatures that live on earth; afterwards they live on food (*Anna*), and in the end (when they die) they return to it.... Let a man worship food (*Anna*) as his self". In the *Adi Granth*, *Anna* has been called a god (*Anna Devatā*) (Var Asa M.1, p. 473). Those who think that the cereal food causes an obstruction in spiritual advancement are mistaken. Those who abstain from such food, they lose all relish (Var Asa M. 1, p. 467) and cause anguish to their bodies (Ramkali M.1, p. 905 and Prabhati M. 5, p. 1348). A hymn of Kabir on this subject will be of great interest: "Praise be to the Lord and the Preceptor. Praise be to *Annadi* (*Annadi—Anna*—cereal food), which blossoms the lotus heart of the hungry. Praise be to those saints who know this and thus realise the Lord. The cereals were born out of the primal Purusha and through the relish of the cereals, the Name of the Lord is remembered. With the remembrance of the Name, the cereals may also be remembered, which when mixed with water give a fine taste. Those people who abstain from cereals lose their honour in the three worlds. Those who forsake cereals are practising heresy; they are neither good wives nor widows. Those who claim to live on only milk, in fact eat lot of food secretly. There can be no prosperity without cereals. None can meet the Lord by forsaking cereals. I have known it like this; Praise be to the *Anna*, which enables me to enjoy the blessings of the Lord" (Gaund Kabir, p. 873). *Anna-Homas* are food oblations. Since the Guru was against all rituals, the *Anna-Homas* (offering of grains) have no significance in Sikhism.

Annihilation: In Sikhism, the word 'annihilation' is used in respect of ego. The emphasis has been laid on the effacement of the lower-self i.e. ego.

Anras: Other pleasures; other enjoyments. All the sensuous pleasures are insipid and futile. Our body enjoys many pleasures: ornaments of gold and silver, beautiful wife, fragrances, vehicles, bedecked beds, sweets, meat etc., how can the Name of the Lord abide in this body? (Sri Rag M. 1, p. 15). Guru Ram Das says, "All the other pleasures which we have enjoyed, they are all insipid. When we tasted the ambrosia of the Name of the Lord on meeting the True Guru, it was sweet like the sugarcane juice" (Gauri M. , p. 169).

Antam-Saṁskāra: The funeral sacrament. In Hinduism, some ceremonies are performed on the death of a person. The *Adi Granth* rejects all the sacraments. See: *Sacraments*; *Sraddha*.

Antarjāmī: See: *Antaryamin*.

Antar-Khoj: According to the *Adi Granth*, there is everything within our home and nothing outside it. Through the Grace of the Guru, the inner door is opened and we realise the inner things (Asa M. 3, p. 425). That person may be considered a scholar and a wise Pundit, who gives thought to the Word of the Guru. After searching the interior of his self, he realises the essence and attains salvation (*Moksha*)—(Var Sorath M. 4, Shlok M. 3, p. 650).

Antaryāmin: The internal ruler; the internal check. This word is used for the Supreme Being, who guides and regulates mankind. He knows the internal feeling of an individual and guides him. "The Immortal Higher Brahman and Supreme Ishwara is *Antaryāmin*" (Maru M. 5, p. 1082).

Ants: The ant, though a small common insect and ordinarily considered very insignificant, can become a mighty force, if God Bestows power on it. It can destroy millions of troops (Gauri Sukhmani M. 5, p. 285). Guru Nanak Dev considered an ant better than a mighty and wealthy king, if it remembers the Name of the Lord (Japuji, p. 5). What can a created being do, if the Creator is the Protector? Even the ant can conquer the whole world (Ramkali M. 5, p. 888).

Anushāsan: Discipline; Advice; Instruction laying down rules or precepts. The *Adi Granth* presents a discipline for the perfection of an individual and creation of an ideal state and society. Therefore it lays down rules or precepts (*Anushāsan*) for a common man, so that he may rise higher on all the planes i.e. physical, mental and spiritual. The *Anushāsan* (discipline) for a saint is given in the following manner: "Listen, my brother, the discipline for a saint, the merits of which are indescribable. The Name of the Lord alone is his occupation. His rest is the enjoyment of the Praises of the Lord. The friend and the enemy are the same for him. He does not know any other besides the Lord. He absolves himself of millions of sins. He removes anguish and bestows life. He is heroic and true to his promises. He subdues the helpless *Lakshmi* (*maya*). Even the gods seek his company. His sight is efficacious and his service bears fruit. I pray with folded hands to the Treasure of Qualities to Bestow on me the service of the saints" (Asa M. 5, p. 392).

Aparsa: Without touch; Without impact. A Sadhu, who is beyond the touch/impact of *maya*. Ordinarily, that Sadhu is called *Aparsa*, who does not touch any metal etc., but Guru Arjan Dev calls only that

Sadhu *an Aparsa,* who sees the Lord everywhere and absorbs the Name of the Lord in his heart. Falsehood does not touch his tongue. He does not see the beauty of another's woman with his eyes, his ears do not listen to the calumny of others and considers himself the lowliest. With the Grace of the Guru, he conquers vices and has full control of his senses. (Gauri Sukhmani M. 5, p. 274).

Apas: Water. One of the five gross elements, the other four being Ether, Air, Fire and Earth. In the *Adi Granth Apas* is written as *Apu* (Maru M.1, p. 1031). See: *Water.*

Apostasy: It is the abandonment of one's religious faith or moral allegiance. In the *Adi Granth,* this term has been used for those persons, who have abandoned the Path of the True Guru. Such persons of ill-luck always remain in anguish and experience birth and death repeatedly. They do not have any comfort, even in their dream (Sri Rag M. 3, p. 30). Such apostates can have no peace like a deserted evil woman (Var Sorath M. 4, Shalok M. 3, p. 645).

Apostles: The prophets or messengers of God. The Arabic equivalents of this word are *Rasūl, Nabī* and *Hawārī.* The chief *Apostles* recognised by the holy Quran are Abraham, Ishmail, Isaac, Jacob, Moses and Jesus. Mohammad is called the *Rasūl* of God. The twelve witnesses who were sent by Jesus Christ to preach his gospel were known as *Hawārīs.* The Persian and Hindustani translation for *Rasūl* and *Nabī* is *Paighambar.* In the *Adi Granth,* this word occurs as *Paikāmar* (Sri Rag M. 1, p. 53), *Paikānbar* (Asa M. 1, p. 358), *Pikānbar* (Var Gujri M. 5, p. 518) and *Paikābar* (Var Maru M. 5, p. 1100). The Sikh Gurus have emphasised that the gods of Hindu Pantheon and also the holy men of Islam including *Pīrs*, Prophets, *Darveshes* and Saints sing the Praises of the same Lord (Var Gujri M. 5, p. 518). *Jagannātha* and *Gopāl* of Hindus is the same as *Maulā* (*Allah*) of *Pīrs, Paighambars* and *Sheikhs* (Ramkali M. 5, p. 897).

Apsarās: According to Hindu mythology, they are young and charming damsels of heaven, ruled by god Indra. They are of two kinds i.e. worldly and divine. The latter are said to interrupt the penances of holy sages. They are also known as the wives of *gandharvas*, the musicians of gods. They are said to be offered to valiant heroes fallen in the battlefield. It is said that whenever God Indra feared that a particular sage might occupy his seat because of his severe penances, he used to send these charming damsels to cause the fall of the sage. Guru Nanak Dev says, "Even if the charming women of heaven be found everywhere, the Love for the Lord be not diminished and He be Praised constantly" (Var Majh M. 1, p. 142). In his poem "Anand" Guru Amar Das has shown the families of fairies (*Parīs*) joining the Divine Music (Ramkali M. 3, p. 917). The Perisan word *Parī* seems to have been used for *Apsarā*.

Archangels: See: *Angels*.

Archdevils: Demons. In the *Adi Granth Kāma* (lust), *Karodh* (anger), *Lobh* (greed), *Moh* (attachment) and *Ahamkāra* (ego) have been shown as the chief demons enticing the *Jīva* away from God (Var Gujri M. 3, p. 513). See: *Demons*.

Archery: The practice of shooting with bow and arrow. There is the figurative use of the art of archery in the *Adi Granth*. Sheikh Farid says, "Let the bow be the forbearance and the bending of the bow be also of forbearance, then the arrow will not miss the target—such is the Will of the Lord" (Shlok Farid, p. 1384). Kabir says, "The Guru-warrior shot such an arrow as made me fall on the ground and the heart was pierced" (Shlok Kabir, p. 1374). Guru Ram Das says, "The arrow of Lord's Love has pierced my heart" (Gaund M. 4, p. 861).

Architecture: The art of constructing edifices for human use. In the verses of the *Adi Granth*, there is mention of several types of constructions: small huts, houses, palaces, resting places and temples. There is also mention of the upper storeys of houses. Namdev, the Maharashtrian saint giving an account of the carpenter, who constructed his house, says, "O Lady, listen to the qualities of the carpenter. He has, by his construction, kept the sea under control and fixed the Pole Star in the firmament." (Sorath Namdev, p. 657). According to Guru Ram Das, those temples, palaces, resting houses are all holy and auspicious, where the disciples get comfort (Var Sorath M. 4, p. 648). Guru Nanak Dev says, "Only the fools consider the pacca and beautiful buildings as their own (Var Majh M. 1, p. 141) because they will have to leave them on their death".

Ardās: Derivative from Persian word *Arz-Dāsht* meaning Prayer, or earnest entreaty. A prayer is a bridge connecting the devotee with the Lord. A prayer sincerely performed never goes waste (Asa M. 5, p. 819). Everybody begs benedictions from the Lord through prayers (Var Sri Rag M. 4, p. 81). See: *Prayers*.

Arrogance: Aggression; Conceit; Haughtiness. Arrogance is the cause of ruin. Anyone who indulges in arrogance is soon humbled by misfortunes (Gaund M. 5, p. 868). The Lord dislikes arrogance (Var Maru M. 3, p. 1089).

Artha: Wealth; Riches; Property. It is considered one of the four ends of human existence, the other three being *Dharma* (righteouness), *Kāma* (fulfilment of worldly desires) and *Moksha* (final liberation). By God's Grace *Dharma*, *Artha*, *Kāma* and *Moksha* are bestowed in no time (Bilawal M. 5, p. 816).

Ārtī: See: *Circumambulation.*

Artisan: A handicraftsman. Several types of crafts prevalent in the times of the Sikh Gurus and the saint-poets of the *Adi Granth* have been mentioned in their compositions. In *Japuji*, Guru Nanak Dev has figuratively described the workshop of a goldsmith. Other artisans who have been depicted are blacksmith, potter, weaver, cobbler, calico-printer and carpenter. Some of the saints were themselves artisans: Kabir was a weaver, Ravidas a cobbler and Namdev a calico-printer.

Arts: Several fine arts have been mentioned in the *Adi Granth* e.g. the art of writing poetry, the art of singing, the art of dancing and the art of painting. The poetry should depict the profound love for the Lord, which ought to be set to Music. One may dance with the tune of Divine Music. All other dancing and music are meaningless. Kabir says in great wonder: "Which painter has painted those stars in the firmament?" (Gauri Kabir, p. 329).

Āsā Mansā: *Āsā* means hope and *Mansā* means desire (*Trishnā*). The *Jiva* has been bound down by *Āsā Mansā*. Every one in the world lives with hopes and desires. Such a person is rare, who forsakes them (Var Ramkali M. 3, p. 956). One is born in the world of hope and desire and enjoys savoury foods. Because of his hopes, he is bound down and punished (Sri Rag M.1, p. 61). The whole world has been deluded by *Āsā Mansā* (Sri Rag M.1, p. 59). He who forsakes all *Āsā Mansā* and lives in the world sans hopes and desires, he who rises above lust and anger, the Lord abides in his heart (Sorath M.1, p. 633). The Word of the Guru (or the Name of the Lord) burns away *Āsā Mansā* (Asa M. 1, p. 413). There are many who are sleeping in hope; only that person awakes, whom the Lord wants (Asa M. 3, p. 423).

Āsan: The Yogic posture. It is one of the eight limbs of *Raja Yoga* as enunciated by the sage Patanjali in his *Yoga Sutra*. There are eighty-four different *Āsanas* (postures), which contribute to physical fitness, and considered a necessary base alongwith *Prānāyāma*, for the control of the mind. But the Sikh Gurus are averse to this type of Yoga. Guru Arjan Dev says, "I became tired of practising eighty-four *Āsanas*: Though I got a long lease of life, but I could not be united with Hari"

(Sorath M. 5, p. 642). Guru Amar Das says, "If one learns the *Āsanas* of Siddhas and tries to subdue his senses, still the dirt of ego is not cast off from his mind" (Vadhans M. 3, p. 558). See: *Yoga Sutra.*

Asapati: The Lord of the regions; The Lord of the horses. This is the name of Sun used by Namdev in one of his hymns. Alongwith *Asapati*, the *gajapati* (the Lord of the elephant i.e. Indra) has been used. Speaking about the Lord, Namdev says that the Master of Sun, Indra and Brahma is also his Lord and Redeemer (Tilang Namdev, p. 727).

Asceticism: The practice of rigorous self-discipline and austerities. A hermit who retires into solitude to exercise himself in meditation and prayer and practises rigorous self-discipline by celibacy, fasting etc. is called an ascetic. Such a discipline has been rejected by the *Adi Granth*, which expounds a religion of householders. The Sikh Gurus have emphasised the practice of such discipline as prepares one for God-realisation, while fulfilling all the worldly obligations. Guru Arjan Dev says, "He sits by the side of the fire of *dhūni* (smouldering ashes) and wears ochre-coloured clothes. Overburdened with sufferings, he runs away from his house. He leaves his own country and moves to a foreign land, but brings the five demons with him. He gets his ears pierced, begs for alms from various houses and is not satisfied. He leaves his wife and fixes his evil eye upon another woman. Nothing is gained except suffering by changing guises. He does not speak and has become a *Munī*, who practises silence. He undergoes births and deaths repeatedly because of his bad thoughts. He does not eat cereals and puts his body in agony. Because of his attachments, he does not understand the laws of God" (Prabhati M. 5, p. 1348).

Ashes: The powdery residue after the combustion of any substance. The remains of a human body after cremation are called ashes (Var Majh M.1, p. 138). According to Sunder, the grandson of Guru Amar Das, the Guru in his last instructions asked his family to consider the assemblage of holy congregation as the fulfilment of the final rites including the immersion of ashes (Ramkali *Sad* of Sunder, p. 923).

Ashramas: The four stages of life viz. 1-*Brahmacharya Ashrama,* i.e. the life of the student, 2-*Grahasthya Ashrama,* i.e. the life of a householder, 3-*Vanaprastha Ashrama,* i.e. the life of a hermit in the forest, and 4-*Sannyasa Ashrama,* i.e. the life of an ascetic. Hinduism is also called *Varnashrama Dharma,* because it believes in four major castes (*varnas*) and four stages of life (*ashramas*). Sikhism is a religion of the householders, therefore it has only one *ashrama* i.e. *Grahasthya.*

About the *varnas* and *ashramas* of Hinduism, Guru Ram Das has remarked that out of the four *varnas* and four *ashramas*, that person may be considered prominent, who remembers the Lord (Gaund M. 4, p. 861), otherwise the Sikh Gurus have rejected the division of *varnas* and *ashramas*. Guru Nanak Dev has given his own definition of a *Sannyasī*: "That person may be called a *Sannyasī*, who remembers the True Guru and destroys his ego, who rises above the hopes about the procurement of food and clothes and who accepts whatever is received by him without effort" (Maru M.1, p. 1013).

Ashvamedha: The horse-sacrifice. This sacrifice was of a politico-religious character. The claimant to the position of a supreme ruler used to send a selected horse all around. If the same was seized, there was a war. If it remained untouched, then the horse was sacrificed. The ruler who performed a hundred of such sacrifices raised himself to the level of Indra. The saint-poets of the *Adi Granth* rejected all types of sacrifices and rituals. Namdev said, "The horse-sacrifice, charity equal to the weight of the donor and taking a bath at Prayag—all these cannot equal the singing of the Praises of the Name of Hari" (Gaund Namdev, p. 873).

Assassins: Persons who undertake to put others to death by treacherous violence. "They move out during the night with nooses; God knows such beings" (Var Gauri M. 4, Pauri of the 5th Guru, p. 315). "The highwayman loots on the highway and the robber robs another's house and in this way the criminals satisfy their hunger" (Sarang Parmanand, p. 1253).

Assault: An unlawful attack; A violent hostile attack by physical means. "He has not foresaken violence from his mind and has not practised mercy" (Sarang Parmanand, p. 1253). The *Adi Granth* decries violence and assault.

Assembly of saints: Called *Sādh Sangat* or *Satsang* in the *Adi Granth*. According to the *Adi Granth*, this holy congregation only sings and repeats the Name and the Praises of the Lord. (Sri Rag M.1, p. 72). He who goes into this assembly, crosses the ocean of *Saṁsāra* (Jaitsri M. 5, p. 701). Guru Arjan Dev says, "Listen, O Friends, the Glory of the assembly of saints—all the dirt is washed away, the effect of millions of sins is removed and the *cit* (mind) becomes pure" (Bilawal M. 5, p. 809). In this assembly all the jealousies are forgotten and none remains an enemy (Kanra M. 5, p. 1299).

Asterism: A cluster of stars. Guru Nanak Dev has metaphorically depicted the *Tārikā Mandal* (the sphere of stars) as the gems in the salver of the sky (Dhanasari M.1, p. 663). Kabir asks in wonder: "Which painter has painted those stars in the sky?" (Gauri Kabir, p. 329). Guru Arjan Dev has talked about millions of suns, moons and stars. The same Lord is present everywhere (Gauri Sukhmani M. 5, p. 274 and p. 294). Hari is like a shooting star; how can we see Him? (Tukhari M. 1, p. 1110).

Astrologers: Those who judge the occult influences of the stars on human affairs. The Sikh Gurus have no faith in the foreboding of the astrologers. Guru Nanak Dev says, "O Pundit, do not tell lies, speak truth... you make calculations and prepare horoscopes. You read and make your customers listen, but you have not understood the reality. Above everything else is the concentration on the Word of the Guru. I do not talk about anything else, because the same is of no significance. (Ramkali M. 1, p. 904).

Astrology: The application of astronomy for prediction of events. The *Adi Granth* rejects the practice of astrology. Guru Nanak Dev says, "All calculations about stars and signs of Zodiac create doubts and apprehensions" (Ramkali M. 1, p. 904). The reading of the horoscope of the mind brings ease and tranquility (Var Maru M. 3, p. 1093).

Astronomy: The science which treats of the constitution and motion of the heavenly bodies, including the planets of our solar system. Guru Nanak Dev has referred to the motions of the sun and moon, which traverse millions of miles (Var Asa M. 1, p. 464). The sun is seen moving during the day and the moon during the night. Lakhs of stars move and vanish (Sri Rag M. 1, p. 64).

Asur, Asura: An evil spirit; a demon. In Rig Veda, this term is used for the Supreme Spirit and gods like Indra, Agni and Varuna and carried the sense of "divine", but afterwards, it acquired an entirely opposite meaning and signified an evil spirit. Other equivalent words used for *Asura* are *Daitya, Danava* and *Rakshasa*. The first three words occur in the *Adi Granth*. God has been described as the killer of demons (Maru M. 5, p. 1082). His Praises are sung by *Devas* (gods) and *Danavas* (demons) alike. The examples of mythological *Daityas* prominently given in the *Adi Granth* are of Ravana (Ramkali M. 1, p. 942), the king of Lankā and Hiranyakashipu, the father of Prahlad (Bhairo M. 3, p. 1133). According to the saint-poets of the *Adi Granth*, the lust, anger, greed, attachment and ego are the *Asuras* (demons). Those who kill these demons pass their lives comfortably (Sri Rag M. 3, p. 30).

Ātam-Cīnaṇā: Search of the self. See: *Ātman*.
Ātam-cintan: Self-study. See: *Ātman*.
Ātam-giān: Knowledge of the self (soul). See: *Ātman*.
Atharva Veda: The fourth Veda belonging to *Kali Yuga* (the Iron age), the other three Vedas being Rig Veda, Sām Veda and Yajur Veda. Guru Nanak Dev says, "The Veda of *Kali Yuga* was *Atharban* (Atharva) and the Name of God became *Allah*. The clothes of blue colour were worn and the way of life was that of Turks and Pathans" (Var Asa M. 1, p. 470). This Veda mostly contains incantations, which aim at long life, recovery from sickness, downfall of enemies, success in love etc. Whitney writes about this Veda in the following manner: "It seems in the main that the *Atharva* is of popular rather than of priestly origin; that in making the transition from the Vedic to modern times, it forms an intermediate step rather to the gross idolatries and superstitions of the ignorant mass, than to the sublimited pantheism of the Brahmanas". All the mantras and charms (of the Vedas) have been decried by the *Adi Granth*.
Atheism, Atheists: Atheism is the denial of the existence of God. Even the first Word in the *Adi Granth* is *Ik-Omkār*, which emphasises the existence of God, Who is the One and One Alone. The attitude of the *Adi Granth* is as follows: "Those who do not believe in God, they remain separated from Him for many births successively (Majh M. 5, p. 135).
Atithya: Guest. According to Guru Arjan Dev, the human being comes into this world as a guest for night's stay (Sri Rag M. 5, p. 50). Sheikh Farid considers the angel of death as a guest (Shalok Farid, p. 1381).
Ātmā, Ātman: The self; the soul. In Indian philosophy, *Atman* as higher self, is soul and as lower self, it is "I" or ego. In the *Adi Granth, Atman* as soul, is a part and parcel of Brahman (*Param-Atma*—Higher Soul). In metaphorical language, Atman is a ray and Brahman, the sun, Atman a drop and Brahman, the ocean (Bilawal M. 5, p. 846). The relation of Atman and Brahman has been expressed by Guru Arjan Dev in the following manner: "He (Brahman) does not die, I (Atman) have no fear. He does not perish; I have no worry. He is not poor; I am not hungry. He is without sorrow; I am without grief... He has no ties; I am not bound... He is not Impure and I am not tainted. He is Blissful. I am always ecstatic. He has no worry; I have no anxiety. He is Uninfluenced; I am without any effect. He is not hungry; I am not thirsty. He is Pure; I am deemed holy. On meeting the Guru,

the illusion has been removed. He and I have become one, imbued with the same hue" (Asa M. 5, p. 391). The following thoughts about the nature of Atman are found in the *Adi Granth*: "Neither it is human body nor a god, nor an ascetic practising restraint, nor a Shaivite; neither a Yogi nor an ascetic renouncing all worldly achievements. Neither it has a mother, nor it is a son. Who lives within this temple? Nobody knows its specifications. Neither a householder, nor a hermit, neither a king, nor a begger, neither it has a body nor blood, neither a Brahmin, nor a Kshatriya, neither an ascetic practising austerities, nor a Sheikh; neither it is alive nor it dies. If anyone weeps on its seeming death, he loses the grace of his personality (Gaund Kabir, p. 871). Atman is the master of the body-chariot, which is driven by the horses of senses and controlled by the intellect, with the reins of the mind. (Kathopanishad). Atman gives consciousness to the body, which becomes the playground of senses and sense-organs. It lives within the innermost sheath of the body called *Anandmaya Kosha* (the sheath of bliss), the outer sheaths being *Vigyanmaya Kosha* (intellectual sheath), *Manomaya Kosha* (mental sheath), *Pranamaya Kosha* (Vital sheath) and *Annamaya Kosha* (gross body sustained by food). It transmigrates from one body to another in accordance with the merits and demerits of its actions. When the egg of illusion bursts forth with the help of the True Guru, it merges in Brahman, being its part and parcel.

Ātma Vidya: Knowledge of the self; Spiritual knowledge. The True Guru is the giver of the spiritual knowledge (Gauri Sukhmani M. 5, p. 293). *Satsangat* (the holy congregation) is the school of the True Guru, where the disciple learns to imbibe the godly qualities (Var Kanra M. 4, p. 1316). *Atma Vidya* may also be called *Brahm Vidya* or *Para Vidya*. Before the realisation of Brahman, the self is to be known. The self is known only through the discipline of the Guru, when one realises that Brahman is within Atman and Atman is within Brahman (Bhairo M. 1, p. 1153). He who knows his self, knows all the godly qualities (Maru M. 3, p. 1056). He realises the State of Supreme Bliss (Asa M. 5, p. 375).

Atoms: The ultimate particles of matter. According to modern science the atoms spin around and are in constant motion. Guru Nanak Dev has talked about motion in respect of material objects and *Jivas*. According to him, there is no end to this motion (Var Asa M. 1, p. 465). Guru Arjan Dev says with regards to the motion of an atom: "One may move like an atom through the spheres and regions of the skies in the twinkling of an eye, but he cannot get final liberation without the company of the saints (Gatha Shlokas M. 5, p. 1360).

Atonement: Propitiation of God by expiation of sins. Through atonement, the consciousness of one's sins is expressed. It is the reconciliation between God and sinful man. The sinner gets satisfaction through this act. In Christianity, the atonement was effected through Christ, the Saviour of Humanity, through his sufferings. In Hinduism, it is effected through sacrifices, fasts etc. The *Adi Granth* has no faith in such atonements. The saint-poets believe in the Grace of the True Guru and the Lord which can be effected by sincere prayer. Guru Arjan Dev says, "I prayed to my True Guru, who became merciful and through his intervention all my anguish and fear vanished. We are sinners, heretics and greedy. He bore all our merits and demerits" (Devgandhari M. 5, p. 533).

Attachment: A tie or bond especially for material objects. See: *Moha*.

Audhoot: A Yogi. See: Avdhoot.

Augan: Vices: Bad qualities. See: *Avgun*.

Auguries: Divinations, Omens drawn by auguries. The *Adi Granth* has no belief in auguries or divinations. The disciples of the True Guru do not make calculations for a lucky hour. They consider God over and above all omens (Ramkali M. 1, p. 904).

Auspicious Marks: Good omens, betokening success. According to the *Adi Granth*, the auspicious marks, tites and sights are meaningless for a true disciple. For him, only the Love of the Lord is the *Shastra* of auspicious marks. For him, the spiritual ecstasy is within his home (Bhairo M. 5, p. 1137).

Austerity: Severe self-discipline. It is the meditation connected with the practice of personal self-denial or bodily mortification. Such a discipline has been rejected by the *Adi Granth*. Guru Arjan Dev says, "Severe austerities were performed on the body, but the mind ran in all the ten directions (Maru M. 5, p. 1003). He considers a disciple attending the holy congregation (*Sādh Sang*) the real *Tapasavī* (ascetic)—(Basant M. 5, p. 1180). According to Guru Amar Das "the best of the austerities is the service of the Guru, when God, the remover of all anguish, resides in the heart" (Asa M. 3, p. 423).

Avadhoot, Avadhūt: In the *Adi Granth*, he has also been called *Audhū*. An *Avadhūt* is a Yogi. Guru Nanak Dev says, "Listen, O Machindra (Matsyendra), an *Avadhūt* is one who remains firm and has full control over the five vices. He follows the Yogic discipline in such a way that he not only swims across the ocean of *Saṁsāra* himself, but also all his clan gets release. He receives the alms of Love and Fear of the Lord and always remains contented. His posture is of Contemplation and he concentrates on the Name of the Lord (Ramkali M. 1, p. 877).

Āvāgaun: Lit. Coming and going; Birth and Death. See: *Transmigration.*

Avarice: Greed; Covetousness. It is one of the five major vices, the other four being lust, anger, attachment and ego. Guru Nanak Dev has figuratively depicted greed as darkness of the prison-cell and the vices as the fetters (Basant M. 1, p. 1191). Whatever actions we do under pressure of greed, we further bind ourselves (Jaitsri M. 9, p. 702). Greed destroys human beings just as the green scum over water makes it stagnant (Var Ramkali Satta and Balwand, p. 697).When there is greed, there can be no sincere love (Shlok Farid p. 1378). Those who are subdued by the evil of greed, they forget the Benign Lord. They are called *Manmukh* because they follow the dictates of their mind. They are foolish and ignorant; the writ on their foreheads is inauspicious (Todi M. 4, p. 711). The wave of greed is like the madness of a dog (Nat M. 4, p. 983). As far as possible, a greedy person should never be trusted... such persons are black-faced and waste away their precious lives (Shlok Varan te Vadhik M. 3, p. 1417).

Avgun: Immoral practice; Vice. See: *Vices.*

Avidya: Ignorance; Nescience. *Avidya* is the source of all evil and suffering. Through ignorance one considers his body, vital air, mind or intellect as self. Through ignorance, the ego or the lower-self is considered the real self. In ignorance, there is no comfort, the king and the poor both shall weep (Gauri Kabir, p. 325). He who is in ignorance, is like a dead body in the world (Var Sri Rag M. 3, Shlok M. 4, p. 88). This nescience disappears with the knowledge obtained from the Guru, just as the darkness vanishes, when the lamp is lit (Sri Rag M. 3, p. 39).

Avtār, Avataras: Incarnations; Descent of deities on earth. Hinduism believes in several incarnations of Vishnu, but ten of them have been significantly mentioned viz. four of *Kritya Yuga* i.e. *Matsya* (Fish incarnation), *Kurma* (Tortoise incarnation), *Varāha* (Boar incarnation) and *Narsingh* (Man-Lion incarnation); three of *Treta Yuga* i.e. *Vāman* (Dwarf incarnation) *Parasurama* and *Ram Chandra*; one of *Dvapara Yuga* i.e. *Krishna* and two of *Kali Yuga* i.e. *Buddha* and *Kalkī*, the incarnation yet to come. These ten incarnations are said to take birth from *Shunya*. (Maru M. 1, p. 1038). The Sikh Gurus have no faith in incarnations, because their God does not incarnate. It has been clearly stated by Guru Arjan Dev: "That mouth may be burnt, which says that the Lord incarnates (Bhairo M. 5, p. 1136).

Avyakta: Unmanifest. This word has taken the form of *Abigat* in the *Adi Granth*. It is used for Unmanifested Brahman, Who is without any quality (*Trigunatīta*), Who is beyond the world of Name, Speech and senses (*Agocar*). Guru Arjan Dev says, "When there was only *Avyakta* (Unmanifest Lord) and *Agocar* Lord, from whom did Chitra and Gupta enquire about the account of actions?" (Gauri Sukhmani M. 5, p. 291).

Azrāīl: The angel of death in Islam. He is one of the archangels. See: Angels.

B

Backbiting: The act of talking ill of another person in his absence. The backbiter is a secret calumniator. Backbiting has been considered a great vice and a great sin. Even if one may perform many virtuous acts, he will not receive any reward for them, if he indulges in backbiting. Ravidas says, "If one takes a bath at the sixty-eight holy shrines, if he worships the twelve genuine *Jyotir-linga* or 'effulgent phalluses', if he gives a well or a tank in charity—all this will be useless, if he indulges in backbiting. How can the calumniator of a saint attain final beatitude? He will definitely go to hell. If he performs rituals at Kurukshetra, at the time of the solar eclipse, and offers his wife with all embellishment. If he listens to the recitation of all the *Smritis* with his ears—all this will be useless, if he indulges in backbiting. If he presents many offerings, gives land in charity and erects a public building and receives ovation for that. If he executes the works of others at the cost of his personal errand— he will transmigrate repeatedly, if he indulges in backbiting. O People of the world, why do you indulge in backbiting? The position of a calumniator is quite evident. I have pondered over it in depth. The sinner goes away to hell" (Gaund Ravidas, p. 875). Therefore one should totally abstain from backbiting. Whosoever calumniates, pollutes his inner self (Sri Rag M. 3, p. 88). The face of a calumniator is blackened in both the worlds (Dhanasari M. 5, p. 674). He is always in agony, greatly deformed and darkened (Var Sarang M. 4, p. 1244). He washes away the dirt of others and is punished for his act of slandery. He is comfortless in this world and propless in the next.... He wastes away his precious birth (Asa M. 5, p. 380).

Baikunth: Heaven. See: *Vaikuṇtha*.

Bairāg, Bairāgī: *Bairāg* is the state of non-attachment. One who rises above the desire for material objects, is a *Bairāgī*. One of the orders of the Yogis is also called *Bairāgī*. Guru Ram Das says, "My mind is in the state of *Bairāg*, for the sight of my Lord and Friend Hari" (Asa M. 4, p. 369). Kabir says, "If you are a householder then perform the acts of *Dharma*, otherwise practise *Bairāg;* if a *Bairāgī* binds himself in worldly desires consider him as most unfortunate" (Shlok Kabir, p. 1377). See: *Vairagya*.

Baisno: A Vaishnava. According to Guru Arjan Dev, the real *Baisno* (Vaishnava) receives the blessings of the Lord and is free from any impact of *maya*. He performs actions without any desire for their fruit and is always absorbed in the devotion of the Lord.... He himself is firm on the Name of the Lord and makes others remember the Name. Such a Vaishnava attains the Supreme State (Gauri Sukhmani M. 5, p. 274).

Bājīgar: A juggler. In the *Adi Granth*, the Lord is likened to a juggler, Who starts His Play and ultimately assembles it (Sorath Kabir, p. 655). See: *Jugglers*.

Balance: A weighing apparatus consisting of a beam poised so as to move freely on a central pivot, with a scale pan at each end. In the *Adi Granth*, three words have been used for balance viz. *Takrī, Tarāzū* and *Kandā*. When anything is weighed in the balance, that scale pan is heavy, which lowers down (Var Asa M. 1, p. 470). The scale which lowers down, exhibits humility (which brings weightage for the person observing it).

Bandā, Bandagī: *Bandā* means a person and *Bandagī* is worship. That person is called a real person, who binds himself in a discipline for the Sight of the Lord (Var Asa M. 1, p. 465). Kabir says, "O *Bande* (Man, Person), you must worship the Lord, even if He Loves or Forsakes you" (Gauri Kabir, p. 338). Sheikh Farid requests the Lord for the alms of *Bandagī* (worship, meditation)—(Asa Farid, p. 488).

Bānī: The Word or Composition of the Guru, which is a verbal testimony for the devotee. See: *Gurbānī*.

Banishment: A state of enforced absence. Even the great ones are sometimes punished for some lapse. The god Indra, Parasurama, the incarnation of Vishnu, Ajai, the grandfather of Lord Rama, Ravana, the king of Lanka, Pandavas, the friends of Lord Krishna, Janmeja etc. suffered because of their ego or sin. Even Lord Rama was banished from Ayodhya and during his exile, he suffered the separation of his wife Sita and his brother Lakshman. "The whole world is subject to suffering" (Var Ramkali M. 3, Shlok M. 1, pp. 953-54).

Banner: An ensign or flag. While the kings or States have their banners declaring their distinct entity, the saints and the Gurus are also said to have banners of higher ideals and *Dharma*. The bards (*Bhats*), whose verses have been included in the *Adi Granth*, have stated this in their Eulogies of the Sikh Gurus. Guru Amar Das is said to have been blessed by the Lord with a white banner on the bridge of *Vaikuntha*. (Swayyas of III Guru, p. 1393). The banner of *Dharma* of Guru Ram Das flies for ever (Swayyas of the IV Guru, p. 1404). Guru Arjan Dev, the son of Guru Ram Das, also holds the banner of *Dharma* (Swayyas of the V Guru, p. 1407).

Barbarians: Rude, wild, uncultured and uncivilised persons. In Sanskrit the word *malecha* has been used for a barbarian. The Aryans called non-Aryans *malechas*. For Hindus all the foreigners including Muslims were *malechas*. Guru Nanak Dev said, " (The Hindus) worship the Puranas, but take the materials from the *malechas* or Muslims. They eat the meat of a he-goat killed by people speaking foreign languages, but forbid their people from entering the cooking ground (Var Asa M. 1, p. 472). The Guru lashed at the Kshatriyas who forsook their *Dharma* and spoke in the language of the *malechas*. (Dhanasari M. 1, p. 660). Those who caluminate the Guru, transmigrate like the barbarians (*malechas*)—(Bilawal M. 1, p. 832). Even a *malecha* with his whole-hearted devotion for the Lord, becomes holy (Bilawal Ravidas, p. 858).

Basant: In Indian terminology the spring season is called Basant. According to Guru Angad Dev, those ladies always live in spring (*Basant*), whose Lord lives with them (Var Suhi M. 3, Shlok M. 2, p. 791). See: *Seasons*.

Bath, Bathing: The act of immersing the body in water for washing and purifying it. The *Adi Granth* enjoins a disciple to take bath every day in the early hours of the morning. Guru Arjan Dev says, " Take a bath and remember your Lord; your mind and body will become healthy" (Sorath M. 5, p. 611). It is stated in *Khādira-Grihya-Sutra*: "...Having sprinkled his feet (with water), let him besprinkle his head. Let him touch the organs of his senses (i.e. his eyes, his nose and his ears) with water (i.e. with a wet hand). When he has finally touched (water) again, he becomes pure.... If the word *Snāna* (or bathing) is used, this refers to the whole body including the head". Talking about Jaina monks, Guru Nanak Dev says, "None other can protect the Jivas, it is only the Lord, who kills and gives life to Jivas. Ashes may be thrown on the hair-plucker, who remains without charity and bath. When the gods made the churning-stick of Mount Sumeru, several gems were created from water. The gods have established sixty-eight holy places, where fairs are held and discourses are delivered. By taking bath, the Muslims perform the prayers and the Hindus their worship; the wise men always take a bath. Salvation is attained if the water is poured on the head at the time of birth and death.... If these hair-pluckers do not take a bath then seven handful of ashes be thrown on their heads. (Var Majh M. 1, p. 150). Self-willed fools, showing worldly wisdom attain nothing even if they wash their bodies (Majh M. 3, p. 114). By washing the body, the dirt (of ego) is not removed (Ramkali M. 5, p. 893). Guru Nanak Dev says, "They go to the holy places to take a bath, but their minds are full of deceit and their bodies work like thieves, in this way, if they shed one part of their dirt, they get two parts more of their dirt of ego. Though the gourd is washed from outside, it has the poison within it. The saints, even if they do not bathe, they are saintly and the thieves even if they bathe, are thieves (Var Suhi M. 3, Shlok M. 1, p. 789). Even if a person takes a bath and tattoos signs or circles on the body, his inner dirt cannot be removed (Bibhas Prabhati M. 5, p. 1347).

Bathing Places: Holy Places or *Tīrthas* (places of pilgrimage or dedicated to some holy object). It is written in *Baudhayana Dharma Shastra*: "All mountains, all rivers, holy lakes, bathing places, the dwellings of *rīshis*, cowpens, (holy) plains and temples of the gods (are) places (which destroy sin)". Hence all the holy bathing places purify a disciple. This contention has been refuted by the *Adi Granth*. Namdev, the Maharashtrian saint says, "A visit to the Ganges, Gaya and Godavari is a worldly act (Basant Namdev, p. 1195). If one resides on the banks of the Ganges and drinks its pure water, he cannot get salvation without the devotion of the Lord (Shlok Kabir, p.1367). If one gives alms in *Makkar Rashi* at Prayag and cuts half of his body, he cannot attain salvation without the Name of the Lord (Mali Gaura M. 4, p. 986). The pilgrimage at holy places is one of the twelve virtuous *karmas*. Kabir does not consider a visit to Varanasi a virtuous act and Maghar an evil act. He considers them *at par* (Gauri Kabir, p. 326). He says, "If the interior of a person is full of dirt and he takes bath at a holy place, he will not go to heaven. No useful purpose will be served by pleasing the people. God is not ignorant. Therefore worship only one Lord and the true bath is the service of the Guru. If one gets salvation by bathing at holy places, the frogs always take a bath there. That person is just like a frog and will transmigrate repeatedly. A hard-hearted person, who dies at Varanasi cannot escape hell. A saint of the Lord, even if he dies at Maghar, will cause the release of all his people" (Asa Kabir, p. 484). Hinduism recognises sixty-eight holy places, but the *Adi Granth* considers the presence of sixty-eight holy places in the heart of a God-intoxicated person, where the Lord Himself resides (Gujri M. 3, p. 491). Wherever the saint sets his feet, the sixty-eight holy places are there (Ramkali M. 5, p. 890). The Guru shows his disciple all the sixty-eight *Tīrthas* (Ramkali Namdev, p. 973), and even the Word of the Guru does that (Suhi M. 3, p. 713). The Name of the Lord itself symbolises sixty-eight *Tīrathas* (Maru M. 1, p. 1009). For the devotee of the Guru, the *Tīrtha* is the Name of the Lord (Dhanasari M.1, p. 687). Bathing at the worldly *Tīrthas* puts the dirt of ego in the mind of a seeker (Dhanasari M. 1, p. 687). The real *tīrtha* is the Guru himself, in whose company all the dirt is removed. (Suhi M.3, p. 713).

Battle: A hostile encounter between opposing forces. God is not pleased with the engagement of warriors in battle (Var Sarang M.4, Shlok M. 1, p. 1237). They may not be called kings, who die fighting in battles and undergo transmigration (Var Vadhans M. 4, Shlok M. 3, p. 590). God has Created two opposing forces of *Shiva* (the Conscious soul) and *Shakti* (*maya*), God Willed it, therefore *Shiva* was defeated by *Shakti*, but someone was protected by the Lord by uniting him with *Sādh Sangat* (the company of the saints)—(Var Maru Dakhne M. 5, p. 1096). In the battle between good and evil, the ultimate victory is of the former. The Guru, with open arms, takes the disciple out of the well of attachment (*Moh*) and makes him conquer the precious birth, never to be defeated again (Gauri M. 5, p. 291). Kabir says, "The True Guru met me and discharged one of his arrows, which pierced my heart and threw me on the ground (Shlok Kabir, p. 1374).

Beasts: Animals. The *Adi Granth* considers the beasts better than human beings, if they perform actions without remembring the Name of the Lord. Guru Nanak Dev says, "The animals deserve appreciation because they eat grass, but give the nectar (i.e. milk). Fie on the life and actions of those people, who do not remember the Name of the Lord" (Gujri M. 1, p. 489). Without the remembrance of the Name, the self-willed persons (*Manmukh*) are far removed from Truth and move like ghosts. They are like animals enveloped in human skin and are dark from inside (Var Malar M. 1, p. 1284). Though seemingly they are human beings, but they act like animals (Gauri Sukhmani M. 5, p. 267). They have come into this world, but without higher understanding, they are like animals (Gauri Bawan Akhri M. 5, p. 251).

Beatitude: Supreme Happiness. According to the *Adi Granth*, the Supreme Happiness is attained on realising the Lord. Guru Arjan Dev says, "When we meet the Beloved Lord, Who is the Ocean of Happiness, we experience Supreme Bliss. On meeting the Lord, Who is Supreme Bliss, all our sufferings end (Asavari M. 5, p. 431). Supreme Happiness consists in the concentration on the Word of the Guru. Whosoever listens to it and practises it, crosses the ocean of *saṃsāra*. (Asa M. 5, p. 370). The State of Bliss is obtained on becoming attuned to the sayings of the Guru. Guru Amar Das says, "Every one talks about Bliss, but realises it only on meeting the Guru. When the Guru showers his Graces, all our sufferings end and we are blessed with the antimony of knowledge (Ramkali M. 3, Anand, p. 917).

Beauty: The quality or combination of qualities, which affords keen pleasure to the senses especially, the sense of sight. According to the *Adi Granth*, whereas the Lord is the embodiment of Truth and Goodness, He is also Beautiful (Japuji, p. 4). Guru Nanak Dev addresses the Lord as "my Beautiful and Incomprehensible Lord" (Basant M. 1, p. 1169). Guru Ram Das says, "Please tell me, how can I meet my Beautiful Lord?" (Devgandhari M. 4, p. 527). Guru Arjan Dev says, "I was wonder-struck on having the Most Beautiful Sight of the Lord. My Lord is Most Beautiful and I am the dust of His Lotus Feet (Suhi M. 5, p. 784). The Abode of the Beautiful Lord is also Beautiful studded with precious stones (Sri Rag M. 1, p. 17). Guru Amar Das says, "O my mind, you were full of the dirt of ego. My Lord is Beautiful for ever; you can only be adorned by the Word (Sri Rag M. 3, p. 35). The Beautiful Lord is the rest-house for the saints (Sri Rag Chhant M. 5, p. 80). Guru Arjan Dev says, "They are indeed beautiful, who sit in the company of the saints (Majh M. 5, p. 132). The physical beauty is indeed no beauty without the remembrance of the Name of the Lord (Devgandhari M. 4, p. 528).

Bed: Veda. See: *Vedas*.

Begam Purā: The City of Bliss. It has also been called *Abical Nagar* (Eternal City). Ravidas says, "*Begam Pura* is the name of the city. There is neither grief nor anxiety there. There is neither trouble nor any tax on commodities. No fear, no blemish, no downfall. Now I have achieved entry in this good land, where there is always peace, where rule is steadfast and eternal. None is of second or third status, all are equal. The fame of this habitation is eternal, where every one is affluent and contented. The residents move freely according to their will. They are acquainted with the abode and no one stands in their way. I enjoy freedom here and whosoever is the fellow-citizen, he is my friend" (Gauri Guareri Ravidas, p. 345).

Begging: The habit of asking for alms. The action or habit of begging has been condemned in the *Adi Granth*. Speaking about the Jaina monks, Guru Nanak Dev says, "They keep bowls fastened to their waists"; the main purpose of keeping such bowls is begging. Similarly the Yogis and *Jangams* (Shaivites) beg for their livelihood (Var Majh M. 1, pp. 149-50). To the Yogi, the Guru says, "Are you not ashamed of begging in many houses? (Ramkali M. 1, p. 903). Guru Arjan Dev says, "You beg for bread and do not feel satisfied, you beg forsaking the real *Nāth* (Master). Are you not ashamed of it? (Ramkali M. 5, p. 886). Guru Nanak Dev strongly condemned the begging because it encourages parasitism in society. He advocates for honest labour, honest earnings and help for the indigent and disabled. He says, "Without any knowledge, he sings hymns. For the sake of bread, he becomes a *Mullah* (priest) and turns his house into a mosque. Shirking work, he gets his ears pierced. He becomes a *fakīr* and loses all his identity. He is called a Guru or *Pir*, but goes abegging. None should fall at his feet at all. One should be absorbed in work and give something (for the indigent). Such persons can only realise the Path of God" (Var Sarang M.4, Shalok M. 1, p. 1245). People condemn a begging person and he receives no respect (Ramkali M. 1, p. 878). One should beg only from the Munificent Lord and receive everything desired. If he begs from any other, he should die of shame (Var Vadhans M. 4, p. 590). The best begging is the begging for Lord's Praise from the Guru (Maru M. 5, p. 1018). He who is absorbed in the Formless Lord, why should he go for begging alms? (Var Ramkali M. 3, Shlok M. 1, p. 953).

Behaviour: Etiquette; Manner of conducting oneself. The behaviour of a person depends upon the nature of his thinking, his company and the performance of his actions. "A person who performs righteous actions is called a virtuous person and a person who commits sinful acts is called a sinner" (Var Majh M.1, Shlok M. 2, p. 138). The thinking of a person manifests his personality (Gauri M. 1, p. 224). He who examines his self, imbibes all the virtues (Maru M. 3, p. 1056). Though the performance of sinful act is bad, it is liked by the sinner (Ramkali M. 1, Dakhni Omkar, p. 935). The vice and virtue both reside within the body and they are together the cause of creation (Majh M. 3, p. 126). Guru Arjan Dev exhorts a person to perform such actions as keep him away from the dirt of vices (Gauri M. 5, p. 199).

Being: That which is; That which exists. Being also connotes Truth as well as entity. In the *Adi Granth*, it has been called *Sat*, which pertains to *Param Atman* or Brahman. Being is *Purusha*, that which fills the

Universe. It is different from gods and is beyond the ken of senses. In ordinary sense, the word 'being' is used for a *Jiva/Atman*, because *Atman* is also ever-existent like Brahman. As a modern philosophical concept, 'being' denotes the objective world or the world of matter, which is recognised as primary, considering *Atman* as secondary.

Beings: The *Jivas*, who are alive; The creatures who are in existence. Hinduism believes in the four divisions of creation viz. 1-*Andaj*, the beings created from eggs, 2-*Jeraju*, the beings created from foetus, 3-*Svetaju*, the beings created from sweat and 4-*Udhibhija* or the earth-born vegetation. Guru Nanak Dev says, "The egg-born, the foetus-born, the sweat-born and the earth-born—all the creation is Thine, O Lord" (Sorath M. 1, p. 596). Guru Ram Das says, "The Lord Himself is in the egg-born, womb-born, sweat-born and the earth-born" (Sorath M. 4, p. 605). There are innumerable *Jivas* of various classes and categories living on various planes of existence. There are gods, demons, men, animals,Yakshas, Gandharvas, Kinnaras, ghosts, spirits etc. The animals of the earth have been divided into three categories viz. the animals moving on earth, the animals living in water and the animals who can fly. The Guru says, "All the animals moving on earth, living in water and flying remember none else than Hari" (Malar M. 4, p. 1265). Jainism holds that there are six kinds of living beings viz. earth-bodies, water-bodies, fire-bodies, wind-bodies, plants and animals. Islam believes in three different species of created intelligent beings: 1-Angels who have been created by light, 2-Genii, who have been created by fire and 3-Human beings, who have been created of earth. Besides these intelligent beings, there are unintelligent beings. Writing about various species of creation Guru Arjan Dev says, "There are millions of Siddhas, Yogis and celibates... birds, poisonous snakes, trees, elements—water, air, fire-gods, demons, Kinnaras, Pishachas, spirits, swines, tigers, deer, dwellers of the underworld and dwellers of heaven and hell (Gauri Sukhmani M. 5, pp. 275-76).

Bell: Prayer-bell used at the time of service in Hindu temples. It has been used in calling the worshippers for the observance of the ceremonies. Through its sound, the gods are invoked and the demons and evil-spirits are warned. Guru Arjan Dev has talked about the Bell in God's Temple (Ghantā) ringing throughout the four corners of the universe (Asa M. 5, p. 393).

Bemukh: A person whose face is turned away from the Lord. In the *Adi Granth*, it has also been written as *Vemukh*. "Those who turn away from the Lord are separated from Him for several births" (Baramaha Majh M. 5, p. 135). See: *Manmukh*.

Benediction: The utterance of a blessing; Solemn invocation of blessedness upon a person. Guru Nanak Dev asks for the blessings for the Union with the Lord (Gauri Purbi Dipki M. 1, p. 157). In one of his hymns, Guru Arjan Dev has recorded the benediction received by him from his mother: "O son, this is the blessing of the mother that you may never forget the Lord and on Him you should contemplate for ever. By remembering Him all the sins are destroyed and the ancestors attain release. You should always contemplate on Him. The True Guru may always be kind towards you and you may love the saints. May God clad you in the robes of honour and give you the food of the Praises of the Lord. May you drink the nectar of the Lord and live eternally with Him. May you ever remember the Lord and remain in the state of Bliss. May you remain ever in Happiness, your desires be fulfilled and you remain free from care. May your mind, like the black bee, hug the Lotus-Feet of the Lord..." (Gujri M. 5, p. 496). The *Adi Granth* contains such like benedictions.

Benevolence: Kindness; Generosity; Charitable feeling. In many hymns of the *Adi Granth*, the Benevolence of the Lord has been depicted. He is Kind, Generous, Gracious and Merciful. His Bounties are enormous. Through His Grace we receive a beautiful and healthy body, bloom of youth, delicious foods and other pleasures. Through His Grace, we revel with the sons, brothers, friends, wife and other relatives. Through His Grace, we drink cool water, breathe the life-giving air, enjoy the warmth of fire. He gave us hands, feet, ears, eyes, tongue and other parts of the body (Gauri Sukhmani M. 5, p. 267). The sixth *ashtapadi* (octavo) of *Sukhmani* gives a comprehensive survey of the Bounties of the Lord. An example will suffice: "By Whose Grace, your ears hear the music, the eyes see the wonders of the world, the tongue speaks sweetly, the life is led in pleasure and peace, the hands move and work, why should we forget that Lord? Awaken your mind towards Him by the Grace of the Guru (p. 270). Like the Lord, the Guru is also Benevolent. He gives the wealth of the Name to the disciple and releases him from the bondage of transmigration (Gauri Sukhmani M. 5, p. 286). The Guru is Beneficent, the house of peace and the light of three worlds (Var Majh M. 1, p. 137). Having been absorbed in the Name of the Lord and the discipline of the Guru, the *Brahm-Giānī* (the Knower of Brahman), the saint, the

Sadh, the *Jivan-Mukta* and the *Gurmukh*—all imbibe the quality of benevolence. About *Brahm-Giānī* it is said that he is the spring of kindness and benevolence (Gauri Sukhmani M. 5, p. 273).

Bhāe Bhagtī: Devotion with love. It is also known as *Premā Bhagtī*. See: *Bhakti*.

Bhagat: Devotee; One who surrenders totally before the Lord. See: *Devotee*.

Bhagautī: An adherent of Bhagavat Dharma. While talking about his contemporary Sadhus, Guru Arjan Dev considers the *Bhagautī* as one who ever remains absorbed in devotion towards Bhagwant (the Lord) and has totally discarded the company of the evil forces" (Gauri Sukhmani M. 5, p. 274).

Bhagavad Gītā: In the *Adi Granth*, the word 'Gītā' occurs once in the verses of Namdev in Raga Gaund (p. 874), where he refers to the authority of *Gītā*, while stating that he holds fast to the Name of the Lord through the Guru's Word. There are several poems under the title 'Gītā viz. Shiv Gita, Ram Gita, but the popular Gita in the mediaeval age was *Bhagavad Gītā*. Gyan Dev, the noted saint of Maharashtra wrote a commentary on it. It is one of the scriptures in *Prasthana Treyi* besides *Brahm Sutra* and *Upanishads*. The eminent Acharyas wrote their commentaries on this eternal song. It consists of 650 verses divided into eighteen chapters. It is the part and parcel of *Mahabharata*, the great epic and covers 25th to 45th chapters of the *Bhīshma Parva*. It is a *Goshta* or conversation between Arjuna and Lord Krishna. Arjuna, one of the mighty Pandava heroes, on seeing the armies of Pandavas and Kauravas arrayed for mortal combat in the field of Kurukshetra, feels a great agony in his mind, because his kinsfolk on both the sides were preparing to kill one another. He seems unwilling to start the fight, but Lord Krishna, his charioteer, beckons him to fulfil his duty as a warrior in right earnest. The dialogue between Arjuna and Lord Krishna propounds the philosophy of three Yogas viz. the *Karma Yoga* (the Yoga of action), *Gyan Yoga* (the Yoga of knowledge) and *Bhakti Yoga* (the Yoga of devotion). Some modern thinkers have argued that the *Gītā* was composed during the third or fourth century BC and was later on interpolated into the *Mahabharata* in the second century AD.

Bhāgavat, Bhāgavatas: The word 'Bhāgavat' is found in the *Adi Granth* in the verses of pre-Nanak saints viz. Kabir (Bhairo, p. 1162) and Beni (Prabhati, p. 1351). It has been used for the Lord. In Vaishnava terminology it refers to Lord Vishnu or Krishna. In the *Adi Granth,* the word *Bhagautī* has been used for the adherent of the Lord, also called *Bhagvant.* In a hymn of Ravidas, the word *Bhāgavat* is written as *Bhāgautu.* A *Bhāgavat* is an adherent of *Bhagvān/ Bhagvant.* The sect preaching devotion for *Bhagvān* is also known as *Bhāgavat.* The followers of this sect are knows as *Bhāgavatas.* The most popular Purana i.e. *Bhāgavat Purana* belongs to this sect. This Purana is divided into twelve *skandhas* and contains eighteen thousand shlokas. In *Japuji,* Guru Nanak Dev talking about the limitless universe has referred to the Vedas, *Katebs* (*Taurat, Zabūr, Anjīl* and *Qurān*) and eighteen thousand shlokas of *Bhāgavat Purana.* There is description of all the incarnations of Vishnu in the *Bhāgavat Purana.* The tenth *skandh* describes the life and activities of Lord Krishna.

Bhakti: Written as *Bhagtī* in the *Adi Granth.* Bhakti or devotion takes its birth from faith. For every individual, the first requisite of religious and devoted life is faith. A Muslim must have the prayer-mat of faith (Var Majh M. 1, p. 140) and a Yogi, the staff of faith (Japuji, p. 6). Without faith there can be only deceit and no devotion. Devotion demands complete self-surrender. The devotee cannot question the Will of the Lord (Asa M. 3, p. 440). Those who question, can never find a place in the Heart of the Lord (Ibid). Therefore the devotee must resign completely to the Will of the Lord. Fear of the Fearless Lord is a pre-requisite for devotion (Bilawal M. 5, p. 829). Ordinarily fear and love are two antagonistic factors in the devlopment of human personality, but in the domain of devotion, they go side by side. The devotee (*Bhakta*) is full of undefiled fear and pure love, fear of the Omnipotent and Love of the Merciful and Compassionate Lord. The real devotion of Hari is His Love (Sri Rag M. 3, p. 28). There are two types of devotion i.e. *Laukika* and *Anurāga* or *Behrang* (outward) and *Antarang* (inward). The *Laukika* devotion is outward and formalistic and *Anuraga* devotion is inward. The Sikh Gurus have rejected the outward form of devotion and laid great emphasis on inward devotion i.e. pure love. There are nine types of Bhakti called *Naudha Bhakti,* which includes the devotion through 1-listening (*Shravan*), 2-Music (*Kīrtan*), 3-Remembrance (*Simran*), 4-washing the Feet of the Lord (*Pād-seven*), 5-service (*archā*) 6-bowing (*vandanā*), 7-obedience (*Das Bhāv*), 8-Friendship (*mitratā*) and 9-self-surrender (*ātam-nivedan*). Suitable quotations regarding each type of Bhakti can be found in the verses of the Sikh Gurus, but prominence is given to *Bhāe Bhakti* or

Premā Bhakti or devotion through love. The path of devotion can be attained through the Grace of the Guru and the Lord (Asa M. 3, p. 440). When the disciple meets the Guru and receives instructions from him, the real devotion begins at that time. Bhakti is the real path of *Nirvāna*. The final emancipation can never be attained through learning and guises. The world is mad without Bhakti (Asa M. 3, p. 440). Without Bhakti, the human being looks like a dog or a swine (Shlok M. 9, p. 1428). Bhakti is a type of Yoga, which unites a devotee with the Lord. The word of the Guru is the treasure-house of devotion, whosoever sings, listens or practises it, attains the objective (Asa M. 5, p. 376).

Bhakti-Yoga: The union with the Lord through devotion. See: *Bhakti*.

Bhānā: The Will, Order or Judgment of the Lord. See: *Hukam*.

Bharm: Corrupted form of *Bhram*, which means illusion. "He who is lost in illusions, does not know the essence" (Majh M. 3, p. 114). "The wall of illusion falls down, when we meet the mighty Guru" (Asa M. 5, p. 454).

Bhavānī: One of the names of the mother-goddess Parbati (Parvati) or Durga. Namdev has addressed the goddess in the following manner: "You are called Bhavānī, the Primal goddess. When one asks you for salvation, where do you hide yourself?" (Gaund Namdev, p. 874).

Bhedabheda: Bheḍa (different) and Abheda (non-different). It is the Vedantic philosophy propounded by Nimbarka. It expresses the relation of the soul to Brahman as neither absolutely different nor absolutely non-different.

Bhekh: Guise, Guises; external appearance. "One is worldly-wise and adopts several guises. His mind speeds in all the ten directions. He is absorbed in ego and does not search for the Word; therefore he transmigrates repeatedly" (Suhi M. 4, p. 732). "The Lord cannot be attained by adopting several guises and without real instructions" (Var Maru Dakhne M. 5, p. 1099).

Bhikkhu: It is a Pali word meaning a monk. The Pali word *Bhikkhunī* means a nun. The Sanskrit equivalent for these words are *Bhikshū* and *Bhikshunī*. A *Bhikshū* is an almsman or a mendicant monk and a *Bhikshunī* is an almswoman or a mendicant nun. They are the members of either Buddhist *Saṃgha* or Jaina *Saṃgha*. The *Adi Granth* rejects such orders in society; because they preach renunciation. Guru Ram Das says about a Jaina monk: "When the hatred of the world arises in his mind, he becomes a *Digambara* (a Jaina monk), but his mind becomes a store-house of desires. Though he wanders extensively, his desires remain unfulfilled (Bilawal M. 4, p. 835). Guru Nanak Dev has also admonished such monks in the following words: "He does not wear clothes and groans all the time. Having sunk in silence, he wastes his life. How can he wake up from sleep without the Guru? He walks with bare feet and reaps the fruit of his actions. He eats dirty food and throws ashes on his head. Thus this foolish and ignorant person loses respect (Var Asa M. 1, p. 467).

Bhūta: In the *Adi Granth*, the word *Bhūta* is followed by the word *Preta*, in *Sukhmani*, where Guru Arjan Dev has mentioned them as a distinct class of creation (p. 276). Ordinarily, the word *Bhūta* signifies a spirit, a demon or a hobgoblin. In Punjabi speech it is very often preceded by the word *Jinn* (*genii*). This word also occurs in the *Adi Granth* (Var Bihagra M. 3, p. 556). The son of a *jinn* has been called *jinnūrā* and the daughter, a *jinnūrī*. *Jinn* is an Arabic word of Islamic origin. It is believed in Islam that the *jinn* are aerial animals with transparent bodies. They can assume various forms and are invisible to men. When their form becomes condensed, they are visible. Trilochan has used the word *Preta* in one of his hymns: "The person who remembers the house-property at the time of death, becomes a *Preta* after death". Thus a *Bhūta, Preta* or *jinn* is the ghost of a deceased person. *Bhūtas* are said to be mostly violent, injurious and destructive, but there are said to be good *Bhūtas* as well. "Bhūta" also means an element. There are five elements viz. air, fire, water, earth and ether, known as 'Panch Bhūtas'. Guru Nanak Dev (p.14) and Guru Ram Das (p. 983) have referred to the human body's composition from five elements.

Bibek Budh: The intellect (*Budh*) saturated with spiritual knowledge (*Bibek*). *Bibek Budh* can only be attained from the True Guru (Todi M. 4, p. 711). *Bibek Budh* is the purest in the world (Kalyan M. 1, p. 1325). Guru Arjan Dev says, "I have finally surrendered at the Door of the Lord. O Lord, give me *Bibek Budh*" (Sorath M. 5, p. 641).

Bible: New Testament or *Injīl*. The word 'Kateb' in the *Adi Granth* includes this scripture of Christianity.

Bidhātā: The Lord, Who writes and Controls our destinies. "The Lord, Who is *Antaryamin* (Inner controller) and also *Purusha*, Who controls our destinies; only He can fulfil the desires of our mind. I beg of Him only this boon that He may make us the dust of the Feet of the saints" (Gauri M. 5, p. 13).

Bindu: The creative power; the semen. *Nāda* and *Bindu* occur in Yogic terminology and have also been used in the *Adi Granth*. (Asa M.1, p. 352). The body is created out of one drop of *bindu*. (Asa Kabir, p. 481). A Yogi is required to preserve the *bindu*, even in a dream (Var Ramkali M. 3, Shlok M. 1, p. 952). Kabir says, "If one swims across the world-ocean by preserving *bindu*, then why the eunuch does not attain final emancipation?" (Gauri Kabir, p. 324).

Birds: The beings, who have wings and can fly. In the *Adi Granth*, the word 'pankhi' [a being with *pankh* (wings)] has been used for a bird. When the soul leaves the body, which is its bondage, it has the power to fly and moves freely, therefore it has been likened to *a haṁsa* (swan). According to the Will of God, the body (kāiā) and the *haṁsa* (soul) have been united (Var Majh M. 1, p. 139). But when the time is up, the body and the swan-soul have to undergo separation (Vadhans M. 1, p. 579). The imagery of birds has been frequently used in the *Adi Granth*. Sheikh Farid has likened a virtuous person to a swan and the evil-minded person to a crane (baglā). Other birds include sparrows, crows, chakvis, chatriks, peacocks, kites, falcons, hawks, koel etc. The sparrows chirrup, when the day dawns (p. 319), the crows live in dirt (p. 239), the koel resides in mango trees (p. 157), the kites fly down on dead bodies (p. 322), the falcons and hawks pounce upon cranes (p. 1383), chatriks (*papīhās*) drink the rain-drops (p. 454), chakvi loves the sun (p. 60) and the peacocks dance in the month of *Sāwan* (p. 557). The mythological bird *Garuda* has been mentioned as the vehicle of Vishnu (p. 1166). According to Namdev, the Lord cannot be known just as the trail of the flying bird cannot be cognised (Gujri Namdev, p. 525). Guru Nanak Dev says, "If I were a bird and trailed across a hundred skies and if I remain invisible and eat and drink nothing, it will still be not possible to Evaluate Thee and Thy Name, O my Lord" (Sri Rag M. 1, pp. 14-15). Guru Arjan Dev says, "If the wings be on sale and I purchase them paying the price equal to my own weight, I would fix them on my body and fly away to find my Lord" (Shlok M. 5, p. 1426).

Birhā: Separation; pangs of separation. "We talk of *birhā*, but O *Birhā*, you are the ruler (over the hearts of the people). That body, which does not experience *birhā* (pangs of separation), the same may be considered as dead (Shlok Farid, p. 1379).

Blessedness: The state of being blessed, especially with divine favour. Such a blessedness is mentioned in the *Adi Granth* in the context of saints and God-intoxicated persons. Guru Ram Das says, "Those devotees are blessed, who recite the Name of the Lord. Those saints are blessed, who listen to the Praises of the Lord. Blessedness is for those holy persons, who sing the Praises of their Lord and become virtuous.... Blessedness is for those God-conscious persons who have subdued their minds by the Grace of the Guru. Blessedness is for those devotees who fall at the Guru's Feet." (Var Sorath M. 4, p. 649).

Blessings: Benediction; Authoritative declaration of divine favour. The *Adi Granth* lays emphasis on the blessings of the Guru for unification with the Lord. "Through the blessings of the Guru, the True Name is received" (Sri Rag M. 5, p. 71). "With the blessings of the Lord, the world is rid of its afflictions" (Suhi M. 5, p. 746).

Blind: Without the sense of sight. "By mere listening, how can a blind person find his path? He can reach his destination safely, if the hand of another person is held by him" (Gauri Sukhmani M. 5, p. 267). When the Guru gives the collyrium of knowledge, the darkness of ignorance is destroyed (ibid., p. 293). The *Adi Granth* lays stress on the spiritual perception, which comes by following the Guru's discipline. Guru Nanak Dev says, "O ye blind persons, abandon the greed, because it brings immense anguish" (Asa M. 1, p. 419). Similarly for the spiritual sight, all the sinful and evil acts are to be abandoned. In the words of Guru Ram Das, the mind of the blind person is illumined on meeting the Guru (Var Bihagra M. 4, p. 551).

Blindness: According to the *Adi Granth*, the world is blind. It acts in blindness, because the darkness persists without the Guru (Sorath M. 3, p. 600). The intellect of the blind one is enveloped in blindness (Maru M. 1, p. 1033).

Bliss: (*Ānanda*). For the saints of the *Adi Granth*, bliss is not merely blitheness or gladness, it is beatitude that is Supreme Blessedness or Happiness. Whereas God is Truth and Consciousness, He is also Bliss, therefore Bliss is godly or divine ecstasy. The state of Bliss is attained after meeting the True Guru. Guru Amar Das says in *Anand*: "Everybody talks of Bliss, but the Bliss is realised on meeting the Guru" (p. 917). Guru Arjan Dev has described the state of Bliss in the following way: "Whom should I describe that Bliss? On Seeing the Lord, the state of Utter Joy has been attained; the mind sings the Praises of the Lord. On Seeing the Wonderful Lord, I have been wonderstruck. The Beneficent Lord pervades all. I drink the priceless nectar, but cannot describe its taste like the smiling mute" (Sarang M. 5, p. 1205). Guru

Ram Das says, "I have been engrossed in Bliss, as I have Seen the Lord. I have tasted the Sweet Essence of my Lord" (Asa M. 5, p. 452). In the words of Guru Arjan Dev "the Lord has come to Abide in my heart, therefore the Music of Bliss resounds within me. Having come under the discipline of the Guru, I have practised Truth and the false illusion and fear have been dispelled (Suhi M. 5, p. 781).

Blood: The red liquid circulating in the arteries and veins of human being and higher animals. Sheikh Farid after austere ascetic practices, became very weak, when he said, "If one dissects my body, he will not find a drop of blood in it. Those who are absorbed in the devotion of the Lord, all their blood is sapped" (Shlok Farid, p. 1380). In his rejoinder to Baba Farid, Guru Amar Das says, "This body exists because of blood. Without blood, the body cannot live. Those who are absorbed in the devotion of the Lord, do not have the blood of greed" (ibid). The human body is a compound of marrow, blood, bones and foul odour. The ignorant one is proud of this body (Gatha M. 5, p. 1360). Guru Nanak Dev says, "In the iron age, the kings are like lions and the courtiers like dogs. They go to awaken those who sleep in peaceful slumber. The servants of the king tear and wound the subjects with their nails and like dogs they lick their blood" (Var Malar M. 1, p. 1288).

Bloodshed: The shedding of blood; Slaughter. Guru Nanak Dev has described the scenes of the battlefield and the plight of the people captured during the war, in his hymns relating to the invasion of Babur. In one of his hymns, he says, "(Babur, the Mughal king) has come from Kabul with the wedding party of sins.... The wedding-songs of bloodshed are being sung and the wedded ones are anointed with blood and not saffron" (Tilang M. 1, p. 722).

Body: The *Adi Granth* recognises the human body as the abode of God (Dhanasari Pipa, p. 695). It is the temple of God, wherein the Light of the Lord can be seen. The human body is a microcosm, wherein we can peep into the macrocosm and realise the Creator (ibid). Like other temples, the temple of human body has to be kept neat and clean with full veneration. It should be made a befitting Abode for the Lord. The cleanliness of mind and body takes the individual self nearer God (Var Asa M. 1, p. 472). It has been well said by the wise people that cleanliness is next to godliness. A healthy mind lives in a healthy body. The health of the mind becomes the basis and cause of a healthy body. Guru Arjan Dev says, "That body is pure, which does not commit sin

(Gauri M. 5, p. 198). Ordinarily the night passes in sleep and the day in eating, and in this manner, the diamond-like body is wasted (Gauri M. 1, p. 156). The human body is a rare phenomenon, we do not get it repeatedly like the ripe fruit of the forest, which when drops down, cannot be united with the bough (Shlok Kabir, p. 1366). The gods are said to have a burning desire for the human body, which is the only medium through which the soul reaches the desired goal (Bhairo Kabir, p. 1159). When the body is without disease and old age and without the effect of death, the individual should concentrate on the Lord (ibid). All the other *yonis* are subservient to human body, which eats, drinks, plays, laughs and acts in several ways (Gauri Sukhmani M. 5, p. 261). The *Adi Granth* lays emphasis on limited diet, which keeps both the mind and body quite fit. The Sikh Gurus have forbidden the use of intoxicants, which destroy sanity and bring madness and one loses hold on his senses (Var Bihagra M. 3, p. 554). The body should be washed clean every morning (Basant M. 5, p. 1185). One must do all the work with his hands and feet and keep his mind in tune with the Lord (Shlok Kabir, p. 1376).

Bond: That with which one is bound; a shackle, chain or fetter. The individual is bound with the world through several bonds. They are *maya* (wealth), property and relatives. All the worldly-wise are ultimately affected by one or the other bond. "One is consumed by the love of *maya*" (Bhairo M. 5, p. 1140). Man is subjected to agony by the malady of ego (ibid). Kabir says, "Mother, father, wife, son and wealth, none of them accompanies you on leaving the world. The life is being wasted, therefore, O fool, remember the Lord" (Sarang Kabir, p. 1152). The fool considers the solid and beautiful mansions as his own. A large accumulation of wealth can be emptied in no time (Var Majh M. 1, p. 141).

Bondage: According to Guru Nanak Dev, the individual self, bound in bondage through actions, experiences births and deaths (Ramkali M.1, p. 903). None else is to be blamed for bondage. Only our *karmas* are to be blamed. We are the recipient of the fruit of our actions. Why should we blame others? (Asa M. 1, Patti, p. 433). The ego and *maya* are the main factors causing bondage. Guru Arjan Dev says, "By observing mineness (ego) they experience bondage. On being involved in maya's struggle, they are either born in heaven or hell" (Suhi M. 5, p. 761).

Bones: Besides flesh and blood, the bones form an important part of the body. The distinct parts which unitedly make up the skeleton are called bones. Sheikh Farid after great austerities became very weak and a mere skeleton. He addresses the crow in the following manner: "My body has withered and has become a skeleton. The crows are pecking at my palms. God has not come as yet. This is my fate. O crow, you have searched all my skeleton and eaten all my flesh. Do not touch both the eyes because I long to see my Lord. O crow, do not peck at my skeleton. If you have perched on it, then fly away. Do not eat the flesh of the body in which my Lord resides" (Shlok Farid, p. 1387). The angel of death forces the helpless soul out of the body, striking the bones (Shlok Farid, p. 1377). The soul-bird resides in this skeleton composed of bones, flesh and veins (Sorath Ravidas, p. 659). When the soul leaves the body, it is put on the funeral pyre for cremation. The bones burn like the faggot of wood and the hair like the bundle of grass (Gaund Kabir, p. 870).

Books: In the *Adi Granth*, there is mention of religious texts and scriptures of various religions and sects. The equivalent for the books of Middle Eastern religions is *Kateb* and for Hinduism and its sects, it is *Pothian*. The Arabic word *Kateb* refers to the scriptures of Judaism (*Taurāt* and *Zabūr*), Christianity (*Injīl*) and Islam (*Quran*). The word *Pothian* refers to Vedas, Puranas, Smritis etc.

Boon: A boon is a blessing. It is an antonym of curse (sarāp). The austerity and whole-hearted devotion elicited a boon from a god or a sage, as is apparent from the myths and old stories. The saints of the *Adi Granth* have no faith in such boons. The only boon that they seek is the prayer of the devotee to the Lord to be Merciful and his earnest desire to always tread the path leading towards the Lord (Suhi M. 5, p. 781).

Brahmā: One of the gods of Hindu Trinity, who is said to be the creator of the world. In the *Adi Granth*, there are some references regarding Brahmā from the Puranas viz "Brahmā talked in ego without knowing the consequence. He became repentent, when he suffered the loss of the Vedas" (Gauri M. 1, p. 224). In *Bhagavata Purana*, it is recorded that during his repose one night, Brahmā lost the Vedas, which had been carried away by the demon Haya-Grīva. Vishnu assumed the form of a fish (*matsya*), slew the demon and restored the Vedas to Brahmā. "Brahmā was born in the lotus emerging from the navel of Vishnu and began to recite Vedas in a melodious voice. But he could not know the limits of the Lord and moving to and fro remained in darkness (of ignorance)" (Gujri M. 1, p. 489). Since Brahmā the creator of the world (Sansārī) is the disciple/son of *maya* alongwith Vishnu and Shiva, he is impure (Bhairo Kabir, p. 1158). All the four Vedas, uttered through the mouth of Brahmā, involved the world in the *maya* of three qualities, (Maru M. 1, pp. 1037-38). Brahmā is the first to study and dwell upon the teachings of the Vedas. From him issued forth the gods, with an urge of attachment and desire. They wandered within the three modes (Gauri M. 3, p. 230). Brahmā reads the Vedas, but is absorbed in quarrels. Within him is the quality of morbidity and he does not recognise his self (Gauri M. 3, p. 231). Though the light of the hymns of the Vedas dawned through Brahmā, he himself was involved in maya and attachment (Vadhans M. 3, p. 559).

Brahmacharin: Out of the four stages of life *Brahmacharya* is the first stage, when a young '*dvija*' practised sacred study, after having been initiated into a new spiritual life through *Upanayana* ceremony. He was required to adopt a rigorous discipline up to the age of twenty-five, as a student, living in the house of his Guru. He had to beg for alms and practise austerity in addition to his studies. He had to remain absolutely chaste during this period. According to the *Adi Granth*, the *Brahmacharin* practises his rigorous discipline, but there is ego within his heart (Maru M. 5, p. 1003). The *Brahmacharin* forsakes the company of another's woman, but the man of God, in humility, desires the company of Hari (Gauri Guareri M. 4, p. 164). In fact, the life of a *Brahmacharin* has been rejected by the saints of the *Adi Granth*. The detail of the discipline of a *Brahmacharin* is given in Manu Smriti chapter 2.

Brahmaloka: The word 'loka' signifies a division of the universe, therefore, *Brahmaloka* is the highest heaven or the Abode of Brahman. Out of the seven upper worlds, the highest i.e. *Satyaloka* has also been called *Brahmaloka*. The superior deities are said to live on this *Loka*. In the *Adi Granth*, the highest region has been called *Sach Khand* (the region of Truth), but *Satyaloka* or *Brahmaloka* has no similarity with this region.

Brahm, Brahman: In Indian philosophy, the Ultimate Reality is called *Brahman*. In Sikh scriptures, this word occurs very often. It is pronounced as *Brahm*. Guru Arjan Dev says, "Whatever I see, is Brahman; whatever I hear, is Brahman" (Bilawal M. 5, p. 846). In fact, the whole of the *Adi Granth* talks about Brahman and His Divine Will. The real motive of our birth in this world is the realisation of

Brahman. The real nature of this Ultimate Reality has been summed up in *Mūl Mantra*, the fundamental sacred prayer, wherein it is recorded: "God (Brahman) is One. His Name is Truth. He is the Creator. He is without any fear and enmity. He is Immortal, Unborn and Self-existent. He can by realised through the Grace of the Guru" (Japuji, p.1). The words *Brahm* and *Pāra Brahman* occur in the *Adi Granth* for the Lower Brahman and Higher Brahman respectively. The Higher Brahman is devoid of attributes. He is Indeterminate and Incomprehensible. He is Transcendental Being, called Truth. This Truth is without Beginning and End. He is Consciousness and Bliss. He is non-phenomenal, non-spatial, non-temporal, non-causal, Impersonal and devoid of all sensible qualities. He is "Neti Neti" and can be described by method of negation. He is called *Nirguna Brahman*. The Lower Brahman is also called *Saguna Brahman* and Ishwara. He is endowed with attributes. He is Immanent in the phenomenal world. He is the Lord of the spatial and temporal world, governed by causality. He is Infinite, Eternal, Omnipresent, Omnipotent and Omniscient. He is the Creator, Preserver and Destroyer of the universe. He is the Lord of the Law of Karma and is the Inner Controller. He is Truth, Consciousness and Bliss. He is the Higher Soul and Supreme Self (Parmātamā)—(Sorath M.1, p. 597, Maru M. 1, p. 1035 and Maru M. 1, p. 1038).

Brahmānda: The egg (*Ānda*) of Brahman (*Brahm*). See: *Brahman-Egg*.

Brahman-Egg: *Brahmānda* is the Sanskrit equivalent of *Brahman-Egg*. According to Hindu mythology, there was nothing in the beginning except an egg. When the egg was split, a male child came out. He had the radiance of innumerable suns. This helpless child was "*Virāt Purusha*", because of his materiality. From each pore of the body of this *Purusha*, a world came into being. Each world had its own Trinity of Brahma, Vishnu and Shiva. It had the seven nether regions and the seven upper regions. In the *Adi Granth*, the word *Brahmānda* occurs several times. "The Lord of the Universe is the master of millions of *Brahmāndas*" (Sorath M. 5, p. 612).

Brahm-Giānī: (Knower of Brahman). One complete *ashtapadi* (octavo) has been composed on *Brahm-Giānī* by Guru Arjan Dev in his poem *Sukhmani* in Raga Gauri. One whose mind is absorbed in the True Lord and in whose mouth the Name of the Lord abides and who sees only the True Lord everywhere, is, indeed, a *Brahm-Giānī* (Gauri Sukhmani M. 5, p. 272). *Brahm-Giānī* is for ever unattahced, is free from evil, looks alike on all, has even patience, is the purest, has illumined mind, treats the friend and foe alike, is the highest, but most humble, knows the essence of the self, is merciful, sheds nectar from his eyes, has his fetters cut off, is always in bliss, leans on the One Alone, is for ever eternal, seeks pleasure in doing good, is free from shackles, holds his mind from wanderings and his actions are holy and good (ibid, pp. 272-74). Etc.

Brahmin: "He is only a Brahmin, who realises Brahman" (Shlok Varan te Vadhik M. 1, p. 1411). See: *Varnas*.

Brahmopasanā: Meditation on Brahman. The *Adi Granth* lays stress on the meditation on Brahman only and rejects devotion to all other gods because Brahman is the Highest Divinity and the Creator of all. Brahman cannot be comprehended by any other symbol except His Name, on which stress has been laid in the *Adi Granth*. Innumerable ascetics, sages, Brahmas, men of wisdom meditate on Brahman through contemplation, austerity, self-control, moral-code, worship, obeissance and other purifying acts. All dwell on Him—the human beings, the vegetation, the animals and the birds. Innumerable Vishnus and Shivas meditate on Him and also the gods, siddhas, the attendants and musicians of gods, yakshas, dancers in the court of the god of wealth and innumerable Indras, myriads of goddesses, Lakshmis, the seen, unseen, air, water, day and night, stars, moon, sun, earth and the sky sing His Praises. All the divisions of creation and the divisions of speech-sound, Smritis, Vedas, Puranas, Shastras and all others both known and unknown, meditate on Him (Asa Chhant M. 5, pp. 455-56).

Brahm-Vidyā: Knowledge of Brahman. In the Vedas, the knowledge of Brahman is revealed through *Upanishads*. Similarly, the knowledge of Brahman is revealed through the *Adi Granth*. Both are texts of *Brahm-Vidyā*, containing revelations about the Reality and Nature of the Supreme Being. *Brahm-Vidyā* is also called *Parā-Vidyā*. One who is an adept in *Parā-Vidyā* (*Brahm-Vidyā*) is known as *Brahm-Giānī*.

Breath: The air received into and expelled from the lungs in the act of respirations; a single respiration. The breath (*prāna*) gives life to the body. "We are the men of a single breath and do not know the time of our death" (Dhanasari M. 1, p. 660). Being uncertain about the next breath, Guru Ram Das says, "Do not delay in the remembrance of the Lord even for a moment, nobody knows whether the next breath will come or not" (Bihagra M. 4, p. 545). The remembrance of the Lord with every breath is enjoined in the *Adi Granth*. "All the breaths that I breathe, I cherish the Name of the Lord as advised by the Guru. All the breaths that go without the Name, they pass away in vain" (Nat M. 4, p. 981).

Breathings: *Prānas*. The following five breathings have been mentioned in Indian philosophy: *Prāna, Vyāna, apāna, samāna* and *udāna*. They are the *five Pranas*. The *Prana* means the vital breath. In *Brhadaranyaka Upanishad* it has been identified with *atman*. The association of breath with life is very obvious. See: *Prāna*.

Brother: A male child related to the other male or female children of the same parents. Guru Arjan Dev says, "Mother, father, wife, son, relatives, bosom friends and brothers meet in this life, as determined by Destiny in a previous birth, but they are not of any assistance in the last hour (Jaisri M. 5, p. 700). This word is also used for fellow members of the same religious order and is also a term of address.

Buddha: The founder of Buddhism. He is considered Vishnu's ninth incarnation. Guru Nanak Dev says, " When it was the Lord's Will, He created Ten Incarnations" (Maru M.1, p.1037). In the *Adi Granth,* the word 'Buddha' occurs several times and is conjoined with the word 'Siddha'. Whereas Buddha may have been used for Gautam Buddha, the founder of Buddhism, it also means 'Wise one'. In *Japuji,* the Guru says, "There are several Siddhas, Buddhas and Nathas" (p. 7).

Buddhī: Intellect. Also called *Budh.* The *Adi Granth* has laid great stress on the discriminating intellect (*Bibek Buddhi*). Ordinarily, the mind overshadows the intellect and defiles it. Because of the impure intellect, the devotee says in great humility, "O dear, I cannot meet Him in this way; I have done many pious deeds; ultimately I have fallen at the Door of the Master and pray: 'Bless me with the discriminting intellect'" (Sorath M. 5, p. 641). The devotee asks for such intellect as creates Love for the Lord (Todi M. 5, p. 712). The intellect is responsible for the remembrance of the Lord, receipt of honours, realisation of the discriminating knowledge and performing charitable deeds. This is the real path. All else is under the influence of the devil (Var Sarang M. 4, Shlok M. 1, p. 1245). In the daily prayer of the Sikhs, it is said: "The mind may remain low and the intellect may rise higher".

Buddhism: The religion founded by Gautama Buddha, who taught the Four Noble Truths, the Eight-fold Path and the doctrine of *Pratītyasmutpāda* (Dependent Origination). The Four Noble Truths are: 1-That there is suffering, 2-That there is cause of suffering, 3-That there is cessation of suffering and 4-That there is a way leading to the cessation of suffering. The eight-fold Path consists of 1-right faith, 2-right resolve, 3-right speech, 4-right action, 5-right living, 6-right effort, 7-right thought and 8-right concentration. The doctrine of *Pratītyasmutpāda* is related to two Noble Truths, the Second and the Third, therefore it deals with *Saṃsāra* and *Nirvāna* both. From one angle it is *Saṃsara* and from the other, it is *Nirvāna*. Everything appears relative, conditioned and dependent. It hangs between nothingness and reality or between nihilism and eternalism. This is Buddha's "middle path". On the one hand, there is life of pleasure and on the other, the life of mortification. The middle path brings enlightenment. The two major sects of Buddhism are *Hīnayāna* and *Mahāyāna*. *Hīnayāna* or the 'Lesser Vehicle' confined its salvation to a select few, but *Mahāyāna* or the 'Greater Vehicle' extended salvation to a much larger number of people. *Hīnayāna* is agnostic idealism and follows the simple morality of Buddha, but *Mahāyanā* is a speculative theistic system and sophistic nihilism. The goal of *Hīnayāna* is *Arhathood* and a negative cessation of misery, but the goal of Mahayana is a positive state of bliss. *Shūnyavāda* is one of the most important schools of Buddhism. The followers of the 'Middle Path' or *Madhyamikas* belong to this school. According to them *Shūnya* is not an empty void, it means 'indescribable'. The world and the Absolute both are *Shūnya,* because the world is neither existent nor non-existent and the Absolute is transcendental. Thus everything is *Shūnya*. Buddhism like Jainism is a religion without God. Karma takes the place of God in *Hīnayāna*. Gradually several other schools arose in Buddhism and image-worship became prevalent. Guru Nanak Dev agreed with the Four Noble Truths and the Eightfold Path, but he rejected agnosticism, image-worship and asceticism of Buddhism. According to him, the liberation can only be attained through the Grace of the Lord. *Nirvāna* of Buddhism is different from the spiritual ideal of the Guru. For the Guru, the final emancipation consists not only in the cessation of misery, but also in the merger in the Absolute. In the poem *Siddh Goshta,* the Guru has elucidated his concept of *Shūnya*. There is *Shūnya* inside, outside and in the three worlds, but the knowledge of *Shūnya* in the fourth state i.e. *Turiyā* is essential. The secret of the immortal *Shūnya* can only be known through the remembrance of the Name of the Lord.

Buildings: Guru Nanak Dev says that the man of the world is lured by the mansions built of earth and decorative stones and forgets about his spiritual responsibility (Suhi M.1, Kuchajji, p. 762). Those who remember their houses and buildings at the time of death, become ghosts (Gujri Trilochan, p. 526). The fools consider their buildings as their own, because the limit of our stay in them is uncertain (Var Majh M. 1, p. 141). Those houses, buildings, palaces and rest-houses (*sarāis*) are pure, which are dedicated to the devotees of the Lord (Var Sorath M. 4, p. 648). The houses, halls and mansions are the display of the men of the world (Var Asa M. 1, p. 472). Sheikh Farid says, "Those who built houses and mansions also left the world. They made a false deal and met their end in the grave. O Farid, be not fond of your houses, halls and mansions, because they are a heap of dust and do not accompany you" (Shlok Farid, p. 1380).

Bull: Nandi, the Bull, is the vehicle of Lord Shiva. Namdev says, "Those who repeat the Name of Lord Shiva, they will get the bull to ride upon in their next birth" (Gaund Namdev, p. 874). In India a bull has been widely used, from the very ancient times, for tilling the land, though its mother, the cow, has been receiving utmost respect. The bull is the symbol for the support of the world, therefore, he is often symbolised as *Dharma*. Guru Nanak Dev does not believe in the Pauranic myth that the earth is supported by the Bull. For him, it is *Dharma*, which supports the world. (Japuji, p. 3). The bull toils very hard. Kabir is of the view that without contemplating on the Lord, one is like a stray bull, with a torn nose and bruised shoulders fed upon the straw of coarse grain (Gujri Kabir, p. 524).

Burial Grounds: Whereas the Hindus cremate their dead, the Muslims bury them in the graves. For the Hindus, the deposit of the dead is in the cremation ground, the Muslims dig the graves for the dead in the burial grounds. Two words '*Masān*' and '*Jīrān*' have been used for the grounds meant for the deposit of the dead. The Hindus burn their dead, the Muslims bury them, some throw their dead to the dogs, some cast them in the waters, while others are thrown into the wells (Var Sorath M. 4, Shlok M. 1, p. 848). Guru Nanak Dev says, "My beautiful friends have gone to sleep in the burial ground, I am also going with anguish and cry in my weak voice" (Sri Rag M. 1, p. 26). Sheikh Farid has talked about graves in his Shlokas. He says, "The lowly grave calls me saying "O homeless one, come to your home; ultimately you will come to me, then why do you fear death?' " (Shlok Farid, p. 1382).

C

Caj Ācār: The way of living; The qualities and character. Guru Arjan Dev says, "I had no *caj ācār*, I did not know anything, but the Lord, through His Grace, brought me to His bed" (Asa M. 5, p. 372).

Cākar, Cākarī: *Cākar* means servant and *Cākarī* is service. Guru Nanak Dev says, " If a servant acts according to the instructions of the Master, he receives great respect and double remuneration" (Var Asa M. 1, p. 474). "If on the one hand, the servant is engaged in service, but on the other he is egoistic and quarrelsome, he does not receive the respect of the Master" (Var Asa M. 1, Shlok M. 2, p. 474). "The service of another is very difficult. One sells himself at the cost of his *Dharma*" (Gauri M. 3, pp. 246-47).

Calamities: The conditions of grievous affliction or adversity; deep distress arising from some adverse circumstances or events. A grievous disaster or misfortune may befall an individual or society or a country. For a child or children, the death of the parents or the breadwinner is a grievous calamity. The death of the husband brings the calamity for the widow. The persecution of a distinct society because of religious fanaticism is a calamity for the society. Natural calamities may befall a country in the form of drought, famine, flood, earthquake etc. An ant can destroy a myriad of hosts, if the Lord grants power to her. (p. 285, Gauri Sukhmani). The Lord turns water into desert and desert into a well and from a well he makes a mountain. From the earth he raises man to the sky and from thence dashes him down. He makes a beggar rule an empire and a king is turned into a beggar. He makes an idiot a scholar and a scholar a fool. He transforms a woman into a man and a man into a woman (p. 1252, Sarang Kabir). Thus the saints of the *Adi Granth* believe that the calamities befall by the Will of the Lord.

Calumny: Slander; a false and malicious misrepresentation to the injury of another. The vice of calumny has been highly deprecated in the *Adi Granth*. Because of slander, no merit accrues from the accomplishment of all the good works or deeds. The slanderer roars and bewails (Asa M. 5, p. 373). A hymn of Ravidas amply elucidates the point. He says: "The merit of bathing at sixty-eight holy places, worshipping all the twelve *lingams* and digging up wells and tanks for others go in vain, in the face of calumny. The merit of bathing at

Kurukshetra at the time of eclipse, making an offering of bedecked wife to the gods and hearing attentively all the Smritis go in vain, in the face of calumny. The merit of giving abundantly in charity, giving away lands, building castles and doing good to others at one's own cost, go in vain, in the face of calumny. The calumniator is cast into the womb many a time and is thrown into hell. Then why the saints should be slandered. The malice of the slanderer is always exposed." (p. 875, Gond Ravidas). See *Backbiting*.

Cangiāī: Virtue. According to Guru Arjan Dev, one becomes lazy in the performance of *cangiāī* (virtues), but is always ready to commit *buriai* (vices)—(Var Gujri M. 5, p. 518).

Capital Punishment: It is the verdict of death by any means. This is a legal term. We find the idea of punishment at several places in the *Adi Granth*. The worldly rulers being unjust could give death penalty on account of religious fanaticism. There is mention of the threat of such punishment to the Maharashtrian saint Namdev by the king Muhammad Bin Tughlak. On the death of his cow, the Sultan wants Namdev to show the miracle and revive the cow. "Bring back the cow to life, otherwise I shall strike off your head at this very spot".—Such was the order and verdict of death for Namdev (p. 1165, Bhairo Namdev). Kabir has also mentioned his persecution on the orders of Sikandar Lodhi in the following manner". Binding me in a bundle, they cast me before the elephant, who in rage trumpets and runs about, as if saying "I am a sacrifice to this image" (p. 870, Gond Kabir). Regarding the punishment, Guru Nanak Dev says, "If the Lord Wills, He blesses with glory and if he Wills, he punishes. If one remembers the Lord in time, then why should he be punished?" (p. 413, Asa M. 1). The Lord blesses or punishes the beings according to their *karmas* (actions). Guru Arjan Dev says, "Those who commit sins, are assuredly plundered. Izrail, the angel of death seizes and tortures them. They are thrown into hell by the Creator and asked to render the account by the Just Judge" (pp. 1019-20, Maru M. 5).

Caran Kamal: The Lotus-Feet. In the *Adi Granth*, the words *Caran Kamal* are very often repeated with reference to the Lotus-Feet of the Lord. The saint takes refuge at the Lotus-Feet of the Lord. He neither wishes for a kingdom nor salvation and is always absorbed in the love for the Lotus Feet of the Lord. (Devgandhari M. 5, p. 534). Kabir rises above the ideas of heaven and hell by the Grace of the True Guru. He is always in Bliss at the Lotus-Feet of the Lord. He cannot describe such a Bliss which can only be visualised (Shlok Kabir, p. 1370).

Cār Jug: The four Yugas. See *Yugas*.

Cār Padārath: Four ends of human action viz. *Dharma* (duty or virtue), *Artha* (wealth), *Kāma* (pleasure or enjoyment) and *Moksha* (emancipation). *Moksha* or final emancipation is the highest end. Kāma, *Artha* and *Dharma* are inter-dependent. While pursuing *Kāma* and *Artha,* the observance of *Dharma* is necessary. "If one asks for all the four ends of human action, he should absorb himself in the service of the saints" (Gauri Sukhmani M. 5, p. 266).

Caste, Castes: Hinduism is a caste-ridden religion. It is called *varnashrama dharma,* because it is divided into *varnas* (castes) and *ashramas* (stages of life). The four major *varnas* are: *Brahmins* or priestly class; *Kshatriyas* or military caste, *Vaishyas* or merchants and *Shudras* or artisans and labourers. The *Adi Granth* has rejected both the divisions of *varnas* and *ashramas.* Guru Nanak Dev says, "In the House of the True Lord, no enquiries are made about the caste or birth. The actions of the person determine his caste or birth" (p. 1330, Prabhati M. 1). It is the Lord God, who gives shade to all, therefore the pride of caste and glory is vain (p. 83, Var Sri Raga, Shlok M.1). Guru Amar Das says, "None should be proud of his caste. He who knows Brahman is in reality a Brahmin. O fool and idiot, do not be proud of your caste. Several vices crop up from this pride" (p.1128), Bhairo M. 3) For the saint-poets of the *Adi Granth,* the whole humanity is one and indivisible. Therefore, their instruction is for all the four *varnas* (p. 747, Suhi M. 5). Kabir is very critical about Brahmins (p. 324, Gauri Kabir).

Categories: According to Vaisheshika Shastra of Kannada, there are six categories called *padarathas* in which all objects can be thought or named. These categories are: 1. Substance 2. Quality 3. Movement and action 4. Generality and association 5. Particularity or difference and 6. Inherence. Later Vaisheshika theoreticians added the seventh category of non-existence. The *Padarathas* mentioned in the *Adi Granth* are the four ends of human life. There is no mention of the *Padarathas* of Vaisheshika. However, the idea of soul as a *Padarath* is not acceptable to the saint-poets of the *Adi Granth.*

Cattle: Livestock; a collective name for the bovine genus and for live animals held as property and who are reared to serve as food, or for their milk, skin, wool, etc. The *Adi Granth* considers cattle of better worth than the human beings. If a man dies, he is of no use, but when an animal dies, it can be used in many ways (p. 870, Gond Kabir).

Guru Nanak Dev says, " Blessed is the cattle, that eat grass, but yield nectar-like milk. Cursed is the life of that man, who performs works, but does not remember the Name of the Lord (p. 489, Gujri M. 1). He who does not hear the praises of the Lord, is worse than the animals, birds and reptiles (p. 188, Gauri M. 5).

Caturāī: Worldly wisdom. One cannot search the Lord with worldly wisdom (Gauri M. 1, p. 221). "O man, attune your mind with the Lord. The Lord cannot be attained through worldly wisdom" (Gauri Kabir, p. 324).

Cauthā Pad: The Fourth State. It is also called *Param Pad,* Supreme State or *Turiyā Avastha*, which is beyond the three states of *Jagrit* (awakening), *Svapana* (dream) and *Sushuptī* (dreamless sleep). In *Chautha Pad, there is* Sahaj (*Sahaj Avastha*), which is attained only by *Gurmukh* (Sri Rag M. 3, p. 68).

Cave: Cavern; a hollow place opening under the ground. In India, the hermits, living in solitude, used to reside in caves for meditation. But in the *Adi Granth,* the heart in the body is mentioned as a cave. Guru Amar Das says, "Within the cave of the heart is an inexhaustible treasure. The Unknowable Infinite resides within it" (p. 124, Majh M. 3), and again "Through the Word of the Guru, one should search this cave and find that holy Name of the Lord abides within it" (p. 126, Majh M. 3).

Celibacy: The state of living unmarried. There are rare examples of people practising celibacy. In Indian religious literature six prominent celibates have been mentioned. They are Bhairo, Hanuman, Lakshman, Gorakh, Bhisham and Dattatreya. Kabir says, "The six celebates (men of chastity) are the slaves of maya" (p. 1160, Bhairo Kabir). In the *Adi Granth*, there is mention of *Brahmacharins* practising celibacy (p. 164, Cauri Guareri M. 4). Guru Nanak Dev is critical about the fake celibates. He says, "They call themselves celibates, but they do not know the way and abandon their homes" (p. 469, Var Asa, Shlok M. 1).

Cemetery: A place set apart for the burial of the dead. See: *Burial Ground.*

Ceremonies: Performance of religious rites. The saint-poets of the *Adi Granth* are critical about the ceremonies and rites observed in Hinduism and Islam. They have decried all the ceremonials. Guru Arjan Dev says, "The men of the world are engaged in the observance of six types of works, but the dirt of ego is not cleansed from their hearts and without the Guru they lose the game of life" (p. 495, Gujri M. 5).

Cessation: Ceasing, discontinuance, stoppage. On the attainment of final emancipation, there is total cessation of suffering. The cause of suffering is *trsna* (craving for worldly objects). The bliss can be attained with the cessation of *trsna*. Guru Nanak Dev says, "There is the fire of *trsna* in the body which can be made to cease with the *Word* (Name of the Lord) (p. 147, Var Majh M.1). The ignorant craving is epitomised by the fetters in the chain of karmic causation. The ignorant *trsna* be burnt down from this body. Its cessation can be accomplished through the Word of the Guru (p. 1067, Maru M. 3).

Cetāvanī: Warning. Most of the hymns of the *Adi Granth* are a warning for the man of the world, who is absorbed in the worldly objects and vices and who will consequently undergo transmigration. Guru Arjan Dev gives this warning: "Sing the Praises of the Lord and meditate on him with every breath, there should be no delay in it, because there is no certainty about the life of our mortal body.... This world is not our permanent abode. The fool clings to it, whom myriads have already left" (Gauri Bawan Akhri M. 5, p. 254). Sheikh Farid says, "Where are your parents, who gave birth to you; they have left you, but you are still not satisfied about the impermanence of the world" (Shlok Farid, p.1381).

Chaos: A state of utter confusion and disorder. Whenever there is absence of government in the country, there is a state of chaos and anarchy. Due to the absence of the supreme power or its inefficiency, there is a state of lawlessness. When the kings lose their heads and revel in revelries, there is a revolution and not even the princes get bread to eat (p. 417, Asa M. 1). When Babur invaded India and the Pathan government failed, the riches and beauty of the ladies of high gentry became their enemies and the soldiers were told to dishonour them and carry them off (*ibid*).

Chariot, Charioteer: A chariot is a wheeled vehicle; its driver is called charioteer. The idea of the chariot is given in the verses of Guru Nanak Dev. He says, "For the bead of the human body, there is a chariot and a charioteer. They change in every age. Only the wise know this fact. In the age of *Satya* (truth), contentment is the chariot and the righteousness is its driver; in the *Treta* age, continence is the chariot and the power is its driver; in the *Dvapar* age, austerity is the chariot and charity is its driver; and in the *Kali* age, the chariot is of fire and falsehood is its driver" (p. 470, Var Asa M. 1). The idea of the chariot and charioteer has been taken from *Kathopanishad*, wherein it has been stated that the human body is the chariot, which is driven by the horses of senses. The intellect is the charioteer and mind is the reins. The soul is the owner of this chariot. The chariot moves smoothly, if the intellect (*buddhi*) properly controls the senses through the reins of mind. If the reins are let loose, the chariot is sure to move towards its destruction.

Charity: Benevolence especially to the poor; alms-giving. According to the *Adi Granth*, a devotee strictly observes the trio of Nam (remembrance of the Name of the Lord), Dan (charity) and Ishnan (the purity of mind and body). Dan consists in the sharing of one's earnings with the deserving and the needy. In Hinduism, it is one of the good works. It has also a great significance in Muslim ethics. According to the saint-poets of the *Adi Granth*, the real Donor is God Himself, who continues to give and never stops, though the recipient may even feel tired in receiving the gifts of God (p. 2, Japuji). The charity should be without any sense of repayment. The donors, ordinarily, though satisfied with the idea of giving away in charity, beg hundred times repayment from God and want the approbation of the world (p. 466, Var Asa M. 1).

Charms: Incantations; magic spells. The use of charms, spells and incantations has been condemned in the *Adi Granth*. For Guru Nanak Dev, *maya* is the charmer, who has charmed the whole world tying the many-coloured thread round every one's neck (p. 582, Vadhans M. 1). The attachment of *maya* is like the attachment with a condemned woman; she is an ugly charmer, practising charms and spells (p. 796, Bilawal M. 1).

Chastity: The quality or state of being chaste; Continence; Celibacy; Purity from unlawful sexual intercourse. A chaste woman has been called *Suhagan* (true bride) in the *Adi Granth*. "She is imbued with the Lord's colour and equipoise and is merged night and day in His Love. She is Beauteous, Glorious, Brilliant, Wise and Awake" (p. 722, Tilang M. 1). A *Brahmacharin* or Vedic student has been enjoined to observe chastity (p. 164, Gauri Guareri M. 4).

Chatter: Incessant trivial talk. The saints talk very little. Guru Amar Das in his *Anand*, speaking about the way of life of a devotee, says, "They shed their greed, ego and craving and speak but little" (p. 918, Anand, Ramkali M. 3). Bhai Gurdas, the elucidator of Gurbani, talking about the instructions of the Guru, says that a Sikh eats less, sleeps less and talks less.

Child, Children: The metaphor of a child has been used for a devotee in the *Adi Granth*. Guru Ram Das says, "O my Lord, we are the ignorant children of Hari. Blessed is the Guru-teacher, who by giving instructions regarding Hari, has made us wise" (p. 168, Gauri Bairagan M. 4). "There are three stages of life: A child, a youth and an old man. All of them are vain, if the Lord is not remembered" (p. 1428, Shlok M. 9). The Lord provides the infant child with milk. (p. 266, Gauri Sukhmani M. 5). "When a child dies, his sports are remembered" (p. 1027, Maru M. 1).

Cintā: Anxiety. The people who appear to us great, are engrossed in the malady of anxiety (Gauri M. 5, p. 188). He, who is short of wealth, is always in anxiety (Maru M. 5, p. 1019). Everybody seems to be afflicted. Only He is in comfort, who remembers the Lord (Ramkali M. 1, Dakhni Oamkar, p. 932). Guru Angad Dev says, "Do not feel anxious because the Lord is anxious about you" (Var Ramkali M. 3, Shalok M. 2, p. 955). He, who has taken refuge in the Lord, is never in anxiety (Asa M. 5, p. 380).

Chiromancy: Divination by the hand, palmistry. There is no mention of the practice of chiromancy in the *Adi Granth*.

Church: A building for public Christian worship—applied in general to public place of worship of any religion. The place of public worship is Islam is known as *masjid* (masjid and masīt as mentioned in the *Adi Granth*) in Hinduism as *mandir* and in Sikhism as *Gurdwara*. Kabir says, "If God resides in the mosque, to whom the rest of the world belongs? If a Hindu finds the Lord's presence in the idol, then the quintessence is not known to both (the Muslims and the Hindus) (p.1349, Prabhati Kabir). For Guru Nanak God's Grace is the mosque for a true Muslim (p.140, Var Majh M.1). Guru Arjan Dev says, "There is the light of the Word within my *mandir* (temple)" (p. 384, Asa M. 5).

Circumambulation: Walking round about; performing *Aarti*. In India there has been practice of worshipping the sacred objects by going round them towards the right. In Hindu temples, the idols were circumambulated and sacred hymns called *Aarti* were chanted during circumambulation. When Guru Nanak visited the famous temple of Jagannath at Puri in Orissa, the priests were performing *Aarti*. But the Guru did not join them and instead sang his *Aarti* hymn. According to him the *Aarti* for Jagannath (the Lord of the World) cannot be appropriate by merely putting lighted earthen lamps in a platter and showering petals over the idol while circumambulating. For him, the sky is the platter and sun and moon are the lamps; the stars are the pearls. The fragrance of the sandalwood makes the incense, the winds act as fan and all the vegetation showers its flowers (p. 663, Dhanasri M.1, Aarti). The Muslims also circumambulate their most holy shrine *Kaabah* in Mecca. On the model of the *Aarti* in Hindu temples, Dhanna, a saint-poet of the *Adi Granth* has composed his *Aartī.*

Circumcision: Cutting off the foreskin or prepuce of males, practised as religious rite by Jews and Mohammedans. This practice is known as *Sunnat.* Kabir says, "If circumcision makes one a Muslim, then what we can say of a woman?" (p. 477, Asa Kabir) Guru Nanak asks the Muslim to make effort his circumcision. (p. 140, Var Majh M. 1)

Civilization: The process of being civilised i.e. coming out of the state of barbarism. The civilised nations are elightened and refined. Guru Arjan Dev has addressed the civilised man in the following words: "All the other creatures of the world are at your service. You are the lord of this earth. You have gold, silver and wealth with you, but the lust has disturbed your conduct of life" (p. 374, Asa M. 5). Ravidas, a saint-poet of the *Adi Granth* talks about an ideal civilised city: "The name of my city is Begumpura (the city without any affliction). There is neither anguish nor care. There is no agony of taxes on goods. There is neither any fear, nor error, dread or decline" (p. 345, Gauri Guareri, Ravidas).

Civil Law: The law of any city or state regulating the private rights and duties of the inhabitants. In Islam, the law including both the teaching of the Quran and the traditional sayings of Prophet Muhammad is called *Shariah* or *Shariat.* Guru Nanak Dev says, "A Muslim dwells on *Shariat* or the Prophet's way" (p. 84, Var Sri Raga, Shlok M. 1).Here Guru Nanak Dev refers to the Muslim religious code. Guru Arjan Dev has also referred to it in one of his hymns (p. 1083, Maru M. 5). Hindu religious code is contained in the *Smritis* and *Sutras.* There is mention of several Hindu sacred books in the *Adi Granth.* Guru Arjan Dev says, "The Smritis, the Vedas, the Puranas and other sacred books proclaim that everything else is a vain prattle except the Name of the Lord" (p. 761, Suhi M. 5). The main concern of the *Adi Granth* is regarding the religious and spiritual discipline of the devotees.

Clothes: Covering for the person; wearing apparel; dress; vesture. A Jaina sect known as Digambra discards the use of clothes on the body.

Guru Nanak Dev has refuted this practice. He says, "(The Jaina) does not wear clothes and is always in a state of agony (p. 467, Var Asa M. 1). "Discarding the clothes one becomes a Digambara" (p. 1169, Basant M. 3). Guru Arjan Dev says, "The more I embellish myself, I crave for more.... I consider the raiments, ornaments and alluring pleasures of no avail" (p. 373, Asa M. 5). For a lover there can be no sleep and no hunger without the Lord. Even the clothes are of no comfort to the body (p.1108, Tukhari Baramaha M.1). If one dyes his robes in ochre and dons the distinctive coat of a mendicant; if he tears off his clothes and wears a wallet and spreads it to collet money; in this way he begs from door to door, but instructs the world; he is blind in mind and loses all his honour" (pp. 1012-13, Maru M. 1)

Cloud: A visible mass of condensed water-vapour floating at various heights in the upper air. The image of cloud is found at several places in the *Adi Granth*. Guru Arjan Dev, says, "There are flashes of lightning and the dark clouds thunder. Heavy rain is showered from the clouds. Those who are united with the Lord, are, indeed, blessed" (p. 1102, Var Maru, Shlok M. 5). When the *Papiha* cries early in the morning, his prayer is heard in the House of the Lord. The cloud is ordered to show mercy and shower rain. (p. 1285, Var Malar, Shlok M. 3). The bird (*Papiha or Chatrik*) mentioned here is the seeker and the cloud is the Guru. In the month of *Shravan*, the rainy season begins. It continues in the month of *Bhadon*, when the clouds burst and the earth is covered with water, the seas are full to the brim. This is the time to enjoy the company of the Beloved. It rains during the whole dark night, but there is no peace for the young bride. The peacocks shriek and the frogs croak. The *Chatrik* also cries out for the beloved (raindrop); the snakes sneak out to bite, the mosquitos sting. The pools overflow, but where is peace for the bride without the Lord (p. 1108, Baramaha Tukhari M. 1).

Cock: The male of the common domestic fowl. The crowing of the cock, early in the morning, informs the early-risers about the dawning of the day. There is mention of its short flight in the *Adi Granth*. Guru Arjan Dev says, "One plays the game of polo, but does not know how to ride. One wants to fly with the swans, but has only the flight of a cock (p. 322, Var Gauri M. 5, Shlok M. 5).

Cognition: Knowledge; Consciousness. According to M. Winternitz, the Sanskrit word *vidya* is the equivalent of *cognition*. Guru Nanak Dev says, "He who dwells on *vidya*, becomes a benefactor of all" (p.

356, Asa M. 1). Without the wisdom of *vidya,* one cannot attain emancipation (p. 903, Ramkali M. 1). One is the recipient of honour and glory, if he dwells on *vidya* by the grace of the Guru" (p. 1329, Prabhati M. 1). *See : Knowledge.*

Cohabitation: Living together as husband and wife. According to the *Adi Granth,* the soul is the bride and the Higher soul or God is the bridegroom. There are several hymns which indicate the relationship of the devotee with the Lord with the imagery of wife and husband. Guru Amar Das says, "The bride and bridegroom are not they who pose as one whole. They are the two bodies with one soul" (p. 788, Var Suhi M. 3, Shalok M. 3) The Guru addresses the bride in the following way: "O bride, Bedeck yourself only after you have pleased the Lord lest your bridegroom does not come to your bed and thus you waste away your life. The real embellishment consists in the mutual affection. The embellishment is of avail only when the bridegroom loves the bride. Let the bride embellish herself with the Fear of the Lord and have His Love as her food and betel-chewing. If she surrenders her body and mind to the Lord, only then the Lord embraces her" (p. 788, Var Suhi M. 3, Shlok M. 3). In the words of Guru Nanak Dev "If the bride in the temple of her mind lights the lamp and makes her body a couch, the Lord , who is the king of knowledge, comes to her bed and enjoys her" (p. 359, Asa M. 1).

Commotion: Mental perturbation; agitation. The mind is encircled by vices and performs evil deeds. As a result of this it remains in an agitated state. Its perturbation can cease only if it concentrates on the Lord's Name. Guru Ram Das says, "O my mind, always dwell on the Lord's Name because it brings peace night and day, it washes off all the sins, it drives away the poverty, pain and hunger. This is the only great good destiny" (p. 88, Var Sri Rag M. 4, Pauri 13)

Compassion: Suffering together with another; Fellow feeling, sympathy. Compassion is a godly quality. One must be conscious of compassion towards other beings. *Daya* or compassion is the mother and *Dharma* or righteousness is its son (p. 3, Japu). Thus compassion is the basic Virtue. Guru Arjan Dev says, "Do not injure any one and go to your true Home with honour" (p. 322, Var Gauri M. 4).

Concentration: Bringing towards a common centre or focus. Concentration or *dharana* is a significant step of Yoga, mentioned by Patanjalli in his *Yoga Sutra.* It consists in giving full attention of the mind to any one thing or idea. According to the *Adi Granth,* the mind is to be concentrated on the Name of the Lord. *Simran* or remembrance of the Lord is the first requisite of concentration. Guru Nanak Dev says: "Our life is like a tree on the sea-shore. Its roots can be eternal, if its top is absorbed in concentration on the Lord" (p. 840, Bilawal M. 1, Thitti). According to Guru Amar Das the body is of little worth without true concentration" (p. 917, Ramkali M. 3, Anand).

Conception: The action of becoming pregnant. According to the *Adi Granth* when it is the Will of the Lord, one is conceived. It thrives in the womb, standing on its head. When it is the Will of the Lord, one takes birth" (p. 636, Sorath M. 1). On the birth of the sixth Guru Hargobind, Guru Arjan Dev wrote thus: "God has blessed me with the boon of the son.... The son when conceived in the womb, brought immense pleasure in the mind of the mother" (p. 396, Asa M. 5)

Conduct: Behaviour. Conduct is the voluntary behaviour of any sort, actual or intended. It pertains to an action for which a person may be held responsible. The action may be good or bad, therefore, conduct is the subject-matter of ethics. In the *Adi Granth*, a definite ethical code of conduct has been laid for an individual, who has triple responsibility, in relation to his self, in relation to the society and in relation to God. The mind, speech and actions are to be disciplined. Guru Arjan Dev says, "He who realised the Lord in thought, word and deed, has his mind illumined and awakened.... Greed, falsehood, sins and affliction infest our lives. Peace can come only through the grace of the Guru, when the nectar of the Name of the Lord is drunk" (p. 259, Gauri Bawan Akhri M. 5).

Confession: Acknowledging of sin or sinfulness. The confession brings purification in the mind of the sinner. It induces him to perform penances (*prayaschittas*). The *Adi Granth* has no faith in penances. Guru Arjan Dev says, "All the *Prayaschittas* (acts for the atonement of sins) are effaced by joining the company of the saints" (p. 621, Sorath M. 5).

Congregation: A body of persons assembled for religious worship. The holy congregation is called *Satsang* (The true company) and *Sadh Sangat* (The company of the saints). The Sikh discipline lays great emphasis on attending the holy congregation regularly every day. The congregation is presided over by the Guru. Since the personal Guruship ended with Guru Gobind Singh, the Guru in Sikhism for all the time is Guru Granth Sahib. Therefore the congregation is held in the presence of Guru Granth Sahib (The *Adi Granth*). The musicians sing the praises of the Lord through the hymns of the Guru. Guru Nanak Dev has defined *Satsangat* as the congregation where only One Name of the Lord is recited. The Lord Wills the remembrance of the Name, which can be realised through the True Guru" (p. 72, Sri Rag M. 1) "If one is in search of eternal bliss, the Guru has advised him to join the company of the saints, where only the Name is remembered" (p. 1182, Basant M. 5). *Satsangat* is the school (instruction centre) of the True Guru, where the devotee learns to imbibe the godly qualities (p. 1316, Var Kanra M. 4).

Conjunction: (Samjoga): Union. The conjunction and separation are the functionaries and the destiny of all is taken into account (p. 6, Japuji). With the creation of conjunction and separation, came the origin of the world (p. 509, Var Gujri M. 3). My Lord has created both conjunction and separation. He has endowed us with pleasure and pain. But the people who are God-conscious are detached from both—joys and sorrows (p. 1032, Maru M. 1).

Conjurers: Magicians; Jugglers. The *Adi Granth* has no belief in the *mantras*, spells and incantations. Guru Arjan Dev says, "He who dwells upon the Name of the Lord is always awake. The *Tantras* and *Mantras* have no effect upon him" (pp. 817-18, Bilawal M. 5). According to Guru Nanak Dev: "The religious hypocrisy of *Tantra* and *Mantra* is now known to me. I only cherish my Lord..." (p. 766, Suhi M. 1).

Consanguinity: Blood-relationship. Several verses in the *Adi Granth* speak of blood-relations. At the time of death none of the blood relations are of any help. Kabir says, "Whose are the father and mother and whose is wife? When the pitcher of the body breaks, every one says, "Take him away". The mother weeps at home, the brothers take away the bier, the wife cries shaking off her relationship, but the soul goes alone" (p. 478, Asa Kabir). Guru Arjan Dev says, "When one is in utter distress and there is no one to support him... and his kinsmen have left him alone.... If he then remembers the Lord, he will not be touched by the hot wind (agony)" (p. 70, Sri Rag M. 5).

Conscience: Inward knowledge; internal conviction. The internal recognition of the moral quality of one's motives and actions. The faculty or principle which pronounces upon the moral quality of one's actions or motives, approving the right and condemning the wrong. When one is in full youth, he cannot discriminate between right and wrong; his mind is intoxicated with ego (p. 77, Sri Rag M. 5). So long as one is in duality, he speaks of right and wrong, but the enlightened person recognises One Lord everywhere and merges in Him (p. 757, Suhi M. 3). The self-willed persons do not know what to say. They are engrossed by lust, anger and ego. They always think of evil and cannot discriminate between good and bad (p. 1248, Var Sarang M. 4, Shlok M. 3). Thus the voice of the conscience of the sinner becomes very feeble and is not heard.

Consciousness: Knowledge to which one has the testimony within oneself. In Indian philosophy, the soul is pure consciousness The term "consciousness" is applied to the conscious mind. Guru Amar Das has addressed the mind thus:" You are the embodiment of Light; recognise your base. The Lord is ever with you. Enjoy His Love through the Word of the Guru... O my mind, you are absorbed in ego, you are lured by *maya*, therefore you undergo transmigration... enjoy bliss by losing your self-entity and abiding in humility" (p. 441, Asa M. 3). The consciousness, of course lies at the root of all knowledge. In the state of consciousness, the mind abides in the state of awakening.

Consecration: Dedication or devotion to some purpose or pursuit. According to Hindu thought, consecration brings merit in the next world. But the saint-poets of the *Adi Granth* have no belief in this act. The Maharashtrian saints Namdev says, "If one consecrates horses, elephants, lands or even one's woman; if he offers himself to gods or gives away gold equal to his weight—all this does not equal the contemplation of the Name of the Lord" (p. 973, Ramkali Namdev).

Consideration: Regard for the circumstances, feelings, etc. of another. Keeping into consideration the contemplation of the devotee on Lord's Name, he is welcomed everywhere and is short of nothing. The Lord blesses him with the Robe of Honour (p. 631, Sorath M. 5). When the mind is dyed in Lord's Love and the tongue utters the Lord's Name,—in consideration of this, no one will be impolite to you in the court of the Lord and every one will welcome you to your exalted seat" (p. 252, Gauri Bawan Akhri M. 5).

Contamination: Rendering impure by contact or mixture. Kabir says, "The whole world is soiled and contaminated. Only (the Name of) the infinite Lord is the One Immaculate Thing" (p. 1158, Bhairo Kabir). The grease of ego stuck to the mind was completely cleansed by the dust of the feet of the saints. If the body is bathed in many waters, the contamination does not leave it and it is not cleansed (p. 200, Gauri M. 5). If the mind is contaminated, everything is contaminated; by bathing the body, the mind is not cleansed (p. 558, Vadhans M. 3)

Contemplation: Meditation; Religious musing. Out of the eight steps of Yoga mentioned by Patanjali in *Yoga Sutras*, contemplation or *Samādhi* is the final step. In this state, the entity of the Individual ceases and there is unity of the perceiver and perceived. The flow of thought comes to a natural end. According to the *Adi Granth*, the Lord was in abstract meditation (contemplation)—Shunya Samadhi—before the creation the world. In the state of contemplation, the Yogi enters the state of deep trance. But according to Kabir, the true devotee enters into deep contemplation through the four ages, if he makes the rake of compassion, the fire-place of the body, the kindling of the fire as the stilling of the eye's craving and breathing in the Lord's Love within himself (p. 477, Asa Kabir). Such a trance, in fact, is the greatest awareness. It is a state of perfect happiness.

Contentment: The process of being satisfied. Contentment and compassion are the two great virtues, whose contact gives birth to *Dharma* (righteousness) (p. 3, Japuji). Without contentment, no one gets satisfaction (p. 279, Gauri M. 5, Sukhmani). Persons who observe contentment, truly serve the Lord and dwell only on Truth. Their feet do not traverse the path of evil. They perform good actions and practise *Dharma*. They remain unattached with the world; they eat less. The Lord blesses them more and more and His Grace is showered on them. They praise the Lord and realise Him (p. 466-67, Var Asa M. 1). The real performance of a devotee consists in the practice of Truth, contentment and compassion (p. 51, Sri Rag M. 5).

Contracts: Mutual agreements between two or more parties. In the verses of Kabir, the word *Patta* has been used, which signifies a contract or a title deed. A deed is an authoritative document. According to Kabir, the *Yama* or the messenger of death has been authorised through a contract or a deed to take away the souls from the bodies at a particular time. Kabir says, "The Yogis, the followers of Vedas, men of one word and the men of silence—all come under Yama's contract" (p. 654, Sorath Kabir).

Convents: A religious association; A body of monks, friars or nuns forming one local community. In Christianity the Convents signify monastries and in Buddhism Viharas. The *Adi Granth* does not believe in asceticism and ascetic practices. The Jainas had also their convents where the Bhikshus lived and came to habitations in order to beg for their food. Guru Nanak Dev has decried the practices of these Jaina monks. He says, "They fold their blanket like a cowl over their heads and appear like a mourner and do not attend an assembly of persons". (p. 149, Var Majh M. 1).

Converts: Persons brought over to any religious faith. The *Adi Granth* does not believe in forcible conversions. A Muslim should remain a True Muslim, a Brahmin should adopt the qualities of a Brahmin etc. All the religions are valuable. Guru Amar Das says, "The world is burning, O Lord, protect it with your Grace. Save it, through whichever door it can be saved" (p. 853, Var Bilawal M. 4, Shlok M. 3).

Cor: A thief. "None is pleased with his Praises by a thief. If the thief commits vice, it has no effect on the other person. Nobody stands surety for a thief. None of the acts of a thief is considered good" (Dhanasari M. 1, p. 662). "The thief, the immoral person and the gambler are crushed in a crusher (by Yama)"—(Var Malar M. 1, p. 1288).

Cosmogony: A theory, system or account of the generation of the universe. Cosmogony describes the way in which the universe was created. Several mythological cosmogonies deduce the creation of the Universe from a single material principle or from a spiritual and abstract principle. The genesis is believed to be a slow development and the creation process is divided into periods. It is held that the universe had a beginning in time. The oldest Hindu myth of Brahman—egg has been mentioned in the *Adi Granth* (p. 839, Bilawal M. 1). The Greek philosophers considered one or the other element as the origin of the Universe, but the *Adi Granth* believes in the Sankhyan, evolutes which in order are Ether, Air, Fire, Water and Earth (p. 19, Sri Rag M. 1). The Transcendent Lord (*Nirguna*) became Immanent (*Saguna*) as Ishwara and created the Universe according to His Will. The process of evolution has been very slow.

Cosmology: The theory of the universe as an ordered whole, and of the general laws which govern it.

Cosmology is a branch of philosophy which treats of the origin and structure of the universe. Western philosophers have given divergent views about cosmology. Greek philosophers are of the view that the universe is limited in space. It is governed by a set of laws, but has no beginning and no end. The philosophers of the Middle ages introduced the concepts of divine creation and annihilation. Kant believes that the cosmological problem is insoluble. The modern philosopher Peirce believes in three cosmic principles of chance, law and continuity. But the *Adi Granth* does not limit the creation of the Infinite Lord. There are innumerable spheres and universes. "In the Domain of

Truth, the Transcendent Lord abides. He watches His Creation with Bounteous Eyes. In this Domain there are regions, spheres and universes, of which there is no end, if they are to be described" (p. 8, Japuji). There are millions of regions, divisions of creation, skies and universes" (p. 276, Gauri Sukhmani M. 5).

Costume: A complete set of outer garments. The equivalent for costume in the *Adi Granth* is 'VES'. Guru Nanak Dev says, "The Lord as Creator wears many costumes" meaning thereby that the Lord appears in many forms. Guru Arjan Dev says that *maya* wears many garbs (costumes) and assumes many forms (p. 371, Asa M. 5).

Courage: A quality of mind which shows itself in facing danger without fear. It is considered one of the cardinal virtues in Ethics. It exhibits firmness in the face of threats, temptations and dangers. It is enjoined as a moral duty in the *Adi Granth*. "Live courageously; work and abide in joy. Contemplate on the Lord and meet him. There will be no worry" (p. 522, Var Gujri M. 5). Beckoning for courage, Guru Arjan Dev says, "Look and move forward. Do not look back. Make this birth fruitful, so that you may not transmigrate (p. 1096, Var Maru M. 5).

Covetousness: Culpable desire of that which is another's. Covetousness or greed is one of the five major vices. A greedy person runs in all the directions like a mad dog. He does not discriminate and eats all the permitted and forbidden food (p. 50, Sri Rag M. 1). Those who are engrossed in the vice of covetousness, forget the Beneficent Lord. (p. 711, Todi M. 4). Covetousness is like a dark prison, a vice that enchains our feet (p. 1191, Basant M. 1). It destroys the human beings, just as the moss pollutes the water (p. 967, Var Ramkali Satta and Balwand).

Cow: In Hinduism, cow is considered a sacred animal. In Satapatha Brahman, the gods are said to have spoken thus about the cow: "Verily, the cow and the ox support everything here; come let us bestow on the cow and the ox, whatever vigour belongs to other species". In Hindu mythology, the cow has been symbolished as Kamadhenu, the cow who fulfils all the wishes of the devotees. For Guru Arjan Dev, the singing of the attributes of the Lord are a real Kamadhenu for the devotee (p. 265, Gauri Sukhmani M. 5).

Creation: The action of making, forming, producing or bringing into existence. The Transcendent Lord (Higher Brahman) became Immanent (Lower Brahman) and created the Universe as Ishwara. The material of Creation, both the souls and the matter, was within Him.

When it was His Will, He created the world of name and form. Since the Lord is Infinite, His Creation cannot be limited. The upper and the lower worlds cannot be counted. Besides the human beings, there are innumerable species of beings. There are innumerable elements, gods, kings, spheres, suns, moons, demons, sages, divisions of creation and sound etc. (p. 7, Japuji).

Creator: The Supreme Being who creates all things. Whereas, according to the *Adi Granth*, God is Omnipresent, Omnipotent and Omniscient, He is also the Creator of the Universe. Guru Nanak Dev says, "You are the Creator, O Lord, the Unknowable. You created the Universe of diverse kinds, colours and qualities. You know your own Creation. All this is your Play" (p. 138, Var Majh M. 1)

Crime: An act punishable by law. Guru Arjan Dev says, "Man readily commits a crime but he falls asleep, at the time of the remembrance of the Name of the Lord. He, the ignorant one, misses the opportunity and is always engrossed in the love of *maya*. He gladly rides the wave of greed" (p. 738, Suhi M. 5). Since the body commits crimes, Guru Nanak Dev instructs it to maintain discipline: "O my body, listen to my advice. You indulge in slandering other people, telling lies and losing your trust. You look at other women and commit theft and crimes. When the soul leaves you, you are left behind like a deserted woman" (p. 155, Gauri Cheti M. 1).

Criminal Law: Law relating to crime or its punishment. There is mention of the criminals in the *Adi Granth* who receive punishment not only in this world according to the criminal Law but also they receive punishment by the god of Justice. Guru Arjan Dev says, "Carrying a noose in their hands, some move in the night in order to strangle others; the Lord knows the culprits. Some look at the beauty of other women, hiding themselves; they break into houses, which are hard to break and taste the sweet wines. If such are their deeds, they come to grief and repent. The angel of death presses them like sesame seed" (p. 315, Var Gauri M. 4, Pauri M. 5).

Cripples: Those who are disabled from the use of their limbs. Guru Angad Dev considers the man of the world as mentally crippled. He says, "How can the lame, handless and the blind person clasp the Lord in his embrace?" (p. 139, Var Majh M. 1, Shalok M. 2). "How can a cripple scale over a mountain? He cannot go up to that place. O Lord, the Merciful, I your humble servant pray to you to ferry me across by your Grace" (p. 267, Gauri Sukhmani M. 5).

Cruelty: Disposition to inflict suffering. Cruelty of any kind on weak and helpless beings is condemned in the *Adi Granth.* Guru Nanak Dev says, "There can be no grievance if a powerful man overpowers a powerful man, but if a powerful lion attackes and kills a flock of sheep, then the Master must answer" (p. 360, Asa M.1). In the same hymn, the Guru is seen beseeching the Lord for Compassion. He says, "You have sent the Mughal (Babur) as the angel of Death. With such intense suffering the people cried; did you not feel compassion on them?" (p. 360, Asa M.1). The saint-poets of the *Adi Granth* have laid emphasis on Compassion and non-injury to the beings.

Cullī: Mouthful of water for rinsing; sacred rinsing. According to Guru Nanak Dev 'the sacred rinsing consists in knowledge for the wise, self-control for a Yogi, contentment for a Brahmin, charity for a householder, justice for a king and concentration on Truth for the educated (Var Sarang M. 4, Shalok M. 1, p. 1240). Such practices have been decried in the *Adi Granth.* See: *Ablutions.*

Customs: Habitual or usual practices. In the texts of Confucianism it is recorded that the customs in different countries differ according to the soil. In every country, the people have their peculiar customs. Those who migrate to another country retain their customs observed in their original country. The converts from one religion to another observe the customs of their society in the previous religion. In order to win favours from the conquering authority, the subjects generally imitate the customs of their masters. In the *Adi Granth*, the Hindu subjects of Muslim Kings are shown imitating the living pattern of their Muslim masters. Guru Nanak Dev says, "In the time of Atharva Veda, i.e. in Kaliyuga, Allah has become the name of God. He is clad in blue attire and has assumed the attributes of Turks and Pathans" (p. 470, Var Asa M. 1). (The Hindus) seek approval of the Muslim rulers by wearing blue clothes" (p. 472, Var Asa M. 1).

Curse: A profane oath; an imprecation. According to the *Adi Granth,* the old age, death, fever, headache, curse etc. are in the power of the Lord, none other except the Lord can inflict them (p. 168, Gauri Bairagan M. 4) The Boon and Curse of a sage can have effect only if the Lord desires. In one of the shlokas of Guru Nanak Dev, there is mention of a curse regarding Lakshmana, the younger brother of Lord Rama, but the Lord had pre-ordained the recovery of Lakshmana. It is written: "Though himself very sad, Rama collected his army and gathered his prowess. He became greatly zealous of war and had also the army of monkeys at his command. Sita had been carried away by Ravana and Lakshmana died of a curse. The Creator and Doer watches his acts of creation and destruction. Within his mind Ramchandra grieved for Sita and Lakshmana. He remembered Hanuman, who appeared as pre-ordained. The misguided demon did not know that the Lord did everything. The carefree Lord rewards all for their deeds" (p. 1412, Shlok M. 1).

D

Daityas: Demons; Antonym for *Devas*. According to Hindu mythology, *daityas* existed alongwith *devas* in times of yore and there had been frequent wars between them for supremacy of the one over the other. Both the *devas* and the *daityas* have been referred to in the *Adi Granth. Devas* represent godly forces and *daityas*, the evil forces. Ultimately, the egoistic evil forces surrender. The prominent demons mentioned in the *Adi Granth* are Bālī, Hiranayakashyapa, Rāvana, Sahasarbahu, Madhu, Kaitabh, Mahishasura, Jarāsandh, Rakat Bīj, Kālnem and Kesī (Gauri M. 1, pp. 224-25). All these demons were destroyed, because they were puffed up with ego and duplicity. All the *devas* and *daityas* remember and worship God (Maru Solhe M. 5, p. 1079). In the company of the saints even the *daityas* get release (Malar M. 5, p. 1269). He who remembers the Lord, cannot be harmed by a *daitya* (Bhairo M. 5, p. 1150). It is only the Lord, who sends evil *daityas* to the saints on the one hand and protects them on the other (Bhairo M. 3, p. 1133). Prahlad, the saint was the son of Hiranayakashyapa and has been referred to as *daitya-putra* in the *Adi Granth*.

Dakshinā: Sacrificial gift; the alms given to Brahmins on auspicious occasions. The *Adi Granth* has no belief in such a ritual. The only *dakshina* that Guru Nanak Dev begs is the bestowal of the Name (Prabhati M. 1, p. 1329). The following alms is requested: "The rice of celibacy and Truth, wheat of mercy, milk of good actions and ghee of contentment" (*ibid*).

Dambh: Deceit; delusion; duplicity. This word is very often used with reference to *Pākhand* (heresy), which is in fact deceit and duplicity. See: *Heresy*.

Damsel: A young unmarried girl—In the *Adi Granth*, the human being is symbolised as a damsel. Just as a damsel, has to leave the home of her parents and has to reside in the house of her Lord after marriage, in a similar manner, the human being has to leave this world and enter the abode of the Lord after death. Guru Nanak Dev says, "Do you not listen to the murmuring in your ears, O damsel, that you have to come ultimately in the abode of the in-laws, as the home of your parents is not your permanent abode" (Sri Rag M. 1, p. 23).

Dān: Charity. See: *Charity*.

Dānavas: Demons. The words *Dev* and *Dānav* are used together in the *Adi Granth*; *Dev* having been used for a god and *Dānav* for a demon (*daitya*). Both of them sing the praises of the Lord (Japuji, p. 6). Both are the creation of the Lord (Japuji, p. 7). Both act according to their Writ (Maru M. 1, p. 1038). See: *Daityas*.

Dancing: Guru Nanak Dev considers dancing and playing as an excitement of the mind (Var Asa M. 1, p. 465), therefore even the devotion involving dance or physical movements is not liked. However, he has suggested his own dancing poses in a figurative manner. "Let intellect be the musical instrument and love the drum and the mind be in the ecstatic mood. This is the real *bhakti* and the ascetic-practice; dance only in this pose with your feet (Asa M. 1, p. 350).

Dangers: There are several dangers which confront the human being. Guru Nanak Dev considers violence, attachment, desire and ego as great dangers (Gauri Guareri M. 1, p. 151).

Dar: Door, Gate. Guru Nanak Dev has described the appearance of the Door of the Abode of the Lord in one of the stanzas of *Japuji*. This hymn has also been included as the first hymn of the evening prayer called *Rahirās*. All the gods and goddesses, the adepts, the saints, heroes, Pundits, sages, the holy shrines etc. are standing in obeissance at "That Door" (Japuji, p. 6).

Darbha Grass: Sheikh Farid has made a mention of this grass figuratively. He says, "Be the darbha grass (*dabbu*) of the path, if you want to find the All-Pervading Lord" (Shlok Farid, p.1378).

Darkness: In the *Adi Granth*, knowledge is depicted as light and nescience as darkness. Just as the lighted lamp dispels darkness, the intellect bearing knowledge devours the sins (Var Suhi M. 1, p. 791). Kabir says, "When the lamp is lighted in the house, the darkness is destroyed, similarly where the Fearless Lord resides, the illusion vanishes (Kedara Kabir, p. 1123). The body without the Name of the Lord is like a dark cell (Asa M. 1, p. 354). The world is likened to a dark well. Guru Arjan Dev says, "The sinner is in the frightful dark well, O Gracious Lord, bring him out (Gauri Sukhmani M. 5, p. 267).

Darshan: This word has two connotations viz. 1-The sight and 2-The philosophy. There are many hymns in the *Adi Granth*, in which a strong desire for the Sight of the Lord has been expressed. The Gurus and Saints are said to have visualised the Wonderful Sight of the Lord. Regarding the philosophy of the Gurus, Guru Amar Das says, "The six philosophies (of the six Shashtra) are in vogue, but the philosophy of the Guru is incomprehensible and boundless (Asa M. 3, pp. 360-61).

Darvesh: A *fakīr* (hermit), who stands and begs at the door. In the *Adi Granth*, a *darvesh* has been defined by Sheikh Farid as having tree-like forbearance (Shlok Farid, p.1381). The humble men of the Lord are the real *darveshes,* who are received reverently at the Door of the Lord (Maru M. 5, pp. 1083-84). He is a *darvesh*, who fixes his mind on the Praises of the Lord (*ibid*). According to Sheikh Farid, the *derveshī* (the practice of a *dervesh*) is very difficult (Sheikh Farid, pp. 1377-78).

Dās, Dāsī: *Dās* means a servant and *Dāsī*, a maid servant. In the *Adi Granth*, the Gurus and the saint-poets have called themselves as *Dās* or servant of the Lord. The word *Dāsī* has been used for *maya*. Guru Amar Das says, "*Maya*, the maid-servant, is in the service of the saints" (Gauri M. 3, p. 231).

Dasam Dvār: The Tenth Door. The nine doors of the body i.e. two eyes, two ears, two nostrils, one mouth and the two organs of procreation and elimination are quite apparent but the tenth door is hidden from our sight. Guru Amar Das says, "Nine doors (of the body) are kept open, but the tenth one has been concealed (Ramkali M. 3, Anand, p. 922). The Lord is said to Abide within the Tenth Door. He can be visualised on the opening of the Tenth Door. This Door can be opened through the discipline of the Word of the Guru. Within this Door resounds the Unstruck Music. According to Guru Amar Das, 'within the nine doors of the fort of body, the tenth door has been kept concealed. This very strong door cannot be opened except the Word of the Guru. We hear the resounding unstruck Melody, when the door is opened' (Var Ramkali M. 3, p. 954).

Dāt, Dātā: *Dātā* or *Dātār* is the Beneficent and Munificent Lord, Who is the Giver of everything. Whatever He Gives, is His *Dāt*. The human being is ungrateful that the Lord Who bestows all sorts of gifts on him, he does not remember Him or express his gratitude towards Him. Guru Arjan Dev says, "The man loves the Gift (*Dāt*), but forgets the Lord (*Dātār*)"—(Dhanasari M. 5, p. 676).

Daughters: The *Adi Granth* shows no distinction between sons and daughters. The relations of mother, father, son (and daughter) have all been made by the Lord (Gujri M. 4, p. 494), therefore all the members of a family have their own individual significance.

Dawn: (The first appearance of light before sunrise)—In the *Adi Granth* this time is considered most suitable for concentration for spiritual advancement. This is the time for the attainment of nectar of the Name of the Lord (Japji, p. 2). Sheikh Farid considers such persons as living dead who do not rise at the final hours of the night.

(Shlokas of Farid, p. 1383). Guru Arjan Dev has beckoned the seeker to meditate on the Name of the Lord, if he wants to be free from ailments (Gauri Bawan-Akhri, p. 255). At day-dawn one should take a bath and remember the Lord (Basant M. 5, p. 1185). At dawn the sparrow chirps and the saints are absorbed in the Name (Var Gauri, M. 5, p. 319).

Day: In the *Adi Granth* that day is considered auspicious, when one, singing the praises of the Lord, attains the final beatitude (Asa M. 5, p. 395). Ordinarily the day is wasted in eating (Gauri Bairagan M. 1, p. 156).

Dayā: Mercy. See: *Mercy*.

Dead: Guru Angad Dev says, "The living meets the living and the dead meets the dead" (Var Suhi M. 3, Shalok M. 2, p. 788). In Hinduism the dead elders are known as *Pitr*. *Pitri-Puja* or ancester-worship was prevalent among Hindus. The Sikh Gurus were against this practice. The charity in the name of dead forefathers has been condemned by Guru Nanak (Var Asa M. 1, p. 472). Kabir has criticised the funeral oblation and meal given in the name of the manes. He says, "While alive, the forefathers were never given respect, but when they were dead and gone, the funeral oblations were arranged. What do the poor manes obtain? The crows and dogs eat away the meals (Gauri Kabir p. 332). The earthen lamp lighted for the dead was of no avail (Asa M. 1, p. 358).

Death: Sheikh Farid has personified death as the bridegroom, who weds the bride of life (Shlokas, p.1377). Death is like a falcon, who pounces upon the crane suddenly (Shlokas of Farid, p. 1383). The edge of death is like the bank of the river. (Shlokas of Farid, p. 1383). Whereas Sheikh Farid talks of Izrail, the god of death, the Hindu saints talk of Dharamraj or Yama. Death is a certainty. Whosoever is born, must die (Shlok M. 9, p. 1429). The fool does not understand that the death is laughing over his head. In quarrels, pleasures and ego, he does not remember death (Bilawal M. 5, p. 809). Death does not consider the age like the farmer's sickle (Asa M. 5, p. 375). The infants, youth and old all are taken away by death (Bilwal Kabir, p. 855). On death, the air merges in air, light in light, earth in earth, then for what should one weep (Ramkali M. 5, p. 794). Emancipation can not be linked with the death at a particular place. Kabir says, "A hard-hearted (sinner) dying at Banaras cannot be saved from hell. But if a saint dies at Haramba (Maghar), all his companions obtain release with him (Asa Kabir, p. 484).

Debts: Debts, if ever taken, ought to be cleared. It is a kind of responsibility. For the disciple, the Guru takes the responsibility and clears his debts (Bilawal M. 5, p. 816). The self-willed person is burdened by the heavy debt of vices which can be cleared by the meditation on the WORD. All these debts and their claimants (the messengers of *Yama*) have fallen at the feet and have become servants (Nat M. 4, p. 981). Before the Guru, we bear marks of slavery, because of our indebtedness to his generosities (Gauri Purbi M. 4, p. 171).

Decay: (Progressive decline). There is continuous decay in the world of matter. The fruit gradually ripens and falls down on the ground. (Shlok Kabir, p.1366). Sheikh Farid says that the faculties of the body gradually decline. The power of the teeth, feet, eyes and ears declines and the body mourns over the dwindling strength of these organs. (Shlok Farid, p.1381). Farid says, "The eyes were weakened by continual seeing, the ears were weakened by continual hearing. When the bough reached maturity, it changed its colour (p.1378). Farid says again, "Look, what has happened, the beard has turned brownish. The end is coming near and the beginning has been left far behind" (p.1378). The season has changed and the forest is trembling, the leaves are falling down. I have sought in all the four directions, there is no permanent abode" (Shlok Farid, p. 1383).

Deeds: *See Works*. In the *Adi Granth*, there is emphasis on good deeds alongwith the right speech and the purity of mind.

Defamation: *See Abuse* and *Backbiting* (The bringing of ill-fame on any one).

Defilement: (The act of rendering dirty). The hands, feet and body get defiled, which can be cleansed with water. The clothes get defiled with urine, they can be washed away with soap. But when the mind gets defiled by the sins, that can be purified by the Name of the Lord. (Japji, p. 4) See: *Impurity*.

Deformities: (bodily malformations) The person with all the bodily organs in proper shape, should be thankful to the Lord every moment (Gauri Sukhmani, p. 270). The company of the good can remove the deformities. The crippled one can cross the mountains, the blind can see the world around him (Bilawal M. 5, p. 809). Those who join the calumniators of the Guru, they suffer physical deformities like those whom they meet (Var Gauri M.4, Shalok M. 4, p. 309). Without the Name of the Lord one is like a leper (Asa M. 4, p. 367).

Dehī: Body. See: *Body*.

Deities: See: *Gods*.

Deliverance: (liberation, release). The attainment of heaven is not considered deliverance. Moreover the traditional deliverance (Mukti) is also rejected by the enlightened one (Maru M. 5, p. 1078). The deliverance is obtained through the remembrance of the Name (Asa M. 1, p. 352).

Delusion: (a deception, anything that deceives the mind with a false impression). Guru Nanak Dev says, "Forsake lust, anger and calumny. Be carefree by forsaking greed. Break the queer chain of delusion and enjoy nectar of Hari within" (Maru M.1, p.1041). When one is absorbed in the Word, the delusion vanishes from the body (Sri Rag M. 3, p. 134). The follower of mammon is always in delusion. He churns water and ends in misery" (Suhi M. 4, p. 739).

Demons: See: *Daityas*.

Departed: See: *Ancestor-Worship and Dead.*

Deposits: The miser, with great labour, becomes the master of the deposits of wealth but it is of no use to him because he neither gives it in charity nor serves the saints (Todi M. 5, p. 712). The deposits of wealth become the property of others on death (Suhi Kabir, p. 792).

Desires: There is no end to desires, therefore there can be no satisfaction. Such a person is rare whose desires have been satiated (Gauri M. 5, p. 213). The desires of great kings and landlords could not be fulfilled (Dhanasri M. 5, p. 672). The desire for the accumulation of wealth is a great malady and because of this disease, one forgets death (Ramkali M. 3, Anand, p. 919). The remedy for this disease is the Name of the Lord (Ramkali M. 3, p. 909). The fire of desires can be extinguished with the Word (Var Majh M. 1, p. 147).

Destiny: (Fate, that which is destined to happen). In this present age (of Kaliyuga) one is destined to reap the fruit of his actions sown in the field of the body (Sri Rag M. 5, p. 78). None is to be blamed for the destiny. The fault lies with our own actions (Asa M. 1, Patti p. 433). One may run continuously hither and thither, but nothing is achieved without *Karmas* (Tilang M. 1, p. 722). There is a writ on the forehead of every individual. God created the brittle vessels and put his light in them. Whatever writ has been put in the beginning by the Creator, the actions were performed in accordance with it (Ramkali M. 5, pp. 822-83). According to this writ the disciple comes to the preceptor (Var Ramkali M. 5, p. 960).

Determination: (resoluteness, a fixed intention). The *Adi Granth* lays stress on determination to go forward and not to turn the shoulder back. In this way the seeker will make his birth meaningful and the cycle of transmigration will cease (Maru Dakhne M. 5, p. 1096).

Devas: (gods). Thirty-three crore gods have been referred to in the *Adi Granth*. They are gods of the Hindus. According to the *Adi Granth*, these thirty-three crore gods are in search of Brahman (Majh M. 5, p. 130). They beg for the generosity of the Lord. (Gauri M. 1, p. 504). All of them are prone to die (Var Maru M. 5, p. 1100).

Devatā: See: *Deva (s)*.

Deva-Worshippers: In the *Adi Granth* the worship of gods has been decried. The supreme bliss can be achieved only by the grace of Brahman (God). The boons of each god are limited. He can bestow the material objects on his worshippers according to his limits. Those who meditate on Shiva repeating his name, they get the bulls to ride upon and the drums to beat upon. Those who worship the great goddess, they may be bestowed womanhood instead of manhood (Gond Namdev, p. 874).

Devī-Devatā: Gods and goddesses. See: *gods and goddesses.*

Devil: Talking about his contemporary religious conditions, Guru Nanak Dev has mentioned the impact of the devil on society. According to him 'the Qadis and the Brahmins have lost their sanctity and the devil performs the nuptial ceremonies' (Tilang M. 1, p. 722). Thirty fasts and five prayers cannot be effective if the devil (Satan) overpowers the individual (Sri Rag M. 1, p. 24). Other things, beyond the true path, belong to the devil (Var Sarang M. 4, Shlok M. 1, p. 1245).

Devil Worshipper: The devil worshippers, in whose mind the devil resides, cannot comprehend the praises of the Lord (Var Suhi M. 3, Shlok M. 1, p. 790).

Devotee: A devotee is one who is absorbed in truth (Prabhati M. 1, p. 1342) and is loved by the Lord (Dhanasari M. 5, p. 677). He feels no difference between pleasure and pain and meditates on the Name of Hari (Vadhans M. 4, p. 574). A devotee is known by the Word and his speech is truthful (Asa M. 3, p. 429). Though very wise, he poses to be ignorant; though very powerful, he poses to be powerless. Even if he had nothing, he sacrified himself; such a devotee is very rare. (Shlok Farid, p. 1384). He acts according to the Will of the Lord. (Var Ramkali M. 3, p. 950). That country is blessed, where the devotee resides (Basant M. 5, p. 1183). He always remains in bliss and sings the praises of the Lord in ecstasy (Asa M. 5, p. 373). The Lord resides in his mind (Asa M. 5, p. 397). The devotee of the Lord is fearless and the messengers of death adore him (Jaitsri M. 5, p. 702). The ways of devotees are strange. They traverse the difficult path. They forsake greed, ego and desire and talk less. Their path is sharper than the double-edged sword and finer than the hair. (Ramkali M. 3, Anand, p. 918). In all ages the devotees take birth and the Lord protects them (Asa M. 4, p. 451).

Devotion: The devotion of the Lord is His Love. There can be no devotion in heresy (Sri Rag M. 3, p. 28). This devotion is sought by the gods, *munis* and men but it can not be attained without the true Guru. (Asa M. 3, p. 425). He who is bestowed with true devotion becomes a god (Var Bilawal M. 3, p. 850). Through the devotion of love the ocean of saṁsāra can be crossed. (Gauri Sukhmani M. 5, p. 290). The delusion does not end without devotion (Bilawal M. 9, p.8 30). There can be no devotion by dancing. Some rare one achieves devotion by dying in the Word (Gauri M. 3, p. 159). Those who indulge in ascetic practices and go to forests do not imbibe the devotion enunciated by Narada (Sorath Kabir p. 654). The devotion liked by Hari consists in remembering Hari with the Word given by the Guru (Majh M. 3, p. 120). There can be no devotion without the Fear of the Lord (Ramkali M. 3, p. 911). There can be no devotion without adopting the qualities (Japji, p. 4). Without devotion one can never go to the abode of the Lord (Dhanasari M. 1, p. 683). The final emancipation can be achieved by devotion through love and remaining humble (Var Asa M. 1, p. 470).

Dewānā: Mad. Another equivalent word is *Baurā*; both have been used in the *Adi Granth*. Guru Nanak Dev says, "I have become *dewānā* for my Lord. I do not know any other except the Lord. One may be called a *dewānā,* if he becomes so in the Fear of the Lord..." (Maru M. 1, p. 991). Kabir says, "O my Baba (father), I am *baurā* (mad); the whole world is wise, but I am mad.... I was not mad, but the Lord has made me mad..." (Bilawal Kabir, p. 855).

Dhādhī: Musician. "He may be called a *dhādhī,* who falls in Love with the Lord and standing at His Gate renders his services by contemplating on the Word of the Guru. If he maintains Truth in his heart, he will receive reverence in the Abode of the Lord. He attains a high rank because of his love for the Name of the Lord. His service consists in the remembrance of the Lord..." (Var Gujri M. 3, p. 516). A *dhādhī* begs at the Door of the Lord and never leaves it (Var Gauri M. 5, p. 323).

Dhamma: (Dharma) (The True Law, the righteous path)—This word connotes righteousness, justice and duty. When personified Dharma is the son of *Daya* (Mercy)—(Japuji, p. 3). Where there is knowledge, there is Dharma (Shlok Kabir, p. 1372). Dharma is the flower and knowledge (Gyan) is the fruit. (Basant M. 1, p. 1168). The ladder of *Dharma* is on the path of the saints (Sorath M. 5, p. 622). To forsake all illusions and to meditate on Hari—This is the eternal *dharma* (Gauri M. 5, p. 196). Of all the duties the best duty is the meditation on the Name of the Lord (Gauri Sukhmani M. 5, p. 266). One who observes dharma is blissful; on the other hand, the sinner is fearful (Var Sri Rag M. 4, p. 84). A devotee without dharma is like a Brahmin without frontal mark, a king without authority and a warrior without arms (Shlok Sahaskriti M. 5, p. 1359). Do not delay in acts of Dharma, delay in committing a sin (Shlok Sahaskriti M. 5, p. 1354).

Dhan: It has two meanings viz. 1-wealth and 2-wife. It has been used in both these senses in the *Adi Granth*. With regard to wealth it has also been used in two senses viz. *Kācā dhan* (the wealth which stays for a short period i.e. *maya*) and *Sācā dhan* (permanent wealth of the Name of the Lord). *Sācā dhan* is also called *Hari dhan*.

Dhan Pir: Wife and Husband. See: *Husband and Wife*.

Dharam: See: *Dhamma* (*Dharma*).

Dharam Khand: The region of Dharma (righteousness). It is the first of the five spiritual regions mentioned in *Japuji* by Guru Nanak Dev. Its base is our earth, which has been called the place of Dharma. Various types and colours of Jivas, doing varied actions and having innumerable names, live on this plane. The actions of these Jivas will be judged in the True court of the Lord.

Dharam Rāj: The Lord of Dharma, who judges the account of the actions of the Jivas and who consults Chitra and Gupta, the two account-keepers of good and bad actions. Dharam Rāj works under the orders of the Lord. He decides according to the Code of True Dharma. He has the authority over all the evil souls, but he receives good souls with great reverence, which are absorbed in the remembrance of the Lord (Sri Rag M. 3, p. 38).

Dharamsāl: The abode of Dharma. Our earth has been called the abode of Dharma (Japuji, p. 7). See: *Dharam Khand*.

Dharma Shastras: Hindu law-book are known as Dharma Shastras. In the *Adi Granth*, besides the Vedas, the Hindu scriptures, mention has been made of Puranas, Smritis, Shastras and Gita. *Katebs*, i.e. the scriptures of Islam and Christianity have also been mentioned. The words Quran and Hadith also occur in the *Adi Granth.*

Dharma Sutras: They are the basis of the metrical Hindu Dharma Shastras. There is no direct reference to Dharma Sutras in the *Adi Granth.* However, a reference to Nārada implies the significance of his Bhakti Sutras.

Dhiān: (*Dhyāna*). Steadfast contemplation without any break. It is one of the steps in *Ashtānga Yoga* (the Eightfold Path of Discipline). It connotes meditation and consists in the undisturbed flow of thought round the object of meditation. Guru Arjan Dev says, "O my mind, fix your *dhiān* (attention, contemplation) on the Guru, who is my *Pāra Brahman* and *Param Ishvara*" (Bilawal M. 5, p. 827).

Dhīrā: (Firm). Only Dharma stands firm in the Iron age (Kaliyuga). Guru Arjan Dev says, "Without His Will, Hari cannot be realised. Without true Guru, the mind cannot be controlled. In Kaliyuga, the *Dharma* only stands firm. The sinner cannot hold long" (Var Maru M. 5, p. 1098).

Dhūṛ, Dhūṛī. The dust. In the *Adi Granth*, the dust of the feet of saints is said to be highly meritorious. "Those who bathe in the dust of the feet of saints, their sins of many births are destroyed" (Bilawal M. 5, p. 828). Even the holy rivers like Ganges try to touch the dust of the feet of saints (Malar M. 5, p. 1263). 'Raj' and 'Ren' are equivalents for 'dhūṛī'.

Dhur Karam: Grace from the very beginning. "Those on whom the Lord has been Graceful from the very beginning, they have remembered the Lord" (Var Asa M. 1, p. 469). Those in whose Writ is recorded the Grace of the Lord from the very beginning, they receive the true instructions and their noose of *Yama* is cut down (Dhanasari M. 5, p. 691).

Dialogues: Dialogue pertains to a literary work in the form of conversation between two or more persons. In Indian poetic tradition such works are found in abundance. In the *Adi Granth*, an example of this type is *Siddh Goshta* wherein we find a conversation between Guru Nanak and the Yogis.

Dib-drishtī: Divine vision; Divine sight. "When there is awakening of divine vision, the illusion is destroyed and with the Grace of the Guru, the devotee attains the Supreme State" (Maru M. 3, p. 1016). Guru Amar Das says, "These eyes were blind, but on meeting the True Guru, the divine insight has been attained (Ramkali M. 3, Anand, p. 922).

Dice: (plural of die). A game played with dies. A die is a small cube, having its faces marked with spots numbering from one to six, used in games of chance by being thrown from a box or hand. The game of dice has been mentioned figuratively in the *Adi Granth*. The game of dice was played earlier between Yudhishtra and Duryodhana, as given in the *Mahabharata*. It was with the help of Shakuni that Duryodhana defeated Dharmaputra (Yudhishtra) in the foul game of dice. Guru Nanak Dev says, "If the dice of ego is played with the dies of falsehood and pride, the whole world is defeated. Only that person wins, who dwells upon Word of the Guru" (p. 422, Asa M. 1). Guru Arjan Dev says, "Let the righteous actions be your game of dice (chess), and Truth be your dies. Conquer lust, anger, greed and attachment—this game is dear to the Lord" (p. 1185, Basant M. 5).

Difference: A dissimilarity—A diversity of opinion, sentiment or purpose. The Servant of the Lord is like the Lord. Do not think of any difference due to his human body (p. 1076, Maru Sohe M. 5). How do those people look like, who do not forget the Name of the Lord? They are like the Lord, do not consider any difference (p. 397, Asa M. 5). Ordinarily, the difference (*Bheda*) is considered of three kinds: the difference between one thing and another, the difference in the same group or class and the difference between a thing and its parts. But in the spiritual world, Brahman has none of these differences. Therefore he is called *Abheda*.

Digesting: The process whereby the nutritive part of the food, in the stomach and intestines, is rendered fit to be assimilated by the system. The enlightened persons eat little (p. 467, Asa M. 1). Hence their food is easily digested. Those who go in for various tastes and eat much, they suffer from indigestion and various other disease (p. 1255, Malar M. 1). All other foods and pleasures are in vain, which fill the mind with evil and make the body full of pain. (p. 16, Sri Rag M. 1).

Dīkshā: It is a Sanskrit world and is used in the sense of initiation, consecration and dedication. In the early Vedic period, the consecration of the institutor (Yajamāna) of a sacrifice was considered important. In the later Vedic period the *brahmacharin* had to undergo a form of dīkshā, called *upanayana*. In the middle ages, *dīkshā* was given by the Guru in the form of a *mantra*. The *mantra* could be used for good or evil purposes. In the *Adi Granth*, the word *Dīkhyā* has been used for *dīkshā*. Guru Angad Dev says, "Those who are the disciples of Guru Nanak Dev and have received instructions of the Guru to imbibe Truth and concentrate on the praises of the Lord, what is the necessity of giving more instructions to them?" (p. 150, Var Majh M. 1, Shlok M. 2). For a true Yogi, the Guru's instructions are the ear-rings, when the Formless Lord is enshrined within (p. 208, Gauri M. 5). The disciple should consider the *dīkshā* (instruction of the Guru) as his food and remedy both (p. 878, Ramkali M. 1).

Dīkshita: A disciple who has undergone consecration or initiation. In the *Adi Granth*, such a disciple is called a Sikh, for whom the Guru has laid down a definite discipline. Guru Ram Das says, "He who calls himself a Sikh of the Guru, should rise early in the morning and remember the Name of the Lord. He should awaken himself in the early hours of the morning and take a bath in the tank of Immortality. He should dwell upon the Word of the Guru, so that all his sins and blemishes are washed away. And when the sun rises, he should sing *Gurubani* and remember the Name of Lord, standing or sitting. He who remembers the Lord with every breath, he is loved by the Guru..." (p. 305, Var Gauri M. 4).

Dimbī Gurū: The deceitful preceptor. See: *Gurū*.

Discussions: A disquisition in which a subject is treated from different sides. In the *Adi Granth*, there is a longer poem of Guru Nanak Dev consisting of discussions on various aspects of Yoga. This poem is *Siddh Goshta* in Ramkali Raga. On one side there is an assembly of saints represented by Guru Nanak Dev and on the other side there are Yogis known as Siddhas. In the disquisition that follows, the Guru is victorious.

Diseases: A condition of the body, or of some part or organ of the body, in which its functions are disturbed or deranged. Most of the diseases are the result of the consumption of delicious and tasty foods (p. 1034, Maru M. 1). The mind becomes dirty in duality (p. 121, Majh M. 3). A dirty mind which is diseased make the body also a prey to various diseases. The whole world is diseased because without Truth it becomes dirty and diseased. The remedy lies in the remembrance of the Name of the Lord (p. 687, Dhanasri M. 1). The most heinous disease considered in the *Adi Granth* is ego, which can be cured by the Grace of the Lord and the Word of the Guru (p. 466, Var Asa M. 1).

Disputations: An exercise in which the parties formally sustain, attack and defend a thesis. Sometimes there are disputations on spiritual matters between the rival religious sects. Some hymns in the *Adi*

Granth were composed because of the disputation on certain themes. Guru Nanak Dev composed his *Aarti* at Jagannath Puri in which the practice of circumambulation being performed in the temple there was rejected. Kabir has attacked the Brahmins for their haughty and vicious attitide (p. 324, Gauri Kabir).

Divination: The foretelling of future events or discovery of what is hidden or obscure by supernatural or magical means. The *Adi Granth* has no faith in divination. Guru Nanak Dev says, "The astrologer makes our horoscope after calculations. He reads it out, but does not realise the essence. Above everything else is the contemplation on the Word of the Guru. I do not speak of anything else, because everything else is dust (p. 904, Ramkali M. 1). One must read the horoscope of the mind—this only brings real comfort (p. 1093, Var Maru M. 3).

Divinities: Deities, gods. Hinduism believes in thirty-three crores of divinities (gods). The *Adi Granth* believes in the eternality of only One Transcendent Lord. The thirty-three crores of gods alongwith Indra will pass away (p. 1100, Var Mar M. 5). These thirty-three crores of gods beg from Lord God, who blesses them out of His inexhaustible Treasure (p. 504, Gujri M. 1). Even if one has command over thirty-three crores of divinities and the Siddhas and ascetics stand at his gate...; this high status and high command will become a dream in the end (pp. 42-43, Sri Rag M. 5). The thirty-three crores of gods seek Him (the Eternal Lord) (p. 130, Majh M. 5).

Divinity: Divine nature; Divine quality, virtue or power. The Highest Divinity is Brahman. "He, our Lord, created Brahma, Vishnu and Shiva and also gods and goddesses and others in innumerable forms" (p. 839, Bilawal M. 1, Thitti). "One worships gods and goddesses, but what can one demand of them and what can they give? One washes the stone-gods in the water. They that sink down, how can they ferry others across?" (p. 637, Sorath M. 1). The source of all other divinities except the Highest Divinity (Brahman) is *maya* (p. 129, Majh M. 3).

Divorce: Legal dissolution of marriage by a court or other competent body, or according to forms locally recognised. The idea of divorce as a legal dissolution of marriage is not present in the *Adi Granth.* There is mention of a deserted woman, who has been driven out of the house of her husband because of some serious deficiencies in her way of life. She has been called a *"Dohagan"*. What are the characteristics of *Dohagans* or deserted women? These poor wretches are without their husbands. Their apparel is soiled and their night passes in great *anguish"* (p. 72, *Sri Rag M.1*). The simile of a deserted woman has been given to a person who turns his back upon the Guru (p. 645, Var Sorath M. 4, Shlok M. 3).

Documents: Something written, inscribed etc. which furnishes evidence or information upon any subject. With the increase of vices, the account has been written on many papers (p. 195, Gauri M. 5). Such documents are in the charge of Chitra Gupta, which are presented when the soul reaches the court of the god of justice. In the *Adi Granth*, there is also mention of a writ on the forehead of every being. According to this writ, one is destined to meet the Guru and his mind is filled with the love of Lord's Domain (p. 13, Gauri Poorbi M. 4).

Dog: A person without devotion towards the Lord has been depicted as a swine or a dog (p. 1428, Shlok M. 9). Allegorically every being has one dog and two bitches with him. The greed is the dog and hunger and thirst are the two bitches (p. 24, Sri Rag M. 1). Speaking about the Iron age, the Guru has used this metaphor about the tyranny of the authorities: "The kings are lions and their officers dogs" (p.1288, Var Malar M.1). These dogs lick up the blood of the subjects.

Dogmas: The body of opinion formulated and authoritatively stated. Dogma is a Greek term which meant a public ordinance of decree. But at present it signifies an established philosophic opinion, accepted without the support of demonstration or experience. In Christianity the dogmas are the interpretation of the revealed truths by the highest authority of the Church and accepted by all the faithful adherents. In the *Adi Granth*, the dogmas of various faiths and sects have been decried. "Leaving the household one became a *vanaprasthi*, but the mind was never peaceful, even for a moment... Leaving his family, the mind of *Sannyasin* craved more and more and never stilled... Because of his indignation for the world, one became a *Digambara*, but his mind wandered ceaselessly... Having learnt many postures, the *Siddha* (Yogi) craved to possess extra- psychic powers and his mind was never content..." (p. 835, Bilawal M. 4).

Dosh: Fault, See: *Fault*.

Dowry: The presents given by the parents to their daughter at the time of marriage. The practice of dowry is very old in India. In the *Adi Granth*, every person is considered a would-be bride. The bridegroom, with whom the bride has to meet ultimately on leaving the house of her parents, would accept only that bride who brings with her the dowry of virtues. Guru Nanak Dev says, "Do you not hear, O lovely maid, the news with your own ears that ultimately, you will go to the in-laws (the house of the Lord) and you cannot live in the parents' house (this world) for ever. If you sleep in your parents' house, you consider yourself robbed in broad daylight; you will lose the bundle of virtues and will go with a bundle of vices (p. 23, Sri Rag M. 1). The bride at her parent's house became ignorant... When she is bedecked with love and fear, she then enjoys the Bed of her Most Beautiful Lord for ever" (p. 357, Asa M. 1).

Drama: A series of actions or course of events having dramatic unity, and leading to a final catastrophe. According to the *Adi Granth*, the state of utter peace and joy can only be obtained in the company of the saints and by remembrance of the Name of the Lord. All the other devices including the watching of the actors and listening to their song and dance in the theatre are of no avail (p. 179, Gauri Guareri M. 5). The Lord's Play (Drama) of the world is like the mimicry or a mime. One sees the show for a very short time, but it passes away immediately (p. 422, Asa M. 1).

Dream: A train of thoughts, images, or fancies passing through the mind during sleep. The world is like a night's dream (p. 808, Bilawal M. 5). Without the True Guru, one is faithless and does not love the Name of the Lord. He does not get peace even in dream (p. 65, Sri Rag M. 3). Out of the three states of consciousness, experienced by all men (*Jagrit, Svapan* and *Sushupti*), the dream state is that in which the man is aware of the flow of images in his own mind. At that time, the senses are asleep. There are mental pictures of things, without any rational control. Ravidas says, "O Lord God, the doubt is such a delusion that it makes us believe that which is not there in reality. It is just as a king falling asleep on his throne and becoming a begger in the dream. Actually he has the kingdom, but he has lost it in the dream, therefore he is in anguish—such is the state of my mind" (p. 657, Sorath Ravidas). Having seen the colourful play of the world, the day of death arrived. All ended like a dream and only our earnings went with us (p. 813, Bilawal M. 5). One is never satiated without contentment. Like the objects of a dream, all the works are in vain. (p. 279, Guru Sukhmani M. 5).

Drinking: The use of intoxicating liquor. The use of all types of intoxicants, including drinking, have been condemned in the *Adi Granth*. Guru Amar Das says, "One person brought the flask full of wine and the other person filled the cup for drinking. The drink which makes one senseless and mad; which makes him lose the sense of discrimination, and is driven out by the Lord, which makes him forget the Lord and receive the punishment in His Court; such a vicious drink should be totally abandoned; attempts be made for it. The true intoxicant (the Name of the Lord) can be obtained by the grace of the true Guru" (p. 554, Var Bihagra M. 4, Shlok M. 3).

Drought: Dryness of the weather or climate; Lack of rain. It is the Lord, who makes the dry lands full of greenery. With His nectar-like Sight, He watered them and brought back to life (p. 191, Gauri M. 5). Thus the Grace of the Lord can only remove the drought. He alone makes the dry wood verdant (p. 1070, Maru M. 4). The drought ends, when the streams are flooded and the signs of famine disappear. (p. 143, Var Majh M. 1).

Drug (S): A narcotic or opiate. The drugs and intoxicants are taboos for the Sikh. The drug-addict continues to live with the use of drugs (p. 1180, Basant M. 5). He thinks only of the drugs (p.613, Sorath M.5). The pills of the drug of falsehood have been given and the egoist-addict has forgotten Death and enjoyed life for a short while. In order to keep them in the court of the Lord, the Sufis (teetotallers) have received Truth (p. 15, Sri Rag M. 1). See Drinking.

Drums: A percussive musical instrument, consisting of a hollow cylinder or hemisphere of wood or metal, with a head of tightly stretched membrane at one or both ends, to be beaten with a stick. The drums and trumpets were beaten during battles by the drummers. The beating of drums was a sure sign of war. A true devotee is considered a warrior in the battlefield where the fighting is going on between the forces of good and evil. Kabir says, "The drum is beaten in the sky (of the body) and the target has been pierced. The hero is engaged in the battlefield and this is the time for him to strike". The drum is also a sign of the royal splendour, which is ephemeral. Sheikh Farid says, "Those who have drums by their side and canopies over their heads; for whom the pipes shriek and the bards sing—in the end they too sleep in the graveyard like the orphans" (p. 1180, Shlok Farid).

Drunkenness: The habit of drinking to excess. The habit of drunkenness has been allegorically depicted in the *Adi Granth*. "The mind drinks deep the wine of lust from the drinking bowl of anger, where ego is the bar-man (p. 553, Shalok Mardana). The wine of ego from the pitcher of the body associated with greed is being served by Death, the bar-man, in the drinking bowl filled with falsehood. One earns great number of vices by drinking such a wine (p. 553, Shlok Mardana) See: Drinking.

Dualism: A system of thought which recognises two independent principles. The Vedantic dualism was expounded by Madhavacharya, a Vaishnava born in South India. According to him, there is eternal existence of God, selves and the world. The selves and the world are subordinate to God, who is identified with Vishnu. The doctrine of *Dvaitavād* (dualism) is maked by five fundamental differences: the difference between God and individual selves and matter and the difference between the material substances. The *Adi Granth* believes in only one Ultimate Reality i.e. Brahman. It does not believe in the eternal existence of the world. Hence the dualism of Madhavacharya stands rejected. Guru Arjan Dev says, "Whatever I see is Brahman, whatever I hear is Brahman, I speak of only One God. The Creator of the expanse of selves is none else but God" (p. 846, Bilawal M. 5).

Duality: The fact of being dual; two-fold condition. Unless duality ceases, one cannot become One with the Lord. On meeting the True Guru, the duality departs (p. 153, Gauri M. 1). He whose sense of duality does not cease, is punished by the god of Justice (p. 491, Gujri M. 3). Those who have forgotten the Name of the Lord and are absorbed in others tasks; they burn in the fire of duality. There is the fire of desire within their minds (p. 19, Sri Rag M. 1). Thus the love of the individual for all else except the Lord is duality. He who kills the duality, enjoys the bliss of *Raja Yoga*. He who kills it becomes fearless, merges in the Name of the Lord, quenches his thirst (of desires), is approved at the court of the Lord etc. etc. (pp. 237-38, Gauri M. 5).

Dubidhā: Duality. Those who are absorbed in other works and have forgotten the Name of the Lord, they are engrossed in *dubidhā* (duality) and have died in agony with inward fire of desire (Sri Rag M.1, p.19). See: *Duality*.

Duhāgan: A deserted woman. "What is the mark of a *duhāgan*? She is separated from her husband and moves in humiliation. She is clad in dirty attire and passes her night in anguish" (Sri Rag M. 1, p. 72).

Dūjā Bhāv: Duality. See: *Dubidhā* and *Duality*.

Dukh: Suffering. See: *Suffering*.

Duniā: (Dunyā)—The world. See: World.

Durgā: The goddess, said to be the wife of Shiva. She is known by several other names viz. Pārbatī, Kālī, Bhavānī etc. Bhavānī is her amiable form and as Durgā and Kālī, she is the destroyer of demons.

She is also called Chaṇḍī. Guru Gobind Singh wrote *Chandi di Var*, in which the goddess Durga is shown fighting with the demons and killing all of them including Mehkhasur (Mahishasur). Sumbh, Nisumbh, Chand, Mund and Rakt-Bīj. The Guru himself had no belief in the goddess, he narrated her heroic deeds in order to instil the heroic spirit in his Sikhs, fighting against the evil forces. The *Adi Granth* has no faith in any other god or goddess except God. Kabir says, "Myriad Durgas caress the Feet of the Lord God" (p. 1162, Bhairo Kabir). Namdev has called Durga: Bhavānī and Maha Maaee (Great Mother). He says, "Thou, who are called the primal Bhavānī, where were you, when one asked for Emancipation" (p. 874, Gond Namdev).

Durmat: It is antonym for *Gurmat*. *Gurmat* teaches virtue and *Durmat* is vice. *Durmat* is evil and immoral practice. "One who does not follow *Gurmat* and is enslaved by *Durmat*, loses all respect (Ramkali M. 1, p. 879). When *durmat* leaves, one is purified and his mind gets absorbed in the Name of the Lord (Asa M. 4, p. 443).The fire of *durmat* burns away the world. Only he, who contemplates on the Word of the Guru, is saved (Gauri M. 1, p. 225).

Duty: That which one ought or is bound to do whatever one is morally obliged to do is called duty. In Greece, the Stoics popularised the idea that man has a duty to live virtuously without any consideration of human happiness. In Hinduism and Sikhism, it is called *Dharma*. *Dharma* is interpreted as piety and righteousness. Hence the duty of an individual is to imbibe piety and righteousness in life. In the *Adi Granth*, there are several injunctions meant for a devotee who has to practise them in life as a duty. Thus the discipline enunciated by the Guru becomes a duty for the Sikh. e.g. "Sing the praises of the Lord day and night, you will attain deliverance while living in your house", etc. etc. (p. 281, Gauri Sukhmani M. 5).

Dvaita Bhav: Dūjā Bhāv; duality. See *Duality*.

Dvāpara Yuga: In Hindu religious literature four ages of the world have been mentioned viz. Sat Yuga, Tretā Yuga, Dvāpara Yuga and Kali Yuga. Dvāpara Yuga lasts for 2400 divine years or 864,000 mortal years. All the four ages have been mentioned in the *Adi Granth*. Guru Nanak Dev says,"In the Dvāpara age, compassion was reduced to half and Dharma, who upholds the world, became two-legged" (pp. 1023-24, Maru M. 1).

Dwelling: A place of residence. The dwellings, mansions and palaces are built, but they do not go alongwith us (p. 648, Var Sorath M. 4).

The dwellings, mansions and shops are elegant if the Name of the Lord abides in them (p. 783, Suhi M. 5). The human body is also a dwelling in which the soul as well as the Lord Himself reside. Guru Amar Das says, "Within our home-dwelling is the 'Thing' and there is nothing without" (p. 475, Asa M. 3).

Dyer: One whose occupation is to dye cloth etc. He who is imbued with the Name of the Lord, how can he be imbued with the colour (of *maya*)? The real Dyer, the True Lord should be remembered whole-heartedly (p. 751, Suhi M. 1).

Dyu: This word occurs at a few places in the *Adi Granth*. Its origin seems to be *Dyaus*, who is a masculine Vedic deity. He is occasionally called *Dyaus Pitri* meaning 'heavenly father'. In the *Adi Granth*, the word *Dyu* has been used for Brahman, who is the most Beneficent Heavenly Father. "It is painful to forget *Dyu*. Without Him, there is none else" (p. 133, Barahmaha Majh M. 5).

E

Eagle: A bird of prey. In the *Adi Granth,* three kinds of birds of prey have been mentioned. They are Bāj, Charag and Kūhī. Guru Nanak Dev says: "If the Lord Wills, He may make the tigers and the birds-of-prey eat grass and the grass-eating animals may be made to eat meat" (p. 144, Var Majh M. 1)

Ear: The organ of hearing. For the saint-poets of the *Adi Granth* the ears are meant to hear the praises of the attributes of the Lord (p. 631, Asa M. 5) and listen to the *Kirtan* (the divine music) (p. 1200, Sarang M. 4) and listen to the *Katha* (the religious preaching). One attains a great merit by listening to the Name of the Lord, which ends the afflictions and evil effect of the sins (pp.2-3, Japuji). The ears should never hear the calumny of any one (p. 274, Gauri Sukhmani M. 5). Guru Amar Das has addressed the ears thus: "O my ears, you were sent to listen to the praises of the Lord" (p. 922, Ramkali M. 3, Anand).

Earth: According to Guru Nanak, the Earth has been set as the seat of Dharma (righteousness) in the midst of air, water, fire and nether regions (p. 7, Japuji). The True Lord created the Earth for the God-conscious persons (p. 941, Ramkali M. 1, Siddh Goshta). Kabir says, "The Earth was created for the saints, but it is being trampled by the thieves" (p. 1375, Shalok Kabir) The Earth has been called the Mother, because of her motherly care of all her creation. When Water as father comes into contact with Earth, the mother, various types of beings take their birth (p. 8, Japuji). The Earth is one of the five elements and is an evolute from water (Sri Rag, M. 1, p. 19). That Earth becomes evergreen, where the true Guru sits (p. 310, Var Gauri M. 4). The Earth becomes holy, where the Praises of the Lord are sung (p. 801, Bilawal M. 5).

Earthquake: A convulsion of the earth's surface produced by volcanic or similar forces within the crust. When it is God's Will, He causes the Earth to appear out of water and a well to appear in a dry land. From a well, He makes a mountain (p.1252, Sarang Kabir). Such changes in the Earth's crust take place on account of earthquakes.

Easing Nature: Guru Nanak Dev has said of Jaina monks that after easing nature, they rake up the filth and suck bad odours. They hate natural water (p. 149, Var Majh M. 1).

Eating: Guru Nanak Dev says, "If one eats more, he increases the dirt within (his body)" (p. 1331, Prabhati M. 1). Guru Arjan Dev says, "If one eats and eats and then commits evil actions, then know this that his life is a field of poison" (p. 105, Majh M. 5). For a devotee, the listening of the Name of the Lord is like tasting salty foods. "All other foods, that we eat", says Guru Nanak Dev, "are in vain because they fill the mind with evil and create pain in the body" (p. 16, Sri Rag M. 1).

Echo: A repetition of sounds, due to the reflection of the sound-waves by some obstacle; hence a secondary or imitative sound, as distinct from the original sound. It is the Word (Sabda) of the Guru or the Name of the Lord, which is repeated by a true devotee with his tongue, is echoed again in his heart (p. 514, Var Gujri M. 3).

Eclipses: The eclipses of the sun and moon are considered as ill-omens. In Hinduism various rites were performed to ward off their evil influences. The *Adi Granth* decries such observances. Guru Arjan Dev says, "Clean yourself with a bath in the Name of the Lord, because its merit is very great, much more than the merit of the charity practised on crores of eclipses" (p. 97, Gauri M. 5). Ravidas says, "If one takes a bath at Kurukshetra at the time of eclipse and makes an offering of his adorned wife to the gods, and listens to all the Smritis with his own ears,—all his works are of no avail if he calumniates the saints" (p. 875, Gond Ravidas).

Economy: Management of expenditure. Talking about the Trade and the Traders, Guru Nanak Dev syas, "O Traders, trade in true merchandise. Such goods be purchased as last with you. The Trader at the other end is all-wise, He will receive the goods under His Care. O Brother, concentrate yourself on the Name of the Lord. Take with you the goods of the Praises of the Lord. He will see it with pleasure" (p. 22, Sri Rag M. 1). The Guru says at another place: "Trade with the true Traders and dwell on the Lord through the word of the Guru" (p. 56, Sri Rag M. 1). The goods mentioned by the Guru never diminish. Guru Arjan Dev says, "When I opened treasure of my father and grandfather, I was pleased immensely at the find... You may expend at your will with all your company, but this treasure does not diminish and is always on the increase" (p. 186, Gauri Gaureri M. 5).

Ecstasy: The state of rapture, in which the soul is engaged in the contemplation of divine things. Guru Nanak Dev says, "The Abode of the Lord is very high; His Glory crowns the three worlds. I am in ecstatic mood, seeing his qualities and hearing the Unstruck Melody of the Word" (p. 765, Suhi M. 1). Guru Arjan Dev says, "Seeing the Wonderful Lord, I am in ecstasy. He, the Beneficent Lord, pervades all. I drink the invaluable Nectar of the Name, smiling like the dumb person, unable to express its taste" (p. 1205, Srang M. 5).

Education: According to the *Adi Granth*, the real education is imparted by the Guru (religious preceptor) in his school of holy congregation, where the devotee learns the practice of godly qualities (p. 1316, Var Kanra M. 4). Such an education makes the recipient a philanthropist (p. 356, Asa M. 1). Without the wisdom of such education, one cannot attain salvation (p. 903, Ramkali M. 1). One who sells education, for the sake of *maya* (money), wastes away his life (p. 1103, Mary Kabir). The secret of the Lord cannot be known by mere reading; it can only be known by understanding (p. 148, Var Majh M. 1). It is through the practice of the remembrance of the Name of the Lord, that both the educated and uneducated become One with the Lord (p. 197, Gauri M. 5). Here the word "educated" refers to the worldly education. We may become a great Pundit of such education, still we are impure because we are seized by ego (p. 39, Sri Rag M. 3). The educated one is a fool, if he indulges in greed and ego (p. 140, Var Majh M. 1). If the Pundit is well-read and wise, and well-versed in the Name of the Lord; if attuned with the True Lord, he can ferry across the ocean of the world (p. 1171, Basant Hindol M. 1).

Ego: The I; the conscious thinking subject. The term "Haumai" is used for ego in *Adi Granth*. It is also called *Aham* or *Ahamkāra*. It is a disease given to man (p. 1140, Bhairo M. 5). In ego none can realise God; forgetting his source, he wastes away his birth (p. 664, Dhanasari M. 3). If we get free from ego, we attain final emancipation (p. 226, Gauri M. 1), and we merge in the Lord (p. 750, Suhi M. 1). See: AHAM, AHAMKĀRA.

Egoism: The theory which regards self-interest as the foundation of morality; systematic selfishness. Ethically speaking when an individual seeks as an end only for his own welfare, it is known as egoism. Deluded by egoism, a man thinks himself the doer of actions. Guru Arjan Dev says, "So long as a man thinks that he is the doer, he has no peace; so long as he thinks that he is the doer, he is cast into the womb again and again" (p. 278, Gauri Sukhmani M. 5). Egoism is the cause of creation (p. 946, Ramkali M.1, Siddh Goshta). It is also the cause of the destruction of the world (p. 33, Sri Rag M. 3). See ego, Aham, Ahamkāra.

Ekādshī: The eleventh lunar day, when the Hindus observe fast. Namdev says, "In the company of the Lord, the *Ekādashī* fast is not observed any more. Why should I visit a holy place (*Tīrtha*)?" (Todi Namdev, p. 718). Guru Arjan Dev says, "On the Ekādashī day, see the Lord quite nigh. Control your senses, listen to the Name of the Lord. Have contentment in your mind and show mercy towards all the Jivas; this is the way of completing your fast" (Gauri M. 5, p. 299).

Ekankār: *Ek* (The One) *Oamkār* (Lord). The One Lord.

Elder: A senior; a parent; a forefather hence a predecessor; a member of a senate, governing body or class, consisting of men (supposed to be) venerable for age. One may be called elder because of old age. Every one becomes a prey to *Yama* (the god of death), be he a child, a young one or an elder (p. 855, Bilawal Kabir). One amy be called an elder because of his position. Whosoever becomes an elder of the court of the Lord, is accepted at all courts (p. 87, Var Sri Rag M. 4).

Elements: The whole world is made of five elements. Guru Ram Das says, "O Lord, you have created the whole world out of five elements. Let any one try his hand with the sixth element, if he can" (p. 736, Suhi M. 4). Guru Tegh Bahadur says, "This body is made of five elements, know O Wise ones" (p. 1426, Shlok M. 9). Kabir has questioned about the origin of these five elements. He says, "The body is made up of five elements, then how were the elements created? (p. 870, Gond Kabir). Guru Nanak Dev says, "These five elements came out of *Shunya* (Absolute Lord). They were assembled in the body, which practised actions (p. 1038, Maru M. 1). These elements are earth, air, fire, water and other. The mind was born out of these five elements (p. 415, Asa M. 1). The mind is the essence of five elements (p. 342, Gauri Kabir). These gross elements (Mahābhūtas) were born out of the five subtle elements (Tanmatras), which are *Shabda, Sparsh, Rupa, Rasa* and *Gandha.* The evolute from *Shabda* (sound) was *akasha* (other), from *Sparsha* (touch), *Vayu* (air), from *Rupa* (form), *Agni* (fire), from *Rasa* (taste), *Jal* (water) and from *Gandha* (smell), *Dharti* (earth).

Elephants: In the *Adi Granth*, there is mention of the mythological elephant whose supreme devotion for the Lord saved him from the clutches of *grah* (a water animal of enormous strength). Mind puffed up with ego, appears as an elephant to the Gurus and saint-poets of the *Adi Granth.* Guru Nanak Dev says, "The elephant eats a hundred maunds of ghee and jaggery and five hundred maunds of grain. He belches and breathes loudly and scatters dust, but he repents when the breath fails him. In fact, the mad breath of ego died down (p. 1286, Var Malar M.1). The Guru also says, "The mind is a wild elephant wandering in the woods of maya and attachment" (p. 415, Asa M. 1).

Elixir: According to the *Adi Granth*, the real elixir is the Name of the Lord. "The elixir of the Name satiates the mind" (p. 99, Majh M. 5).

Emancipation: The action of setting free from bondage, which has been called *Bandhan Mukt* in the *Adi Granth*. Guru Arjan Dev says, "O Saints, we achieve emancipation through the Lord and our ego leaves us" (p. 52, Sri Rag M. 5). See *Beatitude*.

Emptiness: Philosophically this word is used in the sense of Shunyavada or void or nihilism or nothingness. In the *Adi Granth*, the word *Shunya* has been used for the Absolute. Who is the source of all creation. The *Adi Granth* believes that both the emptiness and Fullness -are the work of God. Guru Tegh Bahadur says, "This is the Way of my Lord; He fills those which are empty and empties those which are full (p. 537, Bihagara M. 9).

Enlightenment: The action of imparting knowledge, wisdom or spiritual light. It is the Guru who enlightens the devotee regarding the discipline for final emancipation. "The Guru blessed me with the collyrium of knowledge and dispelled my darkness of ignorance. With the Grace of God, I met the saint and my mind was enlightened (illumined)" (p. 293, Gauri Sukhmani M. 5).

Entanglements: The involvement in anything from which extrication is difficult. In the *Adi Granth*, there is a great emphasis for a devotee to free himself from the entanglements of *maya* and vices. They are the major hindrances in the path leading towards the Lord. "Bound down by many entanglements of maya, the release is obtained by contemplation on God" (p. 976, Nat M. 4).

Entity: Being: Essence. A real being is an entity. Hence God and souls are entities. A Purusha is an entity. Guru Nanak Dev says, "O Lord, Thou art Unfathomable, Unperceivable and Unknowable Entity. Thou art seen only through the knowledge imparted by the Guru" (p. 1291, Var Malar M. 1).

Equanimity: Evenness of mind or temper; the quality of being undisturbed by good or ill fortune. The state of equanimity is a means for final emancipation. Guru Tegh Bahadur has described this state in the following manner; "He for whom pain and pleasure are alike, honour and dishonour are alike and who has risen above joy and sorrow, he only knows the Quintessence. He neither praises nor calumniates, but is only in search of the state of *Nirvana*" (p. 219, Rag Gauri M. 9). A *Jivan-mukta* (one who attains deliverance in life) lives in such a state. Guru Arjan Dev says in Sukhmani, "For a *Jivan-mukta,* pleasure and pain are alike. He is never in woe and is ever in bliss. For him gold and dust, poison and nectar, honour and dishonour, king and beggar are alike" (p. 275, Gauri Sukhmani M. 5).

Esoteric Doctrine: It is the secret lore, not openly avowed. It is communicated to or intelligible by the initiated only. The doctrine related to the soul (Atman) and Higher Soul (i.e. Param Atman or Brahman) is the secret or esoteric doctrine. The doctrine related to the World is the exoteric doctrine. Buddha said, "I have preached the truth without making any distinction between exoteric and esoteric doctrine; for in respect of the truth, Ananda, the Tathagata has no such thing as the closed fist of a teacher, who keeps some things back" (Buddhist Suttas). The same can be said of the teachings of the *Adi Granth.* Guru Ram Das says, "I am a sacrifice to the True Guru, who has revealed to me the secret Name of the Lord (p. 697, Jaitsri M. 4). The holy scripture of the Sikhs is the True Guru in the Iron Age; the seeker can find the spiritual secrets scattered in it.

Essence: The spiritual entity. Guru Nanak Dev says, "The mind is satiated, when the essence merges in the essence" (p. 943, Ramkali M. 1, Siddh Goshta). The essence in the first place is the soul and the essence in which it merges is the Higher Soul or Brahman. Essence is also essentiality. For example: "One finds the Essence of Brahman in His Nectar-Name" (p. 1146, Bhairo M. 5).

Eternal: Without beginning or end. That which has always existed and will always exist. Eternality is an attribute of Brahman. The soul being part and parcel of Brahman is also eternal. The Eternality of Brahman has been revealed in the following manner in the beginning of Japuji: The Truth (GOD) existed in the beginning and in the beginning of the ages. He exists now and shall exist hereafter (p.1, Japuji). Kabir says: "This soul is the part of Brahman and abides like the indelible ink on paper" (p. 871, Gond Kabir).

Ether: The fifth element; the clear sky; the Space. Ether is one of the five gross elements. It is the evolute of *Shabda* (sound), one of the subtle elements. Kabir says, "The amalgam of five elements is our body, but how were the elements created?" (p. 870, Gond Kabir). Guru Nanak has mentioned the process of creation in brief in Sri

Raga, where he says: "From the True Lord came the wind, from the wind came water; from the water came the three worlds" (p. 19, Sri Rag M. 1). This process was earlier elaborated in Hindu religious literature according to which the True Lord first created Ether or the space (sky), from which the air, fire, water and earth is the order of the evolutes.

Ethics: The science of morals. According to the *Adi Granth*, the Ethics or morality is the basis of religion. The main objective of human life is to attain the unity with Brahman. For this purpose, the godly qualities are to be imbibed in life. Without the practice of virtues, there can be no devotion (p. 4, Japuji). In fact, the foundation of Dharma (righteousness) is essential for all our activities in order to achieve the prime objective. The positive injunctions regarding mind, action and speech must be followed. Guru Nanak Dev says, "Abandon the vices, imbibe the virtues and thus realise the Essence" (p. 418, Asa Kafi M. 1). According to Guru Amar Das, "Do not do the deeds, which make you regretful in the end" (p. 918, Ramkali M. 3, Anand). Guru Arjan Dev says, "Practice the deeds, which make you bright-faced" (p. 397, Asa M. 5). There is great significance of the moral code or moral discipline in the life of a devotee. The *Adi Grnath* is against all formalism, ritualism and symbolism. The works or deeds which a devotee is expected to perform are the practice of qualities and virtues and doing away of all vices including lust, anger, greed, attachment and ego.

Etiquette: The conventional rules of behaviour and ceremonies observed in polite society. In every society the rules of behaviour and ceremonies are followed closely. When a Hindu goes to the house of a Hindu, he makes him wear the sacred thread, reciting the mantras". The first Hindu is a Brahmin (p. 951, Var Ramkali M. 3 Shlok M. 1). According to Guru Arjan Dev, the etiquette of a Muslim consists in the tenderness of his heart and cleansing of the inner dirt from the heart (p. 1084, Maru M. 5).

Evidence: Statements or proofs admissible as testimony in a court of law; a witness. In the iron age, the Qadis or judges, whose duty it is to do justice, commit sins by accepting false evidence or false witnesses. For this purpose they accept bribes (p. 951, Var Ramkali M. 3, Shlok M. 1).

Evil: The antithesis of GOOD; Bad in a positive sense. Man is ever ready to commit evil, but when it comes to contemplation on the

Name, he falls asleep (p. 738, Suhi M. 5). At the time of full-blooded youth, when mind is intoxicated with ego, man does not distinguish between good and evil (p. 77, Sri Rag M. 5). The Lord knows good and evil in us (p. 735, Suhi M. 4). Out of the Absolute Lord came the five elements—the body was assembled from them and one practised deeds. And good and evil were written on the forehead of the man and the seeds of virtue and vice were sown (p. 1038, Maru M. 1). The devotee looks upon good and evil alike (p. 432, Asa M. 1, Patti).

Evil Eye: Talking about a Yogi, Guru Arjan Dev says: Though his ears are pierced, he begs for crumbs and alms from door to door and is never satisfied. Though he has abandoned his own wife, he casts an evil eye upon another woman. By donning a mendicant's garb, one cannot attain unity with the Lord (p. 1348 Prabhati M. 5). According to the Guru's discipline, a devotee should never see another's woman with an evil eye (p. 274, Gauri Sukhmani M. 5).

Evil Spirits: There is mention of several types of evil spirits in the *Adi Granth.* In Sukhmani, Guru Arjan Dev has mentioned *Bhutas* and *Pretas,* while numerating the Creation (p. 276, Gauri M. 5). *Bhutas* are malignant fiends. They are represented as ghosts, spirit bands, goblins, serpent-spirits, vampires and the like. *Bhutas* cast no shadow. They haunt forests and desolate places. *Pretas* are the ethereal forms assumed by dead men. Some *pretas* may haunt their former homes. A person who remembers his house at the time of death, becomes a *Preta* (p. 526, Gujri Trilochan). Two words *Jinn* and *Shaitan* from Muslim vocabulary have been used in the *Adi Granth.* The *Jinn* are said to appear in the shapes of serpents, dogs, cats and human beings. Guru Nanak Dev says, "The Jinns have taken birth in the iron age. The son is the Jinn, the daughter is the Jinn and the woman is their leader" (p. 556, Var Bihagra M. 4, Shlok M. 1). The *Shaitan* or devil (also called Iblis) is the master of the evil forces, opposed to God. The disciples of *Shaitan* are also *Shaitan.* A *Shaitan* also belongs to the order of *Jinns*, but they are distinguished by a longer existence. Farid says, "Though you were always goaded and advised (to follow the right path), but being misled by the *Shaitan,* how could you change your mind (p. 1378, Shlok Farid).

Evil Works: There are certain works which are considered evil in every society, and every religion. They are considered sinful acts. According to the *Adi Granth*, sinners undergo punishment for their sins (evil works). "The sinners who commit evil works are assuredly looted. Azrāil, the god of death seizes them and tortures them to death. They are cast into hell by the Creator. They are asked to render the account by the Just Lord (pp. 1019-20, Maru M. 5). The sinners commit sins (by doing evil works). They weep and wail because of the sufferings. They are punished by the god of *Dharma* (righteousness), just as the churners churn (the curd) (p. 1425, Shlok M. 5).

Evolution: Evolution has been described differently in different religious philosophies. The *Adi Granth* believes in the Vedantic theory of evolution. The evolution in respect of creation is in the following order: Akasha—air—fire—water—earth (p. 19, Sri Raga M. 1) The spiritual evolution has been described by Guru Nanak Dev in *Japuji*. The soul rises from *Dharam Khand* (the region of piety) and enters *Gyan Khand* (the region of knowledge). Then it moves further into *Saram Khand* (the region of effort) and then into *Karam Khand* (the region of Grace). Finally it enters *Sach Khand* (the region of truth). This evolution is accomplished through proper discipline laid down by the Guru. (pp. 7-8, Japuji).

Excrements: Faeces; refuse. About Jaina monks, Guru Nanak Dev has said that they rake their excrement after easing nature and suck bad odours. The self-willed (those who follow the dictates of the mind) are always absorbed in falsehood and are deluded by illusion. They live like the worms in the excrement and do not know the taste of the Lord's Grace. Without the Name of the Lord they suffer and transmigrate" (p. 144, Var Majh M. 1). The idea of a worm in the excrement is repeated many times in the *Adi Granth* for those who are evil-minded and who fall so low as to become a worm in the excrement.

Existence: According to the *Adi Granth*, the world is not an illusion. It is real and actually exists. Since the Lord pervades the whole existence, it has an entity. The soul being a part and parcel of the Lord is immortal like Him, but the world of matter, because of its transitory existence, is relatively real. The Light of the Lord is the life-giving power. Whenever this Light leaves the body, it falls down as a dead mass. This body wears off and age creeps in upon it (p. 584, Vadhans M. 3).

Exorcism: The action of expelling an evil spirit by adjuration. In Islam, the word used for exorcism is *Da'wah*, which literarlly means "A call, an invocation i.e. of God's help". This term is used to express a system of incantation, which is held to be lawful by orthodox Muslims. It is lawful to use charms and amulets on which the Name of the God only is inscribed. The *Adi Granth* has no belief in mantras, charms and incantations. Guru Nanak Dev says, "The egocentric (*Manmukh*) is strayed by doubt and wanders about in wilderness. He recites set incantations at the cremation grounds. He strays away from the Path and is deluded. He does not know the Name of the Lord and utters useless charms" (p. 941, Ramkali M. 1, Siddh Goshta). Only the Name of the Lord's is the remedy for the world full of ailments (p. 687, Dhanasari M.1). The Name of the Lord (Narayana) breaks the teeth of the evil spirit (p. 868, Gond M. 5).

Expiatory Rites: The rites by means of which atonement is made. The religious rites for purification. The religious ceremonies for averting the threatening affliction. All rites and ceremonies have been decried in the *Adi Granth*, because they create ego. Guru Arjan Dev says, "The good deeds, acts of piety and hypocrisy that we see are looted through taxation by Yama. Therefore, sing the immaculate praises of the Lord, because it brings release, even though dwelt upon for a very short time (p. 747, Suhi M. 5).

Eye: The eye is the organ of the sense of sight. For the attainment of final emancipation, it is necessary that all the sense-organs should remain under discipline, which is enunciated by the Guru. Guru Amar Das addresses the eyes in the following manner in his poem *Anand*: "O my eyes, God has placed His Light within you, do not see anything else except Him. Only see the Lord. This world that you see is the manifestation of the Lord. It is the Lord that you see.... These eyes were blind, but when I met the Guru, I began to see intuitively" (p. 922, Ramkali M. 3, Anand). Our eye should never become evil. Guru Arjan Dev says, "Do not see the wife of another person with evil eye" (p. 274, Gauri M. 5, Sukhmani). It is only the Guru who gives the antimony of knowledge in order to dispel the darkness of ignorance from our eyes (p. 293, Gauri Sukhmani M. 5).

F

Fables: The Gurus and saints whose verses have been included in the *Adi Granth* were folk-poets. Their religious fervour exhibited itself through the folk-idiom and folk-imagery. They illustrated their thoughts according to the folk-tradition. Hence their references to the animals and their characteristics are mostly based on the prevalent fables. Guru Nanak Dev has compared the kings of his time to lions and his officers to dogs. There is a reference to a fable in *Panchtantra* in the hymn of the saint Sadhna, wherein he says, "In order to marry a king's daughter, a person assumed the garb (of Vishnu) and though he was lured by lust and self-interest, you, O Lord, fulfilled his wish" (p. 858, Bilawal Sadhna).

Falcon: A family of the smaller diurnal birds of prey, characterised by a short-hooked beak, strong claws and great distinctive power, especially trained to the pursuit of other birds or game. Two warrior Gurus of the Sikhs, namely, the sixth Guru Hargobind and the tenth Guru Gobind Singh use to carry a falcon or a hawk on their hand. In the *Adi Granth*, the falcon symbolises death. Sheikh Farid says, "The crane, sitting on the river-bank, is busy in its sport. But the falcon pounces upon the sportive crane unawares. When the falcon of God pounces upon him, all his sportiveness ends. That which never was in his mind, occurred; such are the ways of God" (p. 1383, Shlok Farid).

Family: The group consisting of parents and their children, whether living together or not. The egocentric gives supreme importance to the worldly relations and is thus always in anguish. But real comfort and peace lie in the Name of the Lord, which only a God-conscious person understands. Guru Nanak Dev says, "The parents like their son. The father-in-law likes the son-in-law. The children like their father; the brothers like their father; the brother likes his brother. When the Lord commands, one leaves every one and all become alien to him" (p. 596, Sorath M. 1). Guru Arjan Dev has described an ideal family, where the pivot is the good-natured lady: "She is accomplished with all the qualities. Truth is her family and her sons. She is obedient, wise and charming. She fulfils all the desires of her Lord and has given full satisfaction to the younger brother of her Lord and also his elder-brother's wife. She is considered supreme in her family. She advises superbly her husband's younger and elder brothers. Blessed is that home in which she lives, because she abides in peace and bliss" (p. 371, Asa M. 5).

Fares: A passage for which a price is paid; hence the cost of conveyance. The load-carrier gets only the fare i.e., whatever is due to him. Guru Arjan Dev says, "Through unjust actions one hoards wealth consisting of gold, silver and coins, but as a load-carrier, he gets only the fare (i.e. bare sustenance), and the remaining wealth becomes the property of others" (p. 497, Gujri M. 5).

Fasting: Abstinence from food. Fasting is prevalent in several religions. It is called "vrata" in Hinduism and "rozah" in Islam. *Vratas* are controls ordained by Vedic-Samhitas. They are solemn vows for the purification of mind. When it involves the mortification of the body, it is called *tapas* or penance. When they control the organs of sense, it is called *niyama*. But ordinarily they are abstinence from food on certain occasions. Several types of *Vratas* are mentioned in Hindu religious books. One of them is *Chandrayana*, which is mentioned in the *Adi Granth* (p. 1099, Var Maru Dakhne M. 5). In Islam, fasting is highly commended as an atonement for sin. There is thirty days fasting in the month of Ramazan. The Muslims resort to fasting on other occasions also. But the *Adi Granth* has rejected the practice of fasting. Guru Amar Das says, "On the ninth day of the moon if one practises Truth and eats up lust, anger and desires; if on the tenth day he closes all the ten doors of the body and on the eleventh day believes in Unity, on the twelfth day controls the five vices, then only the mind is at peace. O Pundit, observe these fasts; no other instruction is required" (p. 1245, Var Sarang M. 4, Shalok M. 3). Kabir addresses the Qazi in the following manner". You keep the fast to please Allah, but slay life for your relish... But you do not reflect on the Lord, Who is within you" (p. 483, Asa Kabir).

Fatalism—Predestination: The doctrine that all things are determined or arbitrarily decreed by fate. In Islam, the word "Taqdir" is usually employed for predestination in theological works. It means "preordering". Undoubtedly, the *Adi Granth* believes in the writ on the forehead of every individual, but it also exhorts him to be up and doing in order to be worthy of the Grace of the Lord. God showers his graces on those, who surrender to him completely. "Those who seek the Lord's Refuge, they are emancipated by him like Prehlad" (p. 834, Bilawal M. 4). Whereas the law of Karma asserts that one is answerable for every action and has to reap the fruit of his actions in various births, his *agami* (forthcoming) karmas done under the directions of his spiritual preceptor (Guru) can save him. "The Guru saves his disciple both here and hereafter" (p. 286, Gauri Sukhmani M. 5).

Fatalists: Those who hold the doctrine of fatalism. The adherents of the *Adi Granth* are not fatalists because their Gracious Guru guides them and the Graceful Lord listens to their prayers. "The *Jiva* has fallen into the blind well and is bound down by illusion and attachment. When the Lord is Merciful he meets the Guru, who catches his arm and pulls him out" (p. 823, Bilawal M. 5).

Fate-Destiny: The principle, power or agency by which events are unalterably predetermined from eternity. The doctrine of fatalism has been rejected by the saint-poets of the *Adi Granth* because they believe in a Lord, who is Graceful and a spiritual preceptor, who has the welfare of the whole humanity in his mind. All the gods and goddesses, all the planets supposed to be guiding our destinies have been rejected. "He is the True Guru, who unites every body with the Lord" (p. 72, Sri Raga M. 1). Fate loses its sting before the Benevolent, Generous and Kind True Guru.

Father: A male parent. In the *Adi Granth*, God has been mentioned as the Father of all. "There is One Father and we are all His children" (p. 611, Sorath M. 5). "O my Father, you are the Supreme and Unknowable Master" (p. 507, Gujri M. 5). "How may the son know (visualise) the birth of his father?" (p. 284, Gauri Sukhmani M. 5). My God-Father is eternal and the Father and the Son have met together to become One" (p. 1141, Bhairo M. 5).

Fathers: The ancestors; the elders. In the *Adi Granth*, the ancestor-worship of the Hindus has been rejected. Kabir says, "In the lifetime the elders are not cared for, but offerings are made to them after death. The ancestors, of course, do not get the offerings, which are eaten by crows and dogs" (p. 332, Gauri Bairagan Kabir). Guru Nanak Dev says, "If a robber robs a house and he offers the booty in order to propitiate the ancestors. The thing is recognised in the other world and the ancestors are charged with theft. The Justice of he Lord demands the chopping off the hands of the mediator (Brahmin)" (p. 472, Var Asa M.1). Guru Arjan Dev says, "When we contemplate on God, we are rid of all our sins and even our ancestors are redeemed" (p. 496, Gujri M. 5).

Fault: Defect; Flaw. Guru Nanak Dev says, "Do not find fault with others. The fault lies in our actions. I have received the reward of my actions. Do not blame anyone else" (Asa M. 1, Patti, p. 433).

Fear: A state of alarm or dread. The emotion of pain or uneasiness caused by the sense of impending danger. It is the Fear of the Lord which makes the Wind blow, rivers flow, fire burn, the earth overburdened, the clouds roam, the sun blaze, the moon shine etc. Everyone is under the Fear of the Lord. Only the Lord is Fearless (p. 464, Var Asa M. 1). Because of the Fear of the Lord, our self is revealed and all other fears are driven out (p. 151, Gauri M. 1). Without the Fear of the Lord, there can be no true devotion. When there is a mingling of the Fear and love, we realise our objective in devotion (p. 911, Ramkali M. 3). Guru Arjan Dev says, "The earth, sky and the stars are in the Fear of the Lord who is the only Fearless Entity.... The life led in all the three modes (qualities) is in the Fear of the Lord. The beguiling *maya* is also in His Fear like the *Dharmaraja*" (pp. 988-99, Maru M. 5).

Female: According to the sacred law of the Aryas "in childhood a female must be subject to her father, in youth to her husband, when her Lord is dead to her sons; a woman must never be independent". Such an attitude regarding the female members of the family is not in accordance with the spirit of the *Adi Granth*. Undoubtedly, the female as wife has to serve her husband to the best of her abilities, but in society she has to be accorded a rightful place. She is the most important member of the society and is not to be considered inferior in any way. "None should talk ill of her as she gives birth to the kings and the most high" (p. 473, Var Asa M. 1).

Festivals: According to the movements of the planets certain dates were considered auspicious for celebrating festivals. One such festival was "Abhich", when the Hindus used to take bath in the Ganges. Guru Ram Das has made a mention of this festival in his hymns (p. 1116, Tukhari M. 4). He has referred to the visit of the third Guru Amar Das to a holy place on the bank of the Ganges where this festival was being celebrated. According to Guru Nanak Dev, the knowledge given by the Guru is the true and eternal holy place of pilgrimage, where the festival of Dasahara (Dusehra) is celebrated for ever. Ordinarily Dusehra is celebrated only on one day that is the tenth day of *Ashwin Shukla Paksha*, but under the discipline of the Guru, there is eternal celebration (p. 687, Dhanasari M. 1).

Fetters: A chain or shackle for the feet. The actions (*Karmas*) of a *Jiva* become his fetters. According to the *Adi Granth* each action of an individual adds a link to the existing chain caused by the actions. Guru

Arjan Dev says, "When one commits actions in ego, they add to the links in the chain on the neck. When one dwels on "mineness", his actions add links to the fetters on his feet" (p. 1004, Maru M. 5).

Fiend(s): The evil spirits. Because of evil actions in the world, one takes different forms, one after the other, after his death. One may become a ghost and an evil spirit. Guru Arjan Dev says, "One becomes an animal, a bird, a ghost or an evil spirit and being sinful, passes through myriad births. Wherever he goes, he does not remain there and without an abode runs from place to place. Since his mind and body are filled with expanding vicious desires and are defrauded by ego, he suffers great grief and is punished grievously and thrown into hell by the Priceless Lord Whom he has forgotten..." (p. 10005, Maru M. 5).

Filial Piety: Of or pertaining to a son or daughter. According to the *Adi Granth*, all human beings are children of God. Just as it is the duty of the child to show filial respect to their parents, it is the duty of all the human beings to show great respect for God-father. Kabir has very beautifully depicted this filial piety in one of his hymns: "My Father has comforted my mind and blessed me with a comfortable seat... How can I forget such a Father?... I am Thy son, Thou art my Father. We both abide in the same place..." (p. 476, Asa Kabir).

Final Beautitude: The Ultimate Supreme Bliss. There are many hymns in the *Adi Grnath*, in which there is mention of the attainment of the final emancipation. The discipline of the True Guru is to be followed for the achievement of this state. Guru Nanak Dev says, "If one practises Truth through the True Word, and if through the True Word one sings the praises of the Lord, and also abiding in his self, he attains the Supreme state, then and only then he looks Glorious at the court of the Lord". The state of final beatitude is also called the Fourth state, Supreme state of *Turiya*. It is the Guru who gives the True Word (or the Name) to the devotee. See: *Emancipation*.

Fine(s): Fine is a penalty of any kind. Guru Angad Dev says, "If under compulsion, one pays as though fined, it is of no merit at all. "If the action is performed with one's heart, then it is the real action" (p. 787, Var Suhi M. 3, Shlok M. 2). Guru Arjan Dev says, "He suffers the penalty in vain and is deemed of no account in the court of the Lord. He did not attempt those works, which would have saved his honour". (p. 408, Asa M. 5). The calumniator is penalised by the messengers of Yama (p. 1145, Bhairo M. 5).

Fire: One of the five elements. It is an evolute from air in the process of creation. The Hindus and Zorastrians are fire-worshippers. Guru Nanak Dev has called the *Agni-devata* of the Hindus as *Baisantar-devata* (p. 473, Var Asa M. 1). The fire is the latent power in the wood (p. 1323, Kalyan M. 4). By adopting the discipline of the Guru, the devotee crosses the ocean of fire (*Saṁsāra*) (p. 865, Gond M. 5); by the Grace of the Guru, the fire of desires is extinguished (p. 732, Suhi M. 4). The womb of the mother is an abode of fire for the conceived being and *maya* is also fire for the being in the world (p. 921, Ramkali M. 3, Anand). See: *Agni*.

Fire-Altar: While commenting on meat-eating, Guru Nanak Dev has made a mention of the fire-altars prepared during *Yajnas*, when the rhinoceros was sacrificed to please the gods (p. 1289, Var Malar M. 1). According to the *Adi Granth*, the sacrifices made at the fire-altar are of no value in comparison to the remembrance of the Name of the Lord (p. 265. Gauri Sukhmani M. 5).

Firmament: The Omnipresent Lord is over the firmament, in the underworld and all over (p. 870, Gond Kabir). In the *Adi Granth*, the word *Gagan* (literally meaning the firmament) also connotes *Chidākāsh* (the firmament of *Chitta* (mind)) and *Dasam Dvar* (the Tenth Door). The visible sky is studded with stars. Kabir says: "Those stars which are visible on the firmament—who has created them?" Guru Nanak Dev says, "The Lord separates the earth and the firmament and spreads the canopy of the heavens over the world. He upholds the firmament without pillars" (p. 1279, Var Malar M. 1).

Fish: Any animal living exclusively in water. If separated from water, it perishes. In the *Adi Granth*, the metaphor of fish has been used several times. Just as the fish writhes, when it is separated from water, in a similar manner the devotee writhes when the Lord does not respond to his entreaties. "Just as the fish is in distress without water, so is poor Namdev without the Name of the Lord" (p. 874, Gond Namdev). The mind is mercurial like the fish and it is to be held through equipoise (p. 991, Maru M. 1). The love of the fish for water is so intense that when it is caught, cut up into bits and cooked, and then eaten up, still it craves more and more for water. Such is the intensity of love of the devotee for the Lord (p. 658, Sorath Ravidas). Just as the fish is trapped in the net for its own folly, so is the man caught by death unawares (p. 55, Sri Rag M. 1). When entrapped by the fisherman's net, the fish realises that though her love with water was sweet, her world was *maya*; similarly the man caught in the noose of death has the same realization (p. 439, Asa M. 1). Guru Nanak Dev says, "I would be a fish abiding in water, if in this way I remember the Lord and receive Him in my embrace with open arms and visualise Him everywhere" (p. 157, Gauri Bairagan M. 1).

Five People: In the *Adi Granth*, these five people are called "Panch Janaa" and these five people are the five vices viz. lust (*Kama*), anger (*Karodh*), greed (*Lobh*), attachment (*Moha*), and ego (*Ahankāra*). Guru Arjan Dev says, "I recited the holy texts and ruminated on the Vedas: I cleansed through yoga the inner-physical system; but I could not abandon the compnay of the five people and was thus bound to egoism more and more" (p. 641, Sorath M. 5). When one makes an effort and makes his mind pure; when he dances the dance of selflessness and controls the five people, the one Absolute Lord is Enshrined in his mind (p. 81, Asa M. 5).

Flamingoes (Haṁsās): Flamingo is a bird with bright scarlet plumage, long and slender legs and neck and a heavy bent bill. The Indian equivalent for flamingo is *haṁsa*. Some English scholars have translated the world *haṁsa* as swan, but the "Wild Goose" may be the proper translation for it. The flamingoes or *Haṁsas* breed on the lakes of central Asia like Manasarovar and migrate to India in winter. In the *Adi Granth*, the metaphor of *Haṁsa* has been used several times. In the Shlokas of Sheikh Farid, it is used as a symbol for a saintly person and a crane as a symbol for a self-willed man (p. 1384, Shlok Farid). The word *Haṁsa* also symbolises 'the soul' (p. 794, Suhi Farid) and the life-force conveying "He am I" (p. 60, Sri Rag M. 1).

Flesh: The soft substance, especially the muscular parts, of an animal body; that which covers the framework of bones. Guru Nanak Dev says, "One's life is tied to the flesh all around... one is conceived in flesh, born in flesh, feeds upon the flesh... one's relationship is with the things of flesh". Guru Nanak Dev has not touched the controversy of eating or avoiding flesh. He says, "People do not know what is flesh and what is vegetable; which food is sinful and which is not. Wherefrom all this flesh has come. It has come from water like other eatables..." (pp. 1289-90, Var Malar M. 1). In olden days animal flesh was offered as sacrificial food to the gods in the *Yajnas*.

Flood: The idea of flood-water has been used metaphorically in the *Adi Granth*. Guru Arjan Dev says, "O mother, *Maya* is a delusion. Without the Devotion of the Lord, it is like the straw-fire, cloud-shadow and flood-water" (p. 717, Todi M. 5).

Flowers: The idea of short life of flowers has been used figuratively in the *Adi Granth*. Guru Arjan Dev says, "Why are you enticed away by the worldly life? It is all the garden of flowers" (p. 50, Sri Rag M. 5). Guru Nanak Dev says, "The wealth, youth and flower are the guests for only four days (i.e. for a very short period" (p. 23, Sri Rag M. 1). The flowers disappear when the fruit takes shape. Ravidas says, "The whole vegetation is flowering. When the fruit appears, the flower disappears" (p. 1167, Bhairo Ravidas). Talking about the flowers of the *Simmal* tree, Guru Nanak Dev says, "Its fruit are insipid and its flowers are nauseous" (p. 470, Var Asa M. 1).

Folklore: The beliefs, legends and customs current among the common people. The Gurus and saints whose hymns have been included in the *Adi Granth* were folk-poets, hence they came under the impact of folklore. We find in their verses various illustrations of folk-idiom, folk-sayings, folk-tales etc. They were, of course, imbued with Pauranic lore. They composed their verses in folk-metres and folk-tunes. An example from Namdev: "O Pundit, I saw your Gayatri grazing in the field of Lodha, who was beating her with a stick and she was going away limping. O Pundit, I saw your Mahadeva riding on the white bull; his meal was prepared in the house of Modi (Store-keeper), whose son was killed. O Pundit, I saw your Ramchand arriving, opposing and fighting against Ravana and losing his wife" (p. 875, Gond Namdev).

Food: Guru Nanak Dev says, "To believe in Your Name is like tasting the sweets, to hear Your Name is like tasting the saltish foods, to utter Your Name is like tasting the sour, to sing Your Name is like tasting the spicy foods and to love single-mindedly is like tasting thirty-six kinds of delicacies... all other foods and all other pleasures are vain and useless" (p. 16, Sri Rag M. 1). All those foods and drinks are pure, with which the Compassionate Lord has blessed us (p. 472, Var Asa M. 1). A person, who eats well but commits evil, his life is like field of poison (p. 105, Majh M. 5). The men of contentment loosen their worldly bonds and eat and drink sparingly. (p. 467, Var Asa M. 1). If one eats more food he increases the waste-matter within his body (p. 1331, Prabhati M. 1). The first food for the baby is mother's milk and in youth one is absorbed in eating and drinking and other pleasures (p. 137, Var Majh M. 1). The foodgrains, sugarcane and cotton grow where the earth comes into contact with water (p. 1290, Var Malar M. 1).

Fools: Guru Amar Das has defined a fool. He says, "A fool is one who believes a fool. He is unwise and dies on account of his ego. He earns sorrow and always abides in pain" (p. 953, Var Ramkali M. 3). The fool does not know the truth, he wastes away his life (p. 467, Var Asa M. 1).The fool asserts his ego and does not know the True Deed (p. 1343, Prabhati M. 1). He is most foolish who does not believe in the Name of the Lord (p. 1015, Maru M. 1). None should argue with a fool (p. 473, Var Asa M. 1) The fool is blind and runs after darkness; the more he utters the more he exposes himself. (p. 1239, Var Sarang M. 4, Shlok M. 1). If one speak with the fools, he wastes his time and energy (p. 870, Gond Kabir). The fool is mended only on being struck in the face (p. 143, Var, Majh M. 1).

Forefathers: Ancestors. In Hinduism, there is the practice of worshipping the forefathers, but the *Adi Granth* rejects such practice. Kabir says, "In the lifetime, the fathers were not looked after, but when they passed away, people performed *Sraadhs* (made offerings in their names) but these offerings do not reach the dead, because the crows and the dogs feed on them" (p. 332, Gauri Bairagan Kabir). Talking about an enlightened person Guru Nanak Dev says, "With the Lord's Fire, he burns the snares of *maya* and death. He slays age, death and ego. He not only swims across the ocean of *Saṁsara*, but also saves his forefathers (p. 223, Gauri M. 1) See: *Fathers*.

Forest: The hermits renounce the world and go to the forests, but the Sikh Gurus are against the renunciation. Guru Tegh Bahadur says, "Why do you go to the forest? The Omnipresent Lord, though ever detached, abides within you like the fragrance in the flower and the reflection in the mirror" (p. 684, Dhanasri M. 9). Since the *Adi Granth* adopts only the householder's path, it has rejected other *ashramas* (stages of life acccording to Hinduism) i.e. *Brahmachara, Vanaprastha* and *Sannyasa*. But "leaving their homes, the *Vanaprathis*, go to the forests and eat the roots of the plants, but still the evil mind does not forsake the vice (p. 855, Bilawal Kabir). The world is identified with a dreadful forest. Guru Arjan Dev says, "In the dreadful forest, I have found a lone companion in the Name of the Lord. It is the dispeller of sorrow (p. 519, Var Gujri M. 5).

Foresters: The foresters or forest-dwellers are the hermits roaming in the forests in search of God. They may be Hindu vanaprasthis, Buddhist or Jaina monks, the Yogis or others who believe in renunciation and asceticism. Such hermits and ascetics, according to the *Adi*

Granth, never realise their objective. Sheikh Farid, had been wandering in the forests, but ultimately, when he settled down, he said, "Why do you wander in the forest making way through the bushes? The Lord resides in the heart, why do you search him in the forest?" (p. 1378, Shlok Farid). See: *Forest*.

Forgiveness: Forgiveness is a great virtue. Guru Nanak Dev says, "Without forgiveness, innumerable people have been wasted away. It is not possible to count them" (p. 937, Ramkali Dakhni Oamkar, M. 1). He who practises forgiveness, for him it is the keeping of the fast, good conduct and contentment. No ailment touches him (p. 223, Gauri M. 1). Guru Nanak Dev advises the devotee to cling to forgiveness in the refuge of the True Guru (p. 1030, Maru M. 1). If the bride is decked with the jewel of forgiveness, she enjoys her Lord (p. 359, Asa M. 1). Kabir says, "Where there is knowledge, there is *Dharma* (piety), where there is falsehood, there is sin, where there is greed, there is death, where there is forgiveness, there is God (p. 1372, Shlok Kabir).

Form: Our world, in which we live, is the world of Form, Action and Name. The Transcendent Lord, who has created it, is Formless. Every object in the world has some form. Such forms, big or small, are infinite (p. 5, Japuji). All the Forms come into being under the Will of Lord (p. 1, Japuji). There are forms upon forms in waters, on lands and in three worlds (p. 466, Var Asa M. 1). All the forms work under the Fear of the Lord (p. 585, Var Vadhans M. 4, Shalok M. 3).

Fornication: Voluntary sexual intercourse between a man and an unmarried woman. In scriptures this term is used in respect of adultery. Guru Amar Das says, "If we enjoy a hundred thousand of women and rule over the nine divisions of the world, we do not receive the Grace of the Lord and the True Guru and we are cast in the womb repeatedly (p. 26, Sri Rag M. 3). Not only fornication, but also looking at other woman is a taboo in Sikhism. Guru Arjan Dev says, "Some feed their eyes on the beauty of other men's women, hidden from the eyes of the world they come to grief" (p. 315, Var Gauri M. 4, Shlok M. 5). "O fool, being a devoted husband, you have not to touch another woman (p. 1095, Var Maru Dakhne M. 5).

Fortune: In Hinduism *Bhāga* is Fortune personified. *Bhaga* is the god who gives human beings their share of happiness. *Bhaga* is sometimes associated with the lunar asterism, astrologically considered to be favourable to marriage. In the *Adi Granth*, only the saints are considered fortunate, who treasure the riches of the Name of the Lord (p. 748, Suhi M. 5).

Fortune-Telling: In Hindu Pantheon, the stars and planets are personified, all of which have power over the lives of men. It might have been the origin of Indian horoscope astrology. Guru Nank Dev has scoffed at the practice of fortune-telling. He says, "The astrologer makes our horoscope calculating this and that; he reads it out to us, but does not realise the reality himself....Calculations about one's future creates doubt and sorrow within him, but one is ever at Peace, if he reclines in the Guru's refuge" (p. 904, Ramkali M. 1). The true devotees forsake all fear of the inauspicious aspects of the planets and totally surrender to the Will of the Lord (p. 813, Bilawal M. 5).

Free-Will: The doctrine of free-will is opposed to determinism. It ascribes freedom to the human will. According to the *Adi Granth*, the Will of God is supreme. Every one works under the Will of the Lord and none is out of it. (p.1, Japuji). There is, however, freedom regarding the *Kiryaman karmas* (the Karmas, which are to be done by an individual). In this respect the analogy of the hunter is given, who is standing armed with the bow and arrow. He is in the process of shooting the arrow, but still he can think of the validity or invalidity of the act before releasing the arrow. Because of this freedom, the Sikh Gurus and the saints of the *Adi Granth* have laid stress on effort. Guru Arjan Dev says, "Live your life, always making an earnest effort, abide in comfort while earning and meet the Lord by contemplation on Him, so that you are absolved of all anxieties" (p. 522, Var Gujri M. 5).

Friars: A Friar is a brother or member of any religious order. The word "Friar" is used for a member of the Christian monastic order and the word *Bhikkhū* for the member of the Buddhist monastic order. *Bhikkhūs* or *Bhikshūs* are mendicants. The religion of the *Adi Granth* lays stress on the life of the householders and is against renunciation and asceticism.

Friend: The only Real Friend is the Lord Himself. Guru Ram Das says, "O Brother, The Lord is my Friend" (p. 41, Sri Rag M. 4). Guru Arjan Dev says, "I accept that whatever my Friend Does. His works are a source of pleasure to me, My mind takes refuge in the One Lord. He, my Friend, Does everything. My Friend is Care-free. My love with Him is through Guru's Grace. My friend is the Inner-knower of all, He, the Omnipotent and Supreme Lord" (p. 187, Gauri M. 5). Guru

Nanak Dev says, "There are many friends in the worlds, but there is no real friend without Guru and God (p. 1028, Maru M. 1). All the relatives, friends and brothers whom we see in the world, meet us only with their self-interest. The day, when their hopes are shattered, none comes nearby (p. 860, Gaund M. 4). They are the real beloved friends, who make us remember the Name of the Lord (p. 739, Suhi M. 5). A friend in need is a friend indeed. He alone is our friend, who goes alongwith us in the Yond. And whatever account is asked from us, he stands there as our surety (p. 729, Suhi M. 1). Guru Arjan Dev says, "I have befriended every one—I am a friend to every one" (p. 671, Dhanasari M. 5). Such is the social attitude in Sikhism.

Friendship: With whom should we have friendship, when the whole world is ephemeral? (p. 468, Asa M. 1). The friendship with a *Manumukh* (self-willed person) lasts only for four days. It will break in an instant; several vices accompany such a friendship (p. 587, Var Vadhans M. 3). The Real Friendship is with him, who controls everything (p. 312, Var Gauri M. 5). The friendship with the self-willed persons consists only in relation to *maya*; but whenever they see one is suffering, they break relations and speed away. Their relationship lasts only up to that time, when they can get some necessities for themselves. But when there is nothing for them, they talk ill. These egocentric persons, unwise and blind, do not know the state of their souls (p. 959, Var Ramkali M. 5). The friendship with the unwise and love with the egoists is like a line drawn across water, of which no sign or mark is left (p. 474, Var Asa M. 1).

Frog: The man of the world is identified with a frog in a well. The saint Ravidas says, "I am like a frog in the well; I know nothing of this or that world. My mind is enticed by the vices..." (p. 346, Gauri Poorbi Ravidas). Using the metaphor of a frog, Guru Nanak Dev addresses the man of the world in the following manner: "Out of the clear waters sprouts the lotus as well as the filth. The lotus lives with both, but keeps detached from them. But, O frog, you do not know and eat only the dirt, discarding the pure nectar. You always live in waters, but do not know the love like the black bee... O Frog, you deem yourself clever living with mere water, but in nectar sweet milk are also treasured honey and sugar, which the tick does not taste and sucks only blood, considering itself wise like you" (p. 990, Maru M. 1). It is in the rainy season, in the month of *Shrāvan* and *Bhādon*, the frogs shriek (p. 1108, Baramaha Tukhari M. 1).

Fruits: When the fruit appears, the flower disappears (p. 1167, Bhairo Ravidas). Since the fruit is the resultant in the vegetation, it idiomatically connotes the 'result'. The word "Phal" in Indian vocabulary is also used in that sense. A few fruits have been mentioned in the hymns of the *Adi Granth* e.g. grapes in the Shlokas of Sheikh Farid (p. 1379), mango and lemon in a hymn of Kabir in Ramkali Raga (p. 972).

Fumigation: The action of generating odorous smoke or flames especially in incantations. It was the practice of the yogis to besmear their bodies with the ashes created by kindling a fire in order to extort a favour. The Indian equivalent of fumigation is "Dhūnī", ordinarily a small ignited pile of chaff. It was a method of exorcising demons and evil spirits, and removing the influence of an evil eye or securing one against the influence of witchcraft, by burning aromatic substances. In the *Adi Granth*, there is mention of the practice of besmearing their bodies by the Yogis. Guru Nanak Dev says, "He walks on the path of *maya* and besmears his body with ashes and wallows in dust (p. 1013, Maru M. 1).

Funeral Rites: The Sikh Gurus have rejected all the sacraments performed by the Hindus. On the death of Guru Amar Das, as recorded in the *sadd* of Sunder in the *Adi Granth* in Ramkali Raga (pages 923-24), the praises of the Lord were sung and the scriptures were read. "In any of the three ways the dead body is consumed—by the waters, the dogs or the fire" (p. 609, Suhi M. 50) "Some are cremated, others buried, still others thrown to the dogs. Some are cast to the waters, while others are thrown into the wells. But, O Nanak, no one knows where does one's soul merge in the end" (p. 648, Var Sorath M. 4, Shlok M.1). The traditional method of burning the dead is followed by the Sikhs. "Of what avail are the embellishments to the dead?" says Guru Arjan Dev. All the rituals being performed by the Hindus for their dead have been rejected in the *Adi Granth*. Nothing else except the good deeds of the dead person are helpful in the next world (p. 472, Var Asa M. 1). It is useless to light earthen lamps at the holy places like Gaya (p. 358, Asa M. 1) or perform *Srādh* (p. 332, Gauri Kabir).

Future Life: There have been several speculations about the future life or the life after death. The *Adi Granth* believes that the air mingles with the air, the light (of the soul) merges in the Light (of the Lord), the earth becomes one with the earth, then why should a man grieve?... Who knows what will befall one in the Yond?... one comes and goes according to the Unfathomable Will of the Lord. Neither one dies nor is one capable of dying. No one perishes; the soul is eternal (p. 885, Ramkali M. 5). Though the soul is eternal, the *Karmas* committed by it in the earthly life give it the new form. The actions are like seeds and any seed that sprouts forth brings the soul to the new existence. This is according to the theory of Karma and Tansmigration, which has been accepted by the *Adi Granth*. Guru Arjan Dev says, "Stung by the greed you are cast into the ditch. You do not know what is going to happen to you in the Yond. You are thus born to die and die to be reborn again and again. There is no end to this journey.... When the Lord is Merciful, one contemplates on Him and is blessed with the Nectar-like Name of the Lord..." (p. 1020, Maru M. 5). With the remembrance of the Name of the Lord, the cycle of transmigration ends, with the Grace of the Guru. The inner darkness of the devotee is dispelled and also his coming and going (p. 1348, Prabhati M. 5).

G

Gambling: Playing game of chance for money. Gambling is a very old game, which was also prevalent in the times of the Sikh Gurus. Guru Arjan Dev says, "Some pass their lives in gambling" (p. 914, Ramkali M. 5). Just as a gambler loses his money and other possessions through gambling, the man of the world, like him, loses the precious human birth. He has been asked not to gamble away his invaluable life (p. 80, Sri Rag M. 5), and (p. 212, Gauri M. 5).

Games: Ravidas has identified the world with a game or play (p .487, Asa Ravidas). There is a mention of a few games, which were prevalent in the times of the Sikh Gurus e.g., gambling (p. 914, Ramkali M. 5), dice (p. 434, Asa M. 1, Patti) and polo (p. 322, Gauri Ki Var M. 5). Guru Nanak Dev has given the characteristics of the game of love. He says, "If you want to play the game of love, then come to my path with your head on your palm. Once you set your feet on this path, then do not hesitate to lay down your head (p. 1412, Shlok Varan te Vadhik, M. 1).

Gana: *Gana* connotes troop or multitude of demi-gods. They are the attendants of Shiva and Parvati. The ganas are generally grouped into various classes viz. Adityas, Vasus, Sadhyas, Rudras etc. In the *Adi Granth* mention has been made of these demi-gods alongwith Kinnars, Gandharvas, and other mythological beings. All of them have been shown as singing the praises of the Lord (p. 249, M. 5, Chhant). The ganas also die like other beings (p. 64, Sri Rag M. 1).

Gandharvas: The gandharvas are celestial beings, having their dwelling in the sky or atmosphere. They are said to prepare some heavenly juice for the gods. It is said that they are skilled in medicine, regulate the asterisms and are fond of women. Those who belong to Indra's heaven are musicians and singers, who attend the banquets of gods. In the *Adi Granth* they have been mentioned as singing the praises of the Lord. Kabir says, "A myriad of Gandharvas shout Thy Victory, O Lord," "The Lord, in whose House sing the Gandharvas and the seers and the gods and the attendants of gods in utter humility" (p. 1292, Malar Namdev).

Ganesha: A Hindu god, also known as Gana-pati, or Lord of the Ganas (or troops of inferior deities). He is the son of Shiva and Parvati. He is said to have sprung from the scurf of Parvati's body. Shiva did not know it. Ganesha was guarding the door, when Parvati was taking a bath. Shiva wanted to enter. When opposed by Ganesha, he cut off his head. Because of the lamentations of Parvati, Shiva replaced the head with an elephant's head. He is the god of wisdom and remover of obstacles. Therefore, he is propitiated during all important errands. He is also invoked in the very beginning of the account books. It is said that he was the scribe, when Mahabharata was dictated by Vyasa. The rat is his vehicle. In the *Adi Granth*, Bhagat Beni has mentioned the name Ganesha, while describing a fake devotee of God of his time. He says, "The devotee worships the stone-image and paints on his body the signs of Ganesha" (p. 1351, Prabhati Beni). In the times of Sikh Gurus, Ganapatya cult was prevalent in India alongwith other Bhakti cults. All these cults which advocated the worship of gods and goddesses, have been rejected in the *Adi Granth*.

Ganga: The sacred Indian river Ganges. It had been brought down from heaven, by the prayers of the saint Bhagiratha, to purify the ashes of the sixty thousand sons of king Sagara, who had been burnt down by the angry glance of the sage Kapila. Due to its origin on the earth by the saint Bhagiratha, the river is also called Bhagirathi. It is said that the descent of the Ganges disturbed the saint Jahnu, because he was performing a sacrifice and in his rage, he drank up the waters, but on relenting he allowed the river to flow through his ear. Therefore the river is also called Jahnavi. This episode is mentioned in the *Adi Granth*. Guru Ramdas says, "Bhagiratha, the seer, had brought the Ganges into life and Kedara was established by the saints of the Lord" (p. 1263, Malar M. 4). Ganga is personified as a goddess. The waters of Ganga are sacred and pure. The waters of other streams which mingle with it, also become pure. "The stream lost itself in the Ganga, but it also turned into Ganga" (p. 1158, Bhairo Kabir). "As the rain-water received by the drains and streams becomes pure by falling in the Ganga, such beneficence is also in the True Guru..." (pp. 854-55, Var Bilawal M. 4).

Garb: Ego; Pride; Ahamkāra. See: Ahamkāra.

Garbh: Womb. Guru Arjan Dev syas, "O my Lord, You protected me in the womb of the mother by enabling me to remember you. Kindly ferry me across the ocean of fire and its boundless waves" (Sorath M. 5, p. 613).

Garbhādhāna: It is one of the Hindu sacraments. The *Adi Granth* has rejected all the sacraments (Samskaras). In Hinduism, Garbhadhana is a purificatory rite, which is performed after menstruation in order to ensure both conception and the right development of the embryo. On this occasion, the prayers addressed to various gods are recited. The *Adi Granth* has rejected all the gods and goddesses, because their origin is *maya*. The prayers for the well-being of individuals are addressed only to the One, Supreme and Eternal Lord. On the conception of the sixth Guru Hargobind, the fifth Guru, Guru Arjan Dev wrote: "God has blessed me with a boon.... The son was conceived in the womb and brought immense happiness to the mind of the mother... As I had wished, so was I blessed by God..." (p. 396, Asa M. 5).

Garībī: Poverty; humility. In the *Adi Granth*, this word has been used in the sense of humility and modesty. Guru Arjan Dev says, "There is bliss in the humility observed in the company of saints, where the Lord is remembered" (Suhi M. 5, p. 745).

Garments: Articles of dress.... According to Guru Arjan Dev, the Lord blesses His Devotees with the Robe of Honour (inclusive of the garments from the head to the feet) and in this manner the Glory of the Lord is Revealed (p. 631, Sorath M. 5). Our body is a garment of the soul. Guru Nanak Dev says, "My body (physical garment) is mercerised by *maya* and is dyed in the colour of greed, but this skirt is not liked by the Lord and He cannot accept me as His Bride on His Bed... If the body is dyed and imbued with the fast colour of maddar (i.e. the Name of the Lord). And if the Dyer is the Master Himself, then rare and wonderful will be the colour. They whose skirts are dyed red in this way, the Lord is ever with them" (pp. 721-22, Tilang M. 1).

Garuda: A mythological bird, said to be the vehicle of Lord Vishnu. He has the beak and talins of the predatory bird and the body of man. He is the devourer and destroyer of serpents. Depicting his personal harassment at the hands of the king, who wanted immediate resurrection of the dead cow, the saint Namdev says, "Here comes Govind (the Lord) seated on Garuda" (p. 1166, Bhairo Namdev). The Lord comes to the rescue of his saints, seated on his vehicle Garuda. "Though Aruna is the charioteer of the sun and his brother Garuda is the king of the birds, yet Aruna due to his own actions, was rendered a cripple" (p. 695, Dhanasari Trilochan). There is also a mention of the *Garuda Mantra* in the *Adi Granth*. Guru Arjan Dev says, "As the poison of the snake does not affect the one who knows the Garuda Mantra, similarly the Name of the Lord helps the devotees" (pp. 986-87, Mali Gaura M. 5).

Gathas: A Gatha is primarily a song or a religious recital. It also connotes a tale or a narration. There is also a stanza-form of this name. A language named Gatha was also prevalent. Though it contained Sanskrit words, mixed with Deshi words like Sahaskriti, it was neither Sanskrit, nor Prakrit. A few Shlokas in this language are given at the end of the *Adi Granth.* One of the Shlokas gives the following characteristics of Gaths: "Gatha is very deep and rare is the person who knows it" (p. 1360, Gatha M. 5). In the Gatha dialect is woven the praise of the Lord (p. 1360, Gatha M. 5).

Gaya: It is a city in Bihar and is one of the seven sacred cities of Hindus. Therefore it is a place of pilgrimage. It is said that an *asura* (demon) named Gaya, called Gayasura, sacrificed himself at this place for the welfare of humanity. This city is called *Pitr-tiratha* (a holy place of the *Pitrs* (ancestors). The Hindus make offerings to their ancestors at this shrine, which directly benefits them. Grierson is of the view that Gaya was originally a holy place for the Hindus with a sacred tree (called akshayavata) which granted offspring; later on it became sacred for Buddhists, because it was here that the Buddha attained Enlightenment under the *ashvattha* tree. There is mention of this city in the *Adi Granth* in a hymn of Namdev. He says, "The pilgrimages to the Ganges, Godavari and Gaya are only worldly works. If the Lord is pleased, only then one is the True Servent" (p. 1196, Basant Namdev).

Gayatri: It is the name of a metre in Sanskrit. Several hymns of Rig Veda were composed in this metre. The most sacred hymn is the prayer known as *Gayatri Mantra,* an invocation to Sun, the supreme generative force. This *mantra* is repeated every morning and evening by the *dvijas* (twice-born). Gayatri is personified as a goddess, who is the wife of Brahma. Guru Amar Das says, "One offers the daily prayer *Sandhya* and makes water-offerings to the gods and ancestors (called *Tarpan*); he also repeats *Gayatri Mantra,* but without knowing the Lord, he undergoes suffering" (p. 603, Sorath M. 3).

Gems: Jewels. In the *Adi Granth*, Guru Arjan Dev syas, "The Name of the Lord is precious like the gems and jewels" (p. 134, Baramaha Mahj M. 5). The same thought has been expressed in the following Shloka, "O my mother, my Lord has blessed me with a gem, which keeps my heart cool and comfortable" (p. 1098, Var Maru Dakhne M. 5). Guru Nanak Dev says, "The ego of the mind is destroyed by the gem of the Name of the Lord (p. 992, Maru M. 1). Thus the word gem is used metaphorically in the *Adi Granth*. For Sheikh Farid every heart is like gem because it is the abode of the Lord. It should never be hurt (p. 1384, Shlok Farid).

Generation: Procreation; propagation of species. According to the *Adi Granth*, the Lord is the only generative power. Guru Nanak Dev addresses the Lord thus: "The egg-born, the foetus-born, the sweat-born and the earth-born, all are there because of your generative power. And this is your Glory that you pervade all" (p. 596, Sorath M. 1). In Gauri Sukhmani Guru Arjan Dev says, "He Expanded Himself like myriad of waves" (p. 275). The Lord has spread out Himself in innumerable ways. The expanse was created repeatedly, but He is ever the One Absolute Lord. He has Created millions in myriad ways. Created by Him, they merged in Him" (p. 276).

Ghar: Home; the spiritual home. The Enlightened Person (*Gurmukh*) understands and remains in tune with the One Lord. He abides in his own real home and merges in Truth (Gauri Guareri M. 1, p. 222).

Ghee: Clarified butter. Ghee is an essential article of food in Indian meals. The saint Dhanna has begged the Lord to provide him with the necessities of life. They include ghee besides others like pulses, flour, shoes, clothes, grains of various types, the cow, the buffalo, the horse, good wife etc. (p. 695, Dhanasari Dhanna). It is recorded in the Var of Satta and Balwand that in the free kitchen of Guru Angad Dev rice-pudding mixed with ghee was distributed abundantly (p. 967) and in the free kitchen of Guru Amar Das, ghee was served with refined flour and sugar (p. 968). The wise housewife churns the curd for ghee (p. 1167, Bhairo Ravi). Just as fire is in the wood and ghee in the milk, similarly the Lord pervades all (p. 617, Sorath M. 5). No one curses ghee or silk, similarly no one cares for the caste of the devotee of the Lord (p. 721, Tilang M. 1).

Ghosts: An incorporeal being called *Bhūta* or *Preta* in Indian vocabulary. While mentioning various beings in the creation, Guru Arjan Dev says in Sukhmani that there are millions of *Bhūtas* and *Pretas* (ghosts). Kabir says, "The house in which a saint is not served, nor God is remembered, that house is like a crematorium populated by ghosts" (p. 1374, Shlok Kabir).

Ghouls (Demons): An evil spirit supposed to prey upon the human corpses. It is a species of Jinn (Genii). Though the Jinn, Bhutas and Pretas have been mentioned in the *Adi Granth*, this word (ghoul) has not been used.

Giān, Giānī: *Giān* is knowledge and a person having knowledge, especially spiritual knowledge, is a *Giānī*. See: *Knowledge*.

Giant-Giantesses: Supposed beings of human form but of super-human stature. Describing various types of created beings Guru Arjan Dev says in *Sukhmani*: "There are millions of gods, *Danavas* (giant-like demons) and Indras shaded by a canopy" (p. 267, Gauri Sukhmani M. 5). In Japuji, Guru Nanak Dev has written: "The *Devas* (gods) and *Danavas* (giant-like demons) sing the praises of the Lord (p. 6, Japuji).

Gifts: The Lord is Most Beneficent and Munificent. The gifts that He has given to the human being are innumerable. He has bestowed the individual soul with a body, which has been given ears to hear music, eyes to see world's wonders, tongue to speak sweetly, hands to move and work..." (p. 270, Gauri Sukhmani M. 5). Why to forget such a Lord, who has given you all the good gifts of life? (p. 290, ibid). Guru Nanak Dev says, "The Giver is giving everything, but the recipients may get tired (p. 2, Japuji). The Giver has kept all the bounties in His Own Hands and He Gives whomsoever He Pleases" (p. 604, Sorath M. 3). The Gifts of the Lord are many, which cannot be put in writing. The Great Giver Himself does not covet anything. Many warriors beg at His Door.... There are many who after receiving the gifts say that they have received nothing.... There are many who are ever afflicted with sorrow and hunger, O Giver, this is also your bounty (p. 5, Japji).

Girhī: The householder; Grihasthi. "The men of the Lord always remain unattached while living as householders and contemplate on the essence of knowledge" (Sorath M. 3, pp. 599-600).

Girls (Women): The girls who imbibe virtues in their life, are neither at pains in their parents' house nor in the house of their in-laws. Guru Arjan Dev says, "O bride, when your groom is with you, you are honoured by all, but when he goes away, there is no one to care for you. You are blessed both at your parents house and the house of your in-laws; if you learn the right way, you are never in anguish. O girls, you all will go one day to your in-laws, all of you will be given in marriage. But that bride is blessed who adores her spouse" (p. 550, Sri Rag M. 5). The boys and girls love their father (p. 596, Sorath, M. 1). Guru Nanak Dev addresses the young girl thus: "O ignorant girl, why are you egoistic? In your own house why do you not enjoy the love of your Lord? The Lord is near you, why do you seek Him outside? Apply the collyrium of Fear to your eyes and bedeck yourself with love. When your Lord loves you, then you will be the real bride. O ignorant girl, what can you do if the Lord likes you not. You cry out in vain, and do not enter the palace of the Lord" (p. 722, Tilang M. 1). The *Adi Granth* gives the image of a girl to a human being, who has to leave this world (parental home) and go to the Lord (the house of the in-laws).

Gita: Its full name is *Srimad Bhagavad Gita*, and is said to have been composed by Vyasa in the fifth century B.C. It forms part of the famous epic *Mahabharata*. It is in the form of a dialogue between Lord Krishna and Arjuna and, in the main, presents the philosophy of triple yoga i.e. *Gyan Yoga*, the path of knowledge, *Bhakti Yoga*, the path of devotion and *Karma Yoga*, the path of action. The emphasis is on selfless action for the sake of righteousness. In the *Adi Granth*, there is mention of *Gita* in the verses of Maharashtrian Saint Namdev. (p. 874, Gond Namdev). See: *Bhagavad Gita*.

Glory: Exalted and merited praise, honour, or admiration accorded by common consent to a person. According to the *Adi Granth* mortals cannot be glorious. Their praise or honour is short-lived. Such a glory of position or worldly honour becomes a dream (p. 42, Sri Rag M. 5). The *Adi Granth* elucidates the glory of God and others who have become one with Him e.g. The True Guru, *Brahm Gyani*, Saint, Sadh and Gurmukh.

Goal: According to the *Adi Granth*, the goal of human life is the unity of the soul with God from whom it has been separated, having been ensnared by *maya*. This goal can be achieved with the help of the Guru. The Guru gives the Name of the Lord to his disciple and under his guidance leads him towards the goal. The disciple has to shed away all his ego and sense of duality and follow *en toto* the discipline ordained by the Guru. Guru Amar Das says, "Their life is fruitful, who follow the discipline of the Ture Guru. They save their family and blessed is their mother. They absorb themselves in the Name, on whom the Lord is Graceful" (p. 28, Sri Rag M. 3).

Gobind: See: *Govind*.

Goblins: Fiends. They are mischievous and ugly demons. In Indian vocabulary they are called "Bhutas" and "Pretas". See "Fiends" and "Bhutas".

God: Brahman: The Lord. The nature of Ultimate Reality has been summed up in the *Mul Mantra* in the very beginning of the *Adi Granth*. The translation of this sacred text is as follows: "God is One.

His Name is Truth. He is the Creator. He is without any fear and enmity. He is immortal, Unborn and Self Existent. He can be realised through the Grace of the Guru. "God is both Transcendent and Immanent. He is Omnipresent, Omnipotent and Omniscient. In His Transcendent aspect He is devoid of attributes and in His Immanent aspect He is Ishvara and treasure-house of qualities. See: *Brahman*.

Gods and Goddesses: The *Adi Granth* has rejected all the gods and goddesses, because they are not immortal and shall pass away ultimately (p. 237, Gauri M. 5). Moreover they are within the fold of *maya* (p. 129, Majh M. 3) and hence cannot realise Brahman (p. 7, Japuji). They are soiled and unclean (p. 1158, Bhairo Kabir).

Gold: Gold is a precious metal, but the saints of the *Adi Granth* have no love for gold. They love the Lord, whom they consider invaluable. Kabir says, "The Lord is too precious to be bought for gold. Therefore I gave my heart away to Him and realised Him" (p. 327, Gauri Kabir). To a saint or a real devotee of the Lord, the gold and dust are equal (p. 2755, Gauri Sukhmani M. 5). In the *Adi Granth*, human body is considered golden. Guru Ram Das says, "Within the fortress of my golden body resides the Lord" (p. 449, Asa M. 4).

Good: A term of general or indefinite commendation. It also connotes moral excellence. Its antonym is evil. *Adi Granth* considers that man good, who follows the discipline of the True Guru. "He who follows the saints of the True Guru, that Purusha is true and good... O Lord, everything is your creation and so all is good" (p. 304, Var Gauri M. 4).

Good Conduct: According to the *Adi Granth* "That conduct is good, glorious and fortunate, which makes one live in his heart with the Word of the perfect Guru" (p. 290, Gauri Sukhmani M. 5).

Goodness: The quality or condition of being good. Guru Ram Das says, "He who seeks his own goodness must surrender completely before the Guru" (p. 1310, Kanra M. 4). If one wants his goodness, he should do good and be humble (p. 465, Var Asa M. 1).

Good Works: The sacraments and rituals enjoined by Hindu Shastras have been rejected by the *Adi Granth*. The only good works according to the *Adi Granth* are the ethical qualities. Guru Arjan Dev says, "I bedeck myself with Truth, contentment, compassion and righteousness; thus my bridehood becomes fruitful and I realise my Lord" (p. 812, Bilawal M. 5). The truthful conduct is considered supreme by the *Adi Granth* (p. 62, Sri Rag M. 1).

Gopāl: The Preserver (Pāl) of the world (Go). It is one of the Vaishnave names of the Lord. The word 'Go' also means "cow", therefore this name is also used for Lord Krishna.

Gosāīn: The Lord (*Sāin*) of the world (Go). Name of the Lord.

Goshta: Conversation; dialogue. In the *Adi Granth*, one of the compositions of Guru Nanak Dev is *Siddh Goshta*, which contains a dialogue between Guru Nanak Dev and the Yogis.

Government: Only the Government/rule of God is eternal. He neither comes nor goes. His servants serve Him ever... (p. 592, Var Vadhans M. 4, Shlok M. 3). The Government of the Lord abides for ever. He is the sole ruler of the Universe (p. 769, Suhi M. 3). Guru Nanak Dev addresses the Lord thus: "I am a sacrifice to your True Name. Your Government is eternal, it never ends. Your rule is everlasting and stays for ever" (p. 5567, Vadhans M. 1). The *Dharmaraja* has God's instruction to administer Law, but his rule (dominion) is over those evil souls, who are torn by duality" (p. 38, Sri Rag M. 3).

Govind: The Preserver (*Bind*—the seed of preservation) of the world (Go). It is the Name of the Lord.

Govinda: Literally it means the "protector of Cows" and is an epithet of Lord Krishan. But in the *Adi Granth*, this word has been used for Lord God. Guru Ram Das says, "My Govind is Great, Unknowable, Unapproachable, the Primal, Immaculate and Absolute" (p. 448, Asa M. 4, Chhant).

Grahas: Seizure. Literally the word *Grah* means 'To sieze or overpower', but this name is given to a class of demons, who seize their victims and inflict various types of troubles. Various types of *grahas* have been mentioned in Hindu literature. They have also been associated with planets, giving rise to the science of astrology. The positions of the planets at the time of the birth of a person are said to exert favourable or malevolent influences. The *navagrahas* or nine planets are the sun (Surya), moon (Soma), Mercury (Budha), Jupiter (Brihaspati), Venus (Shukra), Mars (Mangala), Saturn (Shani), Rahu (ascending node of the lunar orbit) and Ketu (descending node of the lunar orbit). In the *Adi Granth* there is mention of *nine Grahas*. Kabir says, "The nine *Grahas*, in millions, stand at Your Gate" (p. 1163, Bhairo Kabir). Guru Arjan Dev says, "The Guru has blessed me with his WORD and thus has vanquished the evil *Grahas*" (p. 400, Asa M. 5). Guru Nanak Dev says, "If my body writhes in pain, under the influence of evil *Grahas*...even then my desire to utter Your Praises will not diminish" (p. 142, Var Majh M. 1).

Grain: A hymn of Kabir amply gives the concept of the *Adi Granth* regarding grain (Ann, Anaj). He says, "The Lord and the Guru both be praised. The fooograins be praised which satisfy the hunger. Those saints be praised, who know thus. In their company one realises the Lord. It was the Primal man, who bequeathed the foodgrains to us. By enjoying the taste of the foodgrains we contemplate on the Name of the Lord. We may contemplate on the Name and also on the grains, which mixed with water, become very tasteful. Those who do not enjoy the taste of the grains, they lose respect in all the three worlds. Those who give up the foodgrains are hyprocrites. They are neither this way nor that way. They announce to the world that they drink only milk, but in secret they eat a good load of grains. Without foodgrains, life cannot be easygoing. By giving up grains we cannot meet the Lord. Thus I have come to know, says Kabir, that the foodgrains be praised, the consumption of which has pleased our Lord" (p. 873, Gond Kabir).

Grants: The gifts or assignments of money. The gifts and grants of the Lord are innumerable. According to the *Adi Granth*, the Lord grants not only material objects and prosperity to an individual, but also he grants virtues to the non-virtuous. There is none who can do some good in return to God (p. 2, Japuji). One should not depend on human beings for favours. It is only the Lord, who can grant him everything (p. 281, Gauri Sukhmani M. 5). See: *Gifts*.

Gratitude: Gratefulness; a warm feeling of goodwill toward a benefactor. The benefactor, according to the *Adi Granth* is either God or the Guru. God gives all the bounties to His created beings and the Guru gives a discipline to the devotee, on account of which all his sufferings cease. Guru Arjan Dev says, "The Lord takes care of each one of his own creatures. He is our Eternal Protector and Ever-Compassionate Lord. I am for ever a sacrifice unto Him (p. 1271, Malar M. 5). He says in another hymn: "I am a sacrifice unto my perfect Guru, by whose Grace I always utter the Name of the Lord. On hearing this Nectar-like word, I have become blessed and all my involvements with the illusion have ceased" (p. 1340, Prabhati M. 5).

Grave: A place of burial: an excavation in the earth for the reception of a corpse. The Muslims bury their dead in the graves. Guru Nanak Dev has addressed a Muslim thus: "You recite your prayer five times and read the Quran and other holy texts, but you do not know that your eating and drinking will be of no avail, when the grave calls you" (p.

24, Sri Rag M. 1). Sheikh Farid says, "The humble grave calls me, O homeless person, come to your home. One day you will come to me, then why to fear death?" "The mansions are rendered vacant and one resides under the earth. The humble graves have been occupied by the souls" (pp. 1382-83, Shlok Farid).

Great One: Two Sanskrit words "Mahat" and "Pradhan" convey the sense of "Great One". Both these words occur in the *Adi Granth*. The word "Mahat" has been used in the closing Shloka of Japuji. "Mahat" is, in fact, a Sankhyan term meaning Buddhi or intellect. The word "Pradhan" has been used in Sukhmani. "Pradhan" is again a Sankhyan term, meaning *Prakriti*. Guru Arjan Dev says, " 'Purusha' and 'Prakriti' (Pradhan) are manifest in the whole world" (p. 295, Gauri Sukhmani M. 5).

Greed: It is one of the five basic vices, the others being lust, anger, attachment and ego. Greed, like a mad dog, bites and infects every one (p. 983, Nat M. 4). When there is greed, there can be no love. The love created in greed is false. How long can a person stay in a hut with a leaking thatched roof?" (p. 1378, Shlok Farid). One is bound down, when his actions are goaded by greed (p. 702, Jaitsri M. 9) The greed is a dark prison-house, and the sins committed out of greed are the fetters round one's feet (p. 1191, Basant Hindol M. 1). Greed destroys men in the same manner as the moss pollutes water (p. 967, Var Satta Balwand). One should forsake the false greed and remember the Unknowable Lord whole-heartedly (p. 468, Var Asa M. 1).

Grihasthya: One of the four stages of life, the other three being Brahmacharya, Vanaprastha and the Sannyasa. This *Ashrama* has been given preference over the others in the *Adi Granth*. "One should remain unattached like the lotus in water in *Grihasthya*" (Maru M. 4, p. 1070). *Grihasthya* is better than lives of various guises, wherein one attains something (Vadhans M. 3, p. 587).

Guests: Guru Nanak Dev says, "The wealth, youth and flowers are the guests only for four days (i.e. for a very short time)" (p. 23, Sri Rag M. 1). The human being born in the world is like a night-guest. Guru Arjan Dev says, "Like the night-guests, you will depart in the morning. Why are you then absorbed in the household. It is all like a garden of flowers" (p. 50, Sri Rag M. 5). The saints are welcome as guests (p. 452, Asa M. 5, Chhant). In one of his hymns Kabir has mentioned the reception of the rich and poor guests. He says, "No one shows consideration to the poor...if the poor man goes to a rich man, he turns his back upon him. But if a rich person goes to the poor one, he is called in with great respect. The rich and poor are both brothers..." (p. 1159 Bhairo Kabir).

Gun: Quality; Virtue. "There can be no devotion without the practice of virtue in life" (Japuji, p. 4). Without *gun*, one clings to the dirt of *maya* and transmigrates in ego (Asa M. 4, p. 367).

Gunas: They are the three constituent elements or qualities of *Pradhan* or *Prakriti* (*maya*). These three qualities are: *Sattva* (rhythm), *Rajas* (motion) and *Tamas* (resistance). When these qualities are in equilibrium, there is inactivity and the *Maya* of the Lord is asleep. When it is the Will of the Lord, the state of equilibrium ends and the process of creation begins. In His Transcendent aspect, the Lord is devoid of these qualities. He is called *Nirguna* or *Trigunatita*. In His Immanent aspect, the Lord adopts these qualities and is called *Saguna*. Guru Nanak Dev says, "The three *gunas* (*Rajas*, *Tamas* and *Sattva*) are under the shade of Your Power" (p.1038, Maru M.1). Kabir says, "O Lord, the three Modes of *Rajas*, *Tamas* and *Sattva* are all your *Maya*" (p. 1123, Kedara Kabir).

Gur-Asthān: The place of the Guru; the abode of the Guru. "Wherever my Guru goes and sits, that place becomes sacred" (Asa M. 4, p. 450).

Gurbānī: The Word of the Guru; the utterance of the Guru. According to the *Adi Granth*, *Gurbānī* is the light in this world, which is instilled in our mind through the Grace of the Lord (Sri Rag M. 3, p. 67). He in whose mind the *Bānī* of the Guru abides, all his troubles vanish away (Prabhati M. 5, pp. 1339-40). All the dirt is removed by listening to *Gurbānī* (Dhanasari M. 3, p. 665). *Gurbānī* is the store-house of devotion. He who sings it, listens to it and practises it, attains bliss (Asa M. 5, p. 376).

Gur-mantra: The *mantra* of the Guru; the Word of the Guru; the Name of the Lord. "Remember Gur-mantra, then there will be no suffering (Var Gujri M. 5, p. 521).

Gurmat: The discipline of the Guru. "*Gurmat* is the highest rung of the ladder, where the gem of knowledge is contained and the ego is destroyed" (Maru M. 3, p. 1050). The mind is stilled by *Gurmat* and then it never wavers (Bihagra M. 4, p. 538). In Gurmat, by remembering the Name of the Lord, one attains *Dharma* (righteousness) and forbearance (Gauri M. 1, p. 225).

Gurmukh: He whose face is turned towards the Guru; An enlightened person; One who is engrossed in *Grumat*. "The *Gurmukh* destroys his ego. Absorbed in the love of the Lord, he rises above attachment" (Asa M. 3, p. 362). He wakes in *sahaj* and sleeps in *sahaj* (the highest spiritual state). He is always absorbed in the Praises of the Lord (Var Sorath M. 4, Shlok M. 3, p. 646). There is peace in the heart of *Gurmukh.* The Name of the Lord is absorbed in his mind and body (Var Sorath M. 4, p. 653). In several stanzas of *Siddh Goshta,* Guru Nanak Dev has eulogised the personality of a *Gurmukh.* There is love in his heart and he has realised the Sight of the Lord. He has great affection for *Gurbānī.* The All-pervading Pure Light of the Lord is lit within him and visualised by him (*Gurmukh*) (Maru M. 1, p. 1032).

Guru: The religious preceptor. In every walk of life we need a guide. For our spiritual uplift we need a Guru or religious preceptor. The institution of Guru is very old in India. In Upanishads, the last part of the Vedas, we find the Guru instructing the disciples. The Guru is the pivot of the whole Sikh thought. In the *Adi Granth,* nearly every hymn talks directly or indirectly about the Guru. The Primal Guru is God Himself. Guru Nanak Dev and Guru Gobind Singh talk of Him as their Guru. The enlightened souls through whom the Word of God or the Name spreads in the universe are called Gurus. The ten Gurus of the Sikhs are the ten manifestations of the Guru-Soul. When the personal Guruship ended with Guru Gobind Singh the Guruship was bestowed on the *Adi Granth,* the treasury of *Guru-bani.* "The *Bani* is the Guru and all the ambrosias exist in the *Bani*" (p. 982, Nat M. 4). "The word is the Guru" (p. 943, Ramkali M. 1). The attributes of the Guru have been mentioned in the *Adi Granth.* He has realised Brahman (p. 1264, Malar M. 4). He is anxious to get the release of all humanity. He is merciful. He forgives the sinners (p. 302, Var Gauri M. 4). He is the field of piety (p. 302, Var Gauri M.4). He is without enmity. He sees Brahman all around. Everybody is equal in his eyes (p. 302, Var Gauri M. 4). He is the giver of comfort and the destroyer of evils (p. 559, Sri Rag M. 1). Whosoever meets him finds bliss (p. 168, Gauri Bairagan M. 4). He is like Himalayas (p. 137, Var Majh M. 1). He gives the knowledge of Brahman (p. 469, Var Asa M. 1). He gives Name of Word to the disciple (p. 250, Gauri Bawan Akhri M. 5). For his disciple, he is like father, mother, master, God, friend, relative and brother (p. 250, Gauri Bawan Akhri M. 5). He is the key-bearer of the house of the Lord. Only he can open it (p. 124, Majh M. 3).

H

Hadīs: This word is generally used by both Muhammedan and Christian writers for the collections of traditions. They are records of the doings and sayings of the Prophet Muhammad. They also include the sayings and doings of the Companions of the Prophet. This word occurs in the *Adi Granth* in one of the hymns of Guru Arjan Dev in Raga Maru. The Guru says, while addressing a Muslim: "Let good deeds be your body and faith your lady. May you revel in the joys of the Truth of your Lord and your *hadīs* be the purging of the mind of all the dirt, while living in the presence of the Lord, with the untarnished body and the turban on the head" (p. 1084, Maru M. 5).

Hail: Ice or frozen vapour falling in pellets or masses in a shower from the atmosphere, usually accompanying a thunder-storm. There is mention of snow in the *Adi Granth*, but an equivalent of hail has not been used. Guru Ram Das says, "If it snows or if there is frost and chill, I, as a devotee, will still go out to see the Guru" (p. 758, Suhi Ashtpadi M. 4).

Hair: Guru Nanak Dev has thus depicted the beauty of the hair, of women: "I have woven my wavy hair in lovely plaits and filled the parting with vermillion" (p. 558, Vadhans M. 1). When Babur invaded India, such beautiful women were humiliated. "Those who had bedecked their hair in plaits and vermillion was filled in the partings, their hair were cut with the scissors..." (p. 417, Asa M. 1). But when a person dies and the body is cremated, the bones will burn like the faggot of wood and the hair will be burnt like the bundle of grass" (p. 870, Gond Kabir). The devotee bows his head before the saint and in great humility wipes his feet with his hair (p. 810, Bilawal M. 5).

Haj: This Arabic word literally means "setting out" and pertains to the pilgrimage to Mecca performed in the month of Zul-Hijjah or the twelfth month of the Muhammedan year. It is an incumbent religious duty for a Muslim enjoined by the holy Quran. This word occurs in the Verses of Guru Arjan Dev and Kabir in the *Adi Granth*. Guru Arjan Dev says, "Some one takes a bath in a holy place, some one goes on a Haj. Some one performs worship and some one bows down in prayer" (p. 885, Ramkali M. 5). "Neither I take a bath at the Hindu holy place nor I perform the Haj" (p. 1136, Bhairo M. 5). Kabir says, "I went to perform the Haj at the Kaaba and on the way I met the

Lord. He quarrelled with me saying, "Who told you, I was there" (p. 1375, Shlok Kabir).

Halāl: The Muslim method of killing an animal. According to Muhammedan law, an animal is slaughtered, for the sake of food, by drawing the knife across the throat and cutting the windpipe, the carotid arteries and the gullet. The meat prepared in this way is called *kuṭhā* (killed in Muslim fashion). By such killing, the animal writhes in so much agony, that the Hindus condemned it. Kabir says, "By using force, you exhibit cruelty and you call it *halāl*. What will become of you when you will be asked to render the account (Shlok Kabir, p. 1374). The word *halāl* also connotes the permissible method of preparing meat.

Hans, Haṁsa: Swan. In the *Adi Granth*, the Enlightened Person (Gurmukh) is likened to a swan and the evil person to a crane (Bag, Baglā) (Shlok Farid, p. 1384). The metaphor of *haṁsa* is used for the soul (Var Majh M. 1, p. 139).

Haoma: or Homa. It is an oblation by fire. All the oblations are thrown into the fire, which forms a ladder to the world of gods and spirits. It is a name of a part of the worship and was originally connected with the *Yajna*. It is also called *Havana*. Guru Nanak Dev has mentioned the sacrifice of rhinoceros as sacrificial food in the *Yajnas* in olden days (p. 1289, Var Malar M. 1). Human sacrifice in *Homa* fire has been mentioned by Guru Arjan Dev in Sukhmani, where he says, "He offers his life to the fire of Homa)... He gets himself cut up, bit by bit, but the dirt of ego does not leave him" (p. 265, Gauri Sukhmani M. 5). The *Adi Granth* has rejected all such sacrifices.

Happiness: The *Adi Granth* believes that there can be no happiness without the worship of the Lord (p. 210, Gauri Cheti M. 5). There can be no happiness without the remembrance of the Name of the Lord (p. 1145, Bhairo M. 5). There can be no happiness in earning great wealth; there can be no happiness in seeing dance and drama; there can be no happiness in possessing many lands. One attains all the happiness in singing praises of the Lord (p. 1147, Bhairo M. 5). It is further said regarding eternal bliss: "If you want eternal bliss, then remember the Lord always" (p. 714, Todi M. 5).

Haqīqat: This is the spiritual stage, when the Sufi merges in the Lord and comprehends Reality. In order to reach this stage, the seeker has to pass through *Sharīat, Tarīqat* and *Mārfat*. Guru Arjan Dev says, "Attain the stage of *haqīqat*, so that you may never die again (Maru M. 5, p. 1083).

Hara: Literally this word means the "destroyer". In this sense, it is an epithet of Lord Shiva. But in the *Adi Granth* it means the destroyer of ignorance, sins and sorrows. Guru Ram Das says, "O Lord, your Name is Har(a/i), the Destroyer of sorrows" (p. 725, Tilang M. 4). While writing the Name of the Lord, no distinction seems to have been made in the words Hara and Hari in the *Adi Granth*.

Harem: also Harim or Hareem. This word is used for the female apartments of a Muslim household. This word is mostly current in Turkey, Egypt and Syria. In India, the term *zananah* is generally used instead of Harem. In the *Adi Granth*, this word has been used by Guru Nanak. He says, "He is the master of the saddled horse which are swift like wind and the harems which are bedecked colourfully. He is the lord of the houses, halls and mansions.... He indulges in pleasures to his heart's content. But he does not know the Lord and thus he is lost" (p. 472, Var Asa M. 1). In these verses the Guru has pointed out towards the luxurious life of the Muslim chiefs of his time.

Hari: One of the names of the Lord-God, mostly used in the *Adi Granth*. In the religious literature of the Hindus, this epithet is used for several gods e.g. Indra, Yama, Shiva; but mostly it is used for Vishnu. In Vishnu Purana, Hari is said to be composed entirely of the essence of Brahman and from Him and in Him is the universe. He is the Supreme Lord of all and comprises all that is perishable and imperishable. In the *Adi Granth*, this name has been applied to God, the Lord of all the gods. Guru Arjan Dev says, "None is so Powerful except Hari" (p. 1323, Kalyan M. 5). Guru Nanak Dev says, "Read only about Hari, Know Him and Love Him" (p. 937, Dakhni Oankar, Ramkali M. 1).

Hari-bhajan: Remembrance of the Lord.

Hari-dhan: The wealth of the Name of the Lord.

Hari-gun: The qualities/attributes of the Lord.

Hari-jan: The man of God.

Hari-Kīrtan: Singing of the Praises of the Lord.

Hari-mandir: The Temple or Abode of the Lord i.e. the body.

Hari-nām: The Name of the Lord.

Harlot: An unchaste woman; a prostitute. Guru Nanak Dev says, "Thieves, illicit lovers, harlots and touts—all of them keep company together" (p. 790, Var Suhi M. 3, Shalok M. 1). Guru Arjan Dev says, "One does not delay in thinking of sin and is not ashamed of running to a harlot. He works hard for the whole day for earning his bread, but when he has to meditate, he shuns it as though hit by lightning (p. 1143, Bhairo M. 5). Namdev says, "As in the house of a harlot, people gather for the show. She bedecks herself with beautiful ornaments. When she dances, the lewd lover counts her breaths. Around his neck falls the noose of *Yama*" (p. 1165, Bhairo Namdev).

Harmlessness: Harmlessness or *Ahimsa* connotes the friendliness for all. He who does not cause any suffering to any creature, is received with respect in the abode of the Lord (p. 322, Var Gauri M. 5). According to Guru Amar Das, an enlightened person dies himself, but does not kill others (p. 1128, Bhairo M. 3). Sheikh Farid says, "Those who give you blows, do not strike them in return; you may go home after kissing their feet" (p. 1378, Shlok Farid).

Hate, Hatred: He whose mind is absorbed with the One Lord, forgets the hatred of others (p. 189, Gauri M. 5). The Guru says, "Now I do not hate anyone, when I have attained the society of the saints. None is my enemy or stranger, I am the friend of all" (p. 1299, Kanra M. 5). Guru Ram Das says, "He who harbours jealously or hatred against any one, he never gathers good. He has no following, and always weeps and wails in the wilderness" (p. 308, Var Gauri M. 4).

Haṭh: It means forcefulness. It also means persistence in one's behaviour. Such an attitude is rejected in the *Adi Granth*. "He who practises the persistence of the mind, it is utterly of no avail..." (Dhanasari M. 5, p. 687). Inspite of efforts made by many, none has been able to realise the Lord with the persistence of the mind (Sri Rag M. 4, pp. 39-40).

Haṭh-Yoga: In Yogic terminology, the word *haṭh* has been derived from the roots *ha* (sun) and *ṭha* (moon). It is the equalisation and stabilisation of the sun-breath (which flows through the right nostril) and the moon-breath (which flows through the left nostril). The principal steps of *Haṭh-Yoga* are *Āsana* and *Prānāyāma*. *Āsana* is the bodily posture and *Prānāyāma* is the regulation of breath. This Yoga forcibly releases the dormant energies of human personality. The *Adi Granth* has rejected the practice of *Āsana and Prānāyāma*. See: *Āsana* and *Prānāyāma*.

Hau, Haumai: The ego. See *Aham, Ahamkāra*.

Head: The uppermost part of the human body, which is the seat of brain, the thinking principle and also the mouth and special sense-organs. The nine apparent doors of the human body are two ears, two eyes, two nostrils, one mouth and the two organs of excretion and procreation. Out of these the first seven exist in the head, through which the senses of hearing, sight, smell and taste work. The secret door called *Dasam Davar* also exists in the head. Thus the head not only performs the physical and mental functions, it also performs the spiritual functions. On the forehead of every human being, there is a writ of the Lord, which determines the actions of the individuals. "The Lord, who has placed the writ in the head of every individual, has no Writ on His Head" (p. 4, Japuji). The head bows at the feet of elders, saints, preceptor and Lord, but Guru Nanak Dev says, "A mere bowing down of the head is useless, if the heart is impure" (p. 470, Var Asa M. 1). The faculties in the head are the gifts of God, therefore, the human being should always express his gratitude. Guru Nanak Dev says, "The Lord should be remembered, who has blessed us with ears, eyes and nose and also the tongue which speaks presently" (p. 611, Dhanasri M. 1). The Head and face should have a complete form with the natural hair and turban on it (p.1 084, Maru M. 5).

Heart: Whereas the head is the seat of intellect in the body, the heart is the seat of emotions. In the widest sense, this word is used for mind. The Persian equivalent for heart is "Dil" and the Indian equivalent "Hirda". Kabir says, "O man, search your heart every day and do not remain upset" (p. 727, Tilang Kabir). Guru Arjan Dev says, "If the Lord abides in the heart, one is cool-comforted" (p. 1078, Maru M. 5). He says in another hymn, "The dark well of the heart is immediately illumined with the Light of the Lord" (p. 1212, Sarang M. 5). He says again, "The Master of our hearts speaks to us (from within)" (p. 897, Ramkali M. 5).

Hearth: The floor of a fireplace. Talking about the fake saints, Kabir says, "They are the cheats of Varanasi and not the Saints of the Lord—They scour their utensils and place them on the hearth. They wash the wood before burning it. They dig the earth and make double fire-places; but they devour the men completely" (p. 476, Asa Kabir).

Heat: Heat is produced by sun or fire. In the summer months, scorching heat is produced by the sun. Guru Nanak Dev says, "In the month of Asarh, the sun blazes in the sky and the earth is roasted with heat.... The sap of the earth is sapped by the heat of the sun" (p. 1108, Baramaha Tukhari M. 1). Fire creates enormous heat in the hell, where the sinners undergo sufferings. Guru Arjan Dev says, "Izrāīl, the angel of death seizes and slays the sinners. He casts them into the hell-fire. They are asked to render the account by the Lord-Justice" (pp. 1019-20, Maru M. 5). The fire in the mother's womb is identified with the hell-fire. "The fire rages in the womb of the mother. There is utter darkness and one lies upside down" (p. 1107, Maru Anjali M. 5). The world is like fire in which the Name of the Lord is cool (p. 1291, Var Malar M. 1). The Guru is like Himalaya. He makes one cool amid the heat of the fire of passions. One lives in joy and the sorrows depart (p. 287, Gauri Sukhmani M. 5).

Heathen: One who holds a religious belief which is neither Christian, Jewish, nor Mohammedan. Mostly restricted to those holding polytheistic beliefs. A pagan. In India, the Muslims used to call the Hindus "Kafirs" (heathens). The word *Kufr* has been used in the *Adi Granth* by Guru Nanak Dev. He says, "He may be considered blessed who considers the two paths (of Hinduism and Islam) as one. But he, who is heathen with the belief that God lives only among Muhammedans and not among Hindus, burns in his own inner fire" (p. 142, Var Majh M. 1).

Heaven-Heavenly: The Indian equivalent for heaven is Svarga. Out of the fourteen worlds—seven upper and seven nether, which constitute the whole universe, *Svarga* or *Svah* is one of the seven upper worlds. According to the Hindu belief, one enjoys material happiness in this world as a reward for his meritorious actions on earth. It is the heaven of Indra and is supposed to be situated on Mount Meru. In the post-Vedic Hindu mythology *Vaikunth* is the name given to the heaven of Vishnu, which is eternal and built of gold and precious stones. In the *Adi Granth*, both the words *Svarga* and *Baikunth* have been used, but the concept of such heaven has been rejected. The God-man (*Gurmukh*) does not want to reside in heaven (p. 1078, Maru M. 5). For an enlightened person the holy congregation is a heaven (p. 1161, Bhairo Kabir). Islam believes in seven heavens, through which the Prophet passed during *merāj* or night journey. These are 1. The heaven of pure silver, where Adam resides. 2. The heaven of Pure gold, where John the Baptist and Jesus reside. 3. The heaven of pearls belonging to Joseph. 4. The heaven of white gold of Enoch. 5. The heaven of silver of Aaron. 6. The heaven of ruby and garnet of Moses and 7. The heaven of Abraham. Heaven is also called *Jannat* by Muslims, a term used for the regions of celestial bliss. In the Paradise, the faithful is served by beautiful damsels, called houries with large dark eyeballs. The word *Bahisht* is used in the *Adi Granth* for Muslim heaven.

Hell: The Indian equivalent for the hell is "Naraka". It is a place of torture, where the souls of the evil persons are sent. Manu has enumerated twenty-one hells. Other authorities vary greatly regarding the number and the names of the hells. Twenty-eight different divisions of hell are described. They are said to be situated below Pātāla, where there is darkness and terror. They are particularly described in Vishnu Purana. These hells lie one above the other, each having one hundred and forty-four sub-divisions. The keepers of these hells have the faces of jackals, cats, vultures, owls, etc. These hells are not the places of eternal sufferings. After due punishment, the souls take birth according to their karmas. The Muslims use the word "Dozakh" for hell. Seven divisions of hell have been described in Muslim commentaries: 1. *Johannum*, the purgatorial hell, 2. *Laza*, blazing fire, 3. *Al-Hutamah*, an intense fire, 4. *Saeer*, a flaming fire, 5. *Saqar*, a scorching fire, 6. *Al-Jahim*, a huge hot fire, and 7. *Hawiyah*, a bottomless pit. Different types of souls categorised by their actions are sent to different hells. Both the words "Naraka" and "Dozakh" have been used in the *Adi Granth*. Guru Nanak Dev says, "One is drowned in the well of hell (*Naraka*)...the worshipper of *maya* passes through the hells of eighty-four laks species" (p.1028, Maru M.1). Guru Arjan Dev says, "How can he be saved from hell (*Dozakh*), who does not keep the Prophet in his mind (pp. 319-20, Var Gauri M. 5).

Hemp: A narcotic drug obtained from the Indian hemp; bhang; hashish. The *Adi Granth* has condemned the use of all types of intoxicants. Guru Nanak Dev wants spiritual intoxication. He says, "O Lord, your fear is my hemp and my mind is the container. In this way I have become intoxicated..." (p. 721, Tilang M. 1). Kabir says, "Whosoever eats the fish, the hemp and the wine, loses the merit of all pilgrimages, fasts, rituals and observances" (p. 1377, Shlok Kabir).

Herbs: The plants, of which the leaves, or stem are used for food and medicine, or for their scent or flavour. In the *Adi Granth*, mention has been made of those herbs whose roots and stem are eaten as food by the hermits. In the *Siddh Goshta*, the Yogis say that they live in the forests and eat the roots and stem of certain herbs. The word *mool* is suggestive of the roots of these herbs (p. 939, Ramkali Siddh Goshta M. 1).

Heresy-Heretic: Opinion or doctrine in philosophy, politics, science, art, etc. at variance with what is orthodox. For example the Muslims considered the Hindus as hereitcs, because they believed in several gods instead of THE ONE ALLAH. The Hindus were the idol-worshippers, while the Muslims were the idol-breakers. Similarly a *Sākat*, the worshipper of *māyā* was an heretic in the eyes of the saint-poets of the *Adi Granth*. Guru Arjan Dev says, "Do not seek the company of the worshippers of *māyā*, as far as possible. On meeting them one abandons the Lord and leaves the world with a black face" (p. 641, Sorath M. 5). Kabir says, "Do not associate with Sākats (the worshippers of *māyā*) because they will ruin you in the end" (p. 1369, Shlok Kabir).

Hermit: A beadsman; a person living in solitude. Guru Nanak Dev has described various types of hermits of his time in one of his hymns in the *Adi Granth*. He says, "There are some who go to the forests, and observe silence. There are others who suffer the pangs of wintery frosts and become like ice in snowy waters. There are others who besmear their bodies with ashes and do not remove the dirt from their bodies. There are others who keep matted hair and look dreadful and thus bring a bad name to their families. There are others who wander naked day and night and do not sleep. There are others who burn their limbs and thus waste themselves. Without the Name of the Lord, there body is like dust. Why and how to grieve for such people? They alone will look beautiful in the House of the Lord, who serve the True Guru" (pp. 1284-85, Var Malar M. 1).

Heroes-Heroism: A hero is an illustrious warrior, who exhibits extraordinary bravery, firmness, or greatness of soul, in connection with any pursuit, work or enterprise. Guru Amar Das says, "They are not heroes, who die of ego and always weep in anguish" (p. 1089, Var Maru M. 3). Kabir says, "That person may be called a hero, who fights for the oppressed. Though he is cut into bits, he does not leave the battlefield" (p. 1105, Shlok-Maru Kabir).

Heterodoxy: The quality or character of being heterodox; deviation from orthodoxy. The Sikh Gurus and the saint-poets whose hymns have been included in the *Adi Granth* were opposed both to the Hindu and Muslim orthodoxy. Guru Nanak Dev has addressed a Kshatriya thus: "He alone is Kshatriya, who is a hero in actions and makes his body of compassion and charity" (p. 1411, Shlok Varan te Vadhik, M. 1). To a Muslim he says, "Let mercy be your mosque, faith your prayer-mat, and honest living your Quran, effort your circumcision, and good character your fast. In this way you can become a real Muslim" (p. 140, Var Majh M. 1).

Highest Being: Brahman is the Highest Being. He is described as "Ucho Ucha" in the *Adi Granth*. Guru Arjan Dev says in *Sukhmanī*:

"O Lord, no one knows your limits. O Lord, the Maker of our Destiny, you are the Highest of the High" (p. 268, Gauri Sukhmani M. 5). He says in another hymn, "He is the Highest of the High and always described as Companion of all" (p. 812, Bilawal M. 5).

Highest Good: It is also called the "summum bonum". Eternal happiness, Supreme Enlightenment and the Perfect Enjoyment, (Bliss) may be called the Highest Good for the human being. Its basis is *Dharma*, which leads to *Moksha*. The Highest Good lies in "all joy, all comfort, all poise and all bliss, which is in the meditation on the Supreme Bliss in the holy congregation" (p. 295, Gauri Sukhmani M. 5).

Highest Self: Brahman is the Highest Self. He is the Immaculate Purusha, the Lord of all other Purushas. He is also the Supreme Self. He is the Highest Being; Whose Court is the Highest of the High. He is Infinite and Limitless" (p. 562, Vadhans M. 5).

Hiṁsā: Violence. Antonym of *Ahiṁsā* (non-violence). The *Adi Granth* has laid stress on *Ahiṁsa*, i.e. non-injury to animals and human beings (Vay Gauri M. 5, p. 322). *Hiṁsa* is one of the streams of fire (Var Majh M. 1, p. 147).

Hindrances: There are several hindrances in the way of the spiritual advancement. They are, primarily, the five vices namely lust, anger, greed, attachment and ego. That is the reason why a devotee makes the following supplication to the Guru, "O Holy Guru, Bless me with your Grace, I seek your refuge. May my lust, anger, greed, attachment and ego be destroyed" (p. 269, Gauri Sukhmani M. 5). Out of these five vices, the ego is considered a chronic malady (p. 466, Var Asa M.a). These five dreadful demons run away, when the Lord blesses one with His Grace (p. 866, Gond M. 5).

Hindu: A votary of Hinduism. This word has been used in the *Adi Granth* by the Gurus and Bhaktas both. Namdev says, "The Hindu worships in a temple and the Muslim in a mosque, but I worship, Him, Who is beyond a temple and a mosque" (Gaund Namdev, p. 875). Guru Nanak Dev says, "Hindus have forgotten the Lord and are following a wrong path. They worship idols as instructed by the sage Narada. They are blind and dumb and are in the darkness of ignorance. The fools instal stones and worship them. How can those stones ferry you across the world-ocean, when they themselves sink down" (Var Bihagra M. 4, Shalok M. 1, p. 556). The Guru says elsewhere: "When a Hindu comes in the house of a Hindu, he recites mantras and puts the *yagyopavita* (cotton thread) around the neck of the incoming

Hindu. Though he puts the sacred thread around his neck, he commits evil actions, all his efforts of purification are of no avail (Var Ramkali M. 3, Shlok M. 1, p. 951).

Holiness: Holiness connotes purity. Purity is one of the godly attributes. He whose mind becomes pure is a saint and a holy person. The Guru is the creator of these holy persons, therefore, he is Most Holy. Wherever the True Guru sits, that place becomes holy (p. 450, Asa M. 4). Guru Ram Das says, "Even the Ganges, Yamuna and Godavari crave for the dust of the feet of the holy persons and pray: "O Lord, we are sinful and are not delivered till the holy persons come to anoint us with the dust of their holy feet" (p. 1263, Malar M. 4). He who believes in the holy Name of the Lord, is considered True at the Gate of the Lord (p. 140, Var Majh M. 1).

Hom (Haoma): Hom or homa is "oblation by fire". It is also the name of a part of the *puja*. Originally, however, it was connected with the *yajna*. See: *Haoma*.

Home: The fixed residence of a family or household. In every home, the call for leaving is always received. Therefore, the Lord from whom the call comes should not be forgotten (p.1557, Guri Poorbi Deepki M.1). Since the body is the abode of the soul, the word home is also used for body in the *Adi Granth*. Guru Nanak Dev says, "The bride who bedecks herself with the Word, finds her Spouse at home" (p. 61, Sri Rag M. 1). "He, who shows us the Home within our Home, is the Guru, the Wise Purusha" (pp. 1290-91, Var Malar M. 1). The first Home in this verse is the abode of the Lord and the second Home is the abode of the soul.

Homicide: The action, by a human being, of killing a human being. Guru Arjan Dev says, "With a noose in their hands some go out in the night to strangle others, but the Lord knows all" (p. 315, Var Gauri M. 4, Shalok M. 5). Kabir says, "When nights are dark, some men of dark deeds, wander and run with their nooses...such people are cursed by God" (p. 1365, Shlok Kabir). When Babur invaded India and people were slaughtered, Guru Nanak Dev said, "Such great is the suffering, O Lord, why do you not feel compassion?... If a powerful lion falls upon a flock of sheep, then the Master has to answer about it" (p. 360, Asa M. 1).

Honesty: Uprightness of disposition and conduct. Guru Amar Das says, "The honest and dishonest are adjudged in the True Court" (p. 5570, Vadhans M. 3). While addressing a Muslim, Guru Nanak Dev has urged him to make honest living his Quran (p. 140, Var Majh M. 1).

Honey: Though honey is sweet, God is the sweetest (p. 1379, Shlok Farid). The bee gathers honey in her bee-hive, but man throws dust in her face and escapes with the honey (p. 1252, Sarang Namdev). Just as bee collects honey, in a similar manner the fool-hardy gathers his riches (p. 654, Sorath Kabir).

Hope: The world builds hopes and dies but the hopes neither go nor die. He, who rests his hopes on God, they are fulfilled. The hope and desire will die away, if their creator so wishes. Nothing is eternal except the Name of the Lord (p. 517, Var Gujri M. 3). All the people build hopes and consider the life to be long. They want to live for ever and bedeck their mansions. They practise fraudulent ways and gather wealth. But the *Yama* keeps his watch on every breath and thus the life of such wretches decreases every day. Those who come under the refuge of the Guru are protected by the Guru and the Lord (p. 1248, Var Sarang M. 4).

Hospitality: Guru Arjan Dev says, "Dye your mind in the Colour of the Lord. Utter the Name of the Lord with your tongue. Then none will be impolite to you in His Court. Every one will be hospitable..." (p. 252, Gauri Bawan Akhri M. 5). In another hymn, the Guru says, "Everywhere there is complete hospitality and I am short of nothing. The Lord has Blessed His Devotees with the Robe of Honour, thus Revealing His Glory (p. 631, Sorath M. 5).

House: "The men of the world expand their property in the form of houses, halls and mansions.... They are defeated ones because they have not recognised the Lord" (p. 472, Var Asa M. 1). The houses, halls and mansions may be painted from without; but if they fall they are useless..." (p. 729, Suhi M. 1). It is only the unwise who are attached to their houses, halls and mansions (p. 788, Var Suhi M. 3). Kabir says, "Within the house (of the body) is the house (of the mind) which may be considered as the Great House" (p. 970, Ramkali Kabir).

Householder: (*grihasti*) One of the four stages of a man's life as prescribed in ancient Vedic culture, namely *brahmacharin* (the student—a celibate), *grahasthya* (the householder—married man), *vanaprastha* (the forest-dweller—the recluse) and *sannyasin* (wandering monk). This division of the span of life into *ashramas* has been rejected by the *Adi Granth*, which lays emphasis on the life of a householder. All the ascetic orders have been decried. One must work hard to earn his livelihood and not depend on the mercy of others. Guru Nanak Dev says, "Those who work hard for their livelihood and give something in charity to the deserving, they only recognise the path leading towards the Lord" (p. 1245, Var Sarang M. 4, Shalok M. 1). Guru Amar Das says, "It is better to be a householder than to wear the robes of a recluse because the former gives (something to the needy) (p. 587, Var Vadhans M. 4, Shlok M. 3).

Housewife: The saint Dhanna begs for a good housewife from the Lord (p. 695, Dhanasari Dhanna). In one of his hymns Guru Arjan Dev has depicted the qualities of a good housewife. He says, "She is accomplished in all ways. Now her family is Truth. She is obedient and wise and of utmost grace.... In her family she is now considered supreme. Her hope and desire are well-instructed. That home is blessed in which she resides, because she always passes her day, in bliss" (p. 371, Asa M. 5). There are two hymns in the *Adi Granth*, entitled *Suchajji* and *Kuchajji*. The former describes a cultured housewife and the latter an uncultured housewife. A cultured housewife is called *Suhagan* (who is loved by the Lord) and the uncultured one is called *Dohagan* (who has been forsaken by her Lord).

Hukam: *Hukam* is an Arabic word which means Order or judgement of God, Prophet, ruler or a judge. In the holy Quran, it pertains to the Order or Judgment of God. In Muslim Theology, it includes the Order of Prophet as well. With the advent of Muslims, the word was adopted in India. Guru Nanak Dev says, "Everybody is under the *Hukam* of the Lord; there is none outside it (Japuji, p.1). This *Hukam* is an over-all Order of the Lord. This Order is a set of commandments or a set of the Laws of God. These Laws are True for all times and work in all the three fields i.e. physical, moral and spiritual. All the creatures in the world are bound by these Laws. The order of a worldly ruler can be unjust, but the *Hukam* of God is always Just. Hukam may be identified with *Bhāna* or the Divine Will. If we are subjected to several kinds of reverses in life, they are the result of our own actions and are not the resultant of sudden anger of the Lord because the Lord is Kind and Merciful. Guru Arjan Dev says, "Through His *Hukam*, He creates and dissociates; everything is created and also dissolved. Through His *Hukam*, He becomes high up and also lowly and also Manifests Himself in several ways (Gauri Sukhmani M. 5, p. 277).

Humanity: According to the *Adi Granth*, humanity is one. All the differentiations of caste, colour and creed are only due to the distinctions in geographical and historical conditions in various regions, but it is the only One Lord, who has created all the humanity and He is the Father of all. Guru Arjan Dev says, "There is only One Father and we are all His Children" (p. 611, Sorath M. 5). All have been created of the same air, the same earth and the same Light. Only one Light pervades all (the diverse forms) and none other has mingled in it (p. 96, Majh M. 4). The Creator is in the humanity and the humanity is in the Creator, who pervades everywhere. The Creator fashioned the same earth in a myriad ways: no fault can be found either with the earthen vessels or with the Potter. The True Lord is within all, and everything happens under His Will. He who recognises His Will, he knows the One alone. God alone is beyond the castes and names, because on every body there is only one shade of God (p. 83, Var Sri Rag M. 4, Shlok M. 1).

Human Life: According to the *Adi Granth*, the human body is attained after many births and ages (p. 631, Sorath M. 9). Through the Service of the Guru, devotion was practised and the human body was obtained. Even the gods want to be born as human beings. Then why do you not contemplate on the Lord through this invaluable body? Do not forget to remember the Lord, this is the real objective of human life (p. 1159, Bhairo Kabir). Guru Arjan Dev addresses the human being thus: "All the other forms of existence are your slaves and you are the overlord of this earth. You have the gold, silver and wealth with you, but the lust has perturbed your good nature" (p. 374, Asa M. 5). There are eighty-four lakhs of species, but the man has been blessed with a position above all others. Whosoever misses the opportunity in this birth, he undergoes suffering in transmigration (p. 1075, Maru M. 5). The human life is invaluable; it will not come to you again, like the ripe fruit, which after falling down, does not stick to the branch again (p. 1366, Shlok Kabir). The human body has been obtained. This is the only time to meet the Lord. No other works are of any avail. Remember only the Name of the Lord in the company of the saints (p. 12, Asa M. 5).

Human Sacrifice: There has been practice of Purusha-yajna, Purushamedha or human sacrifice in olden times according to the religious literature of the Hindus. The Shaivas use skulls as drinking vessels and practise other cruel rites. The Sikh Gurus and the saint-poets of the *Adi Granth* have rejected such rites and yajnas (sacrifices). They advocate non-injury to all the beings of the world. The human body is considered as *Hari Mandir* or the abode of the Lord, therefore its destruction for any rite is condemnable.

Humility: Humility is considered a great virtue. According to Guru Nanak Dev humility is sweetness and is the essence of virtues (p. 470, Asa M. 1). He, who considers himself the lowest, is, in fact, the highest (p. 266, Gauri Sukhmani M. 5) If one wants his good, he should do good and be humble (p. 465, Var Asa M. 1). You will come up if you fall below the feet; serve your Lord in this way. Consider every one else to be above yourself, in this way, the bliss can be attained in the Court of the Lord (p. 883, Ramkali M. 5). Kabir says, "I am the worst of all, Everyone else except me is better. He, who believes in this way, is alone my friend" (p. 1364, Shlok Kabir). Sheikh Farid says, "Become like the grass, if you want to find the All-pervading Lord. Firstly the grass is cut and then crushed under the feet. In this way, it enters the Door of the Master" (p. 1378, Shlok Farid).

Hunger: There is suffering of separation and also of hunger (p. 1256, Malar M. 1). It is through suffering that one gathers wealth in the world, but there is also suffering when it leaves; without the True Name of the Lord, the hunger is never satiated. The beauty also does not end one's hunger; the more one sees it, the more one hungers for it. All the joys of the flesh afflict us with suffering (p. 1287, Var Malar M.1). The hunger does not go, even if we gather loads of riches of several worlds (p. 1, Japuji). When one's thirst and hunger bark, one puts food in his mouth. All that one eats becomes dust, still we are attached to the victuals (p. 146, Var Majh M. 1). Guru Arjan Dev says, in his hymn entitled *Gunvanti* (A virtuous lady): "I have been blessed with the treasure of the Devotion of the Lord; such is the mercy of Guru Nanak Dev upon me. Now I hunger no more and thirst no more. I am completely sated and satiated" (p. 763, Suhi M. 5).

Hunting: Our life wears off gradually day by day, quarter by quarter and hour by hour. The death is like a hunter who walks about. What is to be done in order to save oneself? (p. 691, Dhanasri Kabir). Guru Arjan Dev says, "I go out hunting with the saints of God and catch the deer without the horses and arms. My mind always went out hunting before, but now I find the catch in the abode of the self. I have caught the deer and brought them back to their home. I have shared every bit of them with the saints. This is my share in the hunt. The Name of the Lord resounds within me" (p. 1136, Bhairo M. 5). In the beginning of this hymn, the Guru has described the hunting of the ten she-deer (ten organs of action and perception) and the five deer (lust, anger, greed, attachment and ego). These deer have been pierced through with the never-failing arrow-heads of the Guru's word.

Husband and Wife (Family-Marriage): The husband (bridegroom) and the wife (bride) are not they, who sit down together. The husband and wife are they who are two bodies with one soul. In the *Adi Granth*, God is the husband and the soul is the wife. Guru Ram Das says, "The bride and the bridegroom live together, but there is a hard wall of ego between them. The Perfect Guru broke this wall of ego and the soul realised the Lord" (p. 1263, Malar M. 4). In another hymn, the soul has been symbolised as husband and the body as the wife. Guru Arjan Dev says, "The bride (body) prays with folded hands, "O Lord, do not go to the foreign lands and live with me. Engage yourself in such business within your abode, as absolves you from hunger and thirst"... The bridegroom (soul) says, "I have to submit to the Will of my Lord (God). My Master is Supreme and is not Dependent on any one. I will live with you so long as the Lord Wills and when He Calls me, I shall go away" (pp. 1072-73, Maru Solhe M. 5).

Hymns: Meterical compositions adapted to be sung in a religious congregation. They are essentially the songs of praise in honour of the Lord. The *Adi Granth* is a great anthology of hymns, composed by the Sikh gurus and the radical saints. Besides the hymns in praise of the Lord, there are a good number of hymns in praise of the Guru and the true devotee (*Gurmukh*), who follows the discipline enjoined by the Guru in letter and spirit. All the hymns of the Sikh Gurus are in the name of Nanak, whose spirit pervades all and who is the light of all. The parts of the hymn are called *padas*. The hymns in the *Adi Granth* are generally arranged according to the *padas*.

Hypnotising: Artificially producing a state in which the subject appears to be in a deep sleep, without any power of changing his mental or physical condition, except under the influence of some external suggestion or direction. On recovering from this condition, the person has usually no remembrance of what he has said or done during the hypnotic state. Such a practice was not prevalent in the centuries when the Gurus and saints composed their hymns. There were other charms and spells, called "Kāman", which the brides practised on their grooms for their subjugation. The *Adi Granth* rejects such practices. Guru Nanak Dev says, "One should know the Will of the Lord and apply the *Chandan-Scent* of fear to the mind. One should charm the beloved with the charm of merit and in this way attain Him" (p. 725, Tilang M. 1).

I

I: "I" in Sanskrit is "Aham", which gives the sense of individuality. "I" is the conscious subject. It is "Haumai" or ego. The Sanskrit word "Soham" means "I am That" or "He is me" conveys the identity of the soul with Brahman. This word occurred in the *Adi Granth* also. Guru Nanak Dev says, "Without the Guru, the Love of the Lord does not crop up and the dirt of ego does not go. When the Word of the Guru pierces through the body, one is satiated and cries out: "I am That" (p. 60. Sri Rag M. 1). Kabir says, "Take your bath in the *Mansarovar* of the Lord. There contemplate on Him whose mantra is "He is me" (p. 1162, Bhairo Kabir). "When one destroys his I-ness or Mine-ness from his self, and effaces the duality, he can become one (with the Lord) (p. 943, Ramkali M. 1, Sidh Goshta).

Iblīs (Satan): There are two words used in the Quran to denote the Devil: 1-*Shaitān* and 2-*Iblis*. *Shaitān* is one who is far from the truth and *Iblīs* is one who is without hope. The word *Shaitān* has been used in the *Adi Granth*. Farid says, "You were goaded frequently to follow the path of God, but still you chose the Devil (Shaitan). Why do you not leave the Devil?" (p. 1378, Shalok Farid). It was *satan* in garb of *Iblīs*, the serpent, who persuaded Eve to eat the forbidden fruit.

Īd: The Muslim Festival. There are two chief festivals of Muslims, called *Idu'l Fitr* and *Idu'l Azha*. *Idu'l Azha* is also called *Idu'l Zuha* (The feast of sacrifice and *Baqarah-Id* (the cow festival). *Idu-l Zuha* is *Idu'l Kabir* or the great festival and *Idu'l Fitr* is *Idu'l saghir* or the minor festival. *Idu'l Zuha* is celebrated on the tenth day of Zu'l Hijjh. It is observed both as a day of sacrifice and as a great festival. *Idu'l Fitr* (The festival of the Breaking of the fast) commences as soon as the month's fast in Ramzan is over and thus on the first day of the month of Shawwal. In the *Adi Granth*, the words Īd and Bakrīd have been used by the saint Ravidas. He says, "He, in whose family cows were sacrificed on the occasion of Īd-day, and whose ancestors believed in the Sheikhs, divines and martyrs; in the family of such Muslims, Kabir took birth and became renowened because of his contemplation on the Name of the Lord" (p. 1293, Malar Ravidas).

Idā: It is one of the three important *nādīs* or channels. It is situated in the human body on the left of the chief channel *Sushumnā*. It has been described as coiling round the *Sushumnā* and ending at the left nostril or at the *Ajna Chakra*. The saint Beni says, "*Idā, Piṅglā* and *Sushumnā* converge at one place, where there is the confluence of Ganga (Ganges), Yamuna and Saraswati. My mind bathes at this place" (Ramkali Beni, p. 974).

Idealists: According to the *Adi Granth*, the real ideal of the human being is the realisation of Lord-God, from whom we have been separated because of the evil influence of *maya* and ego. In this sense all the Gurus and saints whose verses have been included in the *Adi Granth* were idealists. Their idealism may be called pure idealism or immaterialism which identifies the ontological reality exclusively with the ideal. The *Adi Granth*, while mixing monotheism and monoism inclines towards a personalistic idealism and a corresponding ethics of selfless devotion (bhakti).

Ideas: Ideas are the reflections in the mind. They are the class concepts of the human mind. Ordinarily, the ideas that crop up in the mind are influenced by our surroundings and the company that we keep. That is the reason why the *Adi Granth* lays emphasis on good company (*Satsang*) and the surroundings unimpaired by vices. One should reflect in the mind on the Name of the Lord (p. 1090, Var Maru M. 3). Kabir says, "The ignorant fool does not dwell on the Name of the Lord. Then what is it that he should reflect upon again and again?" (p. 655, Sorath Kabir).

Idiots: A blockhead; an utter fool. It is out of utter humility that the Sikh Gurus call themselves devoid of knowledge, lowly and devoid of intellect and understanding. Guru Ram Das says, "We, the ignorant and idiotic people have sought your Refuge; meet us, O Lord, in your Love" (p. 449, Asa M. 4). Guru Amar Das says, "We are ignorant and idiotic, O Lord, our minds are filled with ignorance and we always act in ego" (p. 666, Dhanasari M. 3).

Idolaters: Those who worship the idols. The *Adi Granth* has condemned the idol-worship. Therefore, the practices of the idolaters have been rejected. Guru Arjan Dev says, "He does not see the Lord within his self and hangs the stone-god around his neck. The Sakta (worshipper of *Maya*) wanders in delusion. He merely churns the water and wastes away his life in agony" (pp. 738-39, Suhi M. 5). Kabir says, "Those who speak of the stones as gods, their service (to the Lord) is of no avail. He, who falls at the feet of the stone-god, his efforts for the spiritual life bear no fruit" (p. 1160, Bhairo Kabir).

Idolatery: The Gurus and saint-poets whose verses have been included in the *Adi Granth* have condemned image-worship, which was prevalent among the various Bhakti-cults. Guru Nanak Dev says, "If one worships a stone and resides in the woods or at holy places, if he becomes an ascetic and wanders about he does not become pure, if his mind is unclean. He attains Honour only, if he attains the Truth" (p. 686, Dhanasari M. 1). The saint Namdev says, "When we meet the True Guru, we are rid of the delusion. Whom should I worship, when I see none other. We worship one stone as an image and we tread upon the other stone. If one is a god, the other one may also be considered a god. Therefore, I am in the service of the Lord alone" (p. 525, Gujri Namdev).

Idols: Images . According to the *Adi Granth,* a stone-image cannot be called a god. If one stone is a god, then why the others are not gods. (p. 525, Gujri Namdev). Guru Arjan Dev says, "The stone he (a Sakta) calls his god, in the end, drowns him with itself... How can one reach the far-end on the boat of stone?" (p. 739, Suhi M. 5). Kabir says, "The stone neither speaks nor gives anything. Therefore its service is fruitless and its worship is of no avail" (p. 1160, Bhairo Kabir).

Ignorance: (Nescience): In Indian philosophy, it is known as *Ajnana* or *Avidya.* Because of this ignorance, the Absolute appears as many. It leads one to suffering and bondage. It can be destroyed by knowledge or *Jnana.* Guru Nanak Dev says, bereft of knowledge, one worships ignorance. Lured by duality, he gropes into darkness (p. 1412, Shlok Varan te Vadhik M. 1). Guru Arjan Dev says, "With the consciousness of "mine and thine", one was held in bondage; the Guru effaced the ignorance and freed him from the bonds" (p. 400, Asa M. 5).

Ik: The one; the one Lord. The Lord is Only One, O Brother, the Lord is Only One" (Asa M. 1, p. 350).

Ikantī (or *Ekantī*): One who abides in solitude. "He may be called an *Ikantī* who keeps his mind at its own place" (Basant M. 5, p. 1180).

Illusion: Deceptive appearance, belief or statement. "The person from whose mind the illusion is destroyed, he has no fear of *Yama*" (Gauri M. 5, p. 186). On remembering the Name of the Lord , the illusion and fear run away (Gauri M. 5, p. 190). See: *Bharm (Bhram).*

Immortality: The Lord-God is immortal. The soul, which is the part and parcel of the Lord is also immortal (p. 188, Gauri M. 5). In one of his hymns, Guru Arjan Dev says, "O mother, God is true and ever-existent. His saints are also True... Night and day, galaxy of stars, the sun, the moon, the earth, the mountains and the seas, all will pass away, but the Word of the saint will abide for ever. The egg-born, the foetus-born, the sweat-born and the earth-born, the Vedas and the six Shastras, all will pass away, but the Word of the saint will abide for ever. The three modes of *maya* will also pass away, but immortal and infinite is the Word of the saint" (p. 1204, Sarang M. 5). Kabir says, "Death, which has terrified all, has been revealed to me through the Word of the Guru. How should I die now, when my mind has accepted death? Those who do not know their Lord, die again and again. Everyone says that he has to die, but he alone becomes deathless, who dies in the state of equipoise (p. 327, Gauri Kabir). One attains immortality by stilling his self; but he is rare who reflects on this knowledge (p. 689, Dhanasari M. 1).

Impediments: Obstacles. There are several obstacles/impediments in the path leading towards the Lord. Guru Nanak Dev says, "The night and the day are the nets cast for us; all the time is like a snare. We are ever put in bondage by the pleasures of the world; then, O fool, how can we be saved?" (p. 990, Maru M. 1). The more one involves himself with the mundane, the impediments become stronger than before. The five main impediments are the five vices viz., lust, anger, greed, attachment and ego. The hunger and thirst are also big impediments. Moral depravity in any form takes us away from the Lord and we become soiled and impure. All the impediments are destroyed when our mind becomes pure. Guru Arjan Dev says, "we are released from bondage and our wanderings end when we achieve victory on conquering the mind" (p. 258, Gauri Bawan Akhri M. 5).

Imperishable: The Lord God is called *Akshara* (*Akkhar*), the imperishable. He is also called *Abnashi,* the One who never perishes. He is *Amar*, the One Who never dies. He is *Achhed*, the One Who is invincible. He is *Akal,* the One Who is deathless and Who is Sat, the One Who is Ever-Existent.

Impermanence: Temporary and Short-lived. The world is impermanent. Only the Lord is Ever-Existent. He who is born in the world, comes and goes (p. 352, Asa M. 1). All that is created, dies in the end (p. 227, Gauri M. 1). Whatever is born, passes away like the shade of the cloud (p. 1231, Sarang M. 9). He, who has come, must also depart (p. 1047. Maru M. 3). He that came must pass away, the turn of every one will come (p. 474, Var Asa M. 1).

Imprecations: The acts of invoking evil upon any one. Though there are imprecations against the one who kills a Brahmin, a cow, a daughter and who accepts the offerings of an evil person, he who is an egoist and is afflicted with the leprosy of similar sins, but such sins afflict those who forget the Name of the Lord" (p. 1413, Shlok Varan te Vadhik, Shlok M. 3). Everyone imprecates a beggar and none gets glory for begging (p. 878, Ramkali M.1). The ascetic was imprecated by the True Guru (p. 316, Var Gauri M. 4).

Impurity: Everything else except the Lord-God is impure. Even the gods are impure. Those who are soiled with *maya* and ego, become impure. Those who become one with the Lord, also become pure. In the words of Kabir, "Brahma, Indra, the sun, the moon and the whole world, is impure. Only the Infinite Lord is Immaculate. The kings of the world, the day and night, the thirty days of the month, the pearl, the diamond, the air, the water, the fire, Shiva, Shankara, Mahesha, Siddhas, the seekers, the pretenders, the Yogis, the Shaivites wearing matted hair, the bodies and the souls are all soiled. Only those who have realised the Lord are pure" (p. 1158, Bhairo Kabir). If the mind is impure, everything is impure; by bathing the body the mind is not cleansed (p. 558, Vadhana M. 3). Guru Nanak Dev says, "O mind, you are cleansed from within through the Pure Word and thus you know your True Home" (p. 1113, Tukhari M. 1).

Inanimate Things: Whereas there are living beings in the world, there are inanimate things also. Kabir addresses a lady-gardener in this manner: "Why do you tear off the leaves? The life is also in them. But the stone-gods, to whom you make your offerings of leaves are inanimate (p. 479, Asa Kabir). Guru Ram Das says, "The foolish unbelievers wander in illusion and thus deluded, they make offerings of flowers to their gods. They worship inanimate stones and tombs and in this manner waste away their human birth" (p. 1264, Malar M. 4).

Inauspicious Objects: In all societies, people have belief in omens, good omens as well as bad omens. The objects that they see are auspicious as well as inauspicious. Some of the stars in the horoscopes are considered inauspicious. But the saint-poets of the *Adi Granth* have decried such a tendency. Guru Arjan Dev says, "Only that person is affected by omens, aupicious or inauspicious, who does not enshrine the Name of the Lord in his mind" (p. 401, Asa M. 5).

Incantations: Charms; Spells; formulas or words spoken or chanted to produce a magical effect. The *Adi Granth* rejects the use of incantations. Guru Nanak Dev says, "The one, who strays from the path, recites incantations at the crematoriums, wastes away his life. He does not know the Word and speaks evil" (p. 941, Ramkali Siddh Goshta

M. 1). These incantations are of no avail. At the time of the invasion of Babur, the *pirs* (divines) of the Muslims recited incantations in order to check his advance, but the temples were burnt and princes were murdered (p. 417, Asa M. 1).

Incarnations: According to the *Adi Granth,* God does not incarnate. Guru Arjan Dev says, "O ignorant one, you have kept aside all other lunar dates and believe that God was born on the eight day of the Moon. This belief is utterly false, because God neither takes birth nor dies...That tongue be burnt, which says that the Lord is cast into the womb" (p. 1136, Bhairo M. 5). It is the gods like Vishnu, Shiva and Brahma, who incarnate. Guru Amar Das says, "Vishnu is engaged in reincarnating himself. Who will then emancipate the world?" (p. 559, Vadhans M. 3). There is mention of ten incarnations of Vishnu. "The ten incarnations played the kingly role" (p. 747, Suhi M. 5). These ten incarnations are Matsya, Tortoise, Boar, Man-Lion, Vaman, Parasu-rama, Ram Chandra, Krishna, Buddha and Kalki.

Incest: The crime of sexual intercourse between persons related within the degrees within which marriage is prohibited by law. The *Adi Granth* wants the devotee not to see another's woman with lustful eyes (p. 274, Gauri Sukhmani M. 5), hence incest is condemnable. There is a clear injunctions: "He who does not covet another man's wealth or woman, the Lord abides near him" (p. 1163, Bhairo Namdev).

Indestructible (Imperishable): The Infinite Lord is immortal, Imperishable and indestructible. The created world is prone to destruction. Thus the world of matter perishes, because it is not everlasting. But the scientific assertion that matter is indestructible is also not wrong in the sense that everything in the material world is subject to change. When a body perishes, its elements return to the elements. "The air mingles with the air...the earth mixes with the earth" (p. 885, Ramkali M. 5). "Nothing is born and nothing dies. The Lord enacts His Own plays. Coming and Going, visible and invisible and the entire world, He has made obedient to Himself" (pp. 281-282, Gauri Sukhmani M. 5).

Indifference: Unconcern; apathy; absence of feeling for or against. The saints and the worldly-wise men are generally indifferent to each other (p. 147, Var Majh M. 1). The saints are indifferent to the worldly pursuits and are always attuned with the Lord (p. 711, Todi M. 5).

Individualism: Self-centred feeling or conduct as a principal; free and independent individual action or thought; egoism. This doctrine emphasises the reality of the individual. Every person has his own aspirations and objectives in life. Primarily, he looks towards his own comforts. "In the world, the love (of individuals) is false. Everyone is absorbed in one's own welfare, whether it is the wife or a friend" (p. 536, Devgandhari M. 9). In political philosophy, the doctrine of individualism expounds that the state exists for the individual. In this sense, it must fulfil the needs of the individual, but the rulers of the Iron Age (*Kaliyuga*) lead a luxurious life without caring for the welfare of the subjects, which results in their own ruin (p. 417, Asa M. 1).

Individuality: Separate and continuous existence. Every being has a distinct individuality or entity. This is the result of individual ego. The constitution of a reality as a singular member of a species is called individuation. According to D.D. Runes 'Dictionary of philosophy, in the context of the matter and form theory it is difficult to explain how either prime-matter (which is in itself the same in all physical things), or substantial form (which is the same in all members of the same species) can be the cause or principal of individuality. Guru Nanak Dev says, "O my Master, Wonderful is your Play... you have but one Form, though concealed, and yet in your creation no one is like another" (p. 596, Sorath M. 1). This shows the separate entity or individuality of every being.

Indra: The king of the gods. He is the wielder of the *vajra* (the thunderbolt), therefore he is called *vajrapani*. He is the deity of the atmosphere and governs the weather and the rain. A good number of hymns have been addressed to him in the Vedas. He reigns over Swarga, the heaven of gods and of beautified spirits. He loves to drink Soma juice. There are several examples of his incontinence and adultery. He seduced Ahalya, the wife of the sage Gautama for which he was cursed to have on his body a thousand marks resembling the female organ. After great austerities and penances, these marks were changed to eyes. The reference to this story is found in the *Adi Granth* in the hymns of Guru Nanak (p. 1343, Prabhati M. 1), Namdev (p. 988, Mali Gaura Namdev) and Ravidas (p. 710, Jaitsri Ravidas). There are several stories of Inḍra's rivalry with Lord Krishna. It is said that Krishna went to Swarga to bring the *Parijata* tree for the Gopi, which was resented by Indra. Indra was defeated in the ensuing war and Krishna carried away the *Parijata* tree. This story is mentioned in the *Adi Granth* in the verses of Guru Nanak (p. 470, Var Asa M. 1). His wife is called Indrani or Sachi. According to Guru Nanak, Indra works in the Fear of Lord-God (p. 464, Var Asa M. 1). His vehicle is the white elephant Airavata and he possesses the wonderful horse Ucchaisravas. Both these rose out of the milk ocean. The Swarga of Indra is also called Amravati.

Indre: The senses; five senses of perception and five sense-organs. Five senses of perception are the sight, the hearing, the smell, the taste and the touch. The organs represented by them are the eyes, the ears, the nose, the tongue and the skin. The five organs of sense are the hands, the feet, the mouth and the organs of procreation and excretion. The *Adi Granth* lays emphasis on the control of these senses. They should perform their real duty. Guru Arjan Dev says, "He who keeps the ten organs under control, his soul experiences the unfoldment of the Light of Knowledge" (Gauri M. 5, p. 236. Also see Gauri M. 5, Sukhmani, p. 268).

Industries: Branches of productive labour. In the *Adi Granth,* the idea of honest labour has been prominently exhibited. Though the Gurus and saints were men of God, they were also workers. Some of the saints were workmen of particular industries, for example Kabir was a weaver, Namdev a dyer and Ravidas, a cobbler. There is mention of farming, milk-churning and gold-smithy in the verses of Guru Nanak Dev.

Infanticide: The killing of infants. Since the *Adi Granth* lays emphasis on love and mercy towards all beings, injuring or killing any being is prohibited. There has been the practice of killing newly-born daughters in Hindu society, but the Sikh Gurus preached equality of all human beings, whether men or women, sons or daughters and had great respect for women being the mothers of great men, they were against such heinous crime as infanticide. Guru Nanak Dev said, "Why to talk ill of women, who give birth to kings?" (p. 473, Var Asa M. 1).

Inference: That which is inferred, a conclusion drawn from data or premises. According to Nyaya, it is one of the four valid means of knowledge. Its Sanskrit equivalent is "anuman". It is defined as that cognition which presupposes some other cognition. No inference can follow in the absence of perception. Guru Arjan Dev has inferred: Just as the fish cannot live without water, the *Chatrik* is not satisfied without the rain-drop, the deer is enticed by the music and the black-bee by the fragrance of flowers, similarly the saints love the Lord and are only satisfied with his sight (p. 708, Var Jaitsri M. 5).

Infidels: Unbelievers. In Muslim terminology a *Kāfir* is an infidel or an unbeliever or heretic. The saint Namdev says, "Those who do not contemplate on their Lord-God, I would not like to have their sight" (p. 1163, Bhairo Namdev). Guru Nanak Dev says, "He who does not believe, burns in his own inner fire" (p. 142, Var Majh M. 1). See: *Heretic*.

Infinite: Limitless. Guru Nanak Dev says in one of the *pauris* of *Japuji*: "Infinite are the Praises of the Lord, Infinite are the ways of Praising, Infinite are the Workings of the Lord and Infinite are His Gifts. Infinite are His Sights and Sounds. Infinite are the mysteries of His Mind. Infinite is his Creation and Infinite the Expanse" (p. 5, Japuji).

Ingratitude: Ungratefulness; indisposition to acknowledge or reciprocate benefits received. Guru Arjan Dev says, "He, Who gives us food to eat and clothes to wear, how can we be lazy in showing our gratitude to Him?" (p. 195, Gauri M. 5). In another hymn the Guru says, "He, Who denies the Lord's Gift of food and clothing, the messengers of death keep a watch on him. If he turns his back on Him, Who gave him body and life, he wanders through millions of births" (p. 195, Gauri M. 5). None can save the ungrateful person; he is thrown into the horrible hell (p. 1086, Maru M. 5). The ungrateful persons forget the Lord and thus transmigrate (p. 706, Var Jaitsri M. 5).

Inherence: The state or quality of being inherent; existing in something as a permanent attribute or quality. According to Nyaya-Vaisheshika, the whiteness of a cloth is different in essence from its stratum, the cloth. The former resides in the latter by a special relation called *samavaya* (inherence). By virtue of that peculiar relation, the whiteness appears to be identical with the cloth. The two, the cloth and its whiteness, are, however, two different entities. Similarly, the light (*jot*) of the soul is not different from the soul. It is the inherent quality of the soul. The soul is a part and parcel of the Lord, Who is "All-Light". When the soul realises the Lord, the smaller light merges in the "All-Light". "The light merged in Light and the self realised the Higher Self" (p. 1111, Tukhari M. 1).

Inheritance: Hereditary succession to property; natural derivation of qualities or characters from parents or ancestry. In every society there are set rules of inheritance. In Islam, the subject has been dealt with to some extent in the scripture. In Hinduism, the Smritis and Sutras enlighten us on the subject. In the *Adi Granth*, there is only mention of the spiritual inheritance. Guru Arjan Dev says, "When I opened the treasures of my father and grandfather, my mind felt immensely pleased" (p. 186, Gauri Guareri M. 5).

Initiation: Formal introduction by preliminary instruction or initial ceremony into some office, society etc., or to participation in some principles or observances. There is initiation ceremony in every religion. The Christian initiation is known as baptism. A *dvija* is initiated by *Upanayana Samskara* or the sacred thread ceremony. In Sikhism, the initiation ceremony is called *Amrit Chhakna*. At the time of initiation, the religious discipline is explained to the disciple (initiate). He is instructed to recite daily the three *banis* from the *Adi Granth* and two from the *Dasam Granth*. The *banis from the Adi Granth* are *Japuji*, the morning prayer, the *Rahiras*, the evening prayer and *Kirtan Sohila*, the prayer to be recited before going to sleep.

Injunctions: Authoritative or emphatic admonitions or orders. The *Adi Granth* holds that morality is the basis of spiritual advancement, there are several injunctions for an individual in the scripture. For example, Guru Nanak Dev says, "There can be no devotion without the practice of qualities" (p. 4, Japuji). The sweet humility is the essence of virtues (p. 470, Var Asa M. 1). Do not be inimical to any one, because the Lord resides in every heart (p. 259, Gauri Bawan Akhri M. 5). etc.

Insanity: Madness; lunacy. The state of insanity comes if one resorts to drinking. Guru Amar Das says, "One man brings the vessel full of wine and the other man fills in his cup with it. By drinking it one loses intellect and the state of insanity comes over him. He cannot discriminate between his own and another's and is kicked by the Lord..." (p. 554, Var Bihagra M. 4).

Insight: Mental vision or perception. According to the *Adi Granth*, the insight comes through the Grace of the Guru and the Lord. The saint Ravidas says, "I am like a frog in the well. I know nothing of this place and that place. I am so much enticed by the vices that I have no insight for good or bad (for this end and that end). O, the Hero of the Whole World, bless me with Thy sight for a moment" (p. 346, Gauri Poorbi Ravidas). Guru Tegh Bahadur says, "Lured by the wealth and women of others one wastes away his life. Having been intoxicated by the wine of *maya*, he loses insight for wisdom. He does not know the mystery of the Absolute Lord, who resides within him" (p. 633, Sorath M. 9).

Instructions: Making known to a person what he is required to do; a direction. The *Adi Granth* lays emphasis on the instructions of the

Guru, which lead the devotee towards the Lord. The devotee should feed himself upon the instructions of the Guru, which are, in reality, the proper medicine for him (p. 878, Ramkali M. 1). Guru Angad Dev says, "What instructions can be given to him, whose Guru is (Guru) Nanak Dev. Those who have become wise getting instructions from him, they are absorbed in the Praises of the True Lord" (p. 150, Var Majh M. 1, Shlok M. 2).

Intellect: Power of thought; understanding. In Indian terminology, intellect is *Buddhi*. The Sankhyan term for this is *Mahat*. When Purusha and Prakriti come into contact with each other, *Mahat* or intellect is born. The *Adi Granth* has laid emphasis on "Bibek Buddhi" (discriminating intellect), which is recieved from the True Guru (p. 711, Todi M. 4). The mind is conquered with such intellect, otherwise generally the mind subdues the intellect. The Sikh Prayer begs for the victory of the intellect over the mind, which generally leads the individual towards the vices. (*Man nivan rahe, mat uchchi rahe*). In *Saram Khand* (the region of effort) the mind and intellect both become pure. This is a higher spiritual state.

Intelligence: Intellect; understanding. Guru Nanak Dev says, "It is not wise to destroy the intelligence in strife. It is through intelligence that one serves the Lord and receives honours. It is through intelligence that one knows what he reads. It is through intelligence that one practises charity. This is the True Path, everything else leads towards Satan" (p. 1245, Var Sarang M. 4, Shlok M. 1). See: *Intellect*.

Intercourse: The sexual intercourse is valid only with one's wife. To have such relation with any other woman is strictly prohibited in the *Adi Granth*. "The egocentric (*manmukh*) is enticed by another's wife. The noose falls around his neck..." (p. 226 Gauri M. 1). The ravishing of another's woman is like the company of a snake (p. 403 Asa M. 5). For a moment's pleasure in lust, one incurs the grief for a million days (ibid). He closes all doors and behind many curtains, he ravishes another's woman. But when the account-keepers Chitra and Gupta ask for the account, then who will protect him? (p. 616, Sorath M. 5). Those who enjoy other's woman have to suffer shame (p. 1362, Phunhay M. 5).

Intermediate Place: Intermediate place is the state of dreams falling between the waking state and the state of dreamless sleep. The daylight experience comes in dreams in various forms. Many images arise from the sub-conscious mind, which is a vast store-house of such images. A king may become a beggar in a dream. The saint Ravidas says, "The king fell asleep on his throne and became a beggar in the dream. Even being a ruler (in his waking state), he was separated from his kingdom in his dream and was in agony—such is the state of my mind also" (p. 657, Sorath Ravidas).

Internal Organ: The *manas* or mind is called the internal organ. Guru Amar Das says, "Only the Enlightened one (Gurmukh) looks into the mind within the body. He absorbs himself in devotion of love and his ego is dried up. All the adepts, seekers and men of silence concentrate, but can not visualise the mind in the body" (p. 124, Majh M. 3). According to Guru Nanak Dev, "the mind is within the body and True Lord is within the mind" (p. 686 Dhanasri M. 1). The Guru says in another hymn, "The five evil passions dwell within the mind. The mind does not remain fixed and wanders like a deserter" (p. 359, Asa M.1). Kabir says, "It is through the mind that everyone speaks. Without destroying the wickedness of the mind, there cannot be any devotion of the Lord" (p. 329, Gauri Kabir).

Intoxication: Drinking of spirituous liquor is forbidden in the *Adi Granth* (p. 554, Var Bihagra M. 4, Shalok M. 3). It is the false intoxicant according to Guru Amar Das. The use of hemp is also prohibited (p. 1377, Shlok Kabir). In fact, all the intoxicants have been forbidden and all those foods have been decried which create vices in the mind and pains in the body (p. 16, Sri Rag M. 1). The Gurus and saints are for God-intoxication created by the remembrance of the Name of the Lord. Guru Arjan Dev says, "O my mother, my mind is intoxicated with God..." (p. 1225, Sarang M. 5). The madness due to the intoxication of *maya* has been decried. "Madly intoxicated by the wine of *maya*, one does not utter the Praises of the Lord (p. 536, Devgandhari M. 9).

Intuition: The immediate knowledge ascribed to Angelic and spiritual beings, with whom vision and knowledge are identical. Guru Nanak Dev says, "When one knows the Lord through the Grace of the Guru, his intuition awakens" (p. 725, Tilang M. 1). Kabir says, "Knowing his Essence, I attuned myself to my Immaculate Lord and then my intuition was awakened..." (p. 328, Gauri Kabir).

Invisibility: It is an attribute of Brahman. Kabir says, "You only see whatever is prone to destruction. You contemplate on Him Whom you do not see. When you open the tenth door then you will see the Compassionate Lord" (p. 341, Gauri Bawan Akhri Kabir). Through equipoise, the invisible Lord is realised (p. 68, Sri Rag M. 3). The Lord Who is Invisible, Imperceptible, Unknowable and Immaculate is seen with eyes by the Grace of the Guru (p. 87, Var Sri Rag M. 4).

Īrakhā: Jealousy. Kabir says, "O my mind, do not be jealous of others. Make your earnings through right effort" (Asa Kabir, p. 479). Guru Arjan Dev says, "He, whose mind is absorbed in the Lord, he forgets the jealousy for others" (Gauri M. 5, p. 89).

Iron: A metal, whose name is used figuratively in the *Adi Granth.* Guru Ram Das says, "The sinners are ferried across by the saints, just as the iron is ferried across in a wooden bark (p. 1297, Kanara M. 4, See also page 1309, Kanara M. 4). Guru Nanak Dev says, "Just as iron becomes gold when rubbed with the philosopher's stone, in a similar manner, the individual is transformed by the society of the saints" (p. 303, Var Gauri M. 4).

Irrigation: The process of irrigation is used figuratively in the *Adi Granth.* Guru Nanak Dev says, "The Word is the tree within the beautiful garden and land is irrigated with the waters of love. They bear only the fruit of the Name of the Lord. But without karmas (actions), how can one get the fruit?" (p. 354, Asa M. 1). Kabir says, "If one irrigates the neem tree with nectar, will it change its nature?" (p. 481, Asa Kabir). Guru Arjan Dev says, "One's mind is purged of its evil, if it is irrigated with the Name of the Lord" (p. 893, Ramkali M. 5).

Ishwara: The Name of the Lord. Brahman is said to have two aspects viz. Transcendent Brahman (*Nirguna*) and Immanent Brahman (*Saguna*). When *Nirguna* or unmanifested Lord becomes *Saguna* or manifested, He is called Ishwara. The origin of this word is from the Sanskrit root Ish, which means "to have power". Thus *Ishwara* denotes the Powerful Lord, Who is a Cosmic Purusha. The derivative from *Ishwara*, the word *Ishar* is used for Shiva in the *Adi Granth.* For Ishwara, the words *Īs* or *Īsai* have been used in the *Adi Granth.*

Islam: Muhammedanism or the religion preached by the Prophet Muhammad. Literally the word Islam means the resignation to the Will of the Lord. The Prophet explained it to mean the observance of the five duties: 1-Bearing witness that there is only one Lord, 2-Reciting daily prayers, 3-Giving the legal alms, 4-Observing the Ramazan or month's fast and 5-Making the pilgrimage to Mecca once in the lifetime. Those who profess the religion of Islam are called Mussalmans or Momins. In the *Adi Granth* the hymns of Muslim saints like Kabir and Farid are included. Guru Nanak Dev has elucidated in several of his hymns his ideas about Islam. He has defined a Muslim like this: "Make the Mercy of the Lord your mosque, the faith your prayermat, honestly-earned income your Quran, the effort your circumcision, the character your fast—in this way you can become a Mussalman" (p. 140, Var Majh M. 1).

Island: The word *Dīp* has been used for the island in the *Adi Granth.* But when mention is made of *Sapt Dīp,* it cannotes seven continents.

Isnān: (Ishnān). Bath, Bathing. See: *Bath.*

Istrī: Woman. Other words used for woman in the *Adi Granth* include *Bhand, Dhan, Nari, Triya* etc. Mention has been made of *Suhagan* (the woman, who enjoys the love of her Lord) and *Duhagan* (the deserted woman). Guru Nanak Dev has asked his contemporary society not to talk ill of the woman, who gives birth to the greatest of men (Var Asa M. 1, p. 473). See: *Woman.*

Itihāsa: Ordinarily, this word means history. But it has also been used for popular literature, when it has been associated with *Purana.* In Indian literature, this word has been used for the two epics: *Ramayana* and *Mahabharata.* Both Itihasas and Puranas were current in the early Vedic period. We find several references to *Ramayana* and *Mahabharata* in the *Adi Granth.*

J

Jackal: An animal of the dog kind, about the size of a fox, hunting in packs by night with wailing cries. A symbol for cowardice. The saint Sadhana says, "Why to seek the refuge of a lion, when one is to be seized by a jackal?" (p. 858, Bilawal Sadhna).

Jagat: (*Duniā*). World. See: *World.*

Jaina, Jainism: Mahavira, the twenty-fourth Tirthankara, is considered, the founder of *Jainism*. His followers are called *Jainas*. They are divided into two main sects i.e. *Svetambra* and *Digambra*. The former wear white clothes and the latter remain naked. The latter were very rigid in their practices. Guru Nanak Dev has condemned their practices. They used to rake up their night soil, breathe continuously, keep off from water, pluck their hair, drink impure water and eat impure food obtained by begging. They always remained dirty and remorseful and did not attend congregations. They moved in a queue with cups hanging by their waiste and dusters in their hands. They did all this because of jiva-mania. In order to save the minutest jivas they passed very unhygienic lives. The Guru told them: "God kills jivas and gives life to them. None else can save them". Therefore he advised the Jaina monks to desist from unhealthy practices. The *Digambaras* have been specially mentioned in the *Adi Granth*. Jainism believes in the doctrines of *Anekāntavada* and *Syādvāda*. The first is the doctrine of manyness of reality and the second the doctrine of the relativity of knowledge. A close study of the doctrines of Jainism shows that it is an ethical teaching. Its aim is the liberation of the soul from the *karmic* matter, but the teachings of Guru Nanak Dev take us to the spiritual domain, where we attain unity with *Godhead*. Jainism is a religion without God. This is the basic difference between Jainism and Sikhism (See Var Majh M. 1, pp. 149-50 and Var Malar M. 1, p. 1285).

Jam: Yama; the god of death.

Jamdūt: The messengers of Yama.

Jan: man; person; man of God.

Janeū: The sacred thread; *Yagyopavīta*. See: *Sacraments*.

Jant: That which is born; the creature.

Jantar: (*Yantra*) The mystic diagram; a distinct form of *mantra* used as a charm. When the *mantra-sound* is given a form, it is known as *Yan-*

tra. Whereas a *Yantra* is the form of a sound, it is also a point of contact with the source of the sound. There has been a practice among the Tantriks to use the *Yantra* as a *kavac* (coat of mail) for the protection of an individual from impending dangers. Guru Arjan Dev says, "The Mantra of the Name of the Lord is the coat of mail (*kavāc*) for the devotee" (Gaund M. 5, p. 868). A *Yantra* within an amulet was tied round the neck of an afflicted person with a thread by the Tantrik in order to create the desired effect. The *Adi Granth* is averse to such practices (See Vadhans M. 1, p. 582).

Jap: Repetition of spiritual formula. It is a time-honoured method of concentration. It is believed that one can realise the Lord by its constant practice. The *Adi Granth* lays great emphasis on *Jap* or repetition of the Name of the Lord. The very first poem of the *Adi Granth*, composed by Guru Nanak Dev, is *Japu*.

Jat, Jatī: *Jat* is self-control and chastity. A *Jatī* is a celibate or man of chastity. See: *Yatī*.

Jāt-varan: (Jāt pāt). The castes: See: *Caste*.

Jesus: There is no direct reference to Jesus Christ in the *Adi Granth*, but the usage of word "Kateb" (Books) refers to the Christian scripture *Injil*, which contains revelations made by God to Jesus. But some Christian Missionaries have mistook the word *Isai* used in the *Adi Granth* for Christ, though it is a derivative from Sanskrit "Īsh", Which means Ishwara or God (p. 1072, Maru M. 5).

Jewels: A precious stone; a gem. Guru Nanak Dev says, "The Guru is an ocean full of jewels. There is therein the inexhaustible pearly treasure of Truth" (p. 933, Dakhni Oamkar, Ramkali M. 1). In another hymn, the Guru says, "The Guru is the ocean full of jewels and pearls. The enlightened persons and saints, eat them like swans. They remain near the ocean (p. 685, Dhanasari M. 1). Guru Arjan Dev identifies the Name of the Lord with a jewel (p. 893, Ramkali M. 5).

Jews: The Jews are called *Yahudi*. There is no reference to Jews in the *Adi Granth*, though there is mention of their scriptures, the *Taurat* and the Zabur in the word "Kateb" (Books). Like Muslims, they are also known as *Ahl-i-Kitab* (the people having a Book or scripture).

Jīvan-mukta, Jīvan-muktī: The state of final emancipation, while one is alive in this world, is known as *Jivan-muktī* and one who has achieved this state is a *Jīvan-mukta*. See: *Moksha; Mukta; Muktī*.

Jivātman: The embodied soul. See: *Atman*.

Jog, Jogī: (*Yoga, Yogī*). See: *Yoga* and *Yogin*.

Judaism: The religion of the Jews. In the word "Kateb"(Books) used in the *Adi Granth*, there is reference to the two scriptures of Judaism, called *Taurat* (The Book of Moses) and *Zabur* (The Book of David). See: *Jews, Books*.

Judge(s): In the times of the Sikh Gurus, the Muslim *Qazi* was the judge about whom, Guru Nanak Dev says, "The Qazi sits in judgement upon others. He tells rosary and mutters the Name of God. He accepts bribe and passes unjust orders. If any one enquires from him, he quotes the verses from the Quran (p. 951, Var Ramkali M. 3, Shlok M. 1). But the real judge of our Karmas is *Dharma Raja*, who sits in judgement on the accounts of the mortals. His scribes, Chitra and Gupta present the books containing an account of the actions of the soul during its life on the earth. "The sinners are cast into the hell by the Creator and they are asked to render the account by the Lord-Justiciar" (pp. 1019-20, Maru M. 5). The Muslims believe in Last Day of Judgement.

Jug: (Yugas). The four ages of the world. See: *Yugas*.

Jugglers: A magician; a wizard; a sorcerer. In the *Adi Granth* The Lord has been depicted as a great juggler. Guru Arjan Dev says, "When the Lord, as a Juggler, starts His Play, He exhibits many forms and guises and when He Assembles His Play, He alone remains absorbed in Himself" (p. 736, Suhi M. 5). The same thought has been expressed by Kabir (p. 655, Sorath Kabir).

Jūn: The birth in one of the eighty-four lakh species of creation. In Sanskrit, it is called *yonī*. Unless and until the soul attains release, it migrates into a series of bodies. The release is obtained, when the cycle of *karma* is broken through. Guru Arjan Dev says, "The jiva was born several times as worm and flying insect...an elephant, a fish and a deer.. a bird and a snake...a horse and a yoked bull...a stone and a mountain...germs...plants. It strayed into eighty-four lakhs of physical forms (Gauri M. 5, p. 176).

Justice: For the king the mind is cleansed through justice (p. 1240, Var Sarang M. 4 , Shlok M. 1). Since Lord alone is True, His Justice also is True (p. 84, Var Sri Rag M. 4). His Justice is in accordance with His Law (p. 84, Var Sri Rag M. 4). He Himself adjudicates and drives away the false (p. 89, ibid). Perfect is the Justice of the Creator (p. 199, Gauri M. 5). If a self-willed fool fights with the saintly person, the Just Lord condemns him (p. 148, Var Majh M.1, Shlok M. 2). In the Lord's Court, the adjudication is based on Truth (p. 621, Sorath M. 5).

Jūth: Impure and unclean used articles. "If mind is unclean, the body is unclean and also the tongue becomes unclean. He, who utters falsehood from his mouth, how can he become pure?" (Sri Rag M. 1, p. 56). "When the interior is unclean, how can we purify it? Such a person is rare, who purifies it with the Word" (Prabhati M. 1, p. 1344).

K

Kaabah: Literally this word means "A cube". Kaabah is the cube-like building in the centre of the mosque at Mecca, which contains the black stone (Hajaru'l-Aswad). It is the most sacred shrine of the Muslims. Every Muslim performs his prayer in the direction of the Kaabah. According to the Traditions, the Kaabah was first constructed in heaven. It was Adam, who erected the Kaabah on earth exactly below the spot its perfect model occupies in heaven. During the Deluge, this sacred house was destroyed. The Lord instructed Abraham to rebuild it. In order to mark the corner of the building, the black stone was provided by the angel Gabriel. Kabir says, "One keeps fast and mutters his daily prayers and the Kalimah, but he does not go to heaven. There are a good number of Kaabahs in the heart, only if one knows it (p. 480, Asa Kabir). Addressing a Muslim, Guru Nanak Dev says, "Let pious deeds be your Kaabah" (p. 141, Var Majh M. 1). Kabir says, "O Sheikh, why do you go to the Kaabah without patience in your heart. He, who does not have a whole heart, how will he realise the Lord" (p. 1374, Shlok Kabir). He says again, "I was going to the Kaabah and on the way I met the Lord. He quarrelled with me Saying "Who told you that I had gone thither" (p. 1375 Shlok Kabir).

Kāiā: (*Kāyā*). Body. See: *Body*.

Kāla: Death, the destroyer of all creatures. It also means Time. Guru Arjan Dev Says, "Whomsoever one sees, will be taken away by *Kāla* (death)" (p. 740, Suhi M. 5). *Yama* is called *Kāla Kantaka* (The thorn of death) (p. 742, Suhi M. 5). Death is also called *Kāla Kanyā*, the daughter of *Yama*". The terrible and the destroyer *Kāla* (death) stands over the head of the world (p. 147, Var Majh M. 1)". You believe in the illusion as true and do not remember *Kāla* (death)" (p. 267, Gauri Sukhmani M. 5). *Dharma Raja* (the god of *Dharma*) is called *Kāla Purakh* (p. 1159, Bhairo Kabir). The noose of death is called *Kāla Jaal* or *Kāla Phaas*.

Kali Age: (*Kali Yuga*). It is called the Iron Age. The action which merits most in the Kali Age (Kaliyuga) is the remembrance of the Name of the Lord. Guru Arjan Dev says, "The Kali Age has come and now sow the seed of the Name of the Lord. This season is not suitable for any other crop. Have no doubt about it" (p. 1185, Basant M. 5). In Kali Age the chariot of body is made of fire and its charioteer is falsehood (p. 470, Var Asa M. 1) About Kali Age Guru Nanak Dev says, "That time has passad away when the people knew the real Yoga and practised Truth. All the places of worship are now defiled and the world is being drowned. In the Kali Age, the most meritorious action is the remembrance of the Name of the Lord. (In this age) people beguile others by closing their eyes and holding their nostrils. They hold the nostril with their three fingers and say that they have visualised three worlds, but they can not see the things lying at their back—this is a strange lotus-posture. The Kshatriyas have forsaken their religion and speak the foreign language. The world has adopted the same hue and there are no more the religious values. With the knowledge of grammer, they study the Vedas and Puranas, but they cannot obtain release without the Name of the Lord (pp. 662-663, Dhanasari M. 1).

Kalpas: A period of time mentioned in the religious books of the Hindus. One Kalpa is equal to one day of Brahma or one thousand Yugas. This period is equal to four thousand three hundred and twenty millions of years of human beings. In another Puranic system, a kalpa is divided into fourteen periods, known as *Manvantaras*, each *Manvantara* containing 71 mahayugas. Thus in total a kalpa consists of 994 mahayugas, including six mahayugas as the dawn and twilight of mahayugas, the total comes to 1000 mahayugas. In the *Adi Granth*, there is mention of yugas, but not of kalpas.

Kāma: Ordinarily, means "desire for" or "longing for". Generally, this word connotes lust, one of the five main vices. When personified, it is used for 'god of love'. The god of love or lust has been addressed thus: "O Lust, you are the cause of landing men in a hell and making them transmigrate, you deceive all minds, away in all the three worlds and destroy the merits of all austerities and meditation; your pleasure is illusory, you make men unsteady and poor and punish the persons of various status alike" (p. 1358, Sahaskriti Shlokas M. 5). Kama weakens the body (p. 932, Ramkali Dakhni Oamkar M. 1). Kama lives within the sinning mind, therefore being mercurial it can not be steadied. A Yogi, a Shaivite or a Sannyasin all are caught within the noose of Kama (p. 1186, Basant M. 9) For a moment's pleasure of Kama, one suffers for a million days, He enjoys for a short while but repents again and again (p. 403, Asa M. 5). *Kama* as worldly desire is one of the four ends of human life, the other three being *Dharma, Artha* and *Moksha*. "The Lord blessess us with Dharma (righteousness), Artha (wealth), Kama (worldly desires) and Moksha (emancipation). The person on whose forehead it is written, all his desires are fulfilled" (p. 927, Ramkali M. 5).

Kamal: The Lotus. In Indian literature and also in the *Adi Granth*, the lotus flower symbolises purity and non-attachment. Various nerve-centres in the body are called lotuses by the Yogis. When various parts of the body of a saint are described, the word *kamal* (lotus) is added to them e.g. *caran-kamal, hast-kamal, nain-kamal* etc. Here the beauty and purity of the parts of body are kept in view. The feet, hands and eyes are identified with lotus flower. Guru Nanak Dev says, "Though the lotus is thrown hither and thither by the waves, still it blossoms in love" (Sri Rag M. 1, p. 60). The Guru also says, "Just as the lotus remains unaffected by water, similarly we remain unaffected by the world, if we concentrate on the Name of the Lord and in this way, we can cross the ocean of *saṁsāra*" (Ramkali M. 1, Siddh Goshta, p. 938).

Kamma-Karma: Action. The personality of a person is formed according to his *karmas* (actions) (p. 730, Suhi M. 1). The body is the field of actions; whatever one sows, one eats (p. 78, Sri Rag M. 5). Because of one's Karmas, he is either near or far away from the Lord (p. 8, Japuji). The Lord moves all according to His Will and His Writ is according to the actions (p. 1241, Var Sarang M. 4, Shlok M. 1). Every one would be fortunate, if he gathers everything with his own efforts. Though we may crave for everything, we only get according to our actions (p. 157, Gauri Bairagan M. 1). We cannot find fault with others. The fault lies with our actions. We receive the reward according to our actions, why to blame others? (p. 433, Asa M. 1, Patti). "O Brother, Look at the Greatness of our Lord, One gets only whatever one deserves according to his actions (p. 653, Var Sorath M. 4). If one performs virtuous actions, he is known as a virtuous person, if one commits sin, he is known as a sinner (p. 138, Var Majh M. 1, Shlok M. 2). Only your deeds will accompany you on death. Whatever you have done cannot be effaced (p. 460, Asa M. 5). All the actions committed in ego are like the links of a chain on one's neck. The sense of possession which grips our mind, is like the fetters on one's feet (p. 1004, Maru M. 5).

Kapat: Deceit. Kabir says, "O my misled mind, do not practise deceit. Ultimately your soul will be answerable for that" (Sorath Kabir, p. 656). He says again, "You have deceit in your heart, but you speak like a knowledgeable person. O lier, why do you churn the water?" (ibid).

Karam: This word, whose root is in Sanskrit, connotes action (or karma). See *Karma.*

This word, which comes from Persian stock, connotes Grace. See: *Grace.*

Karāmāt: Miracle. See: *Miracles.*

Karam Khand: The region of Grace. It is one of the five regions, which Guru Nanak Dev has mentioned in *Japuji*, the other four regions being the region of piety, the region of knowledge, the region of effort and the region of truth. It is the fourth region and precedes the region of truth. In this region, the Grace of the Lord is bestowed on the devotee, on account of which he attains Power. He becomes Immortal and is always in Bliss (Japuji, p. 8).

Karma-Bhūmi: Literally the field of actions. (See p. 717, Todi M. 5). But considering the law of Karma, the worlds where the rewards for actions are reaped are known as the *Karma-Bhumis* and the worlds where the souls are sent for sensual enjoyments, are known as *Bhog-Bhumis*. Our world, for instance, is the *Karma Bhumi*, where we reap the reward of our past Karmas. For Muslims, the *Jannat* (heaven) and for Hindus *Swarg Loka* is the *Bhog Bhumi*. Guru Nanak Dev has referred to the *Karma-Bhumis* in *Japuji*, while talking about the expanse of the universe (p. 7, Japuji).

Karma Kānda: The *Adi Granth* rejects all kinds of Karma Kanda, i.e. ritualism. Guru Amar Das says, "They practise rituals and works of pious conduct, but cursed is the ego regarding them. They neglect the Name of the Lord" (p. 162, Gauri M. 3). "One may perform the karmas (action) enjoined by Smritis and Shastras, but there can be no peace without the Vision of the Lord" (p. 408, Asa M. 5). Without the remembrance of the Lord all other actions are useless. The merit of all contemplations, austerities, disciplines and actions are even robbed away in this world. The fasting and regular observance and disciplines are all in vain. Hereafter, the discipline is different and no works and rituals are of any avail there (p. 216, Gauri M. 5). All the seeming actions, pieties and hypocrisies are subject to taxation by *Yama* (p. 747, Suhi M. 5).

Kapālas: Kapalīka is a South Indian medieval Tantric cult. It was later on associated with Kalamukha cult. Both these cults are regarded as offshoots of the Shaiva Pashupata cult. Both the words *Kapala* and *Kalmukha* are found in the verses of the *Adi Granth*. The saint Beni in his hymn has used the word Kapala with reference to the frontal mark on the forehead. Since the saint talked about Vaishnavas and Ganapatyas in this hymn, probably he is referring to Shaivites by using the word Kapala (p. 1351, Prabhati Beni). Though the word *Kalmukha* means "black-faced", but in all probability its origin is the name of the Shaivite cult (p. 1207, Sarang M. 5).

Karmans: The performance of actions and deeds is meant to get knowledge, but when knowledge is attained, of what avail are the actions and deeds? (p.1167, Bhairo Ravidas). The couriers of Yama are dreadful. Chitra and Gupta, know all our karmans and bear witness to them day and night. Therefore I seek Thy Refuge, O Lord" (p. 838, Bilawal M. 5). You say, that this soul is bound to its karmans, but who is it who gave life to karmans?" (p. 870, Gond Kabir). See: *Kamma-Karma*.

Karma Yogi: A Karma-Yogi is one who believes in re-integration through action. He applies his mind constantly to the actions ordained by the religious texts. According to the *Adi Granth* a Karma-Yogi is one who performs the deed, but does not care for its fruit. He has no desire for the fruit of his actions, but is absorbed solely in devotion and the praises of the Lord" (p. 274, Gauri Sukhmani M. 5).

Karnī: Karma; Deed; Action. The word *Karnī* is often used in good sense, when it connotes good actions. Guru Nanak Dev says, "Where there is good deed, the intellect is fully mature, and wherever there is no good deed, the intellect dwindles down (Sri Rag M. 1, p. 25). Guru Arjan Dev says, "The action, for which you are feeling ashamed, you have performed the same act. You have firmly taken up the wrong path of the calumny of the saint and the worship of Sākat (the follower of mammon)—(Dhanasari M. 5, p. 673).

Karodh: Anger. See: *Anger*.

Kartā Purkh: The Purusha, Who is the Creator. Describing the Nature of Brahman in the *Mūl Mantra*, Guru Nanak Dev has mentioned this attribute of Brahman.

Kateb: The Four Books of Middle-Eastern Religions i.e. *Taurāt* and *Zabūr* of Judaism, *Injīl* of Christianity and *Quran* of Islam. See *Books*.

Kathā: The learned exposition of scriptures and religious books. In the *Adi Granth*, there is an emphasis on the listening of the learned exposition of scriptures and the Divine Music (*Kīrtan*). (Bilawal M. 5, p. 820). The learned expositions of lives of saints lead us on the Path of Peace. Those who are destined to listen to them according to their Writ, actually receive them (Var Maru Dakhne M. 5, p. 1101).

Kathnī: The speech; the talk. Kabir says, "With mere speech, the illusion does not end, though all the world has been speaking constantly (Sorath Kabir, p. 655). The Yoga (union) is not achieved by mere talk" (Suhi M. 1, p. 730).

Kesava: Name of Lord. Many names used for various incarnations have been used in one of the hymns of Guru Arjan Dev in the *Adi Granth*, which has been given the title of "Sahansar Nama" in various manuscripts of the scripture. It is written in this hymn that Keshava (the Lord) is the performer of mysterious wonders. "Whatsoever He seeks to do, Will happen" (p. 1082, Maru M. 5). *Keshava* literally means "Long-haired" and is an epithet of Lord Vishnu/Lord Krishna. This word has also been used as Keso/Kesau. Kabir says, "if we cry out "Keso, Keso" and have no wink of sleep, and crying out repeatedly throughout day and night, he may at last listen to our cries" (p. 1376, Shlok Kabir).

Khand: Region. "The regions and universes created by the Lord are real" (Var Asa M. 1, p. 463). Guru Nanak Dev has mentioned five spiritual stages in *Japuji* and has called them *khand* (pp. 7-8).

Khasam: The Lord; the husband; the Master. "Those who have forgotten the *Khasam* (Lord) and have indulged in pleasures, their bodies are subjected to several diseases (Malar M. 1, p. 1256). "When the *Khasam* (husband) dies, the wife (i.e. *maya*) does not weep, because she is taken over by another one (Gaund Kabir, p. 871).

Khat Darshan: Six philosophies; Six systems of Indian Philosophy. These systems are Samkhya (of Kapila), Yoga (Of Patanjali), Nyaya (of Gautama), Vaisheshika (of Kannada), Pūrva Mimansā (of Jaimani) and Uttara Mimansā (of Vyasa). The philosophy of the Guru is quite different from these philosophies (Asa M. 3, p. 360). Another phrase "Che Updes" has been used for Khat Darshan in the *Adi Granth*.

Khat Karam: Six Karmas. According to Hindu Shastric injunctions, a Hindu has to perform six karmas in order to obtain salvation. These *karmas* (works) are *Pathan* (reading of the Vedas), *Pāthan* (teaching the Vedas), *Yajan* (to perform Yajnas), Yajan (to make others perform the Yajnas), *Dān* (to give in charity) and *Pratigraha* (to take charity). Guru Arjan Dev says, "One performs six karmas and adopts Yogic postures and kiryās; he recites the scriptures at the houses of wealthy persons; he tells the beads of the rosary and begs money from others. O brother, no one has been able to cross the ocean of *Saṁsāra* in this way" (Ramkali M. 5, p. 888). The *Adi Granth* rejects such works.

Khatrī: Kshatriya. See: *Kshatriyas*.

Khema (Nibban-Nirvana): "Emancipation. "Emancipation, peace, wealth, nine treasures, wisdom, knowledge and all miraculous powers, education, austerity and Yoga are all contained in the contemplation of the Name of the Lord" (pp. 295-96, Gauri Sukhmani M. 5). Guru Arjan Dev says, "If you want the eternal emancipation/bliss, then always remember the Lord" (p. 714, Todi M. 5).

Khimā: Forgiveness. This is a godly quality. Kabir says, "Where there is knowledge, there is *Dharma* (righteousness), where there is falsehood, there is sin, where there is greed, there is death and where there is *Khimā* (*kshimā*), there is God Himself" (Shlok Kabir, p. 1372). "When we hold fast to *kshimā* (forgiveness), the anger is destroyed (Gauri M. 3, p. 233).

Khoj, Khojī: *Khoj* is search and *khojī* is one, who searches and is absorbed in research. "The searcher is absorbed in search and the saint (searcher, seeker) has ultimately realised the Lord (Bilawal M. 5, p. 845). Guru Nanak Dev says, "He who indulges in research creates something and he who is absorbed in quarrels destroys something (Malar M. 1, p. 1255).

Kindness: It is an attribute of the Lord. He is Merciful, Graceful and Kind. Great emphasis is laid on this attribute of the Lord in the *Adi Granth*. The fourth Guru addresses the Lord as the Beneficent Lord and Merciful Lord (p. 669, Dhanasari M. 4). Guru Arjan Dev says, "My Lord is Gracious and Kind and Blesses all with His Grace" (p. 724, Tilang M. 5). The kindness towards all beings is exhibited in the following verse: "Do not injure any one and go to your real Home with honour" (p. 322, Var Gauri M. 5).

Kindred: Related by birth or descent. Guru Arjan Dev says, "When one is in utter distress and there is none to support; when the enemies have come down upon him and his kindred have left him alone; when all the support has ended and props finished; if he then remembers the Lord, he will still be safe" (p. 70, Sri Rag M. 5). Whose is the father? Whose is the mother? All these kindred are in name (p. 188, Gauri M. 5), "Dwell on the Lord, by whose Grace your kindred and friends came to your help in old age and fed you in your bed" (pp. 266-67, Gauri Sukhmani M. 5).

Kine: Plural of cow. Guru Nanak Dev says, "Residing in the citadel of gold, if you give fine horses and elephants in charity, and lands and a good number of kine, the ego will not leave your mind" (p. 62, Sri Rag M. 1).

King: The rule of that king is enduring, who follows the democratic ideals (p. 992, Maru M. 1) The king is proud of his kingdom (p. 679, Dhanasari M. 5). In the iron age, the king administers justice if he is bribed, but he is not moved in the Name of the Lord (p. 350, Asa M. 1). In the iron age, the king is like a lion and his officials like dogs (p. 1288, Var Malar M. 1). At the time of the advent of Babur, the kings had lost their heads and were absorbed in revelries (p. 417, Asa M. 1). The kings are not those who are ever engaged in battles and transmigrate repeatedly (p. 590, Var Vadhans M. 4, Shlok M. 3). The king cleanses his mouth through justice (p. 1240, Var Sarang M. 4, Shlok M. 1). From a king to a worm and from a worm to the god of gods, all fill their bellies giving agony to the others because they abandon God and worship others (p.1267, Malar M. 5). If the king makes a demand, he is satisfied, if his demand is met (p. 143, Var Majh M. 1). The real and true king is the Lord Himself, Whose rule is eternal (p. 567, Vadhans M. 1). Neither kings nor beggars would remain. They all come and go (p. 931, Ramkali M. 1, Dakhni Oamkar). The king is not satisfied with his kingdom (p. 148, Var Majh M. 1). He is the king of the whole world, whose mind is saturated with the Name of the Lord (p. 707, Var Jaitsri M. 5).

Kingly Glory: The *Adi Granth* sings only of the kingly Glory of the Lord, because He is the only Immortal King. The glory of the worldly kings is short-lived (p. 645, Var Sorath M. 4). Addressing the Lord-God, Guru Arjan Dev says, "Thou art the King of kings; I cannot describe all Thy Attributes" (p. 761, Suhi M. 5).

Kinnaras: They are mythological beings having human bodies, but heads of horses, or vice versa. They are said to be the musicians of Kuber alongwith the *gandharvas*. Mentioning the creation, Guru Arjan Dev says, "There are millions of Kinnaras and Paishachas" (p. 276, Gauri Sukhmani M. 5). In another hymn, the Guru says, "O Lord, the gods, Siddhas, Ganas, Gandharvas Worship Thee and the Yakshas and Kinnaras sing your attributes" (p. 455, Asa Chhant M. 5).

Kinship: Relationship by descent. The moral law of causation is the cause of various kinships. Guru Nanak Dev says, "One becomes now a father, now a son, now a Guru, now a disciple; one cannot count them, how many there are and how many there have been (p.1238, Var Sarang M. 4, Shlok M. 1). See: *Kindred.*

Kirpā: (Kripā) Grace. See: *Grace.*

Kirt: Out of the three jewels of Sikh Faith, the first one is: "Work hard". The second is the remembrance of the Name of Lord and the third is to share the earnings with the deserving and needy. Guru Nanak Dev has said. "Work to sustain (yourself) and share with the needy" (Var Sarang M. 4, Shlok M. 1, p. 1245).

Kīrtan: The singing of *Gurbanī* is known as *Kīrtan*. The word *Kīrtan* literally means the singing of the Praises of the Lord, therefore literally, *Kīrtan* is divine music. It is like invaluable diamond, full of bliss and profound in qualities (Gauri M. 5, p. 893). Whosoever listens or sings the *Kīrtan* of Hari, no trouble can come near him (Gauri M. 5, p. 190). It is a significant mode of devotion. It brings bliss and comfort to the devotee (Var Sarang M. 4, p. 1250). He who performs the *Kīrtan* and sings the Praises of the Lord is loved by the Lord Himself (Var Sorath M. 4, p. 650). The disciple who listens to the *Kīrtan* of Hari casts off enmity and jealousy from his mind (Gauri Bawan Akhri M. 5, p. 259). "Perform such actions, by which the dirt (of ego) is removed and the mind is awakened in the *Kīrtan* of Hari" (Gauri M. 5, p. 199).

Knife: The Iron-age has been identified with knife, which is held by the kings in the garb of butchers. Guru Nanak Dev says, "The Kali-age is the knife and the kings are the butchers. Dharma (righteousness) has flown away. There is the dark night of falsehood and the moon of Truth is not visible anywhere" (p. 145, Var Majh M. 1). Talking about his times the Guru says, "The man-eaters mutter the prayers and those who hold the knife, wear the sacred thread....On their foreheads is the saffron-mark and they have the Dhoti's folds around their loin. But in their hands is the knife and they are the butchers of the world. (pp. 471-72, Var Asa M. 1).

Knowledge: The *Adi Granth* lays emphasis on the knowledge of the Divine. The knowledge of the soul leads towards the knowledge of God. This is done only through the Guru (p. 1030, Maru M. 1). The mind is held by knowledge and there can be no knowledge without the Guru (p. 469, Var Asa M. 1). The knowledge is figuratively called the antimony (collyrium), which when applied to the eyes gives us an insight into the nature of things. "Applying the collyrium of knowledge of the Supreme Essence, I visualise the Lord of the three worlds" (p. 764, Suhi Chhant M. 1). Everyone talks of knowledge, but mere talk leads to discursiveness and suffering (p. 831, Bilawal M. 1). The substance of knowledge (*Gyan Padarath*) is the Name of the Lord, which is obtained through the Grace of the Guru. Through it, one knows the secrets of the three worlds (p. 60, Sri Rag M. 1).

Krishna: One of the ten main incarnations of Vishnu. He was a Yadava prince and son of Devaki and Vasudeva. The tradition announces him as the incarnation of Dvapara age, just before the advent of Kali-age. He was born at Vrindavan and ruled over his dominions in West India, having his capital at Dvaraka. He played a significant role in the great war of Mahabharata fought between Kauravas and Pandavas. He was an ally of Pandavas and his exposition of Vedanta addressed to Arjuna, in the field of battle, is contained in Bhagavad Gita. His maternal uncle Kansa had usurped the throne of his maternal grandfather Ugrasena. It was Krishna, who killed Kansa and restored the kingdom to his grandfather. There are many miracles attributed to him. Several stories are current about his love for the *gopis*. In the *Adi Granth*, there are several allusions to him. Besides *Krishna* (meaning black), he has been given the names like "Gopal", "Govind", "Keshava", "Madhusudan", "Vasudeva" etc. Guru Nanak Dev says, "Krishna may be the gods of gods, but still higher is the *Atmann* (self). The self is Vasudeva" (p. 469, Var Asa M. 1). The doctrine of *Avatara* (incarnation) has not been recognised in the *Adi Granth*. The saint-poets used popular mythological names of God like Krishna, Gopal, Govind in their verses. Guru Arjan Dev says, "Krishan, the slayer of Mur demon is the friend of *Gurmukh*, the Enlightened person (p. 98, Majh M. 5).

Krita Age: Name of the first of the four ages of the world. It is also known as *Sat-Yuga* (the age when truth prevailed in the world). Guru Nanak Dev says, "In Satyuga, the Truth and Contentment permeated the human bodies...." Everybody says, "True was this age of truth and the True Lord Manifested Himself as Truth. The human being had Truth in his speech and mind" (p. 1023, Maru M. 1). Guru Amar Das says, "In the Satyuga, everyone spoke Truth. There was Love of God in each heart by the Grace of the Guru. The *Dharma* had all the four legs to stand upon" (p. 880, Ramkali M. 3).

Krodha: Anger. One of the five major vices, the other four being Lust, Greed, Attachment and Ego. Guru Arjan Dev says, "O Anger, the origin of strife, you know no compassion. You have a powerful sway over vicious people, who dance to your tune like monkeys and thereby you have to face punishment at the hands of the messengers of Yama" (p. 1358, Sahaskriti Shlokas).

Kshatriyas: Those belonging to one of the four major castes, i.e. Kshatriya. In a wide sense, they are warriors. According to *Dharma Sutra* of Vasishtha "the lawful occupations of a Kshatriya are three: studying, sacrificing and bestowing gifts". In the words of Guru Nanak Dev "a Kshatriya is one who is a warrior of actions and makes his body of compassion and charity. He sows the seed of charity in the appropriate field. Such a Kshatriya is approved in the Court of the Lord" (p. 1411, Shlok Varan te Vadhik, M. 1). According to Guru Ramdas a Kshatriya performs the action of bravery and is called a warrior (p. 164, Gauri Guareri M. 4). In the times of Guru Nanak Dev, the Kshatriyas had forgotten their Dharma (duty) and taken to the foreign tongue. The distinction of good and bad was no more there and none thought of religious values" (p. 663, Dhanasari M. 1).

Kucajjī: The housewife, who spoils everything by her inappropriate and wrong actions. In the hymn entitled *Kucajjī*, a negligent woman is shown enduring the pangs of separation (Suhi M. 1, p. 762).

Kūṛ, Kūṛiār: *Kūṛ* is an antonym of *Sac*. *Sac* is Truth and eternal. *Kūṛ* is falsehood and mortal. One who indulges in falsehood, is *Kūṛiār*. Guru Nanak Dev says, "The king, his subjects and all the world are false and mortal....The false objects are sweet like honey and they have drowned innumerable beings. O Lord, except you everything is false and mortal" (Var Asa M. 1, p. 468). "Those who are *Kūṛiār* and indulge in falsehood will never achieve any position; they will go to hell with blackened faces (Var Asa M. 1, p. 463).

Kurukshetra: Though a town is situated at this place now, originally it was the battlefield, where the great war i.e. Mahabharata was fought between Kaurvās and Pāndavās. The details of this war are contained in the epic Mahabharata. Bhagavad Gita, the prominent Hindu scripture, took its birth in this battlefield, when Lord Krishna addressed Arjuna beckoning him to perform selfless action (Karma Yoga). In the *Adi Granth* the word Kulkhet has been used for Kurukshetra. The saint Ravidas says, "If one bathes at Kurukshetra at the time of eclipse and makes an offering of his bedecked wife to the gods and listens to all the Smritis with his own ears; but if he calumniates the saints, all these works are of no avail" (p. 875, Gond Ravidas). In one of his hymns, Guru Ramdas has mentioned the visit of Guru Amar Das to Kurukshetra for the spiritual welfare of the visitors (p. 1116, Tukhari M. 4).

Kurus: Kaurvas. The great Indian epic, the Mahabharata mentions two Bharata clans, Kauravas and Pandavas. Out of these two clans, the former was evil-minded and consisted of the family of the blind prince Dhrtarashtra. Pandu, the younger brother of Dhrtarashtra was the father of five sons, who were known as Pandavas. Duryodhana was the eldest of the sons of Dhrtarashtra, who was responsible for the ordeal of Daropadi, whose mention has been made in the *Adi Granth*. Daropadi was the wife of Pandavas, the five brothers; the eldest among them was Yudhishtra.

Kusangat, Kusangī: *Kusangat* is bad company. The person who joins this company is *Kusangī* "Those who sit in a bad company, will always suffer and remain in anguish" (Maru M. 3, p. 1068).

Kūṭan: He who brings together evil persons. According to Kabir, the real *Kūṭan* is one, who repeatedly strikes the mind and in this way releases himself from Yama (Gaund Kabir, p. 872).

L

Lab: Greed. See: *Greed.*

Labour: Bodily or mental toil. One indulges in all kinds of labour and then feels sorry, because he gets no peace without the worship of the Lord (p. 254, Gauri Bawan Akhri M. 5). He who falls at the feet of the stone-god, his labour is of no avail (p. 1160, Bhairo Kabir). Why should we forget the Lord, who gives due reward for our labour? (p. 289, Gauri Sukhmani M. 5). In the society of the saints, the labour is not hard, because you are saved by the mere sight of the saint (p. 272, Gauri Sukhmani M. 5). He alone knows the Path, who labours and shares his earnings with others (p. 1245, Var Sarang M.4 Shlok M. 1).

Labourer: Man, as a labourer, toils all day long just as one threshes the chaff with the thresher and like the labourer forced to toil, he is of no use to his home (p. 712, Todi M. 5). The labourer toils the whole day for his living, but when asked to meditate on the Lord, he shuns it as though a weighty stone has fallen on his head (p. 1143, Bhairo M. 5). The Pandavas wept, when they became labourers (p. 954, Var Ramkali M. 3, Shlok M. 1).

Lachan, Lakhan: Qualities; attributes. The word *Lakhan* has been used in the *Adi Granth* in connection with a housewife. One who is bedecked with (thirty-two) qualities is called *Battīh Sulakhanī* (Asa M. 5, p. 371). The word *Sulakhani* is used for a good housewife and the word *kulakhani* is used for a bad one.

Lakshmī: The consort of Vishnu and goddess of wealth and prosperity. She is said to have arisen from the ocean as one of the fourteen gems, when its waters were churned by the gods and demons together. She is also called "Sri" and, therefore, her husband Vishnu is known as *Srīpatī*. As Lord of Lakshmi, Vishnu is called *Lakhmī Bar*. In the *Adi Granth*, the word Lakhmi has been used several times as meaning 'wealth'. The Lord-God has been described as the Lord of Maya and hence of Lakshmi (which as wealth connotes Maya). Kabir says, "He who loves the Lord of Lakshmi, his sufferings end and he attains bliss" (p. 342, Gauri Bawan Akhri Kabir).

Lālā: Servant; slave. "My mother is your slave (*lālī*) and my father is your slave (*lālā*) and I am the son of your slave (*lālā*). *Lālī* dances and *Lālā* sings and thus I perform your devotion" (Maru M. 1, p. 991). "*Lālā* has forsaken greed and has obtained the Name of the Lord....

Lālā has abandoned ego...*Lālā* has recognised the Lord...Lālā is the slave of the Lord..." (Maru M. 1, p. 1011).

Land: The Landowner is attached to his land just as the addict is attached to his substance of addiction (p. 613, Sorath M. 5). The landowner always fights over his land (p. 288, Gauri M. 5). Guru Arjan Dev says, "If you give away gold in charity and also offer land; if you purify your mind in many ways, but nothing equals the Name of the Lord (p. 1229, Sarang M. 5).

Languages: Several languages and dialects have been used in the *Adi Granth*. Dr. Trumpp is right when he says that the *Adi Granth* is the treasury of the old Hindui dialects. The Sikh Gurus wrote their hymns in various languages and dialects, keeping in view their devotees, who belonged to different areas. They have composed their hymns in Eastern Punjabi, Western Punjabi (Lehndi), Southern Punjabi (Sindhi), Western Apabhramsa i.e. Sahaskriti, Sant Bhasha (Saint Language), Braj Bhasha (Western Hindi), and colloquial Persian. The radical saints, whose verses have been included in the *Adi Granth* lived in different parts of India, therefore even if they composed their verses in the common saint-language, the impact of their regional languages is clearly visible. Jaidev has used Eastern Apabhramsa and Namdev and Trilochan used Southern Apabhramsa. For more information see "A Critical Study of the Adi Granth" by Dr. S.S. Kohli.

Law: According to the *Adi Granth*, the law is *Dharma*. Those who act according to Dharma are called *Dharmī* (lawful) and those who violate Dharma are called sinners. The Lord of Dharma punishes the sinners (p. 138, Var Majh M. 1, Shlok M. 2). For example one who harbours enmity against the person who is never inimical to anybody, violates the law (i.e. Charma), therefore, *Dharma Raja*, in his justice, destroys him (p. 317, Var Gauri M. 4, Pauri M. 5). Only Dharma stands firm in the Iron age and the sinner never lasts long (p. 1098, Var Maru M. 3). Dharma is the flower of the tree of Karma with branches of the Name of the Lord. The fruit, thus, is the knowledge of the Lord (p. 1168, Basant M. 1). The ladder of Dharma is the path of the saints (p. 622, Sorath M. 5). None is Greater than Hari, who considers only the Law (Dharma) (p. 90, Var Sri Rag M. 4).

Law Books, Law Courts, Law Suits: The Law-Books are Dharma Shastras. For a devotee of the Sikh Gurus, the Law-Book is the Sikh Scripture, i.e. the *Adi Granth*, which contains the injunctions enjoined by the Gurus and the Saints. The Law-Court is the Court of the god of

Justice (*Dharma Raja*), before whom the good and bad deeds are presented by the scribes Chitra and Gupta. The merits of the case are judged by the god of Justice himself, who gives due reward for the actions. Guru Amar Das says, "The Dharma Raja, who dispenses the Law of the Lord, has instructions from the Lord to administer the Law, but his dominion is over those guilty souls, who are always absorbed in duality. The enlightened person meditates in his mind on the One Lord, Who is the treasure-house of qualities. The Dharma Raja even serves him..." (p. 38, Sri Rag M. 3).

Lay Devotees: The Buddhist and Jaina devotees, who do not follow the rigorous discipline meant for *Sramanas* are called lay devotees. The life-style of *Sramanas* is brought under criticism in the *Adi Granth*. There is no separate category of laymen according to the discipline enunciated by the *Adi Granth*. This discipline is meant for all. Guru Ram Das says, "The True and Gracious Guru is for ever compassionate. He is without envy and looks upon all as the creatures of the Lord. He wishes well to every one..." (p. 302, Var Gauri M. 4).

Learning-Knowledge: If one learns about the *Tariqah* (Path), then he is a Muslim and if one acquires the learning of Vedas and Puranas, he is a Hindu; but some learning must be attained for the instruction of the mind (p. 340, Gauri Bawan Akhri Kabir). If we have cart-loads of learned books and if our whole company carries nothing else except the loads of books...if we read many of them month after month and year after year, read throughout life with every breath. Only one thing is of account, the remaining is all the futile exercise in ego" (p. 467, Var Asa M. 1). The learned men read and argue in vain, because they do not know that the Substance is within them (p. 152, Gauri M. 1). One reads the text of the Smritis and listens to and studies the Vedas and the Puranas in order to hold his mind, but not knowing the Essence, his mind wanders in many ways (p. 226, Gauri M. 1). By learning alone, the impurities do not leave, you may ask any man of learning.... As the light dispels darkness, similarly the Divine Learning destroys ignorance (p. 39, Sri Rag M. 3).

Legends: An unauthentic story handed down by tradition and popularly regarded as historical. The story of the life of a saint is also called a legend. In the *Adi Granth*, there are several allusions to the old and Pauranic legends which concern the incarnations, sages, saints, good kings, heroes, heroines, bad kings and tyrants. For some references we may see the hymn of the Guru Nanak Dev in Var Ramkali (p. 954,

Var Ramkali M. 3, Shlok M. 1). There is also mention of some incidents from the lives of the saints. e.g. the legend regarding the revivification of the dead cow concerning the saint Namdev (p. 1163, Bhairo Namdev).

Lekh: The Writ on the forehead of each being born in the world. The life is led according to this writ. "Whatever the Creator has recorded in this Writ, must happen" (Ramkali M. 1, Dakhni Oamkar, p. 937). "The Writ of the Lord is there in the head of every being from the very beginning and there is none without this Writ. Only the Lord is without this Writ, Who Creates, Perceives and Orders" (Sorath M. 1, pp. 498-99).

Lekhā: The account of good and bad actions, recorded by Chitra and Gupta, who present this account before *Dharmaraja* (god of Justice). Guru Nanak Dev says, "Listen, O mind, the right instruction. God will call you to render the account, keeping the account-book before Him..." (Ramkali Ki Var M. 3, Shlok M. 1, p. 953). Kabir says, "The life has come to an end and you have to render the account of your actions. The ferocious messengers of Yama have come to take you. What have you gained? and what was your loss?..." (Suhi Kabir, p. 792).

Lepers: Those affected with leprosy, a disease which slowly eats away the body and forms shining white scales on the skin. According to the *Adi Granth*, the mind and body may be said to be afflicted with leprosy (p. 1064, Maru Solhe M. 3). He, who does not seek the Lord, is like the leech which is applied to the body of a leper (p. 1253, Sarang Surdas). Without the Name, one is a leper and blinded by attachment (p. 367, Asa M. 4).

Letters: In the *Adi Granth*, hymns like *Bawan Akhri, Dakhni Oamkar* and *Patti* are based on letters of alphabets. The *Bawan Akhris* of Kabir and Guru Arjan Dev are based on fifty-two letters of Devanagari script, the *Patti* of Guru Nanak Dev is based on Gurmukhi script, the *Patti* of Guru Amar Das is based on Landa Alphabet. *Dakhni Oamkar* is also based on fifty-two letters. For the word 'letter' the word *Akkhar* (Sanskrit *Akshara*) has been used in the *Adi Granth*. Literally, the *Akshara* (that which cannot be destroyed) is the Name of the Lord. According to *Bawan Akhris* and *Dakhni Oamkar*, *om*...(AUM) is the primal letter. Guru Nanak Dev says, "*Oamkar* is He, who created Brahma,...the mountains, the *Yugas* (ages), Vedas, the word...Listen to the meaning of the letter OM, it is indeed the Essence of the three worlds" (pp. 929-30, Ramkali Dakhni Oamkar M. 1). The significance of letters is conveyed by Guru Nanak Dev in *Japuji*: "The Name and Praises are through the letters. The knowledge, songs and eulogies are through the letters; the speech and writings are through the letters and writs of union in our heads are also through the letters" (p. 4, Japuji). The three worlds created by God are manifested through the letters. The Vedas are discerned through the letters. The Shastras, Smritis and Puranas are revealed through the letters. The sounds of subtle Music and the discourses are described through the letters. The path of release and the thoughts of Fear and Doubt are depicted through the letters. The actions, purity and religion are described through the letters. Whatsoever is visible, it is within the sway of letters. Only the transcendent Lord (*Para Brahman*) is unattached (p. 261, Gauri M. 5).

Liar: One who lies; an untruthful person. The devotees are blessed by the Lord and the liars are condemned by him (p. 851, Var Bilawal M. 4). The liars are left behind; having falsehood in their hearts, they are in anguish (p. 302, Var Gauri M. 4). The liars mix with the liars, while the truthful get a seat close to the Guru (p. 314, Var Gauri M. 4). They, who harbour falsehood within themselves, do not love the Truth. If some one utters the Truth, the liar is burnt. Just as a crow feeds upon ordure similarly the liar is satiated with lies (p. 646, Var Sorath M. 4). He, who practises falsehood, transmigrates. (p. 352, Asa M. 1).

Libations: A drink-offering. The libations through mouthfuls of water can be real, if one knows (the significance). The libation of a Pundit is knowledge and that of a Yogi is continence. The libation of a Brahmin is contentment and a householder is charity. The libation of a king is justice and the learned is the concentration on Truth (p. 1240, Var Sarang M. 4)

Liberality: Generosity; munificence. It is a godly quality and the seeker must practise it in order to attain nearness of the Lord. "How can the Giver be evaluated, whose liberality cannot be evaluated" (p. 157, Gauri Poorbi Deepki M. 1). "O Lord, through your Liberality, the interior is illumined and the moon of knowledge shines forth within the body" (p. 765, Suhi Chhant M. 1). But the liberality of human beings is criticised, who while giving alms beg for more and more and seek more honours in this world (p. 466, Var Asa M. 1).

Liberation: Final Emancipation. In Indian philosophy it is termed *Mukti* or *Moksha*. Guru Nanak Dev says, "He can only be called a

Brahmin, who knows Brahman, who practises austerity, contemplation, self-control, good actions, contentment and culture. It is he, who breaks the bonds and attains liberation" (p. 1411, Shlok Varan te Vadhik M. 1). If some one turns his back on the Guru, he does not get liberation.... The liberation can be attained only when he falls at the Guru's feet and the Guru gives him the Word (p. 920, Ramkali Anand M. 3). Kabir says, "The door of liberation (salvation) is narrow, narrower than one-tenth of the sesame seed. The mind is inflated like an elephant, how can then it pass through this door? If one meets such a Guru who, in his Grace blesses him, then the door of salvation opens wide and he passes through it with ease" (p. 509, Var Gujri M. 3, Shlok Kabir). But Guru Amar Das says, "The door of liberation is narrow and he who is very humble passes through it. The mind has become gross on account of ego, how can it pass through this door? When the True Guru meets, the ego leaves and one is illumined with the Light of God. The soul then attains liberation and the state of equipoise" (pp. 509-10, Var Gujri M. 3, Shlok M. 3).

Lie: A false statement made with intent to deceive; a criminal falsehood. Guru Nanak Dev says, "One who tells lies, in fact, eats ordure, but still he goes to preach to others. He, who himself is deceived, will deceive his companions also (p. 140, Var Majh M. 1). How can a mouth, which tells lies, be pure? Cleanliness comes only with the water of the Word. Purity comes with Truth (p. 56, Sri Rag M. 1). The liar loves the liar and forsakes the Lord. (p. 468, Var Asa M. 1).

Life: Life is the bride and the death is the bridegroom, who will marry her and take her away (p. 1377, Shlok Farid). That life is fruitful which ever listens to and remembers the Name of the Lord (pp. 1018-19, Maru M. 5). True life is life in God, contemplation on the Name and the society of the saints (p. 684, Dhanasari M. 5). The life is meaningful only if we see the Lord (p. 1221). You crave for life, while the *Yama* keeps watch on every breath of yours (p. 481, Asa Kabir). Shed your desire for life. The surest sign for the iron age is its approval of the tyranny over life (p. 902, Ramkali M. 1). He, who wants to live life in doubt and attachment, he is a fool of fools (p. 254, Gauri Bawan Akhri M. 5).

Light: In every one there is the Light of the Lord and every one is lighted because of this Light. This Light is revealed through the Guru (p. 663, Dhanasari M. 1, *Aarti*). The Light of the soul ultimately merges in the Light of the Lord (p. 446, Asa M. 4). The Word of the

Guru reveals that it is through the Light of God that all hearts are illumined (p. 509, Var Gujri M. 3). With the collyrium of knowledge given by the Guru, the darkness of ignorance is destroyed (p. 293, Gauri Sukhmani M. 5). Thus knowledge is light. The journey (after death) on which you go in utter darkness, there the Name of the Lord is the Light (p. 264, Gauri Sukhmani M. 5). If a hundred moons and thousand suns arise, with such enormous light, there will still be utter darkness without the Guru (p. 463, Var Asa M. 1, Shlok M. 2). There can be no (light of) knowledge without the Guru (p. 469, Var Asa M. 1).

Likhat Lilār, Likhat Lilāt: The Writ on the forehead. See: *Lekh.*

Lion:The Omnipotent Lord has kept the opposites at the same place for example earth and water, wood and fire, the goat and the lion (p. 735, Suhi M. 4). So long as the lion lives in the forest, the forest does not blossom. But when the Jackal devours the lion then the forest yields the flowers and fruit (p. 1161, Bhairo Kabir). In these verses the lion is the ego and the Jackal is humility. When one is puffed up with ego, there are no blossoms of godly qualities and when it is subdued, the qualities spring up (p. 1161, Bhairo Kabir). Can the rider of a cow pursue a tiger? (p. 198, Gauri M. 5). When the Lord showers His mercy, the cow is led to the pasture by the tiger (for grazing) (p. 898, Ramkali M. 5). If the Lord desires, the lions are made to eat grass (p. 144, Var Majh M. 1). The powerful lion kills hundreds of deer and many others eat his leavings. Becoming powerful, he does not contain himself in his den, but when he breathes his last, he regrets (p. 1286, Var Malar M. 1). If the powerful kills the powerful, there can be no grief in the mind, but when a powerful lion pounces upon a herd of cattle and kills it, the Master must be answerable (p. 360, Asa M. 1)

Liv: Concentration. "The body is abased without the true concentration (*Sāci Liv*)" (Ramkali M. 3, Anand, p. 917). The concentration (*Liv*) ends, when the order of desire and *maya* prevails (Ramkali M. 3, Anand, p. 921).

Lives-Souls: Plural of life connoting living beings. The proper Indian term for 'lives' is "jivas". Guru Amar Das says, "The Word is the life of all the lives, because through it, one realises the Lord" (p. 1250, Var Sarang M. 4, Shlok M. 3). In all lives, the Lord/Sovereign Pervades, keeping Himself Detached (p. 1038, Maru M. 1). O Lord, Being Life of all lives, you know everything (p. 965, Var Ramkali M. 5).

Living Beings-Beings: Jivas. See: *Jivas* and *Lives*.

Lobh: Greed. See: *Greed*.

Logic: The branch of philosophy that treats of the forms of thinking in general, and especially of inference and scientific method. The *Adi Granth* deals with metaphysical and mystical content, hence it is concerned with logic. However, some statements here and there in support of mystical contentions are logical. For example: "O saints, See the Glory of the Lord that one is rewarded according to his actions" (p. 653, Var Sorath M. 4). In the Iron Age, the body is the field of Karma; whatever one sows in it, one reaps accordingly. The Justice of the Lord is not based on mere talk; if one takes poison, he dies instantly" (p. 308, Var Gauri M. 4).

Logos: In classical Greek *Logos* signifies both the "Word" and "Reason". When it is God's Word, it denotes the declaration of revelation of the Divine Will, and specifically the Christian Gospel as the utterance of the Divine Plan of Salvation. In respect of the *Adi Granth*, Logos connotes the revelation of the Divine Will through God's Word. Guru Nanak Dev has called the bani "the Word of God" (p. 722, Tilang M. 1). The *Bani* (Word) has come from God, which has dispelled all my woes (p. 628, Sorath M. 5). "The Lord has Uttered the Word, which has dispelled all my woes and Truth and righteousness have flowed within me" (p. 781, Suhi M. 5). Thus the *Adi Granth* is Logos-incarnate.

Loka: The world; a part of the universe; the sphere of a god or goddess. It is also called a loa or bhavan. The popular Hindu idea of three Lokas or Bhavanas is found in the *Adi Granth* (See p. 328, Gauri Kabir and p. 931, Ramkali M. 1). There is also mention of spheres of various gods (p. 692, Dhanasari Kabir). The seven upper and seven nether regions of the universe are mentioned as the fourteen Bhavanas (or Lokas) (p. 840, Bilawal M. 1).

Lokapalas-gods: Literally *Lokapala* means the Guardian of the region. According to Hindu mythology, there are four guards of the cardinal and four of the Intermediate points of the world. The Lokapalas are Indra in the East, Agni in the Southeast, Yama in the South, Surya in the Southwest, Varuna in the West, Vayu in the Northwest, Kubera in the North and Soma in the Northeast. There is direct or indirect reference to nearly all these gods in the *Adi Granth*, but there is no mention of their authority as Lokapalas. It is only the Lord Himself Who is the Protector, Sustainer and Guardian of the Universe. "O Lord, you are my Protector at all the places" (p. 103, Majh M. 5).

Lokayata: A Charvaka; a materialist. The word "Lokayata" literally means "belonging to the world of sense". Lokayata is a staunch materialist and regards only the four principal elements i.e. earth, water, fire and air as valid. He has no belief in the soul and God. Thus he is basically and hypothetically far removed from the thought of the *Adi Granth.* Namdev says, "Those, who do not meditate on the Lord, I do not like to see even their sight" (p. 1163, Bhairo Namdev).

Longevity: Long life. Even if one lives for a hundred years, ultimately the body will be reduced to dust (p. 1380, Shlok Farid). Even if one lives to eat for a whole century, only that day is approved, when he realises the Lord (p. 350, Asa M. 1). Even if one lives a hundred thousand years and loves a hundred thousand people, there may be many pleasures and desires, but when separation comes, it comes in an instant and ends all pleasures. Even if one tastes sweets for a hundred years, thereafter he has to taste the bitter (p. 1243, Var Sarang M. 4, Shlok M. 1).

Lord: In the *Adi Granth*, God has been addressed as Sahib, Malik, Khasam, Thakur etc., which are the equivalents of the Lord. The Lord or Brahman, is the Lord of the whole Universe. He is beyond time and space, therefore He is called the non-temporal and non-spatial Lord. He is Omnipresent, Omnipotent and Omniscient. He is the only Lord and all the individuals are his wives (p. 933, Ramkali M. 1). See: *Brahman.*

Lord of Beings: Guru Arjan Dev, addressing the Lord, says, "You are the Master (Lord) of all, all are under your shelter" (p. 520, Var Gujri M. 5). The Lord of all Abides with all at all times, but that person is rare who realises Him by the Grace of the Guru (p. 112, Majh M. 3).

Lotus: It is a symbol of purity in life. In the *Adi Granth*, we have its figurative usage. Since the lotus remains unstained by the water on which it floats, that person is identified with lotus, who remains unsoiled in the world of *maya.* "The knower of Brahman remains for ever unattached like the lotus, which abides in water quite detached from it" (p. 272, Gauri Sukhmani M. 5). "As the lotus abides detached in water and the duck floats on the streams, similarly one crosses the ocean of *Saṁsāra*, by attuning his mind to the Word" (p. 938, Ramkali M. 1, Siddh Goshta). The feet, hand and eyes of the Lord and other Pure ones are often identified with the Lotus. The Tantriks describe the psychic centres in the body with coloured lotuses. The mother-goddess Lakshmi has been called *Kavalā* (lotus-goddess) and thus her husband Vishnu is *Kavalā-Kant*. Since the Lord is the Master of *maya* (Lakshmi), He has been called as *Kavalā-Kantā* in the *Adi Granth* (p. 650, Var Sorath M. 4).

Love: The poetry of the *Adi Granth* is the poetry of love. It is the love of the Lord, which the seeker/devotee should imbibe for love's sake and without any other motive. It is selfless love. Such love is manifested through various moods of the devotee. But the highest form of love, according to the *Adi Granth*, is the remembrance of the Name of the Lord. "Love the Lord like the lotus and the water...like the fish and the water...like the *Chatrik* and the cloud...like the milk and the water...like the *Chakvi* and the sun" says Guru Nanak (p. 59, Sri Rag M. 1). Such mystical love is called *Bhakti* (devotion). The devotion of Hari is the love of Hari (p. 28, Sri Rag M. 3). In Bhakti, love and Fear of the Lord abide side by side (p. 911, Ramkali M. 3). If you want to play the game of love, then place the head on the palm of the hand. If one sets his feet on the path of love, he should not hesitate to sacrifice his life (p. 1412, Shlok Varan te Vadhik M. 1). The lover, who wants to have a sight of the Lord, has no desire for the heaven or mukti (p. 360. Asa M. 1). The cup of Lord's Love is received only by His Grace (p. 947, Var Ramkali M. 3). "One who is in love, he is ever awake; he feels the pangs of separation. He, whose heart is pierced through with the shafts of love, no physician can cure him (p. 993, Maru M. 1). The sight of the Lord is the only cure.

Lust: Sensuous appetite or desire, as sinful. The lust and anger weaken the body (p. 932, Ramkali Dakhni Oamkar M. 1). The sinner keeps lust in his heart, therefore the mercurial mind cannot stabilise. One may be a Yogi, a Jangam or a Sannyasi, he is caught in the noose of lust (p. 1186, Basant M. 9). One must run away from lust, anger and the company of the wicked (p. 219, Gauri M. 9). See: *Kāma*.

Luminaries: The sun, moon and stars are the luminaries in the sky. Kabir says, "Who has painted those stars which we see in the sky?" (p. 329, Gauri Kabir). The Lord Creates the sun and the moon, which are Illumined by his Own Light (p. 1279, Var Malar M. 1). The Lord Created the sun and the moon, which are ever on the move (p. 580, Vadhans M. 1). He, whose canopy extends to all the corners of the Universe...his lamps are the sun and the moon... (p. 1292, Malar Namdev). "O Lord, the sun and the moon are your two lamps, and the moon merges in the house of the sun" (p. 1033, Maru M. 1). He (The Lord) is the One Alone in the sun, moon and stars (p. 294, Gauri

Sukhmani M. 5). The sun and the moon move millions of miles in the Fear of the Lord (p. 464, Var Asa M. 1).

Lunar: Pertaining to the moon. There are two poems in the *Adi Granth* entitled *Thitti*, whose stanzas are based on the lunar days—the first is by Kabir in Raga Gauri (pp. 343-344) and the second is by Guru Nanak Dev in Raga Bilawal (pp. 838-840). The poem of Kabir ends on the fifteenth day as the full moon day, but the poem of Guru Nanak Dev ends on the fifteenth day as Amavasya (the dark night). The fasts kept on lunar days are of no avail (p. 1099, Var Maru M. 5).

Luxury: Something which conduces to enjoyment over and above the necessities of life. Anguish is the result of attachment to pleasures and luxurious life. Becoming diseased with indulgence, one is wasted away (p. 1034, Maru M. 1). One who indulges in luxuries, gets agony and disease (p. 1189, Basant M. 1).

Lying: Telling lies. Those who indulge in lying, they do not like the truth. If anyone speaks truth, they feel hurt. They are satiated with the food of lying (p. 646, Var Sorath M. 4). Those who indulge in lying, they are like dogs and swines (p. 1029, Maru M. 1). Their dirt of lying can be washed away by the Name of the Lord (p. 950, Var Ramkali M. 3). One who has been given the pill of lying and is thus intoxicated, he forgets death and revels only for a few days (p. 15, Sri Rag M. 1).

M

Mādhava: (Mā—Maya+Dhava=Lord, husband). The Lord of Maya or Lakshmi i.e. Vishnu. This word is also used for Krishna, an incarnation of Vishnu. But in the *Adi Granth*, this Name is given to Brahman, who is considered the Lord of Maya. In the verses of the saint-poets of the *Adi Granth*, this word has taken the form of 'Mādhav' or 'Madhau'.

Madhūsūdan: (Madhu=the name of Rakshasa+ Sūdan=the killer). The killer of the Rakshasa named Madhu i.e. Lord Krishna. But in the *Adi Granth*, this Name is applied to God.

Mad Man: According to Guru Nanak Dev, the mind of the individual is maddened by the mad duality (Prabhati M. 1, p. 1342). He who goes astray towards delusion becomes mad (Ramkali M. 1, p. 935). But the true seekers really become mad in the Love of the Lord. Guru Nanak Dev became mad in his Love for the Lord (Maru M. 1, p. 991). People say that Kabir has become mad, but the Lord knows the secret of his madness (Bhairo Kabir, p.1158). Kabir says again, "If I am mad, I am Thine, O Lord! how can the people know my secret? (*ibid*). Guru Nanak Dev says, "He may be considered mad, who becomes mad in the Fear of the Lord.... He may be considered mad, who has only one task; he recognises the *Hukam* of the Lord and has no other second wisdom. He may be considered mad, who Loves the Lord and who, in utmost humility, considers the whole world superior to him" (Maru M. 1, p. 991). The devotee, who is mad in Love for the Lord, does not care for anyone else. He laughs in Love and weeps in Love and also observes silence (Var Asa M. 1, p. 473).

Magi: In the *Adi Granth*, God is said to be the Magi, whose jugglery can only be visualised through the help of the Guru (Maru M. 3, p. 1061). He (God) as a Juggler sounded his drum and the whole world came to see His Jugglery. When the Juggler ended His Show, He became absorbed in Himself (Sorath Kabir, p. 655).

Magic: The world is a magical show of the Lord (Asa Kabir, pp. 481-82). Ravidas also thinks in the same manner (Asa Ravidas, p. 487). On human level, the charms, spells and incantations have been decried by the Gurus and the saint-poets. Guru Nanak Dev says, "The self-willed (Manmukh) wanders uselessly in the solitude. By reciting the charms and incantations in the cremation ground, he is being misled and robbed (Ramkali M. 1, Siddh Goshta, p. 941).

Magician: See: *Magi*.

Mahabhūtas: The five gross elements i.e. Ether, Air, Fire, Water and Earth. Kabir wants the human beings to adopt the peculiar quality of each element i.e. detachment from Ether, equal treatment and service from Air, contentment and enlightenment from Fire, purity and serenity from Water and a modesty and forgiveness from the Earth (Gauri Kabir, p. 327). The Samkhyan and Pauranic doctrine about the evolutionary creation of the five elements has been accepted by Guru Nanak Dev. From the True Lord arose Ether, air was created from Ether, fire from air, water from fire and earth from water. Guru Nanak Dev describes this process in a couplet. He says, "From the True Lord came the air, from air the water and from water the three worlds" (Sri Rag M. 1, p. 19). After creating the five elements, the Lord created the whole world (Suhi M. 4, p. 736). The human body is composed of five elements (Maru M. 1, p. 1030). The mind was created from the five elements (Asa M. 1, p. 415).

Mahādeva: The name of Rudra or Shiva, the god of destruction in the Hindu Trinity. The Gurus and saint-poets of the *Adi Granth* are devotees of Brahman or the Supreme Lord. They have no faith in gods and goddesses. Therefore, they have critically viewed the actions and also the heritage of the priests of Vaishnavas, Shaivas and Shaktas. Namdev addresses the Pundit about Mahādeva: "O Pundit! I saw your Mahādeva riding on a bull. The meal was prepared at the house of Modi. Not relishing the food, the god caused the death of his son (through a curse)—(Gaund Namdev, p. 875). Guru Arjan Dev says that the hermit Mahādeva, who smeared his body with ashes, could not know the limits of Brahman (Suhi M. 5, p. 747).

Mahat: According to Samkhya, *Mahat* (i.e. *Buddhi* or intellect) is the resultant evolute, when *Purusha* and *Prakriti* came into contact with each other. This term has been used by Guru Nanak Dev in the Shaloka at the end of *Japuji*. He says, "The Air is the Guru, the Water is the Father, the Earth is the Mother. When they and the *Mahat* come together, the whole world, being nursed by day and night, appears in action"(p. 8). The activity starts, when the conscious energy is infused in the combination of elements.

Mahavratas: It is the name of the vow taken by the Shaiva Kapalikas and because of this they are known as Mahavratins. Vrata is a solemn vow for practising chastity and performing meritorious acts. Many types of vows and observances of meritorious actions cannot equal the meditation on the Name of the Lord (p. 265, Gauri Sukhmani M. 5).

Mahayajna: The Great Sacrifice. The following *Yajnas* are considered *mahayajnas—Brahmayajana* (sacred study), *pitriyajna* (libations to the manes), *devayajna* (burnt offerings to the gods), *baliyajna* (offering to all creatures), *uriyajna* (hospitality), *Prajapatiyajana* (propagation of offspring) and *satyajna* (observance of truth). In the *Adi Granth*, no significance is attached to any *yajna* or *Mahayajna*. Only Guru's Word is supreme. King Bali perfomed the *yajnas* in ego, he was condemned to the underworld because he was bereft of the Word of true Guru (p. 224, Gauri M. 1). The *Yajnas, Havana*, the pious conduct and austerities subject one's body to suffering. One is not emancipated without the Name of the Lord..." (p. 1127, Bhairo M. 1).

Maheshvara: The Great Lord. This epithet is generally applied to Lord Shiva. Guru Arjan Dev addresses the Lord thus: "You alone are Brahma, *Shiva*, Mahesh, Indra, the Siddha and the Muni. They are all contained in your presence alone" (p. 534, Devgandhari M. 5). "Neither Brahma, nor Mahesh (Shiva), nor Indra, nor Siddhas, nor Munis have found your end" (p. 822, Bilawal M. 5). Even Brahma, Mahesh (Shiva), Indra, the Siddhas, the Munis all seek to be blessed with the devotion of the Lord" (p. 1322, Kalyan M. 5).

Maheshvari: The Supreme goddess or the Shakti of Maheshvara (Lord Shiva). She is known by several names e.g. Durga, Parvati etc. The *Adi Granth* has rejected all the gods and goddesses. For Guru Nanak Dev, only the Guru is his Shiva, Vishnu, Brahma and the Mother Parvati (p. 2, Japuji). Guru Arjan Dev says, "O Lord, Your mystery was not revealed to the goddesses" (p. 894, Ramkali M. 5).

Māiā: (Maya). See: *Maya*.

Maiden: Maid; a young unmarried woman; virgin. Farid says, "A maiden has a longing (to be married) but after marriage she suffers because of her involvement (in worldly affairs). Now she repents, but she cannot become a maiden again" (p. 1381, Shlok Farid). Talking lovingly to her friends about her would-be Lord, the maiden feels shy and covers her face, when the Lord comes to her house. Similarly I have obtained my Lord-God through the word of the Guru (p. 1203, Sarang M. 5). The maiden, who bedecks herself, cannot enjoy without her Lord (p. 792, Suhi Kabir).

Male and Female Creation: Guru Arjan Dev says, "O Lord, You have Created both the sides—*Shiva* (the Male creation) and *Shakti* (the female creation)". *Shiva* and *Shakti* also mean *Purusha* and *Prakriti* (p. 1096, Var Maru Dakhne M. 5). Man and woman are lured away by lust and do not know the way of the rememberance of the Name of the Lord (pp. 245-46 Gauri M. 3). When man and woman meet at night, they enjoy the flesh. We are conceived in flesh and born in flesh....All men, all women are born of flesh (pp. 1289-90, Var Malar M. 1).

Mamtā: Mineness. See: *Ego*, *Aham*, *Ahamkāra*.

Man: Human being. He is the best creation of the Lord. Guru Arjan Dev addresses the man thus: "All other forms of existence are at your service; you are the overlord of this earth. You have gold, silver and wealth with you, but the lust has disturbed your way of life" (p. 374, Asa M. 5). O Man, Your Lord has created your body in accordance with his Order, but you know that it will certainly be reduced to dust. Why are you then proud of such a possession? You are a guest of three seers of cereals per day. Other things are with you only as a trust. You are Ordure, bone, blood wrapped up in skin. Can this be the object of ego?" (p. 374, Asa M. 5). Guru Tegh Bahadur says, "O man, imbibe this truth that this world is a dream. It takes no time to shatter it. This wall of sand built with care can only stay for a very brief period. O ignorant one, do not involve yourself in short-lived pleasures of *maya*. Become wise, because still nothing has gone wrong. Contemplate on your Lord" (p. 633, Sorath M. 9).

Manas: Mind. The dirt of ego puffs up the mind and it becomes like an elephant. It cannot pass through the door of Nirvana, which is much narrower than the sesame seed" (p. 1367, Shalok Kabir). The mind in its original form is identical with the soul. The Guru says, "O mind, you are light, realise your source" (p. 441, Asa M. 3). The dirt of ego has blackened the mind in the course of several births (p. 651, Var Sorath M. 3). In order to control the mind, its reins should be tightened. It should be held tightly in grip like the ends of churning rope (p. 728, Suhi M. 4). It is not an easy job to bring the mind under control. The great sages have even failed in their attempts. It is mercurial in nature and always flies like a falcon (p. 776, Suhi M. 4). When the devotee follows strictly the discipline ordained by the Guru, he comes to know the real nature of mind. He realises that the mind is like an intoxicated elephant and only the goad of the Guru can give it a new life (p. 221, Gauri M. 1). The Grace of the Lord and the Guru plays a great part in the conquest of mind (p. 298, Gauri M. 5). When the mind is conquered. The Lord is realised and the whole world is conquered (p. 256, Gauri M. 5). This is the real act of bravery. The Guru is very emphatic about the purity of mind. Kabir says, "My mind has become pure like the waters of the Ganges. The Lord follows me calling 'Kabir, Kabir'" (p. 1367, Shlok Kabir).

Mānav Ektā: (*Manukhī Ektā*). The oneness of all the humanity. "We are the children of the same One Father" (Sorath M. 5, p. 611). "All are called co-sharers, because none is without Thee" (Majh M. 5, p. 97). Firstly the Lord Created Light and all are the beings of His Creation. The whole world emerged from That Light. Whom should we call good or bad? (Prabhati Kabir, p. 1349).

Manes: The defied souls of the departed ancestors. Kabir says, "No respect was given to the manes, when they were alive, but after death the people make offerings in their name" (p. 332, Gauri Bairagan Kabir). The fearless Yogi himself swims across and saves even his manes" (p. 223, Gauri M. 1). Whereas contemplating on the Lord, we are rid of all our sins, even our manes are also redeemed (p. 496, Gujri M. 5). See: *Fathers*.

Mankind: According to the *Adi Granth*, the whole mankind should be considered as one. The same Lord abides in humanity, irrespective of the regional difference in physical forms, therefore none is superior to others. Sheikh Farid says, "The Creator lives in His Creation and the Creation lives in God." Whom should we call bad, when there is none without God" (p. 1381, Shlok Farid). Guru Angad Dev says, "The Lord Himself Creates all and makes everyone a distinct entity, then whom should we call bad, when the Same one Lord Pervades all" (pp. 1237-38, Var Sarang M. 4, Shalok M. 2).

Manmat: Instruction of mind. "Fear of the Lord is of great weight, but *manmat* is light and babbling (Gauri Guareri M.1, p.151). "One does not get peace in ego. *Manmat* (full of ego) is false. Only the Lord is True (Gauri Guareri M. 1, p. 222).

Manmukh: One who follows the instruction of the mind. The word *Manmukh* meaning self-willed person is an antonym of *Gurmukh* (who follows the discipline of the Guru). *Manmukh* only talks and is without discipline (Bilawal M. 1, p. 831). According to Guru Amar Das, the conduct of *Manmukh* is this: He does not remember the Name of the Lord and does not concentrate on the Word (Var Gujri M. 3, p. 509). *Manmukh* is absorbed in *durmat* (evil designs) and duality. There is darkness of attachment within him (Gujri M. 4, p. 507). *Manmukh* is the field of suffering; he sows suffering and eats suffering (Var Ramkali M. 3, p. 947). The friendship of *Manmukh* depends on *maya* (Var Ramkali M. 5, p. 959). He who moves in the company of a *Manmukh*, his face is blackened and stained (Shlok Varan te Vadhik

M. 3, p. 1418). *Manmukh*, the poor one, does not know the *Hukam* (Laws) of the Lord and always acts in ego (Shlok Varan te Vadhik M. 4, p. 1423).

Mantar: (Mantra). See: *Mantras*.

Mantras: The *Adi Granth* has decried all those mantras (incantations; spells), which are recited for the fulfilment of certain worldly wishes. The mantras of the Tantriks are nothing more than hypocrisy or guile. Guru Nanak Dev says, "I do not know the hypocrisies of Tantras and Mantras. My mind is only pleased with the Name of the Lord" (p. 766, Suhi M. 1). The real *mantra* is the Name of the Lord. Since the Guru gives this mantra to the devotee, it is known as Guru-mantra. A few words mentioning the attributes of Brahman, which are given in the very beginning of the *Adi Granth* and form a part of *Japuji* are called *Mool Mantra* (the preliminary mantra). This mantra occurs hundreds of times in the *Adi Granth*. There is also mention of *Bīja Mantra* in Sikhism. This word occurs in the Sukhmani and the Swayyas of the bards. Guru Arjan Dev says, "He who listens to and contemplates on the Name of the Lord, all his maladies disappear. He recites the great Mantra and sings the praises of the Lord" (p. 814, Bilawal M. 5).

Mard: The man; the ideal man. "He is indeed a *Mard* (an ideal man), on whom the Graces of the Lord have been showered (Maru M. 5, p. 1084).

Mārfat: Knowledge; divine knowledge. This is one of the spiritual stages of a Sufi. Guru Arjan Dev says, "O *Abdālā* (devotee), *Mārfat* is the annihilation of the mind (Maru M. 5, p. 1083).

Mārg (Mārag): The Path. Guru Nanak Dev says, "If you want to tread the Path of Love, you should not hesitate to sacrifice your head" (Shlok Varan te Vadhik, p. 1412). Sheikh Farid says, "Our road is very disappointing. It is sharper than the double-edged sword and very narrow. My Path lies on that road" (Suhi Farid, p. 794). "The Path on which the soul treads after death quite alone, there the Name of the Lord gives comfort....The Path whose mileage cannot be counted, there the Name of the Lord sustains you" (Gauri Sukhmani M. 5, p. 264).

Market: In the *Adi Granth*, there is mention of the market place, where the actors play their part singing like kings and queens and talking rot (p. 464, Var Asa M. 1). Guru Arjan Dev has identified this world with a canopied market where the traders, are busy in their trades. There is one most precious commodity. He, who purchases it, is most fortunate

(p. 965, Var Ramkali M. 5). In several verses of the *Adi Granth*, there is mention of those traders, who trade in godly qualities and the Name of the Lord.

Marriage: The day on which the bride is to be married is pre-determined. According to Sheikh Farid, the life is the bride and death is the bridegroom. The bridegroom will come to marry the bride and take her away at the appointed time (p. 1377, Shalok Farid). The life at the parents' home is very short, the virgin has ultimately to go to the house of her in-laws and the Lord (p. 23, Sri Rag M. 1). But at various places in the *Adi Granth*, the marriage of the soul with the Lord has been described. The hymn containing the description of four *lāvān* (circumambulations) by Guru Ram Das mentions the four steps of ascent towards the Lord i.e. the practice of righteousness in the world, the company of the saints, Detachedness and the state of equipoise (pp. 773-74, Suhi M. 4). In the fourth round, the sadhak meets the Lord. Guru Ram Das has described the whole process of marriage in another hymn, mentioning the marriage party and the dowry. (p.p 78-79 Sri Rag M. 4, Chhant). The hymn of Guru Nanak Dev in Rag Suhi (pp. 765-66) also depicts such a marriage. The saint Kabir has also described his own marriage with the Lord in his own distinct style (p. 482, Asa Kabir).

Martial Law: Military Government, by which the ordinary law is suspended and the military authorities are empowered to arrest and punish the offenders at their discretion. According to the *Adi Granth*, the violence of any type is decried. This earth has been created for the saints (p. 1374, Shalok Kabir). The army of the saints consists of unconquerable warriors, whose coat of mail is humility and the praises of the Lord are their weapons. (p. 1356, Shlok Sahaskriti).

Mās: Meat. See: *Meat*.

Mat (Mati): Advice; instruction. "O ignorant one, follow the instructions of the Guru. Without devotion many wise men have been drowned" (Gauri Sukhmani M. 5, p. 288). "Abandon the advice of the mind and forget duality. In this way, you will realise the lord and no trouble will come to you" (Suhi Chhant M. 1, p. 763).

Mate-Wife: A habitual companion; a suitable associate. Guru Arjan Dev says, "In the dreadful forest (of the world), I have found a companion, who is the dispellar of sorrows and He is the Name of the Lord (p. 519, Var Gujri M. 5). The saint Dhanna desires to have good mate (wife) in house (p. 695, Dhanasari Dhanna). The wife with folded hands requests her mate (husband) to remain with her (for ever) (p. 1073 Maru M. 5). In this case the wife is the body and her mate is the soul.

Materialists: Those who believe that nothing exists except matter and its movements and modifications. For the materialists there are only four elements i.e. earth, air, fire and water. They have no belief in God, soul and the world hereafter. Such atheists are known as Charvakas. Since the *Adi Granth* believes in the Omnipresent, Omnipotent and Omniscient Lord, it has condemned the materialists who waste away their precious birth. Guru Amar Das says, "The *Manmukh* (egocentric) is ignorant, evil-minded and egoist. There is anger within him; he wastes his intellect in a gamble. He practises falsehood and sin. What does he hear and what does he speak? He is blind and deaf and by missing the right path he wanders in wilderness. Such a blind egocentric comes and goes repeatedly. Without meeting the True Guru he gets nowhere and functions according to Lord's Writ" (p. 314, Var Gauri M. 4, Shalok M. 3).

Matter: The substance, of which a physical object is made. Guru Arjan Dev says, "The matter in the form of precious stones, pearls, gold and silver is like dust (p. 47, Sri Rag M. 5). When the Guru says, "Nothing is born and nothing dies" (p. 281, Gauri Sukhmani M. 5), the Guru seems to suggest the scientific truth that the matter is indestructible.

Maulā: Allah; The Muslim Name of God. Guru Nanak Dev says, "He is *Maulā*, Who has Evolved the world and given it vitality (Sri Rag M. 1, p. 24).

Mauna, Maunī: The vow of silence. Writing about various ascetic orders, Guru Arjan Dev says, "*Maunī* (the man of silence observes *mauna* (silence)" (p. 71, Sri Rag M. 5). Guru Nanak Dev says, "Sunk in silence, the *Mauni* wastes his precious birth. How can he wake up from his sleep without the Guru?" (p. 467, Var Asa M. 1). "Though the ascetic keeps silence and remains aloof but within his heart is the knot of desire" (p. 1003, Maru M. 5). I observed the vow of silence and used my hands as a bowl. I remained naked in the forest. I visited the holy places, the river-banks and the whole earth, but could not absolve myself of the duality (pp. 641-42, Sorath M. 5).

Maut: Death. See: *Death*.

Māyā: An Indian metaphysical concept, giving explanation about appearance and reality. It creates ignorance (*Avidya*) and the false appears as true. According to the *Adi Granth, Maya* is the power which takes us away from Brahman. We forget the Lord because of attachment and duality (p. 921, Ramkali M. 3, Anand). It is not a separate ultimate reality, it has been created by Brahman (p. 480, Asa Kabir). *Maya* is the principal of illusion. The three *gunas* are created through *maya*. When Brahman comes into contact with *maya*, He is called Immanent (*vikaravartin*) and is known as Ishwara. Guru Arjan Dev says, "Whosoever loves *maya* is devoured by it. Whosoever finds comfort in it, is greatly frightened by it. Because of it, the brothers, friends and relatives quarrel with each other. By the Grace of the Guru, I have subdued it. It is subdued by the person with true knowledge (p. 370, Asa M. 5). *Maya* is the bondage for *Jiva* and its main functionary is ego. The world of *maya* is the world of three *gunas*. Brahma, Vishnu and Shiva, being the representatives of three *gunas*, are the children of *maya*, who is called Lakshmi, the consort of the Lord. *Maya* is also said to be clinging to the world like a she-serpent. (p. 510, Var Gujri M. 3). *Maya* as fortune is fickle and the honour gained through it is short-lived (p. 429, Asa M. 3). A serviteur of *maya* is sans eyes and sans ears (p. 313, Var Gauri M. 3). *Maya* leads *Jiva* towards transmigration. It is a noose for the *Jiva*. *Maya* can be described as indescribable (*anirvachaniya*). This shows that it cannot be said whether *maya* is real or unreal. The unreal can serve to awaken us to the real like the snake in a dream.

Māyāvāda: This doctrine came into existence with Shankara in the ninth century AD Shankara's position is: "Brahm Satyam Jagan Mithya Jivo Brahmaiva na parah". It means that Brahman is the only reality; the world is an illusion or a false appearance; the individual soul is identical with Brahman. This principal of illusion is known as *Māyā*. *Maya* performs two function i.e. *Āvarana* (covering up) and *Vikshepa* (throwing out). The first is like a veil which conceals something. The second is the creative or projecting power, which builds upon the defects brought about by the beguiling power.

Māyāvādin: One who holds the theory of illusion. The Māyāvādin, who is lured by *māyā*, gathers the potion of illusion (p. 930, Ramkali M. 1, Dakhni Oamkar). The delusion of *maya* is born of ignorance, then how can one find the Path leading towards the Lord? (p. 247, Gauri M. 3).

Meals: Though there is no mention of the number of meals which an individual should eat during the day, it is clearly stated that too much eating and gluttony should be avoided. Guru Nanak Dev says, "If one eats more he increases the waste matter within (the body) (p. 1331, Prabhati M. 1). According to Guru Arjan Dev, he, who eats well and commits evil, his life is like a field of poison (p. 105, Majh M. 5).

Mean: Occupying a middle or an intermediate place. The doctrine of the mean or the Middle Path had earlier been propagated by Buddhism. This doctrine calls upon the men of the world to avoid two extremes i.e. over-indulgence on the one hand and self-mortification on the other. The *Adi Granth* also gives credence to this view. Whereas it lays down that suffering and agony results from luxurious life (p. 1034, Maru M. 1), it also decries rigorous ascetic practices (p. 1285, Var Malar M. 1). Sikhism follows the mean or the middle path. It does not allow an individual either to renounce the world or to jump in the field like an unbridled horse. Even in the matter of wealth, one should neither have more nor less than the amount required for leading an honourable life. More wealth creates anxiety for its protection and its scarcity results in wanderings in its pursuit (p. 1019, Maru M. 5).

Measures: Size or quantity ascertained or ascertainable by measuring. In the *Adi Granth*, Several measures have been mentioned. The cloth was measured by *Gaz* (Yard)—(p. 475, Asa Kabir), distance was measured by *kos* (about one and a half mile)—(p. 464, Var Asa M. 1), and the corn was measured by *Paaee* (a measure of 25 seers)—(p. 465, Var Asa M. 1).

Meat: The flesh of animals used for food. The *Adi Granth* lays emphasis on non-injury to living beings, therefore killing of animals and fowls for food has no justification. Kabir says, "He says that God is in all, but still he kills life." Guru Nanak Dev says, "The fool quarrels over the idea of 'eating or not eating meat' he is without any knowledge or contemplation. Which is the flesh and which is vegetable? And which food is sinful?...Those, whose teachers are blind eat the uneatables and do not eat what is to be eaten" (pp. 1289-90, Var Malar M.1).

Medicine: A medicament, especially one taken internally. According to the *Adi Granth*, the Name of the Lord is the medicine for the diseased world (p. 627, Dhanasari M. 1). "Pleasures cause the disease, for which suffering is the medicine," says Guru Nanak Dev (p. 469, Var Asa M. 1). A doctor may be said to be wise, who diagnoses the correct disease and knows the real medicine (p. 148, Var Majh M. 1, Shlok M. 2).

Meditation: The religion of the *Adi Granth* is the religion of devotion and meditation. One must meditate on the Lord throughout his life.

Kabir says, "So long as you are not aged and diseased, so long as the death has not overpowered your body, so long as your speech does not fail, O mind meditate on the Lord. If you do not meditate on Him now, then when will you do it? You will not be able to meditate, when the end comes" (p. 1159, Bhairo Kabir). The first Octavo of *Sukhmani* gives in detail the merits of meditation e.g. "Meditation of the Lord is the highest of the deeds, through which myriads obtain release, through which the thirst (of desires) is quenched, through which one becomes all-knowing, through which the fear of death goes away, through which all the desires are fulfilled, through which the dirt of the mind is cleansed and the Nectar of the Name of Lord is absorbed in the mind" etc. (p. 263, Gauri Sukhmani M. 1).

Memory: The faculty by which things are remembered. Guru Nanak Dev says, "Useless are the pleasures of food, drink and other enjoyments, unless one cherishes the memory of the Lord in his heart (p. 351, Asa M. 1). According to Guru Arjan Dev, if one cherishes the memory of the Lord in his heart in diverse circumstances, the hot wind will not touch him, he gets eternal rule, his body and mind become peaceful and he is saved in the twinkling of an eye (p. 70, Sri Rag M. 5). Sheikh Farid says, "Whatever was never in memory that came to pass. Such is the doing of the Lord (p. 1383, Shlok Farid).

Mendicants: Those who live by begging. Since the *Adi Granth* lays emphasis on work and effort, the practice of begging has been decried. The Hindu ascetics, the Yogis and the Buddhist and Jaina monks who resorted to begging as mendicants have been criticised for this act. Guru Nanak Dev addresses the Yogi in the following manner: "Is it not shameful that you beg from door to door?" (p. 903, Ramkali M. 1).

Menstruation: The process of the discharge of menses. There is figurative mention of menstruation in the verses of Guru Nanak Dev in the *Adi Granth*. The Guru says, "Just as the woman has her monthly period again and again, in a similar manner the impurity abides in the mouth of the impure, who is always in distress. They cannot be called pure, who wash their bodies. They are only pure, in whose heart abides the Lord (p. 472, Var Asa M. 1).

Mental Impressions: Mental impressions contribute towards the variety of ideas. The mind being the 'thinking principle' is responsible for various ailments of man. The mercurial mind does not remain under control. It runs in all the ten directions. The impressions created in it cause duality (p. 127, Majh M. 3). It is very difficult to absolve oneself from the mental impressions (p. 800, Bilawal M. 4). One should forsake the sphere of mental impressions and forget the duality (p. 763, Suhi M. 5). Guru Nanak Dev says, "O my mind, stabilise yourself, so that you may not be hurt" (p. 1113, Bārāmāha Tukhārī M. 1).

Merchant: There is good deal of metaphorical use of this word in the *Adi Granth*. The human being is identified with a merchant. In some of the hymns, the man is addressed as "Wanjaria Mittra" (O Merchant Friend). Guru Nanak Dev says, "Make your decreasing age your shop and store it with the substance of true Name. Let the concentration and reflection be the store-house and put the substance in it. Trade with such merchants, reap the profit and be happy. Let your trade be the listening to the sacred books and load with your merchandise the horses of Truth. Carry with you the fare of virtues and do not depend on the morrow. And when you reach the land of the Formless Lord, you will be in the abode of bliss" (p. 595, Sorath M. 1).

Mercy: Dharma (righteousness) symbolised as bull, is the son of mercy (p. 3, Japuji). Mercy on the living beings is the essence of the pilgrimage to sixty-eight holy places and acts of charity (p. 136, Baramaha Majh M. 5). We know the truth, if we receive the true instructions and are merciful to life and give away something in charity (p. 368, Var Asa M. 1). Only he attains permanent austerity of mercy and righteousness in whose writ it is recorded (p. 1101, Var Maru M. 5).

Merit: That which is deserved; the due reward or punishment. The merit of an individual depends upon his Karmans (actions/deeds). We reap the fruit of the merit of our actions (p. 468, Var Asa M. 1). If one performs good actions he deserves to be called a *Dharmī* (righteous person) and if one commits sins, he merits to be called a *Pāpī* (sinner) (p. 138, Var Majh M. 1, Shlok M. 2). He, who merits a throne, sits on the throne (p. 1039, Maru M. 1).

Meru: Or Sumeru. It is the name of a mythical mountain, said to be a golden mountain. It is said to be situated in the centre of the universe. Its height is 84,000 yojanas and its depth below the surface of the earth is 16,000 yojanas. The square city of Brahma, made of gold, is situated on its summit. The Swarga-Loka of Indra is also there alongwith the cities of other gods and celestial spirits. Beneath the mountain are the seven nether worlds. According to Guru Nanak Dev, as mentioned in the *Adi Granth*, there are many Merus in the vast creation visualised in the region of knowledge (Gyan Khand).

Metals: Besides mentioning valuable metals like gold and silver in the context of wealth and riches, other metals like iron and copper are also mentioned in the *Adi Granth*. There is also figurative use of the philosopher's stone, which transforms the base metals into gold. The Guru is like the philosopher's stone, who transforms the iron-like egocentrics into gold-like Enlightened persons (p. 481, Asa Kabir). The Guru also transforms the Enlightened person into a philosopher's stone (p. 689, Dhanasari M. 1). In the boat of Guru's Word, the iron-like egocentric is ferried across (p. 1309, Kanara M. 4). Like iron, the copper also is transformed into gold when it comes into contact with the philosopher's stone (p. 1158, Bhairo Kabir).

Metaphysics: Theoretical philosophy as the ultimate science of Being and Knowing. Thus Ontology and Epistemology are covered under Metaphysics. In the *Adi Granth*, much has been said about God and soul, which is not at all metaphysical speculation, but instead it is a mystic experience of God-intoxicated preceptors and saints. Hence metaphysics and mysticism mingle in each other. The *Adi Granth* is not a philosophical treatise, it is instead a religious and mystical scripture, consisting of hymns of highest mystical fervour and experience.

Milk: Good actions have been identified with milk, which is curdled through disinterestedness, by using the ferment of the conscious mind (p. 728, Suhi M. 1). The cow without milk and the bird without feathers is useless (p. 354, Asa M. 1). I ask for these alms from my Lord: the milk of deeds and the butter of contentment (p. 1329, Prabhati M. 1). Ravidas says, "The calf has defiled the milk in the teats, the black-bee has defiled the flower and the fish has defiled the water; O mother, what shall I now offer to my Lord?" (p. 525, Gujri Ravidas). When the child depends upon milk and cannot live without it, the mother takes care of him and feeds him, in this way he is satisfied (p. 1266, Malar M. 5). Just as the child is attached to the milk, in a similar manner the saint is attached to God (p. 613, Sorath M. 5). In the first watch of the night, the child-mind is unconscious, he lisps milk and is fondled. The mother and father love him because he is their son (p. 75, Sri Rag M. 1). The love of God should be like the love of milk and water. Guru Nanak Dev Says, "O my mind, love your Lord, as the water loves the milk. He suffers the heat but saves the milk (p. 60, Sri Rag M. 1).

Milk-Ocean: It is a mythological reference. Vishnu is represented in the Hindu myth as the milk-ocean, out of which the transient universe arises and in which it is also dissolved. There is a reference to the milk-ocean in the *Adi Granth*. Guru Nanak Dev says, "When the milk-ocean was churned (by the gods and demons), the jewels came out of it. (The gods and demons) said angrily that it was due to their effort. How could that lord be concealed (Who was the cause of all this)" (pp. 350-51, Asa M. 1).

Mind: Mind and intellect are the outer coverings of the soul undergoing transmigration. Kabir says, "If one disciplines the mind, he attains perfection. The mind can only converse with the mind. There is no meeting better than the meeting of minds. This mind is the *shakti*, this mind is the Shiva. This mind is the essence of all the five elements. He who takes this mind to the higher regions, the mystery of the three worlds is revealed to him" (342, Garui Poorbi Bawan Akhri Kabir). Guru Nanak Dev says, "The mind is like a wild elephant lured by attachment, wanders in the woods of *maya*...Without the Guru's word, the mind finds no peace...This mind is ignorant; how will it be saved? Without knowing, it suffers the pangs of death...The mind is born of five elements. It is the mind which performs good deeds and practises righteousness, but when it is puffed up with power, it becomes wild and ignorant...The mind is the king, the hero of many battles. It becomes fearless also by concentrating on the Name through the Grace of the Guru. It overpowers the five vices and kills them" (p. 415, Asa M. 1). Guru Amar Das addresses the mind thus: "O mind, you are light, realise your source" (p. 441, Asa M. 3). If the mind is conquered, the whole world is conquered (p. 6, Japuji). The light of mind is eclipsed by the dirt of ego, which blackened it in the course of several births (p. 651, Var Sorath M. 3). In order to control the mind, its reins should be tightened. It should be held tightly in the grip like the ends of a churning rope (p. 728, Suhi M. 1). It is not an easy job to bring the mind under control. The great sages have failed in their attempts. It always flies like a falcon (p. 776, Suhi M. 4). The mind is like an intoxicated elephant and only the goad of the Guru can give it a new life (p. 221, Gauri M. 1). The grace of the lord and the Guru play a great part in the conquest of mind (p. 298, Gauri M. 5). The Lord follows that True devotee, whose mind has become pure (p. 1367, Shlok Kabir). See "Manas".

Mindfulness: Taking thought or care of. A true devotee, having been absorbed in the Name of the Lord, should also be mindful of his worldly responsibilities. He has not to neglect the work taken up by him as a breadwinner for the family. In one of his couplets, Kabir refers to the advice given by Namdev to Trilochan: "Remember the

Name of the Lord with your mouth, but be mindful about all the work to be done with your hands and feet, while keeping the conscious mind in tune with the Lord" (p. 1376, Shlok Kabir). Guru Tegh Bhadur says, "Be mindful about the fleeting opportunity, therefore remember the Lord". (Jaijavanti M. 9, p. 1352).

Minerals: The substances which are obtained by mining. The kinds of natural inorganic substances, as used in modern scientific terminology. While talking about the creation of the Lord, Guru Arjun Dev says, "There are millions of trees and stones...There are millions of hillocks and mountains of gold" (pp. 275-76, Gauri Sukhmani M. 5). In these verses, the underlying idea of mineral quarries is implied.

Miracles: A miracle is a marvellous event exceeding the known powers of nature, and therefore supposed to be due to the special intervention of the Deity or some supernatural agency. The *Adi Granth* is against the performance of miracles. The Yogis, following their stern discipline, attained the supernatural powers, but Guru Nanak Dev decried the use of such powers. He says, "to work miracles is to create different relish" (p. 6, Japuji). All the miraculous powers are latent in the Name of the Lord. Guru Amar Das says, "On meeting the True Guru, my mind has been turned away from *maya* and I expend the nine treasures of the Name. The eighteen *Siddhis* (miraculous powers) follow me and I reside in my Pure Abode" (p. 91, Var Sri Rag M. 4, Shlok M. 3). Without the Name all miracles, all powers, all foods and garments are useless. That is, of course, the miracle or the power with which the Lord Blesses us spontaneously. The real miracle is the absorption of the Name in the mind through the grace of the Guru (p. 650, Var Sorath M. 4, Shlok M. 3).

Mirror: A looking-glass. There is a metaphorical use of the mirror in the verses of Guru Tegh Bahadur in the *Adi Granth*: "Just as the fragrance abides in the flower and the reflection in the mirror, similarly God abides within us: Search Him within the heart" (p. 684, Dhanasari M. 9).

Misbelievers: Heretics; Infidels. Misbelievers (non-believers) or those who have no faith are called *Manmukh* (self-willed persons). Much has been said about such persons in the *Adi Granth*. They are egoists. Guru Amar Das says, "The egoist is blind, because his conscience is not awakened. He is the killer of himself and also of the world. He is a slanderer and carries this load of slander without the wages....The poor wretch yells and weeps and gets no peace without the Guru" (p.

118, Majh M. 3). Guru Arjan Dev says, "The bond of *maya* binds the misbelievers to one another. But when they see one in odd circumstances, they do not go near him. Their attachment is only up to the time when they can get something out of him. When they do not get anything, they talk ill of him. Being ignorant and blind, they do not know the state of their souls. Their friendship does not last like the two stones joined by mud. These blind ones do not know their Self and are involved in useless quarrels" (p. 959, Var Ramkali M. 5).

Miscarriage: Untimely delivery (of a woman), usually taken as synonymous with abortion. Guru Ram Das says, "He who forsakes the Name of the Lord, he is accursed. May his clan bring forth no child..." (p. 1263, Malar M. 4). In this quotation, barrenness or miscarriage is implied.

Misfortune-Nirriti: Bad fortune; ill luck. Because of good fortune one finds the society of holy persons. Those who are unfortunate, wander about in doubt and agony. In misfortune, One does not find the society of the saints, without which the mind remains defiled (p. 95, Majh M. 4). When one is in utter misfortune and there is no one to support, the opponents have come down upon him and his relatives have left him alone. When all the support has ended and all the hopes are lost; if under such circumstances, one remembers the Lord, the agonising winds will not touch him (p. 70, Sri Rag M. 5).

Mit, Mittar, Mittartā: A *Mit* or *Mittar* is a friend and *Mittartā* is friendship. The virtue of friendship is necessary for the development of character. A saint is a friend of all. He has no enmity with anybody. All the world is his family. Guru Arjan Dev says, "None is my enemy and I am inimical to none. I am friend of everybody, comrade of everybody (Dhanasari M. 5, p. 671). The friendship based for selfish ends is temporary. "Without love it is all tall talk. The love based on selfishness depends upon mutual give and take (Var Vadhans M. 4, Shalok M. 1, p. 594). "Break off with selfish people, seek the saints, who are real friends" (Var Maru M. 5, p. 1102).

Moderation: Avoidance of extremes; Moderation. There are three essentials for a devotee aspiring to tread the spiritual path, viz. Truth, Contentment and Moderation. Guru Amar Das says, "He, on whom, the Lord showers his grace, Faith is Bestowed on him. He imbibes Truth, Contentment and Moderation and the Music of the Word rings in his pure mind (p. 427, Asa M. 3). In the *Adi Granth*, the phrase "Jat Sat Sanjam" has been repeated several times. These attributes viz.

Continence, Truth and Moderation are necessary for a Yogi or a disciplined devotee (See pages 903, 906--Ramkali M. 1).

Moh: Attachment. It is one of the five vices, the other four being lust, anger, greed and ego. "Whatever pleasure we get from attachment, it is all stained with blackness" (Dhanasari M. 1, p. 662). Abandon this attachment; it is all vice (Asa M. 1, p. 356).

Moha: Attachment—one of the five basic vices.

Mokh Duār: The gate of salvation. See: *Moksha.*

Moksha: Emancipation; salvation. According to the *Adi Granth*, *Moksha* is achieved through the Grace of the Lord, though the human body takes its birth according to the karmas (p. 2, Japuji). One has to be humble and should be absorbed in devotion with love (p. 470, Var Asa M. 1). Only that person achieves the door of Mukti, who destroys his egoistic self (p. 1276, Malar M. 3). The True Word (the Name of the Lord) leads one to Mukti (p. 352, Asa M. 1). Everyone desires to go to heavens and attain mukti and hopes to achieve this end, but those who want to have a sight of the Lord, do not implore for mukti, they are satisfied only with the sight of the Lord (p. 1324, Kalyan M. 4). Out of the four ends of human life, the moksha is the final and most important one. It is the ultimate goal of a devotee. Guru Arjan Dev says, "I do not want the kingdom, I do not want mukti, I want only the love of the lotus-feet of the Lord (p. 534, Devgandhari M. 5).

Momentariness: This Buddhist doctrine is known as *Kshanika-vāda* in Indian philosophical terminology. According to this doctrine, there is no continuous self (atman) in our consciousness, because it is only a succession of changes from moment to moment, and is known only in the moment. This doctrine has been refuted by vedantists. The *Adi Granth*, like Vedanta, believes in the continuous existence of the soul, therefore the momentary changes in the outside world cannot have any lasting impact on a permanent entity. The moment dies but the soul lives. After every moment the life dwindles (p. 726, Tilang M. 9), but the soul is not prone to death (p. 188, Gauri M. 5).

Monasteries: The *Adi Granth* lays emphasis on the life of a householder and is against asceticism. Guru Nanak Dev has decribed the life led by Jaina Monks (p.149, Var Majh M.1). The Buddhist and Jaina monks lived in monasteries and followed a rigorous discipline. The Guru advises the ascetics of all types to forsake the habits of recluses and lead an energetic life for the good of family and society.

Money: The worldly money is a play of the Lord; sometimes it comes sometimes it goes. But the money of a Gyani (the knower) is the

Name of the Lord, in which he always remains absorbed (p. 1282, Var Malar M. 1, Shlok M. 3). If money goes, one grieves, because the heart of the ignorant is within his riches. But such a person is rare, who gathers the riches of truth and loves the immaculate Name (p. 934, Ramkali Dakhni Oamkar M. 1). False money is gathered by the foolish and ignorant. These egocentrics and blind persons have strayed away. They are always in anguish, who gather false money, neither it accompanies nor gives any yield. True money is obtained through the instructions of the Guru, but false money comes and goes (p. 665, Dhanasari M. 3). According to the *Adi Granth*, the real money is the Name of the Lord.

Money-Lending: The institution of money-lender and the practice of money-lending is very old in India. According to the *Adi Granth*, the God and the Guru are the true money-lenders or merchants. "The Lord alone is the true merchant and the rest of the world is His pedlar" (p. 140, Var Majh M. 1). "The true Guru is the True Merchant and Blessed is the disciple with the storage of love. The Trader and the Trade are blessed and Guru the true Merchant is Blest" (p. 449, Asa M. 4). "The Lord is the true Merchant and His Traders are also True" (p. 117, Majh M. 3).

Monism: The doctrine that only One Being exists. Whereas the *Adi Granth* preaches monotheism, it also believes in monism. Guru Arjan Dev says, "Your are One alone all over, I do not see any other" (p. 292, Gauri Sukhmani M. 5). "Whatever I see is Brahman, Whatever I hear, is Brahman" (p. 846, Bilawal M. 5).

Monks: Guru Nanak Dev rejected the rigorous life-style of the Jaina monks. He is against their asceticism (see the hymn of Guru Nanak Dev in Var Majh M. 1, p. 149).

Monotheism: The doctrine that there is only One God. The very first letter as well as the word in the *Adi Granth* is a pointer to this basic Sikh belief. Throughout the *Adi Granth,* we find the repetition of this belief. One example will suffice: "My Lord is one and only One" (p. 350, Asa M. 1).

Monster: An animal of huge size. According to the *Adi Granth* a person, who turns his back upon the true Guru is like a swine, a cur, an ass, a cat, a monster (quadruped), a cursed Chandala and an untouchable (p. 832, Bilawal M. 1). Without the Name of the Lord, the body is worse than that of a wild monster, a ghost and a fool (p. 890, Ramkali M. 5). Guru Arjan Dev addresses the Lord thus: "Through

Your Grace, the fools, the monsters, the goblins and the stones are ferried across. I seek Your Refuge, O Lord, and am ever a sacrifice-un-to you" (p. 802, Bilawal M. 5).

Months: There are two poems in the *Adi Granth*, which contain stanzas based on the months of Indian Calendar. One is composed by Guru Nanak Dev in Raga Tukhari and the other is composed by Guru Arjan Dev in Raga Majh. These poems are called *Baramahas*. In the *Baramaha* of Guru Nanak Dev, in each month the change of the season and the mood of the devotee have been depicted. In the poem entitled *Ruttin*, Guru Nanak Dev has mentioned six seasons based each on two months of the year. Guru Nanak Dev says, "Blessed is the month, when there is ever spring for me. O Mind, you also bloom ever like flower and cherish the Lord, who is the Prop of the earth" (p. 1168, Basant, M. 1)

Monuments: Anything that by its survival commemorates a person, action, period or event. Monuments are sometimes set up as testimonials of good conduct. There are monuments in memory of great persons, gods, incarnations, sages, hermits etc...The places of pilgrimage contain such monuments. There are sixty-eight *Tīrthas*, according to Hindu Shastras. Their mention has been made several times in the *Adi Granth*. "Wherever the True Guru takes his seat, that place becomes meritorious, a monument commemorating the memory of the preceptor" (p. 450, Asa M. 4).

Moon: With the rising of the moon, the darkness is dispelled (p. 393, Asa M. 5). The sun and the moon move millions of miles in the fear of the Lord (p. 464, Var Asa M. 1). When the sun rises, the moon is rarely seen (p. 791, Var Suni M. 3). Sushumna channel in the subtle body goes straight into the interior to the spine starting from the basal centre called muladhara, up to a the interior of the head. Outside the sushumna are two other channels, *Ida* on the left and *Pingala*, on the right coiling upward and uniting at the *ajna-chakra*. *Ida* is called the moon channel and *Pingala*, the sun channel. There is mention of these channels in the *Adi Granth* (p. 1106, Maru Jaidev). Kabir says, "The moon (of dispassion) has devoured the sun (of desire) (p. 972, Ramkali Kabir). Guru Nanak Dev says, "When one utters the word, the moon (of the mind) is immensely illuminated. The darkness is dispelled, when the sun abides in the house of the moon (p. 945, Ramkali M. 1, Siddh Goshta). "Meet the True Guru and you will be Ferried Across by the Lord. Within the moon of the sky (of the mind), you will find the sun (of wisdom) (p. 1041, Maru M. 1). The moon has also been identified with Truth". In the dark night of falsehood, the moon of Truth is not visible (p. 145, Var Majh M. 1).

Morality: Ethical aspect. Ethics or morality is the basis of spiritual advancement, according to the *Adi Granth*, "There can be no devotion without the practice of qualities" (p. 4, Japuji). Great emphasis has been laid in the *Adi Granth* on the adoption of godly qualities. God is Truth, Without Fear and Without Enmity according to the *Mool Mantras*, therefore a devotee should be truthful, and without any fear and rancour. With the armour of qualities and virtues, the devotee enters the field of action like a disciplined soldier and no enemy can stay long before him. His actions are controlled by the injunctions laid down by the great Gurus. He fulfils all his worldly duties, but never forgets the Lord. He performs his physical, mental and spiritual duties at the same time. He earns his livelihood. Performing his duties honestly he takes out a portion of his earnings for the service of the needy brethren and while performing all the worldly duties, he remembers the Lord and in the end attains final beatitude.

Mosque: According to Guru Nanak Dev, the Grace of the Lord should be considered as a mosque, and the faith should be made the prayer mat. The honest earnings be made the Quran, effort, the circumcision and character the fast. In this way one can become a Muslim (p. 140, Var Majh M.1). Kabir says, "If God lives only in a mosque, to whom then belongs the remaining world?" (p.1349, Prabhati Kabir). The saint Namdev has identified the body with the mosque and the mind with the Mullah" (p. 1167, Bhairo Namdev). Guru Arjan Dev has said the same thing (p. 1085, Maru M. 5).

Mother: The *Adi Granth* believes that the Lord Himself is the Real Mother. He is also the Real Father (p. 103, Majh M. 5). The Earth is also called the Mother (p. 8, Japuji). The Guru is also the Mother and Father (p. 262, Gauri Bawan Akhri M. 5). The Guru and God love the devotee as their child. They take care of the real devotee as a mother. Since the earth sustains the jiva, therefore she is also called the mother. In this case water is the father, because when earth and water come into contact with each other, the process of creation starts. "The mother is happy, when her son takes his meals (regularly) (p. 164, Gauri Guareri M. 4). As the mother brings up her son and keeps him always in sight, she feeds him constantly and loves him every moment, similarly the true Guru keeps a devotee ever in the Love of the Lord (p. 168, Gauri Bairagan M. 4). Kabir says, "The mother thinks that her son is growing, but she does not know that his age is decreasing. The more she loves him and calls him her own, the angel of death, seeing this, laughs" (p. 91, Sri Rag Kabir).

Mountains: While giving a detail of the creation in his longer poem *Sukhmani* in the *Adi Granth*, Guru Arjan Dev says, "There are millions of mountains and *Merus* of gold" (p. 276, Gauri Sukhmani M. 5). The mountains, vegetation and lands wane away (p. 1354, Shlok Sahaskriti M. 5). The word "mountain" has been used figuratively. In the Var of Satta and Balwand. It is written that the third Guru Amar Das stood firm like the Sumeru mountain, which could not be shaken by the winds (of desire) (p. 968, Var Ramkali Satta and Balwand).

Mourning: The mourning on the death of a dear one is decried in the *Adi Granth.* Guru Nanak Dev addresses the mourner in the following manner: "Why do you cry and weep for the dead? Only the Lord is immortal. While you weep for the dead, who will weep for you? You are engrossed in useless strife and commit falsehood, because the dead does not hear your cries and wails, only the living world does (p. 418, Asa Kafi M. 1). All those who cry and mourn for us, mourn in vain (p. 15, Sri Rag M. 1)

Mritys-Death-Yama: Death is a reality. Whatever is born, must die (p. 1227, Gauri M. 1). That time is never known, when Yama (the god of death) throws its noose. (p. 254, Gauri M. 5). The death as a rat is continuously cutting at the rope of life (p. 41, Sri Rag M. 4). The question arises: who experiences death? (p. 885, Ramkali M. 5). It is only the body which dies, because the soul is immortal. The body is dust (p.152, Gauri M.1) and thus it is reduced to dust. The falcon-death pounces upon its prey unexpectedly (p. 1383, Shlok Farid). The death-end is like the slippery bank of a river (p. 1383, Shlok Farid). Guru Amar Das says, "I know nothing about my end, how shall I die? If the Lord is not forgotten, the death will be easy. The world fears death, everbody wants to live. By the grace of the Guru, one dies while living, he understands it in *Hukam.* If one dies such death, he attains eternal life" (p. 555, Var Bhigara M. 4, Shalok M. 3). The path that the soul traverses after death is dark, difficult and hazardous. The same can be easily traversed with the Light of the Name of the Lord (p. 264, Gauri Sukhmani M. 5). The weeping on the death of a person has been condemned in the *Adi Granth* (p. 579, Vadhans M. 1).

Mugadh: (*Mūṛh*) Fool. "The Lord Bestows Honour upon the humble.

The fool (*Mūṛh Mugadh*) becomes wise and knowledgeable (Bhairo M. 5, p. 1146).

Mukām: Station; resting place. "We have made a home at this station, but there is always the fear of going away. We can recognise it as a permanent station, if it remains for ever" (Sri Rag M. 1, p. 64).

Mukand: The Name of the Lord. Ravidas says, "O world, repeat Mukand, Mukand. Without Mukand, the body will be wasted. That Mukand is the Giver of salvation. That Mukand is our Father and Mother. Repeat Mukand while living and dying. The servant of Mukand is always in bliss" (Gaund Ravidas, p. 875).

Mukta (Mukat): One who is emancipated. According to the *Adi Granth* that person is an emancipated one, who rises above praise and calumny and for whom iron and gold are alike (p. 1426, Shlok M. 9), who is not affected by joy and sorrow and looks upon friend and foe alike (p. 1427, Shlok M. 9), who forsakes ego and knows his Lord (p. 1427, Shlok M. 9) and who concentrates upon his Lord in his heart (p. 1428, Shlok M. 9). That person is called *Jivan Mukta*, who forsakes his ego and attachment and sings the praises of the Lord. That person is emancipated, who conquers the mind and is not overwhelmed by *maya*. He abides in the tenth gate and becomes the knower of the three worlds (p. 490, Gujri M. 3). People seek emancipation through *Karma-kānda*, but the same is attained by Praising the Lord through the Word (p. 1024, Maru M. 1).

Muktī: If one calls himself lowliest, while practising the devotion of love, he attains emancipation (p. 470, Var Asa M. 1). The body comes in the world through the performance of works, but the abode of emancipation is attained by the Grace of the Lord (p. 3, Japuji). See: *Moksha*.

Mullah: The Muslim priest. "He is, in fact, a Mullah, who forsakes vices (Maru M. 5, p. 1084). Kabir says, "O Mullah, why do you ascend the minaret of the mosque for loud announcenent? The Lord is not deaf. He (the Lord) for Whom you make loud announcements, see him within your heart" (Shlok Kabir, p. 1374).

Munī: According to the *Adi Granth*, that person is the *Muni* (*Muni* is a sage and an ascetic, who has taken a vow of silence), who destroys the duality of the mind and after destroying duality, he reflects upon the Lord" (p. 1128, Bhairo M. 3). Kabir says, "Even if one may be a great *Muni*, the ego destroys all his merit" (p. 1372, Shlok Kabir).

Murder: The unlawful killing of a human being with malice aforethought. The *Adi Granth* lays stress on mercy towards all *jivas*, because this has the approval of the Lord (p. 136, Barahmaha Majh M. 5). Also (p. 1322, Var Gauri M. 5). *Himsā* (injury; harm; violence) is therefore condemned. *Himsā* is one of the streams of fire, the other being attachment, greed and anger (p. 141, Var Majh M. 1). Kabir says, "killing of life by force is sheer cruelty, it cannot be called a sanctified deed. For this one is called to account in the Court of the Lord. How will one feel at that time?" (p. 1374, Shlok Kabir).

Mūrtī-Pūjā: Idol-worship. Idol-worship has been condemned strongly in the *Adi Granth*. "The fools worship the stones. When they sink down, how can they ferry (others) across the world-ocean? (Var Bihagra M. 4, p. 556). "The stone, which is addressed as *Thakur* (Lord) by him, the same stone sinks and drowns him with itself" (Suhi M. 5, p. 739). Those who consider the stones as gods, their service (worship) is of no avail" (Bhairo M. 5, p. 1160).

Musāfir: Traveller. The man of the world is likened to a traveller in the *Adi Granth*. For him, this world is just a resting-place (*Sarāī*). He is also likened to a herdsman in the meadow. He is also the guest of the night, who has to leave in the early hours of the morning (Sri Rag M. 5, p. 50). Guru Arjan Dev says, "O traveller, walking on the bank of the stream, there is slippery and muddy ground down below. Be cautious, so that you may not slip away and get a sprinkling of muddy water on your clothes (Var Maru Dakhne M. 5, p. 1095). "This world is like a traveller, even then it is full of ego (Jaitsri Chhant M. 5, p. 705).

Music: The congregational music, singing the praises of the Lord, is called "*Kīrtan*". The *Adi Granth* considers *Kīrtan* an invaluable jewel through which one attains bliss and qualities (p. 393, Gauri M. 5). The Yoga is attained by singing the *Kīrtan* of the Lord (p. 385, Asa M. 5). The mind is asked to perform such *Kīrtan*, as is useful in this and the other world (p. 236, Gauri M. 5). Kingdom, possessions and involvements are of no use: the *Kīrtan* of Hari is our only support. This is an eternal wealth (p. 398, Asa M. 5). He who is absorbed in the *Kīrtan* of the Lord, the yama will have no dominion over him (p. 867, Gond M. 1). He who is absorbed in the *Kīrtan* of Hari day and night, he will not take birth again (p. 624, Sorath M. 5). In the Iron Age *Kīrtan* of the Lord alone is sublime (p. 624, Sorath M. 5). He who listens to and sings the *Kīrtan* of the Lord, he gets rid of his evil nature; all his wishes and hopes are fulfilled (p. 1300, Kanra M. 5). In the home of that person there is spring, where the music of the Lord is resounds (p.

1180, Basant M. 5). He, who listens to the *Kīrtan* of Hari and sings the *Kīrtan* of Hari, he never experiences pain and sorrow (p. 190, Gauri M. 5). The *bānī* of the *Adi Granth* is musical and metrical. It has been arranged according to the *Ragas* and *Raginīs*. It is meant to be sung. Guru Nanak Dev's Var of Raga Āsa is sung every morning in the Gurudwaras.

Muslim, Mussalmān: One who is a follower of Islam, a Muhammadan. In the *Adi Granth*, Guru Nanak Dev has defined a Muslim in the following manner: "He who has the grace of the Lord as his mosque, the faith as his prayer mat, the honestly-earned income as his Quran, the effort as his circumcision, the character as his fast, he becomes a Muslim" (p. 140, Var Majh M. 1). It is difficult to be called a Muslim. If he has these qualities, then he is one. First let the Faith of Allah be sweet to him, then let him scrub his ego and with faith in the Prophet, let him submit to the Will of Allah...and be merciful to all creatures, then he is acclaimed as a true Muslim (p. 141, Var Majh M. 1). Guru Arjan Dev says, "A Muslim should be tender of heart, he should wash away the inner dirt from his heart, he should not indulge in the pleasures of the world and be pure like flower, silk, clarified butter and the deer-skin (p. 1084, Maru M. 5).

Mysticism: The mysticism of the *Adi Granth* is the mysticism of love and devotion and not of rituals and ascetic practices. The hymns of the *Adi Granth* are full of mystic lore. The love and praises of the Lord and the Preceptor are the focal points. Guru Nanak Dev and Kabir, whose verses are included in the *Adi Granth* are the high-priests of Indian mysticism. The essential element of mysticism is the experience of direct communion with God. All the preceptors and saints, whose verses have been included in the *Adi Granth* were God-conscious personalities and had direct communion with the Lord. They have related their spiritual experiences in their hymns. They consider the all-pervading Lord as their spouse, as their Father, Mother and Everything. They believe that the soul is part and parcel of God and can achieve mystic union with The Lord through the discipline ordained by the Guru.

Myths: The myths are the vehicle for popular religious instructions. The truth is symbolically presented through the myths. In the *Adi Granth*, mostly the Hindu myth has been used by the Gurus and saints in their hymns as imagery, allegory and metaphor. They have elucidated their thoughts and experiences by the use of myths, for the general understanding of the populace. The myths were not a part of their belief. Many instances of the use of myth can be quoted. As an example, the 27th Pauri of Japuji may be seen. It has been repeated also as *So-Daru, Rag Asa M.1* on pages 8-9 of the *Adi Granth*.

N

Nābh Kamal: The navel lotus. The Yogis believe that there are several lotuses in various parts of the body. One of them is in the navel. Navel is considered the prop of the breaths (*Prānas*). The Yogis questioned Guru Nanak: "When there was no support of navel lotus, then where did *Prāna* abide?" The answer of Guru Nanak Dev was: "When there was no support of the navel-lotus, then the *Prāna* resided in its own home (*nij ghar*). (Ramkali M. 1, Siddh Goshta, p. 945). Brahma emerged from the navel lotus of Vishnu and began to recite Vedas in a melodious voice, but he strayed in ignorance and could not know the limits of the Lord"(Gujri M. 1, p. 489).

Nāc: Dancing. See: *Dancing.*

Nād: A musical instrument used by Yogis, therefore it connotes divine sound. The syllables of *bija-mantra* are the sound bodies of Brahman. They reproduce in human speech the original sound-vibrations that accompany the manifestation of *Ishvara.* When repeated, these sounds act as evocations to *Ishvara* and provide the body of *Ishvara* for manifestation to the aspiring devotee. The sound-bodies of *Wahe Guru*, the *bija-mantra* in Sikhism, manifest before the disciple "the wonderful *Para Brahman*" and the Unstruck Melody (*Nād*) is heard.

Nadar: Grace. See: *Grace.*

Nādis: Nerve-channels. They are the channels in the subtle body. There are seventy-two thousand nādis in the human body. Kabir says, "Within the body of seventy-two (thousand) nadis, there abides one Purusha (Soul)" (p. 793, Suhi Lalit Kabir). The body in which there are seventy-two (thousand) nādis, there is but one opening (of the Tenth Door) (p. 477, Asa Kabir). There are three principal nādis in the body viz. Idā, Pingalā and Sushumnā. See: *Idā, Pingalā and Sushumnā*

Nāgas: A Naga is a snake, but there is also a tribe of that name. Guru Nanak Dev says, "When it rains in the month of Shrāvana, these four feel great joy: The Naga (Snakes), the deer, the fish and the indulgers (p. 1279, Var Malar M. 1). There is mention of Seshnaga and Kali in the *Adi Granth.* According to Kala, the bard, the praises of Guru Nanak are sung with devotion by Seshnaga with his thousand tongues" (p. 1390, Swayye Mahle Pehle Ke). Namdev says," The Lord as Krishna destroyed Kesi and Kansa and blessed Kali the serpent with eternal Life" (p. 874, Gaund Namdev). Kala, the bard says again, "The praises of Guru Nanak are sung by the devotees of the Naga clan in the underworld" (p. 1390, Swayye Mahle Pehle Ke). While describing the process of creation, Guru Nanak Dev has mentioned the birth of the jivas of the Naga clan (p. 156, Gauri M. 1).

Nail-Paring: Namdev calls Ganges as the nail-sweat of the Lord (p. 1292, Malar Namdev). The man-lion incarnation of the Lord, known as Narsingh (With lion's head and man's body) tore Hirnayakashyapa (Harnā-kash) with Nails (p. 1133, Bhairo M. 3 and p. 224, Gauri M. 1). There is no mention of nail-paring or wearing nails unclipped in the *Adi Granth*.

Nakedness: The jiva is born naked in the world and also he is naked when he quits the world (p. 1247, Var Sarang M. 4, Shalok M. 3) (p. 1157, Bhairo Kabir). There is also mention of the naked Jaina monk, known as *Digambara*. Guru Nanak Dev says, "He is, in fact a *Digambara*, who has the virtue of compassion and examines his self" (p. 356, Asa M. 1). The Guru has condemned the practice of remaining naked by Jaina monks or other hermits: "One who does not wear clothes, groans day and night" (p. 467, Var Asa M. 1).

Nakshatras: Constellations or lunar mansions. They represent the 27 divisions of the lunar zodiac. About these stars, the *Adi Granth* says that the same Lord pervades the sun, moon and stars (p. 294, Gauri M. 5). The sun, moon and stars meditate on the same Lord (p. 456, Asa M. 5). These *nakshatras* also represent the phases of the moon during the monthly orbit of the earth. Going into the detail of the creation, Guru Arjan Dev says, "There are millions of suns, moons and *Nakshatras*" (p. 275. Gauri Sukhmani M. 5).

Nakshatra Vidya: The science of the stars, i.e. Astronomy. This science treates of the constitutions, relative positions and motions of the heavenly bodies including the earth. The *Adi Granth* mentions the beauty and the movement of the heavenly bodies in long distances (p. 329, Gauri Kabir and p. 464, Var Asa M. 1).

Nāmadheya: or Nāmakarana; the rite of name-giving to the child. The *Adi Granth* does not believe in any rite or sacrament. Guru Arjan Dev says, "Having been named a devotee of the Lord, God saved my honour" (p. 624, Sorath M. 5).

Nāmarūpa: Name and Form. According to the Vedantic concept of Nāmarūpa, *maya* manifests in innumerable names and forms the objects of the relative world. Nāmarūpa *maya* be interpreted as the mind and matter. Through the world of Nāmarūpa, Brahman appears as many, "There are innumerable names and places" says Guru Nanak Dev (p. 6 Japuji). He also says, "Wherever I see, I see your Light. O, What kind of Form is Yours? You have One Form only, but you Move, Hiding Yourself, where none (in the Creations) is like another" (p. 596 Sorath M. 1).

Namāz: The Muslim Prayer, which is performed five times a day. Sheikh Farid has beckoned a Muslim devotee to come to the mosque for morning prayer (Shlok Farid, p.1381). The five prayers, according to Guru Nanak Dev, should be Truth, Honest earning, God's Grace for All, Purity of mind and the Praises of the Lord (Var Majh M. 1, p. 141). According to Guru Arjan Dev, these five prayers are: 1. the Praises of the Lord, 2. Forbearance, 3. Humility, 4. God's Grace for All, and 5. Full control over passions (Maru M. 5, p. 1084).

Names: There are innumerable names (p. 6, Japuji). Guru Arjan Dev addresses the Lord thus: "My tongue utters only your acquired Names, but your age-old Name is "SAT" (which means Ever-existent)" (p. 1083, Maru M. 5). The Muslim tradition mentions ninety-nine Names of God. In Hinduism, *Sahansar-Nāmās*, mention one thousand Names of the Deity. There is a hymn in Raga Maru, which contains a few Names of the Lord, but has often been called a *Sahansar-Nāmā* after the Hindu tradittion (pp. 1082-83). Guru Nanak Dev says, "O Lord, many are your Names and many your Forms" (p. 358, Asa M. 1). The *Sesha Naga* utters countless Names of Lord, but there is no end to His Names. Even Shesha Naga has not been able to know the mystery of the Lord (p. 691, Dhanasari Kabir).

Nar: Man.The man of the world is sometimes addressed as "Re Nar" in the *Adi Granth*.

Nārada: A mythological sage, who works very often as a messenger of Lord Vishnu is several myths. He also acts as a teacher. He is said to be a descendent of Kana and also reckoned amongst the ten sons of Brahmā. Like Mercury, he is said to carry the behests of the gods to men. In folk-tradition he is shown as one who promotes quarrels. As regard his appearance, he has a bald head with tuft of hair in the centre. He carries a Vīnā (lute) in his hand. He dances while singing the praises of the Lord. There is mention of Nārada in the *Adi Granth*. "O Lord, Nārada and Saraswati are also in your Service" (p. 1028, Maru M. 1) (p. 478, Asa Kabir). Nārada is also shown as the author of *Bhakti Sutras*. The type of devotion taught by Nārada has been called

Bhakti of Nārada (p. 655, Sorath Kabir). In the poetry of the bards, Nārada, Dhruva, Prahlada, Sudama have been mentioned as the devotees of God in the past (p. 1405). Guru Nanak Dev has also said, "Nārada dances to the tune of the Kali age" (p. 349, Asa M. 1).

Narak: Hell. See: *Hell.*

Nārāyana: It literally means the abode of the Creator, who Moves upon waters. According to Hindu mythology, Vishnu is said to rest on the cosmic serpent Shesha, who floats on the primeval waters. Hence the epithet "Nārāyana" is used for Vishnu in Hinduism, but in the *Adi Granth,* it is the Name of the Lord, who is all-Pervading. Guru Arjan Dev says, "My Lord Narayana is with me, therefore the couriers of Yama do not come near me" (p. 630, Sorath M. 5).

Nasadīya Sūkta: It is one of the Sukta of Rig Veda. It is a hymn of Creation. Before the Creation, the Lord was in abstract meditation. This state is known as *Sunn Samādhi*. The earliest description of this state is contained in the *Nasadīya Sūkta*. This very ancient hymn is very similar to the hymn of creation composed by Guru Nanak in Raga Maru, p. 1035. We find that the Vedic hymn even expresses doubt about the creative activity of Brahman, but the *Adi Granth* is very positive about it.

Nashā: Intoxication. See: *intoxicants.*

Nāstikas: Infidels; those who do not believe in God. The primary and fundamental belief of the *Adi Granth* is the Eternality of God, the Creator and the duty of beings to worship Him. Therefore the *Nastikas* have been outrightly condemned. "By turning his back on the Lord, man suffers separation continously in various births" (p. 135, Baramaha Majh M. 5). "They who have turned their back on the Lord are like a thief at the gallows (p. 319, Var Gauri M. 5). See: *Nihilists, Infidels.*

Nat, Nātak: *Nat* or *Natuā* is the actor, who takes part in a *Nātak* (Play). "The contentment is not obtained by seeing the actors and the play and listening to their songs" (Gauri Guareri M. 5, p. 179). Just as an actor adopts various guises, but he himself remains the same as ever, similarly the human being adopts various bodies on account of illusion, according to the law of karma. He does not attain peace (Asa M. 5, pp. 403-04).

Nature: The equivalent of nature in Indian philosophy is *Prakriti. Prakriti* is also *māyā*. Guru Nanak Dev has used the word *Qudrat* for *prakriti* or *māyā*. His Shloka on *Qudrat* in Asa ki Var (p. 464) contains his views about Nature: "The Nature (of the Lord) is manifest in seeing and hearing; it is manifest in the Fear, which is the essence of happiness. The Nature is there in under-worlds, in heavens and in all forms. The Nature is manifest in Vedas, Puranas, Semitic scriptures and in all knowledge. The Nature is there in eating, drinking and wearing and also in all love. The Nature is manifested in all species, colours and the living world. The Nature is there in goodness, evil, honour and dishonour. The Nature is manifest in the wind, water, fire and the dust of the earth. All the Nature is of the Pure Lord. "*Qudrat* is an Arabic word, which means Divine Power. Guru Nanak Dev says, "O Lord, Your Nature is your Throne on which you sit and Adjudicate" (p. 580, Vadhans M. 1). "The Lord Creates Nature and then Pervades it" (pp. 83-84, Var Sri Rag M. 4, Shlok M. 1).

Nav: Nine. In the *Adi Granth*, there is mention of *Nav graha* (nine planets) of our solar system, *Nav Khand* (Nine *Khands* or regions of the world which include *Bharat Khand*), *Nav Nāth* (nine famous Yogis of *Nāth* sect including Matsyendranath, Gorakhnath, Charpat Nath etc.) and *Nav-Niddh* (nine miraculous treasures).

Nectar: A beverage of immortality called *Amrita* in Indian terminology. It is the ambrosia of the gods. This celestial elixir has also been called soma, but the same is derived from a plant, while Amrita was brought in a chalice by Dhanvantari, when the ocean was churned by gods and demons. In the *Adi Granth*, wherever the word Amrita occurs, it is generally used for the Name of the Lord. Guru Amar Das says, "The gods, men, and hermits are in search of nectar, that nectar I have obtained from the Guru (p. 918, Ramkali M. 3, Anand). Guru Nanak Dev says, "Where chastity is the workshop and patience is the goldsmith, where understanding is the anvil, the hammer of knowledge, fire of austerity and the bellows of fear, there the nectar melts in the pot of devotion" (p. 88, Japuji).

Neo-Platonism: It is a school of philosophy said to have been established by Ammonius Saccus in the second century AD in Alexandria. It ended as a formal school with Proclus in the fifth century. According to Plotinus the idea of Beauty is One and Perfect. All the lesser beauties are part and parcel of the one Supreme Beauty. The attribute of the beautiful consists in the glow of the spiritual essence of the beautiful thing. Guru Nanak Dev has said, "In everything moves the same Light" (p. 663, Dhanasari M. 1). According to Plotinus, the man must turn his mind away from the inferior things of sense and move towards the inner reality of his own soul. He should achieve communion with the One, which is his ultimate good. Such thoughts are also found in several verses of the *Adi Granth*. Such similarities can be visullised in Neo-Platonism and the *Adi Granth*.

Nescience: Ignorance; *Avidyā* (in Indian terminology). Nescience is the source of all evil and suffering. Two words connoting nescience i.e. *Avidyā* and *Agyān* have been used in the *Adi Granth*. Ravidas says, "O Lord, man is in love with Avidyā (nescience) and his lamp of knowlege is very dim" (p. 486, Asa Ravi Das). Guru Ram Das says, "Through nescience, one is put to sleep and through the knowlege of the Guru, one is awakened" (p. 1309, Kanra M.4). Guru Arjan Dev says, "The Guru has given the antimony of knowledge and the darkness of nescience has been destroyed" (p. 293, Gauri Sukhmani M. 5).

Nether-World: According to Hinduism, there are seven Nether regions. The Nether-world is called *Pātāla*. The seven regions are named Atala, Vitala, Nitala, Gabhastimat, Mahatala, Sutala and Pātāla. Each region has a depth of 10,000 leagues and has its own administration. Islam also believes in seven nether *tabaks*. But Guru Nanak Dev says that the creation of the Infinite Lord cannot be limited. According to him, there are lakhs of nether-worlds (p. 5, Japuji). These nether-worlds are also under the Command of the Almighty like other spheres and regions (p. 1060, Maru M. 3). Guru Arjan Dev says, "The Lord is over the mountains, in the seas, across the deserts, plains, earth and forests, in the fruits and caves, and in the nether-world and over the skies and also in every heart" (p. 1101, Var Maru Dakhne M. 5).

New Moon: In Raga Gaurī Kabir has mentioned fifteen lunar days in his poem *THITTĪ*. He has decried the idea of claiming some days auspicious and others inauspicious. Ragarding the day of the New Moon, Kabir says, "Think about the Lord. The Formless Lord Plays in the body. Always remain Merged in the Primal Lord. The thought of death will never haunt you" (Gauri Thitti Kabir, p. 343).

New Testament: In the *Adi Granth*, the word Kateb (plural of Kītāb meaning Books) has been used for four books i.e. Taurāt or the Book of Moses, Zabūr or the Book of David (These two books are in Old Testament), Injīl (The New Testament) and the Quran (the scripture of Islam). New Testament is the Christian scripture, which deals with the life and injunctions of Christ.

Niāe: Justice. It is a godly quality. Guru Arjan Dev says, "I have seen this wonder of the Lord. He does everything according to His Laws of

Dharma and Justice" (Bihagra M. 5, p. 541). "The Lord decides in accordance with Truth and Justice. For Him, the preceptor and the disciple are equal" (Sorath M. 5, p. 621).

Nibbāna: (Nirvana). Final Emancipation. Nirvana is a term for final beatitude in the Buddhist philosophy. It has been used in other religious systems, but the concept varies. In the *Adi Granth*, this term has also been used, where it connotes the highest mystical state, where the soul merges in the Higher Soul. Guru Ram Das says, "He who is devoted towards the Lord in his mind, he gets eternal bliss and realises the Lord and the state of Nirvana (Asa M. 4, p. 444). Guru Tegh Bahadur says, "He who neither praises nor calumniates and is in search of the state of Nirvana, is the rare one" (Gauri M. 9, p. 219).

Night: When God was in Abstract Meditation, there was neither night nor day (p. 1035, Maru M. 1). The night and day were created by the Lord and thereby the world goes on (p. 948, Var Ramkali M. 3). The day passes in strife and the night in sleep (p. 948, Var Ramakali M. 3). One sleeps by night and works by day, but he does not utter the Name of the Lord even for a moment (p. 326, Gauri Kabir). The Shaktas who forsake the Lord's Name do not pass the night of life in peace (p. 1284, Var Malar M. 1, Shlok M. 5). In the night God showers musk, but they who are asleep do not get a share (p. 1382, Shlok Farid). When the night is young, it yields flower, when it gets old, it yields fruit. They who keep ever awake in devotion for the Lord, are alone blessed (p. 1384, Shalok Farid).

Nigurā: One who is without a Guru. A *Nigurā* does not attain anything (Asa M. 3, p. 361). "He is a *Nigurā*, who transmigrates repeatedly" (Majh M. 3, p. 117).

Nihilism: Total rejection of current religious beliefs or moral principles. According to this doctrine nothing, or nothing of a specified and very general class exists, or is knowable or is valuable. It denies the validity of all distinctions of moral value. Since the religious philosophy of the *Adi Granth* is based on ethical principles and qualities, this doctrine of nihilism has no justification.

Nihilists: Those who profess nihilism in philosophy or religion. They are atheists and have no belief in the soul and Over-Soul like Charvakas. According to the *Adi Granth*, such people are worthy of condemnation. They are calumniators of religious and moral values and for such calumniators, the Guru says, "The slanderer's face is blackened before God and man (p. 674, Dhanasari M. 5). The Lord is the

Father and Mother and protector of His Devotees and the Face of their slanderer is blackened both here and hereafter (p. 1137, Bhairo M. 5)

Nihkaram: Without any consideration for the result of action. Guru Arjan Dev says, "He who performs the action, but has no desire for its fruit, such a Vaishnava has pure *Dharma*" (Gauri Sukhmani M. 5, p. 274).

Nij Ghar: The real home. "The *Gurmukhs* abide in the Fourth state and thus in their real home. By the Grace of the True Guru, they have destroyed their ego" (Bhairo M. 3, p. 1130). Guru Nanak Dev says, "When the devotee destroys the poison of ego with the Word of the Guru, then he abides in the real home (*nij ghar*)" (Ramkali M. 1, Siddh Goshta).

Nimratā: Humility. See: *Humility*.

Nindā, Nindak: *Nindā* is calumny and *Nindak* is calumniator. See: *Calumny*; *Back-biting*.

Nindrā: Sleep. Sheikh Farid says, "During the night, when the musk is being distributed, those who are asleep, do not get a share. How can they obtain anything, whose eyes are laid down with sleep" (Shlok Farid, p. 1382). He says in another Shloka: "We are helpless regarding the gifts of God. Even those who are awake, do not receive anything, but there are others, who are Bestowed with the gift by awakening them from sleep" (Shlok Farid, p. 1384). Guru Nanak Dev says, "The night passes in sleep and the day in eating. Thus the precious birth is being wasted" (Gauri Bairagan M. 1, p. 156).

Nirākār, Nirankār: The Lord without Form; The Transcendental Lord.

Nirbhaitā, Nirbhau: Fearlessness, Fearless. The word *Nirbhau* occurs in *Mul Mantra*. It is an attribute of Brahman.

Nirdhan: Without wealth; poor. "The wife, friends, sons and relatives are all associated with wealth. Whenever they find the person *Nirdhan* (without wealth), they all run away from him" (Sorath M. 9, p. 633).

Nirguna: The Higher Brahman, called Para Brahman. He is without any qualities and attributes. He is indeterminate and incomprehensible. He is without beginning and end. He is consciousness and Bliss. He is non-phenomenal, non-spatial, non-temporal, non-causal, impersonal and devoid of all sensible qualities. He is Unborn, Eternal, Infinite and Self-Existent.

Nirleptā: The quality of being non-attached. "*Brahm-Giānī* (The Knower of Brahman is always unattached like the lotus in water" (Gauri Sukhmani M. 5, p. 272).

Nirmal: Pure. Purity is a godly quality. "All this world is full of dirt. Only the Lord is Pure and Immaculate" (Bhairo Kabir, p. 1158).

Nirt: Dancing. Physical dancing has been rejected in the *Adi Granth*. Guru Amar Das wants the mind to dance and lose its ego with the Grace of the Guru (Gujri M. 3, p. 506). "This mind should dance before the True Guru" (Bilawal M. 4, p. 834). See: *Dancing*.

Nirvair: Without enmity. This word occurs in *Mūl Mantra*. It is an attribute of Brahman.

Nirvāna: In Buddhist theology, the extinction of individual existence, or the extinction of all desires and passions and attainment of perfect beatitude. See: *Nibbāna*.

Niyoga: During the Vedic period, the custom permitted those who had no child to procreate a child in another woman or beget children by another man. This custom fell into disuse after the vedic period. Niyoga could be performed on widows and also on a living husband's request. The *Adi Granth* believes in legal weddings and lawful issues, therefore Niyoga is rejected.

Nobility: The diginity of mind or character; a noble class. The *Adi Granth* does not recognise any caste, therefore no nobillity is recognised on the basis of the dignity of mind or character. According to the *Adi Granth* Truth is the highest but still higher is the practice of Truth (p. 62, Sri Rag M.1). Guru Arjan Dev says, "My character, my way of life and my caste consist in singing the praises of the Lord" (p. 715, Todi M. 5). Such is the concept of nobility in the *Adi Granth*.

Noble-Ones: According to Buddhism, the Buddhas and Arahats are the Noble ones. According to the *Adi Granth*, the saints (Sādhs, Gurmukhs, Brahm Gianīs, Jivan-Muktas) are the Noble Ones. Guru Ram Das says, "Blessed are the saints in whose heart resides the True Guru. My mind blossoms on seeing them, I am a sacrifice to them" (p. 1264, Malar M. 4). Kabir says, "We should serve both the Lord and the saint. The Lord emancipates us and the saint makes us Cherish our Lord" (p. 1373, Shlok Kabir). Thus the Noble ones are the saints of the Lord.

Non-Being: Non-entity, non-existent; *Asat* in Indian terminology; indeterminate; unreal. Guru Arjan Dev says, "He who is Ever-Existent, seems bitter to you and he, which is non-being, is sweet to you; you are burnt by the fire of *maya*" (p. 823, Bilawal M. 5). Guru Tegh Bahadur says, "The world is false like a deer's delusion but the man runs after the (non-existent) mirage all the time (p. 219, Gauri M. 9).

Non-Duality (*Advaita*): The doctrine of non-duality in Vedanta teaches the oneness of Brahman, self and the universe. This doctrine, propounded by Shankara, was based on the famous passage "That Thou Art". He declared that Brahman and self are not to be regarded as subject and object, but as identical, without difference. But this view of Shankara was not accepted by Ramanuja who declared that Brahman and self (atman) are not identical. They are the whole and the part. The *Adi Granth* follows the line of Ramanuja. Kabir says, "This self (atman) is a part of Brahman" (p. 871, Gond Kabir).

Non-Ego: The outer world that has no independent self-existence. The ego is related only to the self which has an individuality of its own. The *Adi Granth* has laid emphasis on the extinction of ego.

Non-Entity: See: *Non-Being.*

Non-Existence: See: *Non-Being.*

Non-Human Beings: See: *Demons.*

Non-Sentient: That which does not have the power or function of sensation, or of perception by the senses. See: *Nature, Pradhān* and *Prakriti.*

Nothingness: The Buddhist theory of nothingness is called Shunyavāda. It was propounded by Madhyamikas, a sect of Mahāyāna Buddhism, which is said to have been founded by Nāgārjuna in the second century A.D. Shūnya ordinarily means Void or zero; but the theory of nothingness is not true nihilism, it connotes the indescribable real nature of things. Nagarjuna is of the view that the external world is void of characteristics and does not really exist as it is experienced. The word *Shūnya* has been used in the *Adi Granth* by Guru Nanak Dev and Kabir. The Guru says, "Shunya is within us and Shunya is outside and the Shunya is in the three worlds. He who realises Shunya in the fourth state (of equipoise) is uninfluenced by virtue or sin" (p. 943, Ramkali M. 1, Siddh Goshta). In these verses, the word Shunya has been used for God, who is Indescribable. In another hymn, the Guru has talked about Shunya (the Indescribable Lord) as the source of all creation (p. 1037, Maru M. 1).

Novices: The new converts; Those who have entered a religious house and are under probation. For such novices Guru Ram Das says, "If some one slanders the true Guru and then comes under his refuge, his past sins are forgiven by the Guru who blesses him with the company of the saints" (p. 854, Var Bilawal M. 4). It is also said, "Whosoever seeks the refuge of the Merciful Lord, he is ferried across the ocean of

Saṁsāra (p. 1204, Sarang M. 5). Bound by pleasure and pain, one is subjected to transmigration. But when he clings to the Feet of the Guru, his soul gets peace (p. 804, Bilawal M. 5).

Numbers: In the *Adi Granth*, several numbers have been mentioned e.g. *One* for the One Lord; *Two* for duality, two worlds (this world and the next world); *Three* for Trinity and the modes; *Four* for the Vedas; *Five* for five types of musical sounds; and five vices; *Six* for six systems of Indian Philosophy; *Seven* for skies, nether-worlds, days, continents, and oceans; *Eight* for regions and sons of major Ragas; Nine for regions, Eminent Yogis of Nāth sect, planets and miraculous treasures; *Ten* for directions; *Eleven* for Ekadashi fast; *Fourteen* for subtle shops (*Hat*); *Sixteen* for *Shingār* (types of bedecking); *Eighteen for Puranas* (Das-Asti); *Thirty* for Muslim fasts; *Thirty-two* for good signs or virtues in a housewife; *Thirty-three* qualities and (crores of) gods; *Sixty-eight* for Tirthas; *Eighty-four* (lakhs) of species etc. etc. Ten, Twenty, Thirty, Forty, Fifty, Sixty, Seventy, Eighty, Ninety are used regarding the age of man.

Nymphs-Apsarās: A class of semi-divine beings, imagined as beautiful maidens inhabiting the sea, rivers, fountains, hills, woods or trees, or attending on superior deities. In Hindu mythology, there is mention of Apsaras or the dancers in the court of Indra, the king of gods. In the Muslim mythology, there is mention of *houris*, the beautiful damsels of Paradise. In the *Adi Granth*, the word *Hūr* has been used (p.1084, Maru M. 5) in connection with the tenets and principles of Islam. Though the word *Apsarā* is not found in the Sikh scripture, there is mention of the beautiful maidens of heaven (p. 142, Var Majh M. 1) Guru Nanak Dev says, "If the fire and snow be my garment and wind be my food and if there be the beautiful maidens of heaven at all the places, even then I may Praise Thee and the zeal for Thy Praise may never diminish" (Var Majh M. 1, p. 142).

O

Oath(s): An act of swearing; a statement or promise corroborated by such an appeal or the form of words in which such a statement or promise is made. According to the *Adi Granth,* he who makes a statement or promise and later withdraws from it is punished by the Lord. Guru Amar Das says, "He who pledges his word but does not keep it, speaks everything falsely. He is false from within, quite hollow and involved in falsehood. He is inimical towards truthful persons and is lured by greed. The true Lord punishes him" (p. 1099, Var Maru M. 3).

Obedience: The Indian wife is obedience-incarnate. An ideal lady is accomplished in all ways, Truth is her family; she is obedient, wise and charming (p. 371, Asa M. 5). Raiments, jewels, pleasures, honour, splendour, grandeur and obedience are of no avail. If the Beautiful Lord responds to the love, then alone the lady feels blessed (p. 373, Asa M. 5). The lady who is obedient to her Lord, enjoys ever the wedded life (p. 785, Var Suhi M. 3). Guru Arjan Dev says, in *Sukhmani* about the Lord: "Coming and going, visible and invisible, all the creation is Obedient to Thee, O Lord" (281). "The poor Jiva is obedient to Thee, O Lord" (p. 277). The Lord created the Obedient *Maya* (p. 294).

Objects: Material things; Things presented to the sight or other sense. The material objects and the pleasures derived out of them are short-lived. The men of God do not have any attachment with them. Guru Arjan Dev says, "All the material objects have bitter taste. The Lord's Name alone is sweet for them" (p. 321, Var Gauri M. 5). For Sheikh Farid though several sweet things exist, but the sweetest is the Lord Himself (p. 1379). The appropriation of any object, which belongs to another, is strictly forbidden (p. 141, Var Majh M. 1). All other tastes are insipid, because they make the body and mind insipid. All riches, treasures and homes are like a ruined house. The Feet of the Lord are the only Treasure (p. 218, Gauri Majh M. 5).

Obsequies-Funeral Rites: In the *Adi Granth,* there is mention of the disposal of the dead bodies: Guru Nanak Dev says, "Some are cremated, others are buried and still there are others who are thrown to the dogs. Some are thrown in the waters and some are cast into the wells. But no one knows where does one's soul merge in the end" (p. 648, Var Sorath M. 4, Shlok M. 1). When one dies, the relatives cry and weep. But every one weeps for the loss of his or her own interest. In his dirge Guru Nanak Dev says, "If one weeps, because of his involvement, then all his wailing is in vain. One wails truly, if one wails in love" (p. 579, Vadhans M.1). See: *Funeral rites.*

Obstacles-Hindrances: The main obstacles in the spiritual path are the five vices namely lust, anger, greed, attachment and ego. All the human suffering is due to them. These vices are committed through mind, body and speech. Guru Arjan Dev has prayed to the Guru to be Graceful, so that these five vices are destroyed. (p. 269, Gauri Sukhmani M. 5). See: *Hindrances.*

Occult Sciences: The occult sciences like divination, Omens and witchcraft have been condemned in the *Adi Granth*. Guru Arjan Dev says, "He alone is affected by the omens, either good or bad, who does not enshrine the Lord in his heart" (Asa M. 5, p. 401). One should pursue the discipline of the spiritual sciences. This is the crux of the religion of the *Adi Granth*. Guru Tegh Bahadur says, "He who does not have the devotion of the Lord in his mind, his body is like the body of a swine or a dog (Shlok M. 9, p. 1428).

Occupations: There is figurative use of several occupations in the *Adi Granth*, e.g. the workshop of a goldsmith, the farmer and his fields, the trader and his trade, the trades of calico-printer, cobbler, weaver, butcher, barber etc. The saints of the *Adi Granth* were men of various trades and occupations, about which they have given hints in their compositions. For example, the weaver saint Kabir of the *Adi Granth* says, "My mother sobs and weeps regarding the sustenance of her grandchildren saying that her son has given up spinning and weaving. So long as I pass the thread through the shuttle, I forget my Beloved Lord. My mind is lowly and I belong to weaver's caste, but I have earned the Profit of the Name of the Lord. O mother, listen to me. The Beneficent Lord sustains us and our children" (p. 524, Gauri Kabir).

Ocean: In the *Adi Granth*, the world is likened to an ocean, which has to be crossed by the man of the world. The Guru says, "The ocean of Saṁsāra is impassable and vast, which can be crossed through the WORD of the Guru" (p. 962, Var Ramkali M. 5). The mythological churning of the ocean by both the gods and the demons has been figuratively depicted in the Var of Satta and Balwand about the Pontificate of Guru Amar Das, "He made Bāsak-Nāga of contemplation, the churning string and his spiritual prowess the churning pot and made the Sumeru mountain of consciousness the churning stick, and thereby churned the ocean of the world. He also obtained the fourteen jewels of knowledge with which the whole world was enlightened" (p. 968, Ramkali ki Var of Satra and Balwand).

Offences: The acts or facts of offending, wounding the feelings of or displeasing others. "Millions of our offences are washed off in the company of the saints" (p. 296, Gauri Sukhmani M. 5). One is purged of millions of offences (sins) in an instant by the Lord (p. 1337, Prabhati M. 5). He who offends the man of God, is reduced to dust instantly (p. 683, Dhanasari M. 5).

Offspring: Progeny; Issue. The Beloved Bride of the Lord is blessed with thirty-two kinds of embellishments. Truth is her family and offspring (p. 371, Asa M. 5). The offspring should not quarrel with the parents (p. 1200, Sarang M. 4). Guru Nanak Dev says, "The Iron Age gives birth to ghosts. The woman is their master and their offspring (sons and daughters) are also and like goblins" (p. 556, Var Bihāgṛā M. 4, Shalok M. 1).

Ogres: Giants; Demons. According to Guru Nanak Dev, the protagonists of religion became like ogres and demons. He says, "These man-eaters (ogres) say the prayers. Although they wear the sacred thread, they carry the killer-knife. The Brahmins blow the conch in their homes; they also relish the same taste" (p. 471, Var Asa M. 1).

Old-Age: There are three stages of life viz. Childhood, Youth and Old age (p. 1428, Shlok M. 9). The hair turn grey when one becomes old. (p.1378, Shlok Farid). The body begins to shake (p. 1380, Shlok Farid). The teeth, feet, eyes and ears gradually cease to function (p. 1381, Shlok Farid). The old age is a must and none can prevent its arrival. It comes in various ways (p. 465, Var Asa M. 1). The True Yogi slays old age, death and the ego (p. 223, Gauri M. 1). "Through poise, when the Lord merges in the soul, the true devotee is not subject to death, old age, woe or pain" (p. 808, Bilawal M. 5). The saint Bhikhan says, "Water wells up in the eyes, the body becomes weak, the hair turn grey. The throat is choked and one cannot speak. In such a stage of life what one should do?" (p. 659, Sorath Bhikhan).

Old Things: The material objects grow old and become useless. "The cloth when worn off, is torn and the needle mends it, but after some time (may be a month or half month, a few hours or even moments) it becomes useless and is thrown away but the truth is never old and never torn" (p. 955, Var Ramkali M. 3, Shlok M. 1). According to Guru Nanak Dev, the sacred thread, on becoming old , is thrown away and a new one is worn instead (p. 471, Var Asa M. 1). One's beauty, breath and body, on becoming old, wither away (p. 1025, Maru M. 1).

Old Times: The texts belonging to old times in India are *Itihāsas* and *Puranas*. The *Itihāsas* include two great epics i.e. *Ramayana* and *Mahābhārata*. There are several references in the *Adi Granth*, which are drawn from thoughts of these old works. There are even some from the oldest Veda i.e. Rig Veda. The thoughts contained in the Nāsadīya Sūkta and the Pūrusha Sūkta are found in the Verses of Guru Nanak Dev. The personages of old times *drawn* from the above-mentioned texts have been mentioned in the *Adi Granth* in various contexts. Whereas there is no change in the human nature in old times and modern times, there is also no change in the natural phenomena. Guru Nanak Dev says, "The same moon and same stars rise, the same sun produces heat. There is the same earth and the same blowing winds; how do the various places affect the working of jivas in the context of time?" (p. 902, Ramkali M. 1).

Om: (Aum, Aumkāra). The very first word that occurs in the *Adi Granth* is Ik Omkara. Oam or Om is the primal letter. It has also been written as Onam in the *Adi Granth*. Guru Nanak Dev says, "Omkara is He, who Created the mountains and the ages. Omkara is He, who Created the Vedas. Omkara is He, who through the Word, Emancipated all. Omkara is He, through whom, the God-Conscious beings were saved. Listen to the connotation of the Word "OM" (Onam),Which is the Essence of the three worlds" (p. 930, Ramkali M. 1, Dakhni Omkara). In the Upanishads, the word OM means the Manifested as well as Unmanifested Brahman. The same meaning has been carried forward in the *Adi Granth*. Om is the sacred syllable. The *Mul Mantra* (primary formula) begins with the word Ik Omkara. It is the primal Name of the Lord and is called *bīja mantra*. The devotee repeats it and meditates on it. In Sikhism, more stress is laid on the remembrance of Waheguru, another *bīja-mantra*.

Omens: Circumstances supposed to portend good or evil; Prophetic signs. The *Adi Granth* holds that only that person is affected by omens, good or bad, who does not enshrine the Lord in his heart (p. 401, Asa M. 5). In Hindu religious literature, there is mention of *Shakuna* (good or bad omen). Shakuna (Dhisthatri) is the name of the goddess who presides over the omens. Shakuna-gyān is the divination of omens by the movements of birds and animals.

Omnipotence: The quality of being Omnipotent; Almightiness. The Lord is All Powerful. Guru Nanak Dev says, "If it is the Will of the

Lord, He may make tigers, hawks, kites and falcons to eat grass and cause the grass-eating animals to feed on meat. He may dry up the streams and show their beds and (if He Wills) He may establish a worm in kingship and reduce the forces to dust. All the jivas live by breathing, but the Lord may keep one without it. The man abides according to the Will of the True Lord" (p. 144, Var Majh M. 1). Guru Arjan Dev says, "The Lord has Created His Power and with that Power, He has upheld the Earth and upheld the sky on His feet according to His Will. He Created fire, imprisoned in wood. He provides sustenance to all His Creatures. He is the only Doer and the cause of all things. He is the All-Powerful Lord. He creates and Destroys in an instant. He provides sustenance in the womb of the mother. He may Reduce the kings and chiefs to the position of worms and Bless the poor with Sovereignty" (p. 1071, Maru M. 5).

Omnipresence: The fact of being present in all places at the same time. The Lord is All-Pervading. "He the Infinite Lord, is both inside and outside of us. He Pervades all hearts. He is on the earth and in the sky and the underworld. He completely fills the whole universe. He is in all vegetation and over the mountains. He is in the air, water and fire. He is in all the four quarters and ten directions. There is no place without Him" (pp. 293-94, Gauri Sukhmani M. 5). "Just as the fire is locked in the wood and the ghee (clarified butter) in the milk, so the Lord Pervades all hearts and His Light enlightens both high and low. O Saints, the Lord abides in all hearts. The Perfect Lord fills all, in the waters and on the land" (p. 617, Sorath M. 5).

Omniscience: The quality of knowing all things. Guru Ram Das addresses the Lord thus: "You are both inside and outside of us. You are the knower of my inmost secrets. You know, Whatever I do" (p. 84, Var Sri Rag M. 4). "O Creator Lord you know everything, then what shall we say unto You? You know the good and bad in us. You know my inner state" (p. 735, Suhi M. 4).

Opposites: This term refers to the pairs of opposites such as heat and cold, pleasure and pain. The soul in its purity is free from all such opposites. "Our Soul is the image of the Transcendent Lord. It is neither old nor young. It neither knows heat nor cold neither it is in joy nor in pain" (p. 868, Gond M. 5). Kabir also sings in the same strain (p. 871, Gond Kabir). The embodied souls (jivas) experience these opposites under the impact of *māyā*. The true saint or the knower of Brahman rises above these opposites. "He who is above praise and calumny and for whom iron and gold are alike, He alone is emancipated and saved. He who is neither affected by joy nor sorrow and looks on the friend and foe alike, He alone is emancipated and released" (pp. 1426-27, Shlok M. 9).

Oracles: Vehicles or mediums of divine communication. In this sense, the Guru and saints, whose hymns have been included in *Adi Granth*, were oracles, because the Lord spoke through them. Guru Nanak Dev says, "I utter only the Word of the Lord, which I receive from Him" (p. 722, Tailing M. 1). "I said, what You, my Lord, inspired me to say" (p. 566, Vadhans M. 1).

Oral Tradition: The act of transmitting or handing down, from one to another or from generation to generation; Transmission of statements, beliefs, rules, customs, or the like, by word of mouth or by practice without writing. Sometimes there is a reference to the utterances of the elders. For example: As I have heard from others about the merits of the True Guru, so I have seen" (p. 957, Var Ramkali M. 5).

Ordeal(s): An ancient mode of trial, in which a suspected person was subjected to some physical test fraught with danger, the result being regarded as the immediate judgement of the Deity. In the *Adi Granth*, the devotee is shown as passing through the ordeals regarding the sincerity of his love for the Guru. Sheikh Farid says, "The streets are muddy, the house of my beloved is far away, but I am in love with him. If I go out in the rain, my blanket is wetted and if I stay behind, I lose my beloved. Let my blanket be wetted in the rains created by God, but I must meet my beloved, so that my love survives the test" (p. 1379, Shlok Farid). The same resoluteness is shown by Guru Ram Das: "If it snows and the weather is frosty and wintry, the seeker will still go out to see the Guru" (p. 757, Suhi M. 4).

Orders: It pertains to four orders or stages of life viz. *Brahmacharin* (student), *Grahasthi* (householder), *Vanaprasthi* (hermit) and *Sannyasi* (ascetic). The *Adi Granth* rejects asceticism and renunciation. Therefore it is only in favour of the life of a householder. Guru Amar Das says, "It is better to be a householder than to clad oneself in some guise, because as a householder one is able to give something to others (Var Vadhans M. 4, Shlok M. 3, p. 587). See: *Ashramas*.

Ordination: The action of conferring holy orders. One does not meet the Lord through effort or through service, but meets Him spontaneously. He who receives the ordination through the Mercy of the Lord, practises the mantra of the Guru (p. 672, Dhanasari M. 5). If one has to cling to someone, then let his mind cling to the Feet of the Guru. He alone, who is so destined (by ordination), attains to this state (p. 1018, Maru M. 5).

Organic Beings: Beings having organs or organised physical structures of animals or plants. There are four classes of organic beings, each class known in Indian terminology as "Khānī". The *Adi Granth* also believes in the four classes of creatures evolved according to their karmas. See: *Creation*.

Organs: There are five organs of perception (*Gyan Indrīyas*) and five organs of action (*karma Indrīyas*) in the human body. Mahat or Buddhi (Understanding) is another one. The mind belongs to both the organs of perception and action. Guru Arjan Dev says, "He who holds in control the ten organs, his soul is undoubtedly illumined" (p. 236, Gauri M. 5). The five organs of perception are eyes, ears, nose, tongue and skin. The five organs of action are hands, feet, mouth and the organs of procreation and elimination. These organs have been identified with ten ladies, whom every individual has to keep in check (p. 1083, Maru M. 5).

Oriental Alphabets: There are a few original alphabets on whose letters, the stanzas of five poems of the *Adi Granth* are based. These poems are Two *pattīs* in Raga Asa, Two *Bawan Akhrīs* in Raga Gauri and *Dakhnī Oamkar* in Raga Ramkali. The *Pattī* of Guru Nanak Dev is based on Gurmukhi alphabet and the *Pattī* of Guru Amar Das is based on Landā, though a few vowels and consonants are in accordance with Devanagari alphabet. *Bawan Akhrīs* of Guru Arjan Dev and Kabir are based on fifty-two letters of Sanskrit alphabet. Dakhni Oamkar of Guru Nanak Dev is also based on the fifty-two letters of Sanskrit alphabet.

Orphans: The children deprived of their parents by death. Sheikh Farid has used the word *Atīmā* (the corrupted form from *Yatīm* (Persian) meaning orphan). He says, "They for whom the drums beat, and the canopies wave over whose heads, whose praises are sung by the bards and in whose honour the pipes shrieck. In the end they also find rest in the burial ground and are buried in the graves like orphans" (p. 1380, Shlok Farid).

Outcast: Cast out from home and friends, hence forsaken, homeless and neglected. Guru Amar Das says, "They who turn their back upon the Guru, do not get any refuge and like an outcast woman go from door to door having been of low character and having earned a bad name (p. 645,Var Sorath M. 4, Shlok M. 3). They who were cursed and outcast by the perfect Guru from the very beginning, the curse of the Guru is even now upon them. They want to be reunited with the Guru, but the Lord does not wish it. They find no refuge in the company of the saints because the Guru has so proclaimed. Whosoever goes to meet them, he will be destroyed by the terrific *Yama*" (p. 307, Var Gauri M. 4).

Owl: There is no use of the word "owl" in the *Adi Granth* but the *Indian* terms "*Andh*", "Andh Ghor" and other similiar terms and phrases are suggestive of the quality of the owl. When there is light of the sun, the owl cannot see. Similarly, that individual can be identified with an owl, who cannot see the light of knowledge. In *Japuji*, Guru Nanak Dev has talked about such fools, when he says, "There are countless fools groping in the dark" (p. 4, Japuji).

Ox: The *Adi Granth* identifies a man without the Love of the Lord with an Ox or a Bull. Kabir says, "Without the Love of the Lord, one is like a stray ox. His nose is torn, his shoulder bruised and he is fed upon the straw of coarse grain. He wanders in the forest the whole day, but his hunger is not satisfied. Since he does not listen to the advice of the devotees of the Lord, he receives whatever is due to him" (Gujri Kabir, p. 524). There is also mention of the mythological Bull personified as *Dharma*, who is the son of (the cow personified as) Mercy (Japuji, p. 3).

P

Pad: The state; position. This word is generally used in the *Adi Granth* in connection with the Supreme spiritual state such as *Chauthā Pad*, *Param Pad* and *Jīwan Pad*.

Padārath: Substance; Valuable article. See: *Cār Padārath*.

Pain: The opposite of pleasure; the sensation which one feels when hurt (in body or mind): suffering. Guru Nanak Dev says, "Pleasure comes out of pain and pain comes out of pleasure" (p. 1328, Prabhati M. 1). "Pain is the cure and pleasure is the malady" (p. 469, Var Asa M. 1). "The pain is the door and anger is the guardsman. The two planks of this door are hope and fear" (p. 877, Ramkali M. 1). Guru Arjan Dev says, "Pain comes when we forget the Lord" (p. 813, Bilawal M. 5). To earn happiness, one goes through pain, but the self-willed does not know it (p. 57, Sri Rag M. 1). The Name of the Lord is the dispeller of pain (p. 830, Bilawal M. 9). The God-conscious person rises above both pain and pleasure. "He looks upon both pain and pleasure alike" (p. 879, Ramkali M. 1).

Pairs of every species created: The Lord created the bodies with the mother's ovary and the father's sperm (p. 1026, Maru M. 1). There are eighty-four lakhs of species, but man is honoured above them all (p. 1075, Maru Solhas M. 5). There are pairs of all these species.

Pākhand, Pākhandī: Heresy/Heretic. See: *Heresy, Heretic*.

Palmistry: (Divination). The *Adi Granth* does not believe in chiromancy or any other practice relating to divination. The astrological observations cannot touch the spiritual phenomena, therefore they are fruitless on this account (p. 904, Ramkali M. 1).

Panc: It has two connotations: 1-five and 2-The selected person; the ideal man. Guru Nanak Dev has mentioned the qualities and attributes of *Panc* in *Japuji*, wherein he says, "He receives respect not only in the court of a king, but also in the Court of the Lord. He concentrates fully on the discipline of the Guru" (p. 3).

Panc Dokh: The five blemishes. The five *Tanmātrās*. "The deer, fish, bumble bee, a moth and an elephant, each one of them is destroyed by one *Tanmātrā* (deer by *Shabad* (*Sabda*), fish by *Rasa*, bumble bee by *Gandh*, moth by *Rupa* and elephant by *Sparsha*) and the man who has all the five *Tanmātrās*, how can he be saved?" (Asa Ravidas, p. 486).

Panc Shabda: Five types of sounds heard by a Yogi during concentration. These sounds are produced by musical instruments working with strings, skin metal, pitcher and breath. But according to the *Adi Granth*, the unstruck and unlimited sound (Anhad Nad) resounds on the realisation of the Lord (Suhi M.1, p. 764).

Panc Tat: Five elements. See: *Elements*.

Panc Vikār: Five vices i.e. Lust, anger, greed, attachment and ego.

Pāndhā: Teacher; Pundit. "That *Pāndhā* is really educated, who is absorbed in studies spontaneously. He studies profoundly and obtains the essence and concentrates on the Name of the Lord...*Pāndhā* may be considered enlightened (Gurmukh), who gives this advice to the students: 'Remember the Name and always remain with the Name, because in this way you will be benefitted in the world'" (Ramkali M. 1, Dakhni Oamkar, pp. 437-38).

Pantheism: The belief that God and the universe are identical, implying the denial of the personality and transcendence of God; the doctrine that God is everything and everything is God. Though the *Adi Granth* believes that God is everything and everything is God, but it does not deny the personality and transcendence of God. It is said: "Whatever I see is Brahman, whatever I hear is Brahman, I speak only of the One Lord" (p. 846, Bilawal M. 5). It is also said, "O Lord, You are Unaccountable, Unapproachable and Detached" (p. 1038, Maru M. 1).

Pāp, Pāpī: Sin, Sinner. See: *Sin*.

Parables: Fictitious narratives (usually of something that might naturally occur), by which moral or spiritual relations are typically set forth. An example or illustration to follow or to avoid. In the *Adi Granth*, several parables from old works have been narrated as examples for particular actions or deeds (p. 954, Var Ramkali M. 3, Shalok M. 1).

Parā Brahman: Transcendental Lord; Nirguna Brahman. See: *Brahman*.

Parādhīnatā: Subservience; slavery. Sheikh Farid says, "O Lord, do not make me sit on another's door. If you want this, then take out the soul from my body" (Shlok Farid, p. 1380).

Paradise: Heaven; the abode of God, saints and the righteous. The *Adi Granth* has rejected the concept of the Hindu Paradise (*Svarga*) or of Muslim Paradise (*Jannat/Bahisht*). "Do not seek the abode of Paradise" (p. 337, Gauri Poorbi Kabir). "Everyone seeks Emancipation or Paradise and rests all his hopes on it, but I seek no deliverance and want only to see Your Vision" (p. 1324, Kalyan M. 4). The countless heavens cannot equal the Name of the Lord (p. 1078, Maru M. 5).

Paradox: A statement seemingly self-contradictory or absurd, though possibly well-founded or essentially true. The *Adi Granth* is a repository of spiritual truths some of which may appear to the non-spiritual and heretical people as paradoxical, because they are the experiences of the mystics of a very high order.

Parāī Vastū: The thing belonging to another. He who considers as his own the articles belonging to others, he suffers in ego (Var Majh M. 1, p. 139). He who weeps for things belonging to others, he loses all his merit (Dhanasari M. 5, p. 676).

Paramātman: It is a combination of two words *Param* and *Atman* which means Supreme Soul or Over-Soul i.e. Brahman, Who is the Creator, Preserver and Destroyer of the universe.

Paramgat: Salvation. See: *Salvation.*

Paramitas: These are cardinal human virtues according to Buddhism, which guide the disciple on the path to Nirvāna. According to some they are six in number and according to others they are ten. The six are the following: charity (*dāna*), morality (*sīla*), patience (*ksantī*), energy (*vīrya*), meditation (*dhyāna*) and wisdom (*prajna*). The remaining four are expediency (*upāya*), vow (*pranīdhāna*), strength (*bala*) and knowledge (*jnāna*). In the *Adi Granth*, the word *Paramita* is found in the verses of Kabir, wherein he says, "Let contemplation and remembrance be your two ear-rings and let *Paramita* (gnosis) be your coat." *Paramita* here signifies *Prajna* (wisdom) and *Jnana* (knowledge).

Param Pad: Supreme State. See: *Cauthā Pad.*

Parāpatī: Attainment. Only He attains this treasure of Hari (the Lord), who enjoys the savour of the Name of the Lord within his self (Maru M. 5, p. 1085).

Pardon: Forgiveness of sins. Guru Arjan Dev says, "As a child commits a lakh of mistakes innocently, the father reprimands him in various ways and hugs him to his bosom, in the same manner, the Lord pardons us for our past sins and shows us the path for the future" (p. 624, Sorath M. 5). Guru Amar Das says, "O Lord, pardon me for past sins and now show me the path" (p. 994, Maru M. 3). In the words of Guru Ram Das "if some one calumniates the True Guru and then seeks his refuge, the Guru pardons his past sins and blesses him with the society of the saints" (p. 854, Var Bilawal M. 4).

Parents: According to the *Adi Granth*, the Guru is both the father and the mother (p. 250, Gauri Bawan Akhri M. 5). The girl who wastes her time in the house of her parents is robbed of her virtues and goes to the house of the Lord with a bundle of vices (p. 23, Sri Rag M. 1). The mother and father are mere attachment and one is involved in such attachment (p. 571, Vadhans M. 3). The mind of the child is mercurial and it does not mind playing even with fire or snake. But when the father and mother keep the child under their loving sight, he is not harmed and plays care-free with joy. O Lord, You are the Father, then why and for what Your Children should hunger? (p. 1266, Malar M. 5). Guru Arjan Dev says, "He who has blessed you with father and mother....Cherish Him, in your heart (p. 913, Ramkali M. 5).

Par-Ghar: Another's house. The self-willed person (Manmukh) wavers in his mind about the house (and wife) of another person. He clings to the evils and the noose falls around his neck (Gauri M. 1, p. 266). Going to another's house (with evil intentions) is like the company of a cobra (Asa M. 5, p. 403).

Parkh: Discrimination: judgment; evaluation. Those coins which are put in the treasury after scrutiny and evaluation can never be called counterfeit afterwards (Var Gujri M. 5, p. 520). The evaluator is called *Pārakh* (Var Majh M. 1, Shalok M. 2, p. 148).

Par-Istrī: Another's wife. Guru Arjan Dev says, "One should not see the beauty of another's wife" (Gauri Sukhmani M. 5, p. 274). The taboo for the eyes is the beauty of another's wife and another's wealth (Asa M. 1, p. 472).

Par-Kirt: To work for others. According to Hindu caste system, the *Shudras* are required to serve the three superior castes. The *Adi Granth* is against the division of castes. Guru Amar Das says, "One should leave the mentality of Shudras, who (unwillingly) work for others, but instead he should recognise the essence" (Bhairo M. 3, p. 1128).

Parmārath: Spiritual knowledge. "If one forsakes false greed, he recognises Truth. He is absorbed in the Word of the Guru and comprehends spiritual knowledge" (Asa M. 1, p. 419).

Parmeshwar: Param Ishvara; the Supreme Ishvara; Brahman. See: *Brahman*.

Partition of Property: Though there is no direct mention of the partition of property in the *Adi Granth*, there is mention of the lure of riches, which divide brother from brother (p. 417, Asa M. 1).

Par-Upkār: Doing good to others; philanthropy. "One should destroy all his vices and do good to others" (Gauri M. 5, p. 218). That body is false, which does not do good to others (Gauri Sukhmani M. 5, p. 269). *Brahm-Giānī* (the knower of Brahman) is the spring of philanthropy (Gauri Sukhmani M. 5, p. 273).

Parwān: Accepted; approved. "Those persons are approved by the Lord, in whose mind the Lord abides" (Gauri M. 4, p. 189). He who recognises the *Hukam* is approved by the Lord (Asa M. 5, p. 386). He who visualises the Lord in every heart, he is approved in the world by the Lord (Gauri M. 5, p. 198).

Passion: Any vehement, commanding, or overpowering emotion; in psychology or art, any mode in which the mind is affected or acted upon, as ambition, avarice, desire, hope, fear, love, hatred, joy, grief, anger, revenge. According to the *Adi Granth*, "none has felt satiated amidst passions" (p. 672, Dhanasri M. 5). Guru Arjan Dev says, "Forsake the insipid forest-fruit of passions and drink the Great Essence of Lord's Name" (p. 802, Bilawal M. 5). He says again, "O Fool, you are lured by vain insipid tastes. You are involved in passions, when the nectar is present within you (p. 1017, Maru M. 5).

Pātāla: All the seven nether regions are collectively called *Pātāla*. It is the seventh and nethermost region, other six being Atala, Vitala, Nitala, Gabhastimat, Mahatala and Sutala. Each region is ten thousand leagues deep and has a separate regent. It is of golden hue. The cobra Vasuki is its ruler. The capital is Bhogavati. The *Adi Granth* believes that there are lakhs of Pātāls (nether-regions) (p. 6, Japuji).

Path: In theology, this word connotes a line of conduct or a line of thought. The *Adi Granth* presents a path (*panth*) or discipline enunciated by the Sikh Gurus and radical saints. This discipline has a triple significance and works on three planes viz. physical, mental and spiritual. In its moral aspect, it elucidates the injunctions regarding body, mind and speech. On the spiritual plane, it brings about the merger of the soul in the Supreme Soul.

Pāth: Reading of books especially scriptures and religious books. "The fools read religious books and deceive others, because their motive is to fill their bellies (Var Sarang M. 3, p. 1246). Though one reads religious texts, he indulges in lies, because he has not received the advice of the Guru, being a *Nigurā* (Maru M. 1, p. 1013).

Peace: The peace of mind is essential for a devotee. When the mercurial mind becomes stable, it would not be hurt any more (p. 1113, Tukhari M. 1). It does not become stable because of desires (p. 219, Gauri M. 9). Our task is with the mind; the perfection is attained, when it is disciplined (p. 342, Gauri Kabir). Guru Amar Das says, "Make your mind wise and then know the Lord. No one will listen to you, if you instruct others. Try to understand through the Word of the Guru and you will be at peace for ever" (p. 230, Gauri M. 3).

Pearl: In the *Adi Granth,* the Name of the Lord is identified with a pearl; but this pearl cannot be stolen by any one (p. 134, Baramaha Majh). The Guru is the sea full of pearls. The saints pick up the pearls like swans and remain near the Guru" (p. 685, Dhanasari M.1). The heart of every one is precious like a pearl, it is bad to hurt it. If you seek your Lord, then do not hurt the heart of any one (p. 1384, Shlok Farid).

Peasantry: Peasants collectively. Several working classes have been mentioned in the *Adi Granth*, e.g. goldsmiths, weavers, cobblers, peasantry etc. The saint Dhanna was a peasant. The word "Jat" has been used by him and for him. Guru Nanak Dev in his later years worked as a peasant in his fields, therefore he has mentioned the working of a peasant in his verses. He says, "If your farm be of good actions and the Word be your seed and the Way of Truth your water, then as a peasant you will see the growth of faith" (p. 24, Sri Rag M. 1). At another place he says, "Let the mind be the peasant and actions be the farming; let the body be the field and effort the water, Let Lord's Name be the seed, contentment the furrowing and humility the fencing. If you do the deeds of love, the seed will sprout and then your home will be fortunate" (p. 595, Sorath M. 1).

Penal Law: The law prescribing or enacting the punishment of an offence or transgression. In the *Adi Granth,* the Gurus as well as the saints have mentioned in their hymns the punishment after death in hell by the god of Justice for those who flout the moral canons and also for those who forget the Lord, their Creator. According to Sheikh Farid, those who commit evil actions, are punished like cotton, sesame seed, sugar-cane, paper, kettle and coals. (p.1380, Shlok Farid). Guru Arjan Dev says, "The sinners are wasted away for sure, and Izrāīl, the angel of death seizes and destroys them. They are cast into the hell by the Creator and are asked to render the account by the god of Justice" (pp. 1019-20, Maru M. 5).

Penance: The performance of some act of self-mortification or submission to some penalty, as an expression of penitence. The equivalent of this word in Indian terminology is *Prayaschitta.* The *Adi Granth* has rejected such acts. Guru Arjan Dev says, "All the acts of penance do not ferry you across the ocean of *Saṁsāra*. Only the Name of the Lord washes away millions of your sins" (p. 264, Gauri Sukhmani M. 5).

Perception: It is considered as one of the valid sources of knowledge, the other being inference, comparison and verbal testimony. Its equivalent in Indian terminology is *pratyaksha*. The perception may be physical, mental and spiritual. The physical eyes see the world but are not satisfied (p. 147, Var Majh M. 1, Shlok M. 2). The mind is satisfied if it dwells on the Name of the Lord. Guru Amar Das says, "Having been attuned to the One Lord, my eyes are content and my mind is also content, because it has forsaken the sense of duality" (p. 560, Vadhans M. 3). The spiritual perception is destroyed by the curtain of ego, therefore the perceptible Lord cannot be visualised (p. 234, Gauri M. 4).

Perfect: Only the Lord God is Perfect. "Our Perfect Lord is Eternal Purusha, whose praises are sung by the Vedas and Puranas (p. 783, Suhi M. 5). Guru Nanak Dev says, "You are perfect, O Lord, I am imperfect; You are Deep and Unfathomable and I am shallow" (p. 597, Sorath M. 1). "Perfect are the doings of the Perfect One, they can neither be increased nor decreased. One must realise such a One by the Grace of the Guru and Merge in the Perfect Being" (p. 1412, Shlok Varan te Vadhik M. 1). Since a *Brahm-Gyani* (The Knower of Brahman) is one with the Lord, he is also considered Perfect. Guru Arjan Dev says, "Brahm-Gyani is the Perfect Man, he is the architect of our destiny...He is the Absolute Lord Himself" (pp. 273-74, Gauri Sukhmani M. 5).

Perfection: The state of perfection has been variously described. In Buddhism it is Bodhisattva, in Jainism, it is Arhathood. In Hinduism it is Moksha. According to the *Adi Granth*, it is the state of final beatitude or final emancipation, when the devotee becomes one with the Lord. Guru Arjan Dev says, "The rays have merged in the sun and the water in the water. The Light has merged in the Light and I have attained Perfection" (p. 846, Bilawal M. 5). The saint Ravidas says, "There is no difference between You and me, between me and You like the golden bracelet and gold and like the water and the wave" (p. 93, Sri Rag Ravidas). Kabir says, "Kabir and God have become One, none can recognise them" (p. 969, Ramkali Kabir).

Periods—Ages of the World: The four Yugas and their main features have been discussed in a few hymns in the *Adi Granth*. According to saint Ravidas, Truth prevailed in *Satyuga*, Charity in *Treta* and worship in Dharma in *Duapar*. People held fast to such acts in these three Yugas, but in the *Kali-Yuga* the only mainstay is the Name of the Lord (p. 346, Gauri Bairagan Ravidas). Guru Nanak Dev says, "For the *Jiva*, there is a chariot and a charioteer. They change in every age; this fact is known to all wise people. In *Satyuga*, the contentment is the chairot and righteousness its driver. In *Treta*, continence is the chariot and power its charioteer. In *Duapar*, austerity is the chariot and charity its driver. In *Kaliyuga*, Fire is the chariot and Falsehood its charioteer (p. 470, Var Asa M.1).

Perjury: The crime of wilfully uttering false evidence while on oath. Guru Nanak Dev points to the act of perjury, when he says, "His speech contains false evidence and he eats away what does not belong to him; but still he goes to preach to others" (p. 140, Var Majh M. 1). Guru Amar Das says, "Love of *Maya* is an affliction and its trade is false. Giving false evidence, one eats poison and adds to his evils" (p. 570, Vadhans M. 3).

Perseverence: Constant persistence in an undertaking; continuance in a state of grace leading finally to a state of glory. Self-restraint is an essential basis for perseverence. One must persevere to go forward and not look back (p. 1096, Var Maru Dakhne M. 5). Perseverence is neccessary for dispelling anxiety. Guru Arjan Dev says, "Live by making earnest effort, abide in joy by earning and Meet the Lord by Contemplating on Him...in this way all the anxiety is dispelled" (p. 522, Var Gujri M. 5). One should never be slack in perseverence (p. 1371, Shlok Kabir).

Philosophy: The *Adi Granth* is not a philosophical treatise. However, there is a manifestation of philosophy through its hymns. It is the religious philosophy. Guru Amar Das says, "Six systems of Philosophy are current among the populace, but the Philosophy of the Guru is Supreme, through which the final Emancipation is attained" (pp. 360-61, Asa M. 3).

Physician: One who practises the healing art including medicine and surgery. "A wise physician is one who understands the malady as well as the medicine" (p. 48, Var Majh M. 1, Shlok M. 2). For a devotee, his Master, the Guru, is the physician, who blesses him with the medicine of the Name of the Lord and cuts away the noose of Yama (p. 618, Sorath M. 5).

Piety: The quality of being pious and righteous. It is also equivalent to *Dharma*. A very fortunate person attains the Path of saints and the ladder of piety (p. 622, Sorath M. 5). Where there is spiritual knowledge, there is piety (Dharma), where there is falsehood, there is sin (p. 1372, Shlok Kabir). A householder should perform acts of piety (p. 1377, Shlok Kabir).

Pilgrim: One who journeys to some sacred place as an act of religious devotion. The saint Ravidas, describing his oneness with the Lord says, "If You are the *Tīrtha* (the place of pilgrimage), then I am a pilgrim" (p. 658, Sorath Ravidas). "Should I go as a pilgrim to holy places? My sacred place is the Name of the Lord" (p. 687, Dhanasari M. 1).

Pilgrimage: A journey made by a pilgrim; The course of mortal life figured as a journey. Guru Arjan Dev says, "My pilgrimage has now become fruitful. I have met the saints and my transmigration has ceased" (p. 687, Dhanasari M. 5). "O Lord, Through Your Service is attained the Merit of pilgrimages, fasting, worship, six kinds of works and living at the river-banks" (p. 1153, Bhairo M. 5).

Pind: Body. In the *Adi Granth*, generally *Jīu* (soul) and *Pind* (body) are used together. "He (the Lord) Created the being by bringing together soul and body" (Sri Rag M.1, p. 72).

Pīr: Muslim word for spiritual preceptor or Guru. "He deserves to go to heaven, who recognises the *Pīr* (Guru). *Izrāīl* (god or angel of death) does not push him towards hell (Maru M. 5, p. 1084).

Pishāchas: Demons. Guru Arjan Dev, while talking about the creation, has mentioned *Pishāchas* also. He says: "There are millions of *Yakshas* (attendants of Kuber, the god of wealth), Kinnars (semi-gods, with heads of horses and bodies of men) and *Pishāchas* (demons)" (p. 276, Gauri Sukhmani M. 5). See: *Demons*.

Pitrīs: Forefathers. The *Adi Granth* has rejected the Hindu practice of worshipping and propitiating their manes. Kabir says, "No one cares for their *Pitrīs* in their lifetime, but after death they make offerings in their name. Even these offerings are not obtained by the *Pitrīs*, only the crows and dogs feed on them" (p. 332, Gauri Bairagan Kabir). See: *Forefathers and Manes*.

Pity: A feeling of tenderness aroused by the suffering or misfortune of another, and prompting a desire for its relief. Seeing the people being killed by the hordes of tyrants, Guru Nanak Dev has complained even to the Lord: "There has been such a great holocaust and bemoaning, but did you not feel any pity?" (p. 360, Asa M. 1). Guru Arjan Dev says: "O Lord, You took Pity on me and blessed me; my friend, the True Guru met me" (p. 1429, Shlok M. 5).

Planets: The heavenly bodies distinguished from the fixed stars by having an apparent motion of their own among them. The seven planets, in the order of their accepted distance from the Earth, are the Moon, Mercury, Venus, Sun, Mars, Jupiter and Saturn. Guru Arjan Dev, while talking about creation, says, "There are millions of moons, suns and planets" (p. 275, Gauri Sukhmani M. 5). The planets (stars), Sun, Moon, Earth and Sky—all worship the Lord (p. 456, Asa M. 5).

Plants: Out of the four divisions of creation (*Khānis*) the *Udhibhijja* includes all sorts of plants. Mushrooms are included in the *Svetajja*. Water is the essence of the plants. Guru Nanak Dev says, "The food-grains, the sugar-cane and cotton are produced from water" (p. 1290, Var Malar M. 1). "The spring brought bloom first, but the Lord was in bloom still earlier" (p. 791, Var Suhi M. 3, Shalok M. 1). The unwise one sees mango on the lemon tree and vice-versa, and the bunch of banana seems to him on the bush. He sees the cocoanut on the Simmal-tree. Such is the ignorance of the unwise (p. 972, Ramkali Kabir). The peasant, who sows *Kikar*, how can he get the vine of Bijaur? (p.1379, Shlȯk Farid). I pluck flowers and weave a garland and offer it to the stone-god; but the fragrance of flowers was first sucked by the black-bee. How shall it please my Lord? (p. 485, Asa Namdev). In his *Aarti-hymn* Guru Nanak Dev says, "The Chandan-scented winds from the Malai mountains wave and scatter across the fragrance of the innumerable flowers of the forests (p. 663, Dhanasari M. 1).

Pleasures: The human being wears both the garments of pleasure and pain (p. 149, Var Majh M. 1). Everyone craves for pleasures; no one wants pain. The self-willed do not know that in order to earn pleasures, one goes through pain. But one looks upon pain and pleasure alike, if one comes into contact with the Word (p. 57, Sri Rag M. 1). If one is attached to pleasures, he meets with pain. The indulgence causes disease and one is wasted away. The pain caused by pleasure is not obliterated (p. 1034, Maru M. 1).

Pledge: Anything put in the possession of another, as security for the performance of a contract or payment of a debt, or as a guarantee of good faith, etc., and liable to forfeiture in case of failure. Kabir says, "I have pledged nothing to anybody. O Lord, how can I pull on with you? If You do not Give Yourself, I shall beg of You to give me..." (p. 656, Sorath Kabir).

Poetry: The works of all the Gurus and saints which are included in the *Adi Granth*, are in poetry. The word used for such poetry is "*bānī*".

This *bānī*, which is both metrical and musical, is of great spiritual significance. The *bānī* of the Guru is Guru itself (p. 982, Mat M. 4). This *bānī* of the Guru is the Light in the world (p. 67, Sri Rag M. 3). The *bānī* of the Perfect Guru is liked by the Lord (p. 629, Sorath M. 5). Such person, who will reflect on the *bānī*, will be rare. He will be an Awakened Person (p. 935, Ramkali M. 1, Dakhni Oamkar). O Sikhs, consider the *bānī* of the True Guru as True. The Lord Himself causes it to come from the Guru's Mouth (p. 308, Var Gauri M. 4).

Poets: Kabir says that all those who are without the Name of the Lord are lost and among them the poets reciting their poetry pass away (p. 654, Sorath Kabir). The *bānī* (poetry) of the (*Adi*) *Granth* is the work of Great Men (p. 935, Ramkali M. 1, Dakhni Oamkar). The *banī* uttered by the saint-poets is like the springs of nectar (p. 320, Var Gauri M. 5).

Poison: The Lord's Justice is not upon mere talk; if one takes poison, one dies (p. 308, Var Gauri M. 4). Those who eat and wear well, but do not serve the True Guru, they are accursed in life and death. They talk sweetly in the presence of the Guru, but emit poison at his back (p. 306, ibid). The wicked can do no harm to the true devotees who are protected by the Lord. The wicked brag in vain in their ego, but they are destroyed by the poison of their own minds (p. 316, ibid). O mother, the tyrants have poisoned themselves to death. I have been saved by the Lord to Whom I belong (p. 1269, Malar M. 5). The ship loaded with poison is launched upon the Ocean of Existence; one does not see the Yonder shore nor the Port of sail... (p. 1009, Maru M. 1). If by Guru's Grace, one listens to his Word, the mind's snake is rid of its poison (p. 10009, ibid). According to the *Adi Granth*, the five vices and the *maya* are poison. Ego is poison (p.1169, Basant M.1). *Maya* is poison (p. 257, Gauri M. 5).

Politics: The science dealing with the form, organisation, and administration of a State. The *Adi Granth* has moral and spiritual welfare of individual and society in view, therefore it has denounced those kings or states which have forgotten their responsibility towards the individual and society. The state/king should follow democratic principles (p. 992, Maru M. 1). It should strictly stick to the canons of justice (p. 1240, Var Sarand M. 4, Shlok M. 1).

Pollution: Impurity; defilement. The mind is polluted by covetousness, the tongue by falsehood, the eyes by coveting another's woman, beauty and wealth and the ears by listening to calumniation (p. 472,

Var Asa M. 1). The whole world is soiled and polluted; Only the Infinite Lord is Immaculate" (p. 1158, Bhairo Kabir). The pollution created by ego is washed away by the Word of the Guru (p. 121, Majh M. 3).

Polygamy: Marriage with several, or more than one, at the same time The *Adi Granth* rejects polygamy. It lays down the golden principle of one spouse, which Bhai Gurdas, the chief Sikh theologian, has mentioned categorically in his verses. He says, "One should be a *Yatī* (celibate) with one wife and consider the women of others as daughters and sisters." Throughout the *Adi Granth*, the idea of one spouse, especially a chaste woman, is given prominence. (See the hymns entitled *Suchajji* and *Gunwanti* on pages 762 and 763 in Raga Suhi.... The first one is composed by Guru Nanak Dev and the second by Guru Arjan Dev).

Portend: (Divination; Omens). That which portends or foretells something about to happen, especially of a calamitous nature. Anything or everything which happens, comes about on account of the Will of the Lord. There is no other agency, which brings about the calamities for an individual or society. It is categorically stated in the *Adi Granth*: "O Brothers, know this that all is in the Hands of the Lord. Age, Death, fever, pain and curse are all in the Power of the Lord; none else can do any harm to you" (p. 168, Gauri Bairagan M. 4). See: *Divinations and Omens*.

Possessions: Belongings, property, wealth. Guru Arjan Dev says, "I have wandered through all the places. The wealthy and owners of vast areas have wasted their life crying "This is mine, this is mine." They gave orders without fear and acted in ego. They subdued every one but without the Name of the Lord, they were also reduced to dust. Even if one has command over thirty-three crores of gods and if the miracle men and ascetics stand at his door; If he is a man of such a high status and master of vast dominions, these become a dream in the end" (p. 42, Sri Rag M. 5). "By Whose Grace you get gardens, land and wealth, keep him ever in your heart" (p. 270, Gauri Sukhmani M. 5).

Potter: Guru Nanak Dev says, "The soil from (a Muslim's) grave came in the possession of a potter, who fashioned it into vessels and bricks; while burning the soil wailed." (p.466, Var Asa M.1). The Lord as Potter kneaded the clay and applied many colours to it. He decked some with necklace of pearls and in some he put a defect (p. 479, Asa Kabir).

Poverty: The condition of having little or no wealth or material possessions. The Knower of Brahman gathers poverty in his mind (p. 273, Gauri Sukhmani M. 5). The word "poverty" is used here in the sense of humility. "Blessed is the poverty, if one Cherishes the Lord in the company of the saints" (p. 745, Suhi M. 5).

Power: Since Brahman is Omnipotent, all the Power emanates from Him. The human being or a created being has no power of its own. Guru Nanak Dev says in *Japuji*: "No power to speak or keep silence, no power to beg, no power to give, no power to die, no power to live, no power to rule...He (the Lord) alone has the Power..." (p. 7, Japuji). Guru Arjan Dev says about it: "He (the man) has no power in his hands, because the Lord—Master of all—is the Doer and the Cause. O Lord, the poor wretch (the man) is under Your Command" (p. 277, Gauri Sukhmani M. 5). There are some powers which a man can attain through the Meditation of the Lord, but such miraculous powers have been denounced in the *Adi Granth*. Guru Nanak Dev says, "To work miracles is worldly and also outwardly" (p. 6, Japuji).

Prabhū: The Name of the Lord.

Pradhāna: Chief; As a Sankhyan term it means *Prakritī*, the material cause of the world. In the *Adi Granth*, this word has been used alongwith Purusha and also separately. It means "Chief" for example "Among all the Purushas, he is the chief, whose ego is destroyed in the company of the saints" (p. 266, Gauri Sukhmani M. 5).

Prakriti: Nature; *Maya*. In the *Adi Granth* the Arabic word *Qudrat* has been used for Prakriti by Guru Nanak Dev (p. 464, Var Asa M. 1). *Qudrat* means Nature. But by using the word *Qudrat*, the Guru means *Maya*, which is composed of three qualities i.e. *Rajas*, *Tamas* and *Sattva*. Kabir says, "O Lord, *Rajas*, *Tamas* and *Sattva* is all Your *Maya*" (p. 1123, Kedara Kabir). Purusha and Prakriti of Sankhya are the same as Shiva and Shakti mentioned in the *Adi Granth* (p. 920, Ramkali M. 3, Anand). The saint Jaidev says: "The Lord is the Wonder of Wonders, beyond Prakriti (Nature, Maya)."

Pralaya: Dissolution of the world at the end of each age or day of Brahma (*kalpa*). *Mahapralaya* takes place at the end of Brahma's own life of one hundred years. In the *Adi Granth*, *Dharmaraja*, the doorkeeper of Brahman, has been called the Lord of *Pralaya* (dissolution) (p. 1292, Malar Namdev). Guru Nanak Dev says, "The Lord Creates and Dissolves, but Himself remains detached" (p. 1033, Maru M. 1). Throughout the ages the same True Lord is there. There is none else,

Who Creates and Dissolves (p. 905, Ramkali M. 1). Through the Word (of God), there is the creation (*utpatī*) and dissolution (*Pralaya*)—(p. 117, Majh M. 3).

Prāna: The breath of life. It is also called the Vital Air. There are five vital airs, which function in different directions throughout the human and animal body. They are: *Prāna* (the respiration through the nose and mouth), *Apāna* (the respiration which goes downwards), *Samāna* (It has its seat in the cavity of the navel), *Udana* (It rises up the throat and enters the head) and *Vyāna* (it is diffused through the whole body). Ordinarily *Prāna* means breath. It is also called *Savās*. The *Adi Granth* exhorts the human being to remember the Name of the Lord with every breath (p. 295, Gauri Sukhmani M. 5). The Jivas who breathe are called *Pranī*. Guru Nanak Dev says, "Why should we forget the Lord, who has given *Prāna* (vital air) and soul?" (p. 16, Sri Rag M. 1).

Pranava: The sacred syllable Om (Aum, Aumkāra, Onam). The word Aum (Oam, Aumkāra, Onam) has been used several times in the *Adi Granth*, but the word *Pranava* has been used only as verb e.g. *Pranavai* and *Pranavat*, which means "to speak or bow with reverence."

Prapanc: The expanse of the five elements. "In this expanse of five elements, the Name of the Lord is of great significance, therefore none should be egoistic" (Bilawal M. 3, p. 797).

Prasād: Grace. See: *Grace*.

Pravritti Marg: The path of action. It is antonym of *Nivritti Marg* (The Path of withdrawal). The *Adi Granth* lays emphasis on *Pravritti Marg*. Guru Ram Das says, "In the first round (of *lavan*—the marriage ceremony), the *Pravritti Karma* has been emphasised" (Suhi M. 4, p. 773).

Prayers: According to the *Adi Granth,* the prayers are only to be offered to the Lord-God with folded hands (p. 736, Suhi M. 5) while standing (p. 1093, Var Maru M. 3, Shlok M. 2). There are many hymns of Prayer in the *Adi Granth*, but generally the last stanza of the fourth Octavo (ashtapadi) of *Sukhmani* is read with great reverence before beginning the prayer. Its translation is as follows: I Pray to You, O Lord, You are the Master. Our body and the soul are Your Gifts. You are our father and mother and we are Your children. In Your Grace are great comforts. None knows Your Limits, O Lord, You are the Highest of the High. All Your Creation is bound by Your Laws. Whatever is Created by You, is in Your Command. You alone know All Your Doings. Your Servant Nanak is always a sacrifice to You (p. 268, Gauri Sukhmani M. 5).

Preachers: Those who proclaim religious doctrine by public discourse. Guru Nanak Dev says, "His speech is false and he usurps what does not belong to him, still he goes to preach to others. He, who is beguiled himself, will also beguile his companions. Such are the leaders of men (p. 140, Var Majh M. 1). Even if one utters divine sayings or reads them aloud to others, one does not attain final emancipation (pp. 905-06, Ramkali M. 1). Guru Amar Das says, "The men of merit imbibe virtues and preach to others regarding them; those persons are fortunate, who meet them and always dwell on the Name of the Lord" (p. 755, Suhi M. 3). The men of knowledge and contemplation and the preachers are involved with the world (p. 338, Gauri Poorbi Kabir).

Preaching: The delivering of a sermon. "What should be the preaching to those, whose Guru is Guru Nanak Dev"? (p. 150, Var Majh M. 1, Shlok M. 2). The Guru is Beneficent, whose preaching is about the Name of the Lord" (p. 250, Gauri Bawan Akhri M. 5). One who preaches to others, but does not follow it himself, undergoes transmigration (p. 269, Gauri Sukhmani M. 5). He preaches to others, but does not practise it himself, he does not know the quintessence of the Word (p. 380, Asa M. 5). He feeds on sand, while preaching to others; in this way, his own possessions are depleted, when he keeps watch over the possessions of others (p. 1369, Shlok Kabir).

Precious Things: The precious things according to the *Adi Granth* are virtues (p. 5, Japuji). My youth, beauty and age all have passed, but no meritorious deeds were committed by me. And this precious life, being without any merit, was wasted away (pp. 855-56, Bilawal Kabir). The precious jewel of life is being sold for a trite (p. 156, Gauri Bairagan M. 1). The gems, jewels and rubies are in the mind, if one listens to the instruction of the Guru (p. 2, Japuji) The Guru is like an ocean full of precious things (p. 685, Dhanasari M. 1; p. 933, Ramkali Dakhni Oamkar M. 1). The Name of the Lord is precious like gems and pearls, which none can steal (p. 134, Bara Maha Majh M. 5).

Predestination: It means preordering. The action of God in foreordaining whatever come to pass, is called predestination. *Taqdīr*, or the absolute decree of good and evil, is the sixth article of the Muhammadan creed, and the orthodox believe that whatever has, or shall come to pass in this world, whether it be good or bad, proceeds entirely from the Divine Will and has been irrevocably fixed and recorded on a preserved tablet by the pen of fate. The idea of God-Writ is present in the *Adi Granth*. Guru Nanak Dev says, "The soul works according to the Writ on the forehead" (p. 74, Sri Raga Pahre M. 1). The idea of predestination leaves no scope for the freedom of the will, but the *Adi Granth* lays stress on the effort of the individual and the Grace of God. Guru Nanak Dev says, "The human birth is attained by *Karmas* (actions), but the final emancipation comes through Grace" (p. 2, Japuji).

Pregnancy: The condition of being pregnant. During pregnancy, in the womb of the mother, one stands on its head, praying for the release (p. 251, Gauri Bawan Akhri M. 5). He who abides in Truth..is not cast into the womb again. (p. 415, Asa M. 1). They, who have heard of or seen Guru Nanak, are not cast into the womb again (p. 612, Sorath M. 5). During many births, the embryo, during pregnancy, was destroyed in the womb (p. 176, Gauri Guareri M. 5).

Prem: Love. The religion of the *Adi Granth* is the religion of love. Therefore, the Poetry of the *Adi Granth* is the Poetry of Love. See: *Love*.

Premā Bhagtī: The Bhakti through Love. See: *Bhāe Bhagtī*.

Presents: Gifts. The Lord, whose gifts (presents) cannot be evaluated, how can we evaluate Him? (p. 157, Gauri Poorbi Deepki M. 1). How ignorant is the seeker, who asks for presents, without realising that the Lord gives even without asking. He (the Lord). Gives all He has to...but the man asks not for God, but for goods, which do not bring happiness to any one (p. 258, Gauri Bawan Akhri M. 5). The Lord, by Whose Grace, one gets all the gifts,... wealth, land, gardens etc.... he should weave Him in his heart (p. 270, Gauri Sukhmani M. 5).

Pretas: Ghosts. There are millions of ghosts, demons, swines and tigers (p. 276, Gauri Sukhmani M. 5). While describing the creation, the Guru tells us about the existence of ghosts. He, who remembers houses at the time of his death, he becomes a ghost and resides in them (p. 526, Gujri Trilochan). This is the greatness of the Guru, that he makes a god of an animal or a ghost (p. 1329, Prabhati M. 1). See: *Demons* and *Ghosts*.

Pride: A high opinion of one's own qualities, attainment or estate. One who is puffed up with pride, wears the wear of wind. Like the passing away of the wind, the egoist is also reduced to dust (p. 318, Var Gauri M. 5). When one has not to remain in this world, then why should he waste himself away in pride? (p. 473, Var Asa M. 1). Those who are puffed up with pride because of the honour and glory caused by great beauty and riches, they passed away without attaining the Grace of the Lord, like a mound after the rain (p. 1383, Shlok Farid). The Lord does not like ego (pride), even the Vedas declare it (p. 1089, Var Maru M. 3).

Priests: In the *Adi Granth*, there is condemnation of the contemporary priestly class, not only of Hindus but also of the Muslims. Kabir says, "I have abandoned all my strife because I have abandoned both the Pundit and Mullah....Whatever was written by the Pundit and Mullah, I did not accept and cast it aside (pp. 1158-59, Bhairo Kabir). Guru Nanak Dev says, "The Pundit reads the sacred texts, but being involved in the household, he attains nothing (p. 1012, Maru M. 1). Guru Arjan Dev says, "He alone is a Mullah, who overcomes evil." (p. 1084, Maru M. 5).

Prithivi: Earth, one of the five elements of matter. Kabir says, "Be on the side of God and adopt the ways of *Ap* (water), *Tej* (fire), *Baae* (air), *Prithmi* (earth) and *akash* (sky)" (Bhairo Kabir, p. 327). The water cleanses and cools, the fire purifies and warms, the earth exhibits patience, the air has all-loving nature and the sky is all-pervasive.

Probation: The testing or trial of a person's conduct, character, or moral qualifications. Guru Arjan Dev says, "Testing (all coins) the Lord casts the True ones in His Treasury and they do not become false again" (p. 520, Var Gujri M. 5). The Guru as Jeweller tested him (the devotee) and found him of beauteous colour and testing him thus, he is accepted in the treasury of the Lord and he is not cast into the fire again (p. 1074, Maru Solha M. 5).

Procreation: The action of begetting. The Supreme Being (Transcendent Lord) procreates all beings (p. 1003, Maru M. 5). Through the Word is the procreation and dissolution of the world (p. 117, Majh M. 5). There are myriads of procreations and myriads of dissolutions (p. 1236, Sarang M. 5).

Prodigies-Omens: Which cause wonder, astonishment or surprise; persons endowed with some qualities, which excite wonder. The saints are prodigies. All their actions are done in the state of equipoise. When violence is done unto them, they are protected by the unseen powers, which cause wonder and astonishment. When Kabir is thrown into the waters of the river, he is not drowned (p. 1162, Bhairo Kabir). When Namdev is thrown before the elephant, the elephant salutes him (p. 1165, Bhairo Namdev).

Professions: Occupations. The saints, whose verses are found in the *Adi Granth* followed different professions in life. Kabir was a weaver,

Namdev a calico-printer and Ravidas, a cobbler. Sain was a barber and Dhanna, a peasant. Even Guru Nanak Dev, a farmer in the later years of his life, was a trader at one time. We find a glimpse of their professions in their compositions. See: *Occupations.*

Property: A possession or possessions collectively. Guru Tegh Bahadur says, "The property which I thought was mine, belonged to another in a moment" (p. 1008, Maru M. 9). "The fool thinks the solid and beautiful mansions will remain his property" (p. 141, Var Majh M. 1). Guru Nanak Dev says, "In the pride of your possessions and the glamour of your beauty, you have wasted away your life" (p. 24, Sri Rag M. 1).

Prophets: Those who speak for God or for any deity as the inspired revealers or interpreters of His Will. Guru Nanak Dev says, "The Pirs, the Prophets, spiritual guides, the men of faith and innocence, the martyrs, the Sheikhs, the Qazis, the Mullahs and the Faqirs in the presence of the Lord are blessed the more, the more they say their prayers" (p. 53, Sri Rag M. 1). "The prophets, the seers, the spiritual guides, the faithful also left the world and were Approved by the Lord" (p. 358, Asa M. 1). Guru Arjan Dev says, "The Qazis, Sheikhs, the Pirs, the seers and the Prophets will all vacate their seats" (p. 1100, Var Maru M. 5). In the *Adi Granth*, the word *Prophet* has been used only in relation to Islam.

Propriety: Fitness; suitability. The *Adi Granth* lays stress on the rules of propriety and moral conduct. A Kshatriya is one, who is a warrior in deeds and dedicates his body to compassion and charity (p. 1411, Shlok Varan te Vadhik M. 1). A Muslim maintains propriety, if he makes mercy his mosque, faith his prayer-mat, honest living his Quaran, humility his circumcision and good conduct his fast. (p. 140, Vas Majh M. 1). The rules of propriety serve as instruments to form character. But according to the *Adi Granth*, the character is formed in the company of the saints and by following the instructions of the Guru. Guru Arjan Dev says, "Meet the Guru and learn the right discipline; then you will never be in pain" (p. 50, Sri Rag M. 5). He says again, "Make yourself the servant of the saints and learn their conduct" (p. 400, Asa M. 5).

Prosperity: The condition of being prosperous; good fortune, success, well-being. Without the foodgrains, we cannot have prosperity (p. 873, Gond Kabir). "When the period of prosperity begins, one meets the True Guru (p. 31, Sri Rag M. 3). Guru Arjan Dev says, "In order to be considered prosperous, you should gather the wealth of the Name of the Lord" (p. 288, Gauri Sukhmani M. 5).

Prostitutes: In the words of the saint Namdev "as men gather in the house of a prostitute, she wears fine raiments and bedecks herself and as she dances, the lewd is enraptured, seeing her breaths, but around his neck there is the noose of the *Yama*" (p. 1165, Bhair Namdev). It is a sin to go to a prostitute. But the sinner does not tarry in thinking of sin and he is not ashamed of running to a prostitute (p. 1143, Bhairo M. 5). See: *Harlot*.

Proverbs: A short pithy saying in common use; a concise sentence which is held to express some truth ascertained by experience or observation and familiar to all. There are many pithy sayings in the *Adi Granth*, which come under the category of *Gurmat Akhaotan* (Proverbs and proverbial phrases in the *Adi Granth*). The writer of these lines has compiled a book containing the Proverbs and Proverbial Phrases of the *Adi Granth* which is published by the Department of Languages, Panjab. A few examples:1-None remains here, when the cup of life is full (p. 465, Var Asa M. 1). 2-His mind is blind, but his name is 'wisdom' (p. 471, Var Asa M. 1). 3-They themselves cannot even offer a mouthful of water, but censure those, who have brought the Ganges (p. 332, Gauri Cheti Kabir).

Psalms: Any sacred song sung in religious worship; a hymn. The holy *Adi Granth* is a Book of Psalms. These hymns are set in various musical modes and are sung by the musicians collectively in the Congregations. These psalms are small as well as large in size. *Sukhmani,* a longer poem of Guru Arjan Dev, is very often called "The Psalm of Peace".

Psychology: The science of the nature, functions, and phenomena of the human soul or mind. The compositions of the *Adi Granth* have a great psychological significance. Their main sphere of concern is the body, mind, intellect and soul. The basis of all the functions is the mind, which through its thinking and subsequent deeds can fall into the pit of hell and also through the spiritual discipline, attains the state of final emancipation. The mind is addressed very often, beckoning it all the time to follow the discipline enunciated by the Guru in the company of the saintly persons. For example, "O my dear mind, I ask you to burn your Doubt in the Company of the Saints...O my dear mind, without the Lord, all the show is false...O my dear mind, carry with you the profitable merchandise in the other world. O my dear mind, live in the company of the Saints" (pp. 79-80, Sri Rag M. 5).

Public Buildings: Two types of public buildings are mentioned in the *Adi Granth* : those built by the people themselves, known as "dharamshalas" (the abodes to be used by the public either for religious purposes or as rest houses on special occasions); those either built by the Govenment or philanthropists, which were used by the travellers or traders. Guru Arjan Dev says, "I have built the abode of Dharma and have gathered in it the worshippers after a great search" (p. 73, Sri Rag M. 5). Kabir addresses the Yama in this manner: "Please wait, because I have yet to collect the revenue from a few more villages. Wait only for the night and I shall go with you. I will pay for your stay too, if you stay for the night and then accompanying you, I will pray in the morning in the *serai* (rest-house) on the way (p. 792, Suhi Kabir).

Public Rest Houses: The public rest-houses were known as *serais*, where the travellers and traders used to stay for the night in the times of Sikh Gurus and the radical saints. Guru Ram Das says, "Blessed are their homes, temples, palaces and rest-houses, which are dedicated to the devotees and mendicants of the Lord" (p. 648, Var Sorath M. 4). In a wider sense, this world and the next world have also been called rest-houses. Guru Arjan Dev says, "They whom the Lord makes them worldly instead of religious, they are indeed sinners in both the *serais* i.e. this world and the next" (pp. 742-43, Suhi M. 5). See: *Public Buildings*.

Pūjā: Worship. "I have investigated various types of worship, but the real worship is that which is liked by the Lord" (Kanra M. 5, p. 1304). He who has duality in his heart, his muttering of mantras, his austerity, his fasting and his worship are in vain (Gauri Kabir, p. 324).

Pundit: A teacher; a learned person. "He is a Pundit, who recognises the essence" (Majh M. 3, p. 128). "The Pundit has gone astray and indulges in duality and the trade in *maya*" (Var Sorath M. 3, p. 647). "O Pundit, concentrate on the Veda and destroy the anger of your mind" (Ramkali M. 5, p. 887). According to Hinduism, a Pundit specialises in Vedas and Shastras.

Punishments: According to the *Adi Granth*, the law of Karma and Transmigration brings the rewards and punishments according to the deeds done by the individual. The sinners are punished in the hell. The Lord-Justice asks for the account of deeds (p.1019, Maru M. 5). Izrāīl, the god of death, gives due punishment to sinners. Though the Muslims do not believe in the law of Karma and Transmigration, they believe in the reward and punishment after death. Guru Nanak Dev says, "None else is to be blamed, blame your own deeds. I got the reward according to my deeds, then why blame others? (p. 433, Asa M. 1, Patti). Guru Arjan Dev says "Those who have been put to sleep by *Maya* and practise evil, they are subject to birth and death again and again and are left on the path of Yama. They are in pain and reap what they have sown" (p. 321, Var Gauri M. 5).

Punn: Virtue. "Singing the Praises of the Lord is a virtuous act in Kaliyuga" (Var Ramkali M. 5, p. 962). "If you want your betterment, then perform virtuous acts and be humble before the world"(Var Asa M. 1, p. 465).

Pupil: In his poem *Patti* (an alphabetical poem) Guru Amar Das says, "O teacher, read, whatever is in your Writ and do not teach evil to the others. If you do, you will be bound down and after you, your pupils will also meet the same fate" (pp. 434-35, Asa M. 3, Patti). When Prehlad was a pupil, he taught the Name of the Lord to other pupils. His teachers made a complaint to his father, king Hiranakashyapa. The saint Namdev relates this parable in one of his hymns: "Shanda and Marka cried: O king, your son does not study, we are tired of him. He utters only the Name of God...and has thus spoiled all his fellow-pupils" (p. 1165, Bhairo Namdev). According to Guru Nanak Dev, that teacher may be called a *Gurmukh* (Enlightened one), if he instructs his pupils for cherishing the Name of the Lord" (p. 938, Dakhni Oamkar, Ramkali M. 1).

Pūran: Perfect. Only the lord is Perfect. "The Lord (Supreme Ishwara) is Perfect in the Beginning, in the Middle and at the End" (Var Jaitsri M. 5, p. 705). He is called *Pūran Purkh* (The Perfect Purusha) and *Pūran Jot* (Perfect Light).

Puranas: The Smriti Literature of the Hindus includes Itihasas (Epics) and Puranas. There are eighteen Maha-Puranas and eighteen Upa-Puranas. The Maha-Puranas are *Vaishnava Puranas*: Vishnu, Bhagavata, Narada, Garuda, Padma, Varaha; *Shaiva Puranas*: Shiva, Linga, Skanda, Agni, Matsya, Kurma and *Puranas* adoring *Brahma*: Brahma, Brahmanda, Brahm-Vaivarta, Markandeya, Bhavishya, Vamana. Out of these Maha-Puranas, two Vaishnava Puranas viz. Vishnu Purana and Bhagavata Purana have remained very popular. In the *Adi Granth*, there are several allusions from these two Puranas. The Words *Das-Ashta* refer to the eighteen Maha-Puranas. The Gurus and saints whose compositions are included in the *Adi Granth*, were well-versed in

Pauranic lore, therefore there are many illustrations in the holy scripture from the Puranas. The view of the *Adi Granth* regarding Smritis is as follows: "The Smritis and Shastras discriminate between good and evil, but do not tell about the Quintessence. Without the Guru, no one knows the Quintessence" (p. 920, Ramkali M. 3, Anand).

Purification: According to the *Adi Granth*, the purification of mind and body are necessary for the realisation of the Lord. "The Truth (God) is obtained after self-purification" (p. 472, Var Asa M. 1). In the words of Guru Arjan Dev, "I read the holy texts and dwelt on the Vedas. I controlled my breath and cleansed the intestines through Yogic practices and tried to awaken the Kundalini, but I did not forsake the company of the five vices and was bound down by ego more and more. I took the vow of silence and made the bowl of my hands; I wandered naked through the woods. I visited all the holy shrines and river-banks and even the whole earth, but my sense of duality never left me. As desired by my mind, I lived at holy places and even desired to be sawn alive, but the dirt of mind was never cleansed in spite of my efforts. As a man of charity, I gave away my gold, horses and elephants and even my wife; I offered in alms my lands, clothes and grains, but still I could not reach the door of the Lord. I performed worship and offered flowers to the gods. I prostrated and performed six types of Karmas, but I was bound to my self and did not realise my Lord. I practised Yoga like a Siddha and practised all the eighty-four postures. I achieved long life, and could not meet my Lord. I was born again and again..." (pp. 641-42, Sorath M. 5).

Purity: Purity is a godly quality. For spiritual growth, the purity of mind and body is necessary. The mind should be pure, the speech should be pure and the actions should be pure. When the mind becomes pure, the Lord Himself appears to the person with pure mind (p. 1367, Shlok Kabir). That body is pure, which is sinless (p. 198, Gauri M. 5). Those who are absorbed in the Name of the Lord are indeed pure, others are full of the dirt of ego (p. 570, Vadhans M. 3). He, who dwells on the Pure Lord, becomes pure. The dirt of ego can be washed away with the Word of the Guru (p. 121, Majh M. 3). Those who are pure from within and pure from without and practise the discipline enjoined by the Guru, they do not hear the talk of falsehood and they desire only for Truth...They whose minds are pure, always abide with the Guru (p. 919, Ramkali M. 3, Anand).

Purohita: Priest. Literally the word "*Purohita*" means "one who is appointed or placed in front." There was a time, when the *Purohita* conducted several ceremonies for the Hindu king. He was no ordinary priest but selected because of his special capabilities. In Hindu society, he played a very significant part. The word "Purohita" does not occur in the *Adi Granth*, but the idea of a (Brahmin) priest is found at several places.

Purusha: In common Indian terminology, a Purusha means a person or male. In Samkhya, it is the conscious, but passive principle. When it comes into contact with Prakriti, which is the active principle, the process of creation begins. In Upanishads, the word "Purusha" is used for Supreme Being or the Soul of the universe. But in the *Adi Granth*, the *Jivas* (souls) are also called Purushas, because they are part and parcel of the Supreme Spirit. But unlike *Jivas* (Purushas), the Supreme Being is *Adi Purakh* (who is from the very beginning), *Sat Purakh* (who is all-pervasive and everlasting), *Karta Purakh* (who is the Creator), *Akāl Purakh* (who is uninfluenced by Time) and *Niranjan Purakh* (who is without the influence of *Maya*). Thus both Brahman and Jivā are Purushas in the background of Prakriti, but whereas Brahman or Supreme Purusha is the Creator of Prakriti and does not come under its influence, Jiva or Purusha plunges into the field of action or Prakriti and repeatedly suffers births and deaths, because of its karmas (actions).

Purusha Sukta: The Purusha-Sukta is a hymn of the Rig Veda. In this hymn, the Purusha is depicted as a cosmogonic figure, the male, who envelops the whole earth. The universe is depicted as a Cosmic Man. We find the direct impact of Purusha Sukta on Guru Nanak Dev, whose hymn entitled *Aarti* contains the idea of the Purusha with a thousand eyes, a thousand forms, a thousand lotus-feet and a thousand smells. But alongwith this idea about the Immanence of Purusha, the Guru also gives the idea of His Transcendence (p. 13, Dhanasari M. 1, *Aarti*).

Purushottama: This word occurs as *Purshotam* in the *Adi Granth*, which means the Supreme Purusha or Brahman. Guru Ram Das says, "I dwell upon the Supreme Purusha, who is the source of all Bliss. (p. 800, Bilawal M. 4).

Puzzles: Riddles. In some verses of the *Adi Granth*, we find some puzzling statements, but they carry a very deep meaning. Hence they are like riddles. For example Kabir says: The sheep sucks the milk from its male offspring. Here the sheep is identified with mind, which sucks the milk of wisdom from its own intellect (p. 326, Gauri Kabir).

Q

Qādī, Qāzī: The Judge. *Qādī* is an Arabic word and *Qāzī* is Persian. Both these words have been used in the *Adi Granth*. "*Qādī* indulges in falsehood and accepts bribes" (Dhanasari M. 1, p. 662). "He is, indeed, a *Qāzī*, who practises Truth" (Maru M. 5, p. 1084).

Qādir: Al-Qādir, meaning "The Powerful", is one of the ninety-nine attributes of God. This Arabic word occurs several times in the *Adi Granth*. Guru Nanak Dev says, "All the *Qudrat* (Nature, Prakriti) is Yours, O *Qadir* (Powerful) Creator" (p. 464, Var Asa M. 1).

Qualities: Mental or moral attributes. A great stress is laid on qualities in the *Adi Granth*. "Without the qualities (virtues), there can be no devotion for the Lord" (p. 4, Japuji). Thus the qualities lay down the foundation for the spiritual growth. In order to conquer the five vices of lust, anger, greed, attachment and ego, one has to imbibe the qualities (virtues) of self-control, toleration, contentment, devotion to duty and modesty. In Manu Smriti, ten qualities have been mentioned. They are self-possession, patience, self-control, integrity, purity, restraint, intelligence, learning, truthfulness and absence of anger. They are the marks of *Dharma*. The *Adi Granth* lays great emphasis on godly qualities. If a Jiva adopts truth, goodness, justice, sweetness, purity, fearlessness, brotherly feelings, graciousness and mercifulness, he becomes godlike. These qualities prepare the ground for the realisation of Brahman.

Quarters: The regions lying about or under the four principal points of the compass or divisions of the horizon. There is mention of the four quarters (directions) in the *Adi Granth*. e.g. "I have wandered in all the four quarters and when tired, I have come under the refuge of the Lord" (p. 133, Baramaha Majh M. 5)." I have searched all the four quarters, but there is no permanent abode" (p. 1383, Shalok Farid). Side by side with the mention of four quarters, ten directions have also been mentioned in the *Adi Granth* e.g. "The mind runs in all the ten directions" (p. 565, Wadhans M. 3). "I searched my Lord in all the ten directions, but I found Him in my own Home" (p. 542, Bihagra M. 5). "The Glory of the Lord Pervades in all the ten directions" (p. 783, Suhi M. 5).

Qudrat: Nature; Creation; *Maya*. Guru Nanak Dev says, "Whatever we see and hear is Your *Qudrat*, O Lord... Your *Qudrat* is seen in the nether-worlds, heavens and all creation... Your *Qudrat* is in Vedas, Puranas, Kateb and all the Thoughts...Your *Qudrat* is in air, water, fire and earth. All is Your *Qudrat* (creation), You are its Creator..." (Var Asa M. 1, p. 464). "O True Lord Your *Qudrat* is also true" (ibid, p. 463). "In His *Qudrat*, the Lord adopts many forms in a moment" (Var Gujri M. 5, p. 519).

Queen: Guru Nanak Dev has talked about the miserable plight of the queens and princesses at the time of the invasion of Babur. He says, "They whose lustrous hair sparkled in plaits and were filled in the partings with vermilion, their hair were cut with the scissors and they were choked by the dust (of the marching forces). They who enjoyed the life of the palaces, do not find a seat in the open..."(p. 417, Asa M. 1). At another place, the stories of the kings and queens sung by the bards have been mentioned as vain prattle by the Guru (p. 464, Var Asa M. 1).

Quiescence: Quietness, Quietism. If "quiescence" conveys the sense of peace, it is in accordance with the ideology of the *Adi Granth,* because peace is necessary for spiritual growth. Guru Amar Das says, "The deeds that you do in peace are Approved by the Lord" (p. 551, Var Bihagra M. 4, Shalok M. 3). But if "quiescence" is used in the sense of quietism, then it is not in consonance with the ideology of the *Adi Granth*. Guru Nanak Dev says, "When one is sunk in quietness (silence), he is wasted away. How can he wake from sleep without the Guru?" (p. 467, Var Asa M. 1).

Qurān: The word "Kateb" used in the *Adi Granth,* meaning "Books", includes the Muslim holy book, the *Quran*, besides Taurāt, Zabūr and Injīl. While defining a True Muslim, Guru Nanak Dev says, that he makes the honest living his *Quran* (p. 140, Var Majh M. 1). Guru Arjan Dev says, "One must practise the injunctions of the *Quran* and other texts within his heart" (p. 1084, Maru M. 5).

Qurbānī: Sacrifice. The word *Qurban* has been used several times in the *Adi Granth*. "I am a sacrifice to that auspicious time, when I came to Your Door" (Suhi M. 5, p. 749). "I am a sacrifice to my Perfect Guru, through whose grace, I remember the Name of the Lord" (Prabhati M. 5, p. 1340).

R

Rabb: The Muslim Name of God. See: *Allah*.

Race: A tribe, nation, or people, regarded as of common stock. Guru Nanak Dev says, "Reflecting on the Word of the Guru, I have been rid of the sense of my colour, caste and race" (p. 1198, Sarang M. 1). Guru Arjan Dev says, "I have forsaken my parents and have sold off myself to the saints. I have lost my caste, birth and race and always Praise my Lord" (p. 1230, Sarang M. 5). This shows that there is no consideration of caste, colour, race and birth, when one enters the spiritual domain.

Rāgas: Musical modes. The hymns and other compositions of the *Adi Granth* have been placed under various Ragas (male musical modes) and Raginis (female musical modes). Though the *Rāgamālā* at the end of the *Adi Granth* mentions fifty-four Ragas and thirty Raginis, there are only thirty-one Ragas and Raginis in the scripture. In several Ragas and Raginis, there are more than one tune (*Ghar*). These musical modes have also been personifed and are said to be busy in praising the Lord (p. 917, Ramkali M. 3, Anand).

Rahīm: Merciful. The Name of the Lord in Islam.

Rahu: A demon responsible for the eclipses of the Sun and Moon. When the ocean was churned by the gods and demons, Rahu, the demon, disguised himself as a god, and joined the other gods, when the holy *Amrta* was being drunk by them. It is said that he was recognised by the Sun-god (Surya) and the Moon-god (Soma). Vishnu, on being informed, struck off the head of the demon. His head and tail survived, other parts of his body were destroyed. Since the demon had drunk *Amrta*, he became immortal. The head of the demon, because of his enmity with the Sun and the Moon, tries to seize and swallow the two planets. His head and tail are in heaven as Rahu and Ketu. In his attempts to swallow the planets, it causes the eclipses. Guru Nanak Dev has mentioned the folk-myth of the evil import of the two stars Rahu and Ketu. He says, "If my body writhes in agony under the impact of two evil stars Rahu and Ketu and the blood-sucking kings rule over me, even then I shall Worship You, O Lord..." (p. 142, Var Majh M. 1).

Rain: The rain (of Mercy) has come and I have realised my Lord. All his creatures are now in peace (p. 105, Majh M. 5). By the Will of the

Lord, the rain (of Mercy) comes (p. 104, Majh M. 5). For the devotee, the nectar rains, its drop is delightful (p. 1107, Baramaha Tukhari M. 1). The true devotee going to meet the preceptor does not stop even if the storm or rain comes (p. 757, Suhi M. 4). Sheikh Farid says, "The street is muddy and the house of the Lord is far away, but I am in love with Him. If I go out in the rain, my blanket gets wet and if I stay behind, my love is lost. Let my blanket get wet in the rains sent by God, I must meet my Lord so that my love does not break down" (p. 1379, Shlok Farid).

Rainbow: There is no direct reference to rainbow in the *Adi Granth*. It is also called 'Indra's bow', because god Indra is considered the god of rain. But Indra and other gods do everything in the Fear of the Lord. Rainbow exhibits seven colours—all are the colours of the Lord (p. 134, Baramaha Majh M. 5).

Rainy Season: The rainy season has been depicted excellently by Guru Nanak Dev in his *Bārāmāha Tukhari*. He says, "O mind, be delighful in the month of *Shrāvana*, because the rainy season has arrived. My mind and body are absorbed in the love of the Lord, but He has gone to foreign lands. The Lord has not returned home and I pine in grief. The lightning flashes and frightens me. My bed is lonely and I am indeed in agony. O mother, this state is like death for me. There is no sleep without the Lord. The body does not bear even the clothes. Blessed is the bride, who merges in the Being of her Lord. In the month of *Bhadon*, I am led astray. Though in full bloom, I am in anguish. The earth is flooded and the waters are full to the brim. It was the time to enjoy (the company of the Lord). It rains throughout the dark night, but how the young bride can be peaceful? The peacocks and the frogs are shrieking. The *Chatrik* is calling the Lord in his own language; the snakes are out to bite. The mosquitoes are stinging; the tanks are overflowing, but how can we enjoy peace without the Lord? Ask Your Guru and go towards Your Lord" (p. 1108, Baramaha Tukhari M. 1).

Rajas: One of the three basic qualities, which constitute *maya*. This quality causes things to continue their habits of motion. It is the principle of restlessness, of force, energy, activity and dynamic inertia. The passion, action and the thirst of desire are its evolutes. Guru Nanak Dev says, "O Lord, You have extended the three qualities, but You Yourself reside in the Fourth House (State)" (p. 1038, Maru M. 1).

Raja Yoga: The system of yoga, propounded by Patanjali in *Yoga Darshana* is called *Raja Yoga*. Through this system, the working of the mind is stilled in order to unite the Yogi with Godhead and make him the king (Rājā) of all his physical and mental powers. Patanjali has enumerated eight steps of Rājā Yoga viz. *Yama* (self-restraint), *Niyama* (observances), *Pranayama* (regulation of breath), *Pratyāhāra* (withdrawal of the senses), *āsana* (posture), *Dhyāna* (contemplation), *Dhārana* (fixation) and *Samādhī* (meditative trance). The positive and negative injunctions i.e. *Yama* and *Niyama* have been accepted by the *Adi Granth*. *Pranayama* and *Asanas* have been rejected. The Gurus have defined *Dhyāna, Dhārana* and *Samādhī* in their own way. The *Adi Granth* has its own distinct concept of Yoga. The Raja Yoga of Guru Arjan Dev is as follows: "The one Name be repeated with the tongue...the illness of ego vanishes. You must enjoy this Raja Yoga with the Grace of the Guru" (p. 211, Gauri M. 5).

Rākshasas: (Demons). The Lord of the Universe is the annihilator of Rakshasas (p. 1082, Maru M. 5). There is mention of mythological *Asuras* (Rākshasas) in the *Adi Granth*. Mention has also been made of the churning of the ocean by the gods and Rākshasas. But the five major vices have also been identified with the Rākshasas. "It is the True Guru who kills the Rākshasas (Devils) within you" (p. 30, Sri Rag M. 3).

Rāma (Rām, Rameīa): In the *Adi Granth*, Rama is the Name of Lord-God, who pervades the Universe. The Name of the Lord has been called Rām-Nām. Guru Ram Das says, "Utter the Name of the All-Pervading Rama" (p. 1324, Kalyan M. 4). Kabir says, "He alone can bear the test on the touchstone of Rama (God) who lives after the annihilation of his ego" (p. 1366, Shlok Kabir). Lord Rama, the son of Dasrath, has been mentioned several times in the scripture. Guru Nanak Dev says, "Ram Chandra was full of grief in his heart for the sake of Sita and Lakshmana. He remembered Hanuman, who came as pre-determined. The misguided demon (i.e. Ravana) did not understand that this was the work of God. The Lord is care-free; Rama could not be absolved of the fruit of his actions" (p. 1412, Shlok Varan te Vadhik M.1). There is also mention of Parashurāma in the *Adi Granth*. "Parashurāma also came back home crying, because Ram Chandra had denuded him of his prowess (p. 953, Var Ramkali M. 3, Shalok M. 1). The name of the elder brother of Krishna, Balarama, has been written as Balbhadra in the scripture (p. 165, Gauri M. 4).

Rasa: (*Ras Kas*). Flavour; savour; taste. "All the *rasas* of the body result in suffering" (Var Malar M. 1, p. 1287). "When one forgets the Lord and indulges in rasas and pleasures, he is subjected to ailments (Malar M.1, p.1256). Kabir says, "I considered all the *rasas* insipid and whatever was insipid, I considered it tasteful. After abandoning these *rasas*, that *Rasa* (*Hari Ras*) came. When I tasted that *Rasa*, I disliked this *rasa* (Gauri Bawan Akhri Kabir, p. 342).

Rasātala: One of the seven nether-worlds according to Hindu tradition. These seven worlds are: 1-Atala, subject to Mahamaya, 2-Vitala, ruled by a form of Shiva, called Hatakeswara, 3-Sutala, ruled by Bali, 4-Talātala, ruled by Maya, 5-Mahātala, the abode of great serpents, 6-Rasātala, the abode of demons, and 7-Pātāla, ruled by Vasūkī. Guru Nanak Dev says, "Those, who are without the Name of the Lord, fall like the wall of sand....They fall into Rasātala (hell)" (p. 934 Dakhni Oamkar M. 1).

Rati: Passion; love. In the *Adi Granth*, this word is used in the sense of "love" and 'absorption'. Guru Amar Das says, "His body is not stained even a bit, who is absorbed in love with the Lord" (p. 771, Suhi M. 3). In Hindu tradition Rati is personified as an *apasarā* (nymph) and is not constant to any one man. Rati is also the name of one of the wives of Kāma, the god of love.

Razā: (Bhānā). See: *Volition, Will, Bhānā.*

Reabsorption: At the time of dissolution (Pralaya), the world is reabsorbed into Brahman. Guru Nanak Dev says, "The Lord Creates (the world) and reabsorbs it, but Keeps Himself Detached (p. 1033, Maru M. 1).

Real and Unreal: In philosophy, the word "real" is applied to whatever is regarded as having an existence in fact and not merely in appearance, thought, or language. It is the immediate object of that which is true. The *Adi Granth* considers God (Truth) and the souls which are part and parcel of God as real. The phenomenal world, though transitory and changing, is relatively real. It is not merely an illusion, as described by Shankaracharya, Guru Nanak Dev says, "O True King, all Your Play is True. They, who dwell on Truth, are also True. All that is born to die is false and vain" (p. 463, Var Asa M. 1).

Realists and Idealists: A realist is one, who is devoted to what is real, as opposed to what is fictitious or imaginary. An idealist is one, who has an ideal in view. The *Adi Granth* presents a commingling of realism and idealism. The Sikh Gurus and the Saints were both idealists and realists. Whereas their idea is the realisation of God through the discipline enunciated by the preceptor, they are also realists in the sense that they have practically lived the lives of householders and have immensely contributed towards the welfare of the society by their actual reform movements. The discipline of uttering the Lord's Name through the mouth and side by side doing all the work with hands and feet is an admixture of both idealism and realism (See Shloka 213 on pages 1376-77) of the *Adi Granth*.

Reasoning: Discursive thought. There is no reasoning or rational approach in the *Adi Granth*. The valid means of knowledge is the *Sabda* or verbal testimony. The spiritual experiences of an assembly of saints are brought forth through the scripture. The belief in the One Lord is hypothetical. But this does not mean that there is no discriminating intellect in an adherent of the discipline of the *Adi Granth*. Guru Ram Das says, "I receive the discriminating intellect from the True Guru; the knowledge attained from the Guru is regarding the preceptor-Lord (p. 711, Todi M. 4) According to the Guru, the discriminating intellect is the purest in the world and the one who practises it, sucks the Essence of the Lord" (p. 1325, Kalyan M. 4).

Rebirth: Because of his deeds in the world, man is reborn and undergoes transmigration. Guru Arjan Dev says, "Stung by greed...one is born to die and after death undergoes re-birth repeatedly. In this way, he is punished continuously and does not see the end of his journey" (p. 1020, Maru M. 5). But the true devotees of the Lord do not suffer re-birth. Kabir says, "I shall merge in the Lord like the water in the sea and the wave in the stream. The *Shūnya* (soul) will merge in *Shūnya* (God) and like air I shall look upon all alike. Then why shall I come again? The coming and going is under the Will of the Lord and Realising This Will, I shall merge in the Lord" (p. 1103, Maru Kabir).

Recluse: A person shut up from the world for the purpose of religious meditation; a monk. The life of a recluse is not in accordance with the discipline enunciated by the *Adi Granth*, therefore it has been rejected. Guru Arjan Dev says, "One becomes a recluse and wanders in the pilgrim-stations, but within his mind is the wrath, born of ignorance" (p. 1003, Maru M. 5). The saint Trilochan says, "Within his mind, there is impurity; he does not cleanse it. He does not know the Lord in his lotus heart; then why has he become a recluse? (p. 525, Gujri Trilochan). Only he is considered a true recluse, who keeps his heart steady (p. 1180, Basant M. 5).

Recompense: Return or repayment for something given or received. According to Guru Nanak Dev, generally we do not show mercy to a man in trouble. Without give and take, nobody does a thing for another. The king ministers justice only if he is sufficiently recompensated. But in the Name of God, he is not moved at all. This is the way of the world in the Iron age (Kali-age) (p. 350, Asa M. 1).

Reflection: The reflection (i.e. maya) is an emptiness, but the world is led astray by it (p. 932, Ramkali M. 1, Dakhni Oamkar). Your reflection, (i.e. maya), O Lord, permeates all beings; Your Creation has thus become an illusion (p. 433, Asa M. 1, Patti). Guru Tegh Bahadur says, "Just as the fragrance abides in the flower and the reflection in the mirror, similarly the Lord abides within" (p. 684, Dnanasari M. 9). The word "reflection" is also used in the sense of meditation, deep or serious consideration. Guru Nanak Dev says, "One may reflect a hundred thousand times, but one does not avail through reflection" (p. 1, Japuji). The night of the life passes away in continuous reflections, says Guru Arjan Dev (p. 390, Asa M. 5).

Regicide: Killing of a king. Guru Nanak Dev says, "There are countless rulers, who rule by force and there are countless cut-throats (killers) engaged in the act of killing" (p. 4, Japuji). The killing mentioned in this quotation may be of any type: homicide, regicide etc.

Regions: Guru Amar Das says, "O Lord, You Created the world of nine regions and Embellished it in every way" (p. 1094, Var Maru M. 3). There are many regions of the Universe; the Hindu tradition mentions nine regions (Nav Khand). Guru Nanak Dev has mentioned five regions in *Japuji*, which may be called the regions of spiritual growth viz. the region of *Dharma* (piety), the region of *Gyan* (knowledge), the region of effort (Saram Khand), the regions of Grace (Karam Khand) and the region of Truth (*Sac* Khand).

Relationship: According to the *Adi Granth*, all worldly relationships are false. Our only true relation is the Lord Himself, Who is our Father, Mother, Brother and Kinsman (p. 103, Majh M. 5). Guru Nanak Dev says, "Our sisters, sisters-in-law, mothers-in-law....our paternal and maternal grandmothers, our brothers and sisters-in-law....our maternal uncles and aunts, our fathers and mothers do not remain here. The caravans of our kindreds have gathered upon the sea-shore to cross into the next world. Our Spouse (the Lord) is Immortal and Sports ever in Bliss..." (p. 1015, Maru M. 1).

Relatives: All the relatives leave a person, when he is in distress (p. 70, Sri Rag M. 5). When one breathes his last, the relatives are of no avail.

The soul goes alone. Kabir says, "When the oil of life is burnt...whose are the father and mother and whose is the wife...every one says, "Carry him away". In the home the mother weeps, the brothers take away the bier...the wife cries, but the soul goes alone" (pp. 477-78, Asa Kabir).

Release: Emancipation; Salvation. Release is the freedom from the cycle of births and deaths. One is in bondage as long as there is the sense of duality, created by *maya* and ego. This state is the state of equipoise and is called the fourth state (the other three states being *Jagrit* (awakening), *svapan* (dream) and *Sushupti* (dreamless sleep)). It is also called *Turiya*. According to the *Adi Granth*, the release is obtained by one who destroys his ego (p. 1276, Malar M. 3). He, who after the death of his ego, lives with the Word of the Guru, attains release (p. 942, Ramkali M. 1, Siddh Goshta). We come into life through good deeds, but the release is obtained through the Grace of the Lord (p. 2, Japuji).

Released: Only he is released, on whom there is Grace of the Lord. He always sings the Praises of the Lord (p. 1261, Malar M. 3). They wanted to be released through the practice of works, but the release is obtained by Praising the Lord through the Word. Without the Word of the Guru, none attains Emancipation (p. 1024, Maru M. 1). Consider him released, who rises above praise and calumny and who sees no difference between gold and iron (p. 1426, Shlok M. 9). Consider him released who conquers the mind and remains unaffected by maya. Then he abides within the Tenth Door and gains knowledge about the three worlds (p. 490, Gujri M. 3).

Relic: An object which remains as a memorial of a departed saint, martyr or other holy person and as such is carefully preserved and venerated. According to the *Adi Granth*, wherever the True Guru goes and takes a seat, that place becomes sacred and is venerated as a relic by the devotees (p. 450, Asa M. 4). At another place Guru Ram Das has said, "Their foods, clothes, riches are sacred, who are imbued with the Name of the Lord. Sacred are their homes, temples, palaces and *serais* (rest-houses dedicated to the devotees and Saints of God). Sacred are their horses, saddles and the cloths placed under the saddles, which are yoked to the service of the saints" (p. 648, Var Sorath M. 4).

Religion: Action or conduct indicating a belief in, reverence for, and desire to please, a divine ruling power. The religion of the *Adi Granth* centres round the worship of the Transcendent Lord through the discipline enunciated by the True Guru. This religion does not believe in any formalism, symbolism and ritualism. According to Guru Arjan Dev "Of all religions, this religion is the purest: Do pure deeds and Meditate on the Name of the Lord" (p. 266, Gauri Sukhmani M. 5).

Religious: (Acts-Instruction-Merit-Student). According to the *Adi Granth*, the religious acts are the pure-Karmas (actions). Guru Ram Das says, "By practising many pure actions, the green branch ever sprouts forth with the flower of Dharma (righteousness) and the fruit of Guru's wisdom (Gnosis), which gives fragrance to the world" (p. 1325, Kalyan M. 4). Religious Instruction is the discipline enunciated by the Guru. Guru Arjan Dev says, "O ignorant one, follow the instructions of the Guru, because many clever ones were drowned without the devotion of the Lord" (p. 288, Gauri Sukhmani M. 5). Religious merit is obtained by remembering the Name of the Lord. "Those who meditate on the Lord are blessed with glory, they are the Approved ones, they are the first among beings" (p. 263, Gauri Sukhmani M. 5). In Indian tradition, the Brahmachārī is the religious student, but the *Adi Granth* mentions the school of the True Guru, (which is called *Satsangat*, the company of the devout disciples) from which the student learns and imbibes the godly qualities (p. 1316, Var Kanra M. 4).

Renovation: A change effected by renewal. As a child, innocently commits many errors and the father instructs and reprimands him, but then hugs him to his bosom, in a similar manner the Lord Forgives our past sins and Shows us the Path for the future (p. 624, Sorath M. 5). "If some one slanders the True Guru who then seeks his refuge, his past sins are forgiven by the True Guru who allows him to join the company of the saints..." (p. 854, Var Bilawal M. 4). These quotations depict the renovation of the human mind, but the renovation of the world can also be effected by the Will of the Merciful Lord. Guru Arjan Dev says, "The Merciful Lord has now Given the Command, that no one will dominate and be cause of anguish to another and all will now abide in peace; there is now the Rule of Humility" (p. 74, Sri Rag M. 5).

Renunciation: Renouncing the pursuit of actions. In Indian tradition renunciation was considered a means to attain the knowledge of Brahman. But the *Adi Granth* has refuted this claim. According to Guru Ram Das, "Forsaking the household, one's mind took him to the forest, but it could not get peace even for a moment; but when it sought the refuge of the Saint of the Lord, its wanderings ceased and it returned to its own home. One abandoned his relatives and became a *Sannyāsi*, but the craving of the mind did not cease. One's desires are not finished without the Word of the Guru, which alone can bring peace. When hatred for the world wells up in one's mind, he becomes a *Digambara* (A Jaina, who remains naked), but the mind wanders ceaselessly and these wanderings do not end his desires, but when he meets the saints, he reaches the House of Mercy. One practises many postures like a *Siddha*, but his mind wants to possess extra-psychic powers. His mind is never content..." (p. 835, Bilawal M. 4).

Repentence: Sorrow, regret, or contrition for past action or conduct. One who commits an evil and sinful action ultimately repents for his doing. According to Guru Nanak Dev one repents if he sins or covets (p. 1037, Maru M. 1). Kabir says, "Without the Name of the Lord, one repents in the end and grieves" (p. 524, Gujri Kabir). "Burnt be that tongue, which does not recite the Name of the Lord with Love. When the body's pitcher breaks, one writhes in pain and trapped by Yama, one repents" (p. 59, Sri Rag M. 1). Guru Amar Das says, "The time once lost does not return and one repents, when he passes away" (p. 28, Sri Rag M. 3).

Resignation: A giving up of oneself to God. Resignation is the literal meaning of Islam. It is a state or condition in which a believer becomes "resigned" to the Will of God. A Muslim is one who is 'resigned', that is the reason why Guru Nanak Dev says, "It is very difficult to be called a Muslim; If one is i.e. he has given himself up to God, then he can be called a Musalman" (p. 141, Var Majh M. 1). In the Quran, the grace of resignation is more frequently expressed by the word "Sabr", which has been given prominence in the Shlokas of Sheikh Farid (p. 1384, Shlok Farid). *Riza* is also a word, which expresses resignation. Talking about a Muslim, Guru Nanak Dev says, "He should resign (submit) to the Will of God..." (p. 141, Var Majh M. 1).

Resource: An action or procedure to which one may have recourse in a difficulty or emergency. "Of all the resources, You are the best resource, O Lord," Says Guru Arjan Dev (p. 507, Gujri M. 5).

Rest-House: The popular Indian term for the rest-house is *sarāi*, where the traveller/trader takes rest during the night. Guru Ram Das says, "Blessed are their homes, temples, palaces and rest-houses dedicated to the devotees and saints of God" (p. 648, Var Sorath M. 4).

Restraint: A means of checking persons from a course of action, or of keeping them under control. Self-restraint is considered the best instrument of purification. "Restrain yourself from the company of lust, anger, greed, attachment, ego and the vicious taste of vices" (p. 1118, Kedara M. 4). Thus the restraint is a mental penance.

Resurrection: The rising again of men on the Last Day. It is believed by the Muslims that on the Last Day of Judgment, the body will be raised from the grave and united to its soul. All will have to cross *Al-Sirat*, a bridge across the infernal fire, which is described as finer than a hair and sharper than a sword and is beset on each side with briars and hooked thorns. The righteous will pass over it with the swiftness of lightning, but the wicked will soon miss their footing and will fall into the fire of hell. In the *Adi Granth Al-Sirat* has been written as *Pursalāt* (instead of Pul Sirāt), in the folk pronunciation. Sheikh Farid writes: "The *Pursalāt* (the bridge of hell) is finer than hair" (p.1377, Shalok Farid). The saint Ravidas says, "The path of *Pursalāt* (the bridge of hell) is agonising, where there is no companion and which one has to cross all alone" (p. 793, Suhi Ravidas).

Retribution: Recompense, in another life, for one's good or bad deeds in this world. "One is rewarded for one's own deeds, good or bad", Says Guru Nanak Dev (p. 470, Var Asa M.1). We reap the fruit as we plant the deeds (p. 468, Var Asa M.1). "The body is the field of Karma in this age; whatever one sows, that one reaps" (p. 78, Sri Rag M. 5). One commits the deeds and is then bound to them. He comes and goes and involves himself in *maya* (p. 888, Ramkali M. 5).

Revelation: The disclosure of knowledge to man by a divine or supernatural agency. About his sayings, Guru Nanak Dev says, "The knowledge that I give, is revealed to me by the Lord" (p. 722, Tilang M.1). "I do not know what to say; whatever I say, is under the Command of my Lord". Thus the *bānī* of the *Adi Granth* has been uttered by the divine agency.

Revenge: The act of doing hurt or harm to another in return for wrong or injury suffered. Sheikh Farid says," Those who give blows to you, do not retaliate, go to your home after kissing their feet" (p. 1378, Shlok Farid). Thus the *Adi Granth* is opposed to revenge. Guru Arjan Dev says, "Cherish no evil in your mind for another, then O brother and friend, you will not come to grief" (p. 386, Asa M. 5).

Ridā: (Hirdā). Heart. Kabir says, "You have deceit in your heart, but you are a *giānī* (wise person) in speech. O lier, why do you churn water?" (Sorath Kabir, p. 656). "He who is absorbed in *Har Ras* (spiritual nectar) within his self and has destroyed his ego, the lotus blossoms in his heart and he attains concentration in the supreme spiritual state" (Sri Rag M. 3, p. 26). "If the Lord abides in the heart, the heart is pure" (Sarang M. 5, p. 1212).

Riddle: Something which puzzles or perplexes; a difficult or insoluble problem. Guru Arjan Dev says, "I knew everything, but kept silent. I was never conscientious, being lured by *maya*. I saw with my own eyes the signals of the riddle, but the foolishness and greed with me did not listen to what I was told" (pp. 217-18, Gauri Majh M. 5). The riddle here is about the illusion of *māyā*.

Riddh Siddh: The miraculous powers. See: *Miracles*.

Right: It has two connotations: 1-That which is morally just, 2-That which has due title. Guru Nanak Dev says, "One is rewarded for his deeds—right or wrong (good or bad)" (p. 471, Var Asa M. 1). To deprive one of his right is to eat the forbidden cow for one (Hindus) and the forbidden swine for the other (Muslims)" (p. 141, Var Majh M. 1).

Right Conduct: The discipline enunciated by the True Guru lays great emphasis on the right conduct. Guru Nanak Dev says, "O brother, imbibe truth and contentment and hold fast the quality of forgiveness, remaining in the refuge of the True Guru; and after realising the soul, realise the Lord—this release can be attained in the company of the Guru" (p.1030, Maru M.1). Guru Arjan Dev says, "On meeting the True Guru one fully comprehends the right conduct; one attains release, while laughing, playing, wearing and eating" (p. 522, Var Gujri M. 5).

Righteousness: Conformity of life or conduct to the requirements of the divine or moral law. In Indian terminology, we call it "Dharma". "Do not think of any other Greater than the Lord; He only Considers the Law (Dharma-righteousness). Why should we fear or doubt, when *Adharma* (unrighteousness) does not cast his evil eye on us. The Lord is True, His Justice is True; only the sinner suffers defeat (p. 90, Var Sri Rag M. 4). See: *Dharma*.

Rig Veda: It is the oldest of the four Vedas. It contains 1017 hymns or *sūktas* and is divided into ten books. The dates of the composition of these hymns are not known. The development from the polytheistic religion to monistic philosophy can be discerned in the hymns, therefore they seem to have been composed after long intervals, and were finally compiled into one collection. The seeds of two hymns i.e. *Pu-*

rusha Sukta and *Nāsadīya Sukta* can be seen in the compositions of the *Adi Granth*. While talking about the four Vedas, Guru Nanak Dev has given the following comments about Rig Veda: "The Rig Veda says that the Lord is All Pervading Rama, the Name of the Lord, is Supreme among gods. He who utters the Name, his sins are destroyed and he attains release (p. 470, Var Asa M. 1). "Sam Veda, Rig Veda, Yajur Veda and Atharva Veda, were uttered by Brahma and involved men in the *Maya* of three modes" (p. 1037, Maru M. 1).

Rik: The verses in the Sūktas of the Vedas are known as *richas* or *Riks*. *Richa* literally means "praise" and a sacred verse recited in praise of a deity is also called *richa*. The word "Rig" in Rig Veda is derived from *Rik* or *richa*. Rig Veda thus literally means "The Veda of the stanzas of praise."

Rishis: 'Rishi' literally means a seer. The inspired poet of the Vedic hymns is also called a *Rishi*. The Tadbhava form of *Rishi* in Indian vernaculars is *Rikhi*. Guru Nanak Dev says, "Brahma, Vishnu, Shiva, Indra, and all the *Rikhis* (seers), ascetics and mendicants—whosoever from these submits to the Will of the Lord is blessed with Glory at the True Court; and those who revolt in ego are effaced" (p. 992, Maru M. 1). Namdev says, "In the House of the Lord, the heavenly musicians and the seers (*Rikhis*) and the gods and the attendants of gods sing (His Praises) in utter humility" (p. 1292, Malar Namdev).

Rites: The formal procedures or acts in a religious or other solemn observance; religious ceremonies. Rituals of all kinds have been decried in the *Adi Granth*. "Without the Lord, all austerities, all actions and all Yogic disciplines are robbed on this side" (p. 216, Gauri Mala M. 5). "One practises the way of rituals and pious conduct, but without the Name of the Lord everything is cursed egoism" (p. 162, Gauri Guareri M. 3). The rites and works create ego. Guru Arjan Dev says, "The ritualists are busy in six types of works, but they are not cleansed from the dirt of ego" (p. 495, Gujri M. 5).

Rivers: Guru Angad Dev says, "In the fourth watch of early morning, the conscious minds feel inspired and befriend the rivers, with the True Name in their minds and mouths" (p. 146, Var Majh M. 1, Shlok M. 2). The rivers which are considered sacred because of the holy places on their banks, have been mentioned in the *Adi Granth*. The position of river Ganges is most significant. It is also known as Sursurī and Jaharnavī. The other rivers mentioned are Yamunā, and Godāvarī. The imagery of the rivers and their banks is found in the

Shlokas of Sheikh Farid. He says, "The crane sitting on the bank of the river is busy in sport, when unawares the hawk pounces upon the crane" (p.1383, Shlok Farid). "O river, do not break your banks, because you have also to render the account." (p. 1382, Shlok Farid).

Robbery: The action of depredation. The five vices i.e. lust, anger, greed, attachment and ego have been personified as robbers in the *Adi Granth.* They commit robbery of the moral qualities. Guru Nanak Dev says, "They are five and I have to fight alone with them. O mind, how can I keep my home safe? They always harass me and commit robbery, to whom should I unfold my grief" (p.155, Gauri Chett M.1). The Yama (the god of death) also robs our citadel of body. Sheikh Farid says, "Even when the two lamps of eyes were alight, the god of death seized the body. He captured the citadel and robbed the heart and extinguished the lamps" (p. 1380, Sheikh Farid).

Rog, Rogī: *Rog* is disease and *Rogī* is a patient. "The sufferings become a remedy and the pleasures a disease" (Var Asa M. 1, p. 469). "The human being is inflicted by the disease of ego, the elephant by the disease of lust, the moth by the disease of sight and the deer by the disease of sound. Whomsoever we see, he is inflicted by disease. Only the True Guru is a Yogi and without disease...." (Bhairo M. 5, p. 1140). "The world is *Rogī* (diseased) and the remedy is the Name of the Lord" (Dhanasari M. 1, p. 687).

Rosary: A rosary is a string of beads used to assist the memory in the recitation of the Name of the Lord or sacred formula. In Indian diction it is called "Mālā" and in Persio-Arabic, it is called "Tasbī". Kabir says, "I cannot absorb myself in devotion without satisfying my hunger, take away this *mālā* (rosary) of yours from me" (p. 656, Sorath Kabir). Guru Nanak Dev says," The Qazi sits in judgment upon others. He tells the *Tasbī* (rosary) and recites the Name of God, but on being bribed, he does injustice to the right person. And if anyone asks him, he quotes from the scripture" (p. 951, Var Ramkali M. 3, Shalok M.1).

Royal: Pertaining to the king or queen as civil or military head or representative of the state. Namdev says, "The royal maidens, in the town, bring the pitchers and fill them with water; they laugh, enjoy and talk about (several things), but they keep their minds in the pitchers"—(p. 972, Ramkali Namdev). "The kings indulging in royal pleasures gather the poison of *māyā*" (p. 1245, Var Sarang M. 4).

Rudra: Literally Rudra means "terrible" (p. 1402, Swayyas of the fourth Guru). Mahadeva or Shiva is also called Rudra, because of his destructive character. Guru Amar Das says, "Brahma, Vishnu and Rudra (Shiva) also Serve the One Lord. No one can Fathom the Unfathomable and mysterious Lord" (p. 1053, Maru M. 3). "The God-conscious person serves only the One Lord, Who Created Brahma, Vishnu and Rudra (Shiva)" (p. 1130, Bhairo M. 3).

Ruler-Internal (Antaryamin): "The Lord is the Ruler-Internal and Perfect Master. He blesses us with the dust of the Feet of the Saint" (p. 563, Vadhans M. 5). "Do you not know that the Lord is Omniscient Purusha and the Ruler-Internal of all hearts, therefore lean on His Support" (p. 1140, Bhairo M. 5). "The Lord, who is the Creator and the Ruler-Internal, is the One alone. Whomsoever He Makes His Servant, he also becomes eternal" (p. 1152, Bhairo M. 5).

Rulers: The glory of the (worldly) rulers and kings is only for a few days (p. 645, Var Sorath M. 4). That ruler alone sits on the throne, who is worthy of it (p. 1039, Maru M. 1). The Lord Himself is the Ruler and constitutes His Cabinet. He Sits on the Throne to Administer Justice....(p. 1022, Maru M. 1).

Rules of Conduct (Morality): According to the *Adi Granth*, the human being has to undergo a discipline for the attainment of final emancipation. This discipline contains rules of conduct for an individual, who has threefold duties to perform viz., the duties for his self, the duties in relation to society and the duties in relation to the Creator. The *Adi Granth* has laid down a definite moral code, which enjoins the disciple to do such actions, which can be called higher *Karmas*. The practice of these higher *Karmas* is the practice of virtues in life. Our perception should be devoid of the sense of possession, because it creates worldly attachment and ego. We should look at the world as the Creation of God, its beauty as the beauty of God (p. 922, Ramkali M. 3, Anand). We should hear no evil (p. 922, *ibid*). We should be sweet in speech (p. 921, *ibid*). A true disciple has to avoid all sensuous tastes and intoxicants (p.1287, Var Malar M.1). The *Adi Granth* lays great emphasis on moral qualities in an individual (pp. 765-66, Suhi M.1). The beauty-aids of a personality suggested by Guru Arjan Dev are truth, contentment, mercy and piety (p. 812, Bilawal M. 5). Guru Nanak Dev considers humility as the best quality in an individual (p. 470, Var Asa M.1). It inspires within us a holy sense of service (p. 286, Gauri M. 5). Above all, the godly qualities have to be imbibed (p. 756, Suhi M. 3).

S

Sabar: Patience; forbearance. Sheikh Farid says, "O man, patience is the objective of life; if you can remain firm on it, you will not narrow down to a small stream, but instead grow into a river" (Shlok Farid, p.1384). See: *Patience. Forbearance.*

Sabda: (Shabad)—Word. See: *Word.*

Sac, Saccā, Saciār: *Sac* is Truth, *Saccā* and *Saciār* connote a truthful person. Truth is eternal. It never gets old (Var Ramkali M. 3, Shalok M. 1, p. 955). Truth is God (Japuji, p. 1). How to become a *Saciār* (truthful person)?—This is the theme of *Japuji.* See: *Truth.*

Sac Khand: The region of Truth. This is the fifth and the last spiritual state mentioned in *Japuji.* In this state, the devotee realises the Transcendental Lord, Who sees and Showers His Graces on His Creation, Which is infinite (Japuji, p. 8).

Sacraments: Certain rites held to be generally necessary to salvation. Since the *Adi Granth* has no belief in the sacraments, it has rejected the prevalent ones in the contemporary Hindu society. For example about the *Yagyopavīta Saṁskāra* (The sacrament of the sacred thread), Guru Nanak Dev says, "The thread is bought for four *kauris* and is worn in the sanctified yard. The instruction is given in the ear and the Brahmin becomes the Guru; but when the man dies, the thread is burnt and the soul goes in the next world without the thread...The thread is spun out of cotton and the Brahmin twists it. He who has killed and eaten a he-goat says to all others: "Wear this sacred thread." When the thread wears off, it is thrown away and a new one is worn. If this thread has any strength, it should not break (p. 471, Var Asa M. 1). See: *Saṁskāra.*

Sacred Beings: The sacred beings are gods and goddesses. But the *Adi Granth* does not consider them sacred, because they have originated from *Maya* (p. 129, Majh M. 3). According to the *Adi Granth* "Brahmān is soiled, Indra is soiled, the sun and moon are soiled; the whole world is soiled, only the Infinite Lord is Immaculate" (p. 1158, Bhairo Kabir).

Sacred Books: In the *Adi Granth* there is mention of the sacred books of various religions and religious sects. The sacred books of Hinduism are the Vedas, Smritis, Purānas, Shastras, Bhagavad Gita, Bhakti Sutras and Agamas. The sacred writings of Islam are the Quran and the

Hadis. Alongwith Vedas, the *Kateb* (The Books) have also been mentioned. These Books are Taurāt (The Book of Moses), Zabūr (the Book of David), Injīl (New Testament--Bible) and the Qurān. According to the *Adi Granth* "Do not call the Vedas and Kateb as false; only he is false, who does not give thought to them" (p. 1350, Prabhati Kabir).

Sacred Cow: In Hindu texts, the cow is considered sacred. She is an auspicious purifier; she alone makes the sacrificial oblations possible by producing butter. Prosperity dwells in the urime of the cow and good fortune in cow-dung. Even in the Buddhist texts, the cows are considered the best friends, in which medicines are produced. They give food and strength. Hence the killing of a cow is strictly prohibited. Guru Nanak Dev has mentioned the taxing of the cow by the Muslim king and has also drawn our attention towards the Hindu view about the sanctity of the cow-dung (p. 471, Var Asa M. 1). In the *Adi Granth*, there is mention of the wish-fulfilling sacred cow known as *Kāmadhenu* and *Surabhī* (Surhī). (For Kāmdhenu see p. 1078, Maru M. 5 and for Surhī see p. 1196, Basant Kabir). According to Guru Arjan Dev, "Singing the Praises of the Lord fulfils our wishes like Kamadhenu" (p. 265, Gauri Sukhmani M. 5).

Sacred Duties: According to Guru Arjan Dev, "He who is in love with the Supreme Being, his deeds (works and duties) are pure and also his way of life is pure" (p. 184, Gauri Guareri M. 5).

Sacred Feasts: The *Yajnas* are the sacred feasts. In accordance with the nature of gods, men offer them the meat of rhinoceros as the sacrificial food in the Sacred Feasts (*Yajnas*) (p. 1289, Var Malar M. 1). "*Maya*....destroys the merit of Sacred Feast (*Yajana*), ablution, austerities and pilgrimages" (p. 673, Dhanasari M. 5). "The *Yajnas*, the sacrificial fire, pious conduct, austerity and works subject one's body to pain. One is emancipated only through the Name of the Lord..." (p. 1127, Bhairo M. 1). The *Sraddhas* are also sacred feasts in memory of the manes (Pitrīs). Kabir says, "While living, the manes are not shown reverence, but after death people hold sacred feasts in their name. But the dead do not get the offerings because they are eaten by crows and dogs" (p. 332, Gauri Bairagan Kabir).

Sacred Objects: Some objects are considered sacred according to Indian tradition. Fire, water, wind, sun, moon, idol of gods, Brahmins, cows, some trees (like banyan) etc. are included among them. But the *Adi Granth* considers only those objects sacred, which are associated with the Name of the Lord. Guru Ram Das says, "The foods, clothes and riches of those are sacred, who are imbued with the Name of the Lord. The homes, palaces, temples and rest-houses dedicated to the Saints are sacred. The horses, saddles and horse-cloths which are used in the service of the Saints are sacred. The deeds of those, who remember the Name of the Lord are sacred (p. 648, Var Sorath M. 4).

Sacred Places: Holy Places or *Tīrthas*. Sacred places or *Tīrthas* are generally situated on the banks of rivers or brooks. A *tīrtha* may have a temple with the idols of gods or goddesses relevant to it. There may be a large tree in it and a pool for taking bath. According to Hindu tradition, there are sixty-eight sacred places. Their mention is made several times in the *Adi Granth*. But there is a repeated contention that by bathing at the Sacred Place, one is not purged of his dirt (p. 890, Ramkali M. 5). The real *tīrath* is the Name of the Lord (p. 687, Dhanasari M. 1). They who listen to the Name of the Lord gather the merit of bathing at sixty-eight sacred places (p. 3, Japuji).

Sacred Syllable: *Aumkāra* is the sacred syllable, which has been given as the first letter in the beginning of both the *Bawan Akhris* (of Kabir and Guru Arjan Dev) and the *Dakhnī Oamkar* (of Guru Nanak Dev). Guru Nanak Dev says, "Listen to the merit of the Syllable AUM (OM); it is, indeed, the essence of the three worlds" (p. 930, Ramkali M. 1, Dakhni Aumkāra).

Sacred Times: According to Hindu tradition and belief, some time is considered auspicious and some inauspicious, subject to planetary conjunctious. The *Adi Granth* considers only that time sacred, when one Contemplates on the Name of the Lord (p. 819, Bilawal M. 5). The months, days and the time are auspicious, when there is the Grace of the Lord (p. 136, Baramaha Majh M. 5).

Sacred Twigs: The *Adi Granth* mentions the sacred twigs of the Name of the Lord. Guru Nanak Dev says, "Let there be the tree of (higher) Karmas, with the twigs of the Name of the Lord, the flowers of righteousness and the fruit of gnosis, the leaves of attainment and the shade of the purging of the mind's ego" (p. 1168, Basant M. 1).

Sacrifice(s): Primarily, the slaughter of an animal as an offering to God or a deity; anything offered to God or a deity as an act of propitiation or homage. In ancient times rhinoceros was offered as a sacrifice (p. 1289, Var Malar M.1). The sacrifices and offerings for manes are of no avail (p. 472, Var Asa M. 1 and p. 332, Gauri Bairagan Kabir). Namdev says, "Ashvamedha Yajna, giving charity equal to one's weight, bathing at Prayag—all these cannot equal the merit of the Name of the Lord" (p. 873, Gond Namdev). Guru Arjan Dev says, "Deeds of charity and piety and oblations to the sacred fire, cutting of the body and offering in *havana* each bit in sacrifice, keeping of fasts and other acts of merit—all these do not equal the meditation on the Name of the Lord" (p. 265, Gauri Sukhmani M. 5).

Sacrificer: One who offers sacrifice. "All the works done by the sacrificer to expiate for his sins, do not save him. Only the Name of the Lord washes away innumerable sins" (p. 264, Gauri Sukhmani M. 5). The best sacrifice for the sacrificer is total surrender before the Guru and the Lord. "He who surrenders body, mind and riches before the Guru and following his discipline he realises the Lord" (p. 918, Ramkali M. 3, Anand). The prayer of the sacrificer should be: "I am a sacrifice to You, O Lord, You Protect me like the Mountain, I am a sacrifice to You for innumerable times, because You have raised the curtain of Doubt" (p. 779, Suhi M. 5).

Sacrificial Fee: In Indian terminology, it is called *dakshinā*. It is the honorarium given by the sacrificer to the priest. It is more a present than a fee. The *Adi Granth* rejects priest-craft and thus the *dakshinā* in that sense. The devotee asks for His Name as *dakshinā* from the Lord (p. 1329, Prabhati M. 1).

Sādh: A saint (*Sādhū*). See: *Saint*.

Sādh Sangat: The holy congregation. A great merit is attached to the attendance of a holy congregation in the *Adi Granth*. One attains discriminating intellect in *Sādh Sangat* (Asa M. 5, p. 377). The sleeping mind awakens in *Sādh Sangat* (Asa M. 5, p. 386). I forgot the jealousy of others, when I joined the company of the saints (Kanra M. 5, p. 1299). See: *Congregation*.

Sages: A Sage is a man of profound wisdom. Its equivalents in Indian terminology are *Rishi* and *Muni*. Guru Nanak Dev says, "Out of Brahma, Vishnu, Shiva, Indra, rishis (seers-sages), ascetics and mendicants, whosoever submits to the Will of the Lord, is blessed with glory in His Court" (p. 992, Maru M.1). "Myriads of *Munīs* (sages) Praise Him (the Lord) in love, Enshrining Him in their minds (p. 221, Gauri Guareri M. 1).

Sahaj: The Supreme spiritual state, which is also called *Turiyā* or *Chauthā Pad* or *Param Pad*. "*Sahaj* cannot be achieved without the Guru, though everyone wants to achieve it" (Sri Rag M. 3). See: *Chauthā Pad*.

Sahaj Jog: Sahaj Yoga. The *Bhakti Yoga* of Guru Nanak Dev has been called *Sahaj Yoga* by the Guru in comparison to *Raja Yoga* of Patanjali and *Haṭh Yoga* of Gorakhnath. See: *Yoga.*

Sahanshīlatā: Patience; forbearance. See: *Forbearance.*

Sāhib: The Master; The Lord.

Saibhang:Self-Existent. See: *Svayambhū.*

Saint: He who ever remembers the Lord with every breath and in whose mind there is the *mantra* of the Name of the Lord; he alone is the perfect saint (p. 319, Var Gauri M. 5). He alone is the saint, with whom the Lord is Pleased; the Working of the Saint and the Lord is the same (p. 867, Gond M. 5). The Saint and the Lord are One (p. 486, Asa Ravidas). The routine of the life of the saint is as follows: He occupies himself with the Name alone. He has his peace in the Blissful Song of the Lord. For him friends and foes are alike; he does not know any other except God. He washes away innumerable sins from the tablet of his mind. He is a man of word; his company is sought even by the gods...(p. 392, Asa M. 5).

Saintship: Saintliness of life or character. The real saint does not shed his saintship, even if he meets millions of unholy persons; Though the Chandan tree is enwrapped by the snakes, it does not fail to emit fragrance (p. 1373, Shlok Kabir). Listening to the Lord's Praise and Contemplating on Him are the characteristics of saintship (p. 1222, Sarang M. 5). See: *Saint.*

Sajjan Mittar: The friends; companions. "I want Him as my friend, who is helpful to me in the beginning, in the middle and at the end" (Gauri M. 5, p. 240). "They are my friends, who accompany me wherever I go. Wherever I am called to account for, they stand by my side" (Suhi M. 1, p. 729). "I have befriended everybody and I am the friend of all" (Dhanasari M. 5, p. 671).

Sākat: (Saktā)—the follower of Shakti or *Maya*. Shaktāism is one of the Bhakti cults. *Sākats* have been strongly condemned by the Gurus and the saint-poets of the *Adi Granth*. Kabir says, "Never keep the company of a *Sākat*; run away from him from a distance, because you will be stained if you come into contact with a black utensil" (Shlok Kabir, p. 1371). He considers a swine better than a *Sākat*, because by eating the dirt, it keeps the village clean, but nobody will think of poor *Sākat* after his death (Shalok Kabir, p. 1372). "*Sākat* cannot enter the temple of the Lord and suffers transmigration" (Maru M. 1, p. 1043).

Sāk Sambandhī: The relatives. "Mother, father, wife, son, relatives, dear friends and brothers are all there because of their contacts in previous births, but none of them is helpful at the time of death" (Jaitsri M. 5, p. 700). "Whose is the mother and whose is the father? All the relations are only in name and false" (Gauri M. 5, p. 188). "O my mind, all the seeming family members, friends and brothers, only meet for their self-ends. The day, when their self-interest fails, none will come near you" (Gaund M. 4, p. 860).

Salt: Guru Arjan Dev says, "O Lord, I have betrayed Your Salt, forgive me for this" (p. 195, Gauri M. 5). Guru Nanak Dev has used the word "Salt" in the same sense (p. 991, Maru M. 1). The pepper and salt, if treated with ghee, do not dissolve in water, similarly the devotees of the Lord live in the midst of *Maya* (p. 877, Ramkali M. 1). The grain, water, fire, salt and ghee produce good food, but when such food goes into the body of the sinner, it is polluted (p. 473, Var Asa M. 1). Farid says, "Some have surplus wheat-flour, others have not even the salt; but when both go to the next world, those worthy of punishment will be known" (p. 1380, Shlok Farid).

Saluting: A raising of the hand to the forehead by an inferior, when meeting or leaving. It is an etiquette. Guru Nanak Dev says, "One who salutes and is also impudent to the Master fails to get at anything". Both these aspects are contradictory and the person concerned remains unrewarded (p. 474, Var Asa M.1). Like a king without salutations, the mind is a blind spot without the Name (p. 354, Asa M. 1). Kabir says, "I salute the Lord repeating His thousand Names" (p. 478, Asa Kabir).

Salvation: The deliverance from sin and admission to eternal bliss. In Indian terminology, its equivalents are *Mukti* and *Moksha*. The concept of salvation is different in different religions. According to the *Adi Granth*, an Enlightened Person even forsakes *Mukti* (p. 1078, Maru M. 5). See: *Emancipation* and *Beatitude*.

Samādhī: Comtemplation. It is a form of advanced meditation, beyond the processes of thought. It is the means for reaching the knowledge of the self and Higher Self. In the eightfold limbs of Raja Yoga, it is the final limb. In the *Adi Granth*, it is the Trance of Equipoise (p. 1106, Maru Ravidas). Guru Arjan Dev says, "They who are blessed by the Perfect Guru with a spontaneous trance and bliss, the Lord is ever on their side" (pp.807-808, Bilawal M. 5).

Samarpan: Dedication; Devotion to God's service. The Lord says, "In the first instance accept death and leave all hope of life. Become the dust of the feet of all, then come to me (Var Maru M. 5, p. 1102). "O my Lord, if any one talks about You, what present should we give to him? Cut the head and present it as a seat and the service be performed without the head (ego)" (Vadhans M. 1, p. 551).

Sāma Veda: It is the second of the four Vedas, the others being Rig, Yajur and Atharva. The hymns of the Rig Veda have been recast into it and arranged for singing at the Soma sacrifice. There is mention of Sāma Veda in the *Adi Granth*. Guru Nanak Dev says, "According to Sāma Veda, the Lord is Decked in white; whosoever comes in Truth remains in Truth" (p. 470, Var Asa M. 1).

Samdarsī: He who has the sight of love for everybody; He who rises above duality. He has non-discriminating sight (*Samdrishtī*). According to Guru Arjan Dev, "the knower of Brahman (*Brahm-Giānī*) has non-discriminating sight like wind, which does not discriminate between rich and poor. He is always *Samdarsī*; only the nectar rains from his eyes" (Gauri Sukhmani M. 5, p. 273). "He is, indeed, a Yogi, whose sight considers everyone equal to others" (Suhi M. 1, p. 730).

Saṁsāra: The world. This world (Saṁsāra) is a dream (p. 1231, Sarang M. 9). This *Saṁsāra* is involved in sin (p. 1327, Prabhati M. 1). This whole *Saṁsāra* comes and goes (p. 607, Sorath M. 4). The release from the *Saṁsāra* is attained, when the involvement in *Maya* ends (p. 693, Dhanasari Namdev). If one is absorbed in doubt, this *Saṁsāra* is of no worth for him (p. 13, Gauri Poorbi M. 5). This *Saṁsāra* is like poison, it is the ocean of fear, which the Lord makes us swim across through the word of the Guru (p. 353, Asa M. 1). This world (Saṁsāra), that you see, is the manifestation of the Lord. (p. 922, Ramkali M. 3 Anand). The world is beautiful, but within it is the garden of evil; those who are blessed by the Guru, the thorns do not prick them (p. 1382, Shlok M. 5, in Shlok Farid).

Saṁskāra: The purificatory rite or ceremony, The Sacrament. The members of the three higher castes in Hinduism are sanctified by the *Saṁskāras*. The *Adi Granth* rejects the sacraments. See: *Sacraments*.

Sanctity: Holiness of Life, Saintliness. They only attain sanctity, who remember the Lord. They become pure, who by the Grace of the Guru, Dwell on the Lord. Their father, mother, relatives and the whole congregation are sanctified (p. 919, Ramkali M. 3, Anand). See: *Purity*.

Sandhyā: Twilight. In Hinduism, it is personified as the daughter of Brahmā and wife of Shiva. In the *Adi Granth* this term is used for Hindu prayers. Guru Amar Das says, "He offers Sandhya and makes water-offerings to the gods and manes (Tarpan), he recites Gayatri mantra, but without knowing the Reality, he is in agony" (p. 603, Sorath M. 3). "If an egocentric offers his (Sandhyā) prayers, his mind is unsteady and he is wasted away in transmigration" (p. 553, Var Bihāgṛā M. 4, Shlok M. 3).

Sangī: Companions. See: *Sajjan Mittar* and *Sāk Sambandhī*. "He may, indeed, be called a *Sangi*, who is not separated here and hereafter" (Dhanasari M. 5, p. 677).

Sanjam: (*Sanyam*)-Self-restraint. It is the golden principle. Lust is overshadowed and effaced by self-restraint. The *Adi Granth* rejects both self-gratification and self-mortification, and recommends self-restraint for the growth of a healthy personality. The seeker must remain within limits in order to remain fit. Too much of everything is bad. Too much eating and drinking etc. make one unhealthy. Similarly we endanger our health if we take less than our requirement. The word *Sanjam* accompanies *Sat* (truth) and Santokh (contentment) in the *Adi Granth* (See Asa M. 3, p. 427 and Ramkali M. 1, p. 939).

Sanjog: (*Samyoga*)-Conjunction. In the *Adi Granth*, two words *Sanjog* and *Vijog* (separation) come together. "My Lord has Created both *Sanjog* and *Vijog*" (Maru M. 1, p. 1032). "My Lord has included both *Sanjog* and *Vijog* in the Writ" (Malhar M. 3, p. 1058). "*Sanjog* and *Viyog* exist from the very beginning (Maru M. 5, p. 1007).

Sankalpa: Will; conception. In the *Adi Granth*, the word "Kalpa" has been used after removing the prefix "San". Guru Nanak Dev says, "When I met the True, Carefree Master, I renounced the *Kalpa* (formative will) and the argumentative reasoning" (p. 18, Sri Rag M. 1).

Sannyāsin (Sannyāsi): A renunciate, who belongs to the fourth *ashramā* (stage of life). He renounces all worldly attachments and absorbs himself in meditation and contemplation. He passes his time in spiritual pursuits, scriptural studies and service to humanity. The *Adi Granth* has rejected the life of a sannyasin. One becomes a *Sannyasi* and wanders in the pilgrim-stations, but the vice of anger does not leave him (p. 1003, Maru M. 5). The *Sannyasi* is involved with his self and becomes egoistic (p. 1193, Basant Kabir). The *Sannyasi* smears his body with the ashes and thus decorates it (p. 164, Gauri Guareri M. 4). Guru Nanak Dev says, "I have known by the Grace of the Perfect Guru that the Jangams, warriors, celibates and *Sannyasis* are not rewarded without service and service is the most sublime deed" (p. 992, Maru M. 1). "The Yogis of the twelve sects and the *Sannyasis* of the ten sects...are caught in the noose of *Yama*, if they do not rely on the Word of the Guru (p. 1332, Prabhati M. 1).

Sansā: (*Bharam, Bhram*)...Illusion. See: Bharam, Illusion. "This world is *Sansā* (an illusion), the night passes away in sleep (Sri Rag M. 3, p. 36).

Sansār: (Duniā)—The world. See: *world.*

Sant: A saint. See: *saint.*

Santokh: Contentment. See: *Contentment.*

Sarab-Viāpak: Omnipresent. See: *Omnipresent.*

Sat (Sac): Ordinarily "Sat" means truth, but when it pertains to the Lord, it means "Ever-Existent." The very first Shloka in the *Adi Granth* (in the beginning of *Japuji*) is as follows: "The Ever-Existent Lord is there in the Beginning, He is there in the Beginning of the Ages, He is there in the Present and will be there in Future" (p. 1, Japuji). God being Truth and Ultimate Reality, the reality of His Creation cannot be denied (p. 463, Var Asa M. 1). We know the Truth, when the heart is true...when we love the Truth... if we receive True instruction (p. 468, Var Asa M. 1). Though Truth is the highest, but truthful living is still higher (p. 62, Sri Rag M. 1).

Satan: A derivative from the Arabic word "Shaitān" meaning "Devil". He is the great spirit of evil. According to the *Quran*, Satan was created of fire, while Adam was created of clay. Though the *Adi Granth* does not believe in any such entity, the word *Shaitān* occurs several times in the *Adi Granth*, particularly in respect of Muslim conduct. Guru Nanak Dev says, "Though you keep fast for thirty days and say your prayers five times a day, but you should see that the Satan does not wash away their merits" (p. 24, Sri Rag M. 1). Thieves, illicit lovers, prostitutes and touts keep company together....They do not know the Praise of the Lord, because the Satan abides within them (p. 790, Var Suhi M. 3, Shlok M. 1). Through wisdom one serves the Lord, one attains honour... This is the True Path, everything else leads towards Satan (p. 1245, Var Sarang M. 4, Shalok M. 1).

Satgurū: The True Guru; The true preceptor. See: *Guru.*

Satī: A benefactor. Talking about the sign of Kali-Yuga (Iron-age) Guru Nanak Dev says, "The benefactors (Satīs) give away their riches (in charity), which they gather through sin" (p. 951, Var Ramkali M. 3, Shalok M. 1). In Hinduism that lady is called a *Satī*, who burns herself on the funeral pyre of her husband. Kabir says, "How can a woman become a Sati (True bride) by burning herself on the funeral pyre of her husband without truth (in her heart)?" (p. 328, Gauri Kabir). Guru Amar Das has denounced the practice of *Satī*. He says,

"A *Sati* is one who lives contented and decks herself with good conduct" (p. 787, Var Suhi M. 3).

Satsang, Satsangat: The holy congregation *(Sādhsangat)*. See: *Congregation*.

Sattva: One of the three modes of *maya*, the other two being *Rajas* and *Tamas*. It denotes goodness and purity. This quality predominates in unselfish persons and those absorbed in spiritual pursuits. This quality is the primary requisite for a person aspiring for God-realisation. Even the quality of *Sattva* creates ego, though it is the nobler and purer, therefore the true Devotee of the Lord remains above the three modes (p. 865, Gond M. 5).

Satya: The true and the real. He who considers Higher Brahman as *Satya*, merges in the True Lord (p. 283, Gauri Sukhmani M. 5). God Himself is *Satya* and whatever is Created by Him is *Satya* (p. 294, Gauri Sukhmani M. 5). In Hindu tradition, one of the seven upper regions is *Satyaloka*; it is the uppermost region. It is also known as Brahma-loka, the region of infinite wisdom and truth. In the *Adi Granth*, there is mention of the fourteen regions, seven upper and seven nether. They are called "Bhavan".

Saviour: One who delivers or rescues from peril; He who saves mankind from sin and its consequences. The Lord is the only Destroyer and Saviour. There is no power in man (p. 281, Gauri Sukhmani M. 5). Guru Nanak Dev says, "O my Saviour Lord, He whom you want to save, You lead him to the True Guru and in this way You take care of him; he is then rid of the vice of ego and all his troubles end" (p. 1169, Basant M. 1).

Savitrī-Gāyatrī: The name *Savitrī* is used in the Vedas for the sun. But the holy verse of the Veda is also called Savitrī or Gāyatrī. This most sacred verse of the Veda (Rig Veda) is a sacred mantra, which every Brahmin has to repeat several times in mornings and evenings. Guru Nanak Dev has made a mention of this important Gāyatrī hymn in his hymn of creation, wherein he says, "There were no distinctions of colour and guise, Brahmin and Kshatriya; there were no gods, temples, no sacred cow and no Gāyatrī...(before creation)" (p. 1036, Maru M. 1). This Gāyatrī Mantra is an invocation to the sun-god. In Hindu tradition Savitrī is also personified as the daughter and wife of Brahmā, who is also regarded as a personification of the holy verse.

Scepticism: The opinion that real knowledge of any kind is unattainable; Doubt as to the truth of some assertion or supposed fact. The

Syādvāda of Jainism is the same as scepticism. There is no place for scepticism in the religion of the *Adi Granth*. The *Mantram* given by the Guru is firmly embedded in the heart of the devotee, which neither wavers nor wobbles. (p. 671, Dhanasari M. 5).

Schism: The offence of causing or promoting divisions in the Church, an act of infidelity. Guru Ram Das says, "The infidel or egocentric is led astray by greed and ego. He passes all his time in strife and does not contemplate on the Word (of the Guru). The Creator has taken away his discriminating intellect, everything that he speaks is vicious. He is not content with any gift; there is immense craving and darkness of ignorance within him. It is good to break away from such a self-centred person who is infatuated with the lust for *maya* (p. 316, Var Gauri M. 4). Such a person, who creates schism, remains unhappy and gets no comfort, he transmigrates repeatedly. The True Guru even forgives him, if he is attuned to the Feet of the Guru (p. 652, Var Sorath M. 4). See: Heretics.

Scholar: A learned or erudite person. In Indian terminology, a scholar is a Pundit. According to Guru Nanak Dev, a real scholar (Pundit) is well-read only, if he reflects on the learning spontaneously, if he churns it and finds its quintessence and absorbs himself in the Name of the Lord. The egocentric sells his learning and thereby earns and eats poison. The foolish one does not dwell on the Word and is, therefore, without any knowledge and realisation. A scholar may be called enlightened, if he instructs his followers to cherish the Name of the Lord, live with it and profit by it in the world (pp. 937-938, Ramkali M.1, Dakhni Oamkar). According to Guru Arjan Dev, the renowned Pundit, though laden with many-sided learning, is hard-hearted and his body does not feel satiated. He lives a double life, always having his eye on *maya* (p. 960, Var Ramkali M. 5). He who recognises the quintessence, is indeed, a real scholar (Pundit) (p. 128, Majh M. 3).

School: *Sat Sangat* (The holy congregation) is the school of the True Guru, where the disciple learns and imbibes godly attributes (p. 1316, Var Kanṛā M. 4). When Guru Nanak Dev talks of the six houses of philosophy, he actually refers to the six schools of philosophy pertaining to six Shāstras, each school under a separate teacher (p. 12, Asa M. 1).

Sciences: There is no direct reference to any science in the *Adi Granth*, but talking about learning and wisdom, the word *Vigyān* (a word used for science) has been used. It connotes knowledge (See p. 903,

Ramkali M. 1). The words *Jotik* and *Jotki* pertain to astrology and the word *Ganit* to arithmetic.

Scribe: An official concerned with writing.

: One who writes at another's dictation.

: A copyist or transcriber of manuscripts.

The first scribe of the *Adi Granth* was Bhai Gurdas, the eminent Sikh theologian. The scribe engaged by Guru Gobind Singh for *Damdame wālī Bīr* was the eminent Sikh scholar Bhai Mani Singh. There is mention in the *Adi Granth* of the two mythological scribes *Chitrā* and *Guptā*, who write about the good and bad deeds of a person (See p. 393, Asa M. 5).

Scripture: The Sacred writing. In the *Adi Granth* (which is the scripture of the Sikhs), there is mention of or reference to various scriptures of other religions. *Vedas* (the scriptures of Hinduism) and *Quran* (the scripture of Islam) have been prominently mentioned. The word "Kateb" includes four scriptures viz. Taurāt, (The Book of Moses), Zabūr (The Book of David), Injil (New Testament) and the Quran. Other sacred writings referred to are *Āgams, Tantras, Smritis, Purānas, Gītā,* of Hinduism and *Hadis* of Islam. The six *Shastras* of Hinduism have also been prominently mentioned.

Sea: The Guru is identifed with the sea, which is full of pearls; the saints have been identified with the swans, who pick up the pearls and remain near their Guru (p. 685, Dhanasari M. 1). The world has been called "The sea of existence", which one crosses on singing the Praises of the Lord" (p. 536, Devgandhari M. 9). The true devotee must meet the true Guru, even if the highly saline sea falls in the way (p. 757, Suhi M. 4).

Seasons: In the poem entitled "Ruttīn" (seasons), composed by Guru Arjan Dev in Raga Ramkali, six seasons have been mentioned, viz. *Basant* in Chet and Baisākh, *Garīkham* in Jeth and Asarh, *Rut Baras* (Rainy season) in *Sāwan* and *Bhādon*, *Sard* in Asuj and Kartik, *Sisiar* in Maghar and Pokh and *Himkar* in Magh and Phalgun (pp. 927-929, Ramkali M. 5, Ruttīn). The Guru says, "Blessed is the season, when the mind cherishes the Lord" (p. 1183, Basant M. 5). Sheikh Farid has described a changing season: "The season has changed and the forest trembles, the leaves are falling down" (p. 1383, Shlok Farid).

Secret Doctrines: There are two types of doctrines: the exoteric and the esoteric. The esoteric doctrines concern *Atman* and *Brahman*, therefore they are called secret doctrines. The *Adi Granth* thus, is a scripture of secret doctrines. It is only the Guru, who reveals the secret doctrine to the disciple. Guru Arjan Dev says, "I have heard the secret doctrine from the Guru" (p. 739, Suhi M. 5). "The Lord's Secret Gospel is most sweet and rare is that person, who has witnessed it with his own eyes" (ibid).

Secret Rites: Such rites are associated with witchcraft. The *Adi Granth* has rejected such like charms, spells and rites. Guru Nanak Dev says, "*Maya* and attachment are like the love of a cursed woman i.e. an ugly witch, who is devoid of chastity (p.796, Bilawal M.1). Guru Ram Das says, "Come friends, let us weave the charms of the Praise of the Lord" (p. 173, Gauri Majh M. 4). Guru Nanak Dev says, "Let good deeds be your charm, strung on the thread of the mind" (p. 557, Vadhans M. 1). According to Guru Nanak Dev, the real Charmer is the Lord Himself, who has Charmed the whole world, tying many-coloured thread round every one's neck; being of shallow mind, one eats the sweets alongwith the fly (p. 582, Vadhans M. 1).

Sects: There is mention of various religious sects and cults in the *Adi Granth.* Out of five Bhakti cults of the Hindus, Vaishnavism, Shaivism and Shaktāism have been prominently referred to. There is pointed reference to twelve sects of Yogis and ten sects of Sannyasīs (p. 941, Ramkali M. 1, Siddh Goshta). Out of the two sects of Jainism, there is mention of *Digambaras* (p. 356, Asa M. 1). Different sects of ascetics have been named.

Seduction: The action of inducing a woman to surrender her chastity. According to the *Adi Granth*, great merit is lost, when one seduces another's woman (p. 941, Ramkali M. 1, Siddh Goshta). The five thieves make the mercurial mind wobble, therefore one keeps an eye on the homes of other people. He does not search his inner-self. Without the WORD, he loses honour...(p. 1021, Maru M. 1). The nine organs of the body become impure if one does not remember the Name of the Lord and follows the wrong path. He goes to another's woman and calumniates the saints...such an unfortunate person transmigrates repeatedly (p. 298, Thittī, Gauri M. 5). Guru Arjan Dev has advised a devotee not to see the beauty of another's woman (p. 274, Gauri Sukhmani M. 5).

Seed: In the *Adi Granth*, the *karma* (action) is likened to a seed. Just as a seed is sown in the earth, we sow the *karma* in the field of the body. Guru Arjan Dev says, "As you sow, so shall you reap, such is the field of *karma*" (p. 134, Baramaha Majh M. 5). If the seed is not sown in season, what will the hungry eat hereafter? (p. 450, Asa M. 4). Sowing the seed of Lord's Name at the appropriate time, the devotee reaps the harvest, which never exhausts (p. 734, Suhi M. 4).

Seers: Those to whom divine revelations are made in visions; those gifted with profound spiritual insight. In Indian terminology, they are called *rishis*. Guru Nanak Dev says, "Out of Brahma, Vishnu, Shiva, Indra, Rishis (seers), ascetics and mendicants, whosoever submits to the Will of the Lord, is blessed with glory at the True Court" (p. 992, Maru M. 1). The saint Namdev says, "In the House of the Lord, the heavenly musicians, the *Rishis* (seers), the gods and their attendants sing (His Praises) in utter humility" (p. 1292, Malar Namdev).

Self: The Self connotes the individual self, which is identified with the body, senses, mind and prāna (the vital breath). The lower self is ego and the Higher Self is the soul or *Atman*, which is identical with Brahman. The embodied self (or soul) is called *Jiva*. Following thoughts about the nature of self i.e. *Atman* are found in the *Adi Granth*: "It is a strange story, quite strange. The soul is like God Himself. Neither it is old, nor young. Neither it is prone to misery nor dies. It never dies, but exists from the very beginning. Neither heat nor cold have any effect on it. Neither it has an enemy nor a friend. It neither experiences joy nor sorrow. It is the master of all, the doer, it has no father, no mother but continues to exist from the limitless times. Virtue and sin have no effect on it. It is always awake within every heart" (p. 868, Gond M. 5).

Self- concentration: Self-concentration is the concentration of mind. By exclusive meditation, the devotee attains self-concentration. The meditation may be carried on at any time, and in any place, favourable to concentration of mind. Guru Ram Das says, "The outgoing mind, now in the upper region and now in the nether region is brought back to its only home through concentration on the Name of the Lord..." (p. 443, Asa M. 4). Guru Nanak Dev says, "O mind, wobble not in concentration and walk straight on the Path. In the rear, there is frightful *wolf* and in front there is pool of fire" (p. 1410, Shlok Varan te Vadhik M. 1).

Self-conquest: Victory over ego. Guru Arjan Dev says, "He who conquers his self by the Grace of the Perfect Guru, conquers the whole world (p. 680, Dhanasari M. 5). The same idea has been expressed by Guru Nanak Dev, when he says, "One conquers the whole world by conquering his mind" (p. 6, Japuji). The devotee has to follow the discipline of the Guru for self-conquest.

Self-consciousness: Consciousness of ego; Consciousness of one's own identity, acts, thoughts etc. Guru Arjan Dev says, "So long as one is conscious of the fact that he can do a thing, he does not get peace. So long as one is conscious of the fact that he does a thing, he is cast into the womb repeatedly. So long as one is conscious of the fact that one is his friend and the other his enemy, his mind is not at peace. So long as one is conscious of the fact that he is attached to *māyā*, he receives punishment from the Lord of Justice" (p. 278, Gauri Sukhmani M. 5).

Self-control: Control of one's self, one's desires etc. Guru Nanak Dev says, "There can be no worship without honour, no self-control without Truth and no sacred thread without continence" (p. 903, Ramkali M.1). Guru Amar Das says, "There is the Jewel of wisdom within it, which is embedded in the mind by the Grace of the Guru. By truthful living one gathers the merit of continence, self-control and saintliness and dwells on the Name of the Lord by the Grace of the Guru" (p. 129, Majh M. 3).

Self-correction: According to Sheikh Farid, the Lord says, "You Meet Me through self-correction. On Meeting Me, you are at Peace. If you belong to me, the whole world will belong to you" (p. 1382, Shlok Farid).

Self-culture: The cultivation or development by one's own efforts of one's mind, faculties, manners etc. One has to make efforts for his development. The Grace of the Lord begins, when one tries in this direction. Guru Arjan Dev says, "While living, make an earnest effort and through self-culture, remain in comfort" (p. 522, Var Gujri M. 5).

Self-defence: The act of defending oneself, one's rights or position. Guru Amar Das says, "I am a sinner absorbed in lust and wrath. What can I say in self-defence, O Lord, when I have neither done any service nor have any qualities" (p. 1048, (Maru M. 3).

Self-existent: Existing of or by oneself. Only the Lord is Self-existent (Swayyam-Bhū—p. 1, Japuji), all others are created by Him.

Selfishness: Because of selfishness, there is no durable love in the world. Guru Tegh Bahadur says, "I have seen false love in the world. Due to selfishness all are absorbed in their comfort, whether it is a friend or a wife" (p. 536, Devgandhari M. 9). The *Manmukh* (egocentrics) are selfish, how can they serve others? (p. 643, Var Sorath M. 4, Shlok M. 3).

Self-restraint: Restraint imposed by oneself upon one's actions etc. Lust is overshadowed and effaced by self-restraint (*Sanyam*). The

Sikh Gurus rejected both self-gratification and self-mortification and recommended the self-restraint for the growth of a healthy personality. The seeker must remain within limits in order to remain fit. Guru Arjan Dev says, "If a person leans upon the Support of his Lord, he will remain within his limits and will not lose his strength" (p. 679, Dhanasari M. 5). Too much of everything is bad. Every action should be balanced and under control.

Self-sacrifice: The giving up of one's own interests, happiness and desires for the sake of duty or the welfare of others. The *Adi Granth* lays great emphasis on self-sacrifice. An act of social service is self-sacrifice. Whosoever serves the needy and deserving, assuredly, gets a seat of honour in the Court of the Lord (p. 26, Sri Rag M. 1). The contribution of tithe from one's income is an act of self-sacrifice, though it is obligatory for a Sikh.

Semen: The impregnating fluid of male animals; the seed or sperm. Guru Nanak Dev says, "One calls himself a *Yatī* (a man of continence), but is not able to preserve his semen" (p. 903, Ramkali M. 1). That Pākhandī (Yogī) will not be subject to old age and death, if he does not emit his semen in the dream" (p. 952, Var Ramkali M. 3, Shalok M. 1). The same idea has been given regarding a Qazi by Kabir (p. 1160, Bhairo Kabir). Addressing a man of the world, Kabir says, "The Lord Created your body from a drop of semen and protected you in the fire of the womb. For ten months your mother kept you in her womb, after which you were involved with *maya*. Why do you cling to greed and lose the merit of the precious human birth? (p. 481, Asa Kabir).

Sensations: Perceptions or feelings. Talking about day-dawn, Guru Arjan Dev says, "The sparrow has chirruped, when the day has dawned. Many sensations are spreading. The saints, inebriated with the Name of the Lord, appear in wondrous postures" (p. 319, Var Gauri M. 5). The sensation is an operation of any of the senses. Thus a sensation may be good or bad according to its nature. For example, our sense of hearing may be absorbed in listening to the Praises of the Lord, but it can also become vicious by listening attentively to calumny and back-biting.

Senses: The five senses, usually reckoned are the sense of sight, the sense of hearing, the sense of smell, the sense of taste and the sense of touch. These five senses are present in every human being. Ravidas, the cobbler saint has said that the deer, fish, bumble bee, moth and elephant are doomed to destruction by one sense only, the deer by the sense of hearing (Shabda), the fish by the sense of taste (Rasa), the bumble bee by the sense of smell (Gandha), the moth by the sense of sight (Rūpa) and the elephant by the sense of touch (Sparsha). We can well imagine the fate of the human being, if he becomes a slave of the senses (p. 486, Asa Ravidas). The best use of these senses be made.

Sensuality: The lower or animal nature regarded as a source of evil; the lust of the flesh. The *Adi Granth* has laid emphasis on maintaining a proper check on the evil of sensuality. Guru Arjan Dev says, "He whose tongue does not utter falsehood and loves the Lord and sees the Immaculate One in his mind; whose eyes are fastened not on the beauty of another's woman and who serves the saints and loves the Pure ones; who does not hear calumny with his ears and considers himself as most lowly of all the creatures; who by the Grace of the Guru dispels his evils and shunts out the desires of his mind; who has full control over sexuality and is free from the five evils, such a person is the Purest of the Pure and is very rare (p. 274, Gauri Sukhmani M. 5).

Serpents: In the *Adi Granth, Maya* has been depicted as a she-serpent. Kabir says, "None other is so powerful as the she-serpent (*Maya*), who has deceived even Brahma, Vishnu and Shiva" (p. 480, Asa Kabir). Guru Amar Das says, "*Maya*, as a she-serpent, clings to the whole world. Whosoever serves her, he is devoured by her" (p. 510, Var Gujri M. 3). Guru Arjan Dev says, "I have cut off my ties with the she-serpent. I have been warned by the Guru that she deceives everyone, everywhere" (p. 1347, Bibhas Prabhati M. 5). The Maharashtrian saint Trilochan says, "He who remembers his houses at the time of his death, and dies in this worry, he is born again and again as a serpent (p. 526, Gujri Trilochan). According to Guru Nanak Dev, the snakes, the fish, the deer and the indulgers are in great joy in the rainy season (p. 1279, Var Malar M. 1).

Servants: According to Guru Nanak Dev, that person is the true servant, who merges himself in his Master. That service is of no use which does not absolve one of the fear of the Master (p. 475, Var Asa M. 1). If a servant serves the Master, but is egoistic and disputatious; moreover he talks much, such a servant does not get the approval of the Master. He gets honour only if he loses himself and absorbs himself in service. He who greets his Master and is also impudent towards him, wastes himself completely (p. 474, Var Asa M. 1).

Service: Great stress has been laid in the *Adi Granth* on the service of mankind. Guru Nanak Dev says, "Our service in the world gets us a seat in the Court of the Lord" (Sri Rag M. 1, p. 26). While doing service, one should be selfless, then and only then he will realise the Lord (Gauri Sukhmani M. 5, p. 286). The service in ego is of no avail (Maru M. 4, p. 1070). The service of the Lord without deceit will bring all the comforts (Gaund M. 4, p. 861). The service of *Sādh Sangat* or the society of the saints is considered a great meritorious act. The service of the holy congregation in the form of fanning, providing water for drinking and grinding flour for the common kitchen creates humility and other good qualities in the mind of a Sikh. The best service for the society is free kitchen (*langar*). "He whom the Lord enables to work under His Hukam, is the real serviteur (Sewak) performing service (Sewa) "(Var Asa M. 1, p. 471). The real serviteur is a rare one among millions (Malar M. 5, p. 1269).

Sewā, Sewak: Service, serviteur (servant). See: *Service*.

Shaktī: The word "Shaktī" or "Sakat" is very often used for *Maya* in the *Adi Granth*. Shiva (soul) and Shaktī (Maya, matter) both have been created by God (p. 920, Ramkali M. 3, Anand). "Shaktī" literally means power; thus *Shaktī* as *Maya* is the Power of the Lord. It may be called "Divine Energy" or "Divine Mother," but in the *Adi Granth* the word *Shakti* has been used in the sense of *Maya*. "Through *Shakti* (*Maya*) none has realised the Lord" (p. 1090, Var Maru M. 3).

Shastras: There is mention of six (*khat*) Shāstras in the *Adi Granth*. A Shastra is a treatise or a law-book, but the Shastras, numbering six, as mentioned in the *Adi Granth* are the famous Hindu compilations namely Yoga Shastra of Patanjali, Samkhya of Kapila, Nyaya of Gautama, Vaisheshika of Kannada, Pūrva Mimamsa of Jaimini and Uttara Mimasa or Vedanta of Vyasa. Guru Nanak Dev says, "Six are the ways of the Shastras, but that person is rare who merges in Truth" (p.148, Var Majh M.1). Guru Amar Das says, "The discipline of six Shastras is prevalent, but the discipline of the Guru is boundless" (pp. 360-61, Asa M. 3).

Ships: Kabir says, "Your ship is shattered with a thousand holes. Only those swim across, who are light of weight, but those who are with a load, are drowned" (p. 1366, Shlok Kabir). Sheikh Farid says, "When I could build my ship, I could not do that. And now when the fierce waves are lashing, how shall I be ferried across?" (p. 794, Suhi Lalit Farid). Guru Nanak Dev says, "Build the ship of contemplation and self-control in order to cross the ocean of life unobstructed" (p. 729, Suhi M. 1). The Name of the Lord as also the Lotus-Feet of the Lord are the ship through which we can ferry across the sea of life. Guru Arjan Dev says, "The Lord's Feet are the ship on which the mind crossed the sea of life" (p. 398, Asa M. 5).

Shiva: One of the three deities of the Hindu Trinity, the other two being Brahmā and Vishnu. While Brahmā is the Creator, Vishnu is the preserver, Shiva is the destroyer. Those who worship Shiva, they are known as Shaivites. Their sacred books are called Tantras. Shiva is often depicted as holding a trident in his hand and riding on his bull called Nandi. His wife is called by several names e.g. Pārbatī, Durgā, Satī etc. The *Adi Granth* gives no recognition to gods and goddesses. The saint Namdev says, "Those who worship Shiva and recite his Name, they will ride on the bull and beat hand-drum" (p. 874, Gond Namdev). Shiva is often symbolised as Linga or Phallus, the generative organ. There is mention of Linga and some Shaiva sects in the *Adi Granth.* The scripture has made critical remarks about them. The name Shiva has sometimes been used for Brahman. Whereas Pārbatī is the Shakti of Shiva, *Maya* is the Shakti of Brahman. The Tantras explain the dual principle of Shiva and Shakti. The *Adi Granth* also mentions the phenomenon of Shiva and Shakti. "Shiva and Shakti abide within the body" (p. 1056, Maru M. 3). Here Shiva is the soul and *Maya* is Shakti.

Shiva-Shaktī: The dual principle of Shiva and Shaktī. See: *Shiva.*

Shoes: Guru Nanak Dev says, "He whose speech is insipid is discarded from the Court of the Lord and others spit in his face. Every one calls him a fool and he is punished with shoes" (p. 473, Var Asa M. 1). "If one is of high caste and serves the Lord, no one can narrate his story of praise. If one is of low caste and serves the Lord, I offer my skin for his shoes" (p. 1256, Malar M. 1). Kabir says, "If one utters the Name of the Lord even in a dream, I offer my skin for his shoes" (p. 1367, Shlok Kabir). The saint Dhanna, while asking the Lord to give him the necessities of life, also begs for shoes (p. 695, Dhanasari Dhanna).

Shoh: The Lord (*Shahu*). "The action should be performed according to the wishes of the Lord and the mind and body both be offered to Him" (Tilang M. 1, p. 722). "That day be considered as approved, when the Lord Sees Gracefully (ibid). This word is also written as *Saha* or *Shaha*.

Shooting Stars: Guru Nanak Dev has made a mention of the meteor, a shooting star in his verses in a figurative language. According to him, in the darkness of the night of life, a spiritual meteor can arise, if we contemplate on the Word of the Guru. Within its light no vices can come near us, we become conscious only of virtues (pp. 110-11, Tukhārī M. 1).

Shrine: Guru Arjan Dev says, "Within the shrine of my heart shines the Light of the word, where the Lord plays with me in utter Bliss" (p. 384, Asa M. 5). "Blessed is His Shrine, and Beauteous is His Gate, within which sounds always the Unstruck Melody" (p. 533, Devgandhari M. 5). Guru Ram Das says, "The air, water, earth and sky are the homes and shrines of God, in which He (the Lord) Pervades...." (p. 723, Tilang M. 4).

Siānā, Siānap: *Siānā* is wise and *Siānap* is wisdom. The word *sughaṛ* is also used often with *siānā*, which also means wise. Those persons are, indeed, wise, who have the Love of the Lord in their hearts (Asa M. 4, p. 450). He is really wise, who has abandoned pride (ego) (Gauri Thittī M. 5, p. 297). Worldly wisdom (*siānap*) is of no avail (Gujri M. 5, p. 496).

Sidak: Faith. See: *Faith*. "Make the obeissance to the Lord your faith and the understanding of the mind your objective of life" (Var Shi Rag M.4, Shlok M. 1, p. 84).

Siddhas: There is mention of eighty-four Siddhas in the *Adi Granth*. Guru Ram Das says, "The eighty-four Siddhas, many Buddhas, thirty-three crore gods and the sages all crave for your Name, O Lord, but such a person is rare, who receives it by the Grace of the Guru" (p. 669, Dhanasari M. 40). Guru Nanak Dev says, "The Siddhas (adepts) grapple with their self in their trance, but they see nothing with their eyes" (p. 489, Gujri M. 1). "Even if I become a Siddha, absorb myself in a trance and possess the miraculous powers, at one time I may disappear and at another time I may become manifest; the people may have great reverence for me, But I do not want to lose my head and forget your Name, O Lord" (p. 14, Sri Rag M. 1). Guru Amar Das says, "If one learns the postures of the Siddhas and controls his sex, the dirt of his mind is not washed off and the dirt of ego is not removed" (p. 558, Vadhans M. 3).

Sift Sālāh: The Praise; the Praises of the Lord. "He is, in reality, a king of kings, who has been given the gift of the Praises of the Lord" (Japuji, p. 5). Forsaking the Praises of the Lord, the swan has now fallen down in vices (Var Suhi M. 3, Shlok M. 1, p. 790).

Sikh: Guru Ram Das has defined a Sikh in the following manner: "He who calls himself a Sikh of the True Guru, he gets up early in the morning and remembers the Name of the Lord...He who remembers the Lord with every breath, that Sikh is liked by the Guru. He on whom the Lord Showers His Graces, that Sikh is given the instruction by the Guru. I beg for the dust of the feet of that Sikh, who not only remembers the Lord's Name himself, but also makes others remember it (Var Gauri M. 4, p. 305).

Sikhī: The following of the Guru. "The Guru is the ocean and all his following is like a stream" (Suhi M. 5, p. 763).

Silence: According to Guru Nanak Dev one cannot remain silent even if he tries hard to absorb himself in a trance (p. 1, Japuji). One has to still his mind. At another place, Guru Nanak Dev says, "The silence is good and without the Name of the Lord, whatever one utters is dirt" (p. 1288, Var Malar M. 1). "If one has to face defeat by his utterance, it is good to observe silence" (p. 149, Var Majh M. 1). Guru Arjan Dev says, "The complaint of the plaintiff does not reach the Lord through cries, but justice is obtained in silence" (p. 381, Asa M. 5).

Silver: Gold and silver find sufficient mention as precious metals in the *Adi Granth.* Guru Nanak Dev says "Gold and silver are enjoyable alongwith the pearls and rubies, but they are your Gifts, O Lord, I love them and not You,...therefore I am in agony" (p. 762, Suhi M. 1). "The gold and silver are like poison and dust" (p. 937, Ramkali M. 1, Dakhni Oamkār). "The cooking place and the vessels be of gold, the silver lines of the kitchen square be extended afar. The water be of the Ganges and the fire from the firewood of carissa caranda tree; the food be of fine rice, boiled in milk. O my mind, they are all of no avail, unless you are saturated with the True Name" (p. 1169, Basant M. 1).

Similes-Parables: A simile is a comparison of one thing with another especially, as an ornament in poetry or rhetoric. A parable is also a simile. It is a saying of narration in which something is expressed in terms of something else. We find a good number of similes in the *Adi Granth.* We have an example of lotus, whose similarity is with an enlightened person, who rises above the impact of *maya* (p. 938). But lotus is also used as a metaphor. With regard to the love of the Lord, Guru Nanak Dev has uses the similes of the love of water with milk, the love of *chakvī* with the sun etc. (p. 60). Several myths have been used as parables e.g. while describing the cries in anguish, Guru Nanak Dev has used the similes of Indra, Parashurama, Aja, Ravana, Janmejaya etc, (Var Ramkali M. 3, Shlok M. 1, pp. 953-54).

Simplicity: Freedom from artifice, deceit or duplicity; sincerity, straightforwardness; unsophisticated ways or manners. According to the *Adi Granth,* men of God observe simplicity in their lives. They are humble and modest. "The unbuttered cereal of the saint is a treasure; one cannot remain naked with a torn blanket of the saint..." (p. 811, Bilawal M. 5). "They who have silk within them but dirt outside, they are the good ones in the world.... In love they weep and laugh and keep silence; they do not care for any one else except the True Name of the Lord. They always wait upon the Door of the Lord and whenever He Gives, they eat" (p. 473, Var Asa M. 1). Simplicity also connotes want of ordinary knowledge or judgment. For such persons it is said, "O ignorant one, forsake your sense of mineness" (p. 1168, Basant M. 1). Simplicity in the sense of innocence is necessary for the realisation of the Lord. Kabir says, "The Lord is realised through the innocence of the heart" (p. 324, Gauri Kabir).

Simran: Remembrance; Remembrance of the Name of the Lord. "They (the birds) fly hundreds of miles and leave the young ones behind. Who will feed them in their absence? They remember them in their mind" (Gujri M. 5, p. 495). Guru Arjan Dev has composed one complete *ashtapadī* (octavo) on *Simran* (Remembrance of the Name of the Lord) in his longer poem *Sukhmanī*, wherein he has mentioned the advantages of *Simran.* By remembering the Name one does not transmigrate...the enemies are destroyed, the troubles end...one attains the highest position etc. *Simran* can be done only through the Grace of God (pp. 262-63).

Sin: One who violates the moral discipline commits sins. All the deeds committed under the impact of vices are sinful deeds. "Assuredly, the sinners are wasted away; the angel of death seizes and destroys them. They are cast into hell by the Creator and are asked to render account by the Lord" (pp. 1019-20, Maru M. 5). Though one sees, he is blind, though one hears, he is deaf. The thing which is near, he considers it afar, in this way the sinner commits sins (p. 741, Suhi M. 5). "The sin is bad, but the sinner loves it. He carries the load of sin and is wholly absorbed in sin. If he forsakes his sin and knows his self, he will neither suffer sorrow, nor separation nor pain" (p. 935, Ramkali M. 1, Dakhni Oamkar). "The sinners commit sinful deeds and then wail and weep, they will be churned by the god of Justice" (p. 1425, Shlok M. 5). "The Virtue and Sin, both abide within the body. Both have created the world conjointly. He who kills both and comes to his only home, Merges in the Lord by the Grace of the Guru" (p. 126, Majh M. 3).

Singing: According to the *Adi Granth,* only the Praises of the Lord are to be sung. Any one who sings the Praises of the Lord, never experiences any sorrow (p. 190, Gauri M. 5). Kabir says, "O, my Married-Sisters, sing the songs of marriage, My Lord has come to Abide in the house" (p. 482, Asa Kabir). Guru Nanak Dev says, "Do not sing the songs of separation, but Contemplate on the Name of the Lord" (p. 581, Vadhans M. 1). The Guru says again, "You sing the songs, but do not know yourself. How can you be rid of the anguish that afflicts you?" (p. 903, Ramkali M.1). Guru Nanak Dev has depicted in one of his hymns the Glory of the Door of the Abode of the Lord, where all the gods, sages and other entities sing His Praises (p. 6, Japuji). Guru Arjan Dev says, "O singer, sing the Praises of the Lord, who is the Mainstay of your body and soul..."(p. 395, Asa M. 5).

Sister: The co-disciples are sometimes addressed as sisters in the *Adi Granth*. Guru Nanak Dev says, "Come, dear sisters, hug me in your embrace, you are my closest friends, let us narrate the stories of our powerful Lord" (p. 17, Sri Rag M. 1). In another hymn, the Guru says, "With white clothes and sweet speech, with sharp nose and black eyes, O sister, have you ever seen the Lord?" (p. 1257, Malar M. 1).

Skin: Addressing the man of the world, Guru Arjan Dev says, "Ordure, bones and blood are wrapped up in the skin. This is all you are made of. Can these things be the object of conceit?" (p. 374, Asa M. 5). Kabir says, "If a man dies, his body is of no use. But if an animal dies, its uses are many" (p. 870, Gond Kabir). In these verses Kabir seems to refer to the skin of the animals, which can be brought under various uses.

Sky: Guru Nanak Dev says, "The Lord Himself Creates and Knows Himself. He Separates the Earth and Sky and spreads the canopy of the heavens. He upholds the skies without pillars" (p. 1279, Var Malar M. 1). Sky is one of the five elements, the other four being water, fire, air and earth (p. 1031, Maru M. 1). Guru Nanak Dev circumambulates Brahman with the salver of the sky in his hand, in which the sun and the moon are the two lamps and the stars are like the gems" (p. 663, Dhanasari M. 1). In yogic terminology the word "Gagan" is used to explain the spiritual ascent. The Sky in this case seems to refer to the Tenth Door (p. 1160, Bhairo Kabir). We find the figurative use of the word "Sky" at several places in the *Adi Granth*.

Slander: Calumny, defamation; The utterance of false statements concerning a person in order to defame or injure him. Guru Amar Das says, "It is not good to slander anyone, only the foolish egocentrics indulge in it. Their faces are blackened and they are thrown into the most pernicious hell" (p. 755, Suhi M. 3). Guru Arjan Dev says, "One who slanders, washes off the dirt of others and gets due punishment. He gets no comfort in this world and no refuge in the next. He wastes himself away in the abode of Yama. The slanderer loses the precious birth. He can never reach (the spiritual target) by any means and never gets the Refuge in the next world" (p. 380, Asa M. 5).

Slaughter: The killing of cattle, sheep or other animals for food. Mercy towards all the beings (*jivas*) has been advocated in the *Adi Granth* (p. 299, Gauri M. 5). If one wants to go to the True Home with dignity, he should not injure any one (p. 322, Var Gauri M. 5). The *Adi Granth* has not indulged in the controversial issue of meat-eating. Guru Nanak Dev says, "The fool quarrels over the issue of meat (of animals) and does not know the Wisdom and Meditation" (p. 1289, Var Malar M. 1). See: *Ahiṁsā*.

Slaves: The *Adi Granth* is totallly against the institution of slavery. It advocates the freedom of individuals. But spiritually one must become a slave to the Lord. Guru Nanak Dev says, "I am your Slave, O Lord, I am most fortunate. O Guru, I have sold myself at your shop in exchange for the WORD and do whatever You Order" (p. 991, Maru M. 1). Guru Ram Das says, "I wander about like a mad person, seeking my Lord; whosoever unites me with my Lord, I am the slave of his slaves" (p. 527, Devgandhari M. 4). Guru Arjan Dev says, "The God-conscious person became free from fetters (all worldly bonds) and attained salvation; all his agony and doubts vanished (p. 289, Gauri Sukhmani M. 5).

Sleep: Talking about the Iron Age (*Kaliyuga*), Guru Nanak Dev says, "Those who are in sleep, are called awake and those who are awake are said to be in sleep" (p. 229, Gauri M. 1). "The saints are always awake and do not sleep at all. They dispense only Truth and in this way save their generation" (p. 1025, Maru M. 1). Guru Amar Das says, "The blind world abides in ignorance and men are deceived in sleep" (p. 603, Sorath M. 3). We are asleep, enchanted by duality; being in love with delusion and desire, we do not awake (p. 852, Var Bilawal M. 4, Shlok M. 3). Because of their ego, the Yogi, the Pundit, the householder and the mendicant are all asleep. Having been intoxicated by *maya*, they are in sleep (p. 1128, Bhairo M. 3). Sheikh Farid says, "During the night, the Lord showers musk, but those who are asleep do not get a share; those whose eyes are heavy with sleep, they partake of it (p. 1332, Shlok Farid). None can force God regarding His

Bounties. Some who are awake, do not get them, but there are others, whom He Wakes from sleep and Blesses them (p. 1384, Shlok Farid).

Sloth: Physical or mental inactivity; disinclination to action, exertion or labour. The devotees should be without sloth. The devotee dwells on the Lord in the society of the saints and all his sloth departs (p. 108, Majh M. 5). Guru Arjan Dev says, "Go away my sloth, I pray to the Lord" (p. 460, Asa M. 5). The egocentric, caught in the wilderness (of his mind), is slothful (p. 1011, Maru M. 1). Man is slothful in doing good, but is ever ready to practise evil (p. 518, Var Gujri M. 5).

Smell: The sense of which the nose is the organ. This is one of the five senses, the others being the sense of sight, the sense of hearing, the sense of taste and the sense of touch. All other perfumes and fragrances are of no use except the perfume of the Name of Hari. Of what use are the scents leading to evil actions? (p. 269, Gauri Sukhmani M. 5). A person is known by the perfumes he likes (p. 118, Majh M. 3).

Smoke: The visible volatile product given off by burning or smouldering substances. Guru Nanak Dev says, "When the soul leaves the body, which being dead, appears dreadful. The fire of the body is no more there, the smoke of breath ceases..." (p. 19, Sri Rag M. 1) "I have searched and found that this world is a mansion of smoke" (p. 138, Var Majh M. 1). Guru Tegh Bahadur says that this world is a mountain of smoke (p. 1187, Basant M. 9). Kabir says, "The fire is extinguished and it gives out no smoke" (p. 478, Asa Kabir).

Smriti: The sacred books of the Hindus, which are subsidiary to Vedas. Having been remembered by the priests, they are considered as products of human authorship. They include the *Itihāsas* (epics), *Purānas*, and codes of ethics and jurisprudence. They have been mentioned very often in the *Adi Granth*. Guru Arjan Dev says, "The *Smritis*, the Vedas, the Puranas and the other sacred texts proclaim that without the Name of the Lord all is false and vain prattle" (p. 761, Suhi M. 5).

Snakes: The *Adi Granth* has identified *Maya* with a snake (p. 510, Var Gujri M. 3). (Also see p. 480, Asa Kabir). He, who remembers *Maya* at the time of his death, becomes a snake in the next birth (p. 526, Gujri Trilochan). When it rains in the month of *Shrāvana*, four beings are overjoyed i.e. the snakes, the deer, the fish and the indulgers. (p.1279, Var Malar M.1). The mind of the egocentric is impious and hard, it is not swayed by the WORD. It is like the serpent which is fed upon the milk, but does not lose the sting (p. 755, Suhi M. 3). If one locks the snake in a basket, its poison does not leave it (p. 1009, Maru M. 1). The snake casts off its skin, but not its poison. (p. 485, Asa Namdev).

Sneezing-Omens: A sudden and involuntary expiration of breath through the nose and mouth, accompanied by a characteristic sound. Sneezing at the time of going out is considered a bad omen. In the *Adi Granth*, the idea of good or bad omen has been presented in the following manner: "He alone is affected by good or bad omens, who does not enshrine the Lord in his heart" (p. 401, Asa M. 5).

Snātaka: The word literally means "he who has bathed". A *Snātaka* is a student or a Brahmachārin, who passes his time in religious studies and leads a pure life. The word "Snātaka" has not been used in the *Adi Granth*, but instead, we find the use of Brahmachārin. See: *Brahmachārin*.

Society: The ideal society envisaged in the *Adi Granth* is not Utopia, but a reality. It demolishes all the walls of prejudices between man and man, man and woman, religion and religion, rich and poor, the king and his subjects. It breaks away the shackles of formalism, it gives freedom about food, shelter and clothing. This brotherhood is free from any distinction of caste. No one considers himself superior to the other. Humility and modesty are the virtues imbibed by the member of this society. The service of humanity is the main aim of his life. He is a saint, soldier and scholar, therefore the society is martial in spirit, saintly in character and scholarly in knowledge. In this society all the four values of human life are fulfilled. They are *Dharma* (piety), *Artha* (material gains), *Kāma* (fulfilment of worldly desires) and *Moksha* (final emancipation). Since the religion of the *Adi Granth* is a religion of activity, therefore its adherents are mainly householders. The daily prayer of the members of this society is "the good of all under the Will of the Lord". All the members of this society including women, have an equal status. The ideal member of this society is called *Gurmukh,* who is a God-conscious person (See Siddh Goshta, Ramkali M. 1, pp. 944-946).

So Dar: That Door. In a hymn entitled *So Dar*, which forms part of *Japuji* as well as *Rahirās,* Guru Nanak Dev has portrayed the scene at the Door of the Lord, where all the gods, goddesses, elements, sages, planets, etc. are standing in obeissance and singing the Praises of the Lord.

Sohilā: The literal meaning of this word is 'Praise', but there is a bed-time prayer (after the morning and evening prayers) in the beginning of the *Adi Granth* entitled *Kīrtan Sohilā*. The word *Kīrtan* also means 'praise'.

Soldiers: Those who take part in military service or warfare. Guru Nanak Dev has depicted the contemporary warfare between the Mughals and the Pathans. He says, "The Mughal and the Pathan soldiers grappled with each other, they used their swords freely. The former fired their guns and the latter moved their elephants forward" (p. 418, Asa M. 1). In another hymn He says, "The soldiers have been ordered to dishonour and carry away the ladies of the royal household" (p. 417, Asa M. 1).

Solitude: The state of being or living alone. Guru Arjan Dev says, "My Lord is Ever in Solitude and Detached" (p. 1301, Kanra M. 5). Though the Pundit lives in solitude, the outgoings of his mind do not cease (p. 1003, Maru M. 5). He may be considered in solitude, the outgoings of whose mind have ceased (p. 1180, Basant M. 5). The self-willed transmigrate and wail like the crow in solitude (p. 30, Sri Rag M. 3).

Soma: This is the name of the moon in Hindu mythology. One day of the week is named after this god i.e. Moon-day (Monday—Soma-Vār). (See page 344, Gauri Kabir and p. 841, Bilawal M. 3). Soma is also the name of a particular plant and of its juice. Soma juice is said to be the main drink of gods. The moon is supposed to contain Soma juice or the celestial nectar.

Son(s): The sons and daughters are the Creation of the same Lord. "Our mothers, fathers, sons are all the Creation of the Lord. He Himself has bound us with their bonds" (p. 494, Gujri M. 4). "O son, why do you quarrel with your father. He who has given you birth and brought you up; it is a sin to quarrel with him" (p. 1200, Sarang M. 4). "O son, this is the blessing of your mother, you may not forget your Lord even for a moment; you may ever Contemplate upon Him" (p. 496, Gujri M. 5). Just as the life flows through the veins of the mother on seeing her son, similarly the Servant of the Lord weaves himself into the Lord (p. 198, Gauri M. 5). A *Sannyāsī* abandons his sons and daughters but his mind's cravings do not stop. His desires are not stilled and he does not get peace without the Guru's WORD (p. 835, Bilawal M. 4).

Songs: The hymns of the *Adi Granth* are, in fact, songs meant to be sung in holy congregations. They are composed in various musical modes. Guru Nanak Dev says, "The bride (devotee) hears the Lord's song from the poets and singers and hearing the Name of the Lord, her woes depart" (p. 1109, Baramaha Tukhari M. 1). About worldly songs the Guru says, "I have heard all kinds of songs and melodies, but all of them are insipid, giving rise to disease" (p. 1010 Maru M. 1). Kabir says, "People think that this utterance of mine is merely a song, but this, indeed, contains the Wisdom of the Lord" (p. 335, Gauri Kabir). According to Guru Nanak Dev, the song of separation is not to be sung, but instead the Name of the Lord is to be contemplated. (p. 581, Vadhans M. 1). He has addressed a Yogi in the following manner: "You sing the songs (of the Lord), but do not know the self (p. 903, Ramkali M. 1).

Sophists: In ancient Greece, a scholar engaged in the pursuit or communication of knowledge; one who gave instruction in intellectual and ethical matters in return for payment. For such like Pundits the *Adi Granth* says, "The Pundit reads the books, but gives no thought to them...Many are the Pundits and the diviners of the future, who read the Vedas, but they waste away life in the clash of their cherished arguments" (p. 56, Sri Rag M. 1). The Pundits read and discuss, but without the True Guru they are lost in Doubt (p. 67, Sri Rag M. 3).

So Purkh: That Purusha. There is a hymn entitled "*So Purkh*" in the evening prayer *Rahirās*, in which Guru Ram Das has described the attributes of *Niranjan Purusha*, the Transcendental Lord.

Sorcerers: Magicians. In the *Adi Granth*, the practice of such persons is condemned. Guru Nanak Dev calls the lady sorcerer an ugly witch, who is devoid of chastity (p. 796, Bilawal M. 1). The Lord Himself is considered as a Juggler (p. 736, Suhi M. 5, p. 655, Sorath Kabir). See: *Magicians*.

Sorcery: The use of magic or enchantment. In the *Adi Granth*, God Himself is shown as the Supreme Sorcerer, who has Created the world as a magic show (p. 727, Tilang Kabir). Thus this act of the creation of the world is considered a sorcery. See: *Magic*.

Soul: The Indian equivalent for soul is *Atman*. There are innumerable souls. The Supreme Soul (*Param Atman*) is God Himself. The souls or finite selves are part and parcel of God. Guru Arjan Dev says, "It is a strange story, quite strange, the soul is like God Himself. Neither it is old nor young. Neither it is prone to misery, nor it dies; It never dies, but exists from the very beginning. Neither heat nor cold has any effect on it. Neither it has an enemy nor a friend. It neither experiences joy nor sorrow. It is the master of all—the doer, it has no father, no mother, it continues to exist from limitless times. Virtue and sin have no effect on it. It is always awake within every heart" (p. 868, Gaund

M. 5). In another hymn, the Guru says, "In its company the body has the individuality in all respects. Without it, the body is only clay. It is a *Vairagi*, who lives forever and who acts under the Will of God. God brings both (the soul and the body) together and separates them" (p. 390, Asa M. 5).

Sound: Sound is *Shabda*, an evolute from Ākāsha. *Shabdā* is a mystical sound produced without contact between two objects. When a mantra or the Word of the Guru is uttered, it produces mystical powers. When the bliss of union is attained, the sound of the five strains of unstruck music rings within the body (p. 764, Suhi M. 1). The unstruck melody of the Word rings within the Yogi. The symphony of the five sounds rings sweetly within him. The Divine Music is made by the Lord Himself (p. 1040, Maru M. 1). It is said that five types of sounds created by five types of musical instruments are heard in the state of contemplation.

Sovereigns: Kings. God Himself is considered the Supreme Sovereign of the Universe. Guru Nanak Dev says, "He is the Sovereign of the Sovereigns and Nanak lives in His Will" (p. 348, Asa M.1). It is He, who raises men to become kings and Sovereigns (p. 305, Var Gauri M. 4). The king, who is worthy of the throne, sits on it. He who realises the Truth, is the true king. These rulers of the earth are not kingly in demeanour, because they are torn by duality, therefore they come to grief (p. 1088, Var Maru M. 3). The glory of worldly kings and sovereigns stays only for a few days (p. 645, Var Sorath M. 4).

Sovereignty: Royal authority. Supremacy in respect of power. Guru Arjan Dev says, "Even if one has sovereignty over thirty-three crores of gods and the ascetics and performers of miracles stand at his door, if he is a man of such a high position and master of vast dominions, these become a dream in the end" (p. 42, Sri Rag M. 5). The Guru addresses the human being in the following manner: "All other forms of existence are your slaves and you have the sovereignty over this earth. You have gold and silver and wealth with you but the lust has disturbed the conduct of your life" (p. 374, Asa M. 5).

Space: One of the five Tanmātras, called *Ākāsha* in Indian terminology. It is also called Ether. Kabir says, "The Lord is present over the Space (*Ākāsha*) and in the netherworld. He is present day and night all over" (p. 870, Gond Kabir). The space denotes area of extension. It is an expanse. There are lakhs of skies and netherworlds in space (p. 5, Japuji). Though this world is the world of Time and Space, the Lord Himself is Non-Temporal and Non-Spatial (p. 597, Sorath M. 1).

Species: A class composed of individuals, having some common qualities or characteristics; A group or class of animals or plants. The *Adi Granth* believes in the existence of eighty-four lakh species. Guru Arjan Dev says, "There are eighty-four lakhs of species, but man has supremacy over others; whosoever misses the opportunity of this birth, he suffers agony in transmigration" (p. 1075, Maru Solhe M. 5).

Spectacles: Specially prepared displays of a more or less public nature, forming an impressive or interesting show for those viewing it. Talking about the kings of his day, Guru Nanak Dev says, "The kings had lost their heads in viewing revelries and spectacles" (p. 417, Asa M. 1). In the midst of many joyful spectacles, one forgets the Name of the Lord and thus he lives in a horrible hell" (p. 707, Var Jaitsri M. 5)

Speech: According to the *Adi Granth*, the speech of an individual should be sweet, because insipid speech leads to quarrels and enmities (p. 566, Vadhans M. 1) (p. 745, Suhi M. 5). If harsh and insipid words are uttered, the Lord is displeased (p. 1384, Shlok Farid). One will be punished if his speech is insipid (p. 473, Var Asa M. 1). The speech should be veracious, beneficial and gentle. The tongue often inflicts deep wounds than the sword with harsh and malicious words. A discourteous talk creates unhealthy effect not only on the mind, but also on the body. One should speak less in order to avoid an extravagant and unruly talk. He should utter the Name of the Lord with his tongue. Guru Tegh Bahadur says, "Utter the Praises of the Lord with your tongue" (p. 1427, Shlok M. 9).

Spells: Charms, incantations. Guru Nanak Dev says, "The egocentric recites the set of spells at the crematoriums and straying from the Path, loses all the merits" (p. 941, Ramkali M. 1, Sidda Goshta). There is only one *mantra* (spell) for all the ailments and that is the Name of the Lord (p. 156, Gauri Cheti M. 1). Guru Ram Das says, "O Lord, Give me your *mantra*, which is the cure of my ailments" (p. 95, Majh M. 4).

Spider: Addressing the Pundit, Guru Nanak Dev says, "Like the spider you are caught in your own web, tossed upside down" (p. 635, Sorath M.1). Thus the egoist is identified with a spider, who cannot get out of its web of *māyā*.

Spirit: The animating principle in man and animals; the soul. According to Guru Nanak Dev, those who forget the Name of the Lord, when their bodies return to dust, what would happen to their spirits? Their cleverness will be of no use and they will leave wailing and weeping (p. 17, Sri Rag M. 1). See: *Soul.*

Spirits: Ghosts. In this sense, a spirit is a supernatural, incorporeal, rational being or personality, usually regarded as imperceptible at ordinary times to the human senses, but capable of becoming visible at pleasure, and frequently conceived as troublesome, terrifying or hostile to mankind; a being of this nature imagined as possessing and actuating a person. While describing the creation, Guru Arjan Dev says that there are crores of ghosts and spirits (p. 276, Gauri Sukhmani M. 5). He who forsakes the Name of the Lord, his mind is like a ghost (spirit) in the body, and suffers great agony (p. 1029, Maru M. 1). According to Guru Nanak Dev, the Iron Age (*Kaliyuga*) gives birth to spirits and goblins (p. 556, Var Bihagra M. 4, Shlok M. 1).

Spiritual Insight: All the men have the same spiritual insight. There is none without it (p. 24, Sri Rag M. 1). He who practises falsehood, is subject to birth and death. He cannot achieve his objective through discursiveness. He does not know his spiritual insight (p. 352, Asa M. 1). The self-willed have no perception about their spiritual insight and thus they suffer in Separation (p. 60, Sri Rag M. 1).

Spiritualism: Spiritualism as opposed to materialism is the doctrine regarding the Ultimate Reality (in the Universe) which is All-Pervading. In religious terminology it emphasises that the spirits (souls) correspond with the Holy Spirit (Over-Soul) through worship. The *Adi Granth* totally concerns Spiritualism.

Spiritual Sense: He who has the cognisance of the blissful spiritual sense, enjoys spontaneously the Love of the Lord. "Blessed is such a Person, because he has the Approval of the Lord" (p. 252, Gauri Bawan Akhri M. 5). The Knower of Brahman realises the Blissful Spiritual sense (p. 272, Gauri Sukhmani M. 5).

Spirituous Liquor: Wine. The use of any type of spirituous liquor has been strictly prohibited in the *Adi Granth*, because such liquor makes one crazy and senseless and devoid of all reason. He can not distinguish between his own and that of another (p. 554, Var Bihāgrā M. 4, Shlok M. 3).

Spring: The month of Chaitra is glorious, because the pleasing spring comes and the black bee hums with joy. The forest blossoms and I long for the Union with the Lord (p. 1108, Baramaha Tukhari M. 1). The blossoms of the spring come first, but it was God Who Blossomed much earlier. It is He, through Whom everything Blossoms...Meditate on Him, Who Came before the first spring (p. 791, Var Suhi M. 3, Shloks of M. 1 and M. 2). Spring is within the hearts of those, within whom the Lord Abides (p. 791, Var Suhi M. 3, Shlok M. 2).

Sprites: Super-human beings. See: *Spirits*.

Sraddhā: Faith. Faith is the basis of Bhaktī (devotion). According to Guru Nanak Dev a Yogi must have the staff of faith, a Muslim must have the prayer-mat of faith (p. 6, Japuji and p. 140, Var Majh M. 1). He who has faith in the Guru, the Lord abides in his heart (p. 283, Gauri Sukhmani M. 5). Guru Ram Das addresses the Lord: "O Life of the world, fulfil my *Sraddhā* (faith). O Dear Lord, when I meet You, let my mind be sated with Your Love" (p. 95, Majh M. 4). "On meeting the saint, Sraddhā (faith) wells up and through the Word of the Guru, I taste the Essence of the Lord " (p. 997, Maru M. 4).

Srāddha: It is a supplementary ritual to the *Dah Saṁskāra* (The sacrament pertaining to the funeral). It is performed for a deceased relative. The offerings of funerary cakes are made to the manes and they are supposed to receive the offered objects in the next world. There is mention of this ceremony in the *Adi Granth*. Kabir says, "None gives due reverence to the elders while they are alive, but on their death the *Srāddha* is performed and the offerings are made in their name. Even these offerings are not received by the manes only the crows and the dogs eat them" (Gauri Bairagan Kabir, p. 332).

Srī: Lakshmi, the wife of god Vishnu. She is the goddess of fortune and wealth. Being the husband of Srī or Lakshmī, Vishnu is known as Srīdhar. Guru Arjan Dev says, "He who does not Contemplate on the Lord, who is the Master of *Srī*, he comes to immense grief." Here *Srī* is depicted as *Māyā* (p. 1222, Sarang M. 5). In the *Adi Granth* various Vaishnavite Names of the Lord have been used and Srīdhar is one of them.

Srishtī Racnā: Creation of the World. See: *Creation*.

Sruti: That which is heard. The Hindu scriptures are divided into two groups—the *Srutī*, those which are heard and *Smritī*, which are remembered. Thus *Srutī* are the revealed scriptures and *Smritī* have come into existence through human authorship. Both the words *Srutī* and *Smritī* have been used in the *Adi Granth*. Guru Arjan Dev says, "The *Srutīs* and *Smritīs* also sing the Praises of the Lord like the adepts, seekers and seers" (p. 785, Suhi M. 5). All the four Vedas are the revealed texts, therefore they are *Srutī*.

Stages of Life: In Hinduism, the life-span is divided into four stages, called *āshramas*. They are *Brahmachārya*, the life of a student for the first twenty-five years, *Grahasthya*, the life of a householder for the next 25 years (as a married man), *Vānaprastha*, the life of a forest-dweller for the next twenty-five years and *Sannyāsa*, the life of a wandering monk, for the last twenty-five years. Guru Arjan Dev says, "I underwent the discipline of all the four stages of life, but my mind was not pleased" (p. 687, Dhanasari M. 5). Guru Ram Das says, "There are four castes and four stages of life, but he who meditates on the Lord, is supreme among men" (p. 861, Gaund M. 4). Whosoever, out of four castes and four āshramas, comes to Guru Nanak, he is saved and also his kinsmen and generations are saved" (p. 1297, Kanra M. 4).

Stars: Guru Nanak Dev, while depicting the *Aartī* (circumambulation) of the Lord, considers the sky as the salver, the sun and the moon as the lamps and the stars as the gems in the salver (p. 663, Dhanasari M. 1). Looking at the stars Kabir says in amazement: "Who has planted the stars that are seen in the sky?" "O Pundit, who supports the starry sky? Only the fortunate seer knows the Truth" (p. 329, Gauri Kabir). There are millions of suns, moons and stars (p. 275, Gauri Sukhmani M. 5). The stars, sun, moon, earth, sky—they all worship the Lord (p. 456, Asa M. 5).

Steer: A young ox, especially one which has been castrated, and used for tilling the land or driving the carts. According to Guru Nanak Dev, the five senses work like a steer in driving the cart of the body (p. 879, Ramkali M. 1). Kabir says, "Without the Lord, one is like a stray steer (bull), whose nose is torn and shoulders are bruised and who is fed upon the straw of coarse grain" (p. 524, Gujri Kabir).

Stones: The sinners sink like the stones, but they are saved through the WORD of the Guru (p. 163, Gauri Bairagan M. 3). How can a person swim, with a stone around his neck (p. 267, Gauri Sukhmani M. 5). They who practise rituals are bound down by ego, such men can serve no one better than the idols of stones (p. 324, Gauri Kabir). One stone we worship, but we tread upon another. If one is a god, then the other one is also a god (p. 525, Gujri Namdev). Guru Ram Das says, "Save me, O Lord, I am without virtue, lowly like a stone (p. 799, Bilawal M. 4). Guru Arjan Dev says, "Your Slave, O Lord, has crossed the sea of existance like a stone (in a boat) (p. 913, Ramkali M. 5). If the stone is soaked over and over again, its heart does not get wet and remains dry as ever (p. 1137, Bhairo M. 5).

Store-Houses: In the *Adi Granth*, there is usage of the word "Modī", which means a person incharge of the store-house (See p. 875, Gaund

Namdev). Guru Nanak Dev says, "The store-houses full of wealth, are emptied in a moment" (p. 141, Var Majh M. 1). Guru Arjan Dev says, "The *Gurbānī* (Word of the Guru) is the store-house of the jewels of devotion (Bhakti)" (p. 376, Asa M. 5).

Stories: The stories of great-grand parents are told by their worthy descendants (p. 951, Var Ramkali M. 3). The stories and anecdotes of the Lord were told by the friendly Guru (p. 452, Asa M. 4 and p. 725, Tilang M. 4). In the state of extreme love Guru Nanak Dev says, "Dear sisters, and fast friends, come and clasp me in your embrace; let us narrate the stories of our Powerful Lord" (p. 17, Sri Rag M. 1). Guru Arjan Dev says, "O Lord, I shall walk on Your Path and See You alone with my eyes. If the Guru is Gracious towards me, I shall listen only to Your Stories" (p. 761, Suhi M. 5). Guru Amar Das says, "The egocentrics feed themselves on illusion and utter only the stories of strife" (p. 1091, Var Maru M. 3).

Storm: The devout disciple is adamant to seek his Guru, even if there is thunder-storm and rain (p. 757, Suhi M. 4). The mountain is not shaken by the storm and winds (p. 968, Var Ramkali Satta and Balwand). Guru Nanak Dev says, "In the cloudy weather and storm, there are lakhs of waves surging over the sea; then call the True Guru for help, there will be no fear regarding the sinking of your boat (p. 1410, Shlok Varan te Vadhik M. 1). For Kabir, the knowledge comes like a storm, when the thatched huts of Doubt are swept away, the pillars of duality fall down, the roofing of attachment crashes, the tenement of desire is blown away and the pitcher of false mind is broken. There is welcome rain after the storm (pp. 331-332, Gauri Cheti Kabir).

Stotra: An Eulogy. Most of the hymns in the *Adi Granth* are Prayers and *Stotras* (Eulogies), for the Lord (God), the True Guru and the Enlightened Person (*Gurmukh*). The highest deed is the singing of the *Stotra* (Praise) of the Lord in the Society of the Saints (p. 642, Sorath M. 5). The mouth is unable to utter the *Stotra* of the Lord (p. 261, Gauri Bawan Akhri M. 5). Sing the *Stotra* of the Lord in the mind (p. 281, Gauri Sukhmani M. 5). What *Stotra* and Praises of the Lord be uttered, who is All-Pervading? (p. 1236, Sarang M. 5). An example of the *Stotra* of the True Guru may be seen on page 262 in Gauri Bawan Akhri of the 5th Guru and of the God-Conscious Person (*Gurmukh*) on page 942 in Ramkali Siddh Goshta of the first Guru.

Stridhana: Wife's separate fortune. There is no direct mention of *Stridhana* in the *Adi Granth*. For the Gurus and saints, the real fortune of the woman consists in the accumulation of qualities and virtues in life. The Lord will only be pleased on seeing the ornamentation of virtues like Truth, Contentment, Mercy and Piety (p. 812, Bilawal M. 5). Guru Nanak Dev says, "If you embroider the skirt of the Love of God and wear it, then you are the true bride. If you manage your household well, forsaking all vice, then you are the Beloved of the Lord" (p. 1171, Basant Hindol M. 1).

Student: Guru Amar Das says, "O Pundit, read, whatever is recorded in your Writ and do not teach evil to the others. In this way, as a teacher, you will be bound down first and after you, your students (pp. 434-35, Asa M. 3, Patti). According to Guru Nanak Dev that Pundit is a *Gurmukh,* who instructs his students to Cherish the Name of the Lord" (p. 938, Ramkali M. 1, Dakhni Oamkar). According to Guru Ram Das the Lord Himself is the school, He Himself is the Teacher and Himself Brings the Students (p. 552, Var Bihāgrā M. 4). See: *Brahmchārin.*

Study: The more one writes and studies, the more he is in anguish (p. 467, Var Asa M. 1). One may study for months and years and even for lives, only One thing (i.e. the Name of the Lord) is of account, all else is the Prattle of ego (p. 467, Var Asa M. 1). The Pundits and *Monis* (men of silence) grew weary of studying the Vedas again and again but they did not Cherish the Name of the Lord and thus did not abide within their inner home. The death hangs over their heads and they are wasted away because of their inner deceit (p. 1277, Malar M. 3). The more one studies, the more he is involved in discursive thoughts and attached to *maya* (p. 1131, Bhairo M. 3).

Stupas: Memorial burial mounds. There is no mention of such structures in the *Adi Granth,* which were erected by Buddhists. There was a practice of raising *Marhīs* (the tombs) over the ashes of the dead in Hinduism also. Addressing a Yogi, Guru Nanak Dev says, "Why do you forsake Him, who has Blessed you with body and soul? O fool, the Yoga is not practised at the crematoriums and the tombs" (p. 1190, Basant M. 1). Addressing the Pundit he says, "You instruct the world, but build the tomb for the preservation of your ashes. How can you attain Truth by forsaking your discipline? (p. 903, Ramkali M. 1).

Subjects: Those who are under the dominion of a monarch; one who owes allegiance to a government or ruling power. According to Guru Nanak Dev, the king is false, the subjects are false and the whole world is false (p. 468, Var Asa M. 1). Kabir says, "Death does not care either for rich or poor. It destroys both the king and the subjects. It is so powerful" (p. 855, Bilawal Kabir).

Substance: In Indian philosophical terminology it is called *Padārath*. *Padārath-dharma-samgraha*, a work by Prashastapāda, is considered a commentary on Vaisheshika Sutra of Kannāda; it is an exposition of the Vaisheshika categories. There are seven categories: *dravya* (substances), *guna* (qualities), *karma* (actions), *samanya* (universality), *vishesha* (particularity), *samavaya* (inherence) and *abhāva* (non-existence). The first category *Dravya* consists of nine substances, which are *Prithvī* (earth), *Ap* (water), *Tejas* (fire), *Vayū* (air), *Ākāsha* (ether), *Kāla* (time), *Dik* (space), *Atman* (spirit), and *Manas* (mind). In the *Adi Granth*, *Padarath* signifies four values of human life i.e. *Dharma* (righteousness), *Artha* (wealth), *Kāma* (worldly desires) and *Moksha* (salvation) (p. 266, Gauri M. 5). Guru Nanak Dev considers the Padarath as the Object of life. He says, "Through whose Love one finds the object of life, one should stick fast to His Feet (p. 722, Tilang M. 1).

Subtle Body: In Indian terminology it is known as *Sūkshma sarīra* or *upādhī*. It is also known as *linga sarīra*. In Vedanta, the human being is said to contain five encasements (*koshas*). The first *kosha* i.e. Annmaya kosha is called the *sthūla sarīra* (dense body). The second, third and fourth encasements are called *Prāṅamaya kosha, manomaya kosha* and *vigyanmaya kosha*. They are concerned with vital breath, mind and intellect. These three encasements constitue the subtle body. The fifth kosha called *Anandmaya kosha* is the causal body (*Kāraṅ sarīra*). The subtle body contains seventeen things, i.e. five organs of sense, five organs of action, five vital airs, mind and intellect. When a man dies, his subtle body leaves the dense body and is accountable to *Dharmarāja* (See p. 39, Sri Raga M. 3).

Suc: Purity "Only the Pure one can attain Truth" (Var Asa M. 1, p. 472)

Sucajjī: A virtuous housewife. This word is an antonym of *Kucajjī*. There is a hymn entitled *Sucajjī*, in the *Adi Granth*, composed by Guru Nanak Dev in Raga Suhi, in which a virtuous woman is shown living under the Will of the Lord .

Succā: A Pure person; an immaculate person. "They cannot be called pure, who just wash their bodies. Only they are Pure, in whose mind the Lord abides" (Var Asa M. 1, p. 472). "Those with godly qualities are always Pure" (Asa M. 1, p. 354). "That body is pure, in which there is the True Name of the Lord (Sri Rag M. 1, p. 19).

Sudras: Out of the four *varṅas* (castes) Brahmans, Kshatriyas and Vaishyas are called *dvijās*, who wear the sacred thread. The Sudras can neither wear the sacred thread nor are entitled to study Vedas.

They are only to serve the higher castes. The way of the Vedas is that of Brahmins, the way of heroism is that of Kshatriyas and the Shudras are meant to serve others (p. 469, Var Asa M. 1, Shlok M. 2). The Brahmins, Kshatriyas, Vaishyas, Shudras and even the lowliest are all Emancipated, while meditating on their Lord (p. 300, Gauri Thitti M.5). The Lord's Word is for all the four castes (p. 800, Bilawal M. 4). Of all the four castes whosoever burns the Lamp of knowledge, is Emancipated (p. 878, Ramkali M. 1). Namdev says, 'The custodians of the temple, dubbing me an "untouchable", have driven me out...Even You are being Dishonoured, when the Pundits call me a "low-born". "O wonderful Lord, the temple has turned its back on the Pundits and I have Your Sight" (p. 1292, Malar Namdev).

Suffering: The suffering is universal. Sheikh Farid says, "I thought I suffered alone, but the whole world is suffering. When I saw from the house-top, I saw the whole world in the fire of suffering" (p. 1382, Shlok Farid). Guru Nanak Dev says, "There is suffering of hunger and also of separation. There is also the suffering of Yama, the god of death. Then there is also suffering that afflicts the body.... He who forsakes the Lord and indulges in sensuous pleasures, the suffering arises within him" (p. 1256, Malar M. 1). One is born in suffering, dies in suffering and deals with the world in suffering...The fire of suffering scorches all, but suffering is also the cure of our ailing mind" (p. 1240, Var Sarang M. 4, Shlok M. 1). "There are countless who are afflicted with suffering and hunger. Even these are Your Blessings, O Lord" (p. 5, Japuji). Suffering is the cure and pleasure is the malady (p. 469, Var Asa M.1).

Sugharṛ: Wise. See: *Siānā*.

Suhāgaṇ: The lady whom the Lord likes and loves. This word is an antonym of *Duhāgan* (a deserted woman). Sheikh Farid says, "Those who are called *Suhāgaṇ* do not see anyone else except the Lord" (Shlok Farid, p.1384). "She is, indeed, a *Suhāgaṇ*, on whom the Lord showers His Graces" (Asa M. 1, p. 351). "The *Suhāgaṇ* has bedecked herself with the necklace of virtues" (Asa M. 3, p. 426).

Suicide: The egocentric is blind and not in his senses. He is committing suicide and is also the butcher of the world. He carries the load of calumny and without wages, he carries his load (p. 118, Majh M. 3) This implies the disapproval of the act of committing suicide.

Sukh: Comfort; pleasure. This word is an antonym of *Dukh* (suffering). "We ask for comfort and pleasure instead of sorrow and suffering. But the comfort and suffering are clothes worn by man" (Var Majh M. 1, p. 149). There is no pleasure in earning more wealth, there is no pleasure in seeing plays and dance, there is no pleasure in visiting many lands, all the pleasures consist in singing the Praises of the Lord" (Bhairo M. 5, p. 1147). "There is comfort in the service of the Guru; do not seek comfort anywhere else (Var Bihagra M. 4, Shlok M. 3, p. 548). "According to the instruction of the Guru, there is comfort in accepting the Will of the Lord" (Bilawal M. 5, p. 813).

Summum Bonum: Highest Good; Emancipation. According to the *Adi Granth*, the Highest Good is the Realisation of the Supreme Bliss. Guru Amar Das say, "O my Lord, whosoever Serves You, attains Supreme Bliss" (p. 1172, Basant M. 3). Guru Arjan Dev says, "If you seek Eternal Bliss always Dwell on your Lord" (p. 714, Todi M. 5).

Sun: Addressing the Lord, Guru Nanak Dev says, "The sun and the moon are Your Two Lamps and the moon merges in the house of the sun (p. 1033, Marū Dakhani M. 1). The sun and the moon move in the Fear of the Lord. They traverse millions of miles and yet there is no end (to this movement) (p. 464, Var Asa M. 1). Just as the ray merges in the sun and the drop in the ocean, the light of the soul merges in Brahman (p. 846, Bilawal M. 5). When the sun appears, the darkness of night vanishes (p. 1069, Maru Solhe M. 4). The sun blazes emitting poisonous flames (p. 1029, Maru Solhe M. 1). The *Chakwi* bird knows no sleep without her Love; when the sun rises, she sees him with her eyes...The lotus is in the pond, the sun-rays in the sky, and when the sun rises the lotus blossoms spontaneously (p. 1273, Malar M. 1). Just as the divisions of time, the solar and the lunar day and the changing seasons are all created by the same one sun, the Lord is one, but the garbs are many (p. 12, Asa M. 1). In Yogic terminology, the *Pingalā* channel experiences sun-breathing through the right nostril and *Irā* experiences the moon-breathing through the left nostril (See p. 991, Maru M. 1 and pp. 1105-06, Maru Jaidev).

Sundar: Beautiful, Beautiful Lord. "They are, indeed, *Sundar*, who sit in the holy congregation" (Majh M. 3, p. 132). That person is beautiful, wise and brave, who attains *Sādh Sangat* (the company of the saints (Dev Gandhari M. 5, p. 531).

Sunn: Void; nothingness. See: *Shunya.*

Sunnat: Circumcision. See: *Circumcision.*

Superhuman Beings: Various types of superhuman beings have been mentioned in the *Adi Granth* e.g. gods, goddesses and other creatures connected with these gods derived from Hindu mythology (Brahmā, Vishnu, Shiva, Lakshmī, Pārbatī, Sārdā, Yaksha, Kinnar, Gandharva, Indra, Durgā, Garuḍā, Arun, etc.), others from Hindu mythology e.g. Danavas, Rakshasas, Nagas, Bhutas, Pretas, Pishachas, Siddhas, Daityas, Chitra Gupta, Dharmarājā, Yama etc., angels from Muslim mythology e.g. Izrāīl.

Superhuman Condition: A spiritual experience gained through meditation, which is far above the mundane, physical and mental experience. Such condition is visible in the sayings of the Gurus and saints of the *Adi Granth*. The God-conscious person experiences such a superhuman condition. "He remains for ever alike and always feels the nearness of the Lord.... His soul leans on the Lotus-Feet of the Lord. He is above pleasure and pain" (p. 181, Gauri Guareri M. 5)." He sees only One Lord everywhere. In his heart, He is steadfast on Faith. He hears only the holy words. He merges in the All-Pervading Lord." (p. 294, Gauri Sukhmani M. 5).

Superhuman Powers: The use of superhuman powers has been decried in the *Adi Granth*. Guru Nanak Dev says, "The performance of miracles is vain; it has a separate taste" (p. 6, Japuji). Guru Amar Das says, "Without the Name of the Lord, all miracles and extra-psychic powers, all the meals and clothes are vain. That is only the miracle or extra-psychic power, which is Blessed Spontaneously by the Lord. If the Name of the Lord is Enshrined in the heart, this is the real miracle" (Var Sorath M. 4, Shlok M. 3). "The performance of miracles is all attachment, the Name of the Lord does not reside in the mind" (p. 593, Var Vadhans M. 4, Shlok M. 3).

Superimposition: To place one object upon another. In Indian philosophical terminology, it is called *Adhyāsa*. The superimposition of the snake on a piece of rope is found in the *Adi Granth*. Kabir says, "My mistaking the rope (for the snake) due to the darkness of *Maya* (*Avidyā*) has ended and I now reside in the Eternal Home of the Lord (p. 332, Gauri Kabir).

Superior Man: According to the *Adi Granth*, the true devotee of the Lord is the Superior Man. He is called *Sant*, *Sādh* and *Gurmukh*. He is like a swan. "The Sikhs gather at the Guru's Pool like the swans under the Will of the Guru. They feed themselves on the Pearls, which they find there and this food is never exhausted..." (p. 960, Var Ramkali M. 5). The Gurmukh is never old, because in his conscious mind, he cherishes the Knowledge of God. He always utters the Praises of the Lord and is Attuned to Him in the state of equipoise. He, having the power of discrimination, is always in Bliss. The pleasure and pain are alike to him. He Sees only One Lord, the All-Pervading Spiritual Entity (p. 1418, Shlok Varan te Vadhil M. 3). The views of Guru Nanak Dev on the Superior Man are contained in *Siddh Goshta*, where the Guru has mentioned the attributes of a *Gurmukh* (See pages 941-946).

Superstition: Unreasoning awe or fear of something unknown, mysterious, or imaginary, especially in connection with religion; an irrational religious belief or practice. According to the *Adi Granth*, such superstition ends when we meet the Guru and follow his discipline. Guru Arjan Dev says, "The egg of superstition has burst and my mind is illumined. The fetters have been cut down from my feet. The Guru has emancipated me. (p. 1002, Maru M. 5). The Guru addresses the Lord in this manner: "O Lord, the Treasure of Virtue, meet me so that I shatter the wall of superstition" (p. 543, Bihagra M. 5).

Supreme Being: In Indian Terminology "Param-Atman" or "Param-Ishwara" are the terms for Supreme Being. The Supreme Being is *Param Purusha* (Brahman) in relation to other *purushas* (souls). See: *Brahman*.

Supreme Bliss: In Indian terminology, it is called "Param Ānand." This state is achieved on meeting the Lord, who is also called *Paramanand*. Guru Arjan Dev says, "He, who does not listen to the Praise of *Parmanand* (Supreme Bliss—the Lord), is worse than the quadrupeds, the birds and the crawling creatures" (p. 188, Gauri M. 5).

Sur: god. See: *god*.

Surā: It means spirituous liquor, whose use has been strictly condemned in the *Adi Granth*. The saint Ravidas says, "Even if the waters of the Ganges turn into the spirituous liquor, the saints do not drink it, but if the impure spirituous liquor Sura or other impurities are merged into the Ganges, they are considered not different from it (p. 1293, Malar Ravidas). Kabir says, 'Whosoever eats the fish and takes hemp and wine (*Sura*), they lose the merit of all pilgrimages, fasts and all pious rituals (p. 1377, Shlok Kabir).

Sūrā: Brave; warrior. "He is indeed a brave warrior, who has killed the tyrant ego" (Var Sri Rag M. 4 , Shlok M. 3, p. 86).

Surabhī: In the *Adi Granth*, this Sanskrit word has been written as *Surhī*. It means the cow. Guru Nanak Dev says, "When it rains, the cow (Surhī) has the grass to graze" (p. 150, Var Majh M. 1).

Suras: gods. According to Guru Nanak Dev, in the region of effort (*Saram Khand*), the vision of the devotee is moulded like the vision of the gods and the adepts (p. 8, Japuji). See: *Gods*.

Surg: Heaven. See: *Svarga*.

Sūrmā: Brave; warrior. "The trumpet sounded in the sky and the target was hit. The warrior entered the battlefield, now is the time to strike" (Maru Kabir, p. 1105). See: *Sūrā*.

Surt: Attention, concentration, sense. "All the Jivas have the same one concentration. None could attain anything without it. Whatever grade of concentration one has, one has the cultural attainment according to that" (Sri Rag M. 1, pp. 24-25).

Surt-Shabad: Concentration on the WORD. "The ocean of *samsāra* can be ferried across, with the concentration on the Word and the remembrance of the Name of the Lord (Ramkali M. 1, Siddh Goshta, p. 938). "The Shakta cannot attain the concentration on the Word and without the concentration on the Word, he transmigrates" (Maru M. 1, p. 1042).

Sūrya: The Sun; The Sun-god. The Lord created the sun and moon and they are ever on the move (p. 580, Vadhans M. 1, Dakhni). The sun rises and sets and thereby a day of man's life has gone by (p. 1244, Var Sarang M. 4, Shalok M. 1). Within the mind of a God-Conscious person, there is illumination, but there is no star, no moon and no ray of sun (p. 1033, Maru M. 1, Dakhnī). See: *Sun*.

Sūtak: The uncleanliness supposed to exist in the house, according to Hindu Dharma, for several days at the time of birth and death. Guru Nanak Dev is very critical about this practice. He says, "If we accept Sūtak, then it is present at all places. There are worms within the cowdung and the wood. None of the grain is without a jiva. Primarily water is life, which keeps everything fresh and green. Why to observe the *Sūtak*? It is there in the kitchen. The impact of *Sūtak* cannot be removed in this way, it can only be washed off with knowledge" (Var Asa M. 1, p. 472). "All the *Sūtak* is an illusion which is said to travel from one person to another" (ibid).

Sūtras: They are short aphorisms constituting in their totality a complete body of doctrines upon some subject. There are several types of *Sūtras* in Hinduism viz., Dharma-Sūtras, Grihya-Sūtras, Kalpa-Sūtras, Srauta-Sūtras, Vedanta-Sūtras etc. There is no direct reference to the *Sūtras* in the *Adi Granth*.

Svarga: Heaven. The paradise of Indra. In post-Vedic mythology, Indra, Kuvera and other gods each have their own heaven. In the *Adi Granth*, the word *Surgindū* connotes the heaven of Indra. Kabir says, "What are heaven and hell? The saints of the Lord have rejected both"

(p. 969, Ramkali Kabir). He says again, "I have risen above heaven and hell by the Grace of the Guru" (p.1370, Shalok Kabir). At another place he says, "Do not seek the abode of heaven and do not fear the residence in hell. Do not build hopes regarding them, whatever has to happen is bound to happen" (p. 337, Gauri Kabir). Guru Arjan Dev says, "The whole world works in the three modes and one goes to the heaven and hell again and again" (p. 389, Asa M. 5). Everyone seeks Emancipation or Paradise and rests all his hopes on it, but the devotee does not seek it" (p. 1324, Kalyan M. 4). He who abides in the Will of the Lord, and sees Him everywhere, the heaven, this world and the underworld are sanctified for him (p. 883, Ramkali M. 5). Even if the houris of heaven are enjoyed, they will pass away (p. 142, Var Majh M. 1). See: *Heaven*.

Svayyambhū: The Self-Existent Lord. The Tadbhava formation of this word occurs as *Saibhang* in the *mūl mantra*. The *Adi Granth* clearly states that "The Lord has neither father, nor mother, nor sons, nor relatives, nor wife nor lust" (p. 597, Sorath M. 1) (See also pages 1021 and 1038, Maru M. 1). Guru Amar Das says, "The Lord Created Himself, then there was none other" (p. 509, Var Gujri M. 3).

T

Tales: A tale is a mere story as opposed to a narrative of fact. In the *Adi Granth*, in order to bring home a point a tale or tales have been referred to. For example the Maharashtrian saint Namdev has referred to the folktales about Gayatri, Mahadev and Lord Rama in one hymn and in the other hymn, he has made a mention of Hiranayakashyapa. Ajamal, Ganika, Daraupadi, Ahilya and Kali, deriving tales from Puranas (Gaund Namdev, pp. 874-75).

Talisman: Stone, ring or other object engraven with figures or characters, to which are attributed the occult powers of the planetary influences and celestial configurations under which it was made; usually worn as an amulet to avert evil from or bring fortune to the wearer. Guru Arjan Dev says, "The Talisman of the Name of the Lord is the coat of mail of the devotee (Gaund M. 5, p. 868). See: *Amulet*.

Tamas: It is one of the three modes of *maya*, the other two being *Rajas* and *Sattva*. This quality constitutes inaction, mental darkness and ignorance. It is the cause of dullness, heaviness, immobility and illusion. It is mentioned as *Tam Gun* (Tamas) in the *Adi Granth*. Kabir says, "*Raj gun* (Rajas), *Tam gun* (Tamas) and *Sat gun* (Sattva) constitute your *maya*, O Lord" (Kedara Kabir, p.1123). There is also the use of the word *Tam*, without any reference to the qualities. It means darkness. Guru Arjan Dev says, "O Lord, You are the Dispeller of ignorance and darkness" (Majh M. 5, Din Rain, p. 137).

Tan: Body. See: *Body*.

Tanhā-Trishnā: Desire; craving. "Those who are unclean from within lose their life in a vain gamble. They are inflicted by the great malady of *Trishnā* and because of that they have forgotten death" (Ramkali M. 5, Anand, p. 919). Because of the mercurial desire (*cancal Trishnā*), the mind is never at peace (Gauri M. 9, p. 219). Such a person is rare, who has stilled his desires (Gauri M. 5, p. 213). The world burns in the fire of desire (Maru M. 3, p. 1044). The craving ceases by dwelling on the Name of the Lord. Through the Word of the Guru, one becomes content immensely and is Attuned perfectly to the Lord (Dhanasari M. 5, p. 682).

Tantra: This term literally meaning "warp and woof" is applied to works/texts of the Tantrik Hindu, Buddhist and Jaina cults. The sacred writings of Shaktas are especially called Tantras. They are mostly composed in the form of dialogues between Shiva and his consort on problems of ritualism, magic, philosophy and other types of knowledge. Guru Nanak Dev says, "I do not know the religious hypocrisy of Tantra and mantra; I only Cherish my Lord. (Suhi M. 1, p. 766). Guru Arjan Dev says, "I have received from the Guru the Name of the Lord as the Tantra and Mantra" (Asa M. 5, p. 386). Thus the devotee of the *Adi Granth* has nothing to do with the Tantras.

Tap: Austerity. See: *Austerity.*

Tāp: Ailment. Three types of ailments are: *Ādhi* (ailments of mind), *Biādhi* (ailments of body) and *Upādhi* (ailments caused by illusion). Guru Arjan Dev says, "All the three ailments i.e. *Ādhi*, *Biādhi* and *Upādhi* have been destroyed, the *Trishnā* (desire) has been stilled, the hopes have been fulfilled and all the sorrows have ended" (Sarang M. 5, p. 1223).

Tapā: Ascetic. "Among the selected few he is called a *Tapā,* but secretly he commits sins" (Var Gauri M. 4, pp. 315-16).

Tapas: Austerity; ascetic practice. The word *Tapas* literally means "warmth, heat", but in Indian religious tradition, it signifies the religious ascetic practices. These practices have been rejected in the *Adi Granth.* Guru Nanak Dev says, "Through fasts and ascetic practices, the mind is not subdued" (Ramkali M. 1, p. 905). The Guru lays emphasis on the Name of the Lord. According to Guru Amar Das, service of the Guru is the essence of all ascetic practices and austerities (Asa M. 3, p. 423). Guru Ram Das says, "That is the only contemplation, austerity, worship and fasting, which creates in us the Love of the Lord (Bairari M. 4, p. 720).

Tapsī: Ascetic. See: *Tapā.*

Tarīqat: It is a state of Sufis in their spiritual development. It is the Path leading to *Mārfat* (knowledge). According to Guru Arjan Dev *Tarīqat* is the state of non-attachment when the devotee launches his search for the Lord (Maru M. 5, p. 1083).

Tarpana: It is a rite, in which the water is offered as a libation to the gods and manes. This rite has been rejected by the *Adi Granth.* Guru Amar Das says, "One offers the routine prayer of *Sandhya,* makes water-offerings to the gods and manes and also recites Gayatri mantra (an invocation to the sun-god), but remains in agony without the esoteric knowledge (Sorath M. 3, p. 603).

Taste: This is one of the five senses, the other four being the senses of sight, hearing, smell and touch. The organ representing this sense is the tongue. The taste may be sweet, sour, saltish etc. of the thirty-six kinds of delicacies (Sri Rag M.1, p.16). It may be bitter (Sorath Kabir, p. 656). Guru Amar Das addresses the tongue in the following manner: "O my tongue, you are lured by other tastes and thus your thirst is not stilled" (Ramkali M. 3, Anand, p. 921). Numerous tastes create suffering and because of one's indulgence in them, lead to disease and one is wasted away (Maru M. 1, p. 1034).

Tat: Essence. See: *Essence*.

Tat Giān: The essence of knowledge. See: *Knowledge*.

Taxes: In the *Adi Granth* two types of taxes have been mentioned: those which are levied by the Government and those which are charged by the messengers of Yama (death) from the persons absorbed in duality. Talking about the contemporary Muslim rule in India, Guru Nanak Dev says, "Now that the turn of Sheikhs has come, the Primal Lord is called Allah and the temples of gods have been taxed; such is the way of the world (Basant Hindol M. 1, p. 1191). Guru Amar Das says, "The Yama taxes those, who are deluded by duality (Majh M. 3, p. 127).

Teacher: The teacher is well-read only if he reflects on the Word and churns the knowledge to find its essence...The teacher is *Gurmukh* (God-conscious), if he instructs his followers to Cherish the Name of the Lord (Ramkali M.1, Dakhni Oamkar, pp. 937-38). By good fortune one meets the Guru (Perfect Teacher) who always speaks truth (Var Majh M. 1, Shlok M. 2, p. 146). Blessed is the Guru-Teacher, who by giving Lord's Wisdom, makes us wise (Gauri Bairagan M. 4, p. 168). Without knowing the Reality and led by doubt, life is being wasted away. One calls himself a teacher without cause, when the load of duality is upon his head (Asa M. 3, Patti, p. 434). The Lord Himself is the school, Himself the Teacher and Himself brings the students to the school (Var Bihagra M. 4, p. 552). Blessed are the tongue and the hands of the Guru-Teacher, on meeting whom, one writes the account of the Lord (Var Kanra M. 4, p. 1316).

Teaching: One cannot worship the Lord except through the Guru's teaching (Sri Rag M. 1, p. 22). The teaching of the saints is regarding the True Word (Gauri Sukhmani M. 5, p. 284). There are six systems, six teachers and six kinds of teachings (Asa M. 1, p. 357). Let the Love of the Lord be your teaching (Gauri Guareri M. 1, p. 221). The disciple of the True Guru dwells upon the Lord through the teaching of the Guru and all his sins are washed away (Var Gauri M. 4, p. 305).

Temples: Guru Ram Das says, "Blessed are the homes, temples, places and rest-houses, which are dedicated to the devotees of God" (Var Sorath M. 4, p. 648). The body is the temple of God. Guru Amar Das says, "The temple of God is within you, therefore search Him within your self through the Word of the Guru and enter into this temple cherishing the Name of the Lord....The body is the Temple of the Lord....The Temple of the Lord is embellished only with the Word....This world also is the Temple of the Lord, but without the Guru, one is enveloped by utter darkness....The Temple of the Lord is also the store-house of the Lord, which is bedecked with the Word. In this Temple, the Name of the Lord is sold and it is through the Guru that one buys and bedecks himself with it..." (Prabhati Bibhas M. 3, p. 1346). Within the temple is lighted the Light of the world, where Plays the Lord in utter Bliss (Asa M. 5, p. 384).

Thākur: The Lord; The Master.

That Thou Art: This is the translation of the Sanskrit dictum "Tat Tvam Asi", a phrase which occurs in the Chandogya Upanishad. *Tat* connotes Brahman and *Tvam,* the Atman. It establishes the fundamental identity of Brahman with Atman. It is the central theme in the philosophy of Shankaracharya. The identity of Atman and Brahman is the basic idea in the *Adi Granth*. Guru Nanak Dev says, "The Atman is Brahman and Brahman is Atman" (Maru M. 1, p. 1030). Kabir says, "The soul is part and parcel of God" (Gaund Kabir, p. 871).

That Which Is: In Indian terminology, this phrase is conveyed by the word "SAT". According to the *Adi Granth*, Brahman (the Lord) is *SAT* (Ever-Existent). Shankar believes that Brahman is the only Reality and the world is an illusion, while the *Adi Granth* accepts the first part of this assertion, it rejects the second part. The world is also relatively real according to the *Adi Granth*. According to Guru Nanak Dev: "True are the worlds and True the universes" (Var Asa M. 1, p. 463). Guru Angad Dev says, "The world is the Abode of the True Lord in which He abides" (Var Asa M. 1, p. 463). Guru Arjan Dev says, "True is the Lord and True is His creation" (Gauri Sukhmani M. 5, p. 294).

That Which Is Not: This phrase is conveyed by the term "ASAT" in Indian philosophy. Whatever is false, is "Asat". Guru Nanak Dev says, "False is the king, false are the subjects and false is the whole world....The false ones love the false and abandon their Creator. The whole world will pass away, then with whom should I befriend myself?....O Lord, without You, everything is false" (Var Asa M. 1, p. 468).

Theft: Addressing the body, Guru Nanak Dev says, "Listen to my advice, I say this to you. You slander other people and indulge in talebearing. You behold another's woman and thus commit theft; but when your soul will depart, you will be left behind like a deserted woman" (Gauri Cheti M. 1, p. 155). He says again: "I broke into shops, cities and strong houses and committing theft came home, but though I saved myself from the man's eye, how could I keep my secret from You, O Lord" (Gauri Cheti M. 1, p. 156). Five thieves live in the city of the body. Though they have been warned, they still go out to commit theft (Gujri M. 1, p. 503).

Theogony: The generation of the gods; especially a study of the genealogy of the deities of heathen mythology. Guru Nanak Dev says, "It is He, our Lord, Who Created the Trinity of Brahma, Vishnu and Shiva and also gods and goddesses and other innumerable garbs" (Bilawal M. 1, Thitti, p. 939). "The Lord in His Will, Created His ten incarnations and countless gods and demons....Out of *Shunya* were created Brahma, Vishnu and Shiva" (Maru Solhe M. 1, p. 1037).

Theosophists: An adherent of a system of recent origin, claiming to a knowledge of nature pronounced than obtained from empirical science, and contained in an esoteric tradition of which the doctrines of various historical religions held to be only the exoteric expression... Sometimes called esoteric Buddhism. The religious philosophy of the *Adi Granth* may be called esoteric Sikhism. In this sense, the adherents of the religious philosophy of the *Adi Granth* are Theosophists.

Thief: If a thief praises someone, no one is impressed and if he calumniates someone, then also it is of no account. No one defends a thief and whatever he does, it is of no use...even if a thief is handsome, clever and wise, he remains false and without any respect (Dhanasari M. 1, p. 662). If one abandons his real home and goes to the wrong door, he is caught like a thief. (Asa M. 3, p. 425). He whose mind does not dwell on the Name of the Lord, is bound down like a thief at the abode of *Yama* (Gauri M. 5, p. 240). The city of the body is the abode of five thieves (namely lust, anger, greed, attachment and ego) (Gauri M. 1, p. 503). The others are five and I fight alone with them; how will I be able to keep my home safe? Each day they beat and rob me; before whom should I express my grief? (Gauri Cheti M. 1, p. 155).

Thirst: In Indian philosophical terminology, this word is called *Trishnā*. According to Guru Nanak Dev, the thirst for desire should be shed (Var Majh M. 1, Shlok M. 4, p. 141). They who thirst for the

Love of the True Lord, attain peace of mind (Gauri M. 1, p. 505). The mind of the saint is content, it neither hungers nor thirsts. (Maru Solhe M. 1, p. 1039). The Lord has neither hunger nor thirst (Var Malar M. 1, p. 1279). The *Chatrik* prays, "O my Lord, be Merciful and bless me with the life of the spirit because without Your waters, my thirst is not quenched and I die" (Var Malar M. 1, p. 1284, Shlok M. 3). Kabir says, "O Lord, my thirst for water does not end. The more I partake of it, the more I am athirst. You are the treasure of water and I am your fish. I abide in You and without You I cannot live" (Gauri Kabir, p. 323). It is by the great good fortune that one is imbued with the thirst to sing the Name of the Lord (Dhanasari M. 5, p. 683).

Thou Art That: This is the translation of the phrase "Tat Tvam Asi", which establishes the identity of Atman with Brahman. See: *That Thou Art*.

Thought: The characteristic of mind is Thought. Whatever we are, it is the result of our thoughts. The thoughts are interlinked with our senses. The thought may be good or bad according to our mental make-up. If the thought is good, it leads us to good action, if it is bad, it leads to a bad *karma*. Guru Arjan Dev says, "Abandon all other objects and give your thought to the One Alone" (Asa M. 5, p. 397). Guru Nanak Dev says, "The thinking avails not, even if one thinks for hundred thousand times (Japuji, p. 1). Addressing the Lord, Guru Arjan Dev says, "O Lord the divisions of time Dwell upon You, the *Kāl* (time) and *Akāl* (Timeless) dwell upon you and also the thoughts of purification (Maru M. 5, p. 1079). On ordinary human level, the night passes in anxious thoughts. One thinks endlessly about *maya* and never about the Lord (Asa M. 5, p. 390).

Thoughtfulness: Meditative; contemplative; pre-occupied in mind. Guru Arjan Dev says, "I am thoughtful about this desire in my mind that I should make an effort always to absorb myself in the Praises of the Lord (Var Gujri M. 5, p. 519).

Thoughtlessness: Unreflecting; heedless. The saint Ravidas says, "Wisdom has escaped me and my days pass in thoughtlessness and ignorance. Overpowered by the sense-desires, I am unable to discriminate and meditate upon the Lord" (Sorath Ravidas, p. 658).

Thread-Girdle: The practice of using girdle (thread-girdle) or waist-band is very old. Guru Nanak Dev made a mention of "kamarband" (waist-band) in one of his hymns. He says, "To wear white-coloured costume is to practise purity and charity; to wear blue-coloured costume connotes erasing of black spots; to wear the robes of honour is to meditate upon the Lotus-Feet of the Lord. The waist-band of contentment may be worn and the wealth and beauty of the Name of the Lord may be gathered. To wear anything else is of no use (Sri Rag M. 1, p. 16).

Three: The number three has been used in the *Adi Granth* for the three gods of Trinity i.e. Brahma, Vishnu and Shiva, the three *gunas* (modes) or qualities i.e. *Rajas, Sattva* and *Tamas* (which constitute *maya*), the three *Bhavans* (worlds) heaven, nether-world and our world, three states of awakening, sleep and dreamless sleep, three *tāp* (ailments) namely *Ādhi, Biādhi* and *Upādhi* and three channels of *Iṛā, Pingalā* and *Sushumnā*.

Three Jewels: The three Jewels in Buddhism are: the Buddha, Dhamma and Samgha. The three Jewels in Jainism are the right faith, right knowledge and right conduct. The three Jewels of Hinduism are Karma Yoga, Bhakti Yoga and Gyan Yoga. The three Jewels of Sikhism on the basis of the *Adi Granth* are *Kirt Karo, Nam Japo* and *Wand Chhakko*, which connote 1-Do the work, 2-Remember the Name of the Lord, and 3-Share your earnings with the needy and deserving.

Threshold: The piece of timber or stone which lies below the bottom of a door, and has to be crossed in entering a house; the sill of the doorway; hence the entrance to a house or building. Guru Nanak Dev says, "Those who are Attuned to the Love of the Lord and always seek to see His Vision, who weep, laugh and keep silence in their pleasure; they do not care for anyone except the Lord and wait upon the Threshold of the Door of the Lord; they eat, whenever He gives to them (Var Asa M. 1, p. 473).

Thug: One of the band of robbers and assassins formerly infesting India; a cut-throat, a ruffian. "The deceitful act of a Thug does not remain a secret" (Var Gauri M. 4, p. 303). "The kingdom, wealth, beauty, caste and youth are the five Thugs. These Thugs have robbed the world..." (Var Malar M. 1, p. 1288).

Thunder: The loud noise accompanying a flash of lightening. Guru Nanak Dev says, "When I hear the clouds thunder, my mind is pleased like a peacock and imbued with the Love of the Lord, sings His Praises (Malar M.1, p.1254). Guru Arjan Dev says, "The lightning flashes, the dark clouds thunder, there is heavy downpour, but those souls are Blessed, who are United with the Lord (Var Maru Dakhne M. 5, p. 1102).

Thunderbolt: A supposed bolt or dart believed to be the destructive agent in a lightning flash, when it strikes anything. Guru Arjan Dev say's, "In all the ten directions, the clouds spread over the skies like a canopy and (the supposed thunderbolt of) the lightning fills me with fear" (Sorath M. 5, p. 624). According to Guru Nanak Dev, the clouds burst into showers in the month of *Shravana*, the lightning flashes and terrifies (Baramaha Tukhari M. 1, p. 1108).

Thunderstorm: A storm of thunder and lightning, usually accompanied by heavy rain. The following verse of Guru Ram Das is suggestive of a thunderstorm: "If there is a violent storm accompanied by the rain, I shall still go to see my Guru" (Suhi M. 4, p. 757).

Tiāg, Tiāgī: *Tiāg* is renunciation and *Tiāgī* is one who renounces the world. The *Adi Granth* has rejected renunciation and laid emphasis upon work in the world. Guru Arjan Dev questions: "How can there be a *Tiāgī* without renouncing ego?" (Bhairo M. 5, p. 1140). "Firstly renounce the love for ego, secondly renounce the folk-tradition (formalism), renounce the three *gunas* (modes) and consider the enemies and friends alike; realise *Turiyā* in the company of the saints" (Asa M. 5, p. 370). "It is good to renounce lust, anger and greed" (Maru M. 5, p. 1018). See: *Renunciation*.

Tides: The swelling of the sea, twice in each lunar day, due to the attraction of the moon. In the *Adi Granth*, the sea and the surging waves have been mentioned several times, but the tides produced by the attraction of the moon, find no mention. Guru Ram Das says, "O Lord, the Play of the world is Your Creation and You are the Life of its life, pervading in every pore. It is like innumerable waves rising from the sea and merging again in the sea (Nat M. 4, p. 977).

Tiger: The kings of the Iron age (*Kaliyuga*) have been mentioned as tigers by Guru Nanak Dev (Var Malar M. 1, p. 1288). Why should one seek the refuge of a tiger, if he is to be seized by the jackal (Bilawal Sadhna, p. 858). The tiger is pleased if it is always fed on meat (Basant M. 5, p. 1180). Such meritorious is the devotion of the Lord that the tiger becomes a cat (Bilawal M. 5, p. 810). If the Lord Wills, He may make the tigers eat grass (Var Majh M. 1, p. 144). If a powerful tiger falls upon a herd of cattle, then the Master must answer (Asa M. 1, p. 360).

Time: None knows the time, season, day and month of the creation (Japuji, p. 4). Blessed is the time, when the Love of the True Lord is born in the heart (Majh M. 3, p. 115). Kabir says, "I request for two seers of wheat-flour, a quarter seer of ghee, a pinch of salt and half a seer of lentils, so that I can eat to my fill two times a day (Sorath Kabir, p. 656). Sheikh Farid says, " O prayerless dog, it is not good for you that you have not visited the mosque five times a day (Shlok Farid, p. 1381). When body perishes, you will be called a ghost at that time (Baramaha Majh M. 5, p. 134). Meditate on the True Name at the ambrosial time (in the early hours of the morning) (Japuji, p. 2). Blessed is that auspicious time, when one meets the Lord (Var Jaitsri M. 5, p. 709). One does not think of that time when the thorn of death will pierce through you (Tilang M. 4, p. 723). That Time is approved, when one meets the True Guru (Var Gujri M. 5, p. 520).

Tīrath: Place of Pilgrimage.

Tīrthas: Places of Pilgrimage. For Guru Nanak Dev, the place of pilgrimage is the Name of the Lord (Dhanasari M. 1, p. 687). One who hears, believes in and loves the Name of the Lord, bathes at the sacred *tīrtha* within his self (Japuji, p. 4). If there is dirt inside and one bathes at the *tīrthas*, he does not go to heaven (Asa Kabir, p. 484). Even if one bathes at hundreds of *tīrthas*, the dirt of ego is not washed off (Sri Rag M. 3, p. 39). The Name of the Lord has the merit of the pilgrimage to sixty-eight *tīrthas* (Maru M. 1, p. 1009). The place which is sanctified by the feet of the saint, contains the merit of sixty-eight *tīrthas* and wherever the Name of the Lord is Uttered, that place is a Paradise (Ramkali M. 5, p. 890).

Titans: Superhuman beings; a family of giants. In Greek mythology, *Titan* is the Name of Sun-god. When plural, it connotes a family of giants, the children of *Uranus* (Heaven) and *Gaea* (Earth), who contended for the sovereignty of heaven, and were overthrown by Zeus. In general, this term is used for superhuman beings. See: *Gods, Demons* and *Superhuman beings.*

Tithe: The tenth part of the annual produce of agriculture etc. being a payment for the support of the religious establishments. In Sikhism, the equivalent for this term is *daswandh*, which also means the tenth part. According to Sikh injunctions, the tithe is to be paid to the Guru. In the *Adi Granth*, the verse of Guru Nanak Dev "*ghāl khāe kich hathon dei*" (to use the earnings procured with hard work for oneself and to share it with the others)—(Var Sarang M. 4, Shalok M. 1, p. 1245) is suggestive of the payment of tithe.

Titles: They are applied to both secular and religious chiefs. In the *Adi Granth*, various titles have been mentioned e.g. in administration, the titles used were: *Rājā, mukaddam, mehtā, sikdār, neb (nāib), sultān, khān, mantrī, adlī, Qādī, salār, modī, patwārī, lekhīā* etc. The religious titles used are: *Gurū, Pir, Sheikh, Rasul, Jogī, Sannyāsī, Jatī, sant, sādh, Gurmukh, Brahm Giānī, Jīvan-Mukat, Walī* etc.

Tolerance: The practice of enduring; endurance. The *Darvesh* (religious mendicant) has to have the tolerance of trees (Shlok Farid, p. 1381). God is the Pardoner and Forgiver. Kabir says, "Where there is knowledge, there is purity, where there is falsehood, there is sin, where there is greed, there is death and where there is tolerance, there is God Himself (Shlok Kabir, p. 1372). Forgiveness is linked with tolerance. They are the godly attributes and can be practised by human beings. If one puts the mind under the discipline of the true Guru and imbibes the quality of tolerance, his search is rewarded and he drinks the nectar (Ramkali M. 1, Dakhni Oamkar, p. 932). The anger dies down with tolerance (Gauri M. 3, p. 233). If one observes the fast of tolerance, good conduct and contentment, he will never experience an illness or the agony of death (Gauri M. 1, p. 223).

Tolls: "Toll" is a general term for a definite payment exacted by the state or local authority, by virtue of sovereignty, for permission to pass somewhere, do some act or perform some function. See: *Taxes*.

Tombs: Monuments erected to cover the dead bodies and thus preserve the memory of the dead. Guru Ram Das says, "The unwise agnostics are strayed by suspicion and thus deluded, they make the offerings of flowers to their gods. They worship the lifeless things and tombs and in this way waste their precious human birth" (Malar M. 4, p. 1264). According to Guru Nanak Dev, the Yoga cannot be practised at the crematoriums and the tombs (Basant M. 1, p. 1190).

Tonsure: The shaving of the head as a religious practice. The *Adi Granth* lays emphasis on "Sābat-Sūrat Dastār Sirā" (the completeness of form and a turban on the head), therefore it is against the removal of hair in any way or at any cost. Thus the rite or ceremony of tonsure is rejected.

Topes: (*stupas*). In India and south-eastern Asia, an ancient structure in the form of a dome, for the preservation of relics. This word "*tope*" is of Buddhist origin. See: *Stupas*.

Tortoise: A four-footed reptile, which lives both in water and on earth. Kabir has made a mention of this animal in a very queer way. He says, "Listen to me, O saints, the ant has eaten up a mountain and the tortoise says that he needs the live-coals also (besides water). Listen, I have uttered the word full of mystery" (Asa Kabir, p. 477). By these verses, Kabir conveys the idea that with the Grace of the Lord, the impossible becomes possible.

Touch: One of the five senses, the other four being the sense of sight, the sense of hearing, the sense of taste and the sense of smell. Its sense-organ is the skin. The lust is created by the sense of touch and the elephant is destroyed by this sense (Asa Ravidas, p. 486). Kabir says, "O mad mind, such is the play of the Lord. The fake frame of a she-elephant makes the he-elephant fall into the trap because of lust" (Gauri Kabir, p. 335).

Toys: The children pass their time in playing with toys. They are ignorant about the objective of life. Guru Arjan Dev says, "In your childhood, you were ignorant and blind" (Ramkali M. 5, p. 889). Guru Nanak Dev says "If one dies as a child, his sports are remembered. While crying, the relatives say, "How playful, joyous and beautiful was he" (Maru M. 1, p. 1027).

Trade: They who trade in the Name of the Lord, are priceless, the customers are priceless and the purchase is priceless. The dealers are priceless, their treasures are priceless. Their weights and measures are priceless (Japuji, p. 5). One is a trader only if he gets some profit (Asa Kafi M. 1, p. 418). Guru Nanak Dev addresses the traders in this way, "O traders, trade in true merchadise. Only the lasting goods be purchased" (Sri Rag M. 1, p. 22). Store your ever-decreasing age with the Name of the Lord. Let concentration and reason be the godowns, where the Lord's Name be gathered. The dealings may only be with the saints of the Lord, so that the profit of bliss may be reaped. Let the hearing of the sacred books be your trade; the horses of truth may be loaded with your merchandise (Sorath M. 1, p. 595).

Tradition: A statement, belief or practice transmitted orally from generation to generation. Guru Ram Das says, "O saints, show me the way towards the Lord, which I have to follow. I cherish in my heart the Words of my Lord, this then becomes the right tradition for me. (Devgandhari M. 4, p. 527). Guru Arjan Dev says, "One may have vast riches, glory, culture and tradition, and love of the parents, sons, brothers and friends and men in arms salute him gently —but if he does not remember the Lord, he suffers in hell (Sri Rag M. 4, pp. 70-71). Sheikh Farid says, "O prayerless dog, this is not the right tradition that you do not come to the mosque five times a day" (Shlok Farid, p. 1381). The mind is like a bird and according to its deeds, it becomes good and bad. Sometimes it sits on the sandalwood and sometimes on the poisonous tree. Sometimes it is attuned to the highest tradition—the Lord drives it all under His Will (Var Majh M. 1, p. 148).

Trai Gun: Three modes; three qualities, which constitute *maya*. See: *Modes* and *Maya*.

Trai Vidya: This term is applied collectively for the three Vedas, i.e. Rig Veda, Sama Veda and the Yajur Veda. It connotes the learning of the three Vedas. Such learning has not been commended in the *Adi Granth*. "By reading the Vedas, the egocentrics taste not the taste of the Real" (Majh M. 3, p. 128). One reads the Vedas, but always has strife in the mind (Maru M. 3, p. 1066).

Trance: A state of mental abstraction from external things; absorption; exaltation; ecstasy. Guru Arjan Dev says, "The saints are not affected by delusion and fear and are not caught in the web of *maya*. By the Grace of the Lord, they enter into abstract trance" (Ramkali M. 5, p. 889). When in abstract trance, one hears the unstruck music, which cannot be expressed, so wondrous is its ecstasy" (Gauri Sukhmani M. 5, p. 293).

Tranquillity: Serenity; calmness; peace. Guru Nanak Dev says, "The Shastras and Smritis lay stress on the Name of the Lord. The *Gurmukh*, who performs this sublime action, abides in tranquillity and peace (Bilawal M. 1, p. 831). The *Gurmukh* (God-conscious) is ever in tranquillity and peace, because he always enshrines the Name of the Lord in his heart (Maru M. 3, p. 1055).

Transmigration: Passage of the soul at death into another body. According to the law of Karma in Hinduism, Jiva experiences births and deaths repeatedly by performing actions under the influence of *maya* and ego. This view has been accepted in the *Adi Granth*. The theories of Karma and Transmigration are inter-linked. Jiva experiences bondage, when it enters the field of actions. Every action enchains the human being further. All the physical forms through which the soul passes, are hells. Thus there are eighty-four lakhs of hells. The angels of death take away the sinner before the god of justice (*Dharma Rājā*). The scribes Chitra and Gupta are asked to give an account of the virtuous and sinful acts respectively. The description of hell is Pauranic, through which the Gurus and the saint-poets of the *Adi Granth* wanted to create the hatred in the minds of the individuals against bad deeds and inculcate in them the devotion of the Lord, making it quite clear that even the works performed according to Shastras, could not get the release of the individual self. Transmigration ceases with the exhaustion of desire and remembrance of the Name of the Lord. Guru Arjan Dev says, "The fear of births and deaths ceases with the perfect knowledge imparted by the Perfect Man (Guru). We stray no more, our wanderings cease..." (Gauri Sukhmani M. 5, p. 287).

Travelling: After death, the soul is said to make a journey to the other world. This journey is described by Guru Arjan Dev in the following manner: "The journey, whose mileage cannot be measured, the Name of the Lord sustains the soul in it. The Name of the Lord enlightens it. The path on which there is no acquaintance, the Name of the Lord is the recognition. Where there is wilderness, heat and fire, the Name of the Lord gives the shade. Where the mind is torn by thirst, there the Name of the Lord makes the rain of nectar (Gauri Sukhmani M. 5, p. 264). Even we reach the present birth after a long travel. "Without beauty, wisdom and power, I, the stranger have come from afar. I have neither riches nor pride of youth. I am without support. Merge me, O Lord, within yourself" (Gauri Purbi M. 5, p. 204).

Treasure-Trove: For the devotee, the Name of the Lord is the Treasure-Trove, which the Lord has given to him Himself (Gauri Sukhmani M. 5, p. 265). The Truth is in the Treasure-Trove of the Lord (Suhi M. 5, p. 746).

Trees: The names of some trees have been used figuratively in the *Adi Granth.* The fragrant sandalwood symbolises goodness. Kabir says, "blessed is the Chandan tree, which has been surrounded by *Dhāk Palās* (useless plants), but they having grown near Chandan, become fragrant like Chandan; but no one should become egoistic like bamboo, because though it lives near Chandan, it does not become fragrant (Shalok Kabir, p. 1365). Here bamboo symbolises ego. Another symbol of ego is the *Simmal* tree (Var Asa M. 1, p. 470). The mythological *Pārjāt* tree, which fulfils the wishes of the people, has also been mentioned in the *Adi Granth.* (Basant M. 5, p. 1280). The shade of the trees is a symbol for the short span of life (Gauri Sukhmani M. 5, p. 268).

Tretā Age: Out of the four ages, *Tretā* is the second age, the other three being Satyuga, Dvapara and Kaliyuga. The saint Ravidas says, "In Satyuga, Truth reigned supreme, in Tretā charity, in Dvāpara worship in righteousness. In the three ages, men had such conduct but in Kaliyuga, the only prop is the Name of the Lord (Gauri Bairagan Ravidas, p. 346). According to Guru Arjan Dev, people look upon

Satyuga, Tretā and Dvaparā as great, but Kaliyuga is the greatest, because in this age one reaps only, what he has sown. None is answerable for another (Asa M. 5, p. 406). In the Tretā age, continence is the chariot and the power is the charioteer (Var Asa M. 1, p. 470). The Tretā age was supported by three legs of *Dharma*. Men were then egoistic and considered the Lord far away (Ramkali M. 3, p. 880). In the Tretā and Dvāpara Yugas, one who was rid of ego was rare (Bhairo M. 3, p. 1131).

Trial: That which puts one to the test. Guru Nanak Dev says, "He, the wise lord, puts every one on trial (Maru M. 1, p. 1032).

Trikutī: The confluence of the three channels *Irā, Pingalā* and *Sushumnā*, located between the eyebrows. This word occurs in the *Adi Granth* in the hymn of saint Beni.

Trimūrtī: The Trinity. In Hinduism, this word is used collectively for three gods i.e. Brahma, Vishnu and Shiva. In the *Adi Granth*, these three gods have been mentioned together several times. These gods are in the grip of three modes and act with a sense of 'mineness' (Suhi M. 4, p. 735). *Maya* has pierced through the hearts of Brahma, Vishnu and Shiva (Gaund Kabir, p. 872). Before the creation of the world, the Trinity was not there. And when it was the Will of the Lord, He brought the universe into being. He Created Brahma, Vishnu and Shiva (Maru M. 1, pp. 1035-36). Brahma, Vishnu and Shiva are sublime only if they meditate on the Name of the Lord and are absorbed in it (Maru M. 1, p. 1013). Brahma, Vishnu and Shiva stand at the Glorious Door of the Lord (Maru M. 1, p. 1022).

Trishnā: Desire; Thirst. *Trishnā* is a great malady, which makes us forget death (Ramkali M. 3, Anand, p. 919). *Maya* has spread its net, wherein the bait is placed. The bird of *Trishnā* has been caught in this net and it cannot escape, O mother (Sri Rag M. 5, p. 50). Whether young or old, the *Trishnā* of egocentrics is not stilled (Var Sorath M. 4, Shlok M. 3, p. 649). The land-owner fights over his land always; though he has to leave it, but still his *Trishnā* is not stilled (Gauri M. 5, p. 188). The *Trishnā* is stilled only with the Name of the Lord (Dhanasari M. 5, p. 682). Burnt down by *Trishnā*, the world cries; if it meets the peace-giving True Guru, it is not burnt again (Var Vadhans M. 4, Shlok M. 3, p. 588).

True: Only the Lord is True. He was True in the beginning, True in the beginning of Yugas (ages); He is True in the present and also shall be True (in future) (Japuji, p. 1). The world is the Abode of the True One

(Var Asa M. 1, Shalok M. 2, p. 463). Addressing the Lord, Guru Nanak Dev says, "True are Your Created regions and True are Your universes. True are Your *lokas* (the regions) and their forms...True is Your Will, True is Your Speech. True is Your Grace...They who dwell on Truth are also True" (Var Asa M. 1, p. 463).

Trust: (Property). The condition of having confidence reposed in one, or of being entrusted with something. Guru Amar Das says, "One should pass on another's trust to the one to whom it belongs. There is utter joy in it" (Var Sarang M. 4, Shlok M. 3, p. 1249). Guru Arjan Dev says, "The king bestows his myriad gifts and the recipient enjoys them in joy and peace. If he takes back the things we hold in trust, only the fool grieves over it (Gauri Sukhmani M. 5, p. 268).

Truth: The Truth is the Lord of all and he alone attains it, who is Blessed by the Lord (Ramkali M. 3, Anand, p. 992). He alone merges in Truth, who looks upon the Lord as Truth (Gauri Sukhmani M. 5, p. 283). The Truth never gets old (Var Ramkali M. 3, Shalok M. 1, p. 955). Truth is obtained through the Word of the Guru, which removes all sufferings (Sri Rag M. 3, p. 36). The meritorious one attains the Truth, abundoning the *Trishnā* (desires and vices) (Sri Rag M. 3, p. 36). He whom the Lord Blesses with Truth, practises Truth (Var Asa M. 1, p. 467). We know the Truth, when the heart is True...When we Love the Truth...When our soul knows the way...and when we receive the True instruction (Var Asa M. 1, p. 468). The Truth is obtained, when we become pure (Var Asa M. 1, p. 472).

Truthfulness: Truth is the highest, but truthfulness is still higher (Sri Rag M. 1, p. 62). All the four Vedas are truthful. Those who read and reflect on them, know the distinction between merit and demerit (Var Asa M. 1, p. 470). The truthful devotees serve the Guru well and the false ones do not get an opportunity, even if they try hard (Var Gauri M. 4, pp. 304-05). Those who have turned God-wards are acclaimed as Truthful at the True Gate and Merge in the True Lord (Vadhans M. 3, p. 565). Guru Amar Das says, "I am a sacrifice to those, who are found truthful in the True Court" (Sri Rag M. 3, p. 35).

Truths: The four noble truths. The four noble truths, according to Buddhism are: 1-That there is suffering, 2-That there is cause of suffering, 3-That there is cessation of suffering, and 4-That there is a way leading to the cessation of suffering. According to Buddhist *Suttas*, when these noble truths are grasped and known, the craving for existence is rooted out, that which leads to renewed existence is destroyed, and then there is no more birth. The *Adi Granth* is quite in agreement with the four noble truths, but the way leading to the cessation of suffering is quite different from the Buddhist way. The goal of Buddhism is the end of all desire and the attainment of *Arhathood*, but the goal of the follower of the religion of the *Adi Granth* is the merger in the Absolute through the discipline of the Name ordained by the Guru. Guru Amar Das says, "The God-conscious persons, who are absorbed in the Name of the Lord, are emancipated, dwelling on the Word of the Guru. They are emancipated even in this life, while contemplating on the Name and Cherish the Lord in their hearts. Their body, mind and speech become immaculate. They realise the One and the Only One Lord" (Malar M. 3, p. 1250).

Turiyā Avasthā: The Supreme spiritual state. See: *Chauthā Pad.*

Turks: One is considered a Turk (Muslim) if he follows the discipline of Islam. One is considered a Hindu, if he follows the Vedas and the Puranas (Gauri Purbi Bawan Akhri Kabir, p. 340). In the time of Atharva Veda in Kaliyuga, Allah became the Name of God. The Lord Decked Himself in Blue Clothes and assumed the practices of a Turk and a Pathan (Var Asa M. 1, p. 470). The same Lord is my *Gosāin* and the same is my Allah. I have found release from the Hindus as well as from the Turks (Bhairo M. 5, p. 1136).

Tutelary Spirits: gods; the spirits containing supernatural powers, having the position of Protector, Guardian or Patron. The *Adi Granth* does not recognise such gods and goddesses. Guru Nanak Dev says, "One worships gods and goddesses. What can one ask from them and what can they give? If the idols of these gods are washed in water, they sink there and then (Sorath M. 1, p. 637).

U

Udāna: Out of the five *Prānas* (breaths), this is the ascending breath which is in the heart, throat, palate and skull. Through its action, the contents of the stomach are ejected through the mouth. In the state of *Samādhi*, this vital breath carries the finite self to the head. Guru Nanak Dev says, "He who has the *Prānas* within him, why should he forget the Lord?" (Var Asa M. 1, p. 474). There is no separate mention of *Udāna* in the *Adi Granth*.

Uddam: Effort. Effort is necessary for every achievement and even for the attainment of the Grace of the Lord. "There is happiness in mind, when effort is made; the remembrance of the Name of the Lord results in peace and comfort"(Bilawal M. 5, p. 815). "While living make efforts and through efforts earn comfort and happiness. Meet the Lord by remembering His Name; all your sorrows and sufferings will end" (Var Gaujri M. 5, p. 522).

Udāsī: The condition of being non-attached; one who is non-attached. "One should remain always non-attached in his home like the lotus in the water" (Maru M. 4, p. 1070). "On meeting the Guru, the Name is obtained, which removes the thirst of attachment. The mind is absorbed in the Lord and (the devotee) remains non-attached in his home" (Sri Rag M. 1, p. 26).

Unbelief: Disbelief; incredulity. Those who close their eyes in unbelief for contemplation, their false sense of ego will wear off (Suhi M. 4, p. 734).

Unbelievers: Heretics. He who is unbeliever, burns in his own inner fire (Var Majh M. 1, p. 142). See: *Heretics*.

Unborn: The Lord Who is ONE, Ever-Existent, Creator, without Fear and Enmity, Immortal, He is also Unborn and Self-Existent (Japuji, p.1). Guru Ram Das says, "I am ignorant and unwise, I seek Your Refuge, O my Unborn Lord" (Bilawal M. 4, p. 799).

Unchastity: Impurity. Guru Nanak Dev says, "My mind was unchaste and I was full of demerits without the Guru, no virtue was imbibed by me" (Suhi M.1, p.1763). The unchaste becomes chaste, if it comes into contact with the philosopher's stone i.e. the Guru (Maru M. 1, p. 1012). This whole world is unchaste and unclean, it is only the Infinite Lord, Who is Chaste and Immaculate (Bhairo Kabir, p. 1158).

Uncreated: The whole expanse and the universe has been Created by the Lord, but the Lord Himself is Uncreated and Immortal. Several times this expanse was created, but the One Uncreated Absolute Lord always existed there (Gauri Sukhmani M. 5, p. 276).

Understanding: Intelligence; Judgment. The power of discrimination between right and wrong. According to *Bhagavad Gita*, the five *Prānas*, speech, mind and understanding make up the eight constituents of the universe. However, the Supreme Self is not reached by understanding. Guru Arjan Dev says, "No understanding and cleverness works with the Lord. Whatever He Judges to be right, that alone happens (Gujri M. 5, p. 496). Shed all your understandings and take to the Feet of the Guru" (Sri Rag M. 5, p. 44). The ignorance has been changed into understanding (wisdom), because my Lord is the Knower and Seer (Bilawal M. 5, p. 823).

Undeveloped (Unevolved): Its equivalent in Sanskrit is *Avyaktam*, which connotes the Unevolved and the Unperceived principle. Guru Arjan Dev says, "When the Undeveloped, Incomprehensible Lord was One Alone, then from whom did Chitra and Gupta ask for the account?" (Gauri Sukhmani M. 5, p. 291).

Ungrateful: The ungrateful people forget the Lord and undergo transmigration (Var Jaitsri M. 5, p. 706). None can save the ungrateful person, he is cast into the deep hell (Maru M. 5, p. 1086).

Unity: Oneness; singleness. Guru Nanak Dev says, "Every one utters 'The Lord is One', but every one is afflicted by ego, but He who knows the Unity within and without, he feels the Presence of the Lord" (Ramkali M. 1, Dakhni Oamkar, p. 930). Guru Arjan Dev says "I have shed the sense of duality, because the Unity of the Lord Pervades All" (Bhairo M. 5, p. 1140).

Universal Soul: Brahman is the Universal Soul. He is both Manifested as well as Unmanifested (Gauri Sukhmani M. 5, p. 287). The Unmanifested Brahman is also called Higher Brahman (*Para Brahman*). Guru Arjan Dev says, "He the Infinite Lord is both Within and Without. He Pervades all hearts. He is on the Earth and in the sky and the underworld. He, the Perfect Preserver, is in all the worlds. He is in all vegetation and over the mountains. We act according to His Will. He is in the air, fire and water. He is in the four quarters and ten directions. There is no place without Him. Attain Peace through the Grace of the Guru (Gauri Sukhmani M. 5, p. 294). See: *Brahman*.

Universe: The whole of created or existing things regarded collectively. This world (universe) is the Dwelling-place of the True Lord (Var Asa M. 1, Shalok M. 2, p. 463). The Lord Himself is True and the created universe is also True (Gauri Sukhmani M. 5, p. 294). Whereas it is relatively real, it is also transitory and perishable. "O friend, know it that this world is false. It does not stay like the wall of sand" (Shlok M. 9, p. 1428). The universe Created by the Infinite Lord cannot be delimited. Guru Nanak Dev says, "There is no end to the physical world; there is no end to the Creation of the Lord (Japuji, p. 5). See: *World.*

Unman: The Supreme State. See: *Chauthā Pad.*

Unperceived: Undeveloped; Unmanifested; The Unmanifested Aspect of Brahman. Talking about the Attributes of the Lord, Guru Nanak Dev says, "He has neither form nor colour nor sign and is Revealed only through the True WORD" (Sorath M. 1, p. 597).

Unseen Principle: Its Sanskrit equivalent is *Adrishta.* According to Guru Amar Das, the eyes which see the Unseen and the mind which is attuned to the Unseeable are wonderstruck (Ramkali M. 3, p. 910). Through equipoise, the Unseen Lord is seen (Sri Rag M. 3, p. 68). By the Grace of the Guru, the eyes see the Unseen, the Imperceptible, the Unknowable and the Immaculate Lord (Var Sri Rag M. 4, p. 87).

Untruth: One who speaks untruth, usurps what does not belong to him (Var Majh M.1, p.140). Without the Lord, all is untruth (Var Asa M. 1, p. 467). The egocentric practises untruth, gathers untruth and eats nothing but untruth (Var Bihagra M. 4, Shlok M. 3, p. 552).

Upādāna: The material cause of the world. The unchanging substance or material of which all things are made. Like the gold and golden bracelet or the water and the waves, there is no difference between the Ātman and Brahman Himself. The saint Ravidas says, "Where is the difference between You and me, me and You. Is there any difference between the gold and the golden bracelet or the water and the waves (Sri Rag Ravidas, p. 93).

Upādhī: A limiting or determining adjunct of the soul. It is a distinguishing characteristic. It is a term of Vedantic philosophy denoting limitations imposed upon self or Brahman through ignorance. Shankaracharya has mentioned three *Upādhīs* regarding the human body: the gross body (*sthūla upādhī*), the subtle body (*sūkshama upādhī*) and the causal body (*kāraṇa upādhī*). Guru Arjan Dev says, "Rise early in the morning and meditate on the Name of the Lord and Dwell upon Him night and day, then you will not suffer any sorrow and all your *upādhīs* will dwindle away (Gauri Bawan Akhri M. 5, p. 255). *Upādhī* is thus a woe caused by ignorance.

Upānāyana: One of the significant sacraments in Hinduism. It is the initiation ceremony, in which *dvija* (twice-born—a term used for Brahmins, Kshatriyas, Vaishyas, who can be initiated) is initiated by a Guru. It is the ceremony of the sacred thread and is called *Yajnopavīta*. The sacred thread is worn over the right shoulder, which hangs down over the left. Guru Nanak Dev has criticised the ceremony in this way, "O Pundit, put the sacred thread of the soul on me, if you have it. It has the cotton of compassion, the thread of contentment, the knot of continence and the twist of truth. It neither breaks nor gets dirty, nor burnt nor wasted. They are blessed who wear such a thread around their necks. Ordinarily the thread is bought for four *kaurīs* and the twice-born wears it in the sanctified square. The knowledge is whispered into his ears and the Brahmin becomes the Guru. But when the person dies, the thread is burnt to ashes and the dying person leaves for the next world without the thread" (Var Asa M. 1, p. 471).

Upanishad: This word has been split into three components i.e. *upa* (meaning near), *nī* (meaning down) and *sad* (meaning to sit), which implies "to sit down near (the spiritual teacher)". The spiritual teacher gives and the disciple receives the esoteric knowledge of mystic import. This knowledge pertains to the self and the Higher Self. The Upanishad-like experience is found in the *Adi Granth*. Guru Ram Das says, "If we tell the secret state of our soul to the Guru (teacher), we attain All-Bliss" (Var Bilawal M. 4, p. 850). Guru Arjan Dev says, "I have heard the mysterious gospel from the Guru" (Suhi M. 5, p. 739).

Upanishads: They are the final portion of the Vedas and form the foundation of the Vedantic philosophy. These scriptures, both in poetry and prose, are supposed to have been written in seventh or eighth centuries before Christ. They are said to be more than 200, but traditionally their number is 108. The best known Upanishads are *Īsa, Kena, Kaṭha, Prasana, Mundaka, Māndūkya, Taittiriya, Aitareya, Chandogya, Brhadaraṇyaka, Kaushītaki* and *Shvetashvatara*. Shankaracharya has written commentaries on eleven of the principal Upanishads. There has been great impact of the philosophy of Upanishads on the Gurus and saint-poets of the *Adi Granth*. For example we find a good deal of similarity in the thoughts of Kathopanishad and Asa Ki Var of Guru Nanak Dev. It is written in Kathopanishad: "Through Fear of Hari burns the fire, through Fear of Hari burns the sun, through Fear of Hari runs Indra, the wind and death." In the same strain Guru Nanak Dev says in *Asa Ki Var*: "Through Fear of Him the wind blows, through Fear of Him lakhs of rivers flow, through Fear of Him labours the fire, through Fear of Him the earth remains overburdened, through Fear of Him, Indra walks on his head, through Fear of Him, the *Dharma Raja* stands at His Gate (Var Asa M. 1, p. 464).

Upāsaka: A devotee; a worshipper. An *Upāsaka*, according to the *Adi Granth* is a *Bhakta* (devotee), whose worship of the Lord is the remembrance of the Name of the Lord. They may be called devotees, who are absorbed in Truth (Prabhati M. 1, p. 1342). They are liked by the Lord (Dhanasari M. 5, p. 677). A *Bhakta* is one, who looks upon pleasure and pain alike and is always imbued with the Name (Vadhans M. 4, p. 574). The devotees are always in Bliss and they blossom forth by singing the Praises of the Lord (Asa M. 5, p. 373). The devotee remains uninfluenced by *maya*, whereas the world burns in its secret fire (Dhanasari M. 5, p. 673). The Lord, through His Grace, Protects His devotees (Sri Rag M. 5, p. 46).

Upāsanā: Devout meditation; Worship; Devotion. Guru Arjan Dev says, "O my mind, worship the Lotus-Feet of the Lord (Gujri M. 5, p. 502). The *upāsanā* through works and other external means has been rejected in the *Adi Granth*. Guru Amar Das says, "The fool dances to worship and thus makes himself known, he dances in vain and suffers great agony. The Lord is not worshipped by dancing about. One who dies in the Word and thus worships the Lord is a rare devotee (Gauri Guareri M. 3, p. 150). The devout meditation of the Lord is the most difficult path. That person is rare one, who attains it at the Guru's Door. He on whom the Lord Showers His Grace, is devoted to the worship of the Lord (Asa M. 3, p. 440).

Updesh, Updeshak: *Updesh* is instruction and the one who instructs is *Updeshak*. "He, who instructs others and does not act upon it himself, he transmigrates repeatedly" (Gauri Sukhmani M. 5, p. 269). Those persons are blessed, who instruct for the good of others (Var Gauri M. 4, p. 311). "Firstly one should instruct his own mind and afterwards satisfy others" (Asa M. 5, p. 381).

Upkār: Doing good (to others); selfless service. See: *Service*, *Parupkār*.

Uprightness: Moral integrity; Rectitude. A man of fair dealings is an upright man. A devotee has to imbibe this virtue in life. Guru Nanak Dev says, The uprightness without Truth, is without any balance (Shlok Varan te Vadhik M. 1, p. 1412).

Urine: Guru Nanak Dev has used this word in a figurative way. "If a garment is polluted by urine, we wash it off by the use of soap. If our intellect is polluted by sins, it is only washed off by the love of the Name of the Lord (Japuji, p. 4).

Ushā: In Hindu mythology, *Ushā* is the goddess of the dawn. The word *Ushā*, therefore, connotes dawn. Though the word *Ushā* has not been used in the *Adi Granth*, some words suggestive of the dawn are *Poh phutnā*, *Amrit vela, sabāhi, Jhālānge*, *pichal rāt* and *parbhāt*. This time is considered to be the best for concentration and meditation. Guru Nanak Dev says, "Meditate at *Amrit velā* (ambrosial time) on the True Name" (Japuji, p. 12). The Sufi saint Sheikh Farid says, "If you do not awake in *pichal rāt* (the later part of the night), you will be like the dead, even though living" (Shlok Farid, p. 1383).

Ustat, Ustatī: Praise. See: *Praise*; *Eulogy*.

Usurer: A *usurer* is one who charges an excessive rate of interest. Kabir says, "Now I am not interested in the trade of the *usurer*, in which the interest increases and the capital shrinks (Basant Kabir, p.1195).

Usury: The practice of lending money at interest; the practice of charging excessive or illegal rate of interest for loan. Kabir says, "I put off each day the payment of the Debt of the Lord and the interest increases thereon" (Shalok Kabir p. 1375). Guru Ram Das says, "We trade each day to earn interest and when we earn interest, we are at peace; when we are in loss, our heart breaks (Gauri Bairagan M. 4, p. 166).

Utopia: An imaginary island enjoying a perfect social, legal and political system. Guru Arjan Dev says, "The saints neither seek wealth nor the pleasure of Paradise (Utopia)" (Gauri Bawan Akhri M. 5, p. 251).

Utpatī: Creation. See: *Creation*.

Uttara Mimaṁsā: Another name for Vedanta. The *Uttara Mimaṁsā Sutra* is said to have been written by Vyasa. It systematises *Giān Kānda*. It is the exposition of the later part of the Vedas and is also called *Brahm-Mimaṁsā* and *Vedanta*. See: *Vedanta*.

V

Vaddhī: Bribe. "The egocentrics take bribes and present themselves for false evidence" (Maru M. 5, p. 1032). "The judge (*Qadī*) accepts bribe and commits injustice. Whenever someone asks him about it, he reads out the scriptures" (Var Ramkali M. 3, Shlok M. 1, p. 951).

Vād Vivād: Strife. "One should not indulge in strife with anybody" (Bhairo Namdev, p. 1164). "There is none without strife and opposition. Show me any one, so that I may praise him" (Maru M. 1, p. 1025). "He searches for points of strife and does not concentrate on the Veda. When he drowns himself, how can he ferry across the manes?" (Ramkali M. 1, p. 904).

Vaid: The doctor; apothecary. "One can be called a wise doctor, if he diagnoses correctly the disease and the medicine (Var Majh M.1, Shlok M. 2, p. 148). "He is, indeed a Vaid, who diagnoses the patient correctly (Gujri M. 1, p. 503). "There is no true Vaid except the True Guru (Maru M. 3, p. 1016).

Vaikunṭha: It is the name of the sphere or paradise of Vishnu. It is said to be located either on the northern or eastern peak of Mount Meru or in the depths of the ocean. It is built of gold and precious stones. According to the *Adi Granth* the company of saints is *Vaikunṭha* (Paradise) of salvation, where one attains the Abode of the Lord. (Dhanasari M. 5, p. 682) Wherever the Name of the Lord is Uttered, that place is *Vaikunṭha* (Ramkali M. 5, p. 890). A true devotee has no desire of going to Vaikunṭha. Kabir says, "So long as one hopes to enter Vaikunṭha, he does not abide at the Feet of the Lord. To whom should I say this that the company of the saints is the real Vaikunṭha?" (Gauri Kabir, p. 325).

Vairāg: (*Vairāgya*). Dispassion; passionlessness. "When the Lord instiis His Fear in our heart, then the state of passionlessness is produced. On the attainment of passionlessness, one realises the Lord and remains Merged in Him" (Gujri M. 3, p. 490). One, who is passionless, is a *Vairāgī*. Guru Ram Das says, "Those, who are imbued with the Name of the Lord, they are the true *Vairāgīs* (Var Sarang M. 4, p. 1246). "If everyone desires, none can attain the state of passionlessness without the True Guru" (Maru Kabir, p. 1104). "There can be no *Vairāg* in duality" (Sorath M. 1, p. 634).

Vair Virodh: Enmity and opposition. "Those who listen to the singing of the Praises of the Lord, *Vair Virodh* is destroyed from their mind and body (Gauri Bawan Akhri M. 5, p. 259). "The God-conscious person (*Gurmukh*) destroys *vair virodh* (Ramkali M.1, Siddh Goshta, p. 942).

Vaishnava: A devotee of Vishnu. See: *Baisno*.

Vaishya: It is the trading class and the third of the three upper classes of the Hindu society, the other two being Brahmins and Kshatriyas. Besides trading, Vaisya's occupation is also cattle-breeding and agriculture. The *Adi Granth* preaches the equality of all human beings, therefore its instruction is meant for all the strata of society. Guru Ram Das says, "The instruction is common for all the four castes i.e. Brahmins, Kshatriyas, Vaishyas and Shudras" (Bilawal M. 4, p. 800).

Vaitaraṇī: It is the name of the mythological stream (or river), which flows between the earth and the nether-regions, which is crossed by the dead persons, while going to the abode of *Yama*. It is also called *Mahān Nadi*. In the *Adi Granth*, it is mentioned as *bikham nadī* (a stream hard to cross" (Jaitsri M. 5, p. 702).

Vāk: Speech. The word, the first creative representative of the Spirit. It is the means of communication between men and the gods. Guru Nanak Dev says, "The Word is the Guru, profound and serene. Without the Word, the world goes mad" (Sorath M. 1, p. 635). Guru Arjan Dev says, "I am a sacrifice to the Master, Who has fulfilled the *Vāk* (speech) of His devotee" (Bilawal M. 5, p. 825).

Vaṇaj: Trade. See: *Trade*.

Vānaprastha: Forest-dweller. It is the third of the four Hindu *Āshramas* (stages of life), when after living the life of a householder, one goes to the forest and leads an ascetic life. The other three *Āshramas* are Brahmacharya, Grahasthya and Sannyasa. Kabir says, "One abandons his home and goes to the forest, where he searches and eats the roots, but he does not forsake evil" (Bilawal Kabir, p. 855). Guru Ram Das says, "Forsaking the house, one became a forest-dweller, but he could not hold his mind even for a moment" (Bilawal M. 4, p. 835). In the *Adi Granth*, the three Āshramas i.e. Brahmacharya, Vanaprastha and Sannyasa have been rejected. See: *Āshramas*.

Vanity: Self-conceit and desire for admiration; that which is vain, futile and worthless. Guru Arjan Dev says, "Ordure, bones and blood wrapped up in skin, you are only this much, can this be the object of vanity?" (Asa M. 5, p. 374). "Why are you proud of the little vanities of life? Like the night-guest you shall depart in the morning, why are you then enticed away by your household? Your pleasure-garden will not stay for ever (Sri Rag M. 5, p. 50).

Vāmana: Dwarf. One of the incarnations of Vishnu. He is the fifth of the ten incarnations. He appeared as a dwarf before king Bali and asked for the grant of a piece of land, which could be traversed in three strides. The king agreed, but the dwarf-incarnation swelled himself to enormous size and with two strides, he landed on the head of the king, sending him down to the nether-world. For the magnanimous action of the king, he was made the king of the nether-world. In the *Adi Granth*, there is mention of the ten incarnations of Vishnu, which include the Vāmana incarnation. Guru Nanak Dev says, "The Lord Created ten incarnations under His Will (Maru M. 1, p. 1037).

Varaṇ: Caste. See: *Caste*.

Vart: (*Vrat*). See: *Vrata*.

Vāsūdeva: *Vāsūdeva* is the Name of the Lord. It became prevalent with the propagation of *Krishna-Vāsūdeva* cult, which is said to have remained popular from the fourth to the first century BC In his verses Guru Nanak Dev has used this Name of Brahman or the Supreme Soul. He says, "Vāsūdeva, the Supreme Īshvara Created the universe to witness it. He Sees it and Knows everything and Pervades Within and Without (Asa M. 1, Patti, p. 434). Guru Arjan Dev says, "*Vāsūdeva* is All-Pervading, nothing is without Him" (Gauri Bawan Akhri M. 5, p. 259).

Vāyū: Air; Wind. One of the five gross elements, the other four being ether, fire, water and earth. Guru Nanak Dev says, "From the True Lord came the Air (*Vāyū*), from the air came water and from the water sprang the three worlds" (Sri Rag M. 1, p. 19). *Vāyū* is the evolute from ether and the fire is the evolute from air. This process of evolutes could not be mentioned in the small couplet of Guru Nanak Dev. The world is composed of five elements. Guru Ram Das says, "O Lord, You Created the whole world out of five elements, let anyone try his hand with the sixth, if he can (Suhi M. 4, p. 736). The body is composed of five elements (Shlok M. 9, p. 1426). The Wind blows in the Fear of the Lord (Var Asa M. 1, p. 464). "Air is the Guru, water, the father and earth, the mother" (Japuji, p. 8). *Vāyū* created *Shabda*, therefore it is called the Guru, because *Shabda* is the Guru. *Prāna* (the vital air, breath) is identified with *Vāyū*.

Veda: Veda is a Sanskrit word, which means knowledge. This term was applied to four collections of hymns (*Samhitās*) called Vedas, because they contain "supreme sacred knowledge". These Vedas are: Rig Veda, Sama Veda, Yajur Veda and Atharva Veda. Each Veda contains four parts:1-*Samhitā*, the hymns, 2-*Brahmana*, containing rituals, 3-*Aranyaka*, the forest treatise, and 4-*Upanishad*, which contains esoteric knowledge. The first two portions are collectively called *Karma Kānda*, the third *Upāsana Kānda* and the fourth *Giān Kānda*. The *Adi Granth* has rejected the *Karma Kānda* and *Upāsana Kānda*, but it has close affinity with *Giān Kānda*. Guru Amar Das says, "Though Brahma revealed the hymns of Vedas, but he himself was involved in *maya*" (Vadhans M. 3, p. 559). Kabir says, "Do not call the Vedas and the Semitic texts as false; only he is false, who does not give thought to them" (Prabhati Kabir, p. 1350). Since the Guru is the store-house of knowledge, therefore the Veda (knowledge) is within his mouth (Japuji, p. 2).

Vedānta: Its two components *Veda* and *Anta* connote the final portion of the Veda. Thus *Vedanta* is a philosophical system based upon Upanishads, which form the final part of the Vedas. It is the second part of Mimāṁsā and is called *Uttara Mimāṁsā* or *Brahm Mimāṁsā*. Besides the teachings in the Upanishads, Vedanta also includes the teachings embodied in *Brahm Sutras* and the *Bhagavad Gita*. All the three works are collectively known as *Prasthāna Treyī*. There are three main schools of Vedanta viz., *Advaita* (non-dualism), *Vishishtadvaita* (qualified non-dualism) and *Dvaita* (dualism), which have been founded by Shankaracharya (AD 788-820), Ramanuj-acharya (AD 1017-1137) and Madhvacharya (AD 1199-1276) respectively. The philosophy of the *Adi Granth* is close to the thought enunciated by Ramanujacharya.

Vedānta Sutra: *Brahm Sutra* or *Sarīraka Sutra* (between 500 BC and 200 BC). It consists mainly of an exposition of the doctrines of Brahman. It contains brief aphorisms, each of two or three words, whose different interpretations have been given by various commentators, chief of them being Shankaracharya, Ramanujacharya and Madhvacharya. See: *Vedanta*.

Vedānta Texts: These texts are Upanishads. Brahman is the uniform topic of all the Upanishads. They teach that the cause of the world is Brahman. The nature of the Highest Self is depicted in them. Some of the Upanishads teach the unity of the individual soul with the Highest Self. The Upanishads not only impart knowledge, but also give injunctions on meditation. There is closeness of thought between the *Adi Granth* and the Upanishads. Both are called *Brahm Bānī*. See: *Upanishads*.

Vedāntins: Those who have faith in the religion and philosophy of the Vedas. Since the *Adi Granth* rejects *Varnas* and *Ashramas* of the Vedāntists and the *Karma Kānda* and *Upasanā Kānda* of the Vedas, a disciple of the religion of the *Adi Granth* has nothing in common with a Vedantin except the closeness in the doctrine of Brahman.

Vedī: Altar; the sacrificial ground, an elevated or excavated piece of ground serving for a sacrificial altar. It has receptacles for the sacrificial fire. The Hindus believe that gods descend into the altar. Since the *Adi Granth* rejects all the rituals, the construction of a *vedī* also stands rejected. See: *Hom, Haoma.*

Vehicles: (Yāna). A vehicle is a means by which ideas or impressions are communicated e.g. there are two main vehicles in Buddhism: the Greater Vehicle or Mahāyāna and the Lesser Vehicle or *Hinayāna*. But in another sense, it is a means of conveyance used for the carriage of persons or goods. In this sense, the gods and goddesses in Hinduism have their particular vehicles. The vehicle of Vishnu is Garuda, the vehicle of Shiva is the bull Nandī. Their mention has been made in the *Adi Granth.*

Veils: A veil is an article of attire worn, especially by women, over the head or face; something which conceals, covers or hides. Guru Arjan Dev addresses the Lord thus: "O Lord, when I seek Your Refuge, I am always in peace and by the Grace of the Guru, my veil of doubt is torn" (Asa M. 5, p. 385). Between the Lord and me is a fine veil like the wings of a butterfly, but without seeing Him, I consider him afar (Sorath M. 5, p. 624).

Veins: Speaking about the body, the saint Ravidas says, "The body consists of the wall of water, with the pillar of wind and the plaster of ovary and sperm. The skeleton is made up of bones, flesh and veins, in this (house) lives the poor soul-bird" (Sorath Ravidas, p. 659).

Velā: The time. *Amrit velā* (the ambrosial time of early morning) should be utilised for the remembrance of the True Name of the Lord (Japuji, p. 1). All that time is good, when the Love of the True Lord occupies my mind (Majh M. 3, p. 115). That time has the Approval of the Lord, when we meet the True Guru (Var Gujri M. 5, p. 520).

Veracity: Habitual observance of the Truth. Guru Amar Das says, "Those who are purified by veracity, their glory is True" (Asa M. 3, p. 426). Those who are purified by veracity, their soul merges in the Over-Soul (Var Sorath M. 4, Shlok M. 3, p. 645).

Vetāla: A kind of ghost, demon or ghoul, who frequents burial-grounds and is said to have the power of reanimating the dead. In the *Adi*

Granth, egocentrics and heretics are identified with *Vetāla*. Guru Nanak Dev says, "O Saviour Lord, Kindly Protect me; without Knowing You, we become like animals and *vetāla*" (Gauri M. 1, p. 224). Guru Amar Das says, "The ambrosia is within him, but the fool searches for it outside; the blind egocentric gropes like *vetāla* (Majh M. 3, p. 117).

Viāpaktā: Pervasiveness; All-Pervasiveness of the Lord. See: *Omnipresence.*

Vices: The chief vices considered in Indian religious literature including the *Adi Granth* are five. They are *Kāma* (lust), *Karodha* (anger), *Lobh* (greed), *Moh* (attachment) and *Ahamkāra* (ego). Guru Amar Das says, "Five thieves who live within this body are lust, anger, greed, attachment and ego. They rob us of ambrosia, but the egocentrics do not understand it and no one listens to their cries" (Sorath M. 3, p. 600). Guru Arjan Dev says, "I am in the Refuge of the Lord; Bless me, O Gurudeva with your Grace, so that the lust, anger, greed, attachment and ego may be destroyed" (Gauri Sukhmani M. 5, p. 269). Four vices including violence, attachment, greed and anger have been mentioned as the four streams of fire (Var Majh M. 1, p. 147).

Vidyā: (*Vidiā*). Knowledge. There are two types of *Vidyā*: *Parā vidyā* or spiritual knowledge and *aparā vidyā* or worldly knowledge. The Indian saints and mystics consider *parā vidyā* as the real *vidyā*. According to Guru Nanak Dev, if one understands the real *vidyā*, he becomes a philanthropist (Asa M. 1, p. 356). He who dwells on real *vidyā* by the Grace of the Guru, becomes glorious with such learning. (Prabhati M. 1, p. 1329). He who sells this *vidyā* for the sake of *maya*, loses the merit in his life (Maru Kabir, p. 1103).

Vignāna: Knowledge of various arts and sciences. But in the context of the *Adi Granth*, it means spiritual knowledge. The *tadbhava* formation of this word has been used by Guru Nanak Dev as *vigiān*. The Guru says, "Even if a Yogi wears a quartz ear-ring, with his knowledge and understanding, he cannot attain emancipation" (Ramkali M. 1, p. 903).

Vihāras: Buddhist monasteries. Since monasticism has been rejected by the *Adi Granth*, being a type of asceticism, this word does not find a mention therein.

Vijog: Separation. See: *Sanjog.*

Vikāsa: Expansion (of intelligence); development. The *vikāsa* (development of a devotee) in *Sadh Sangat* (company of the saints), under the guidance of the injunctions of the Guru has been mentioned in the

Adi Granth. Guru Nanak Dev says, "*Gurmukh* (God-Conscious Person) remembers the Name of the Lord, bestows gifts on the needy and achieves purity of mind and body. He is attuned to the Lord in the state of equipoise. He is honoured in the Court of the Lord. He realises the Supreme Being, Who is the Destroyer of fear. He works under the Will of the Lord. Having been United, he unites others with the Lord." (p. 942, Ramkali M. 1, Siddh Goshta).

Violence: Use of force. See: *Himsā.*

Virtues: Qualities; unusual ability, merit or distinction. The *Adi Granth* lays great emphasis on moral qualities in an individual. God as Ishvara is a treasure-house of qualities. He who practises these qualities, becomes godlike. According to Guru Nanak Dev, devotion is not possible without qualities (p. 4, Japuji). The five major vices can be overcome with the practice of five virtues. Lust can be overcome with self-control, anger with toleration, greed with contentment, worldly affection with devotion to duty and ego with modesty. According to Guru Nanak Dev "From the toilet-box of virtues, the fragrance should be taken out" (p. 766, Suhi M. 1). The beauty-aids, according to Guru Arjan Dev are truth, contentment, mercy and piety (p. 812, Bilawal M. 5). With the armour of qualities and virtues, the devotee enters the field of action like a disciplined soldier and no enemy can stay long before him.

Vishnu: One of the gods of Trinity, the other two being Brahma and Shiva. He works as Preserver and represents *Sattva.* For Vaishnavas, he is the Supreme Being. He descends to the earth in various incarnations in order to save mankind from suffering. Rama and Krishna are his chief incarnations. Guru Arjan Dev says, "There are millions of incarnated Vishnus" (p. 455, Asa M. 5). The Lord Created millions of Vishnus (p. 1156, Bhairo M. 5). Vishnu is engaged in reincarnating himself (p. 559, Vadhans M. 3). Vishnu and other gods of Trinity are deceived by *Maya* (p. 480, Asa Kabir).

Vishva: The world. According to Guru Amar Das, this *Vishva* or the world, that you see, is the Manifestation of the Lord (p. 922, Ramkali M. 3, Anand).

Vishva Devas: All the gods of the world. The *Adi Granth* has rejected all the gods, even the highest ones of the Trinity. The Hindus believe in and worship thirty-three crores of gods. "The thirty-three crores of gods seek the Lord" (p. 130, Majh M. 5). "O Lord, the thirty-three crores of gods beg of You and You Bless them" (p. 504, Gujri M. 1).

"The thirty-three crores of gods, alongwith Indra, will pass away" (p. 1100, Var Maru M. 5). "All gods and goddesses are lured away by *Maya*" (p. 227, Gauri M. 1). "The source of all the gods and goddesses is *Maya*" (p. 129, Majh M. 3). What can we demand of the gods and goddesses, whom we worship and what can they give? The stone-gods when washed in water, sink in it (p. 637, Sorath M. 1).

Vishvās: Faith. He who has Faith in the Lord in his heart, there arises the essence of knowledge in his mind (Gauri Sukhmani M. 5, p. 285). Those who have True Faith in their minds, they are always in Bliss, while visualising the Glory of the Lord (Dhanasari M. 5, p. 677). *Sidak* and *Partīt* are other equivalents used for *vishvās* in the *Adi Granth.*

Vismād: Wonder. This word is used in a state of ecstasy. When one sees the wonderful structure and nature of the world, the wonder expressed by him in a state of spiritual ecstasy is called *vismād.* Guru Nanak Dev says, "The sound, knowledge, differences in beings, form, colour, nakedness of beings, air, water, fire, earth, divisions of creation, different tastes, conjunction, separation, hunger, enjoyment etc. all lead me to the state of *vismad* (Var Asa M. 1, pp. 463-64). "Those who Comprehend the Lord and attain the Pleasure of His Sight, they are in the profound ecstatic state of *Vismād* (Gauri M. 5, p. 285). The Lord Himself is called *Vismādī.*

Vital Air: Prana or the breath of life. "The Lord is the Giver of vital air, mind, body and soul. (p. 249, Gauri M. 5). Of what avail is the blessing of the ocean, when the vital air leaves? (p. 858, Bilawal Sadhna). Just as we see the shade of the tree, similar is the case with *Maya.* It goes not alongwith one, when the vital air passes away (p. 325, Gauri Kabir). The vital air is not to be confused with breathing or respiration. It is considered to act from the vital body (*Pranamaya Kosha*) upon the organs of the dense body, which are dependent upon it, but it is itself dependent upon the higher *Koshas.*

Vital Airs: Prāṇas. The Pranas function in different directions throughout the human and animal body. There are five vital airs, the chief of which is *Prāna*, which connotes the respiration through nose and mouth. The other Pranas are: *apāna*, the respiration which goes downwards, *samāna*, the central circulation, which works from the cavity of the navel, *udāna,* the breathing out, rising to the throat and head and *vyāna*, that which works through the whole body. Guru Nanak Dev says, "Why should we forsake Him, Who has given us

Prāṇas and soul (p. 16, Sri Rag M. 1). "The Lord Whose immense Light is within us, has given us life and Prānas (p. 140, Var Majh M. 1). "The Lord Who has blessed us with the body and vital airs (Prāṇas)... Why should we forsake him..." (p. 233, Gauri Bairagan M. 3).

Vivek, Vivekī: *Vivek* is knowledge and *Vivekī* is one who has the knowledge. See: *Giān, Giānī.*

Voice: Sound emitted from the human larynx in speaking, singing or other utterance. Guru Nanak Dev says, "The lovers are united by the sweet voice (speech)" (p. 143, Var Majh M. 1). Guru Arjan Dev says, "O Lord, Which of Your Merits should be sung? With what Voice (words) You are pleased?" (p. 187, Gauri M. 5). Namdev says, "O Lord, how beautiful is Your Turban, how sweet is Your Voice?" (p. 727, Tilang Namdev).

Void: An absolutely empty space. In Indian philosophical terminology, it is called *Shūnya*. *Shūnyavāda* is one of the most important schools of Buddhism. The followers of the Middle Path or Madhyamikas belong to this school. According to them, *Shūnya* is not 'empty void', it means 'indescribable'. The world and the Absolute both are *Shūnya*, because the world is neither existent nor non-existent and the Absolute is transcendental. Thus everything is *Shūnya*. In his poem *Siddha Goshta*, Guru Nanak Dev has elucidated his concept of *Shūnya*. According to him there is *Shūnya* inside and in the three worlds, but the knowledge of *Shūnya* in the fourth state i.e. *Turīyā* is essential. The secret of the immortal *Shūnya* can only be known through the remembrance of the Name of the Lord (p. 943, Ramkali M. 1, Siddh Goshta).

Volition (Will): An act of willing or resolving. The Arabic equivalents for this word are *Hukm* and *Radā* (*Razā*). In Indian terminology, it is called *Bhānā*. These words have been used in the *Adi Granth* in respect of the Will of the Lord. Guru Nanak Dev says in the beginning of *Japuji*: "All the forms are created according to the Will of the Lord, but none can say anything about it. All the beings are created through the Will of the Lord. Greatness is bestowed through His Will. Some are high, some are low, some are in joy and some in pain through His Will. Some are blessed through the Will and some transmigrate through it. All are subject to the Will of the Lord (p.1, Japuji). Farid says, "As is the Lord's *Radā* (Will), the current flows to that side" (p. 1382, Shlok Farid). Guru Nanak Dev says at another place: "When it was the *Bhānā* (Will) of the Lord, He Created the World" (p. 1036, Maru M. 1).

Vow(s): A vow is a solemn promise made to God, or to any deity or saint, to perform some act or make some gift or sacrifice in return for some special favour. Guru Arjan Dev says, "The bread is baked and placed on the platter. Those who have vowed in the name of the Guru, they eat to their fill" (p. 1096, Var Maru Dakhne M. 5). "The corn is ground and cooked and laid it before (the gathering), but if the vow is not offered in the name of the Guru, one waits in vain for the Grace" (p. 1096, Var Dakhne M. 5). In another hymn, the Guru says, "I have attained what I always vowed....That was what I always prayed for and I have attained it by the Guru's Grace" (p. 704, Jaitsri M. 5).

Vrata: It is a religious observance such as making a solemn vow to fast or perform meritorious acts. Ordinarily, this word is used for fasting. Guru Nanak Dev says, "If Truth be the fasting, contentment the holy place, the wisdom and concentration be the bath; the compassion be my god, forgiveness the rosary, then the human being is sublime" (p. 1245, Var Sarang M. 4, Shalok M. 1). Guru Amar Das says, "On the ninth day of the moon, if one practises Truth and eats away his lust, anger and desires; on the tenth day closes all the ten doors of the body; on eleventh day realises the Lord as Unity; on the twelfth day overcomes the five vices, then only the mind believes. O Pundit, observe such *vrata*, no other instruction is of any use" (p. 1245, Var Sarang M. 4, Shalok M. 3). Guru Arjan Dev says "On the day of *Ekādaṣī*, realise this that the Lord is very near. Keep in check your desires and listen to the Name of the Lord. Remain contented in your mind and be merciful to all beings. In this way, your *vrata* (fasting) will be complete" (p. 299, Thitti Gauri M. 5).

Vulture: One of a number of large birds of prey, which feed almost entirely upon carrion and have the head and neck altogether or almost featherless. According to Guru Arjan Dev, the vulture wanders in all the directions, over the seas, the forests and all kinds of vegetation, but it descends only on the dead body (p. 322, Var Gauri M. 5). Here the vulture is identified with an evil-minded person.

Vyāna: One of the vital airs (*Prānas*). It is the pervading breath and through it the vital energy pervades the whole body. See: *Prānas*.

W

Wage(s): Payment to a person for service rendered; the amount paid periodically for the labour or service of a workman or servant. Guru Arjan Dev says, "Through continuous exploitation one collects hoards of gold and silver coins, but the workman gets only the wages and the remaining becomes the property of others" (p. 497, Gujri M. 5). "One toils the whole day (for his wages), but when it comes to contemplation, he shirks away" (p. 1143, Bhairo M. 5). The *Adi Granth* lays stress on honest earnings. Talking about Brahmins, Guru Nanak Dev says, "Himself the Brahmin goes to the next world without a thread (*Yagyopavīta*), but twisting it he puts it upon others. He takes wages and marries off his wards. He reads away the horoscope and shows the Path to all. Listen, O people, this is wonder of wonders. His mind is blind, but his name is "seer" (p. 471, Var Asa M. 1).

War: Hostile contention by means of armed forces, carried on between nations, states or rulers or between the parties in the same state or nation. The conflict of two sides has been mentioned in the *Adi Granth*. Guru Arjan Dev says, "O Lord, You have Created both the sides i.e. Shiva and Shakti (mind and matter). Shakti (matter or *Maya*) loses before Shiva (Conscious mind). This is the Will of the Lord" (p. 1096, Var Maru Dakhne M. 5). The war between the forces of the good and evil is always going on. According to Guru Nanak Dev, all the devices without the Grace and Approval of the Lord are false including the heroic feats in the war and the death in the battlefield (p. 467, Var Asa M. 1). "The saints are the unconquerable armies of God. They are protected by the Coat-of-mail of humility" (p. 1356, Sahaskriti Shlokas M. 5).

Warriors: He is indeed a warrior, who fights for the oppressed. Although he is cut into bits, he never leaves the field of war (p. 1105, Maru Kabir). They alone are acclaimed as warriors, who are Honoured in the Court of the Lord (p. 580, Vadhand M. 1). They are not warriors who die of ego and always weep in agony (p. 1089, Var Maru M. 3).

Water: One of the five gross elements, the other four being Ether, Air, Fire and Earth. Water is the source of all life (p. 472, Var Asa M.1). Therefore water is called the father (p. 8, Japuji). The significance of water has been explained by Guru Nanak Dev in one of his hymns:

"Out of water came the jewels, when the ocean was churned with the stick of the mountain; on the banks of the waters are situated the sixty-eight holy places, where the devotees gather on festivals and talk about the Lord. The wise people always take a bath and afterwards say their prayers. At the time of birth and death the body is washed and water is poured on the head for salvation..." (p. 150, Var Majh M. 1). Just as water merges in water, the soul merges in the Over-soul (p. 278, Gauri Sukhmani M. 5). The association of lotus, fish, milk etc. with water has been depicted figuratively in the *Adi Granth.* In the process of creation, water is an evolute from fire while fire is an evolute from Air (p. 19, Sri Rag M. 1)

Water-Beings: There are forty-two lakh species of beings in water (p. 485, Asa Namdev). The Lord Creates creatures in water and gives them their sustenance therein. There are no farms, no stores and no wares there. No one buys or sells there. There one creature eats another. They who are born deep in the ocean, the Lord Feeds them also" (p. 955, Var Ramkali M. 3, Shlok M. 2). The figurative use of the fish in water has been made in the *Adi Granth.*

Way (Path): The way leading towards the Lord is sharper than a dagger and finer than a hair (p. 794, Suhi Farid). He who believes in the Lord, walks straight on the Path (Way) and lives with honour. He does not wander in the byways and is associated with *Dharma* (p. 3, Japuji). Serving the Almighty Lord, the Way towards Him will be easy to tread (p. 579, Vadhans M. 1). The bride looks on the pathway sighing and with tearful eyes. Her heart is not satiated; she stands with firm step desiring for the sight of the Lord (pp. 337-38, Gauri Kabir). Guru Ram Das says, "I stand always on the wayside, I the beauteous bride of the Lord ask for the Path leading towards the Lord" (p. 449, Asa M. 4). "The fool does not know the Path of Love and goes astray—Forsake the Path of evil and be attuned to the One Lord" (p. 1425, Shlok Varan te Vadhik, M. 5).

Wealth: Abundance of possessions or of valuable products. The *Adi Granth* has deprecated the collection of worldly wealth and has laid stress on gathering the wealth of the Name of the Lord. Guru Ram Das says, "Gather the wealth of (the Name of) the Lord. It is in the society of the saints that one earns the wealth of the Lord...The Lord's Name is the Jewel, Pearl and Ruby....Our Fearless and Infinite Lord blesses us with His Wealth, which no water can drown, no fire can burn, no thief can steal and no death can destroy, no robber can rob it, even the

Yama and the tax-gatherer cannot tax it. The evil persons gather the wealth of poison by commiting sins.... They come to grief in this world and lose their possessions..." (pp. 733-34, Suhi M. 4).

Weapons: Instruments of any kind used in warfare in order to overcome an enemy. According to the *Adi Granth*, the mighty weapon used against the enemy (the vices) is humility. Guru Arjan Dev says, "Humility is my mace and to be the dust of all men is my double-edged sword. No evil person can face these weapons" (p. 628, Sorath M. 5). The arrow of forbearance is to be used, which cannot miss the target (p. 1384, Shlok Farid). In the battle between Mughals and Afghans the swords and guns were used (p. 418, Asa M. 1).

Weather: The condition of the atmosphere with respect to heat and cold, presence or absence of rain etc. In the *Adi Granth* six seasons have been mentioned showing variety of weather. In the summer season, the weather is hot and in the winter it is cold; in the rainy season, the weather is full of dampness and moisture (See Baramaha Tukhari of Guru Nanak Dev and the poem Ruttīn in Ramkali Raga by Guru Arjan Dev). The weather may be stormy. Guru Ram Das says, "Even if there is thunder-storm and squall and even if it rains heavily, I shall still go to see and meet the Guru" (p. 757, Suhi M. 4).

Wedding: Marriage. A marriage song by Guru Ram Das in the *Adi Granth* in Suhi Raga (pp. 773-74) gives the description of four *lavan* (rounds). The four stanzas of the poem are sung at intervals and the marriage couple complete the rounds around the holy scripture (i.e. the *Adi Granth*). This is the wedding ceremony of the Sikhs. Guru Nanak Dev has depicted the wedding of the soul with the Over-soul in one of his hymns: "I marry the Eternal and Immortal Lord. Such is my Marriage, O father, to my Lord by the Grace of the Guru. True is my Lord, O my father, the Marriage-party is of the holy servants of the Lord. At my Mother's place I was happy contemplating on my Lord and at my Lord's place I look Beautiful...On meeting the saints, the Marriage was well-performed and I attained the Lord of Bliss as my Spouse... O father, give me the Dowry of the Name of the Lord" (pp. 78-79, Sri Rag M. 4).

Weeping: Weeping at the time of death has been decried in the *Adi Granth*. Guru Nanak Dev says, "One is born to live for a short while and then he dies. But no one keeps one's company, where his account is settled. All those who cry (on death), they cry in vain" (p. 15, Sri Rag M. 1). "One wails truly, if one weeps in love. If one weeps in involvement, then all the weeping is in vain. Such weeping is useless, when one forgets the Lord and weeps for what is not (i.e. *Maya*)" (p. 579, Vadhans M. 1, Alahunis). Guru Arjan Dev says, "The air (vital air) mingles with the air, the soul merges in the Over-soul. The dust becomes one with the dust, then for what does a man weep?" (p. 885, Ramkali M. 5). "One who weeps, will he not pass away?" (ibid). In one of his hymns Guru Nanak Dev has mentioned several great personages who wept in their most difficult circumstances (pp. 953-54, Var Ramkali M. 3, Shlok M. 1).

Weights and Measures: The weights mentioned in the *Adi Granth* are *Rattī, Māshā, Tolā, Tank, Seer, Maund* and *Bhār*. Eight *Rattīs* make one *māshā* and 12 *māshās* make one *Tolā*. A *Tank* is of four *māshās*, A *seer* contains eight *Tolās*. A *Maund* is of forty *seers*. Eighteen *Bhār* are the weight of the leaves of the whole vegetation. The measures mentioned in the *Adi Granth* are *Gaz* (yard) and *Kos* (about one and a half mile). Kabir says, "Life cannot be measured and it cannot be weighed. Its food is two and a half seers a day (p. 335, Gauri Kabir). Namdev says, "My mind is the yardstick and my tongue the scissors. I measure and measure and cut off the Yama's bonds" (p. 485, Asa Namdev).

Welfare: Prosperity. "He who seeks his own welfare, must surrender completely to the Guru" (p. 1310, Kanra M. 4). If one wants his welfare, one should do good deeds and feel humble" (p. 465, Var Asa M. 1).

West-Quarter: One of the four quarters, the other three being East, North and South. Guru Arjan Dev says, "One resolves to go to the west, but the Lord takes him towards the East" (p. 496). This shows the futility of the human resolution. The Indian Muslims consider the West sacred, because their holy Mecca lies on that side. Kabir says, "(The Hindus) see their God in the South and (the Muslims) in the West; but search Your God in Your heart, because the heart is the seat of the Lord" (p. 1349, Prabhati Kabir).

Wheat: The grain of a cereal, furnishing a meal of flour, which constitutes the chief breadstuff in temperate countries. In the *Adi Granth*, the word *Ann* has been used, which is equivalent for cereal. "Without the cereals (foodgrains) we are not satiated. By forsaking food, we do not Meet our Lord. O man, those foodgrains are blessed, on feeding which we have pleased our Lord; I have realised this" (p. 873, Gond Kabir). "Without cereal, the body is afflicted" (p. 905, Ramkali M. 1).

Wheel: An appliance which supports the vehicle to enable it to move. There is mention of the chariots in the *Adi Granth,* which run either on two wheels or four wheels. e.g. "You leave naked forsaking the chariot, the horse, the elephant and the throne" (p. 1388, Swayyas M. 5). There is also a reference to the potter's wheel (p. 465, Var Asa M. 1). Guru Nanak Dev has figuratively mentioned the wheel of Deeds (p. 878, Ramkali M. 1).

Whore: A prostitute; an unchaste or lewd woman. To go to a prostitute is a sinful act. Guru Arjan Dev says, "One does not wait in thinking of sin. He is not ashamed of running to a whore" (p. 1143, Bhairo M. 5). See: *Prostitute.*

Wickedness: Moral depravity. "The egocentrics love wickedness and argue with the saints" (p. 854, Var Bilawal M. 4, Shalok M. 3). They love wicked people and feel jealous of the saints (p. 755, Suhi M. 3). Guru Arjan Dev say, "O mother, my wicked adversaries have poisoned themselves to death. My Lord, to Whom I belong, has Saved me. My Lord is Merciful towards me" (p. 1269, Malar M. 5). "Who has ever attained release through wicked calumny?" (p. 601, Sorath M. 3).

Widow(s): A woman whose husband is dead. Guru Nanak Dev says, "The widow offers her body to another. Her mind is thus subjugated either for lust or for money. But without her husband, her mind is never satisfied. (p. 226, Gauri M.1). Guru Ram Das says, "He who forsakes the Name of the Lord, is accursed and dishonoured. May his clan never bear any child and may his mother be widowed" (p. 1263, Malar M. 4). Kabir says in the same strain, "Why was that mother not widowed, whose son did not dwell on the Knowledge of the Lord?" (p. 328, Gauri Kabir). He says in another hymn, "When the husband also dies, the wife does not cry, because she has another husband to look after her. And when this second husband also dies, it does not matter how much they enjoyed here, they both fall into hell. There is only one bride, whom every one loves, because she (i.e. *Maya*) is the woman of every living person" (p. 872, Gond Kabir).

Wife (wives): According to Guru Nanak Dev, the husband is One and all others are His wives (p. 933, Ramkali M. 1, Dakhni Oamkar). "The Bride and the Bridegroom are not they who pose as one; But they are indeed Husband and Wife, who are physically two but spiritually one" (p. 788, Var Suhi M. 3). "The same is the bed for the bride and her Lord. The bride is asleep, but the Lord is ever Awake. The bride is intoxicated with the wine of desire, but if the Lord calls her, she awakens" (p. 737, Suhi M. 5). The seeker as Wife meets the Lord only through the Grace of the Guru. "Even if the bride roams through the four ages, she is only wedded to the Lord through the True Guru" (p. 769, Suhi M. 3). "The bride and the bridegroom live together, but between the two there is a strong wall of ego. It is only the perfect Guru, who pulls down the wall of ego and the bride meets her Lord" (p. 1263, Malar M.4) Though within the human body the bride and the bridegroom are the soul and the Over-soul, but at one place the bride is identified with the body and her Lord is the soul. Their interesting conversation is given in one of the hymns of Guru Arjan Dev (p. 1073, Maru M. 5).

Will: In the *Adi Granth*, it pertains to the Will of the Lord, "Everything in the Universe works under the Will of the Lord, none is outside of it" (p. 1, Japuji). See: *Volition*.

Wind: Air in motion. "The wind blows under the Fear of the Lord" (p. 464, Var Asa M. 1). The egoist wears the garments of wind. As it passes away, he too is reduced to dust (p. 318, Var Gauri M. 5). See: *Breath*, *Prānas* and *Vāyū*.

Wine: The *Adi Granth* forbids the use of all types of intoxicants including wine, which make a man insane and brutal. Guru Amar Das says, "One man offers and another pours himself (the wine). It makes him crazy and senseless and devoid of all reason. Then one cannot distinguish between one's own and another's. He is kicked by the Lord (p. 554, Var Bihagra M. 4, Shlok M. 3). See: *Spirituous liquor*.

Winter: One of the seasons, the coldest of the year. Guru Nanak Dev in his Baramaha Tukhari gives the following description of the wintry month *Poha*. He says, "In *Poha*, the snows fall and even the sap of the grass is sapped" (p. 1109). In his poem *Ruttī*, Guru Arjan Dev says, "The season has moon-cooled...in the months of Maghara and Poha...The snow-bound season is pleasing to my mind; how the months of Māgha and Phaguna appear to be meritorious?" (p. 929).

Wisdom: "One cannot find the Lord by intellect or wisdom (p. 107, Majh M. 5). With the Lord no contrivance or wisdom works (p. 496, Gujri M. 5). My ignorance has changed into wisdom, because my Lord is All-wise and the Seer (p. 823, Bilawal M. 5). Guru Nanak Dev says, "Whosoever destroys his wisdom in strife is not wise. Through wisdom one serves the Lord. Through wisdom one attains honour. Through wisdom one realises what one reads. Through wisdom, one becomes charitable. This is the real path, all else leads to the Devil" (p. 1245, Var Sarang M. 4, Shlok M. 1).

Wishes: "All the wishes are fulfilled, when one realises the Unfathomable and Infinite Lord" (p. 747, Suhi M. 5). All my wishes are fulfilled when I repair to my Lord's Feet (p. 1097, Var Maru Dakhne M. 5). My mind dwelt on the Name of the Lord, through the Word of the Guru. All the wishes of my mind and body were fulfilled and the fear of *Yama* was dispelled (p. 731, Suhi M. 4). My Lord Hari, who bestows Bliss, fulfills all our wishes; the *Kamadhenu* (the cow who when requested fulfills all the wishes) is under His Control..." (p. 669, Dhanasari M. 4).

Witchcraft: The exercise of supernatural powers supposed to be possessed by persons in league with the devil or evil spirits. Sorcery or witchcraft has been decried in the *Adi Granth*. See: *Sorcery*.

Witches: Female magicians; women supposed to have dealings with the devil or evil spirits and to be able by their co-operation to perform supernatural acts. Sorcery or witchcraft is condemned in the *Adi Granth*. See: *Sorcerers*.

Witnesses: Those who give evidence in relation to matters of fact under inquiry. Guru Amar Das says, "Great men speak as withnesses; their wisdom is applicable to the whole world" (p. 647, Var Sorath M. 4, Shlok M. 3). Guru Arjan Dev says, "When the Guru became a witness I saw the Lord with my own eyes" (p. 455, Asa M. 5). Guru Nanak Dev says, "If there is no witness for truth then the balance is nil" (p. 1412, Shlok Varan te Vadhik M. 1).

Wizards: Men who are skilled in occult arts; men who practise witchcraft. The use of occult powers has been condemned in the *Adi Granth*, therefore the Yogis and sorcerers and wizards who use miraculous powers or charms and incantations have also been condemned. See: *Sorcerers*.

Wolf (Animals): A somewhat large canine animal, hunting in packs and noted for its fierceness and rapacity. In the *Adi Granth*, the senses have been identified with she-wolves. Guru Arjan Dev says, "The Lord has slain the five tigers (Five vices i.e. lust, anger, greed, attachment and ego) and the ten she-wolves have been conquered (Ten senses i.e. the five senses of perception and the five senses of action) (p. 899, Ramkali M. 5).

Woman (Women): Guru Nanak Dev says, "We are born of woman, we are conceived in the womb of woman, we are engaged and married to woman. We make friendship with woman and the lineage continued because of woman. When one woman dies, we take another one, we are bound with the world through woman. Why should we talk ill of her, who gives birth to kings? The woman is born from woman; there is none without her. Only the One True Lord is without the woman" (p. 473, Var Asa M. 1). There is mention of woman in the *Adi Granth* in various forms i.e. daughter, daughter-in-law, mother, mother-in-law, sister, an approved lady (Suhāgan), a deserted woman (Dohāgan), a prostitute, and a widow. According to the *Adi Granth*, the Lord is Only One, all others are women (p. 933, Ramkali M. 1). *Maya* has been portrayed as a detestable and ignominious woman (p. 394, Asa M. 5).

Womb: A medium of conception and development. Guru Nanak Dev says, "We are conceived in the womb of a woman" (p. 473, Var Asa M.1). Guru Arjan Dev says, "You came into this life to dwell upon the One Lord, but on your birth, the *maya* enticed you away. In the womb of your mother, you stood on your head praying to the Lord for your release. You remembered the Lord with every breath. Now you are involved with *maya*, which you must leave" (p. 251, Gauri Bawan Akhri M. 5). It is the Lord who gives us protection from the fire of the womb (p. 266, Gauri Sukhmani M.1). Guru Amar Das says, "As is the fire of womb within, so is the fire of *Maya* outside. Both the fires are alike. This is the play of the Lord" (p. 921, Ramkali M. 3, Anand). He who sustains us in the womb of the mother, why should we forget Him? (p. 920, ibid). The Jiva was conceived with the father's sperm and the mother's ovary in the fire of the womb, where it stood on its head in the dark, dismal and frightful hell" (p. 706, Var Jaitsri M. 5). I crave for the Vision of God, so that I may not wander again from womb to womb (p. 1323, Kalyan M. 5).

Wood: 1-The firewood used for fuel; a forest. Kabir says, "The wood of the forest, which is already singed, cries out while standing: let me not fall into the hands of a blacksmith, so that he may not burn me for the second time (p. 1369, Shlok Kabir). The wood, unloosed, falls apart and is burnt down by its inner fire" (p. 879, Ramkali M. 1). In the cowdung and the wood also is the life of worms (p. 472, Var Asa M. 1) Just as the fire is locked in the wood and is struck only by one who knows the way, similarly through the knowledge of the Guru, one finds the essence of the All-Pervading Light of the Lord (p. 1323, Kalyan M. 4). The Thing that you have been searching for in the woods, you find in your very home (p. 934, Ramkali M. 1, Dakhni Oamkar). Why do you wander through the woods, keeping away the thorns of the wood; the Lord lives within you. Why do you search for Him in the wood? (p. 1378, Shlok Farid).

Word(s): In the *Adi Granth*, this word has been used in the sense of "the Word of the Guru" or the Name of the Lord. "Through the Word, the Name wells up within us, through the Word we attain Unity with the Lord. Without the Word, the whole world appears insane and wastes away the opportunity of life. The Word is the only nectar, which is attained only through the Guru" (Var Sorath M. 4, Shlok M. 3). The Word itself is the Guru...(p. 635, Sorath M, 1 and p. 43, Ramkali M. 1). In grammatical sense, the letters combine to make words. "With letters, the Name is formed, with letters we Praise, with letters we gain knowledge and sing praises. Through letters we are able to speak and write. Through letters the Writ on the forehead proclaims our union with the Lord. He who has written these letters (words), He does not Have them on His Head..." (p. 4, Japuji). The transitoriness of the world has been described in words (Verbal testimony), but rare is the person, who comprehends this truth (p. 64 Sri Rag M. 1). The primal letter (Word) is *Om* or *Onam* (p. 930, Ramkali M. 1, Dakhni Oamkār).

Works: Actions. The religious actions done according to Shastric injunctions. The *Adi Granth* is averse to all rituals and formal practices. The *Karma Kānda* and *Upāsana Kānda* have been rejected. The works create ego in the mind of the seeker, therefore they have been rejected. Guru Arjan Dev addresses the Pundit in this manner: "O Pundit, sing the Praises of the Name of the Lord, because the way of works and your ego are of no avail" (p. 891, Ramkali M. 5). Guru Amar Das says, "One practises the way of works and pious conduct, but accursed is the ego created by such works devoid of the Name of the Lord" (p. 162, Gauri Guareri M. 3).

World: The world is transient, this should be borne in mind (p. 721, Tilang M. 1). The world which will pass away, should not be praised...The egocentrics who are absorbed in the world, are burnt by the fire of *Trishna* (desire) (p. 755, Suhi M. 3). "This world is quite unstable, where there is no friend and no guide. The brothers and relatives have forsaken all love. It is for this world that I lose even my Faith." (p.1410, Shlok Varan te Vadhik M.1). The world usurps what is due to others... it is the world of animals and ghosts (p. 723, Tilang

M. 5). The world overpowered by greed is thrown into the ditch. It does not know what is going to happen to it in the next world (p. 1020, Maru M. 5). Only the Deeds done in this world are of any avail hereafter...The world dances to the tune of the Devil and you also dance with it. Only he, whom the Lord Protects, does not dance...My heart is attached to the world, but the world is of no avail... (p. 1383, Shlok Farid).

Worms (Animals): "The blind fools are wasted away in duality. They live and lose themselves in dirt like worms (p. 85, Var Sri Rag M. 4, Shlok M. 3). For several births, the Jiva was a worm (p. 176, Gauri Guareri M. 5). The Lord Abides in the worm as well as in the elephant (p. 252, Gauri Bawan Akhri M. 5). In a moment, the Lord can Place the poor worm on the throne (p. 277, Gauri Sukhmani M. 5). For the Lord, the high and low, the elephant and the worm are alike (p. 319, Var Gauri M. 5). Life in all its branches as trees, animals, worms, insects manifests itself in various forms, in several births (pp. 325-26 Gauri Kabir). One, falling from the Grace of the Lord is a worm among worms, a sinner among sinners (p. 2, Japuji). If a person assumes a high position and enjoys to his heart's content. In the eyes of the Lord, he is only a worm eating grains (p. 360, Asa M. 1). Lying on the hard ground (in the grave), with the pillow of brick, (the dead body) will be eaten by the worms (p. 1381, Shlok Farid).

Wrath: Anger. One of the five vices, the other four being lust, greed, attachment and ego. Guru Arjan Dev addresses Wrath in his Shlokas like this: "O Wrath, the origin of strife, you do not know compassion. You have a powerful sway over evil persons, who dance to your tunes like monkeys, who at last face great punishment at the hands of the messengers of *Yama*. In your company men become like devils..." (p. 1358, Sahaskriti Shlokas M. 5). See: *Anger*.

Writing: One should read, write, repeat and sing the Name of the Lord (p. 669, Dhanasari M. 4). While writing about our Lord one exhausts the paper and the ink.... They who write and practise and concentrate on falsehood, they are cast into the fire. The Enlightened Persons write of Truth alone and reach the Gate of Salvation (p. 123, Majh M. 3). The more one reads and writes (about the worldly things), the more one is in agony (p. 467, Var Asa M. 1). One cannot resist the Writ of the Lord, because it is in accordance with one's past actions (p. 582, Vadhans M. 1).

Y

Yajna: Worship through offerings; sacrificial ceremony of Hinduism; an oblation. The motive of the sacrifice was the welfare of the individual or the family or even the community. The sacrifice was an offering to the gods. The aroma of the burnt offerings was considered to rise to heaven. The Tadbhav formation of *Yajna* as *Jag* has been used in the *Adi Granth.* According to Guru Nanak Dev, the king Janmeja performed the *Yajna* and then put to death eighteen impudent Brahmins, therefore he sufffered. No one can escape the Writ of the past actions (p. 1344, Prabhati M. 1). In accordance with the nature of gods, men offer them the meat of rhinoceros as sacrificial food in the *Yajnas* (p. 1289, Var Malar M. 1).

Yajur-Veda: One of the four Vedas, the other three being Rig Veda, Sama Veda and the Atharva Veda. It deals with sacrificial formulas. There are two distinct divisions of this Veda: 1-"Black Yajur Veda", 2-"White Yajur Veda. The Black Yajur Veda prescribes techniques for destorying foes, ending opposition, gaining advantage over others etc. The White Yajur Veda prescribes techniques for the attainment of boons regarding health, prosperity, long life etc. According to Guru Nanak Dev, as the people say, in the time of Yajur Veda, the name of the Lord was Krishna of the Yadava tribe, who seduced Chandraval by force, who brought the *Pārijāt* (the elysian tree) from the heaven for his Gopi and indulged in enjoyments in Vrindavana (p. 470, Var Asa M. 1).

Yakshas: They are earth-spirits, often described as demigods. Kubera, the god of wealth is their leader. Like mysterious genii, they can assume any form, including that of beautiful women. They are either beneficent or malignant. They are regarded as local deities and are the guardian spirits of treasures. They are said to live in forests and mountains. Their favourite haunt is considered to be the sacred tree common to most villages. They are also associated with fertility. In the *Adi Granth*, their mention is made alongwith Gandharvas, Kinnaras and Paishachas. Guru Arjan Dev, while describing the creation of the Lord, says, "There are millions of Yakshas, Kinnaras and Paishachas, there are millions of ghosts, spirits, swines and animals of the forests (p. 276, Gauri Sukhmani M. 5).

Yama: The god of death. His vehicle is the black buffalo and his weapons are the mace (*gadā*) and the noose (*pāsha*). He is attended by two dogs, each having four eyes. He is the lord of paradise and also the keeper of hells, because it is through him that the souls go either to heaven or to hell according to their actions. There is frequent mention of Yama in the *Adi Granth*. Chitra and Gupta, the two scribes accompanying each soul present the account of good and bad actions of the individual to Yama, who is often called *Dharam Raja* (or *Dharam Raj*)—the god of justice. Guru Ram Das says, "Through the Guru's Word...one becomes Beloved of God and the *Yama* does not come near him and the *Dharmaraja* does not call him to account" (pp. 980-81, Nat M. 4). The saint dwells only on the One Lord, therefore the *Yama* does not come near him (p. 869, Gond M. 5). The *Yama* sends his messengers to bring the soul of the dying person. None can escape their grip.

Yatī: A celibate; a man of chastity. According to Guru Amar Das, it is by truthful living, one gathers the merit of celibacy, truth and self-discipline and one dwells on the Name of the Lord by the Grace of the Guru (p. 129, Majh M. 3). The Hindu tradition mentions six celibates viz. Bhairo, Hanumana, Lakshmana, Gorakha, Bhishama and Dattatreya. According to Kabir these six *Yatīs* (celibates) are the slaves of *maya* (p. 1160, Bhairo Kabir).

Yavanas: The word *Yavana* was first applied to Greeks coming from Asia Minor (*Yavana-desha*), who spread to the north and east from the sixth century BC and established settlements in various areas including the areas adjoining the north-western India. Later this term was applied to all foreigners i.e. the Muslims, Europeans and others. The word *Malech* was also used for *Yavana*, a non-Indo-Aryan, who was often regarded as a barbarian. The word *Malech* is used in the *Adi Granth* (p. 4, Japuji).

Year: A year consists of twelve months and six seasons. In the *Adi Granth*, there are two poems called *Baramahas* (one in Raga Majh by Guru Arjan Dev and the other in Raga Tukhari by Guru Nanak Dev) containing stanzas on each month of the year. The poem *Ruttī* by Guru Arjan Dev in Raga Ramkali mentions six seasons, each season of two months.

Yoga: Union; the means for the attainment of the union with the Lord. In the *Adi Granth*, the term Yoga has been frequently used. The practices of Raja Yoga of Patanjali, Hath Yoga of Gorakh, Tantra Yoga and Kundalini Yoga have been rejected by the *Adi Granth*. According to Guru Nanak Dev "Yoga is neither in the patched coat, nor in the staff nor in besmearing the body with ashes nor in wearing ear-rings, nor in removing the hair from the head, nor in blowing the horn; if one remains above all wordly attachments, he attains the real state of Yoga. One does not become a Yogi by mere talk, if one looks upon all the creation alike, he is, indeed, a Yogi..." (p. 730, Suhi M. 1). Guru Amar Das says, "Yoga does not consist in ochre-coloured robes or in soiled clothes. One attains Yoga at home through the Instruction of the Guru" (pp.1420-21, Shlok Varan te Vadhik M. 3). According to Guru Nanak Dev, one cannot attain Yoga without Serving the True Guru... It is only through the True Guru that one attains the Name and the Yoga..." (p. 946, Ramkali M. 1, Siddh Goshta). "Let the Word of the Guru be the ear-rings of the mind, let forgiveness be the patched coat. Let there be complete resignation to the Will of the Lord; in this way, the treasure of the *Sahaj Yoga* (union in the state of equipoise) will be attained (p. 359, Asa M. 1).

Yoga Sutra: The treatise of Yoga by Patanjali; one of the six systems of Indian philosophy, the other five being Samkhya, Nyaya, Vaisheshika, Purva Mimaṁsa and Uttara Mimaṁsa. Yoga Darshana is complimentary to Saṁkhya. They are closely allied to each other. Saṁkhya is called theory and Yoga practice. The metaphysics and epistemology of Saṁkhya has been mostly accepted by Yoga. Yoga Darshana deals with the concept of liberation through concentration. It is known as Raja Yoga. The discipline is called *Ashtānga Yoga*. It includes *Yama* (abstention), *Niyama* (self-culture), *Āsana* (Postures), *Prānāyāma* (regulation of breath), *Pratyāhāra* (control of senses), *Dhāranā* (fixing the mind on the object of meditation), *Dhyāna* (meditation) and *Samādhi* (complete absorption). The *Adi Granth* is in favour of *Yama* and *Niyama*, but rejects *Āsanas* and *Prānāyāma*. Yoga has made an addition to the metaphysics of Saṁkhya and that is the addition of Godhead. But God of Yoga is only a Special *Purusha* and not the Creator like God of the *Adi Granth*.

Yoga Vasishṭha: A sacred Hindu philosophical treatise, containing a dialogue between Lord Rama and the sage *Vasishṭha*. There is mention of this sage in the *Adi Granth*. Guru Ram Das says, "By the Guru's Grace Vasishṭha taught the Wisdom of the Lord" (p. 591, Var Vadhans M. 4).

Yogin: One who practises or attains Yoga or "Union with the Lord". Guru Nanak Dev says, "The Yogi is fearless and dwells on the Immaculate Lord. He always keeps awake in mind and is attuned to

Truth. Such a Yogi pleases my heart. He who serves the True Guru is Yogi. Having been imbued with the Fear of the Lord, he becomes fearless" (pp. 223-24, Gauri M. 1). "He is, indeed, a Yogi, who has the cognizance of the Word of the Guru and within whom flowers the Lotus. He dies to the self and knows everything and Knows within his self the All-Merciful Lord. He achieves the Merit of recognising himself in all beings" (p. 940, Ramkali M. 1, Siddh Goshta). Guru Amar Das says, "He is the Yogi who knows the discipline and attains the Name of the Lord by the Grace of the Guru. In the city of such a Yogi, there is everything; the Yoga is not attained through pretensions. Such a Yogi is very rare, who sees the Presence of the Lord in his heart. (p. 556, Var Bihagra M. 4, Shlok M. 3). Guru Arjan Dev says, "The five disciples (vices) got together and came under the control of one (mind) and the ten ascetics (five organs of sense and five organs of action) became obedient, then the devotee became a stainless and pure Yogi" (p. 208, Gauri M. 5).

Youth: One of the three stages of life, the other two being childhood and old age. At this stage, the *jiva* awakens to the play of love and the desire to eat and drink. The lust arises which knows no caste... At twentyone becomes a youth and at thirty, he/she is called a beautiful (young man or young lady) (p. 138, Var Majh M. 1). The riches and beauty (or the youth) are like the shade of the swallow-wort tree (aak) (p. 689, Dhanasari M.1). "The body remains only till it is in bloom and you breathe; without merit it will all be in vain (p. 20, Sri Rag M. 1). "Meditate on the Name so long as you have the youth and life" (p. 82, Sri Rag M. 4). "Riches, beauty of the youth and flowers are the guests for a few days...therefore love, till the beauty is in ascendancy" (p. 23, Sri Rag M. 10).

Yuga(s): Ages. According to the Hindu tradition, there are four ages. These are 1-Krtā or Satya or 1,728,000 years, 2-Tretā or 1,296,000 years, 3-Dvāpara of 864,000 years, and 4-Kali, the present period of 432,000 years. There is a reduction of physical and moral standards in each succeeding age. The four Yugas together are called Maha-yuga. All these four Yugas have been mentioned in the *Adi Granth*. See: *Ages of the World*.